THE ANGEVIN DYNASTIES OF EUROPE 900–1500

THE ANGEVIN DYNASTIES OF EUROPE 900–1500

Lords of the Greatest Part of the World

Jeffrey Anderson

ROBERT HALE

First published in 2019
by Robert Hale, an imprint of
The Crowood Press Ltd,
Ramsbury, Marlborough
Wiltshire SN8 2HR

www.crowood.com

British Library Cataloguing-in-Publication Data
A catalogue record for this book is available from the
British Library.

ISBN 978 0 7198 2925 3

Typeset by Chapter One Book Production, Knebworth, UK

Printed and bound in India by Parksons Graphics

CONTENTS

PROLOGUE

IN THE 15TH CENTURY, when Richard Duke of York wanted to emphasize his claim to the English throne in opposition to King Henry VI, he took a new name for himself: *Plantagenet*. This resonant name, which referred to a 12th-century ancestor, became – with a little help from Shakespeare – the family name historians use for the monarchs that ruled England from Henry II (1154–1189) until the accession of the first Tudor king in 1485. On Bosworth Field the defeat of Richard III ended the line of Plantagenet kings, but this name remains the most evocative in medieval English history. The greatest exterminatrix in the Plantagenet 'Wars of the Roses', at least according to Shakespeare's plays about Henry VI, was Margaret of Anjou, Queen of England, who not only led troops against her rivals but also murdered Richard Plantagenet with her own hands.

Far away from the civil war in England, Margaret's father, King René of Anjou, presided over one of the most sophisticated courts in Europe. Through genealogy and good fortune, René had become Duke of Anjou, Lorraine and Bar, Count of Provence and titular King of Sicily, Jerusalem and Aragon, and despite military reversals and a chronic lack of funds he had established peerless intellectual and cultural credentials. René held pageants and classically inspired processions in Naples and Lorraine, corresponded with the humanists credited with initiating the Renaissance, wrote (and possibly illustrated) chivalric romances and treatises that are amongst the most sumptuous manuscripts of the 15th century, and founded a chivalric order dedicated to dressing up and telling fabulous stories. Nothing could seem further from the vicious battles of the Wars of the Roses than René's choreographed jousts and his obsession with elaborate costumes. The Plantagenets, who included some of the most effective kings in English history and were now locked in a desperate struggle for supremacy in England, seem to have little in common with the rulers of Anjou – the Angevins – like King René, who amused themselves with literature and learned displays of chivalry.

Yet the Plantagenets were Angevins. King René and Queen Margaret united two Angevin lines, one of which ruled England as the Plantagenets, and another that between the 12th and 15th centuries at one time or another ruled Anjou, Lorraine, Bar, Provence, Catalonia, Piedmont, Florence, Rome, Naples, Sicily, Albania, Greece, Hungary, Croatia, Poland and Jerusalem. Their line included conquerors, saints, philosopher kings, reigning queens, usurpers, reformers and patrons of the greatest art of the Middle Ages.

This is the Angevin story. It encompasses all the major events of European history from the 9th to the 15th centuries, and demonstrates the international sweep and cultural dynamism of Europe's most compelling dynasty.

GENEALOGIES

The Counts of Anjou / Plantagenets

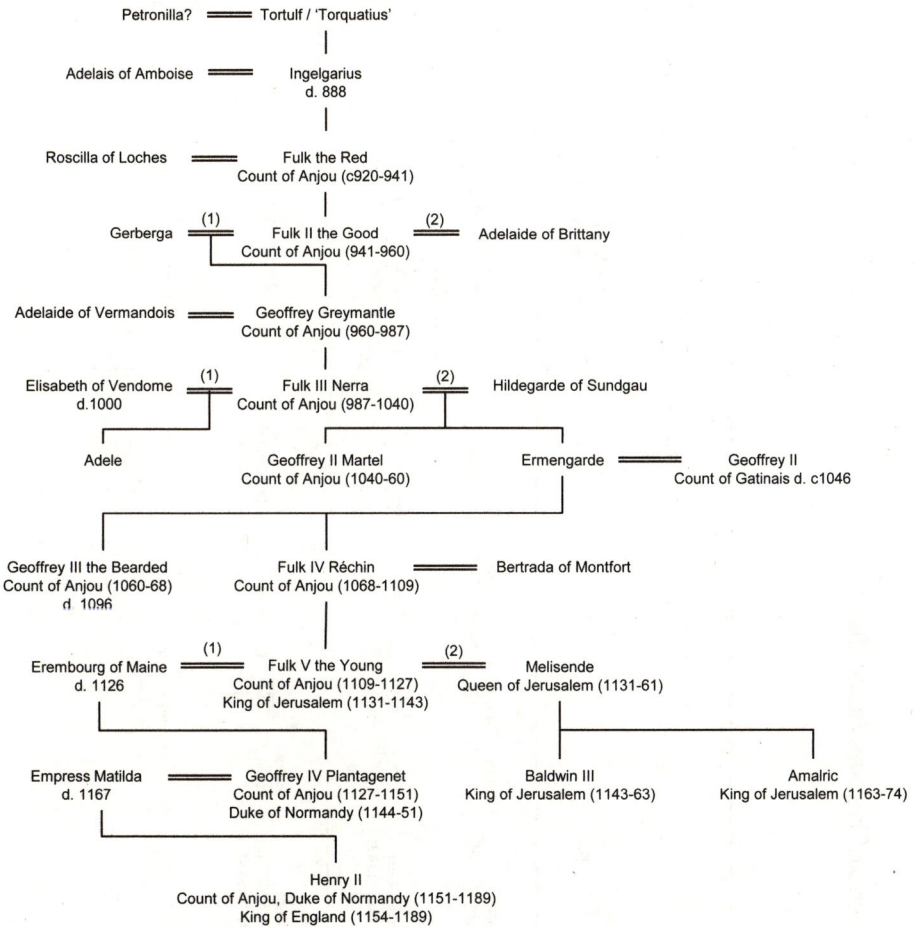

Petronilla? ══ Tortulf / 'Torquatius'

Adelais of Amboise ══ Ingelgarius
d. 888

Roscilla of Loches ══ Fulk the Red
Count of Anjou (c920-941)

Gerberga ══ (1) Fulk II the Good (2) ══ Adelaide of Brittany
Count of Anjou (941-960)

Adelaide of Vermandois ══ Geoffrey Greymantle
Count of Anjou (960-987)

Elisabeth of Vendome ══ (1) Fulk III Nerra (2) ══ Hildegarde of Sundgau
d.1000 Count of Anjou (987-1040)

Adele — Geoffrey II Martel — Ermengarde ══ Geoffrey II
Count of Anjou (1040-60) Count of Gatinais d. c1046

Geoffrey III the Bearded — Fulk IV Réchin ══ Bertrada of Montfort
Count of Anjou (1060-68) Count of Anjou (1068-1109)
d. 1096

Erembourg of Maine ══ (1) Fulk V the Young (2) ══ Melisende
d. 1126 Count of Anjou (1109-1127) Queen of Jerusalem (1131-61)
King of Jerusalem (1131-1143)

Empress Matilda ══ Geoffrey IV Plantagenet Baldwin III Amalric
d. 1167 Count of Anjou (1127-1151) King of Jerusalem (1143-63) King of Jerusalem (1163-74)
Duke of Normandy (1144-51)

Henry II
Count of Anjou, Duke of Normandy (1151-1189)
King of England (1154-1189)

The Angevins of Naples (simplified)

St Louis IX
King of France (1226-1270)

Philip III
King of France (1270-85)

Louis VIII
King of France (1223-1226)
══ Blanche of Castile
d. 1252

Margaret of Burgundy
d. 1308
══ (2)

Charles of Anjou
King of Sicily (1266-1285)

(1) ══ Beatrice of Provence
d. 1268

Charles II the Lame
King of Sicily (1285-1309)

Marie of Hungary
d. 1323
══

Elisabeth
d. 1303
══ Ladislas IV the Cuman
King of Hungary (1272-1290)

Margaret
d. 1299

Charles of Valois
d. 1325
══ (1)

(by 2nd marriage)

Catherine of Valois
Empress of Constantinople
d. 1346

Charles Martel
Claimant to Hungary d.1295

St Louis of Toulouse
d. 1297

Robert the Wise
King of Sicily (1309-1343)

Philip of Taranto
d. 1331

John of Gravina/Durazzo
d. 1336

Charles Robert 'Carobert'
King of Hungary (1306-1342)

Charles of Calabria
d. 1328

Robert
d. 1364

Louis of Taranto
d. 1362

Philip
d. 1373

Charles of Durazzo
d. 1348

Louis
d. 1362

Robert
d. 1356

Louis the Great
King of Hungary (1343-1382)
King of Poland (1370-1382)

Marie of Valois
d. 1332
══ (1)

Andrew
d.1345
══ (1)

Johanna I
Queen of Sicily (1343-1382)

Charles Martel
d. 1348

Catherine
d. 1362

Francoise
d. 1352

(2)

Maria
d. 1366

(1)

Margaret
d.1412
══

Charles III of Durazzo
King of Sicily (1382-86)
King of Hungary (1385-86)

Johanna
d. 1387

Agnes
d.1388

Clementia
d. 1363

Ladislas
King of Sicily (1386-1414)

Johanna II
Queen of Sicily (1414-1435)

The Angevins of Naples, Hungary and Poland (simplified)

Margaret of Burgundy d.1308 (2) **Charles of Anjou King of Sicily (1266-1285)** (1) Beatrice of Provence d.1268

Ladislas IV the Cuman King of Hungary (1272-1290)

Elisabeth d. 1303

Marie of Hungary d.1323 **Charles II the Lame King of Sicily (1285-1309)**

St Louis of Toulouse d.1297

Robert the Wise King of Sicily (1309-1343)

Philip of Taranto d. 1331

John of Gravina/Durazzo d. 1336

Robert of Durazzo d. 1356

Charles of Calabria d.1328

Charles of Durazzo d.1348

Louis of Durazzo d.1362

Charles III of Durazzo King of Sicily (1382-86) King of Hungary (1385-86)

Clementia of Habsburg d. 1293 (or 1295) **Charles Martel Claimant to Hungary d.1295**

Charles Robert 'Carobert' King of Hungary (1306-1342)

Elisabeth of Poland d. 1380

Andrew d.1345 (1) **Johanna I Queen of Sicily (1343-1382)**

Ladislas King of Sicily (1386-1414)

Johanna II Queen of Sicily (1414-1435)

Louis the Great King of Hungary (1343-1382) King of Poland (1370-1382)

Elizabeth of Bosnia d. 1387

Hedwig/Jadwiga King of Poland (1384-99) **Wladyslaw II Jagiello King of Poland (1386-1434)**

Maria King of Hungary (1382-95) **Sigismund of Luxembourg King of Hungary (1387-1437)**

The 'Second House' of Anjou

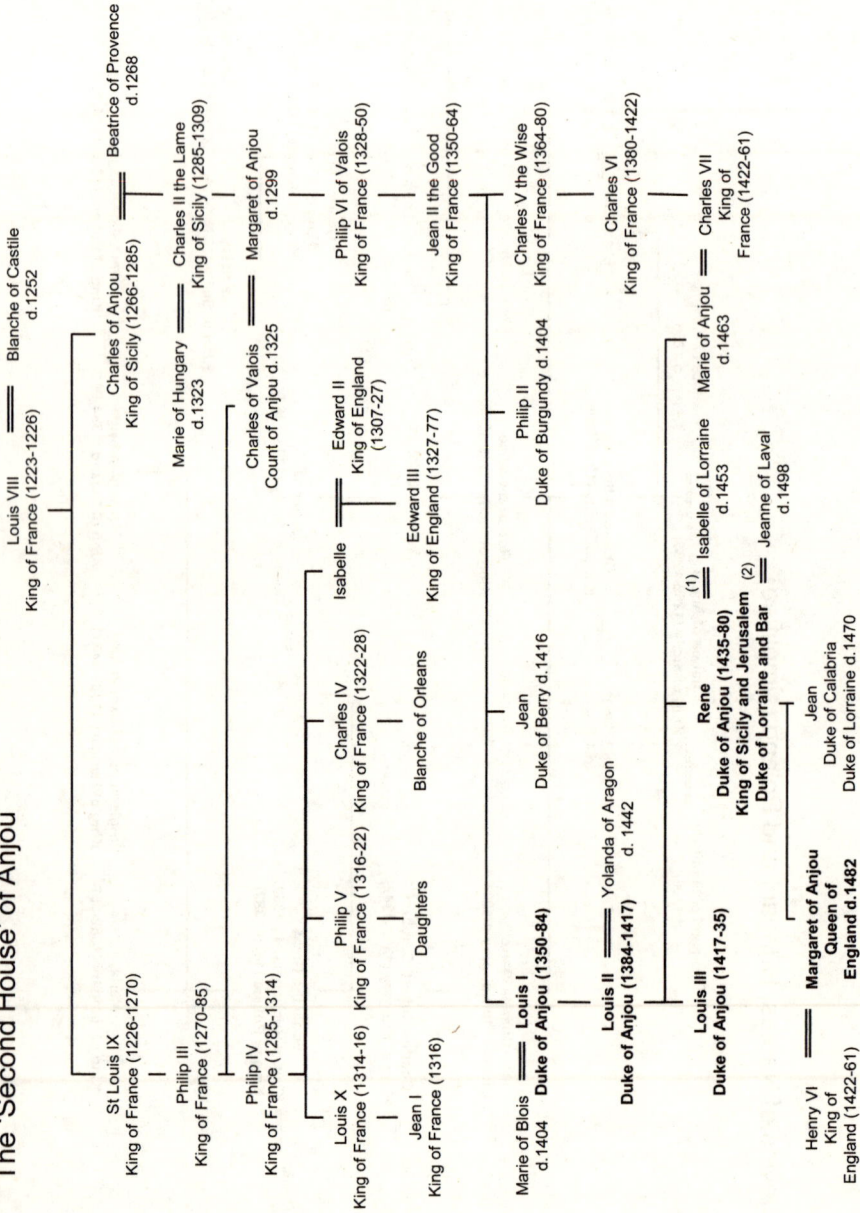

Louis VIII
King of France (1223-1226) ═══ Blanche of Castile d.1252

Beatrice of Provence d.1268

Charles of Anjou King of Sicily (1266-1285) ═══ Charles II the Lame King of Sicily (1285-1309)

St Louis IX King of France (1226-1270)

Philip III King of France (1270-85)

Philip IV King of France (1285-1314)

Marie of Hungary d.1323

Margaret of Anjou d.1299

Charles of Valois Count of Anjou d.1325

Philip VI of Valois King of France (1328-50)

Louis X King of France (1314-16)

Philip V King of France (1316-22)

Charles IV King of France (1322-28)

Blanche of Orleans

Isabelle ═══ Edward II King of England (1307-27)

Edward III King of England (1327-77)

Jean II the Good King of France (1350-64)

Jean I King of France (1316)

Daughters

Jean Duke of Berry d.1416

Philip II Duke of Burgundy d.1404

Charles V the Wise King of France (1364-80)

Charles VI King of France (1380-1422)

Marie of Anjou d.1463 ═══ Charles VII King of France (1422-61)

Marie of Blois d.1404 ═══ **Louis I Duke of Anjou (1350-84)**

Louis II Duke of Anjou (1384-1417) ═══ Yolanda of Aragon d.1442

Louis III Duke of Anjou (1417-35)

Isabelle of Lorraine d.1453 (1) ═══ **Rene Duke of Anjou (1435-80) King of Sicily and Jerusalem Duke of Lorraine and Bar** ═══ (2) Jeanne of Laval d.1498

Jean Duke of Calabria Duke of Lorraine d.1470

Margaret of Anjou Queen of England d.1482 ═══ Henry VI King of England (1422-61)

INTRODUCTION

D IGESTING THE COMPLETE HISTORY of medieval Europe from 900 to 1500 in one volume is perhaps not appealing to everyone, but that is not the purpose here. This book will focus narrowly on the international and cultural connections of the Angevins, albeit over a long period and an extraordinary geographical range, and how they interacted with each other and the other ruling houses of Europe.

It is important to set the parameters of the story first, and that will involve a blizzard of dates, names and places, but we can then move on as quickly as possible. Firstly, Anjou. This was the French province centred on the Loire between Tours and Nantes with its capital at Angers, today probably best known for being the westernmost edge of the great parade of chateaux along the Loire, with Saumur perhaps being its most famous. Anjou corresponds roughly to the current, confusingly named, *département* of Maine et Loire – confusing since Maine is another historic province with its capital at Le Mans, a region just north of Anjou that would be taken by the Angevins. For reasons best known to the French authorities, historic Maine forms the current *départements* of Sarthe and Mayenne. Three historic provinces critical to early Angevin history – Anjou, Maine and Blois – have names referring to their pre-Roman tribal history, giving people from them these designations: *Angevins* from Anjou, *Cenomannians* from Maine and *Blésois* from Blois.

There were three Angevin dynasties in the period 900–1500: the original dynasty founded in the 9th century, which ultimately became kings of Jerusalem, took control of England and lost Anjou in 1204, after which historians refer to them as Plantagenets; next, Charles of Anjou and his descendants who in the 13th and 14th centuries became kings of Sicily, Jerusalem, Hungary and Poland; and finally the 'Second House of Anjou', which was founded by Louis I when he received Anjou in 1350 and essentially ended with King René who died in 1480, after which Anjou reverted to the French Crown.

The initial Angevin line, who were first called counts, began in the 9th and 10th centuries with near-legendary figures like Ingelgarius, Fulk the Red and Fulk the Good, who, although we know they existed, largely figure in fanciful tales. In this period, Anjou was a dynamic county that was one of the main political units in what would become France. After the anarchy of the later 9th century, Viking raiders had settled down to create the 'land of the Northmen' – Normandy – and established what became the most acquisitive and successful power of the 11th and early 12th centuries, while the French kings became so imbecilic that their throne was usurped by a new line that ruled a tiny province centred on Paris. Anjou too emerged as a compact and well governed territory ruled by a series of colourful, ruthless and successful leaders who would ultimately become kings themselves.

Angevin history leaps into focus in 987 with Fulk Nerra, a well-documented figure of European significance because of his multiple pilgrimages to Jerusalem, his pioneering construction of castles and his annexation of territory that would become a permanent part of Anjou. Fulk Nerra's successors in the mid- and late 11th century, Geoffrey Martel and Fulk Réchin, had the misfortune to have as a neighbour Duke William the Bastard of Normandy who would become King William the Conqueror of England, and both were repeatedly bested by the Normans.

Anjou itself seemed to be in peril by the end of Fulk Réchin's reign, but it was from this nadir that Angevin fortunes had an astonishing reversal. Fulk Réchin's son, Fulk V, arranged not one but two historic marriages: his son Geoffrey, the first to adopt the nickname 'Plantagenet', married Matilda, heiress to the English throne, and Fulk himself married Melisende, heiress to the kingdom of Jerusalem that had been established by the First Crusade. The kingdom of Jerusalem was an embattled Christian outpost that needed both clear succession rules and a king to lead the army, so it accepted female succession but gave full royal recognition to the queen's husband, and Fulk became king of Jerusalem. Geoffrey Plantagenet and Matilda had to fight for Normandy and England, and although Matilda's cousin Stephen of Blois usurped the English throne and held it for nearly twenty years, ultimately in 1154 Matilda and Geoffrey's son succeeded as Henry II King of England, Duke of Normandy and Count of Anjou. Moreover, he married Eleanor of Aquitaine, heiress to most of southwestern France, and together they ruled an 'Angevin Empire' that stretched from Scotland to the Pyrenees.

This initiated an Angevin dynasty in England that provided three of the most famous (or in one case, notorious) names in English history: Henry II, Richard the Lionheart and King John. These kings presided over developments that still shape the modern world, and this was a direct result of the methods needed to rule an enormous empire. Although they did move around their domains constantly, they could not possibly visit everywhere frequently, and so were forced to use written documents to send their authority impersonally throughout their dominions, initiating, for better or worse, much of the bureaucracy that is still with us. This also necessitated a more permanent household establishment, and London emerged as the capital of England with its administrative centre at Westminster.

In Jerusalem, the Angevin dynasty ended when the leper king Baldwin IV died without heirs and his sister's husband became the new king, only to lose the kingdom to the great Muslim hero Saladin in 1187. The Crusades continued, most notably for our purposes with the Third Crusade of Richard the Lionheart, but they evolved from religiously motivated wars against Muslims to religiously sanctioned wars against a variety of people – other Christians, such as heretics and political opponents, as well as Muslims and Turks. Most notoriously, in 1204 the Fourth Crusade was diverted to conquer the Christian city of Constantinople and established a Latin Empire there, and the popes began to use Crusades as a routine means of attacking their political enemies.

From the peak of the Angevin Empire, the Angevins nearly lost everything. Richard's successor, King John, lost Normandy and Anjou to the French king, and the English royal line after John is called 'Plantagenet' to distinguish it from subsequent rulers of Anjou. John's loss of his Empire initiated a complex series of responses. The formalization of royal authority begun by Henry II easily slipped into despotism, and this, joined to the need for vast sums of money to defend the Angevin Empire plus King John's inflexible character, culminated in 1215 with revolt and the drafting of Magna Carta, the first document formally curbing royal power, and establishing the principles of limited government and the ultimate responsibility of the king to his subjects. Magna Carta was a consequence of first Richard's, then John's, rapacious behaviour in England to raise sufficient funds to defend the Angevin Empire, and then to attempt to recapture it when it had been lost. The total failure of these schemes despite their vast expense stimulated the barons of England to rise up and demand that the king respect their wishes, the first step on the road to English constitutional monarchy and democracy.

In the 13th century the political entities and struggles that would define Europe for centuries become more clearly defined. France, England, the Holy Roman Empire, Aragon and the papacy came into direct competition, and the focal point of this struggle was Charles of Anjou. Charles was the younger brother of the French king – and future saint – Louis IX, although France and England were so intertwined that Charles was also the great-grandson of Henry II and Eleanor of Aquitaine. Although he had gained Provence by marriage and been given Anjou by Louis, Charles became involved in the great Crusade of the papacy against its enemies in Italy, and at the pope's request he conquered southern Italy and Sicily in 1266.

Charles, more than almost any other medieval figure, had a conscious plan of empire building. He extended his rule over Albania and Greece, and gained the throne of Jerusalem – now an empty title, as the Christians held only one last outpost in the Holy Land – and an interest in the Latin Empire of Constantinople, and prepared for an invasion of the eastern Mediterranean. His great ambition collapsed in 1282 with the revolt known as the Sicilian Vespers, when the people of Sicily, supported by Aragon, rose up against the Angevins. Sicily fell to Aragon, the new great power of the Mediterranean, and the Angevin kingdom of Naples was confined to southern Italy, now ruled by Charles's son, Charles II.

Angevin Naples initially prospered. Charles II's eldest surviving son Louis was a Franciscan who renounced his inheritance and was so renowned for piety in his lifetime that he was recognized as a saint, leaving the next son, Robert, to become king of Naples. Robert 'the Wise' embodied all the qualities of the philosopher king,

composing numerous sermons in Latin, publicly examining the poet and humanist
Petrarch on his classical learning before proclaiming him the first poet laureate since
Roman times, and patronizing two towering artists of the 14th century, Giotto and
Simone Martine.

Naples in the 14th century was the greatest metropolis of medieval Europe except-
ing only Paris, and is brought to vivid life by Giovanni Boccaccio in the *Decameron*,
whose stories describe in detail the rise of the merchant and banking class at the expense
of the old feudal order, prefiguring the course of modern economic and political history.
However, the 14th century was also a time of disasters: the reason the narrators in the
Decameron were staying at an estate in the country and telling stories to pass the time
was that they had fled Florence to escape the Black Death, which killed a third of
Europe's population between 1348 and 1351.

The Golden Age under Robert the Wise proved short-lived. Charles II had married
a Hungarian princess, and the throne of Hungary passed to the Angevins through
Charles II's grandson Carobert, who considered Robert a usurper. Robert's granddaughter, Johanna I, married her Hungarian cousin Andrew to heal the breach, but
despite – or because of – the fact that they had grown up together, the couple disliked
each other, and this, added to Hungarian annoyance that Johanna would inherit the
throne in her own right and Andrew would not be king, meant the marriage was
termed a disaster. Or so it seemed, until a true disaster struck: Andrew was murdered
and Johanna was widely blamed for the crime. Andrew's brother, King Louis the Great
of Hungary, invaded Italy and Johanna fled to Avignon, where she appeared before
the pope in an attempt to clear her name. She succeeded, but the rest of her reign was
blighted by further unhappy marriages and Hungarian invasions, until finally she was
captured by a rival, deposed and murdered.

The Hungarian Angevins can only appear as villains in Naples, yet in Hungarian
history the 14th century under Angevin rule is also considered a golden age. The
warrior king Louis the Great used literal mountains of gold to make Hungary a major
European power and extended his dominion (intermittently) over Naples, as well as
inheriting the throne of Poland. Yet like his ancestor Henry II of England, Louis also
presided over profound political, economic, social and cultural developments that
transformed Hungarian society. His two daughters had the distinction of becoming
kings (not queens, an interesting response to the issue of female succession) in their
own right – Maria became king of Hungary and Hedwig/Jadwiga became king of
Poland – and it is no exaggeration to talk of yet another Angevin 'empire' for a short
time in central Europe.

The Black Death was not the only crisis of the 14th century. The involvement of the
papacy in decades of Italian wars and its complete identification with Angevin political
goals, plus extensive use of the Crusade for these political ends, changed the nature of
the papacy and led to more than a century and a half of disruption. This included the
residence of the popes in Avignon rather than Rome for nearly seventy years, and then

the Western Great Schism, when rival popes reigned in Avignon and Rome, which was only resolved in 1415.

In the 14th century the long conflict between France and England also resumed, this time in the spectacular form of the Hundred Years War. In addition to the remnant of the Angevin Empire they retained in Gascony and their old claims to Normandy, Anjou and Aquitaine, the Plantagenets of England now had a claim to the throne of France, and after a series of spectacular victories they nearly made it good. France was crippled first by a dynastic crisis and change of the ruling line, and then by the madness of King Charles VI.

Still Anjou produced one more dynasty, of warrior dukes who fought in the Hundred Years War and tried to claim Naples. Louis I of Anjou fought at the Battle of Poitiers, served as a hostage in England and then invaded Italy as the adopted heir of Queen Johanna. Louis died on this expedition, but his son Louis II also claimed Naples, fighting against the final branch of the Neapolitan Angevin dynasty represented by King Ladislas and Queen Johanna II. Louis II's wife, Yolanda of Aragon, became a pivotal figure in the Hundred Years War, raising the future king Charles VII and proving a key supporter of Joan of Arc when she turned the tide against the English. This 'Second House' of Anjou made good their claim to Provence, which they would retain for most of the 15th century, as well as intermittently ruling Naples.

Their line culminated with King René of Anjou, himself a figure of European significance through his participation in the Hundred Years War, cultural achievements in literature, art, and chivalric display and most importantly through the geographic scope of his territorial claims. René became Duke of Bar through his mother and Duke of Lorraine in right of his first wife Isabelle of Lorraine even before he became Duke of Anjou, a title he inherited when his older brother died. René then continued the family claim to the throne of Naples, and although he was ultimately unsuccessful, he used the titles King of Sicily and Jerusalem for the rest of his life. Perhaps most importantly, René was also Count of Provence, and it was in Provence that he would spend his final years in calculatedly rustic simplicity, where he and his second wife Jeanne de Laval are still remembered fondly.

René also continued to accumulate titles and claimed the throne of Aragon, a claim his son nearly made good when he captured Barcelona. René's grandson René II was pivotal in the destruction of the duchy of Burgundy as an independent entity and allowing it to be absorbed by France, indirectly strengthening the nation that would also absorb the Angevin dominions.

King René's connection to the French royal family and his otherwise empty titles gave him the cachet to marry his daughter Margaret to King Henry VI of England and France, reuniting the Plantagenet and Angevin lines. Margaret's forceful character and struggles in the Wars of the Roses are well documented both in fiction and fact, and form a powerful narrative in 15th-century English history. Her ultimately tragic end forms part of the final failure of the Plantagenets and Angevins in their royal ambitions.

Although René's descendants through his daughter Yolande of Bar did endure as French nobility, the death of his sons meant that his possessions were taken by the French crown. At the same time, the overthrow of the Plantagenets by the Tudors in England meant that all the Angevin lines had failed as independent political entities, bringing their extraordinary story to a close.

CHAPTER 1 – THE ORIGINS OF ANJOU

The city that became Angers had its origins in the important Roman city of Juliomagus in the province of Gaul, roughly modern France. The inhabitants of the area had been called the Andegavensi, and this older name superseded Juliomagus to give the city and the territory along the lower course of the river Loire the names they keep today, Angers and Anjou.[1] The Roman legacy underpins everything in medieval Europe, since the European provinces of Rome retained a linguistic and cultural affinity that endured throughout the medieval period and beyond. The history we will be examining springs from Roman cities such as Angers, Tours, Poitiers and Le Mans, which retained many characteristics from their Roman origin, and which do not have parallels in England. It was a more organized, urban society than England that produced the Angevins.[2]

In the tumult after the collapse of the Roman Empire and the migration of new peoples to every corner of Europe, Roman institutions and terminology endured as the only way to articulate concepts of government and authority. The Latin words for the Emperor's deputies such as *dux*, *comites* and *vicecomes* stayed in use and became 'duke', 'count' and 'viscount', though with different meanings in a post-imperial age. When in the 8th century a Germanic ruler was successful enough to unite France, Germany and Italy into a very loose but nevertheless real polity, inevitably the conceptual framework and language used to describe him derived from the Roman Empire. This was true in the most literal way when on Christmas Day 800 the king of the Franks and conqueror of the Lombards, Visigoths, Magyars and Huns, known in his own lifetime as 'Charles the Great', was crowned in Rome by the pope as the new Roman Emperor. We know him by the Latinized form 'Charlemagne' and call his empire the 'Holy Roman Empire' to distinguish it from the classical Roman Empire. Charlemagne was able to pass his empire intact to his son Louis the Pious, but by the next generation it had splintered into three pieces, and it is here that we must look for the earliest history of Anjou.

The political system that emerged from the 9th century was focused on the office of the 'count'. This had a particular definition in the kingdom of the Franks, which included Anjou and would become France. The count held an 'honour' – a word still used at the end of the 11th century by the contemporary Angevin count, Fulk Réchin, to describe his inheritance – which was a portion of land providing him with revenues through tolls and taxes to perform his many duties, including defending his county, administering justice to those who lived there and responding to the *ban* or general military summons of the king if he was needed. He swore an oath of loyalty to the king, and despite all the vicissitudes of the French monarchy over the centuries, this idea that the French king had authority over all the lands in what we think of as France, even when they were ruled by another king, never faded away entirely.

In the 9th century, kings still attempted to maintain a centralized authority and the counts were visited by royal inspectors, but this broke down by the end of the century. More importantly, possession of an honour, which had been considered a personal grant by the king, was by the end of the century hereditary, and the great provincial dynasties rose from these honours. The king did seek to exercise some control by granting immunities to comital authority to various bishops and abbeys, and regional counts did still attend the king's court, but for most purposes the counts were independent.[3]

The period from the death of Charlemagne (in 814) until the 11th century was a time of warring states in which territories nominally subordinate to the king or emperor struggled constantly to defend their borders, increase their territory and resist attempts to enforce any kind of suzerainty over them. In this period, there was no king of 'France', only a 'king of the Franks' who directly ruled a tiny area, and political units such as Flanders, Normandy, Brittany, Maine, Anjou, Blois, Champagne, Aquitaine, Toulouse, Provence and Burgundy were of almost equal importance. The history of this period reads as an endless succession of raids, sieges and the occasional battle interspersed with peace treaties and, more importantly, marriage alliances.

This period was formerly known as the 'Dark Ages', a term coined in the 14th century by Francesco Petrarch to compare the enlightened age in which he lived with the primitive period between the fall of Rome and his own time (we shall meet Petrarch again when his ideas about Angevin Naples were expressed in similarly vivid terms). Although we have limited information about what was happening in this period, it did see several important technological developments that would have a profound effect on European history. These included agricultural innovations such as the horse collar, which allowed the use of heavier ploughs to turn the heavy soil of regions like northern France and bring more land under cultivation. This supported a larger population with greater prosperity, and contributed to the formation of population centres for the tiny minority of elites to fight over, in turn promoting more centralized government.[4]

There were also military innovations in this period that had significant social consequences for our story. In the 9th century, local rulers covered northern France with small fortified wooden or stone houses, and the 'castellans' who controlled them used these castles as bases to dominate the surrounding territory.[5] For centuries to follow, castles assumed a dominant position in warfare that was not lost until the 16th century. The castle is the iconic building of the Middle Ages, more so even than the cathedral, and medieval warfare consisted largely of campaigns to take castles and pillaging raids around them.

These technological innovations were matched by a corresponding social innovation with an equally profound legacy: the feudal system. At its most basic, feudalism began as a means by which a leader gave land to a follower in return for military service. This began in the lawless period of Viking invasions when local leaders were given land to finance the defence of their territory. The fact that they now built castles, which needed to be manned and defended, gradually led to the existence of a military class whose primary role was to fight, and thus began a fully realized social structure that provided the framework for medieval Europe until the 15th century.

Perhaps the most important fact about feudalism, and one that may not be readily apparent, is that it was always a reciprocal obligation: the lord had obligations to his vassal as well as the other way round. We may want to assume that one person performing homage to another and becoming a vassal always indicated a subordinate role and by implication a dependent position, but the true situation allowed more ambiguity. For example, a lord's acceptance of his vassal's homage for a fief also indicated his acceptance of the vassal's rights to the fief, and precluded his interfering with its governance except in specific circumstances. Almost all the land that makes up modern France was nominally held from the French king, but the unruly counts of Blois, Anjou, and Flanders, not to mention the more powerful dukes of Normandy, Aquitaine and Brittany, basically ruled their lands as independent territories. They were perfectly willing to involve the king in their constant struggles with each other if they felt it gave an advantage, but they seldom did his bidding in any way and the king could only intervene through military force. These subtleties of feudal law would become decisive in 200 years when the Angevins' complicated feudal relationships shaped the destiny of their empire.

The final technological development to concern us was the technique of a horseman delivering a charge with a fixed lance, exponentially increasing the force of the blow. The programme of training required to learn this technique, with its concomitant developments in horse breeding and military hardware, led to an entirely new kind of warrior, the knight. The technique of charging with a couched lance had a spectacular beginning in the 11th century when the Normans used this innovation to achieve their amazing success in England, Italy and the Holy Land. Its effectiveness was recognized at the time. Anna Comnena, daughter of the Byzantine Emperor Alexius Comnenus (who was first bested by the Normans only to become their uneasy ally on the First Crusade), wrote in her history of Alexius's reign that the force of a Norman cavalry charge could 'make a hole in the walls of Babylon' (although this is often quoted, usually the rest of the sentence is omitted: 'For a Frank on horseback is invincible, and would even make a hole in the walls of Babylon, but directly he gets off his horse, anyone who likes can make sport of him').[6]

Old ethnic divisions remained from the time of the barbarian invasions after the fall of the Roman Empire, and Brittany, Aquitaine and Burgundy retained a distinct cultural identity, as did the two 'Frankish' kingdoms of Austrasia and Neustria. The term

France (*Francia*) was in use by the 10th century, usually to mean the land between the Loire and Lorraine (then known as Lotharingia, the German portion of Charlemagne's former empire), or sometimes in a more restricted sense to mean the land between the Seine and Lorraine, the area actually ruled by the French king until the 13th century.[7] Yet the seeds of what we think of as France were already planted, since despite a lack of ethnic identity some sense of political cohesion remained from the wreckage of Charlemagne's empire. In the 10th and 11th centuries, regional lords recognized that they had political obligations to the king of the Franks, and this would ultimately lead to the unification of almost the entire region into a single entity by the end of the 15th century.

In the charters of the mid-10th century the king was initially called simply *rex*, but by the end of the century he took the title *rex Francorum* or king of the Franks. This change exhibits the tension between two ideas: on the one hand, the king acknowledged that he only ruled the lands of the Franks (between the Loire and Lotharingia), but on the other, and more importantly, that he did in fact rule all the Franks.[8] There would be no king of 'France' until 1254, when the concept arose that the king ruled an abstract political entity rather than a people.[9]

Thus in the 9th century the two great powers of Western Europe were the Emperor and the king of the Franks, a situation that continued until the 11th century when the Norman kings of England became a third great power. The Normans had their origins in the Viking raids, one of the great migrations of peoples that characterized the end of the Roman Empire and the early Middle Ages. Beginning in the 9th century, the Vikings devastated the British Isles and large portions of northern France, and ultimately founded an independent kingdom in England, a substantial colony in Ireland, and most importantly for our purposes, a permanent settlement in France. They gave their name, 'Northmen' or 'Normans', to the land where they settled, Normandy. Their annexation of this territory was formally recognized by the king of the Franks in 911, and their leader given the title of duke. With such an aggressive new enemy permanently established nearby, the count responsible for the vast area around Angers, Tours and Blois could no longer spare any attention for his lands bordering Brittany and delegated his authority to vice-counts or 'viscounts'. This is the origin of the dynasties of Blois and Anjou.

Although we do know something about this early period from ecclesiastical records, charters and a few chronicles, only in the 11th and 12th centuries did anyone attempt to write a history of the region. With the benefit of hindsight, these historians could focus on the regions and figures that would become important and add an extra dash of legend, prophecy and moralizing to highlight key figures. Unsurprisingly, the Angevins, who achieved two crowns in the 12th century, attracted chroniclers eager to show the origins of this great family. What distinguishes the Angevins is the variety of their intriguing ancestors, who inspired richly inventive stories.

Jean of Marmoutier's *Chronica de Gestis Consulum Andegavorum (Chronicle of the*

Deeds of the Counts of Anjou) gives us a very detailed and frequently imaginary account of the early Angevins.[10] Chroniclers at the monastery of Marmoutier had recorded genealogies and short biographies of the Angevin counts over the centuries, and we know the names of Abbot Odo and Fulk V's chaplain, Thomas of Loches, as early authors, but it was the monk Jean who gathered all the previous material and created a new version between 1164 and 1173. It is not coincidental that someone should choose these years, the height of Henry II's power as king of England and ruler of an empire that stretched from Scotland to the Pyrenees, to produce a flattering account of Henry's ancestors, so in addition to the caution that should be applied to trusting an author writing a century or more after the events he describes, we must also consider Jean's natural wish to please the most powerful ruler in Europe. Jean completed his work by producing an even more glowing biography of Henry's father Geoffrey Plantagenet, which we will return to below.

In the 12th century, no less than at the time of Charlemagne, an upstart family in possession of political power must be in want of a pedigree, and this pedigree must inevitably come from Rome. The *Deeds of the Counts of Anjou* (or the *Gesta*, as it is usually known) created an ancestor for them, a forester called Tortulf, though immediately the chronicler takes pains to explain that his name was actually Torquatius as he was descended from a Roman family, and he was called Tortulfus by the Bretons, who were ignorant of the proper use of the old Roman name. He tells us that Tortulf was appointed forester by Charles the Bald, Charlemagne's grandson and the last effective ruler of Francia in the 9th century, in the same year he expelled the Normans from Anjou and from his whole realm. Indeed, throughout the early sections of the *Gesta* the principal enemies haunting the borders of the French king are the Normans.

Jean is correct here, because the Normans, terrifying pagan invaders who caused untold devastation, were the principal enemy of the Frankish lands throughout the 9th century. Yet we must not forget that the *Gesta* was written in the mid-12th century when these same Normans, now Christians, had conquered England with the pope's blessing and established a powerful monarchy that the Angevins had taken through inheritance and battle. These references to the early Norman pillagers can be read in two ways. Certainly the Normans and Angevins had no love for each other: the Normans were the greatest Angevin enemy, even more so than the Bretons or the Blésois (the rulers of Blois), and the Normans were the only enemy the Angevins didn't defeat outright. It would not be surprising if an Angevin chronicler chose to emphasize the unsavoury past of the Normans. Yet Henry II was the son of an Angevin father and a Norman mother, as his mother Matilda was daughter of Henry I and granddaughter of William the Conqueror. Henry II completely assimilated the Norman identity when he took the English throne, a sensible decision since the realm he ruled was emphatically Anglo-Norman, and Anjou formed only a small part of his domains.

This then gives us another reading of the *Gesta*: the wild savagery and invincibility attributed to the Normans is a compliment to Henry II's descent and the strength of the people he ruled. There might have been more need to flatter the Normans at this time than any other, when we consider that Normandy had been conquered by Geoffrey Plantagenet and the Anglo-Norman kingdom had fallen to the Angevins. Normandy's independent history was nearly finished, and by the 13th-century chroniclers found it necessary to make excuses for the Normans' lack of military ability.

The intertwining of Angevins and Normans lay several centuries in the future, so let us return to the very beginning of the Angevin line and Tortulf. The chronicler tells us that Tortulf received a grant of land on the border with Brittany, which could be based on fact, since the aggression of the Bretons in the 9th century led to the creation of a defensive military district based on Angers that was assigned to Robert the Strong (ancestor of the Capetian kings, the future allies, then rivals, of the Angevins), and if there was a Tortulf he may have been Robert's vassal.

The *Gesta* names Tortulf's son as Ingelgarius, and here we are on firmer ground since there is evidence that this person did exist. The Angevins themselves, in the form of Fulk Réchin when he chronicled his family in the late 11th century[11], began the Angevin line with Ingelgarius and said he became the first count of the Angevins in the 9th century, though this seems to anticipate matters. We might think this is direct evidence that Tortulf didn't exist, as Fulk Réchin would certainly have known about him, but in fact Fulk stated that he was listing all the previous Angevin counts, not all his ancestors.[12] We know almost nothing about Ingelgarius and what the *Gesta* says seems designed to weave him into the subsequent Angevin story rather than a true account. Yet what the *Gesta* tells us is instructive: he is said to have distinguished himself fighting the Normans when they attacked Tours. Two key themes of later Angevin history thus come into play: the importance of the city of Tours, and rivalry with the Normans. Typically the *Gesta* embellishes the story, and reports that Ingelgarius performed his heroic deeds against the Normans to gain the favour of the widow of the lord of Chateau-Landon, though this seems more an intrusion of 12th-century chivalric romance than anything genuine. Whatever reward Ingelgarius may have received from the widow, the *Gesta* also tells us that his deeds at Tours were rewarded by the archbishop, who allowed Ingelgarius to marry his niece Adelais and granted him the castle of Amboise.

Although historians have tended not to believe a word of what the *Gesta* says on this subject, the stories are quite important since they delineate from the beginning what will be the most important Angevin concerns for centuries. From the earliest times the Angevins were defined by their territorial expansion. Ingelgarius was given the eastern half of Anjou by the Bishop of Angers and charged with protecting it from the Normans, but he began to look elsewhere. In fact, it is remarkable how seldom Angers appears in the early stories, and this is telling because it shows just how secure the counts were in their capital. Although the old Roman citadel of Angers was the source of the early Angevins' authority, and it was the strength of this base that helps account for their increasing power elsewhere from 920–960[13], we only hear about it when something of significance – which is almost always to say something bad – happens, and that is only rarely. This allowed the counts to turn their attention elsewhere.

This was particularly marked by their desire to acquire Tours. Tours was the metropolis of central France and the site of the shrine of St Martin – the Roman soldier from Pannonia (modern Hungary) who was the founder saint of French Christianity – as well as the seat of Gregory of Tours who wrote the first history of the Franks. Tours was also a vital trading centre and should have become a focus for regional power, which in fact it did, but not for its own region: the religious prestige and financial importance of St Martin's city were harnessed first by the counts of Blois and then the counts of Anjou. Angers too was a prosperous and important city, but Tours was the key to the region, and it was the domination of Tours that gave the Angevin counts the edge in their struggles with their adversaries.

Fulk the Red: the First Angevin Count

These hazy speculations about the origins of the Angevins end with Ingelgarius though, because with his son Fulk the Red the Angevins burst into the verifiable historical record, and in what would become their characteristic name and colour (red hair being a mark of the Angevins for centuries). Fulk the Red appears as a signatory to a charter of 886, and by 898 he was named in another charter as the vicomte of Anjou, though he may not have received the title until a decade or two later. He also refers to himself as the 'son of Ingelgarius', verifying his father's name. By 920 or 930 he styled himself Fulk Count of the Angevins, and is thus indisputably the first Angevin count.[14]

Calling Fulk 'Count of Anjou' would be anachronistic: only in the reign of Geoffrey Martel (1040–1060) do we see that title.[15] As noted above, there was no King of England, only a king of the English, and the same for the King of the Franks (they weren't even 'French' at this point), the Duke of the Normans and the Count of the Angevins. There was a concept of places called 'Francia', 'England' and 'Normandy', but not until later was the ruler seen to rule the land, rather than the people who lived in it. This idea seems to have started from the bottom up, and there were counts of Anjou and dukes of Normandy in the 11th century, but only in the 13th century do we see the shift in perception that the kings of England and France ruled an intangible but real country, rather than being the leader of a particular people. This has enormous philosophical implications as it creates the idea of a country that must be defended and which has borders that become defined, rather than the more flexible of idea of territory that we see in the 11th century.

Fulk the Red was the lay abbot of St Aubin in Angers and treasurer of the abbey of St Martin of Tours, providing a religious and financial dimension to his authority that was a key part of the Angevins' rise from viscount to count. Fulk formalized the

Angevin domination of Tours by adding the title Viscount of Tours to his religious position in St Martin's church no later than 898, which meant he took military responsibility for defending the city.[16] In accepted practice, Fulk also used the revenue of St Martin of Tours to reward his supporters and extend his power.

Compared to Tortulf or Ingelgarius we are in a different realm with Fulk the Red, and although we know little enough about him, what is important is that Fulk's identity is verified in written charters. As well as confirming Ingelgarius's name he tells us the name of his wife, Roscilla, and his sons Guy, Ingelgarius and Fulk 'the Good', who became the next count of the Angevins. Continuing the chain of associations that began with Ingelgarius and the castle of Amboise, the *Gesta* tells us that Fulk the Red obtained castles as his wife's dowry, most notably the castle of Loches. Although rebuilt by Fulk the Red's great-grandson around 1000, this is still one of the oldest castles in Europe, retaining parts of its 11th-century form even now, and one which will become indelibly associated with the Angevins. This association of the Angevins with castles will become one of their hallmarks, and in another century the Angevins would transform castles into the lynchpin of medieval warfare.

The mere existence of written charters involving Fulk the Red is instructive. The Angevin counts, like others in the 10th century, were beginning to arrogate powers to themselves that once had been claimed only by kings. They issued these charters using the monks of St Aubin in Angers as scribes, and the language in these charters is informative as well, as the counts refer to *their* rights and *their* treasury, demonstrating that they no longer believe these things are in any way held from the king, though they still owe him allegiance.[17] However, despite these connections with important ecclesiastical and civic authorities, the Angevins in the 10th century were overshadowed by their rivals in Normandy and Blois until the time of Fulk the Red's son, Fulk the Good.

Fulk the Good: 'an illiterate king is a crowned ass'

Given the later sinister and overtly diabolical qualities that were ascribed to the Angevins, it may seem surprising that the saintly Fulk the Good (941–960) appears among their ancestors, though a cynic would point out that 12th-century chroniclers attempting to compensate for the reputation of contemporary Angevins shrewdly invented him. Fulk was said to have dressed as a cleric and preferred sitting with the canons at Tours to presiding over his court. His devotion to quiet study and reading attracted the derision of King Louis IV, who mocked him, but Fulk responded tartly with the first memorable Angevin quote, 'An illiterate king is a crowned ass.'[18]

Although most of the stories about Fulk the Good come from a version of the *Gesta* prepared 200 years after the event by Geoffrey Plantagenet's chaplain Breton d'Amboise, who copied them from the *Miracles of St Martin of Tours*, the quote was certainly well known to contemporaries and firmly associated with the Angevins. William of Malmesbury, writing before 1129, reports that the youthful King Henry I of England, who was said to be the best educated of his family, frequently cited it to his father William the Conqueror[19] (with what consequences one can only imagine – perhaps it isn't a coincidence that Henry received no territory when his father died).

This quote also highlights a tension that remained throughout the Middle Ages, about what made a good ruler. Was it appropriate for a king (or count) to devote himself to study and sit in a cloister like a monk? Wasn't a king supposed to be a warrior and defend his people? This would frequently be the reason that women were excluded from the throne, as it was believed they couldn't lead armies, and if a king were more interested in books than battle, what use was he? The best example of this tension came 400 years later in relation to the Angevin King Robert the Wise of Naples, a direct descendant of Fulk the Good. Robert produced a vast quantity of sermons and two theological treatises, had the most impressive royal library in Europe and was chosen by the poet Petrarch to examine him publicly to ensure he warranted being crowned as the first poet laureate since Roman times. Critics, including most harshly Dante, mocked Robert for his learning and piety. The situation was almost too neatly summed up, since Robert's elder brother Louis had renounced the throne to become a Franciscan (and was later canonized), whereas Robert became king but chose to give sermons. As Dante said, 'But you wrench to a religious order him born to gird a sword' and 'You make a king of one that is fit for sermons'.[20]

For Fulk the Good, as with Robert, the only thing that matters is how successful a ruler he was, and Fulk was successful in forming an alliance with Theobald of Blois against Brittany. This reversal of traditional Angevin enmity towards Blois gave Fulk a free hand to dominate the important city of Nantes, where he ruthlessly eliminated his rivals in a fashion seemingly at odds with his saintly persona.

So how then did the legend of Fulk 'the Good' arise? We don't know if Fulk really did wear a clerical habit and sit with the canons of the cathedral, and he may or may not have felt that an illiterate king was a crowned ass, but one modern historian of the Angevins believes that what defined Fulk was his resolution of the Angevins' historical strife with Blois. This was sufficient to seal Fulk's reputation as a peacemaker and earn him the sobriquet of 'the Good', and Jean of Marmoutier exercised his creative talents to provide anecdotes emphasizing this quality. Another factor may have been Fulk's progeny, since his second son Guy became bishop of Le Puy in 975 (though only through military intervention), and Drogo, his youngest and favourite son, was highly educated in the liberal arts and succeeded his brother as bishop, perhaps retrospectively bestowing a reputation for saintliness and learning on his father. This reputation – for learning at least, though the saintliness swiftly disappeared – would remain with the Angevins throughout the 12th century. Yet in one of his charters Fulk's son mentioned Fulk's 'bitter and fearful deeds', so we shouldn't accept the legend of the saintly cleric uncritically.[21]

Geoffrey Greymantle: from Myth to Reality

Despite the documentary evidence and legendary material for Fulk the Red and Fulk the Good, it was Fulk the Good's son Geoffrey Greymantle who became the first iconic member of the Angevin dynasty. Geoffrey succeeded as count in 960 and passed into legend as a mighty warrior and mainstay of the first Capetian king in France, Hugh Capet. Geoffrey's relationship with Hugh Capet and participation in the larger affairs of the kingdom are documented, and this connection resonated down the centuries so that Geoffrey became the most important mythic forebear of the Angevins, and every tale whether true or imagined from the Angevin past was attributed to him.[22]

However, in the *Gesta* the deeds ascribed to Geoffrey seem almost wholly fantastical and quite distinct from the facts that are known about him. Take the story of how Geoffrey Greymantle got his name. Jean of Marmoutier relates that the Danes invaded Flanders shortly after Geoffrey's succession as count and laid waste all of northern France, before turning towards Paris. Hugh Capet summoned his nobles to assist him, but before they could arrive the Danish champion, Ethelulf, a giant described as a 'new Goliath', arrived at the gates of Paris and challenged the French to send a champion to fight him. Ethelulf defeated and killed every French warrior sent out to meet him, and Hugh forbade anyone else to face the giant. Geoffrey Greymantle was already en route to Paris to respond to the king's summons when he heard of Ethelulf's challenge. Travelling in secret, Geoffrey crossed the Seine and met Ethelulf in combat; after throwing the giant from his horse with his lance, Geoffrey took his sword and like a 'second David' to Ethelulf's 'new Goliath' beheaded the Dane and gave his head to a miller to take to Paris.

The miller duly delivered the trophy to Hugh Capet and told the king that although he did not know the identity of the giant-slayer, he would recognize him again if he saw him. When all the nobles convened in Paris for the king's court, the miller recognized Geoffrey immediately, and seizing his tunic of coarse grey cloth told the king that the man in the 'grey mantle' was their saviour. Whereupon Hugh Capet decreed that he should henceforth be known as Geoffrey 'Greymantle'.[23] The chronicler's highlighting of Geoffrey's coarse, poor clothing portrays the Angevin counts as plain, old-fashioned warriors in the best Roman fashion.

The *Gesta* then describes Geoffrey's other military adventures on behalf of the king, and states that he was the king's standard bearer. Here there is an interesting conflation between two distinct fictional traditions. In the *Song of Roland*, which was written down around 1100 although it drew on earlier oral tradition, Charlemagne's standard bearer is stated to be Geoffrey of Anjou. This is patently anachronistic since no source names a count of Anjou in the time of Charlemagne, and certainly not one named Geoffrey. The Geoffrey of Anjou in the *Song of Roland* is clearly meant to be Geoffrey Greymantle, despite the epic being set two centuries before Geoffrey lived. Was this because Geoffrey Greymantle was Hugh Capet's standard bearer, and so this epic describing Charlemagne's court drew on contemporary personalities and offices? Or was Geoffrey Greymantle said by Jean of Marmoutier to be Hugh Capet's standard bearer precisely because a Geoffrey of Anjou is reported to have fulfilled that role in the *Song of Roland*? This beautifully illustrates the interplay of fact and fiction that informs early medieval sources.

The *Gesta's* other tales are a repetitive cycle of battles in which Geoffrey is victorious in single combat against various enemies, mixed with the usual pious stories that clerics loved, such as the fact that Geoffrey obtained a piece of the girdle of the Virgin Mary and placed it in the church at Loches. The *Gesta* is also heavily influenced by classical sources, most importantly Sallust. As a partisan of Julius Caesar, Sallust emphasized the importance of new ways of thinking and governing, and how old institutions and rulers could be moribund. This provided a perfect theme for the *Gesta,* which wanted to show how a dynamic new dynasty of rulers deserved their position because of their noble deeds, rather than a long pedigree. This seems to be the reason for ascribing so many adventures to Geoffrey Greymantle, but there is no evidence for any of them being true. Certainly Fulk Réchin, Geoffrey's great-grandson who lived less than 100 years after Geoffrey's death, had very little to say about him in his history of his ancestors.[24]

But what were his tangible accomplishments? Geoffrey's activities seem very similar to his father's; he was victorious in struggles with the counts of Rennes and imposed his will on Nantes, and he also struggled with William Duke of Aquitaine, eventually acquiring the castle of Loudon, which he held as a fief of the duke. This is an example of the ambiguity of the feudal system, since Geoffrey performed homage to William for Loudon, which might be interpreted as an indication that Geoffrey was in an inferior position. Indeed, the contemporary Aquitainian historian Adémar of Chabannes reports that William had defeated Geoffrey and forced him to perform homage. We should think about what this means: Loudon had always belonged to the Dukes of Aquitaine, but now it belonged to Geoffrey Greymantle. Geoffrey's homage to William acknowledged that he held the castle in return for certain services to William, but it also confirmed his hereditary possession of it. This sounds much more like Angevin expansion than a defeat. Geoffrey's son Fulk Nerra in turn inherited Loudon and proceeded to annex further Aquitainian territory, namely the Gâtinais and Saintonge, also performing homage to the Duke of Aquitaine for these lands, but it is useful to compare the obligations Fulk owed with the obligations of the Duke's other vassals. One, Hugh of Lusignan, was required to go on expeditions with his overlord and ask his permission to marry. Fulk did none of this.[25]

We are still in a very murky period historically, yet we can see how Anjou was growing town by town and castle by castle. Most tangibly of all, Geoffrey probably began the first stone donjon at Loches, stamping Angevin power on the southern border of Touraine. Loches is quite far from Angers and is a demonstration of how wide-ranging Angevin ambitions remained.

Fulk Nerra: the Embodiment of His Age

Geoffrey died in 987 during the siege of Marçon, and the process by which, slowly but surely, the Angevin rulers have emerged from obscurity climaxes with Geoffrey's son Fulk Nerra, of whom we have a reasonably well-documented life. As Sir Richard Southern remarked in his *Making of the Middle Ages*, 'by 987 the family was ready to emerge from its legendary and epic age onto the stage of history.'[26] This is not to say Fulk isn't also the subject of fanciful stories, but the events of his long reign can be outlined with some certainty, even if we can't fill in the details. This is a somewhat tepid introduction to one of the towering figures of the Middle Ages, a man not so much wreathed in legend as a man who was a legend.

Fulk's name is one of the most obscure things about him, as he wasn't dubbed Fulk 'Nerra' until the 12th century and no one is quite sure why. In his lifetime Fulk was always called Fulk 'the Pilgrim' or Fulk 'the Jerusalemite' in reference to his pilgrimages to Jerusalem. The new title was adopted by 12th-century chroniclers when it became necessary to distinguish Fulk from his great-grandson Fulk V, who not only went to Jerusalem but also became its king, but no explanation is given for what the word means. 'Nerra' is now always accepted to be some variation of the Latin *nero* or *niger* (that is, 'black'), and in English Fulk is often called 'Fulk the Black'. Yet even if we accept that it means 'black', Nerra seems to be a feminine form.[27]

I wonder if this might not give us a clue to the term's origin. In Occitan, which in Fulk's time was spoken in Poitou up to the borders of Anjou, an area in which Fulk was expanding his power and may have caused considerable fear, the word for black is *negra*. Moreover, in Occitan – uniquely among Romance languages – 'o' is the feminine ending instead of 'a', which may have caused some confusion over the correct form to use, and suggests that we seek the meaning of 'Nerra' in Occitan rather than Latin. Whatever the origin of the word Nerra, modern historians assume that Fulk was called 'the Black' because he was so terrifying: he was ferocious in battle, terrible in his anger and committed horrifying acts of violence. Of course, even if Nerra is a form of 'black', the name could just have easily arisen because Fulk had dark colouring rather than red hair like his ancestors, though this seems unlikely since the name only came about long after Fulk's death.

Kate Norgate, the great 19th-century English historian of the Angevins, adopted a more poetic phraseology and called Fulk the 'Black Falcon'. Pleasing as that designation is, it seems to me a liberty to equate Fulk's name in Latin, *Fulco*, with *falco* or falcon, especially when the French spelling of Fulk's name, *Foulque* is actually cognate with the name of another bird. This is the *foulque macroule* or coot, but calling a figure of Fulk's significance, particularly one so bellicose, the 'Black Coot' is simply unthinkable!

Yet there is a 12th-century precedent for Norgate's choice. Fulk V, who by marrying Queen Melisende became King of Jerusalem and caused Fulk Nerra to receive his new name, may well have been called the 'Falcon', or possibly the 'Coot'. Melisende's sumptuous psalter is in the British Library, and in addition to having a note with the date of her husband's death in the manuscript, on the beautiful Byzantine ivory panels that bind the psalter the word *herodias* is carved like a title above an engraved falcon. In Latin the word for coot is usually *fulica*, but *herodias* is also sometimes used to mean coot – as well as for heron, stork, owl or gyrfalcon. The psalter is believed to have been a gift from Fulk to Melisende after a period of turmoil in their relationship, and given the proud position of the word herodias on the back cover, as well as the image of a falcon, it is much more likely that Fulk was known as the 'falcon' than the 'coot'.

To return to Fulk Nerra, he is always cited as the epitome of the violent, unrestrained medieval character – furious in war, uninhibited in repentance, liable to excesses of violence followed by equal extremes of piety. Perhaps these traits are an accurate representation of Fulk, yet this is just as illuminating about historiography in the modern world as in the medieval. Historians in the 19th century particularly liked to amplify tales of Fulk's violence, especially in a highly influential history of the Crusades by Michaud that features an engraving by Gustave Doré showing Fulk haunted by the spirits of those he has slain, prompting his pilgrimages to Jerusalem. Fulk's terrible reputation became fixed in the 19th century, and now some modern historians casually refer to him as 'terrifying' without any enquiry into what lies behind this.

So what did Fulk Nerra do that made him so terrible and respected? Through his military efforts he elevated Anjou from a lesser county into the first rank of northern French powers, and he began at a very early age. Indeed, in keeping with the medieval love of Roman associations, Fulk would definitely seem to warrant the tag of *adulescens carnifex* (teenage butcher) given to Pompey the Great. Fulk won a great victory against Conan Count of Rennes at Conquereuil in 992 when he was little more than a teenager, and in an age when pitched battles were uncommon occurrences, such a victory enhanced his reputation forever. This is despite the fact that the course of the battle did not flatter his grasp of strategy – the Angevin cavalry fell into a trap, blundering into a concealed ditch filled with spikes, and nearly lost the battle, though they rallied finally to kill the Breton count and inflict great slaughter on their enemies.[28]

Despite this victory over the Bretons, and after Fulk the Good's focus on Brittany and Geoffrey Greymantle's dalliance with Aquitaine, Fulk turned his attention firmly back towards Tours, where he also gained renown for the defeat of the traditional Angevin enemy, the Count of Blois, at the battle of Pontlevoy in 1016. Again, the performance of the Angevins was not entirely convincing: they were completely overwhelmed by their enemies (Fulk himself was wounded and fled) and lost the battle, but in the aftermath when the Blésois had dispersed to pillage the dead, Fulk's allies from Maine led by Count Herbert Wake-the-Dog appeared and utterly routed the Blésois.[29] Yet the circumstances were of little importance to Fulk's reputation when the facts were so stark, as Anjou's enemies to the west and east had been comprehensively defeated in the bloodiest fashion.

Fulk then seized Saumur and later, in what seems to us an act of base ingratitude, he imprisoned his old ally Hebert Wake-the-Dog for two years in the castle of Saintes and demanded his homage for Maine.[30] This was the opposite of Geoffrey Greymantle's homage for Loudon: Geoffrey performed homage for a territory he had seized, confirming that it was his in perpetuity, whereas Herbert was now forced to pay homage to another ruler for a county previously free of obligations. William of Malmesbury said that this betrayal of Count Herbert was the sole stain on Fulk's reputation – a view not taken by any other modern or contemporary historian, who delight in elaborating Fulk's numerous crimes – though as a chronicler of the Normans writing nearly a century after Fulk's death, William had never experienced the full fury of Fulk's aggression. The chronicler of St Florent of Saumur took a different view, saying that Fulk and his son Geoffrey were only just inferior to wild beasts in strength, ferocity and cunning.

Regardless, Fulk's deeds laid the foundation for future Angevin expansion in every direction. The most important component was the final Angevin domination of Tours. This was by no means inevitable, because after Hugh Capet's death the new French king Robert II married Bertha of Blois and inclined to the Blésois, meaning Fulk lost the staunchest ally his father had possessed.[31] Though Fulk himself did not live to absorb Tours into the Angevin domains, he completed all the groundwork and his son finished the task. Fulk's battles played their part, but he achieved this most strikingly through a transformation of medieval warfare that had consequences for centuries: the use of castles for aggression rather than defence.

The use of forward bases was not unknown before Fulk, but Fulk is the identifiable figure who turned the defensive stone fortification into a potent weapon against his enemies. Like all brilliant ideas this seems simple: instead of using castles only for defence, Fulk planted them at points he wished to attack, instantly staking his claim and putting enormous pressure on his opponents. Fulk built Langeais (the earliest known stone donjon in the region, which can still be seen[32]) twenty kilometres from Tours in 994–5, Montrichard in 1005 to threaten the lord of Saumur's castle at Pontlevoy and Montboyau a few kilometres from Tours in 1017, amongst many others.

It can be difficult to appreciate how innovative Fulk's strategy was. Castles had sprung up in the 9th century during the Viking invasions when Charles the Bald struggled to defend his kingdom, and churches built with stone taken from the old Roman fortifications were dismantled in their turn to build new fortresses. The existence of so many castles meant that besieging and taking castles had become a vital component of warfare and territorial control. Yet Fulk made the mental leap that if a castle controlled territory around it, why not also build castles on land you wished to control, rather than only on land you already controlled? Fulk's descendant Richard the Lionheart did something similar when he built Chateau Gaillard, his 'saucy castle', which was so close to Paris that it has been compared to a fist thrust in the face of the French king. Fulk's castle-building activity sealed his reputation as a military genius at an early date: a contemporary called him *elegantissimus bellicus rebus* (most adroit in military matters[33]), and when his descendant Fulk Réchin wrote the history of the Angevins around fifty years later, he included a list of the castles Fulk Nerra built as part of his accomplishments. What was most striking to contemporaries was that these castles were built as part of a coherent policy, and Fulk's flurry of castles set the stage for the moment when Anjou would be in a strong enough position to annex Tours.

The early medieval period is filled with other violent warriors and greedy land-owners, but we have illustrations of another side of Fulk's character: Fulk participated in the unrestrained religiosity of the early Middle Ages. This can seem discordant to the modern reader, but particularly around the millennial year 1000, whatever unsavoury activities a person undertook, a fervent religious devotion was also the norm rather than the exception. Fulk established monasteries and gave his patronage to churches in a conventional medieval fashion, but there is also abundant evidence that he was truly pious when it suited him. His pilgrimages to Jerusalem are the great case in point, as he travelled to the Holy Land at least three times and possibly four. The fact that these pilgrimages were probably motivated – as Doré's illustration shows us – by his awareness of the horrible crimes he had committed would not have seemed incongruous to Fulk or his contemporaries.

Fulk's religious exploits also show that in the early 11th century saints were still viewed as inhabiting their shrines personally and being quite particular about how they were treated. When Fulk took Saumur in 1026, he pillaged and burnt everything in the town, not sparing the church of St Florent. He then immediately promised to build the saint a much better church in Angers, and had the saint's bones put in a boat to be transported. At the point on the river where the boat would have entered Angevin territory it stuck fast and refused to move further, and the monks explained that the saint would not leave his own land. Fulk then built a new church at the spot thus chosen by St Florent, though he decried the ignorance of the saint who refused to be taken to more comfortable surroundings in Angers.[34]

This kind of casual blasphemy is also part and parcel of medieval religiosity, and indeed Fulk's favourite oath gives us a precious example of his direct speech and shows how he was characterized: the *Gesta* begins his biography by saying, 'Fulk Nerra, who customarily swore "by God's souls"', which seems to relate to a mistaken understanding of the Trinity.[35] Yet although Fulk's charters are peppered with references to his fear of hell and his repentance for his terrible temper, the 12th-century Angevin sources preferred to compare him to Roman models and remove inconvenient or embarrassing attributes.[36]

Suppressing any of the stories about Fulk would be a mistake, since they are wonderful. On his first pilgrimage to Jerusalem in c1002, Fulk received a less than hospitable reception from its Muslim custodians, who demanded a large sum from anyone who wished to enter the city, which meant that numerous impoverished Christians were stranded outside the gates unable to complete their journey. We should note that at this time relations between Christians and Muslims were not especially bad: from 1004–1014 there would be a full-blown persecution of Christians under the Fatimid caliph al-Hakim, who ordered the destruction of the church of the Holy Sepulchre in 1009. The pendulum swung back in 1016 when al-Hakim proclaimed his divinity and substituted his own name for that of Allah in prayers, to the utter horror of his Muslim subjects; he became so estranged from other Muslims that he began to heap privileges on Jews and Christians instead. The drama ended when al-Hakim vanished in 1021, most likely murdered by his sister, though the sect of the Druzes believes he will return.[37] Fulk's first pilgrimage came before these difficulties, and he duly paid the toll for himself and the other pilgrims so all could enter the city.

Next, the custodians forbade the Christians to enter the church of the Holy Sepulchre unless Fulk agreed to urinate on the relic of the True Cross and the tomb where Christ had lain. Despite the outrage this must have caused the Christians, compared with later events this was fairly low-level mischief from the Muslims, who must have scoffed at the idolatry of Christians who revered a piece of wood. Nevertheless, Fulk had the last laugh and bested his tormenters with a stratagem. The *Gesta* records that Fulk agreed to the condition but, 'He obtained a ram's bladder, cleansed it of impurities, filled it with the best white wine and placed it in a convincing place between his thighs. Then, after removing his shoes, he approached the Lord's tomb, poured the wine over it and was thus allowed to enter freely with all his companions.' Not only did Fulk visit the tomb, he participated in a miracle when the stone of the tomb grew soft and allowed him to tear out a piece with his teeth and hide it. In addition to the miraculous piece of stone, Fulk also obtained a relic of the True Cross, and founded the abbey at Beaulieu specifically to hold his relics from the Holy Land.[38]

That Fulk's pilgrimages were genuine acts of repentance is borne out by his actions on his final pilgrimage: William of Malmesbury reports that Fulk ordered one servant to drag him around Jerusalem by a halter while another scourged his bare back and Fulk cried out for God's mercy on a miserable sinner. However, there is no denying that pilgrimages also served a political role. When Fulk travelled to Rome around 1007 he wasn't only visiting the holy sites, he was also petitioning the pope to consecrate the new abbey of Beaulieu that he had built illegally in the territory of Tours.[39]

These were his acts of piety, but why was Fulk considered so terrible? Slaughtering enemies and waging constant warfare were absolutely typical for rulers of this period – and for a long time after – and despite Fulk's undeniable success he doesn't seem the most accomplished warrior of the age. He was one of the most persistent though, and his ceaseless attacks on enemies on all sides as well as his pugnacious castle-building programme do mark him out as a bellicose figure even in a time of perpetual aristo-cratic conflict. Fulk was also implicated in less savoury episodes, as when the king's adviser Hugh de Beauvais was murdered while out hunting in 1008, and the assassins fled straight to Anjou, leaving little doubt who was behind the attack. In this case it was Fulk's treason against the king that was much worse than the murder itself, and such revulsion attended the crime that Fulk quickly sued for peace and performed another pilgrimage to Jerusalem to atone.[40]

Fulk had notably bad relations with his son and heir Geoffrey Martel, and although this is not unusual in hereditary states, he punctuated them with characteristically hyperbolic episodes. Fulk lived to such a great and active age that Geoffrey Martel was an adult fighting his own battles long before his father died, which could not have been an easy situation. Yet Fulk did give Geoffrey responsibilities, in sharp contrast to what would happen a century later, when Geoffrey Plantagenet and the Empress Matilda fell out catastrophically with Henry I over his refusal to delegate any responsibility to them as his recognized heirs, and even worse consequences followed Henry II's refusal to delegate sufficient power to his sons in the late 12th century. Geoffrey was active in skirmishes on the border of Poitou with the Duke of Aquitaine, but this was insufficient for his ambitions. When Fulk was away on pilgrimage in 1035, Geoffrey stirred up a rebellion and the count returned to find the gates of Anjou barred against him. Fulk had little trouble suppressing the rebellion, but the punishment he meted out to Geoffrey was terrible indeed, according to William of Malmesbury: 'Saddled and bridled like a beast of burthen, Geoffrey came crawling to his father's feet. "Conquered art thou — conquered, conquered!" shouted the old count, kicking his prostrate son. "Aye, conquered by thee, for thou art my father; but unconquered by all beside!" The spirited answer touched Fulk's paternal pride, and Geoffrey arose forgiven.'[41]

These stories pale into insignificance, though, compared to an event in Fulk's career that is unique, and tainted his memory forever: he burnt his first wife Elisabeth at the stake in the year 1000. It is said to be this act that prompted Fulk's first pilgrimage to the Holy Land.

Fulk married Elisabeth around the time of his accession, and in the usual fashion the marriage was meant to join the interests of neighbouring landowners, as she was the daughter of the Count of Vendôme. After some years she bore a daughter, Adele, and the chronicles all highlight Fulk's disappointment and need for a son. This was a constant feature of medieval marriage, though Fulk's method of dissolving the marriage was unprecedented among the greater aristocracy. Interestingly, Elisabeth's fate, which would seem to be the most lasting stain on Fulk's reputation and possibly the foundation for the later diabolical legends about the Angevins, has not been highlighted by historians and in most cases has been obscured through further elaboration of the legends. The basis for the story is the *Chronicle of St Florent of Saumur*, which says that Fulk accused Elisabeth of adultery and burnt her at the stake. From this statement later authors have spun ever more fanciful elaborations.

Fulk's best biographer, Louis Halphen, claims the text was copied and elaborated by the monks of St Florent from the initial entry in the chronicle of St Aubin.[42] However, the meaning of the text in the History of St Florent is not clear, and modern historians have taken this ambiguity as licence either to embellish the story considerably or simply ignore it. Everything depends on how the text is translated, so giving any translation creates an interpretation of the story. The text, as translated by Fulk's modern biographer Bernard Bachrach, says:

Fulk, the hot-tempered one, killed his wife Elizabeth at Angers after she had survived an enormous fall. Then Fulk burned with fiery flames the same city which
was defended only by a few men.[43]

Bachrach focuses on the details that Elisabeth was killed 'after a great fall' and that
Angers was 'defended by only a few men', and concocts a story that Elisabeth, detected
in adultery, seized the citadel of Angers with her supporters, leading Fulk to besiege
her, whereupon she fell from the battlements and he then publicly burnt her. He gives
no evidence for this elaborate story beyond the brief text cited above.

Halphen bizarrely consigns the episode to a footnote, saying only that Elisabeth
died in 1000 'in a terrible fire'. In the footnote he says that quickly a legend sprang
up to explain her death, as found in the Chronicle of St Florent of Saumur, which is
that Fulk burnt her.[44] Halphen's low-key approach was at least partially in response to
Fulk's previous 19th-century biographer, M. de Salies, who not only cited the story but
gleefully provided more detail: he says that Fulk publicly accused Elisabeth of adultery,
had her solemnly declared guilty by a judge and then burnt her in Angers. Intriguingly
he also repeats a variant story that Fulk stabbed her and drove her off a precipice, trying
to account for the reference to 'an enormous fall'.[45] Halphen took a dim view of Salies'
work, and perhaps this is why he chose to suppress the story, but it does seem incredible
that even the most partial biographer would omit a story like this whether or not he
believed it to be a rumour.

Kate Norgate believes Fulk killed Elisabeth for her 'real or supposed sins as a wife' by
burning her at the stake, and ties this to the universally grim mood in the years leading
up to the year 1000 when everyone feared the world would end, which 'inflamed his
fierce temper almost to madness'.[46] Norgate too loves to hide stories in footnotes, and
in another place she repeats as a separate story a tale from d'Espinay's *Revue Historique
de l'Anjou* of 1874 that was clearly also derived from this incident, though it is applied
to Fulk's second wife Hildegard. This was that Fulk, seeing a potter working, decided
to try his skill and produced a pot that he proudly took home to show Hildegard. As a
joke, he presented the pot to her and said it came from 'the man she loved best'. Taking
this as an accusation, Hildegard 'vowed to disprove it at once by undergoing the ordeal
of water, and flung herself out of the window and into the river'.[47] The point of the story
is that a convent was established at the place where her body came to land, but it shows
that this stubborn second strand of the tale keeps returning, and there is the persistent
idea that somehow one of Fulk's wives fell from a high place.

The chroniclers all agree that at around the same time Angers was destroyed in a terrible fire, and Salies acknowledges that although we might like to believe Elisabeth died
accidentally, there is no evidence for this, though Halphen accepts it entirely. In the
chronicles in which Fulk was said to have killed Elisabeth, the fire that destroyed Angers
was believed to be divine retribution for Elisabeth's execution. We are frustratingly
unable to decide definitively what happened, yet it is clear that Elisabeth died in 1000

and there is a consensus that it was in a fire. It certainly may be the case that the monks of St Florent wanted to defame Fulk because they resented his high-handed treatment of their monastery, and it may be that Fulk's reputation was already so 'terrible' that everyone was willing to believe he might have killed his wife. Whether true or not, this does seem to be the basis for the terrible reputation of the Angevins that later led them to be characterized as diabolical, the 'Devil's Brood'.

By modern standards this may sound ludicrous, but for an 11th-century figure Fulk is rather well documented and leaves tangible reminders of his presence. It is on a charter of Fulk's that we find the first surviving princely – rather than royal – seal[48], and in Loches and Langeais we have buildings constructed for him. Admittedly in this period we don't have contemporary portraits, but we do have one vivid image for Fulk Nerra, and this is intimately bound up with his reputation today. Fulk was a popular figure for 19th-century historians, and as mentioned above, to my mind the entire way we see him was determined by a passage in Michaud's *Histoire des Croisades* from 1825. Fulk died long before the First Crusade, but when Michaud discusses the origins of the Crusade, he includes a study of pilgrimages. Fulk was unquestionably most famous for his pilgrimages to Jerusalem, and Michaud says:

The count of Anjou, Foulque de Nerra ... was accused of having killed his first wife, and of being many times stained with innocent blood. Pursued by public hatred and by the voice of his own conscience, it seemed to him that the numerous victims sacrificed to his vengeance or his ambition issued from their tombs to disturb his sleep and reproach him for his barbarity.[49]

Much more importantly, Michaud's history was illustrated lavishly with engravings by Gustave Doré, and one of the most striking is the one showing Fulk Nerra haunted by the spirits of all his victims. Disappointingly (to me, anyway), I truly believe that despite all his accomplishments and his genuinely important place in medieval history, Fulk's reputation was sealed by Doré's engraving and it is in this way that everyone still seems determined to see him. A better example of the transformative power of art can scarcely be found, despite the fact that this 19th-century engraving has virtually nothing to do with the real Fulk.

There is one medium in which we do get some sense of a person: the funeral effigy. These were still stylized and made no attempt to represent the person's features accurately, but as a three-dimensional form they do convey a sense of presence, a sense reinforced through the connection with a tomb. The later Angevins are spectacularly blessed with funerary monuments, and their necropolis at Fontevraud Abbey contains impressive effigies of Henry II, Eleanor of Aquitaine, Richard the Lionheart and King John's wife Isabella, and Geoffrey Plantagenet's enamelled tomb in Le Mans is both beautiful and of seminal importance to art history with its preservation of a medieval colour scheme and perhaps pioneering use of heraldry. Needless to say we have nothing for Ingelgarius, Fulk the Red, Fulk the Good or Geoffrey Greymantle, but Fulk Nerra's tomb provides tantalising possibilities.

Fulk died on the way home from one of his pilgrimages and was interred in his abbey of Beaulieu. His tomb, like so many others, was destroyed in the unrest following the French Revolution, but there is a drawing of the tomb from 1699 that gives us some idea of what it was like, and preserves its epitaph commemorating his pilgrimages to Jerusalem. However, in 1870 a grave was discovered containing some bones and a perfectly preserved skull, which were believed to be Fulk Nerra's. Perhaps the most fascinating part of M. de Salies's quite peculiar biography of Fulk from 1874 is his discussion of the discovery of the tomb, where he gives a partial transcript of the inquest and discusses interviews with residents of Loches whose parents lived through the events of the Revolution. The tomb had a classical frieze showing Fulk's victory at Conquereuil and an effigy showing Fulk looking like a beardless Roman, though M. de Salies believed that the tomb's characteristics showed it to be a 14th-century reconstruction of Fulk's original tomb. M. de Salies also waxed lyrical about the skull that was believed to be Fulk's (this has subsequently been disproved) and subjected it to anthropological analysis, and he unsurprisingly concluded that the skull must have been that of a great and terrible character.[50]

What, then, should be our final judgement of Fulk Nerra? At the highest level, we cannot disagree with M. de Salies, who states that three people represent the 11th century: their names are mixed in every event, nothing happens without them, nothing is done but by them and their story is, for this period, the history of France: Fulk Nerra, William the Conqueror and Theobald Count of Blois.[51] There is no more accurate statement of Fulk's political centrality to the 11th century, but this fails to identify what makes him such a compelling figure. Fulk Nerra is the first figure in the 11th century who appears to us as a real person with his hopes, fears, faults, victories and defeats. We can see Fulk, however patchily, as an individual who embodied all the trends of his time yet still managed to convey his own personality with all the rough edges later chroniclers would try to polish off.

His foundation of later Angevin success cannot be denied. His grandson Fulk Réchin took an eminently sensible approach when he documented Fulk Nerra's accomplishments and listed all his castles, a roll call of the places such as Loches, Saumur and Chinon that would still be central to the Angevins four centuries later. Fulk's domination of Touraine and Maine made the Angevins one of the great powers of northern France, who within another hundred years would claim the greatest prize of all and become kings twice over. Naturally later myth-makers tried to glorify Fulk by suppressing his perceived faults and embellishing his deeds with fabrications, but what is so extraordinary about Fulk is that his true character still emerges, and shows the Angevin characteristics that would serve the family so well for generations. Even if chroniclers sometimes invented stories to emphasize this continuity, it is amply demonstrated that bottomless energy, a terrible temper and red hair were genetic traits shared by the Angevins over the two centuries from Fulk Nerra to Richard the Lionheart.

Fulk's role as the founder of Angevin greatness was not lost on 12th-century historians, and they were drawn irresistibly to compare him to Henry II, especially as Fulk's greatest test was against the rulers Odo and Theobald of Blois, while Henry II took the throne only after a lengthy war against the usurper Stephen of Blois. As always, Norgate expresses it best:

> The rivalry of Odo and Fulk was a foreshadowing of the rivalry between Stephen of Blois and Henry of Anjou. The end was the same in both cases. With every advantage on their side, in the eleventh century as in the twelfth, in Gaul as in England, the aimless activity of the house of Blois only spent itself against the indomitable steadiness, determination and persistency of the Angevins, as vainly as the storm-wind might beat upon the rocky foundations of Black Angers.[52]

Fulk Nerra provides a brilliant jumping-off point for a discussion of the Angevins who would rule England because he shares so many of their traits, but for me he is perfect for another reason. As Richard Southern illustrates in *The Making of the Middle Ages*, Fulk – and Anjou itself – encapsulates all the key trends of the age, and the purpose of this book is to argue that the other Angevins through the ages did the same. Fulk embodied the consolidation of power by local lords into compact independent states; the restless disorder and unrestrained violence in the age just before national monarchies asserted themselves; the overpowering religiosity that drove pilgrims to the Holy Land and penitents to walk barefoot to saints' shrines; and the impulse that covered first France and then the rest of Europe with the most characteristic medieval building, the castle.[53]

For all that, Fulk Nerra marks only the beginning of the Angevin adventure, and indeed the beginning of a new period in the Middle Ages when Europe was entirely transformed. My focus on the Angevins won't distract us from the achievements of their arch-rivals – not the Blésois, who despite their late resurgence under Stephen of Blois were aimless as ever, but the Normans. Fulk's success had unintended consequences because his expansion into Maine brought his son into collision with Normandy, and if Fulk was the most important figure of the first half of the 11th century then William Duke of Normandy, soon to be called the 'Conqueror', was the most important figure of the second half, as the Angevins discovered to their cost.

CHAPTER 2 – ANGEVINS AND NORMANS

T HOUGH WE HAVE SPENT a chapter looking at the activities of Fulk Nerra, with hindsight the 11th century was actually dominated by two great events, in neither of which the Angevins acted initially, yet which would shape their future decisively. First was the investiture controversy between the popes and Holy Roman Emperors, over the right of lay rulers to invest bishops with their sees, in which the papacy emerged victorious. Despite the vagaries to which Charlemagne's successors to the title were subjected, Charlemagne's legacy ensured that the Emperor still maintained some nominal claim to authority in Europe. The investiture struggle ended with the Emperor's claim for universal power in Europe destroyed and the foundations laid for a papal 'monarchy' that would gather strength over the coming centuries. The investiture struggle was most destructive in Germany and Italy (and it is not a coincidence that it was these regions that remained divided until the 19th century whereas England and France developed into nation-states), but the newly powerful pope would begin to play a much more significant role everywhere in Europe in the coming centuries. The culminating event, which came at the very end of the century and demonstrated that the pope, rather than the Emperor, was the leader of Christendom, was the preaching of the First Crusade by Pope Urban II in 1095. This of course was the second seismic event of the 11th century, and due to the astonishing success of the First Crusade and the foundation of Christian states in the Holy Land, the Crusades became a dominant thread in European society for the next 400 years.

Subsumed within these two events were the great conquests of the Normans in England, Southern Italy, Sicily and the Holy Land, which laid the foundations for kingdoms that would last for centuries or indeed (in the case of England) until the present day. Considering that the Normans were near neighbours of the Angevins, the accession of a warrior as bold as William the Bastard, Duke of Normandy, to the throne of England should have been a catastrophe for the Angevins – and it very nearly was – yet within 100 years the Angevins would conquer Normandy and take the English throne for themselves, plus much more. Angevins also succeeded to the throne of Jerusalem and conquered Sicily/Naples, completing the transfer of power from Norman to Angevin. Though the Normans had played a leading role in the First Crusade, capping what can definitively be called 'the Norman Century', the 12th century would in turn be 'the Angevin Century' and the Third Crusade cemented their dominance.

Geoffrey Martel: 'Showing how much an Angevin can excel a Norman'

Both the investiture struggle and the First Crusade came at a particularly difficult time for Anjou, whose uninterrupted rise was about to meet severe difficulties. Fulk Nerra died in 1040 leaving his son Geoffrey Martel to inherit Anjou, and Geoffrey's reign from 1040–1060 did see the completion of most of the business begun by Fulk Nerra. It also marked the beginning of the Angevin entanglement with the Normans that would have such spectacular consequences, and leaves us at a convenient place to consider the whirlwind of events that would occupy the rest of Europe, while the Angevins sank into relative obscurity for forty years, only to re-emerge at the forefront of European history.

Geoffrey Martel was a belligerent and aggressive figure superficially cut from the same cloth as his father, and contemporaries expected him to add to his father's achievements, as he indeed did. First though, we should consider his name. We are on much safer ground with Geoffrey than Fulk Nerra, since he used the name 'Martel' in his own lifetime and we know that it means 'the Hammer', serving as a warning to his enemies, as well as alluding to Charles Martel, Charlemagne's grandfather and the victor over the Arabs in 747, thus 'saving Europe' from Muslim dominion according to Carolingian family mythology. The *Gesta* relates the story that as soon as Geoffrey was born he was fostered, as noble children always were, but specifically with the wife of a blacksmith near Beaulieu, and Fulk Nerra often visited the forge to see him. This was meant to account for his nickname of 'Martel', though this title was fairly common for those who wished to emphasize their credentials as warriors so the story doesn't really seem necessary. William of Malmesbury, writing eighty years later, also says that Geoffrey took the name Martel in his own lifetime, though he gives his usual unflattering interpretation to this, as below.[1]

Geoffrey was already a successful commander before Fulk Nerra died. One of his first exploits was typical: he met William the Fat, Duke of Aquitaine, in battle in 1033 and captured him, then kept him imprisoned for three years until he managed to extort the region of the Saintonge from him. William died three days after his release, which says something about the nature of Geoffrey's hospitality, but it was undeniably effective in a crude way. Geoffrey was much concerned with Aquitaine, and it is said that this infuriated Fulk Nerra, who wished his son to continue his work in Touraine and Maine. Yet perhaps it is not surprising that as forceful a character as Geoffrey wished to make his own way in a new region while his father lived.

Geoffrey achieved a coup in his Aquitainian policy, though he angered his father further, by marrying Agnes, the young widow of William the Fat's father. William the Fat's half-brother had become the new Duke of Aquitaine, but Agnes had two young sons and a daughter who might one day succeed to the duchy, and Geoffrey must have been hoping to control its affairs by controlling the children. Geoffrey also incurred the displeasure of the church because he and Agnes were third cousins and considered too nearly related to marry[2], but his calculations were correct because Agnes's two sons did become Duke of Aquitaine and Count of Gascony, though they had no love for their step-father. Geoffrey seems to have gained little from this marriage, though the Angevin domination of Poitou (the county just south of Anjou, centred on Poitiers) in this period marked the moment Poitou switched from the *langue d'oc* to the *langue d'oil*, that is from Occitan to French.[3]

Geoffrey had a high reputation with his contemporaries as a warrior and he was even more aggressive, if not as astute and effective, as his father. In the aftermath of Fulk's death, Geoffrey's deeds certainly warranted this reputation, since he completed the annexation of Tours after defeating Theobald III of Champagne and Stephen II of Blois completely at Nouy in August 1044, also capturing Theobald, who gave his full submission. The circumstances of the annexation were part of larger French politics: as the new counts of Champagne and Blois, Theobald and Stephen had rebelled against Henry I of France, who found himself isolated. Duke Robert of Normandy had died in 1035, leaving Normandy in chaos and a beleaguered bastard son to pick up the pieces; Aquitaine was in similar turmoil after several new dukes in succession; and Flanders, Brittany and Burgundy had no interest in the king's difficulties. This left only Anjou, and in an act of inspired diplomacy Henry dispossessed Theobald of Champagne and granted Tours to Geoffrey Martel.

In Maine, the death of Herbert Wake-the-Dog in 1036 left the county to a minor, Hugh III, and a struggle broke out between Gervais the Bishop of Le Mans and Hugh III's great-uncle Herbert Bacon for control of the child. Despite the fact that he was already in rebellion against Fulk Nerra, Geoffrey Martel tried to intervene on behalf of Herbert Bacon, but was defeated and Gervais took over the county. However, once he had become count of Anjou and finished with the conquest of Touraine, Geoffrey returned in force and succeeded in capturing and imprisoning Gervais[4], and he controlled the county in the person of the young count despite being excommunicated. When Hugh III died in 1051, Geoffrey swept into Le Mans by one gate while Hugh's widow Bertha fled with her two children through another. Bertha fled to the court of Normandy, confirming that it was here Geoffrey would find his greatest test, but for the moment he was master of Maine.[5]

It was now that Geoffrey Martel, having so comprehensively defeated Anjou's old rival the House of Blois, annexed Touraine and dominated Maine, met a new rival, William of Normandy, and began a struggle that defined the rest of Geoffrey's life. Of course we know what happened in 1066 and this colours everything we think about the conflict, but Geoffrey Martel died in 1060. Although he had no way of knowing his rival's illustrious future, Geoffrey could certainly see that William was the most powerful enemy he had yet faced. In this struggle, his ally was Henry I of France and the battleground was to be Maine.

Henry I of France was beginning to understand how great the menace that lurked on his border truly was (though he had little idea of how grave the danger would become after 1066), and he chose to continue the alliance with Geoffrey that had proved so fruitful in Touraine. Although their attempts to harass the Normans ended in disaster, the *Gesta* boldly chooses to ignore this, acknowledging that the Angevins had come into conflict with the Normans over Maine, but saying such things as, 'In those days, Duke William of Normandy was greatly harassing Herbert, count of Le Mans. Since Martel was Herbert's ally and protector, Duke William, who later became king of the English, suffered much at Martel's hands.'[6] There is some truth here, because despite various reverses Geoffrey Martel still remained master of Maine in 1060.

Geoffrey is a difficult figure to characterize, falling as he does between Fulk Nerra, one of the most colourful characters in medieval history, and Fulk Réchin, who was the first secular figure to write his own version of events. It isn't that we don't know about his deeds, since we can credit him with one of the greatest accomplishments in early Angevin history, the annexation of Tours, along with the annexation of Saintonge and the domination of Maine. Neither was he a mindless warrior, as it is under him that Anjou developed its own chancery. There isn't even a shortage of anecdotes about him, but these are problematic, and we struggle to disentangle him from the web of legend. What can we say about him?

Geoffrey seems to warrant the adjective 'terrible' as much or more than Fulk Nerra because of his penchant for imprisoning people, his rebellion against his father, his opportunistic marriage to the widowed Duchess of Aquitaine[7] and his pugnacious approach to his neighbours. The horrors of medieval warfare were not specific to Geoffrey, but the *Gesta* gives a graphic description of his callousness when describing the Angevins' complete victory over the Poitevins at Chef-Boutonne: 'The massacre complete, Martel and his men spent the night peacefully in their tents on the plain. Against the bitter north wind which was blowing, they piled up the dead bodies.'[8]

Geoffrey is also much discussed by the English historian William of Malmesbury, who relates several very interesting and highly unflattering stories about him, though his credibility is suspect. Malmesbury's introduction to his discussion of Geoffrey makes it very clear what he thought, as he says of Geoffrey 'who had boastingly taken the surname of "Martel" as he seemed by a certain kind of felicity to beat down all his opponents'.[9] Malmesbury discusses Geoffrey's capture of Theobald of Blois in the context of his abominable behaviour, and mentions that he took Tours, but seems unaware or unwilling to admit that Geoffrey had been granted Tours by the French king after Theobald's rebellion.

This is all a preliminary to Malmesbury's best-known, and most damning, story about Geoffrey. After his seizure of Tours and interventions in Maine, Geoffrey 'insolent from the accession of so much power' seized Alençon, which outraged William of Normandy, who besieged Domfront in turn. Geoffrey rushed to raise the siege, and William sent messengers to meet him. In Malmesbury's description, Geoffrey:

> … immediately began to rage, to threaten mightily what he would do, and said that he would come thither the next day, and show to the world at large how much

an Angevin could excel a Norman in battle; at the same time, with unparalleled insolence, describing the colour of his horse, and the devices on the arms he meant to use.[10]

But when the morning came, Geoffrey did not appear, having slunk back to Anjou. Kate Norgate accepted this story entirely, and believed that it told us everything we need to know about Geoffrey's character, which is what Malmesbury would have intended. As Norgate says,

> … he evaded the risk of open defeat by a tacit withdrawal far more shameful in a moral point of view. It is small blame to Geoffrey Martel that he was no match for William the Conqueror. Had he, in honest consciousness of his inferiority, done his best to avoid a collision, and when it became inevitable stood to face the consequences like a man, it would have been small shame to him to be defeated by the future victor of Senlac. The real shame is that after courting an encounter and loudly boasting of his desire to break a lance with William, when the opportunity was given him he silently declined to use it. It was but a mean pride and a poor courage that looked upon defeat in fair fight as an unbearable humiliation, and could not feel the deeper moral humiliation of shrinking from the mere chance of that defeat. And it is just this bluntness of feeling, this callousness to everything not visible and tangible to the outward sense, which sets Geoffrey as a man far below his father.[11]

This is a striking story that does seem to delineate Geoffrey's character clearly, but we cannot trust Malmesbury, and Norgate herself views this through the prism of future Norman triumphalism.

Malmesbury was writing Norman propaganda, and even William the Conqueror's biographer David Douglas takes a very different view. Before 1066 Angevin control of Maine was not seriously contested, and despite Geoffrey's discomfiture in some skirmishes, he more or less maintained himself against the Normans. This is not consistent with overwhelming defeat or fear of confrontation, but stability. Of course, this is very revealing in its own way: before William the Conqueror, the Angevin story is one of constant steady expansion and the overmatching of competitors such as the Duke of Aquitaine or the Count of Blois. Against the Normans we can only speak of Geoffrey 'holding his own', and Geoffrey's successors fared worse. Still, Geoffrey's record against William is not as bleak as Malmesbury and Norgate make out.

Malmesbury uses his discussion of Geoffrey to initiate a brief history of the counts of Anjou, and though he is highly complimentary of Fulk Nerra (indeed, as we saw in the previous chapter he presented an account that bears little resemblance to the character we find elsewhere), he uses this as another opportunity to condemn Geoffrey and gives us the story of Geoffrey's rebellion against his father and Geoffrey having to wear a saddle.[12] Norgate accepts this story as she does the others about Geoffrey and bases her analysis of Geoffrey's character on it. Yet the *Gesta*, though acknowledging Geoffrey had his critics, reports that when Geoffrey was told that men spoke badly of him because of his aggression, he replied, 'They do what they are wont to do, not what I deserve; they do not know how to speak well.'[13]

The middle of the 11th century was a watershed in medieval warfare. Fulk Nerra may have pioneered the use of castles as offensive weapons, but by the time of Geoffrey Martel this tactic had been adopted by his rivals as well. The Normans adopted the new use of fortifications in their struggles with the Angevins, and it was also a factor in the swiftness and completeness of the Norman conquest of England. The first castles in England seem to have been built by Edward the Confessor's Norman relatives in the mid-11th century, but the custom did not take hold. Orderic Vitalis reports that one of the reasons the Normans conquered England so easily was because 'there were practically no fortresses such as the French call *castella* in the land, wherefore the English, though warlike and courageous, proved too feeble to withstand their enemies.'[14]

The other contemporary development was, as we have seen, the use of the cavalry charge with couched lances. The Bayeux Tapestry shows that the mounted Normans in 1066 were still using their spears in a variety of ways, but it clearly demonstrates that one method was to seat the lance under the arm and use the force of the charging warhorse to give impetus to the blow, which could be made even more effective by having a coordinated group of knights charge together. Within fifty years the Normans would be famous for the unstoppable force of their grouped cavalry charges.

The Angevins also seem to have adopted this method, and an incidental offshoot of this military innovation was the need for teams of knights to practise working together to deliver the shattering charge. This seems to be the origin of the tournament, which in one form or another would become the most popular sport of the aristocracy for the next six centuries. Though it was the Normans who became most famous for the cavalry charge, which played a key role in their conquests of England, southern Italy and in the Holy Land, a fascinating piece of evidence from the *Chronicle of St Martin of Tours* states that the inventor of tournaments was Geoffrey de Preuilly, a baron of Angers, who died in either 1062 or 1066.[15] Sadly the chronicle wasn't written until the early 13th century and has little credibility, but it would be fascinating to think that the tournament originated in Anjou as a means of training the Angevin cavalry in the new method of fighting invented by their Norman enemies.

The Norman Century

With Geoffrey Martel, we are at the high point of Angevin ambition and success, yet it is almost at this moment that Angevin fortunes took a dramatic turn for the worse. Anjou's neighbours, the Normans, had become the most dominant force in Europe, and we will spend a significant part of this chapter discussing them. They also form a vital part of the Angevin story because everything they built would eventually belong to the Angevins.

After being so prominent as the horrifying Viking invaders that coloured early Angevin history, the Normans seemed to have settled down in their new duchy, but in fact they were creating a political and military state whose expansion in the 11th century was unstoppable. Although William the Bastard's disputed succession from 1035–1047 kept Norman aggression focused inward for a time, after 1047 the Normans began to impinge on Angevin designs. This was largely because Fulk Nerra and Geoffrey Martel had completely dominated Maine and now had a border with the duchy. But before that the Normans had already embarked upon the adventures that would see them become a dominant force in the Mediterranean, and indeed in addition to the other factors mentioned above, it was this resurgence of Western Christian power in the Mediterranean through the Normans that gave the First Crusade its impetus.

In the early 11th century, southern Italy was politically fragmented and consisted of independent city-states like Naples, Amalfi and Gaeta; Lombard principalities such as Salerno, Benevento and Capua; and a strong province of the Byzantine Empire centred on Bari that claimed suzerainty over the entire area. Despite the political strength of the Byzantine outpost, the religious influence of Rome dominated much of the region and posed a considerable obstacle to Byzantine hegemony. More importantly, Sicily had long ago been conquered by Muslims, and along with Sardinia, Corsica and certain towns in southern France served as a base for raids on the Italian peninsula.[16]

The advent of the Normans in southern Italy came before 1018 when a small band of adventurers – returning from a pilgrimage to Jerusalem, according to some stories – either helped a Lombard rebel against the Greeks at Bari, or fought off a Muslim siege of Salerno. Though this did not establish a lasting Norman presence in the area, it did show the Italians the benefits of Norman assistance, and showed the Normans what rewards could be won. Within ten years the Normans were called back to help reinstate the deposed leader of Naples, and in addition to money their leader was granted the hill fortress of Aversa with its surrounding land. This was the first Norman state in Italy, and the new Count of Aversa was quick to intervene in the affairs of his neighbours and provide a warm reception for any other Normans who wished to try their luck in Italy.[17]

The most famous of these were the twelve sons of Tancred of Hauteville, a minor Norman landowner whose children would change the history of the Mediterranean world. By 1047 Tancred's elder sons had dominated Apulia and assumed the title of count, and it was also in this year that one of his younger sons, Robert Guiscard (the 'Wily'), arrived in Italy to transform Norman fortunes.[18] Robert Guiscard began his career as a brigand, but he rapidly parlayed this into a more exalted position.

The Normans had become such a force in Italy and also such a threat, that by 1053 Pope Leo IX joined the Byzantines in an effort to expel them from Italy. Leo himself led a combined force to Civitate, but the lords of Aversa and Apulia joined forces, and with the support of Robert Guiscard utterly routed the papal army and captured the pope. Norman supremacy in southern Italy was confirmed, and neither the papacy nor the Byzantines (now thoroughly occupied closer to home repelling constant raids by the Seljuk Turks) had any means of opposing them. Showing the pragmatism that had served the institution for 1000 years, in 1059 Pope Nicholas II decided to ally with the Normans and granted to the lord of Aversa the title 'Prince of Capua', and Robert Guiscard (whose elder brother had died) the title Duke of Apulia and Calabria, and 'in the future, Duke of Sicily'. This gift of territory – which was outside even the nominal control of the papacy – gave the Normans free rein and they were quick to capitalize on their position. Robert Guiscard conquered the remaining portions of Apulia and Calabria, and by 1071 had captured Bari to end 500 years of Byzantine control of the region. It is not coincidental that the pope would approve this, given that in 1054 the Latin and Greek churches finally suffered a breach that could not be repaired.[19]

The papacy's alliance with the Normans marked a turning point for that institution. Leo IX's march against the Normans in 1053 was the action of a local ruler vying for power with local rivals who were his equals. Nicholas II's alliance with the Normans connected him to this rising European power and gave the papacy greater ambition as well. Soon after, we see the pope extending his Norman connection by blessing William the Conqueror's expedition to England, and even intervening in Angevin affairs to sanction the deposition of a count (though he quickly backtracked). The popes had some nominal claim to control secular power through their coronation of the Emperor, but this claim had lain dormant for nearly 300 years. With their new allies the popes were prepared to take a more active role, and this early Norman military support evolved through the participation of the Normans in the First Crusade into a religious and political/military tool that would have profound consequences for European history.

Meanwhile, Robert Guiscard's younger brother Roger had taken an interest in Sicily. Southern Italy and Sicily were the point where the Eastern and Western remnants of the Roman Empire met, with the inevitable tension this caused, and now the rising claims of the papacy and the Norman invasion provided added turmoil. With intermittent help from Robert, Roger had managed to take Messina and establish himself on the island. After Roger assisted in the capture of Bari, Robert Guiscard joined him again and the two managed to take Palermo in 1072, consolidating the Norman hold on the island and creating yet another new state. Roger eventually absorbed southern Italy into a Kingdom of Sicily that was one of the most prosperous states in Western Europe. Sicily also demonstrated the benefits that the peaceful coexistence of Christians and Muslims could bring, as the Sicilians prospered from their participation in the trade of the entire Mediterranean. Thus by the end of the 11th century, the Norman kingdoms of Sicily and England were two of the best organized and most powerful states in Europe, and caused considerable disquiet to their neighbours.[20]

Fulk Réchin, in his own words

Modern historians have arrived at a consensus about the character of the early Angevins, to the extent that these truisms are repeated by most historians now. Fulk Nerra was a force of nature – wild, violent, successful and given to fits of piety – and he is admired as an iconic specimen of 11th-century nobility and taken as an epitome of his age. Geoffrey Martel inspires no love, and is always presented as cold, unpleasant and second best to William the Bastard. As we have seen, this comes from William of Malmesbury, who couldn't have had any first-hand knowledge of Geoffrey and was explicitly a Norman apologist, but it is the view that is always repeated. When we come to Fulk Réchin, or in the words of one modern historian of the Normans on his very first mention of him, 'the repulsive Fulk Réchin'[21] – and why 'repulsive'? – he is usually characterized as odious, but no reason is given. Why does he have this terrible reputation with modern historians? The reasons may lie with his succession to the county.

After a series of such formidable leaders as Geoffrey Greymantle, Fulk Nerra and Geoffrey Martel, it is perhaps not surprising that there must at some point come an ineffective Angevin count. Geoffrey Martel failed in one of the primary responsibilities of a ruler and left no children, though his sister Ermengarde, who was married to Geoffrey Count of Gâtinais, had two sons later to be known as Geoffrey the Bearded and Fulk Réchin. Unfortunately, with the nephews of Geoffrey Martel came not one, but two bad leaders. The *Gesta* states it most succinctly:

> As far as the number and nature of evils which occurred in the county while Geoffrey the Bearded and Fulk Réchin possessed the honour of Martel are concerned, their disclosure is ordered by true history but forbidden by the horror and scale of the destruction. Indeed, I do not know whether it is better for those malefactors if details of their evil accomplishments are omitted or rather whether it does them a disservice to suppress examples of their wickedness.[22]

Geoffrey Martel seems to have divided his domains between his nephews, and the *Gesta* states that Martel gave Geoffrey the Bearded Anjou and the Saintonge, and Fulk Réchin received Touraine and Chateau Landon. It seems incredible that Martel would divide Anjou and Touraine after going through so much to unite them, but William the Conqueror would do the same thing with England and Normandy. This may be the reason the *Gesta* reports the division as it does – it follows the logic that the patrimony goes to the elder heir and any land conquered goes to the younger, even if it is more extensive. Other sources, though, claim that Geoffrey the Bearded received Anjou, Saumur and Touraine, while Fulk Réchin received the Saintonge, which he held as a fief from his brother. We are in the unique position of having a statement from one of the protagonists, and although we may choose whether or not we wish to believe him, Fulk Réchin himself says that Geoffrey Martel knighted him in 1060 when he was seventeen and 'committed to me the county of Saintonge, with its capital Saintes'[23]. Fulk says nothing else about the inheritance – which suggests strongly that everything else was in fact left to his brother – and goes on to say that war broke out between him and his brother, which ended with his brother's imprisonment.

The early relations of the brothers are not clear. The *Gesta* reports that Fulk led a rebellion against his brother in 1066 and that the Duke of Aquitaine took advantage of this dissension to capture the Saintonge. However, the *Gesta*'s chronology seems faulty here, and in fact the Duke of Aquitaine attacked Fulk Réchin first in 1061. Although with Geoffrey's help the Angevins defeated a Poitevin army in 1061, in 1062 Saintes fell to Aquitaine and Fulk Réchin lost his inheritance. Geoffrey the Bearded does not seem to have helped Fulk during the second attack, and an alternative view suggests that Fulk's bitterness over this was what led him to revolt a few years later.[24]

Fulk Réchin's name is sometimes translated as Fulk 'the Quarreller' (more on that below), but Geoffrey the Bearded in his short reign seems to fulfil this designation equally, as he had a genuine talent for alienating people. Geoffrey immediately fell foul of the clergy in Maine, to such an extent that the bishop of Le Mans complained to the pope, who threatened Geoffrey with excommunication. Geoffrey then compounded his religious difficulties in 1064 by demanding that the newly elected abbot of Marmoutier receive his investiture from the count's hands. We have already seen that the conflict over lay investiture had rumbled through the 11th century and would soon rip Italy and the Empire apart, and fatally undermine the Emperor's pretensions to universal authority. Although lay investiture was still practised, Marmoutier had been specifically exempted from comital control in a charter of Geoffrey Martel's from 1044. In the midst of this dispute the canons of Le Mans had to elect a new bishop in 1065, and to Geoffrey's fury chose the Norman Arnaud, a sign of waxing Norman power. Geoffrey tried to block the election and the Cenomannian clergy complained once again to the pope. The pope ordered Barthelmi, the Archbishop of Tours, to consecrate Arnaud immediately and Geoffrey furiously attacked the archbishop's property. Barthelmi wrote to the pope again, calling Geoffrey 'a new Nero' who surpassed all his predecessors in impiety, and with papal support excommunicated Geoffrey and forbade all bishops, especially the bishop of Angers, to have any contact with him.[25] This alone would be sufficient reason for a cleric, particularly one like Jean of Marmoutier whose monastery was involved, to condemn Geoffrey as a monster of wickedness.

It is instructive to look at how the *Gesta* presents Geoffrey the Bearded, since this is the primary source that modern historians use. The section on Geoffrey consists of five pages: the first paragraph is the one quoted above about his legendary wickedness, then four pages follow detailing how badly Geoffrey treated the monks of Marmoutier. The section finishes by stating that Geoffrey was deposed by Fulk Réchin and placed in miserable captivity for more than thirty years, concluding piously that this is what happens to people who oppose God's will. A biography that highlights Geoffrey's oppression of Marmoutier particularly and then describes him as the worst ruler since Nero leaves

us with very little to go on. Geoffrey clearly did have problems with the clergy, but
we are left knowing almost nothing about him other than that he was deposed by
Fulk Réchin. He is an example of the historical figure characterized and caricatured
by a single primary source, leaving later historians nothing to say except to repeat the
slanders of contemporaries and leave it at that.

Geoffrey found himself in a desperate situation by the end of 1066 and Anjou
might have been at the mercy of its hostile neighbours, especially the Normans, but
we know William the Conqueror (as we can now call him) had taken a far larger prize
than Anjou, one that would occupy him for the rest of his life. Closer to home there
was someone willing to take advantage of Geoffrey's troubles, and Fulk Réchin seized
Saumur early in 1067. At this moment a papal legate arrived and convened a council of
bishops, which upheld Geoffrey's excommunication and seemed to give support to Fulk
Réchin's budding coup. Bolstered by this support, Fulk marched on Angers, and thanks
to the support of Geoffrey's leading vassals took Angers and imprisoned his brother. We
need no further evidence of growing papal power in the 11th century than the pope's
apparent support for deposing the count of Anjou so soon after giving his blessing (and
a papal banner) to the Normans who conquered England. However, Pope Alexander II
realized the implications of excommunication becoming synonymous with deposition,
and ordered Fulk to reinstate Geoffrey. Fulk agreed and restored Geoffrey as count due
to this clerical intervention.[26]

Only a year later, in 1068, the brothers were again at war. Fulk seized Brissac and
when Geoffrey besieged him, Fulk and his supporters routed Geoffrey's army and captured the count again, this time imprisoning him in Chinon. Fulk then had to subdue
numerous barons who either supported Geoffrey or had simply used the turmoil to seize
towns or castles for themselves. Fulk showed himself a formidable soldier, besieging
and taking all the rebel castles, but this disruption came at a price: Fulk had to cede
the Gâtinais to King Philip I and pay homage to the Count of Blois for Touraine.
Nevertheless, Fulk was now firmly in power and kept his brother imprisoned for nearly
forty years.[27]

It should be noted that this is a very different story from the one given by William
of Malmesbury, who states that Geoffrey the Bearded was a simple soul who liked to
pray more than fight, although I think this suggests some confusion with the story of
Fulk the Good. Malmesbury then notes that Geoffrey was held in contempt by the
Angevins, 'who knew not how to live in quiet', though he then says that because of
Geoffrey's passivity the county was open to raids, and Fulk Réchin seized power to
protect Anjou, which is a more flattering depiction of Fulk than we usually see.[28]

Despite the fact that Fulk began his reign with the bold action of deposing his
brother, he was curiously ineffective thereafter. This was partially because the method
by which he overthrew Geoffrey was to stir up the barons to rebellion, which unleashed
such a spirit of independence in them that he spent the next decades trying to restore
order. Worse, to ensure his position he made concessions to his rivals that compromised

the security of Anjou for decades and unravelled the work of generations. Fulk lost all influence in Maine, which soon fell to William the Conqueror; performed homage to the Count of Blois for Tours, undoing the work of Geoffrey Martel and Fulk Nerra; and ceded the entire Gâtinais to the French king in exchange for recognition of his title, undoing the work of Geoffrey Greymantle. Even worse, in 1106 his son Fulk V performed homage to the French king for Anjou itself, something which had always tacitly been accepted, but no Angevin count had done such a thing since before the reign of Fulk Nerra.[29] This is certainly sufficient to explain the very low regard in which both contemporary and modern historians hold him, and worse, Fulk had the misfortune to follow the legendary energy of Fulk Nerra and the indisputable success of Geoffrey Martel, and compared to his own son who would become a king he had no accomplishments to recommend him.

He also suffered even more than Geoffrey Martel in being the rival of William the Conqueror. Fulk's natural ally against William was the king of France, who was well aware of the threat the Normans posed, and the two did combine with the Breton lord Ralph of Gael to inflict a defeat on William. Ralph, who was also earl of Norfolk, had rebelled in England and been defeated, so he took refuge in the Breton city of Dol where he was joined by Angevin troops. William besieged them but was then driven away with great loss by King Philip I, in a successful use of the tactics that so often failed for Geoffrey Martel and Henry I of France, where one of the allies acted as the bait and the other arrived to catch William unawares. Despite the victory at Dol Philip I was no match for William, but he successfully lured William's disaffected son Robert Curthose into an alliance against his father in 1078. Robert went so far as to take the field against his father at Gerborai in 1079 and killed his horse, and also wounded both his father and his brother William Rufus. William's defeat prompted an invasion of England by King Malcolm of Scotland, a foreshadowing of events in Henry II's reign when a son would take the field against his father with the assistance of a Scottish invasion.[30]

Whatever balanced approach we may try to take, Fulk's contemporaries were much more scathing, with the *Gesta* pronouncing, 'ill he began; worse he lived; worst of all he ended'[31], and this has little to do with the territory he lost. Why did they think so badly of him? His ill beginning is plain enough, since the overthrow and imprisonment of his elder brother would have shocked some medieval sensibilities. Further, until Fulk Réchin himself, in medieval Europe there were only clerical chroniclers and we must consider what behaviour they would find most offensive. Fulk fell foul of what was becoming one of the signature policies of the 11th-century church, the regulation of marriage. Fulk's first wife died, but after a second marriage to Ermengarde of Bourbon who gave him a son, Geoffrey Martel II, Fulk fell passionately in love with Bertrada of Montfort, a woman 'no good man ever praised save for her beauty', as the *Gesta* says archly, alluding to Sallust.[32] Fulk discarded Ermengarde on the grounds of consanguinity to marry Bertrada, but if the authors of the *Gesta* condemned Fulk for his lechery, imagine the monks' horror at Bertrada, who subsequently abandoned Fulk to marry the king of France!

The author of the *Gesta* is in no doubt about the kind of people these were: 'The lecherous King Philip came to Tours and, having conversed with Fulk's wife, decided to make her his queen. That evil woman abandoned the count the next night and followed the king ... Thus the voluptuous king filled his house with marital crimes committed under the ban of excommunication and begat two sons by the woman ...'[33] William of Malmesbury adds the detail that Philip discarded his previous wife for being too fat and took up with Bertrada 'in defiance of law and equity'.[34] As always, such moral degradation implies that any sin is possible, and concerning the death of Fulk's son Geoffrey Martel II at the siege of Candé, the *Gesta* repeats the rumour that Fulk and Bertrada engineered his death, though the author does qualify this by saying, 'It seems unbelievable to me that the father of such a son should have consented to his death, both when he was an old man and when his son, had he been granted longevity, would have recovered whatever he had lost.'[35] Geoffrey Martel II is unsurprisingly presented as the paragon of all virtues, as is the custom with heirs who seem promising but die before inheriting.

What is interesting is that Fulk Réchin's second son, Fulk V, who would be known as Fulk the Young and later Fulk King of Jerusalem, is also presented as the epitome of goodness, despite being the offspring of Fulk Réchin and Bertrada. Medieval historians enjoyed the chance to present such contrasts, when the child of virtuous parents was wicked, or as in this case, vice versa.

Yet why should we believe what the chroniclers tell us when Fulk himself recounts some of his own story? Fulk Réchin is the first lay historian of the Middle Ages and produced a history of Anjou around the year 1100. We have relied so heavily on the *Gesta* that it comes as a revelation to have a primary source written by one of the protagonists in the story. Sadly only a fragment of Fulk's history remains – some nine pages – which don't address most of the questions we might wish to have answered. Still, it is instructive to see what Fulk wished to have preserved for posterity. The first sentence tells us everything we need to know:

> I, Fulk Count of Anjou, who am the son of Geoffrey of Chateau Landon and Ermengarde, daughter of Fulk Nerra Count of Anjou; and nephew of Geoffrey Martel, who was son of the same Fulk, my grandfather, and brother of my mother, who held the county of Anjou 28 years, and Tours and Nantes and Maine, wished to commit to words how my ancestors acquired this honour and held it until my time, and how I too have held this same honour thanks to divine mercy.[36]

Fulk Réchin refers to 'my grandfather Fulk' (i.e. Fulk Nerra) four times in the first two pages of his history. He is clearly concerned with his legitimacy – or lack thereof – and this is the key to the existence of his history. He wished to set down an account of his ancestors and place himself in this line of succession to justify his usurpation of the county. He also confirms that Geoffrey Martel gave him the Saintonge, though we perhaps have less reason to trust him on this point than any other, and he listed the castles built by Fulk Nerra, proof that two generations later the significance of Fulk Nerra's achievements was well known.

We are incredibly fortunate that Fulk chose to record his thoughts, even if only a fragment remains, since if we rely on the *Gesta* we are left with little more than we had about Geoffrey the Bearded. Worse, the version of the *Gesta* from 1109 had an explicitly didactic purpose in showing all the other counts to be wise and valiant, with Fulk Réchin alone being unworthy and decadent, and warning Fulk V to return to their values. Fulk's failings are illustrated in the episodes narrated: we are told that he overthrew and imprisoned Geoffrey the Bearded, lost Saintes to the Poitevins, alienated property and castles to the French king and finally we are given the lurid details of his three wives.

What we certainly are not told is why he was called Fulk *Réchin*, a term that seems to have been used in his lifetime. This has variously been translated as the 'Quarreller', the 'Growler' or the 'Sour Faced', though in its possible derivation from *rechigner* (to balk) I would also suggest the rhyming 'Fulk the Sulky'. Halphen reports the preposterous story that Fulk bent to kiss a saint's relic and hit his face, which then gave him a *rechigné*, twisted expression, though only to discount the story as being based on a false charter.[37] Disappointingly he then drops the question entirely. Other historians have speculated that Fulk had a stroke, which left him with a twisted expression. William of Malmesbury says explicitly that *Réchin* means 'Growler' because of Fulk's perpetual growling at the ineptitude of his brother. Once again, we really don't know, but at least Fulk has a more interesting name than Geoffrey the Bearded.

Or does he? Why was Geoffrey the Bearded so notable for his beard that he was named for it? Perhaps this is because Fulk Nerra and Geoffrey Martel had been clean-shaven like Romans. The drawings of Fulk Nerra's tomb effigy show that he was beardless, and if Geoffrey Martel was too, then his successor's beard may have been noteworthy. In the conscious association with all things Roman, the Angevins were likely clean-shaven and short-haired. The Romans throughout the Republic and early Empire never had beards, and it was Hadrian (who reigned from 118–138) who first had a beard. Why the change? Some contemporary sources claimed that he had a disfiguring facial scar that he wanted to cover. Whatever the reason, subsequent Emperors were bearded until the 4th century, when Constantine the Great reunited the Empire and self-consciously portrayed himself as the new Augustus, naturally returning to the traditional clean-shaven look as well. The oscillation between beards and no beards in medieval kingship can be quite telling: the politics of facial hair can speak volumes! We shouldn't forget that any given individual may simply have liked having a beard or not, but the point is that his successors would then adopt the fashion and inevitably appearance became a political link with earlier rulers.

Fulk Réchin has another, and arguably more influential, claim to fame than writing a history of his family, and it is utterly extraordinary: the Norman chronicler Orderic

Vitalis claimed that Fulk Réchin invented the long pointed shoes that are such an iconic accessory throughout the medieval period.[38] Indeed, almost every image of the Middle Ages shows an example of this fashion, and it is part of what makes the period seem so alien to us, since they look undeniably silly. It would be unexpected enough for us to know the name of the person who invented the fashion, but for that person to be a particular Count of Anjou is astonishing.

Let us consider the story more carefully. These extravagant shoes were constantly censured by the clergy and secular rulers as a piece of useless vanity, which did nothing to hinder, and in fact increased, their popularity. It is therefore not unexpected that Orderic would locate their origin outside the Norman realm, and attributing them to the enemy Angevins would be sensible. After all, Orderic also claimed that the Angevins were 'barbarians who desecrated churches, slew priests, looted indiscriminately, and ate like beasts'.[39] Why wouldn't they also have been responsible (paradoxically, if they were barbarians) for the quintessential piece of medieval vanity?

But that's not enough, since Orderic also throws in a typically bitchy aside that the reason Fulk invented long pointed shoes was to hide his deformed feet, and this could simply be a scurrilous story to ridicule a Norman enemy. Still, it is reminiscent of the story about Hadrian growing a beard to cover a scar, something which is possible. The Angevin chroniclers are completely silent on this matter, but perhaps that is natural: fashion was always seen as frivolous by monastic chroniclers, so it would hardly be something they would celebrate, especially if it really were because of their lord's deformity. We don't know if Fulk himself might proudly have claimed to be the Manolo Blahnik of the 11th century in the missing part of his history, but it seems unlikely he would have celebrated this for the same reasons as above. We are simply unable to judge whether or not the story is true, but it is an extraordinary claim that must be acknowledged.

The First Crusade

Fulk Réchin lived through the event that marked the climax of the 11th century and shaped Europe for centuries: the First Crusade. The Crusades will now be a constant presence in this book, as indeed they were for the Angevins and all other European rulers. The new movement emerged from key existing themes of the 11th century, the concepts of pilgrimage, penance and holy war against God's enemies.

It is too important to our story, and too good a story in itself, not to set out in some detail, but there are also very good precedents for a digression here on the First Crusade: Fulk Réchin himself, when he decided to write a history of Anjou, included a history of the Crusade, and of the nine pages of Fulk's history that still survive, three and a half are occupied by detailing the events of the Crusade. Fulk couldn't know how important the foundation of the kingdom of Jerusalem would be to his son, but he still found it essential in any history of 11th-century Europe to include a history of the Crusade.

William of Malmesbury did something similar in his history of the Norman kings of England, and spent what amounts to forty-seven pages of one modern edition giving a complete account of the First Crusade including one of the best renditions of Urban II's speech at Clermont that launched the movement.[40]

The story of the First Crusade is compelling. Urban II had continued his predecessor Gregory VII's struggle with the German Emperor, and he had actually been expelled from Rome by the anti-pope Guibert, which is why he travelled to France and convened a council at Clermont. Urban had continued Gregory's reforms, and particularly attempted to implement the Peace and Truce of God, initiatives meant to stop Christians fighting each other by prohibiting violence in certain places (e.g. around churches) and on certain days (e.g. Sunday), and suggested that they should direct their violence towards a worthier goal. He had also received Byzantine ambassadors requesting assistance in the east. The Byzantine Emperor Alexius Comnenus was fighting against the Seljuk Turks, and he needed additional manpower to regain control of lands he had lost in Asia Minor. Finally, on his way to the Council of Clermont, Urban spent time at the abbey of Cluny and would have heard how difficult the pilgrimage to Jerusalem had become. With all this on his mind, Urban spoke at the Council and called for everyone, rich and poor alike, to stop fighting other Christians and march to the east to rescue Jerusalem for Christianity, and assist their Christian neighbours in Byzantium against the Turks.[41] Incidentally he also discussed other church business, including confirming the excommunication of King Philip of France for eloping with Fulk Réchin's wife Bertrada.

There was an immediate and overwhelming response from the audience, both clergy and laymen, and many factors contributed to this. There had been an increase in religious feeling through the 11th century as witnessed by the Peace and Truce of God, the revival of monasticism with the foundation of Cluny and the renewed energy of the papacy. Simultaneously, the growing sophistication of political entities such as Normandy, Anjou and France had moved beyond the disorganized free-for-all of the 10th century and curbed the ability of their nobles to grab land and increase their power, which may have stimulated their desire to look elsewhere.

Urban toured France for a year preaching the Crusade and there was an enormous response. Yet no Angevin representative accompanied the Crusade. Modern historians often point out this absence of Angevin participation, but perhaps this is not surprising, because Fulk Réchin would have been around sixty and his sons Geoffrey Martel II and Fulk the Young would have been too young. Fulk Réchin records in his history that the Crusade was preached by Urban himself in Angers and Tours, and if Fulk can be believed there was certainly no animosity about his failure to respond to the call, for the pope took this opportunity to give him the great symbol of papal favour, the Golden Rose. Indeed, Fulk seems to have taken this honour as the inspiration to write his memoir, and celebrated his own reception of the pope as participation in the work of the Crusade.

Urban's appeal to the aristocracy had been successful, but the movement he launched took on a further life of its own. Itinerant preachers such as Robert d'Arbrissel, the founder of Fontevraud Abbey, which would later be so dear to the Angevins, preached the Crusade, but the most important among their number was Peter the Hermit. Peter was a monk from northern France who possessed incredible charisma and the aura of supernatural authority. Guibert of Nogent, who knew him personally, said, 'Whatever he said or did, it seemed like something half-divine.'[42] Peter progressed northeast on his preaching tour, and by the time he reached Cologne he had thousands of followers. Vast numbers of peasants joined in, perhaps hoping to escape the harshness of their lives, perhaps lured by millenarian fantasies that they would reach a true Promised Land, and began to march east. This 'People's Crusade' was in contrast to the organized bodies of fighting men the pope had hoped for. In their wake, the religious fervour roused by the Crusade led to massacres of Jews in many German towns and cities, despite the opposition of the clergy. Some of the noble Crusaders, most notably Godfrey of Bouillon – later to be revered as the most perfect knight and one of the great heroes of Christian knighthood, the Nine Worthies – used the unrest to extort money from Jewish communities in exchange for protection. A contingent of German Crusaders spread terror along the Rhine and Moselle and massacred Jews in Worms, Mainz, Cologne, Trier and many other places, before marching to the Hungarian border and being slaughtered by the outraged Hungarian king after they devastated the countryside.

Urban had ordered the organized portion of the Crusade to assemble at Constantinople, and the groups led by Peter the Hermit and other itinerant preachers also reached the city. They were cordially received by the Emperor, who recommended that nothing be done until the arrival of the rest of the Crusade, which would consist almost entirely of fighting men. However, ethnic animosities between the French, German and Italian components resulted in the army splitting into various factions and launching raids into Anatolia. This alerted the Turks to their presence and, more importantly, to their disorganization and lack of military experience, and soon the People's Crusade was lured into a trap and almost completely destroyed in October 1096.[43]

The Crusade was thus off to a disastrous start – as many contemporaries, who felt it was a vainglorious and wasteful enterprise, were quick to point out – but the real military forces were about to arrive. The Emperor Alexius Comnenus still hoped for help from the experienced Western armies, and if they were victorious seems to have envisaged them establishing small Christian states on his borders that would be held as fiefs of the Empire. The Crusaders themselves had very different ideas, immediately leading to friction with the Byzantines.

The important contingents of the Crusade included an army from Lorraine led by Godfrey of Bouillon and his brother Baldwin of Boulogne; an army from Toulouse led by Raymond of St Gilles; an army from southern Italy led by the Norman prince

Bohemond; and an Anglo-Norman force led by Robert Curthose, eldest son of William the Conqueror and ruler of Normandy. To raise funds for the journey Robert had pawned the duchy to his brother William Rufus for ten thousand silver marks, leading to the reunification of England and Normandy which would last for another hundred years.

Once all the armies were assembled, the Crusaders set off on their great march across Anatolia. The Turks took a somewhat dim view of the Westerners given the ease with which they had slaughtered Peter the Hermit's rabble, and they quickly paid for their misconception. The Crusaders crushed a Turkish army at Dorylaeum and now marched on to Antioch. It was not entirely clear which road would be the best to take, and the Crusading armies divided. Baldwin of Boulogne took this opportunity to head east, where he became involved in the politics of Armenia and was asked to assist the Christian city of Edessa. Baldwin agreed, and ultimately seems to have connived in the murder of the Byzantine administrator to allow him to take over the city as Count of Edessa. Thus was founded the first of the Crusader States – a city taken from Christians by treachery and murder, and which wasn't even in the Holy Land.[44]

The rest of the Crusaders reached Antioch, but the formidable fortifications of the huge city had been well prepared for a siege. Division among the Muslim rulers of Aleppo, Damascus and Mosul meant that at first the Crusaders could besiege the city without undue fear, but as the siege dragged on for months, and reports spread that Kerbogha, the ruler of Mosul, was about to arrive with a huge relieving army, panic took hold among the Crusaders. Stephen of Blois, whose son Stephen would be the great opponent of the Angevins in the next generation, decided to return home with his men, to his lasting disgrace, and even Peter the Hermit was caught trying to escape. In all this turmoil, one man maintained his singleness of purpose, and this was Bohemond. Bohemond was in negotiations with a traitor within the city, who let the Crusaders sneak into a tower by night and open two of the city's gates. By the evening of 3 June 1098 the city had fallen, and the Turkish population was slaughtered.

After the Crusaders managed to defeat Kerbogha's relieving army of Turks and Arabs due to internal divisions between the Muslim forces (or divine assistance, according to contemporary sources), Antioch was secured as the second new Christian state in the Middle East. Now the Crusaders began to argue over what the next course of action should be. When they learned that Alexius Comnenus had turned back and wasn't coming to join the expedition – this was because the coward Stephen of Blois had convinced him that the Crusaders would be annihilated by Kerbogha and there was no point in continuing – they felt justified in ignoring any nominal authority of the Emperor and carving out new states for themselves. Raymond of St Gilles, the count of Toulouse, who had been one of the first nobles to take the cross and believed that he should lead the Crusade, finally decided to continue the march to Jerusalem, and Robert Curthose and Godfrey of Bouillon, amongst many others, joined him. Bohemond remained in possession of Antioch to rule as his own principality.[45]

The Crusaders reached Jerusalem on 7 June 1099. Their first view of the city came from a hill nearby that the Christians called 'Montjoie' because it was the first place from which pilgrims could see the city. The walls around the city were formidable and a long siege – for which the Crusaders lacked sufficient manpower – seemed inevitable, but there were rumours that the rulers of Egypt, who controlled the city, were sending a large army. The Crusaders began building siege engines, and as news arrived that the Egyptian army was approaching, a timely vision instructed the Crusaders to fast and undertake a barefoot procession around the city, guaranteeing victory if they did.

On 14 July 1099 the Crusaders launched their assault and managed to enter the city. The Muslim commander and his entourage surrendered to Raymond of St Gilles and were allowed to leave, but everyone else was slaughtered, even a group in the Al Aqsa mosque who had surrendered and been offered protection. Reports said that the corpses and rivers of blood were knee-high. The city's Jewish population fled to their synagogue, which was set alight and all were killed. Stories of this ruthless slaughter have repercussions felt to this day.

Yet some modern historians have questioned these reports, and argue that, just as the size of medieval armies was always greatly exaggerated to indicate how important a battle was, so too the slaughter in Jerusalem might have been exaggerated to empha-size the magnitude of the Crusaders' achievement. They note that some contemporary sources claim that large numbers of prisoners were taken and the slaughter may not have been so terrible.[46] The important historical points about this episode are first, that the Western chroniclers would have believed this kind of violence was somehow praiseworthy, and that the extermination of the Jews and Muslims living in Jerusalem was a necessary and fitting climax to the First Crusade. This forms an even more marked contrast when compared with the exemplary behaviour demonstrated by the Muslim hero Saladin when he re-took Jerusalem in 1187. Second, even if the Western chronicles were exaggerating the extent of the slaughter in Jerusalem, the story that the First Crusaders behaved this way is still generally accepted, and forms a part of the way the Crusades are viewed in our own time.

The First Crusade had succeeded beyond all expectation and against the odds, but what now? The Crusaders wished to elect a king, but there were disputes between the clergy and lay lords, and between different factions of the Crusader army. Of the great lords who had set out, Baldwin of Boulogne and Bohemond had founded their own states, and many others wished to return home. This left Raymond of St Gilles and Godfrey of Bouillon. Raymond had made no secret of the fact that he had wished to be recognized as leader of the Crusade, though he was not popular with the other Crusaders. It was decided that he should be offered the position of King of Jerusalem, but Raymond turned this down, saying he could not wear a crown in the city where Christ was crowned with thorns – a popular view among the Crusaders. Probably Raymond hoped to gain credit for this pious attitude and then be begged to take the leadership anyway, but instead the Crusaders took his refusal at face value and offered the crown to Godfrey. Godfrey also refused to accept a crown, but said he would accept the role of leader, and agreed to take the title 'Advocate of the Holy Sepulchre', which was accepted by the Crusaders. Thus in the line of the kings of Jerusalem, Godfrey comes first, though he never used the title.[47]

Godfrey of Bouillon became a talismanic figure in the later Middle Ages and was hailed as one of the Nine Worthies, the most perfect specimens of chivalry. Indeed, he was the only contemporary man to be thus honoured: the others were the great pagan heroes, Hector, Alexander the Great and Julius Caesar; the Jewish heroes Joshua, David and Judas Maccabeus; and Godfrey's fellow Christians Charlemagne and King Arthur. Yet he accomplished nothing of great note on the Crusade and seems to have been chosen simply because he was of high rank and his personal life had no obvious scandal.

Raymond had fallen into his own trap and left Jerusalem in a fury, ultimately returning to Constantinople to visit his ally, the Emperor. Godfrey almost immediately fell ill and died, leaving Jerusalem to his brother Baldwin of Edessa, who became the first king of Jerusalem to be crowned, on Christmas Day 1100. Within five years of the preaching of the Crusade, the Crusaders had met with complete success and founded Christian states in Edessa, Antioch and Jerusalem. The stage was set for the next 200 years of conflict in the Middle East, conflicts that would involve all of Europe, and particularly the Angevins.

CHAPTER 3 – ANGEVIN KINGS

A<small>T THE BEGINNING OF</small> the 12th century the Angevin fortunes seemed to be in decline. Fulk Réchin had usurped the comital title from his brother but in doing so unleashed forces of baronial unrest that blighted the rest of his reign, and worse, after his daring coup he displayed no energy or creativity and seemed sunk in lethargy, aside from making an uncanonical marriage that alienated the clergy. Elsewhere, the dukes of Normandy had surpassed all their local rivals and the French king himself by achieving the throne of England. William the Conqueror had taken Maine from the Angevins, and his son William Rufus had reunited England and Normandy; on Rufus's early death, William the Conqueror's youngest son Henry I had negotiated the difficulties of succession to become the undisputed ruler of a united England and Normandy. Because of the success of the Normans, the French king now tried to tighten his authority over what remained of France, and things looked bleak for entities such as Blois and Anjou. Worse, the Angevins took no part in the greatest event of the 11th century, the First Crusade, and had been left behind in terms of influence.

Within fifty years of Fulk Réchin's death, however, the Angevins had concluded marriages that brought them their own crowns and put them at the centre of the Crusading movement by 1131, and the entirety of Western Europe by 1154, in the process taking over the Anglo-Norman realm and effectively ending the importance of Normandy and the Normans for good. How did they achieve this? The pivotal figure was Fulk Réchin's son, Fulk V.

Fulk V seems to us to possess an energy and determination completely lacking in his father and a prudence alien to his mother, and his contemporaries were not slow to note this. The *Gesta* states, 'It is true that "the father will not bear the iniquity of the son nor the son of the father". Thus it is that after the death of Fulk Réchin, his son Fulk V, count of Anjou, abandoned the ways of his mother and father and led an honourable life, ruling his territory wisely.'[1] This is a case in which the conventional sentiments of the chroniclers – Fulk became king of Jerusalem, therefore he must have every good attribute – can be verified, because Fulk did leave Anjou in a considerably better position than he found it.

The *Gesta* and William of Malmesbury both attribute the same excellent qualities to Fulk's elder brother, Geoffrey Martel II, though it is difficult to decide whether Geoffrey really was perfect or simply shared in the retrospective reflected limelight of his brother. That seems more likely in the *Gesta*, which wished to glorify Fulk as King of Jerusalem, but Malmesbury made it clear that he was writing while Fulk was still Count of Anjou – i.e. before 1129, when Fulk gave the county to Geoffrey Plantagenet – so he had no idea of the greatness that awaited him. Malmesbury's anti-Angevin bias means that he can't resist another dig at his enemies in his brief comments on Geoffrey Martel II:

> Geoffrey obtaining the hereditary surname of Martel, ennobled it by his exertions; procuring such peace and tranquillity in those parts, as no one ever had seen, or will see in future. On this account being killed by the treachery of his people ...[2]

Naturally such a perfect prince couldn't be appreciated by the Angevins!

In 1109 Fulk V married Erembourg, the daughter of Count Hélie of Maine. William the Conqueror had taken Maine from the Angevins under Fulk Réchin, but when England and Normandy were divided after William's death, and during the subsequent struggles between Robert Curthose, William Rufus and Henry I, Maine regained its independence. This was of only brief duration, since the county passed to Fulk and Erembourg when Hélie died in 1110. Although Maine remained a distinct county, it became part of 'Greater Anjou' and with its capital Le Mans became absolutely integral to Anjou; it was in Le Mans that Geoffrey Plantagenet was buried and Henry II was born.

Maine was also of great interest to the Normans, and Henry I retaliated by capturing Alençon and forcing Fulk and his ally Louis VI to sue for peace.[3] However, according to the *Gesta*, which spends pages elaborating on events, it was Fulk who humiliated Henry in a great battle.[4] Fulk was heavily involved in Norman politics at this point, particularly the extended dispute over the succession to England and Normandy. As we saw, Robert Curthose pawned Normandy to William Rufus to pay for his participation in the First Crusade, but when Rufus was killed while hunting in the New Forest in 1100, their younger brother Henry I seized the throne and Robert regained Normandy. Robert failed in his attempts to unseat Henry, and ultimately Henry invaded Normandy and defeated Robert at Tinchebray in 1106. Robert remained a captive until his death in 1134, allowing Henry to rule a united England and Normandy. Robert left a son known as William Clito who would be a threat to Henry, and Clito's existence had a significant influence on Henry's relations with the Angevins.

Immediately after the battle with Henry, Fulk betrothed his daughter Isabel to William Clito, but then quickly broke off the match on the grounds of consanguinity and betrothed her to Henry I's heir William Aetheling instead, with Maine as her dowry.[5] What prompted this sudden rapprochement with Henry I? The marriage alliance was clearly a prize offered by Henry to detach Fulk from a possible grand alliance with France in support of William Clito, which would also have the advantage of securing Maine for Henry.

Unfortunately this Angevin-Norman alliance led to nothing, since William Aetheling drowned in 1120 in the sinking of the White Ship, the 'Titanic of the 12th century'. William and a group of other lively young people from Henry's court, including some of Henry's illegitimate children, were on the recently fitted-out ship sailing from Barfleur back to England, but the White Ship struck a rock and sank. Young Stephen of Blois, the king's favourite nephew – and son and namesake of the cowardly Crusader married to William the Conqueror's daughter – who would later usurp his throne, actually left the ship just before it sailed due to illness; had he died as well this might have altered English history substantially.[6] This disaster was an event of European significance at the time, and had grave repercussions for England, Normandy and Anjou. Had William lived, we would expect him to have ruled England and Normandy plus Maine in right of Isabel, and Anjou to have passed to Fulk's son independently. There would have been no Angevin Empire, but possibly a Norman one. The Normans might also have annexed Anjou if Geoffrey Plantagenet had died young. Yet William, along with all but one of his fellow passengers, did die. Isabel of Anjou, William's widow, did not remarry, instead becoming abbess of Fontevraud.

With the death of his heir, Henry immediately remarried in an attempt to father another son, but when this failed he was forced to think again of alliances. Fortunately for him, his daughter Matilda's husband, the Holy Roman Emperor Henry V, had also died, and so he summoned her home to take up the Anglo-Norman succession. Matilda returned in 1125 to England, a land to which she was almost a stranger, having gone to Germany in 1114 at the age of twelve to marry Henry V. She carried the title of Empress, which she retained for the rest of her life, and various treasures including the crown that would be used by her son and grandsons as kings of England, and more importantly the relic of the hand of St James, which carried enormous prestige.[7] This relic was eventually given to Reading Abbey, Henry I's favourite foundation and his resting place, and, after an eventful history, is now found in St Peter's Church in Marlow.

With the first Norman-Angevin marriage alliance rendered irrelevant by William's death, Henry turned again to Anjou and now had Matilda marry Fulk's son Geoffrey Plantagenet. Henry was determined to have Matilda succeed him, and seemed quite clear that Geoffrey as her husband would not be king, which would have been unacceptable to the Norman barons.

The Kingdom of Jerusalem

Meanwhile another king faced succession difficulties: Baldwin II of Jerusalem, who had four daughters but no son. At this period, rules of succession were still being determined and there was no difficulty about succession passing through the female line, but it was acknowledged that the kingdom needed a strong military leader. Baldwin asked the pope and the king of France for a candidate to marry his eldest daughter,

Melisende, and after due consideration it was decided that Fulk of Anjou fulfilled the criteria. Erembourg had recently died, so Fulk was a widower in the prime of life, successful in war and of good character. He had also been to Jerusalem on a pilgrimage in 1120 and so had some knowledge of the kingdom. We can still read the letter from Pope Honorius II to Baldwin II discussing the issue, and recommending Fulk to him as a powerful and wise man perfect for the job.[8]

The history of the new Crusader states in the Holy Land (or *Outremer*, the land beyond the sea, as it was often known) had been eventful. Though we date the First Crusade as 1095–1099 and treat it as a discrete event, in fact the movement unleashed by Urban II was not quite so tidy. After news of the conquest of Jerusalem reached Europe, a new wave of Crusaders set out. William IX, the Duke of Aquitaine, a powerful noble but also the first known troubadour, and grandfather of Eleanor of Aquitaine, reached Constantinople in 1101 with many other new Crusaders, and even the elder Stephen of Blois returned to make amends for his previous flight. Each of these new expeditions met with catastrophe in Asia Minor, including a German contingent accompanied by Ida the Dowager Magravine of Austria, whom legend said was captured and taken to a harem where she gave birth to the Muslim hero Zengi.[9] The destruction that met the Crusades of 1101, in contrast to the success of the First Crusade, was blamed by Westerners on the treachery of the Byzantines, though the Byzantines took the failure of the new expeditions as proof that the Crusaders were faithless opportunists who only wished to grab as much land as possible, and bad soldiers to boot. The divisions between east and west that would have such catastrophic consequences in 1204 were cemented here.[10]

From the Frankish point of view, Baldwin of Boulogne, first Count of Edessa and then the first crowned King of Jerusalem as Baldwin I, is the real hero of the First Crusade. It was Baldwin who consolidated the kingdom and put it on firm military, political and economic footings. Baldwin's policy was consistent: he wished to retain the trade from the inland Muslim cities such as Damascus for the Mediterranean ports controlled by the Crusaders to build the economy of the Kingdom of Jerusalem, and he saw no difficulty whatsoever in having Muslim vassals and cordial relations with Muslim states when it suited him. Newly arrived Crusaders would find this attitude baffling and insist on attacking all Muslims indiscriminately. Baldwin was also completely pragmatic, and had no qualms about raiding caravans to and from Arabia and intimidating his neighbours with force; in fact, his policy of raiding, castle-building and annexing rich territory is very familiar from what we have seen in Anjou and the rest of France. Though he respected his agreements with Muslims, Baldwin was pitiless to those who resisted him, and in contrast with Godfrey of Bouillon, who reigned briefly enough to be thoroughly idealized, Baldwin appears as a more realistic figure. We are well informed about these details because the Crusader States produced a great historian in William of Tyre, and we have his detailed and critically astute analysis of events from the early history of the kingdom until 1184.[11]

Baldwin I left no heir, and when he died there was some thought of passing the kingdom to his (and Godfrey of Bouillon's) brother, Eustace Count of Boulogne, who actually began the journey to Jerusalem to claim the throne. In the meantime though, the council decided that the throne should pass to Baldwin of Le Bourg, the last of the the leaders of the First Crusade still in the Holy Land, since he was Baldwin I's cousin and had become the ruler of Edessa when Baldwin I became king. Baldwin II was crowned King of Jerusalem on Easter Sunday 1118.[12]

The constant need for military support led to the most famous and lasting creation of the Crusader States, the orders of religious knighthood known as the Hospitallers and the Templars. In 1118, Hugh de Payens, a knight from Champagne, arrived in Jerusalem with a revolutionary idea. He established a group of knights who would take the vows of Benedictine monks, but would also use their military skills to keep the road to Jerusalem free of bandits. Baldwin II granted them quarters in the royal palace that was believed to be the Temple of Solomon, and from this they took their name, the 'Knights of the Temple' or Templars. The Templars, with the support of St Bernard of Clairvaux, received recognition as a distinct religious order at the Council of Troyes in 1128. The origin of the Hospitallers goes back to 1070, when a hospital and inn was founded in Jerusalem for the use of pilgrims, staffed by monks of the Benedictine Order. After the First Crusade, the hospital was raised to an independent monastic order of its own. Inspired by the Templars, the Hospitallers began to take on military functions by the 1150s or 1160s and became a fully fledged military order in 1179.[13]

Succession to the crown of Jerusalem (and indeed all the Crusader States) was always a matter of extreme importance, given the peril that surrounded them. As we saw, Baldwin was to be succeeded by his eldest daughter Melisende, and he arranged for her to marry Fulk V of Anjou. Fulk insisted that Melisende be formally appointed heiress to the kingdom before he married her, and Baldwin also promised that Fulk would be crowned king as a full co-ruler of the kingdom, not merely a royal consort.[14]

With this agreed, and with his son Geoffrey Plantagenet married to Matilda, the heiress to England, and the couple established in Anjou, Fulk was free to take up his role as co-heir apparent to the throne of Jerusalem. He arrived in 1129 and his marriage to Melisende was celebrated immediately. This marriage was, like every marriage among the medieval aristocracy, a political calculation in which personal attraction and desire had no part. This was fortunate for Fulk and his son, since the Empress Matilda was said to despise Geoffrey Plantagenet because he was so much younger (around fourteen), gauche and of only comital rank, despite his great physical beauty, whereas Melisende was said to despise Fulk because he was so much older (around forty), and his appearance (short, wiry, ginger) didn't help. Her feelings were irrelevant – as were Fulk's, for that matter, though we can only assume he must have been delighted with the prospect of a crown, the opportunity to fight as a Crusader and a young wife. It was precisely this reality of marriage as a business and political transaction that would lead to the doctrine of courtly love, which praised the purity of a man's love for an unattainable woman (who was married to someone else), and famously declared that love could not exist in marriage.

Fulk immediately fulfilled the role for which he had been chosen and began to assist Baldwin II in his military enterprises. Baldwin decided to undertake the conquest of Damascus, which would have been a huge prize for the Crusaders. Damascus was in turmoil, having become embroiled in a conflict with the sinister Assassins, a Muslim sect notorious for sending hashish-fuelled killers to murder its enemies (thus giving us the word 'assassin', derived from hashish), and a near civil war had broken out. In 1129, with reinforcements newly arrived from Europe, Baldwin and Fulk marched against Damascus, but due to the indiscipline of the newcomers and torrential rain the expedition had to be abandoned.[15]

Baldwin died in 1131, and had stipulated that Fulk and Melisende should be co-rulers in conjunction with their infant son Baldwin III, which seems to have been an attempt not only to ensure the succession but also specifically to exclude Geoffrey Plantagenet from the crown of Jerusalem.[16] Fulk and Melisende were crowned in the Church of the Holy Sepulchre on 14 September, but the political situation was by no means straightforward. Baldwin I and II had exercised authority over the other Crusader States through prestige and force of personality, but the actual rights of the king were unclear and it could easily be argued that Fulk and Melisende possessed no authority over the other states. The rulers of Edessa and Triopli immediately rejected the authority of Jerusalem, and Melisende's sister Alice claimed the regency of Antioch in opposition to the crown. Fulk responded strongly to these challenges and brought an army against Antioch, and although he defeated a party of rebels and reconciled with Edessa and Tripoli, the matter was clearly not at an end, and this disunity would haunt the Crusader States until their fall.[17]

These important political and military considerations were abruptly overshadowed by a lurid story straight from an Arthurian romance, related by William of Tyre. A young knight and relative of Baldwin II, Hugh of Le Puiset, had inherited lands in Outremer, and had come to live at court where he was close friends with the Princess Melisende. Hugh married a wealthy and much older widow with two sons of her own, and the stepsons hated this young upstart scarcely older than they were. After Melisende's marriage to Fulk, she continued to spend time with Hugh and gossip began to circulate about them. Finally in 1132 or 1133 Hugh's stepson openly accused Hugh of betraying the king and, in a story reminiscent of Malory's *Morte d'Arthur* or Chrétien de Troyes' *Lancelot*, challenged him to single combat to prove his innocence. Hugh accepted the challenge, but on the appointed day he failed to turn up, which was taken as proof of his treason. Hugh fled to the Egyptians at Ascalon and actually returned with a Muslim army to pillage the region around Jaffa, but when Fulk sent a force to oppose them the Egyptians abandoned Hugh and he submitted to the king. Hugh was sentenced to three years in exile, but before he could leave the realm he was attacked and nearly killed by a Breton knight. Suspicion fell on Fulk for organizing the attack, but when put on trial the Breton claimed sole responsibility, and he was executed. Hugh departed for the court of Sicily where he died shortly after, and the sordid affair was at an end.[18]

I have said this episode could be straight from Arthurian literature, but in fact it predates it and may have inspired some of the stories. The first codification of Arthurian legend in a form that we would recognize was by Geoffrey of Monmouth in around 1140, in his *History of the Kings of Britain*. Geoffrey included (or invented) Merlin, Uther Pendragon, Uther's rape of Ygraine in the guise of her husband at the castle of Tintagel to conceive Arthur, Arthur's nephew Mordred usurping the throne, the treacherous queen Guinevere's bigamous marriage to Mordred, and the final war against Mordred in which Arthur was victorious, but mortally wounded and taken to the Isle of Avalon to be healed. What is most striking is the lack of any reference to Lancelot and his love for Guinevere, the Holy Grail and in fact any element of romance.

The romantic elements of Arthurian literature developed later in the 12th century under the influence of troubadour poetry, the cult of courtly love and growing Christian mysticism (as we shall see later), but there is also a distinct possibility that real events such as the accusation against Melisende and the challenge for her supposed lover to prove his innocence in combat also had an influence. We shall return to this when we look at Eleanor of Aquitaine, another queen accused of adultery in the Holy Land, but her involvement with Arthurian literature and courtly culture was much stronger than Melisende's and may have served as a more direct model.

William of Tyre chose to see the episode in personal terms, and believed it confirmed that Melisende cared little for her husband, even being willing to betray him with another man.[19] This fits neatly into traditional medieval attitudes about women's infidelity, and refuses to judge Melisende's motivations as anything other than emotional. However, modern historians view Hugh's revolt in different terms. The details surrounding this episode suggest a political dispute, and that Melisende and her supporters among the nobility were challenging Fulk. Hugh belonged to this party, and although in enlisting Muslim support he went too far and caused his own downfall, it seems that Melisende's party was victorious. Again, William of Tyre chooses to relate this in romantic terms, saying that after the incident Fulk became so uxorious that he would do nothing without consulting his wife first. Yet clearly there had been a struggle and Melisende had successfully asserted her rights as co-ruler.[20]

Queen Melisende is a fascinating figure. She was in fact the first Angevin queen, though it is typical of the Angevins that the first three Angevin queens were all queens in their own right before they married into the family, and Melisende would certainly have objected vehemently to being characterized this way. Melisende was heiress to Jerusalem and gave Fulk his crown; Matilda was an Empress by marriage and inherited the throne of England, though she failed to be crowned and instead passed the crown to her son Henry II; and Eleanor of Aquitaine was queen of France before marrying Henry II to become queen of England. We have striking stories about Matilda and Eleanor, and can form an idea of their characters, but we know very little about Melisende. What we do know comes from chroniclers who used clichéd images of women that must be treated with suspicion. To them, the role of a queen was primarily to bear legitimate children, to intercede with her husband and show mercy to her subjects, and to devote herself to pious and charitable works. If a queen showed too strong a character she would be accused of 'meddling' or dominating her husband in an unseemly way, and if she had powerful friends she was accused of having 'favourites'. All these things Melisende was accused of doing, not only by contemporary chroniclers but also by modern historians who tend to repeat what the primary sources say. This doesn't mean that Melisende didn't have favourites or try to dominate the king, and she might have been selfish, but it is too common for queens to be presented in this stereotypical way for us to rely on these descriptions. William of Tyre chose to describe her after her death as follows:

> Transcending the strength of women, the lady queen, Melisende, a prudent woman, discreet above the female sex, had ruled the kingdom with fitting moderation for more than 30 years, during the lifetime of her husband and the reign of her son.[21]

William's backhanded compliments about Melisende transcending the normal weakness of women do not change the fact that it was she who ruled for more than thirty years.

We also possess, as we do surprisingly often for 12th-century figures, an item that Melisende owned personally. In Melisende's case it is a beautifully decorated ivory and silk cover for a psalter (book of psalms), now in the British Library, and it is indicative of the kinds of beautifully decorated objects that 12th-century aristocrats could own. The embroidered spine has patterns of crosses in silver and silk thread, and the ivory covers show episodes from the life of King David (who was believed to have composed the psalms) and a king performing the Six Corporal Works of Mercy. All the work is in a typical 12th-century Byzantine style, and the king represented on the back cover wears Byzantine dress, confirming the obvious point that the Byzantine Empire was the source of luxury goods for the Kingdom of Jerusalem.[22] Beautiful as it is, the real interest in the psalter comes in its calendar, where there are notes recording the deaths of Baldwin II in 1131 and Fulk in 1143, and as mentioned earlier, the tantalizing graffito on the cover saying 'herodias' may refer to a nickname for Fulk.

We have now seen the first example of Angevin marriage trumping Norman conquest – Bohemond had to endure the siege of Antioch to create his principality, but Fulk V married Melisende and received the crown of Jerusalem. Equally, William the Bastard had to conquer England, but Geoffrey Plantagenet married Matilda and their son gained the throne, then married Eleanor to gain at a stroke the vast domain of Aquitaine.

This contrast was noted by contemporaries. Henry of Huntingdon reports that when the Anglo-Norman army was preparing for the Battle of the Standard against the Scots in 1138, a bishop summarized the Norman achievement as follows:

> No one resists you with impunity; brave France has tried and taken shelter; fierce England lay captive; rich Apulia flourished anew under your rule; renowned Jerusalem and noble Antioch both submitted themselves to you.[23]

There could be no more succinct summary of the Norman achievement in the 11th century. Yet the chronicler Ralph of Diceto made an even more succinct rejoinder when, in commenting on the various ways of gaining territory, he ended by saying, 'And you, happy Anjou, marry'.[24]

The kingdom Fulk and Melisende ruled was still a beleaguered colonial outpost, and now a Muslim ruler emerged who seemed capable of leading a united opposition to the Christian states. This was Zengi, the ruler of Aleppo and Mosul, and the greatest threat to the Crusader States since their foundation. Zengi had designs on Damascus, and the thought of a united Aleppo, Mosul and Damascus was one to terrify the Christians. They were not the only ones to fear this, and the ruler of Damascus also sensed the threat to his independence presented by Zengi's ambitions. In 1138 the Damascenes first approached Jerusalem with the offer of an alliance, which was rejected. However, by 1140 the threat presented by Zengi was much more apparent, and when his army moved to besiege Damascus, the alliance was offered again and it was accepted. Fulk mustered an army and marched on Damascus; Zengi retired without offering to fight.[25]

The earlier kings of Jerusalem had certainly not been averse to accepting Muslims as subjects, but this full-blown alliance with one of the most significant Muslim states was unprecedented. It shows the pragmatism that consistently marked policy in the Crusader States, but this would inevitably cause problems with newly arrived Crusaders who could not countenance such intimacy with the 'infidel'.

The alliance with Damascus was the most important achievement of Fulk's reign, but he did not benefit from it very long, as he died in November 1143 after being thrown from his horse while chasing a hare. He and Melisende had two sons, Baldwin and Amalric. Baldwin was thirteen when Fulk died, but there was no problem of a minority, since the claim to the throne was still Melisende's, and she and Baldwin III were crowned jointly on Christmas Day. This demonstrates the kingdom of Jerusalem's fundamentally different outlook on female succession to the kingdoms of Western Europe, notably England, where Henry I's acknowledged heir Matilda was deprived of her throne and ultimately had to give up her own claim in favour of her son, with no hint of co-rulership. Of course Matilda's son was the Angevin Henry II, so we should leave Jerusalem and return to Anjou to take up the story of Fulk's eldest son, Geoffrey Plantagenet.

Geoffrey Plantagenet and the Empress Matilda

Geoffrey was born in 1113. Jean of Marmoutier wrote a biography of Geoffrey in around 1173, when Geoffrey's son Henry II was established as the most powerful king in Europe, so although it is filled with interesting details it should be used with some caution. Once again we have an Angevin name to discuss, this time one that is instantly recognizable to modern readers. All contemporaries agree that Geoffrey was called *le Bel* ('the Handsome'), but they also state that he was called 'Plantagenet', and both names have followed him through history.

There isn't much need to explain a nickname like 'the Handsome', but why was Geoffrey called 'Plantagenet'? We simply don't know. Later historians in the 16th century – once the name had been adopted for the English ruling family from the 12th to the 15th centuries – claimed that it came about because Geoffrey liked to wear a sprig of the broom plant (*planta genista*, in Latin) in his hat, and this is the definition of the name that is usually given even today. That doesn't explain how this name, without being attributed to anyone else in the English royal family in any written source, somehow persisted for the next 300 years until it was publicly adopted again by the house of York in the 15th century as a way to emphasize their right to rule. A modern historian speculates that there were obscene connotations to the name ('hairy stalk') that celebrated Geoffrey's generative powers in conjunction with his beauty, and that kept prudish chroniclers from mentioning it but allowed it to retain currency in speech, until in the 15th century it was so inextricably connected to the royal line that it could be used openly.[26]

However, if the name does arise from the broom plant, it should be Planta*genest*, not Planta*genet*, and this is clearly what it was in Geoffrey's time, and still is in French. In French the name is written *Plantagenêt*, and the circumflex is essentially an abbreviation for the letter 's'. As an aside, remembering which words in French require a circumflex can be maddeningly difficult when learning the language, but it's easy once you know the circumflex replaces an 's': forêt/forest, côte/coast, bête/beast. In English we have dropped the circumflex, but haven't returned the 's', giving us Plantagenet.

Geoffrey not only gives his name to the royal family, but he is also intimately bound up in the symbols of England. Geoffrey is a key figure in early heraldry as his tomb bears an enamel portrait of him carrying a shield decorated with lions in a distinctly heraldic fashion, making him one of the first figures to be represented bearing a heraldic device and possibly the first to use one. The lion was also used by the Normans, and Geoffrey was given clothing decorated with lions when he was knighted by Henry I. Was Geoffrey simply a person who liked to collect badges and nicknames, though perhaps more systematic in his use of them than his contemporaries?

Geoffrey's biography, while perhaps not particularly accurate about him, does give us an insight into aristocratic life in the 12th century. We have a vivid portrait of Geoffrey's journey to Rouen to be knighted by Henry I before his marriage to Matilda.

The ceremony of knighthood is described in detail, and obviously the Angevin chronicler wants to highlight the respect shown to Geoffrey by the king, not least because Henry gave him a sword made by Weyland, the legendary Germanic smith, who most famously turned his enemies' skulls into drinking cups (and was a great favourite of the Anglo-Saxons, as shown on an exquisite 8th-century casket in the Sutton Hoo room of the British Museum). Already by 1128 the ceremony of knighthood had a defined place in court ceremonial and included such elements as a ritual bath and the public viewing of the knight after the private ceremony.

Of special note in this story is the description of the lion emblems that decorated Geoffrey's shoes and his shield, which were described as 'lion cubs', possibly a reference to the fact that they were lions 'passant', that is walking on all fours with their bodies horizontal, rather than 'rampant', standing on their hind legs. These lions passed from Geoffrey through Henry II to Richard the Lionheart to become the heraldic symbol of England. Geoffrey was one of the pioneers in using such personal imagery, mediating the heraldic representation of England to a substantial degree.[27]

All the Plantagenets were patrons of learning, as well as of conspicuous display. Geoffrey Plantagenet's biographer comments that as much as Geoffrey loved hunting, he loved reading more, and tells the story of how Geoffrey, when the castle of Montreuil-Bellay successfully resisted a siege, consulted the work of the Roman military historian Vegetius and discovered the way to take the castle.[28] Geoffrey was also said to enjoy music like his older troubadour contemporary William IX, and the story was told that when Geoffrey had taken some Poitevin knights prisoner, they composed and performed a song in his praise that pleased him so much that he released them.[29]

Two particular stories in Geoffrey's biography bear repeating, not because they are necessarily true, but because of what they reveal about 12th-century life. The first involves a tournament arranged between the Normans and Bretons near Mont Saint Michel. Geoffrey attended with his new Norman kinsmen William Clito, Theobald of Blois and the future king Stephen to fight on their side, but when he saw that the Bretons were substantially outnumbered, he chivalrously decided to join them.

Naturally Geoffrey was conspicuously the best fighter and 'deprived many of their lives'. Jean of Marmoutier seems to have forgotten that this was a tournament rather than a battle, unless he intended Geoffrey's behaviour, gallant as it was, to be a lesson in the disorder caused by tournaments, which would have pleased the notoriously tournament-hating Henry II. The climax of the tournament came when the defeated Normans challenged the Bretons to single combat, and a gigantic Saxon 'taller than any human by far' appeared and taunted the Bretons. Of course Geoffrey rose to the occasion, impaling the giant with his spear and cutting off his head as a trophy.[30]

This is very similar – too similar? – to the story about Geoffrey Greymantle killing the giant Dane in the *Gesta*, and it may have been a conscious echo to show that Geoffrey followed in his illustrious predecessor and namesake's footsteps. It is also quite striking in its portrayal of the Normans as overpowered and fleeing from the Bretons (and an Angevin) after being defeated, a mischievous touch that surely would have appealed to Henry II.

The second story involves Geoffrey getting lost in the forest when hunting, and finding a charcoal burner who leads him back to Loches without recognizing him. Geoffrey asks the peasant what he thinks about the count, and is given a catalogue of all the ills of the country including oppressive taxation and extortion by Geoffrey's officials, though the peasant says he is sure the count doesn't know about this and is betrayed by his subordinates. Geoffrey promises himself to reform the laws and punish the offenders, then takes the man back to his court and reveals his identity. The man is horrified at having criticized Geoffrey's rule to his face, but Geoffrey entertains him royally and sends him on his way with his freedom and gifts. This is a standard type of tale that shows the good ruler listening to his people (there are similar stories about Haroun al-Rachid in the *Arabian Nights* and James V of Scotland in the 16th century), and shows how Jean of Marmoutier took what was essentially the blank canvas of Geoffrey Plantagenet and shaped him into the image of the model ruler.[31]

Henry I's reasons for turning to Anjou for a marriage alliance can be discerned with some confidence, and it probably wasn't because Geoffrey exhibited the perfection credited to him by Jean of Marmoutier. After the death of William Aetheling, Henry had promoted the interests of his nephews Theobald, Stephen and Henry of Blois. Although the eldest, Theobald, was fully occupied as count of Blois (under the guidance of his mother Adela, William the Conqueror's daughter), Henry I raised Stephen and Henry of Blois at his court. His favour to them culminated in 1125 when he arranged Stephen's marriage to the heiress to the county of Boulogne and in 1126 when he made Henry abbot of Glastonbury. Things were happening very quickly at this point, because it was also in 1126 that Matilda was recalled from Germany and in January 1127 Henry recognized her as his heir.

Also in 1127, Charles the Good, Count of Flanders, was murdered as he knelt in prayer, and William Clito, the son of Robert Curthose, now became count of Flanders through the influence of the French king. With no son of his own, Henry faced the genuine threat that Clito could use his base in Flanders to launch a bid for the English throne after his death. Henry controlled England and Normandy, and Blois was an ally, but France and Flanders were implacably opposed to him, and he needed to secure the succession. Geoffrey was the right age to marry Henry's daughter, and an Angevin alliance would provide a bulwark to Normandy and Blois from the south, neutralizing a potential enemy. As we saw previously, Fulk V had first sought an alliance with Clito, but Henry I proved as adept a diplomat as a warrior, and turned Anjou into an ally.

There may be another factor: Henry at this point was staking everything on Matilda succeeding him. Many contemporary historians noted that Matilda's marriage to an Angevin made her unpalatable to the Normans, and I will argue below that this explains Geoffrey's otherwise inexplicable failure to assist her in England. However, Geoffrey was still a teenager at the time of the marriage. This seems puzzling since we might expect Henry, like Baldwin II of Jerusalem, to choose a strong warrior who could support and defend his daughter's claim. Much is always made of the fact that at the time of their marriage, Matilda was twenty-six and Geoffrey was fourteen[32] and she, with all the haughtiness of an Empress, despised the boy she was forced to marry. But isn't that the point? Norman law was categorical that all a woman's property and rights were controlled by her husband[33], but wouldn't Henry have expected Matilda to dominate the relationship? An aggressive, successful count of Anjou acting as a king would have been repellent to the Normans, but an untried boy who might be dominated by his imperial consort could grow into someone much less objectionable. Henry could hope to shape the character of his son-in-law for some years, especially as Fulk soon left for Jerusalem and Geoffrey was isolated at the Anglo-Norman court. It was for just this purpose that Henry prepared the elaborate ceremonies of knighthood described above.

Unfortunately for Henry, events conspired against him. William Clito died of an infected wound almost immediately after Geoffrey and Matilda's wedding, ending the threat and freeing Henry of the necessity for an Angevin alliance. It is intriguing to speculate about the consort Henry would have chosen for Matilda had the threat of Clito not hung over him, though he had already turned to Anjou before so perhaps things would not have been very different. With Fulk V's departure to become king of Jerusalem in 1129, the young couple took over Anjou, though they seem to have spent more time in Normandy, where their position as Henry's heirs was more prestigious.

By the 1130s Henry had reconciled himself to the fact that he would not father another legitimate son, and he took steps to ensure the succession of Matilda as England's queen. He required all the barons to swear to uphold her succession, which they did so willingly that they even quarrelled for the privilege of being the first to swear, with Henry's illegitimate son Robert of Gloucester losing out, ironically, to Stephen of Blois, who would usurp the throne. When Henry fell ill in Normandy in 1135 (after gorging on too many lampreys, according to tradition) he again called on all his barons present to swear to acknowledge Matilda as queen, then died on 1 December.

Henry I had failed to anticipate the bold action of Stephen of Blois. Stephen was married to the countess of Boulogne, and controlled one of the best places to cross the Channel. Stephen crossed immediately to England and seized the royal treasury at Winchester, which helpfully was controlled by his brother Henry, who was now Bishop of Winchester, and asserted his own right to the throne as William the Conqueror's grandson. With the help of powerful local barons who convinced the Archbishop of Canterbury to break his own oath to support Matilda, Stephen was crowned and anointed on 22 December 1135. Meanwhile, the Norman barons in Rouen had themselves wavered and invited Stephen's brother Theobald Count of Blois, as William the Conqueror's oldest surviving grandson, to be their duke, but when they heard that Stephen was already crowned, they recanted and sent Theobald away. Stephen swiftly took possession of Normandy too, and Matilda and Geoffrey seemed to have been completely defeated. They had been curiously inactive at this critical moment, and it is believed that Matilda was pregnant.[34]

The Anarchy: Civil War in England and the Angevin Conquest of Normandy

Yet they soon took action. Geoffrey launched an attack on Normandy, joined by Duke William X of Aquitaine, but the army contracted dysentery and had to retreat, 'leaving a trail of filth behind them', as Orderic Vitalis eloquently put it.[35] Geoffrey remained committed to the conquest of Normandy, and although the Norman barons resisted fiercely as they had no desire to be conquered by an Angevin, they received little support from Stephen, who faced growing opposition in England.

The conquest of Normandy is Geoffrey Plantagenet's great achievement, and gives the lie to the opinion repeated by many modern historians – which originated with Kate Norgate's several-page demolition of Geoffrey in *England under the Angevin Kings* – that '… one is struck with a sense of something wanting in him. The deficiency was in truth a very serious one; it was a lack of steady principle and of genuine feeling.'[36] This seems overly harsh, especially when the only important 12th-century source about Geoffrey was written after his death and expressly seeks to portray him first as a beautiful teenager worthy of marrying an Empress and then as a dashing chivalric hero. That's the basis for the 'lack of steady principle', and the want of feeling is based on his 'failure' to help Matilda conquer England.

To our knowledge Geoffrey did nothing to help Matilda in England and devoted all his time and resources to Normandy. It may seem that he should have focused on the larger prize, especially as Matilda came so close to achieving it that we might assume that with his help she would have succeeded. This 'want of feeling' in failing to help his wife is taken as evidence that their marriage was loveless.

However, everything is not as it seems. Aside from the brief period when Robert Curthose ruled Normandy, England and Normandy were a unified realm and the aristocracy of both lands had extensive cross-Channel possessions that would be very difficult to disentangle. Stephen ruled both England and Normandy, so an attack on Normandy harmed him just as much as any military activity in England. Indeed, since a key strategic goal of each side in the civil war was to demonstrate that their opponent was incapable of preserving order and that only they could guarantee peace and prosperity for the barons, Stephen's inability to defend Normandy was a major blow to his cause. After his poor start, Geoffrey returned to the attack with much more success and slowly but steadily took Normandy castle by castle, ultimately being recognized as Duke of Normandy in Rouen in 1144.[37] This is astonishing – that the Count of Anjou could be acclaimed Duke of Normandy not as Matilda's husband, but in his own right. Once Geoffrey had conquered Normandy and installed himself as its duke, all the Norman barons with lands in England had a vested interest in seeing Matilda succeed in England.

We must not forget what a liability it was to Matilda's cause to have an Angevin husband. The Normans would not accept an Angevin as their king – not yet, anyway – so having Matilda go to England alone to claim her inheritance made great political sense. Matilda's ways of referring to herself are instructive: in charters she was always 'Lady of the English' or 'Empress', and her seal called her 'Queen of the Romans' (another title from the Holy Roman Empire), but it is notable that her enemies sometimes called her 'Countess of Anjou' or 'Lady of the Angevins' to label her a foreigner.[38] This tactic failed, and it is as 'Empress' that she is best known. Geoffrey and Matilda do not seem to have had much affection for each other, but their divided attack on Stephen is not the evidence for a complete breakdown in their relationship that it is sometimes claimed to be.

Matilda and her forces arrived in England in 1139, where she was welcomed at Arundel castle. In addition to Geoffrey's success in Normandy, the critical factor enabling Matilda's invasion was the support of her half-brother Robert of Gloucester, who in 1138 had repudiated his oath to recognize Stephen as king. Robert also ceded his Norman possessions of Caen and Bayeux to Geoffrey, significantly helping Geoffrey's cause. These were major blows for Stephen, as the previous acquiescence of Robert and almost all the other barons had made the throne Stephen's to lose. This is precisely what Stephen did, alienating key figures in the church and the aristocracy in the years since his accession until as important a figure as Robert finally raised the revolt against him.

Robert had important holdings in the west of England and established a base at Bristol to support Matilda. After Matilda's arrival at Arundel, Stephen arrived with an army to oppose her, but for once her sex was an advantage, because Stephen's chivalric code could not allow him to attack a woman, and so he gave her safe conduct to Bristol, where she joined Robert of Gloucester.[39] There was still no immediate upswell of support for Matilda, and she and Robert were only able to create a base in southwest England from which to harass castles and towns controlled by Stephen, which undermined his authority and helped sow dissatisfaction.

It was also this guerrilla warfare that nearly produced a decisive result. A rebel baron took the castle of Lincoln, and Stephen took a small force to besiege the castle in February 1141. Robert of Gloucester arrived with an army and took Stephen by surprise, and Stephen's bold decision to stay and fight, perhaps prompted by the same chivalric spirit that led him to allow Matilda to leave Arundel, led to his defeat and capture. Matilda would seem to have won and needed only to be crowned in Westminster Abbey.

However, Stephen's supporters did not abandon the fight after his capture. Matilda and Robert moved slowly, rewarding their own followers and trying to gain additional support before reaching London in the summer of 1141. Most notably, Henry of Blois, Stephen's own brother, switched sides to Matilda, presumably since his brother had failed to make him Archbishop of Canterbury, and he thought Matilda would show more gratitude. This allowed Matilda to enter London in triumph to prepare for her coronation in Westminster Abbey. Yet she did not seem to understand how precarious her position still was, and that she could not afford to antagonize anyone in the fragile coalition that might bring her to power.

She first disappointed Henry of Blois in his requests for preferment and excluded him from her advisers, driving him back to Stephen's side. She was unable or unwilling to attract any of Stephen's other supporters, and then she demanded money from the merchants of London to fund her prospective government. London had never been a centre of strength for Matilda, and in fact Stephen's wife controlled Kent with a significant army. Matilda's enemies in London now appealed to Stephen's queen (helpfully also named Matilda, but we'll call her 'Mathilde of Boulogne' to distinguish her from the Empress Matilda, Lady of the English), and as the Empress was preparing for a banquet in Westminster, Mathilde of Boulogne and her army suddenly appeared and drove Matilda from the city before she could be crowned.[40]

Matilda would never again come close to victory. The chroniclers almost universally agree that her 'disgusting' arrogance and pride alienated everyone in London and led to her downfall, but as Helen Castor astutely observes in *She-Wolves*, this was the view of male religious chroniclers who could scarcely imagine being ruled by a queen. Castor argues that male rulers were not criticized for being confident and commanding, and 'arrogant' is not an adjective often used to describe kings. That said, contemporaries openly applied a double standard to male and female behaviour in the Middle Ages, and the fact that behaviour that would have been acceptable in a male ruler was insupportable in a queen should not have been surprising, unfair as it is.

This view is also not entirely true: sixty years later when Richard the Lionheart died without an heir, there was a disputed succession between Richard's younger brother John and his nephew Arthur of Brittany. William Marshal (of whom more very shortly), the leading baron of the time whose support would be decisive for the successful claimant, reports his conversation with the Archbishop of Canterbury and gives as a reason for not supporting Arthur that he was 'haughty and proud'. These are standard criticisms, but it is worth noting that they were also applied to men, and undue pride and high-handedness could damage male rulers as well as female, as King John himself would find to his cost. It should come as no surprise that in the Middle Ages, like our own age, things were never simple. Matilda, and later Arthur, were denied the throne for being too overbearing and proud, but the usual criticism of King Stephen is that he wasn't dominant and commanding enough to be a successful king.

Matilda certainly did not suffer from these defects, as she was in the thick of the action from the moment the civil war began. Modern historians often make the point that one of the barriers to Matilda's succession in her own right was that a woman could not be a commander in an age when kingship was still defined by leadership in battle, but there is no question that Matilda did lead her forces personally, even if she did not fight. She was not the only woman to do so, as Mathilde of Boulogne led

Stephen's armies when he was in captivity. Mathilde also used her control of Boulogne to funnel supplies and mercenaries across the Channel to Stephen's supporters, preserving Stephen's position after he had been captured. The Empress was not one to accept defeat though, and there are amazing stories of her deeds in the civil war, two of which will give some sense of her bravery and daring.

Later in 1141 the Empress and her forces laid siege to Winchester, but suddenly a huge force of Stephen's mercenaries arrived and blockaded the besieging army. Realizing the peril, Robert of Gloucester held off the attackers while the Empress and a small group of retainers fled toward Ludgershall Castle, hotly pursued by the much larger force of the mercenary William of Ypres. Matilda rode sidesaddle, which so delayed her party that they were in danger of being captured. John Marshal, one of Matilda's most faithful and plainspoken retainers, forced the Empress to break convention and ride astride, and they managed to stay ahead of their pursuers. Whether this story is true or not, it shows the Empress's determination to do whatever was necessary to claim her throne, though it could also be a commentary on Matilda's willingness to abandon conventional female roles and assume a more male persona in her quest for power, making her a true 'virago' (in Latin literally meaning a woman who 'acts as a man'). In fact, William of Malmesbury would use just this word to describe her, perhaps the first use of the word in England.[41]

The postscript of the story is equally compelling and appalling, since John Marshal was forced to stay behind and guard the ford of the river Test to cover Matilda's escape; after his small force was overwhelmed by William of Ypres's men, he and a companion retreated to the church of Wherwell Abbey. The mercenaries set fire to the church to drive them out, and after seeking refuge in the tower John Marshal lost an eye in the shower of molten lead that fell on them. Nevertheless he escaped to Ludgershall, where he continued to ravage the countryside as one of Matilda's strongest supporters.[42]

Matilda's escape makes a good story, but there was a much more important event for Matilda that day. The main army was routed and Robert of Gloucester was captured, leaving Matilda without her mainstay. Seeing no alternative, Matilda exchanged Stephen for Robert, thus returning her to exactly the position she had been in before Stephen's capture in 1141. It seems extraordinary that Matilda would release Stephen when his capture should have been a knockout blow to the anti-Angevin party, but her failed coronation and the defeat at Winchester revealed that she still had a long and difficult war ahead of her, and pursuing this without Robert was simply impossible. This also demonstrates the difficulty involved in holding an anointed king captive, because what exactly could be done to him? King John killed his nephew and rival Arthur, who was not even a crowned king, to the horror of his contemporaries. A hundred years later Charles of Anjou would behave with utter ruthlessness and execute his rival Conradin, to widespread condemnation, but again Conradin had not been crowned, and Charles was in a much stronger position than Matilda. Stephen was no use to Matilda in captivity, but releasing him must have been a bitterly difficult decision.

It was at this point, with Stephen once again free and Matilda's bid for the throne in real danger, that an appeal was made to Geoffrey Plantagenet. This is the key piece of evidence for the argument that Geoffrey cared little for his wife, because his response only came after a three-month delay, and even then it was said by William of Malmesbury to have been: 'if the earl of Gloucester would cross the sea and come to him he would do his best to meet his wishes; but for anyone else to make the journey would be a waste of time'.[43] Geoffrey may have believed that leaving Normandy unconquered and diverting his forces to England, where they would have been seen as an invading army and possibly done more harm than good, was the wrong decision. It certainly would have been a quite risky policy. Yet the fact that he refused so categorically to help his wife at her lowest point does indicate that there were no ties of affection that would influence Geoffrey when it came to strategic decisions. Still, Matilda was not one to give up, and she continued the fight.

Her courage and determination were displayed in another incredible escape, when she and her supporters were besieged in Oxford in the winter of 1142. Henry of Huntingdon recounted that a heavy snowfall had covered the area, so the enterprising Matilda and her party slipped over the walls and crossed the frozen river Thames, 'wrapped in white clothes, deceiving the besiegers by appearing so like the dazzling snow.'[44] To further confuse pursuers they wore their shoes backwards.[45] These adventures indicate just how perilous Matilda's position was, but in fact this marked the turning point in her fortunes, because Robert of Gloucester had heard of her peril and returned from Normandy. He brought 300 knights, but also something much more valuable: Matilda and Geoffrey's heir, Henry.

The future Henry II was always a much more acceptable face of the Empress's party than his mother or father. He was only nine when Robert of Gloucester brought him to England in November 1142, and he served only as a figurehead to rally his mother's party after the disaster in London, soon returning to Normandy. Robert and Matilda now seemed content to hold their territory in England until Henry was old enough to fight for himself, and what allowed this strategy was that Geoffrey had broken the Norman resistance by the end of 1142, and within two years he would be recognized as duke. The nobles with cross-Channel holdings would now lose their holdings in either England or Normandy if they backed the wrong side. With Geoffrey in control of Normandy, if Matilda or Henry ever looked like gaining ground in England, there might be a quick surge of support for them. Geoffrey also announced that he would make Henry duke of Normandy as soon as he was old enough, and he began to issue charters in Henry's name as well as his own. If only Matilda had shown some of this diplomacy, the war might have ended in 1141 instead of dragging on for another decade.

Henry was certainly not responsible for any delay. With Normandy secure and the prospect of becoming duke before him in only a few years, Henry nevertheless organized a party of mercenaries and went to England on his own in 1147, when he was only fourteen. There was a brief panic over this invasion and Henry attacked a couple of castles, but the invasion quickly fizzled out when Stephen realized how small Henry's force actually was and moved against him. Worse, Henry's mercenaries, whom he had expected to pay with plunder, now threatened to desert when the money wasn't forthcoming. Henry appealed to Matilda and Robert of Gloucester for money, but they refused, probably so that he would go back to Normandy after this dangerous and unauthorized attack. Henry, in a move that was absolutely typical, then asked for help from Stephen himself – after all, Stephen was his cousin – and incredibly, Stephen produced the money. Contemporary and modern critics attack Stephen for this foolish generosity and attribute it to that most impractical of codes, chivalry, and also use it as evidence that he lacked the necessary ruthlessness to rule. Of course, a perfectly valid reason for Stephen's behaviour could be that he didn't want an unpaid mercenary force on the loose in England.[46]

Yet Stephen's lack of ruthlessness does contrast starkly with Matilda's steely resolution. In 1152 Stephen's forces suddenly attacked John Marshal's castle of Newbury, which was poorly garrisoned. Stephen ordered the castellan to surrender, and when he refused, Stephen vowed to hang every member of the garrison when the fortress fell. As was customary, a day's truce was arranged for the castellan to speak to John Marshal and find out if reinforcements were available; if they weren't, a surrender would usually be arranged with safe conduct guaranteed for the garrison. John Marshal was not in a position to reinforce the castle so quickly, but he asked for a further truce to allow him to speak to Matilda. Stephen grudgingly agreed, but required John to leave his youngest son William, then only five or six years old, as a hostage to guarantee he wouldn't reinforce the castle. John agreed, but once Stephen's army retired he immediately sent a strong force of knights and provisions into the castle.

William's life was forfeit, and Stephen's men prepared to hang him in sight of the castle. Stephen sent a messenger to John demanding that he surrender the castle or his son would be killed. John replied that he had no need of this son since he had the 'hammers and the anvils' to forge another, better son. As Stephen's men prepared to hang him, the child, oblivious to his danger and considering this a very exciting game, begged one of the knights to let him play with his weapons. Stephen was overcome by William's innocence and carried him in his arms back to the camp. This story was told by William Marshal in his old age and seems to have been true, and it is frequently used as evidence that Stephen was simply too gentle to succeed as a medieval king.[47]

Eleanor of Aquitaine

Against the backdrop of the civil war in England and Geoffrey's conquest of Normandy, significant events that would profoundly affect the Angevins were happening in France and Aquitaine. Most important of all is the career of Eleanor of Aquitaine, Henry II's future wife. This is not only because Eleanor brought a huge swathe of territory to the Angevin lands. In addition to ruling Aquitaine personally, Eleanor was fully involved in Henry's reign and at various times acted as regent. It is most instructive that it was only after Eleanor's death, not Henry's, that the French king managed to make significant inroads against the Angevins.

Eleanor's history is as fascinating as Henry's and she is one of the greatest figures of the 12th century. Aquitaine, Gascony and Poitou were her inheritance, and although she is always referred to as Eleanor of Aquitaine, it was Poitou and particularly its capital Poitiers, that was her favourite residence. This area, although not as important politically as its northern neighbours, was a cultural centre of European significance. Eleanor as its heiress had been well known throughout Europe even before her marriage to two kings, but her actions as queen of France and queen of England would make her the most famous woman of the century.

Aquitaine had once been a kingdom and Charlemagne had his son Louis crowned its king in 781, but this honour had long since lapsed, and Aquitaine as a duchy was torn between its more aggressive neighbours in Anjou and Toulouse. By the 11th century Aquitaine had become a coherent region with a stable dynasty and more than a few connections to the Angevins. Duke William IX succeeded in 1086 and married Ermengarde, the daughter of Fulk Réchin[48], though he had the marriage annulled when his wife showed signs of insanity. Perhaps she was only a typical Angevin – chroniclers are quite happy to write about Henry II rolling around on the floor chewing his bedstraw in fury without ever suggesting he was insane, but one suspects a woman behaving this way would have been treated differently. It was William IX who would elevate the duchy to European importance through his cultural influence as the first troubadour.

In 1100, the dominant form of literature in northern Europe was the epic *chanson de geste*, the tale of warfare and military courage that celebrated male virtue in an exclusively male milieu, seen most famously in the *Song of Roland*. In the south the taste ran more to *lais* or love songs, and William IX transformed this into a new style of poetry that celebrated love in a more earthy or even coarse way. The new interest in love fused with the knightly epic to form the signature literary form of the 12th century, the chivalric romance, best demonstrated by the Arthurian romances of Chrétien de Troyes.

William IX had chosen not to join the First Crusade, instead using the absence of Raymond of St Gilles to seize Toulouse in defiance of the Truce of God, which banned attacking the lands of an absent Crusader. After hearing of the stunning success of the First Crusade and the capture of Jerusalem, William reconsidered and led an army to Asia Minor, but it was completely destroyed in battle with the Turks. William visited Jerusalem and Antioch and may have been exposed to the literary traditions of Arabic poetry, and when he returned he began to write a new style of erotic poetry in the southern French dialect, the *langue d'oc*. Poitiers quickly became a literary and cultural capital, and William was highly influential in creating early ideas of chivalry, including the vital ingredient of knights doing daring deeds for ladies.[49] Despite his literary and cultural credentials, political success eluded William and he failed to impose his authority on the rebellious lords of Aquitaine and Poitou.

While William IX celebrated the satisfaction of physical needs and earthly love, his wife Philippa devoted herself to higher concerns. She encountered Robert d'Arbrissel, an itinerant preacher who espoused a more sympathetic message about women than as mere vessels of sin, and she obtained from William land near the border with Anjou for Robert to found a monastery. In 1100 Robert founded Fontevraud as a double monastery for both men and women (though their lodgings were segregated), and under the patronage of Philippa an impressive stone church was started in 1119. This would become the most important monastery for the Angevins later in the century, and serve as the family necropolis. Robert decreed that the abbess should be a noble widow, and Isabella of Anjou, Fulk V's daughter and widow of Henry I's son William Aetheling, became one of the first abbesses. William IX's cast-off wife Ermengarde of Anjou also joined the community at Fontevraud when her second husband died.[50]

William IX must not have shared Philippa's religious preoccupations, because in 1115 he abducted the wife of one of his vassals and installed her in the Maubergeonne Tower at the palace in Poitiers, for which he was excommunicated. Gerald of Wales, writing much later, relates the story that a hermit prophesied that William and all the descendants of his sinful union would never know happiness in their children because of this crime, though this clearly is meant to be a comment on the tribulations of Henry II and Eleanor's family. Certainly it ruined Philippa's happiness because she retired to Fontevraud and died in 1118.

William IX had his son William X marry Aenor, his mistress's daughter from a previous marriage, and these were the parents of Eleanor of Aquitaine, so named because she resembled her mother so much she was *alia Aenor* ('another Aenor'). Like his father, William X struggled to assert his authority in his domains, and this unruliness would remain the defining characteristic of the region for another century. William X's wife and son died in 1130, leaving Eleanor as heiress to all his lands, which amounted to about one-third of modern France.[51] Women in Aquitaine did have a higher status than in other parts of Europe and could inherit and rule their own lands, though it would be unusual for a woman to rule such a large and wealthy territory. William X could have married again and tried to father another son, but perhaps out of genuine grief for Aenor he didn't.

Connections between Aquitaine, Anjou and England-Normandy remained strong, and in 1133 William X's younger brother Raymond of Poitiers, who had been raised by Henry I in the English court almost as his own son, was invited by Fulk the Angevin King of Jerusalem to be the ruler of Antioch. Eleanor's uncle accepted this offer, with interesting consequences for Eleanor's later happiness. Geoffrey Plantagenet invited William X to assist him in the conquest of Normandy in 1136, and William did participate in that ill-fated expedition, which retreated so ignominiously back to Anjou.

Perhaps fed up with fighting, William X decided to go on a pilgrimage to Santiago de Compostella in 1136, but he left careful provisions for his duchy. He had his vassals swear allegiance to Eleanor and commended her to the care of Louis VI of France, expressing the wish that she might also marry his heir, the future Louis VII. William reached Compostella in 1137 but had become ill on the way and knew that he was dying. He confirmed Eleanor as Duchess of Aquitaine and Gascony and Countess of Poitou, and appointed Louis VI as her guardian to rule in her name.[52] William's choice of Louis VI as guardian and the future Louis VII as Eleanor's husband is interesting – why didn't he fear the French would try to seize Aquitaine? Probably he did, but he had few other choices. Geoffrey of Anjou was preoccupied with the conquest of Normandy and either wouldn't be able to devote any time to Aquitaine, or worse, in his expansionist mode might abandon Normandy for easier pickings in the south. The kings of Navarre or Aragon lacked the resources to manage such a sprawling territory, and the count of Toulouse was an enemy. France was the only choice, near enough to intervene yet not obviously greedy, thoroughly occupied with its dangerous neighbours in Anjou and Normandy and the impending civil war for the English throne, and able to provide a royal heir of the right age for Eleanor.

This is also another example of the obligations a lord owed to his vassal, and what to us may seem an act of folly was actually part of feudal custom, since Louis VI was obligated to protect Eleanor as his vassal. That said, William was still fearful that the French king would seize Eleanor's patrimony, so he stipulated that Eleanor's lands could only be inherited by her own children. From Louis VI's point of view, an alliance was more desirable than ever, for after being overshadowed by the Anglo-Norman monarchs on his border he now faced the prospect of the union of Anjou, Normandy and England that would nearly surround the French domains.

Louis VI did not hesitate to cement the alliance, and Eleanor and Louis VII were married at Bordeaux in 1137. It was most likely as a wedding present that Eleanor gave Louis the rock-crystal vase that is now in the Louvre, and gives us a tangible memento of a (future) Angevin queen. The item survives because Louis VII later presented it to the abbey of St Denis and it was modified, yet it shows the kind of gift a 12th-century queen might consider an appropriate wedding present. It is also an example of the cosmopolitanism of the medieval world, since the rock crystal probably comes from Moorish Spain. There were many genuinely towering international figures in the 12th century, including Fulk V and Eleanor, and a pan-European aristocracy and ecclesiastical cultural elite were in contact with each other and travelled frequently. As the newlyweds returned to Paris, word reached them that Louis VI had died and Louis VII was now king. Louis had no need for another coronation because the Capetians always crowned their heirs in their own lifetime, but Eleanor was crowned at Bourges on Christmas Day of the same year.

Despite the fact that Louis VII loved Eleanor 'almost beyond reason'[53] and would be censured for his too fond devotion to his queen, Eleanor does not appear to have enjoyed her time as Queen of France. Paris, despite being the largest city in Europe and its intellectual centre, did not have a comparable social and cultural life to the court at Poitiers. Eleanor seems to have found the fortress-like palace on the Ile de la Cité dank and depressing, especially compared to her light and airy palace in Poitiers, where the 'Hall of the Lost Footsteps', so called because the sound of footsteps was lost in its vastness, was perhaps the largest hall in France at the time. Relaxed southern attitudes towards women and relationships between the sexes were also viewed as scandalous by the more puritanical French clerics and nobles, a stigma that would later attach itself to Eleanor more perniciously. Perhaps worst of all, Eleanor found she had little influence in the court, as Louis was dominated by Abbot Suger of St Denis, an adviser to Louis VI who would remain the most important figure in Louis VII's court until his death.

It is impossible to judge Eleanor's influence on Louis objectively because every contemporary and later source has quite strong views on the subject. The conventional clerical view was that women were instruments of the Devil, and humanity had been condemned to damnation because of the 'sin of Eve'. From this perspective women were always seen as temptresses leading men astray, as well as being weak, foolish, vain and undisciplined. These adjectives are used time and again to describe women who have gone beyond their 'appropriate sphere' or tried to take a more active role in affairs. This was a view particularly espoused by St Bernard of Clairvaux, the most important religious figure of the century and a man who was not afraid to direct the spiritual power of the church against anyone who opposed him: he probably first met Eleanor at Sens in 1140, when the king and queen were present as Bernard secured the condemnation of the brilliant theologian Peter Abelard. Thus on the occasions when Eleanor seemed to influence Louis, or in situations where it was believed she must have been the instigator of his actions, condemnation was universal: she was a 'foolish woman', she 'acted as a man' (a 'virago' like Matilda), she interfered in events about which she knew nothing.

The most notorious example involved Eleanor's sister Petronilla. She began an adulterous affair with Raoul of Vermandois, whose wife was the sister of Theobald Count of Champagne. Doubtless at Eleanor's instigation, Louis supported the couple and found bishops to annul Raoul's previous marriage and marry Petronilla and Raoul, for which the pope excommunicated Petronilla, Raoul and the bishops who performed the ceremony. Louis blamed Theobald of Champagne and invaded his territory, but when Louis's troops assaulted Vitry sur Marne, they set fire to the town as standard medieval practice, only for the flames to spread too quickly and destroy the cathedral in which more than 1,000 townsfolk had taken shelter, killing them all. Louis was so horrified by this that he appears to have suffered a mental collapse, and when Bernard of Clairvaux added his condemnation to the chorus of disapproval, Louis's personality transformed overnight. He abandoned his aristocratic lifestyle to become a penitent with close-cropped hair, wearing sandals and a coarse monk's robe. That Bernard blamed Eleanor for the tragedy is perhaps indicated by Bernard's first references shortly after this event to Louis and Eleanor's consanguinity, and the fact that their marriage might be illegal.[54]

In 1144 the new abbey of St Denis was consecrated, and Suger's lifework was completed. This was the first building in Europe completely in the Gothic style, and began the architectural revolution that would sweep the continent. Interestingly, it was also around this time (c1140) that another landmark of medieval culture was produced, Geoffrey of Monmouth's *History of the Kings of Britain*. Within thirty years Arthurian literature had captivated everyone, and the Angevins played a role in its dissemination. Geoffrey's work was arguably the most successful history in the Middle Ages, and survives in over 200 copies. A third of these copies are found on the continent, showing the success of this Celtic, British story.[55]

Louis, Eleanor and St Bernard all participated in the consecration of St Denis, and Eleanor presumed to offer the saint a deal: if he would lift the excommunication of Petronilla and Raoul, she would convince Louis to make peace with Champagne. Bernard was horrified by her interference and rebuked her harshly, to which Eleanor replied that her marriage was unhappy and God would not bless her with a child. Bernard himself offered a deal saying that if she would cease meddling he would pray for her to conceive. Both sides achieved what they wanted, as Louis did now make peace with Theobald of Champagne, the pope eventually did recognize Petronilla and Raoul's marriage, and Eleanor bore her first daughter, Marie. However, Bernard rather meanly prophesied that Petronilla and Raoul would have only a short time together and their children would never be happy, and obedient to the saint's decree their only son was a leper who died young and their two daughters died childless.[56]

The Second Crusade

All these local concerns were swept away at the end of 1144 when Zengi, whose main threat had seemed to be directed at Damascus, suddenly captured the city of Edessa, which had been the first conquest of the First Crusade. This sent a shockwave through Europe, as after nearly fifty years the states of Outremer were firmly fixed as a part of Western Christendom and it was intolerable that they should be lost. By the end of the next year Pope Eugenius III had called for a Crusade. On hearing this, Louis, without consulting any of his advisers, agreed to go. Suger was highly critical of the king's wish to leave his kingdom when he had no heir (Louis and Eleanor's daughter Marie presumably not counting), and even more critical of Eleanor's desire to accompany Louis on the Crusade, but this was ignored.

Louis wished to take the cross with fitting ceremony, so he invited Bernard of Clairvaux to preach the Crusade formally at the newly built abbey of Vézelay at Easter in 1146. Bernard obliged and before huge multitudes Louis and Eleanor took the cross, followed by legions of their vassals and ordinary people; the priests ran out of crosses and had to make more by tearing up their robes. Bernard was scathing about the usual pastimes of knights – raids, plundering and tournaments – and had punningly called them *malitia* (evil-doers) instead of *militia* (knights), so he had no doubts about the benefits of the Crusade:

> O mighty soldier, O man of war, at last you have a cause for which you can fight without endangering your soul; a cause in which to win is glorious and for which to die is but gain. Are you a shrewd businessman, quick to see the profits of this world? If you are, I can offer you a bargain which you cannot afford to miss. Take the sign of the cross. At once you will have indulgence for all the sins which you confess with a contrite heart. The cross is cheap and if you wear it with humility you will find that you have obtained the Kingdom of Heaven.[57]

At the time, Eleanor's participation in the Crusade did not attract particular opprobrium, and it was only after the Second Crusade failed that her presence was seized on as the reason for divine displeasure. Her presence did add a touch of glamour when the Crusade was launched in Vézelay, and near contemporary sources such as Gervase of Canterbury reported that Eleanor and her ladies dressed as Amazons and rode through the crowd encouraging men to take the cross, and a romance dedicated to Eleanor from around 1156 gives elaborate descriptions of Queen Penthisilea and her Amazons that may be a reference to this event.[58] Eleanor also held tournaments to encourage knightly interest and the troubadours wrote Crusading songs.

Louis encouraged Geoffrey Plantagenet to join the Crusade, not least because King Baldwin III of Jerusalem was his half-brother, but Geoffrey was much more interested in consolidating his hold on Normandy. Geoffrey had completed the conquest of the duchy by 1144 and was recognized as Duke of Normandy by Louis, and he had attempted to build on his gains by proposing that his son Henry marry Louis and Eleanor's daughter Marie. Louis prevaricated because in the absence of a son he did not wish to see Henry attempt to claim the throne of France through Marie, and Bernard of Clairvaux stated that the proposed marriage was prohibited because of consanguinity, so the matter dropped. It was also at this time, according to Gerald of Wales who wrote decades later, that Geoffrey and Eleanor had an affair. Gerald attributes the story to no less a source than St Hugh of Lincoln, who was meant to have had it directly from Henry II, so it is entirely possible that the beautiful Eleanor may have found herself involved with Geoffrey the Handsome.[59]

The Second Crusade set off in 1147, and consisted of the French-Aquitainian force under Louis and Eleanor and a German force led by the Emperor Conrad, which had set out earlier. When Louis and Eleanor reached Antioch, they were welcomed by Eleanor's uncle Raymond of Poitiers in his lovely city that combined the sophistication and culture of the Poitevin court with the fabled luxury of the east.

It is at this point that the most notorious episode of Eleanor's career occurred, one which was to tarnish her reputation forever. Eleanor's close relationship with her uncle led to gossip and ultimately the accusation that she had an affair with him.

John of Salisbury reported in 1149 that the attention Raymond paid to Eleanor and the fact that they were constantly in conversation together aroused Louis's suspicions. William of Tyre wrote in 1179 that Raymond hoped to extend his territories with Louis's assistance and so tried to use Eleanor's influence with her husband, but when Louis refused to attack Aleppo and recapture Edessa, since he preferred to carry on to Jerusalem, Raymond was furious and seduced Eleanor in revenge.

What is indisputable is that for the rest of her life Eleanor was branded an adulteress because of her behaviour on the Crusade. Gerald of Wales alluded to the rumours, saying that how Eleanor had behaved in Palestine was 'well enough known', and Gervase of Canterbury wrote that it was 'best to remain silent about matters best left unspoken'. Richard of Devizes wrote forty-five years later, in 1192, 'Many know what I wish none of us knew. This very Queen was at Jerusalem in the time of her first husband – let none speak more thereof, though I know it well. Keep silent.' Even the troubadour Cercamon may have been referring to this in a song composed during the Crusade when he criticized women who lay with more than one man, saying, 'Better for her never to have been born than to have committed the fault that will be talked about from here to Poitou.'[60] By the 13th century the gossip and rumours became wilder, and in 1260 the Minstrel of Rheims claimed that Eleanor had conducted an affair with Saladin (the Muslim conqueror of Jerusalem who would be the great adversary of Eleanor's son Richard the Lionheart on the Third Crusade) and planned to elope with him by sea, but failed because Louis intercepted her at the dock.

This marks a moment when Eleanor's fame and remarkable experiences served to remove her from the realm of fact and make her a literary figure in her own lifetime. It has been speculated that Eleanor was the model for Queen Guinevere in the Arthurian romances that were becoming so popular in the mid- and late 12th century. Though there is no evidence for this, it is intriguing that Chrètien de Troyes's *Lancelot* of the late 1170s was the first romance to introduce the knight Lancelot and his adulterous love for Guinevere, and Chrètien's patroness was Marie of Champagne, Eleanor's daughter from her marriage to Louis. We have seen that the idea of a knight's perfect love for an unattainable married lady of higher rank was a standard motif of troubadour poetry from the early 12th century, but even if Eleanor wasn't the inspiration for the tale there must have been an unmistakeable resonance between the beautiful adulteresses Queen Guinevere and Queen Eleanor.

Whatever part Eleanor's behaviour played in it, there was a very public rift between Louis and Raymond over the strategy for the Crusade and Louis decided to carry on to Jerusalem. Eleanor refused to go and said that she would keep all her vassals – more than half the crusading army – with her. When Louis insisted that she accompany him, Eleanor for the first time stated explicitly that she felt their marriage was invalid because of consanguinity and should be annulled.[61] Louis ended the dispute and avoided any unpleasantness with Raymond by essentially kidnapping Eleanor and taking her to Jerusalem. Is it extraordinary or commonplace that in the 12th century, on a Crusade launched by a saint that took thousands of soldiers thousands of miles, the marital difficulties of a couple should play so prominent a role?

Though the Crusade was beginning to seem an unmitigated disaster, Louis and Eleanor did reach Jerusalem with their forces, and Louis completed his pilgrimage to the Holy Sepulchre. They were welcomed by Queen Melisende and King Baldwin III, plus the Emperor Conrad, who had travelled to Jerusalem by sea, and a conference of leaders – pointedly not including Eleanor – was held to determine the best strategy. It is fascinating to consider what Eleanor and Melisende might have said to each other, but we have no record of their meeting. Raymond of Poitiers refused to have anything further to do with the Crusade, so recapturing Edessa was out of the question, and the leaders were divided about the best course of action.

At a council on 24 June 1148 the proposal was put forward to attack Damascus, despite its current alliance with Jerusalem. Baldwin III seems to have instigated this plan and gained the support of Conrad, and Louis VII agreed. This could have been at least partially an attempt by Baldwin III to gain a great military victory and eclipse the power of Melisende, who was still wielding the power of regent even though Baldwin was an adult.[62]

Things looked slightly better for the Christians in one regard. Zengi had become a hero of the Muslim world through his conquest of Edessa and was the most formidable opponent yet faced by the Christians, but in 1146 he quarrelled with one of his eunuchs and was murdered while he lay in a drunken stupor. Zengi's ignominious end highlights the limitations of his position: he was a highly capable military leader and politician, but his ambitions were purely worldly and he could not credibly claim to be acting for the greater good. Indeed, this was demonstrated by the willingness of Muslim cities like Damascus to ally themselves with the Christians rather than submit to Zengi. However, what if a ruler arose who was a model of piety as well as military skill? What would happen if a leader appeared who could offer the disparate Muslim territories not only protection, but also a political system based on justice and Islamic ideals? The Christians were about to find out.

Zengi's inheritance was divided, with his elder son taking the more prestigious city of Mosul, and his second son, Nur ed-Din, taking Aleppo. Being *atabeg* of Mosul necessarily involved a ruler in the affairs of the caliph of Baghdad and pulled his attention to the east, something that had reduced Zengi's impact on Syria, but as ruler of Aleppo alone Nur ed-Din did not have this distraction. The rulers of Damascus had no more wish to become subject to Nur ed-Din than they had to Zengi, and thus had remained on very good terms with Jerusalem. It would be catastrophic for Jerusalem if Damascus fell to Nur ed-Din, but the Second Crusade's attack on the city drove it into his arms.

Louis led his men and their allies from the Crusader States to Damascus, but the expedition was a fiasco from the start. The rulers of Damascus were so alarmed at the prospect of a Christian attack that they begged Nur ed-Din for help, and he was more than happy for an invitation to intervene in Damascene affairs. Before he could arrive, the Crusader army had already retreated in disarray and with considerable loss. So inexplicable was the defeat that rumours circulated that Raymond of Poitiers or the emir of Damascus had bribed the barons of Outremer to retreat.[63]

After this latest failure the French army broke up and the Crusaders began to return home. Louis and Eleanor visited Pope Eugenius III in Tusculum, and in a bizarre scene that would be more appropriate to a romantic comedy, the pope played agony uncle to the unhappy pair and personally decorated a bed-chamber with hangings from his own apartment to create an appropriate venue for a reconciliation. Though he was prepared to listen to their marital problems, Eugenius firmly ruled out any possibility of annulling their marriage.[64]

Louis and Eleanor's domestic farce was of minor importance in the face of European reaction to the failure of the Crusade. To understand the shock and horror at its end, we must remember that the First Crusade was seen as a miracle in which God intervened directly to restore the Holy Land to Christianity. For the Second Crusade to fail in such spectacular fashion required an explanation, and William of Tyre struggled to explain how God could permit such a thing to happen. Henry of Huntingdon had no doubts: the army had failed because God was angry at their fornication and adultery.[65]

Other chroniclers agreed: God punished sin, and the presence of fornicators and adulterers – and an adulteress? – as leaders of the Crusade, and indeed the presence of women in the army at all, must be the reason for divine displeasure. Further proof of divine retribution came even before Louis and Eleanor had reached Italy, when the adulterer and alleged traitor Raymond of Poitiers was killed in a skirmish with Nur ed-Din. The emir sent Raymond's head in a silver box as a gift to the Caliph in Baghdad.[66]

If Louis and Eleanor had been unhappy before the failed Crusade and Eleanor's presumed infidelity, the breach between them was now wider than ever despite the pope's best efforts. Louis's knowledge that he had failed in his divine mission to relieve the Crusader States increased his piety and penitence, and Eleanor complained that she had married a monk rather than a king. Nevertheless she became pregnant again and gave birth to a daughter, Alice, in 1150. This more than any other factor undermined Eleanor's position, since she had produced only two daughters in thirteen years of marriage and the Capetians needed a son. During the lifetime of Suger, who had arranged Louis and Eleanor's union and clung to the hope of integrating Aquitaine into the French kingdom, an annulment was unthinkable, but the abbot died in 1151. Bernard of Clairvaux again publicly questioned the validity of the marriage and it was becoming apparent that the ill-matched couple who had failed to produce an heir were ready to part.[67]

Louis returned from the Crusade to more than just domestic problems, because Geoffrey Plantagenet had not been idle in the two years of Louis's absence. The Angevins were now firmly in control of Normandy, and in 1150 Geoffrey passed the title Duke of Normandy to his son Henry.

Henry FitzEmpress, the future Henry II

Despite his initial setbacks, Henry was already known as a vigorous leader (an echo of the teenage successes of his ancestor Fulk Nerra). Indeed he must have been for Geoffrey Plantagenet to hand the duchy of Normandy over to him, as Geoffrey would not have relinquished the duchy he fought so hard to conquer to anyone incapable of ruling it. This was clearly an attempt to make Henry more palatable to the Anglo-Normans as a king of England, and again suggests that rather than ignoring or hindering Matilda's claim to the English throne, Geoffrey was cooperating in a long-term strategy.

Matilda, too, had stepped back from the futile task of conquering England in favour of Henry, and this transformed the civil war entirely. The Anglo-Norman barons who supported Matilda's claim no longer had the public relations disaster of a woman and her hated Angevin husband as their candidates; they now had a dynamic young man of Norman stock with a power base in Normandy who could advance their interests.

Matilda, Geoffrey and Henry were aware that it was the heritage of the Normans that remained talismanic, and the prestige of Normandy that was all important. Geoffrey Plantagenet, once he had conquered Normandy, was always styled Duke of Normandy, a title that trumped Count of Anjou. Henry II, despite his Angevin red hair and epic temper, glorified his Norman lineage above all else, commissioning Wace to write the *Roman de Rou* about Rollo, the founder of the Norman duchy. Yet it was not this rather pedestrian epic that stood the test of time; rather it was the chronicle of the counts of Anjou written at the same time by the monks of Marmoutier that is the more interesting and enduring work. Henry also managed to procure the canonization of Edward the Confessor in 1161 to glorify the English royal line that ruled before the Normans, taking his place in the line of Angevin-instigated canonizations that would reach its zenith in the 14th century.[68]

Despite Henry's wide-ranging interests, England remained a Norman kingdom, and within a generation of Henry II there was no visible disruption in Norman rule. A useful marker of this is found in names – Henry II himself had been given a Norman name in anticipation of his succession, and Henry and Eleanor followed this convention with their own sons William (who died young), Henry and Richard. Only with the fourth son did they allow themselves to use the Angevin 'Geoffrey'. This can be seen in names that remain current today: typical Norman names were Robert, Richard and William, which remain familiar to us. Typical Angevin names were Fulk, Geoffrey and Drogo. I have a particular reason to be grateful that it was Geoffrey (and its variants) among Angevin names that remained in use rather than Fulk (though this is tautological – if Fulk had passed into common use than it would seem as ordinary a name to us as Geoffrey).

The Angevin bid for the English throne was not happening in isolation, and Louis VII was alarmed by the rise of a competitor who might become even more power-ful than the Norman dukes. Louis continued the struggle against his neighbours by leading an army against Geoffrey and Henry in August 1151, but he was ill and had to retreat. St Bernard of Clairvaux attempted to mediate and tried to persuade Geoffrey to go to Paris, but Geoffrey refused outright. St Bernard responded to this snub by prophesying that Geoffrey would die within a month. Henry did agree to perform homage for Normandy to the French king and went to Paris, where he first met Eleanor of Aquitaine.

Gerald of Wales wrote much later that Geoffrey had warned Henry against forming any kind of attachment with Eleanor not only because she was the wife of his lord, but also, Gerald says, because Geoffrey himself had slept with her. The incest taboo covered this eventuality and it was unlawful for a man to marry a woman who had slept with his father. William of Newburgh and Walter Map say that Henry and Eleanor had agreed to marry before he left Paris.[69] This is all speculation and indicates a wish to backdate Henry and Eleanor's relationship to their first meeting, but there is no evidence to support the theory. Eleanor would certainly have been interested in meeting the new duke of Normandy and potential king of England, not least because – whatever the nature of their relationship – she had previously met Geoffrey Plantagenet. She must also at this stage have known that she and Louis would separate, but whether she decided immediately to marry Henry is another thing.

It is curious to speculate about the Angevin family relations at this point. Geoffrey was only forty-one in 1151 and might have lived several decades more. Matilda didn't die until 1167. How might Matilda, Geoffrey and Henry have arranged political matters and Henry's claim to the throne and the rule of England, Normandy and Anjou, and with what difficulties? This was not to be, as Geoffrey Plantagenet went swimming to cool off on a hot day in September 1151, and after catching a chill he died within days, fulfilling St Bernard's prophecy. On his deathbed Geoffrey was said to have ordered that his body not be buried unless Henry agreed to give Maine and Anjou to his brother once he became king of England. Henry was not present and was said to be furious when he arrived to be trapped into an oath such as this. He refused to swear the oath for some time, but the spectacle of his father's rotting corpse finally proved too much, and – weeping with frustration – Henry finally agreed, although he later repudiated his oath.[70]

The speed with which events moved gave rise to the stories that Henry and Eleanor had previously come to an understanding about marrying as soon as she was free of Louis. Eleanor and Louis set off on a tour of Aquitaine in September 1151 amid rumours that the French would leave the duchy by Christmas, and it did seem to be a valedictory tour for Louis, though it wasn't until March 1152 that a synod of bishops dissolved the marriage.[71] Eleanor was now single and once again the wealthiest heiress in Europe, though probably not the most desirable: her connection to Louis, exclusively female children and reputation for adultery would have been grave disadvantages. Yet this did not deter suitors: as Eleanor rode from Paris to Poitiers she had to avoid two attempts to kidnap her, one by the Angevin rival Theobald of Blois and the other by her future husband's younger brother Geoffrey. Nevertheless Eleanor escaped, and in May 1152 she and Henry were married quietly at Poitiers. Despite the lack of ceremony, they did commission a stained-glass window showing the two of them, which is still in the cathedral.

Henry as Count of Anjou and Duke of Normandy, and now de facto ruler of Aquitaine as Eleanor's husband, controlled vastly more territory than his nominal over-lord Louis VII, and he had a very good claim to the throne of England as well. Louis's worst nightmare had come to pass and in the most insulting way possible, since as the feudal overlord of both Henry and Eleanor he should have been asked for permission before they married. He was very well aware that should Henry finally take the English throne things would be worse yet. Henry lost no time in preparing for an invasion of England, showing Louis that his fears were justified. Louis summoned the pair to his court to demand satisfaction for their breach of feudal protocol, but they ignored him.

Louis then used the tactic that Angevin enemies would always use, and which would be so successful for his son Philip Augustus when he fought Henry's son John: he gathered a coalition of Angevin enemies from all sides and organized an invasion of Normandy. The count of Blois was an obvious ally against an Angevin, but Louis also enlisted Henry's younger brother Geoffrey, who was still smarting from Henry's refusal to grant him the lands his father had intended and his failure to capture Eleanor. Henry was forced to postpone his invasion of England to deal with the threat so Louis succeeded in one goal, but Henry – with the seemingly limitless energy that would characterize him until the latter part of his reign – managed to deal with each enemy in turn before they could join forces, and so defeated each one separately. The stage was now set for Henry to become king of England.[72]

By January 1153 Henry was sufficiently secure to accomplish the invasion of England he had planned for so long. In his absence, Matilda took charge of Normandy and Eleanor ruled Anjou and Aquitaine. This set a pattern that would be repeated in later years, when Matilda and Eleanor would often administer parts of the Angevin Empire or act as regent in the king's absence. Eleanor would be somewhat obscured in Henry's early reign, though we should bear in mind that she bore Henry eight children – sufficient proof that her failure to bear many children in her first marriage was entirely due to Louis VII – and would have been pregnant or recently delivered of a child for most of the first twenty years of Henry's reign, and she amply redressed the balance later.

Henry's invasion led to the prospect of England being plunged into the anarchy that had characterized Stephen's struggle with Matilda, which was distasteful to everyone. The Archbishop of Canterbury pressed for the two sides to negotiate. It was at this moment that a death and a birth gave a new complexion to events: Stephen's son and heir Eustace died suddenly from an illness, and Eleanor gave birth to a son, William.[73] Historians always say that Stephen lost the will to fight and agreed to negotiate after Eustace's death since his line had no future, yet Stephen had another son so it does seem curious that he would suddenly lose hope. The Angevins were definitely in the ascendant and Stephen was old by medieval standards, but his capitulation provides ammunition for those who denigrate the listlessness and lack of purpose of the house of Blois when compared with the indomitability of the Angevins.

Henry and Stephen agreed a treaty at Christmas 1153 in which Henry was recognized as Stephen's heir, though Stephen would continue to be king for his lifetime, and Stephen's younger son was entirely excluded. Once the treaty had been confirmed, Henry was free to return to his continental domains and consolidate his position before Louis could provide further opposition. When Stephen died on 25 October 1154, Henry was so secure that he made no attempt to rush to England, and despite the previous years of civil war the succession was uncontested. Henry and Eleanor arrived in England in December, and on 19 December 1154 they were crowned King and Queen at Westminster Abbey.[74]

With his accession to the English throne in 1154 at the age of twenty-one, Henry II, King of England, Duke of Normandy, Count of Anjou and Duke of Aquitaine in right of his wife ruled a greater collection of territories than any other ruler in Europe, an 'Angevin Empire'. He had overcome considerable adversity to inherit these lands, though in fact much of the work had been done by his parents. Henry would spend his entire life defending these territories and asserting every one of the rights that accrued to him, even extending his dominion over Brittany and Ireland and attempting to do so in Wales and Toulouse, and at his death the Empire would pass intact to his son. His grandfather Fulk V was the first Angevin king, but let us now see what this second and much greater Angevin king accomplished.

CHAPTER 4 – THE ANGEVIN EMPIRE I: CREATING THE EMPIRE

I RECALL THAT AS a child I was reading a history of medieval Europe and discovered a map showing the various political components of 12th-century Europe. I was intrigued to see that England and most of France were shaded and labelled the 'Angevin Empire'. I was astonished – what was this Angevin Empire that covered such a significant portion of Europe, including England, and who or what were these Angevins whom I had never previously heard of and how had they conquered so much? I'm convinced that part of the immediate attraction was the 'Ang' prefix, which reminded me of Tolkien's 'Kingdom of Angmar' from Lord of the Rings: the word Angevin felt hard-edged, mysterious and vaguely sinister, and considering that this empire was in the same list of maps that included the Holy Roman Empire, the Byzantine Empire and the Mongol Empire, it was clearly something highly significant.

Of course the term 'Angevin Empire' was only coined in the 19th century and would have been meaningless to Henry II. Henry and his sons Richard and John worked in the period 1154–1204 to retain possession of all their lands and in some cases harmonized legal and political institutions in their territories, yet they never viewed their disparate domains as a single entity. This policy originated with Geoffrey Plantagenet, who had retained the titles Count of Anjou and Duke of Normandy and made no attempt to combine the regions. That this was a specific policy on his part is shown by his advice to Henry II to rule all his domains separately, and never to attempt to govern one by the customs of another. Henry obeyed this injunction for the most part – though with some exceptions – and continued to use multiple titles just as Geoffrey had,[1] though the titles of Count of Maine and Count of Poitou fell into abeyance, subsumed into Anjou and Aquitaine respectively.

Henry and Eleanor had four sons that survived to adulthood, and modern historians emphasize that in the 1180s Henry II planned to divide the Angevin possessions between his sons, with the eldest surviving son Henry inheriting England, Normandy and Anjou; Richard taking Aquitaine; Geoffrey taking Brittany; and John becoming the king of Ireland. The early deaths of Young Henry and Geoffrey along with John's failure to make his lordship of Ireland succeed meant that Richard inherited everything, and Richard's death without heirs meant that John did the same, but this was a genealogical accident. Further, the Angevins avoided imposing a single political system on their various lands and explicitly kept them separate with the only rationale behind the Empire's existence being the family's succession to the various lordships.

What makes further speculation about the relevance of the term Empire pointless is that the edifice collapsed within a matter of five years under John's rule. John is considered one of the worst rulers in English history, but this is insufficient to explain the almost immediate disintegration of his empire. There were other forces at work during the reigns of Henry II and Richard that reached their culmination under John and set the stage for the next chapter of Angevin history.

How useful, then, is the term 'Angevin Empire'? Since Kate Norgate coined it in *England under the Angevin Kings* in 1881 it has become a fixture in medieval historiography and prompted considerable, and profitable, discussion and debate. JC Holt commented:

> The Plantagenet lands were not designed as an 'empire', as a great centralized administrative structure ... They were founded, and continued to survive, on an unholy combination of princely greed and genealogical accident.[2]

However, this could be said of every medieval state, not least William the Conqueror's Anglo-Norman realm, which is never so lightly dismissed.

There is no doubt that the Angevin Empire did not have a centralized administrative structure, but the formation and persistence of the Empire were not accidental. Matilda and Geoffrey Plantagenet fought to make the Empire a reality, and once he had control of his vast domains Henry II fought constantly to preserve their integrity, as did Richard and John. Commenting that they viewed these lands as family possessions that could be divided between family members misses the mark, since this was true of all medieval territories, even France, the most ideologically coherent medieval kingdom. Once the continental portions of the Angevin Empire had been taken by France, some of them were almost immediately apportioned between French princes, including, as we shall see, Anjou. This French use of 'apanages' almost proved disastrous when territories such as Burgundy gained nearly complete independence and became a threat to the French throne in the 15th century, but hindsight allows historians to view the French kings as maintaining some form of central control over them.

The question of fealty and homage raises an interesting point, since Henry, Richard and John owed homage to the French king for the entire Angevin Empire except England, but initially this meant little. This highlights the personal nature of homage, since the fact that one lord performed homage to another could have little impact on who actually ruled the territory. Contemporaries certainly viewed it this way: the troubadour and inveterate troublemaker Bertran de Born commented 'Five duchies has the French crown and, if you count them up, there are three of them missing' – that is, Normandy, Brittany and Aquitaine had been part of France, but now belonged to the Angevins, who were considered completely separate.[3]

Henry II: 'A human chariot, dragging everyone along in fear and excitement'

Henry II is perhaps the most vibrant figure of the 12th century. To enable us to engage emotionally with him we may lack the immediacy of a realistic portrait (though we do have his effigy in Fontevraud Abbey), but we have such finely drawn, intimate descriptions by members of his household that Henry lives for us more than most medieval figures and we can form quite a clear impression of his personality and indeed his appearance.

Our overriding impression of Henry is of violent energy and constant motion, and physical descriptions of him dovetail (too neatly?) with this image. Peter of Blois said he was of moderate height 'appearing neither gigantic among small men nor insignificant among tall ones', and Gerald of Wales and Walter Map said he was 'thick-set, square-shouldered, broad-chested, with arms muscular as those of a glad-iator and highly-arched feet which looked made for the stirrup'. He had the red hair that had characterized the Angevins since Fulk the Red, freckled skin and grey eyes, and though there could be no question that he lacked the qualities that led his father to be called 'the Handsome', his courtier Walter Map said that 'his was a form which a soldier, having once seen, would hasten to look upon again', whatever this means![4] These descriptions are more convincing than Henry of Huntingdon's; when discussing Henry's arrival in England for the final push that established his succession to the throne, he described the future king's appearance: 'The noble youth was at the head of his army, his physical beauty betokening that of the soul, and marked out by arms worthy of him, which suited him so well that we may say that his arms did not so much become him as he his arms.'[5] This might be more calculated to please the new king than calling him freckled or thick-set.

Henry had no use for luxury, dressing plainly and putting gloves over his coarse, rough hands only when hawking, and eating very meagrely, prompting complaints from his courtiers that the ordinary fare at his table even for nobles was half-baked bread, sour wine, stale fish and bad meat.[6] This wasn't a surprise, because Henry had no time to eat sumptuous meals and no call to wear any but practical clothes; he was in the saddle from the break of dawn until nightfall hunting and hawking, and even on his return he was never seated, standing or walking as he discussed business with his courtiers or debated intellectual problems with the clergy.

Here is one key to the existence of the Angevin Empire, because only a king with such energy could have ruled such vast domains successfully, and Henry visited every inch of his territories. Herbert of Bosham described Henry's government as 'a human chariot, of which the king is both driver and marksman, dragging everyone along in fear and excitement'.[7] Henry's energy was so remarkable that Louis VII said that he seemed to fly rather than ride, and it is a commonplace among historians to say that he died 'worn-out' in 1189 at the age of fifty-six; like a shark, when he stopped moving he would die. It is noteworthy that Richard the Lionheart seemed to possess a similar inexhaustible energy – as Norgate called it, the 'demon-blood of Anjou'[8] – but John, who lost the empire, was accused of habitual indolence, though even he could act quickly when necessary. John, if not lazy, sometimes seemed paralysed by the choices he faced and lapsed into inaction.

Henry's constant travel and tireless work on governance were matched by his devotion to learning. Henry had no interest in tournaments or troubadours – as Peter of Blois said, life at court was like school every day, and Henry would often retire to his chamber with a book.[9] It is not coincidental that in his reign we find one of the first medieval treatises, the *Dialogus de Scaccario* ('Dialogue of the Exchequer') of around 1180. England in the 12th century was synonymous with wealth and good government, and the Exchequer was perhaps the key component to this. The Dialogue provides a unique discussion of Henry's fiscal administration, from its origins to the most minute details of receiving and storing money.[10]

What is perhaps most striking to modern eyes is that the Exchequer, which we take for granted as an institution, originated as a machine for counting money. It was a chequered cloth that was placed over a long table, and counters were placed in each square of the cloth to act as an abacus when rendering accounts. It may not stir everyone's heart to ponder developments in mathematics, but this advance in arithmetic made the 11th and 12th centuries immeasurably more like our own time.

Using this technique, the sheriffs could present their accounts on the exchequer cloth easily, with counters being placed to show how much they owed and how much they provided. Soon the term Exchequer came to represent this procedure by which sheriffs publicly rendered their accounts, and then received a receipt in the form of a tally stick to show what they had paid.[11] The most important point was that the accounts were rendered publicly: the sheriff's account was seen to be rendered and the receipt proved what he had paid. This public accountability of government officials was crucial in the development of democracy itself, although this was still an undemocratic society. The sheriff received a tally stick with notches cut to show how much he had paid because he was likely to be illiterate, whereas the literate government ministers wrote the sums on the 'Pipe Roll' (so called because the rolls of parchment looked like pipes when they were stacked) for the government archive. This procedure actually dated to the reign of Henry I (the first surviving Pipe Roll dates to 1130), but is another example of the Angevins taking over Norman procedures and bringing them to new heights of efficiency.[12]

An equally important development that grew from the Exchequer was that it began to be held at a particular place, the Palace of Westminster. As we saw, even in the 1130s Winchester, the Anglo-Saxon capital, was still the kingdom's treasury, although coronations took place in Westminster, but under Henry II we finally see the king's administrative centre of Westminster joining the chief city of London to create a true national capital for England.

Though there were many medieval kings who liked ceremony and pomp – the great Angevin enemies, the Capetians, were masters of this – there was still a rough-and-ready quality to many medieval kings, particularly Henry. Access to the king was relatively easy. Walter Map says, 'Whatever way he goes out he is seized upon by the crowds and pulled hither and thither, pushed whither he would not and yet, surprising to say, he listens to each man with patience, and though assaulted by all with shouts and pullings and rough pushings, does not threaten anyone because of it, nor show any sign of anger; only, when he is hustled beyond bearing, he silently retreats to some place of quiet.'[13] The architecture of the time reflected this lack of privacy, as there was still a Great Hall open to all and the king often moved in the midst of crowds. By the 15th century a distinctly different type of architecture arose with the development of corridors and sequences of private rooms, which was exemplified if not pioneered by those later Angevins, Louis II of Anjou and King René.

Yet Henry's informality was clearly a personal quality and not just typical of the time. Henry was so impatient that he would sometimes eat his meals while standing; he would hunt all day and stop in the meanest lodging he happened to find with no regard for his own comfort or the comfort of those with him; and despite his obsessive concern for royal prerogatives, his ideas of royal dignity did not preclude him flinging himself on the floor in a rage and chewing on his mattress, or having a jester named Roland the Farter, who performed a leap, a whistle and a fart to the delight of the court[14], or rolling on the ground with laughter when St Hugh of Lincoln made a joke at his expense.

The latter episode might be the most characteristic and give us the best insight into his personality. Henry was annoyed with St Hugh, and had gone out hunting but paused in the forest to rest. St Hugh pursued him and demanded to be heard, but Henry's ire was unquenched and he maintained a stony silence. St Hugh sat next to him in silence and decided to wait the king out. Henry could not stand to be idle, and he began to mend a leather bandage that was on one of his fingers. St Hugh then commented to the king how much he resembled his ancestors, the leather workers of Falaise. Henry howled with laughter and rolled on the ground, to the astonishment of his courtiers, who didn't get the joke. Henry explained that Herleva, who bore the bastard William the Conqueror, had been a leather worker in Falaise, as was well known to the Angevins, if not their courtiers. In fact St Hugh was rumoured to be Henry II's own bastard, which perhaps added a bit of spice to his knowledge of that particular bit of family history.[15]

Henry II's Achievements

When Henry became king of England the country must have been deeply weary of war, and the confusion and uncertainty over the disputed succession between Stephen and Matilda. The arrival of a king who could provide strong government and order must have seemed desirable to some, yet others had profited greatly from the anarchy by seizing royal properties and lands from their neighbours, and they may have favoured the current system that essentially devolved power to the barons at the king's expense. Whatever their views, none of the English nobles could have been prepared for just how imposing Henry could be. Henry's immediate goal was to restore the privileges and authority of the monarch to what they were 'on the day when our grandfather Henry I was both alive and dead'. Henry's frequent use of this formula emphasized his connection to the previous Norman monarchy, but it also bluntly stated that the laxity of Stephen's reign and seizure of prerogatives by the nobles (notably the building of unlicensed castles) was over, and Henry intended to regain full royal authority.[16]

Like his great-grandfather William the Conqueror and his ancestor Fulk Nerra, Henry was a prodigious castle-builder. There could be no question that the stone-built castle was the preeminent piece of medieval military technology, and Henry spent enormous amounts upgrading his castles (as well as seizing and demolishing illegal castles erected during the Anarchy). We are uniquely positioned to examine Henry's expenditure because we have the Pipe Rolls giving detailed accounts of almost everything he spent. Henry put £4000 into Dover Castle, which is still one of the foremost medieval fortifications in England, and he commissioned the technologically advanced Orford Castle, polygonal in shape to foil miners who might undermine angles not overseen by the defenders.[17]

Henry was also famous for being able to take castles, as his father had been and his son Richard would be. Contemporaries marvelled at Henry's ability to appear as if from nowhere and capture supposedly impregnable castles within days. This was not because of superior artillery or secret methods, but because Henry and Richard were able to appreciate the changing nature of the medieval army. Although mercenaries had been used by William the Conqueror and King Stephen, there was still an assumption that medieval armies would be composed of knights serving under feudal obligation. These obligations were set out very clearly, and included a strict limit on the amount of time a knight had to serve, which made the feudal levy ill suited for lengthy siege operations. Knights who lived off plunder also had no desire to sit in front of a castle for weeks. Furthermore, many knights owed no duty to serve outside the land of their lord, and so Henry Count of Anjou had no right to summon Angevin levies outside Anjou, just as Henry Duke of Normandy or King of England had no right to summon Norman or English knights to serve in Aquitaine. Henry's solution to this problem was to use armies of mercenaries who would serve wherever and whenever he liked, as long as there was money to pay them. In addition to their unlimited term of service they also might include professional sappers, miners and engineers who provided skills knights had no need or desire to acquire. This transformation of the medieval army constituted a minor military revolution after two centuries of warfare when the advantage lay solidly with the defenders of stone fortifications. Henry's realization – or perhaps the realization of the Exchequer, that precocious embryonic bureaucratic organization – that the single most important factor in conducting war was securing a supply of ready money, and beyond this that a paid professional force that could remain in the field for weeks or months on end might indeed be more useful, if not superior, to a body of aristocrats, changed the face of warfare forever.[18]

However, despite Henry's early success in England, the continental parts of his empire needed attention too. Henry's brother Geoffrey claimed that he had been left Anjou and Maine by Geoffrey Plantagenet, and Louis VII refused to acknowledge Henry's right to Aquitaine. Though Louis may have seemed the more intractable enemy – and in time would turn out to be – Henry quickly pacified him. Henry met Louis at the Norman border in 1156 and did homage for Normandy, Anjou and Aquitaine in exchange for Louis's formal recognition of him as Duke of Aquitaine. Henry's brother Geoffrey refused to come to terms and fortified his three castles of Chinon, Mirebeau and Loudon to raise a rebellion, but he received little support and when Henry marched against him with his already legendary siege train, Geoffrey gave up his castles in exchange for an annuity.[19]

Henry and Eleanor then made a progress around Aquitaine to receive homage from their vassals and dispossess those who had proved troublesome, destroying their castles for good measure. This encouraged the residents of Nantes, Brittany's most important port, to renounce their allegiance to the Count of Brittany and ask for Henry's assistance, and Henry replied by giving them his brother Geoffrey as the new Count of Nantes.[20] Nantes was particularly important as the seaport at the mouth of the Loire, and as such controlled the export of the wines of Anjou and Touraine, which at this time were much more important than the wines of Bordeaux. In fact, it was only because of the collapse of the Angevin Empire and loss of Anjou and Touraine that in the 13th-century Bordeaux became the main port for exporting wine to England, and its position has never faltered in the subsequent 800 years.[21]

Louis VII had demanded the eastern part of Normandy (called the Norman Vexin) in exchange for recognizing Geoffrey Plantagenet and Henry as Dukes of Normandy, but Henry was determined to restore the rights of his grandfather Henry I. He sent Thomas Becket, his chancellor and most trusted adviser, on an embassy to Paris in 1158 with the specific purpose of overawing the French with his power. Though Henry himself had no love of magnificence, he was well aware of its uses, and Becket was the perfect person to fulfil the role. William FitzStephen described Becket's arrival in France and his procession, which included 250 footmen, 200 knights and squires, greyhounds, mastiffs, monkeys, falcons and wagons loaded with gold, silver, books and elaborate garments including twenty-four changes of clothes for Becket. When the enormous retinue had finally passed, the French were at last treated to the sight of Becket himself, and observers said, 'What a magnificent man the king of England must be if his chancellor travels in such great state.'[22] Which was exactly the point, though Louis later quipped to Walter Map, in a quote worthy of an Angevin '... the King of England, who lacks nothing, has men, horses, gold, silk, jewels, fruits, game and everything else. We in France have nothing but bread and wine and gaiety.'[23] At no other time in history can the cheerful rustic simplicity of French royalty have been compared so disadvantageously to English style and wealth.

Becket's mission was a success and it was soon announced that Louis's daughter Margaret would marry Henry's eldest son. Margaret's dowry would be the Norman Vexin, which would thus revert back to Normandy. Since both Margaret and Young Henry were barely out of infancy, Louis would retain the dowry until the marriage actually took place and Margaret was given into Henry's custody, though only on condition that she not be raised by Eleanor, a telling detail showing Louis still could not forgive his former wife, and pointedly questioned her morals.[24]

We can only imagine the anxiety Louis VII must have felt at the growing power of his Angevin enemy, particularly as he was still without an heir. After his marriage to Eleanor ended in 1152, Louis married Constance of Castile, who bore another two daughters. In 1160 she died in childbirth, and nothing could be greater evidence of the pressure for an heir than the fact that five weeks later Louis married his third wife, Adela of Champagne. Without a male heir France risked going the way of England in the reign of Stephen, and this could not be tolerated. So when, in August 1165, the queen of France finally gave birth to a son, it was a cause for national rejoicing. Gerald of Wales was a student in Paris and described being woken in his rented rooms on the Ile de la Cité by the pealing of all the bells in the city and the light of flames shining through his window. He first thought the city was on fire, but when he rushed to his window he saw the streets were filled with people celebrating and declaring, 'By the grace of God there is born to us this night a King who shall be a hammer to the King of the English.'[25] The baby was named Philip, but also called Dieudonné, 'God-given', and in time he would justify these hopes by taking nearly all the Angevin continental possessions for France.

Thomas Becket: The Turbulent Priest

Becket's mission to France and his personification of Henry's majesty was the high point of his chancellorship. Becket and Henry had been close friends since Henry's accession, even engaging in an impromptu wrestling match to decide who would give his cloak to a beggar[26], and Becket ably supported Henry in his attempts to claim (or re-claim, as Henry would have it) royal rights usurped by the Church. For this reason, Henry chose Becket, his most trusted friend and capable administrator, to be the new Archbishop of Canterbury when the position became vacant in 1161. This unleashed a quarrel that ended in Becket's murder and near ruin for Henry.

Historians have explained Becket's abrupt change from upholder of royal rights to defender of the Church by saying that Becket was a single-minded character who believed in inhabiting fully any role he undertook. As chancellor, he indulged in all the ceremony and luxury of the role, yet once he had become Archbishop of Canterbury he changed entirely, wearing a hair shirt and shunning any ostentation. Though as chancellor he had acted to enforce Henry's will, as Archbishop he opposed any action he felt compromised the rights of the Church and fell out with Henry within a year of assuming the office. This view originates with Ralph of Diceto, who said of Becket:

> However, as he put on those robes reserved, at God's command, to the highest of his clergy, he changed not only his apparel but his cast of mind. For he wished no longer to be bothered with the concerns of the chancery but rather that he might be allowed to retire from it and thus have more time to devote to addressing his flock and watching over the affairs of the Church. Therefore, Thomas sent a message to the king of England, then in Normandy, resigning his chancellorship and surrendering the seal. Such a resignation had its sole cause in his own conception of the duties of his new office.[27]

Henry believed that the Church should act to reinforce his authority and good governance of the kingdom, but Becket felt himself bound to a higher power and chose exile in France rather than submission.

Many sympathized with Becket, as best demonstrated in the anonymous song *In Rama sonat gemitus* composed between 1165–1170, which comments on Becket's exile by comparing Henry to King Herod and Becket to a new Joseph in exile in the 'Egypt of France'.[28] There were several attempts at reconciliation, but Becket remained inflexible over what he saw as any infringement of the church's rights, even opposing royal rights that had long been in existence, and no reconciliation could be achieved. Henry then exacerbated the problem considerably: he chose to have his eldest son Henry crowned as king in his own lifetime, a practice the Capetians had long used to ensure the succession, but in Becket's absence he had the coronation carried out by the Archbishop of York. A further attempt at reconciliation seemed successful, but according to Ralph of Diceto, Becket hedged his declarations of allegiance to Henry with phrases such as 'saving my order' and 'saving God's faith', with the result that '… just as our ancestors used to pay very close attention to formulae in law, so the king kept taking issue with certain phrases in the archbishop's words'.[29] Nothing could be more calculated to enrage Henry than a petty legalistic attempt to avoid obligations to the throne.

Nevertheless, the two men finally reached an agreement at the end of 1170, under which Becket returned to England. Becket promptly excommunicated the Archbishop of York and the other two bishops who had crowned Young King Henry. Henry was at his Christmas court in Normandy, and it was here that the most famous episode of his reign unfolded, though it is not clear exactly what he said.

What seems to have happened is that Henry became so frustrated that he expressed his wish that the problem would go away. 'Who will rid me of this turbulent priest?' is the well-known phrase attributed to him, though this is apocryphal. What does seem to be true is that he expressed some sentiment of wanting to be rid of the Becket affair, and four of his knights took this literally. They went to Canterbury cathedral and burst in with drawn swords shouting for Becket. He faced them fearlessly, and knelt before the altar in prayer. The knights then struck him on the head and murdered him at the altar. This was one of the most shocking events in European history and gained wide notoriety. Whatever the merits of his case and his lack of direct involvement, Henry was blamed for the murder. Henry himself was utterly horrified: Becket was killed on 29 December 1170, and when Henry heard the news on 1 January 1171 he locked himself away for three days.[30]

Becket's death reverberated around Europe and condemnation of Henry was universal. Louis VII wrote to the pope to complain and the Archbishop of Sens wrote, 'I have no doubt that the cry of the whole world has already filled your ears of how the king of the English, that enemy to the angels and the whole body of Christ, has wrought his spite on that holy one.'[31]

Becket's death marked the moment when Henry's seemingly unstoppable run of good luck and success came to an end, and he soon faced the most serious threat to his authority he had yet seen. Worse, the threat came from his own family, and Henry had sowed the seeds of this himself by crowning his eldest son Henry as co-king.

Young King Henry: Chivalry and Tournaments

Young King Henry, as he is known, is a figure about whom we know quite a lot, though his early death – and seemingly his character – prevented him from matching the deeds of the other Angevins. Young Henry's character was very different from his father's, and he is the outstanding early link between the Angevins and chivalry. After Geoffrey Plantagenet's precocious use of heraldry, there might have been a notable gap before Richard I's emergence as the perfect troubadour knight, but Young Henry admirably filled it. Young Henry was a key figure in the development of what would become arguably the most iconic activity of the Middle Ages, the tournament, in the period that saw the rise of tournaments and the knight-errant, best described by the contemporary Chrétien de Troyes in his paradigmatic Arthurian romances.

Throughout the early 1170s Young Henry toured Normandy and Anjou to participate in tournaments and perform the traditional monarchical function of magnificent display that was so alien to his father's character. Although many contemporary and modern historians view this as idleness, this role should not be underestimated and there could be serious consequences for rulers unwilling to reinforce their right to rule through display. Although Henry II demonstrated that territorial acquisition, ruthless political control and general success were highly effective, the aristocracy were also expected to be magnificent and generous. Young Henry's reputation did the Angevins no harm in noble circles, even if the Church had other views. The modern view of Young Henry tends to be that he was an idle poseur whose escapades contributed nothing to his father's (and nominal co-ruler's) reign, but we should not disregard the impact his fame as a generous and successful tourneyer may have had.

The brightly coloured image of the mounted knight with couched lance, man and horse draped and crowned with heraldic devices, is perhaps the defining image of the period, although these elaborately choreographed jousts belong to the age of King René in the 15th century. In the 12th century, tournaments were full-scale battles fought with real weapons in which opponents were captured and ransomed, and which differed from outright war only in the existence of refuges where combatants were not allowed to be attacked, and the fact that opponents weren't usually killed, though this is a very grey area. In actual battle, noble opponents were almost always captured for the large ransoms they could provide, so death tolls were very low by our standards, while on the contrary, personal feuds were often prosecuted in the course of tournaments with deadly results, and accidental deaths were also common. Tactics which to us seem most unchivalrous were employed even by such paragons of virtue as William Marshal. Groups of knights fought together in tournaments as teams and might wait until late in the tournament when the other combatants were exhausted, then ride in and take captives. The contemporary response to this behaviour was to applaud it as tactical cunning rather than see it as treachery.[32]

Tournaments were the chosen sport of younger, landless knights who had no employment and nothing to lose, and as William Marshal will demonstrate, the best practitioners could make their fortune and achieve respectability. As with every sport, this only applied to those who performed at the highest level and there are also count-less stories of knights bankrupted by ransom payments or killed ignominiously leaving their families destitute. Famous victims included Henry II's son Geoffrey of Brittany and Robert of Flanders, a hero of the First Crusade who, according to William of Malmesbury in one of the earliest references to tournaments, 'tarnished that noble exploit' by dying in a 'tournament, as they call it' in 1111.[33] This accounts for the Church's unyielding hostility to the tournament and the issuance of decrees forbidding anyone killed in a tournament being buried in consecrated ground.

Secular authorities also opposed tournaments for more practical reasons: the unrestrained mock combat could all too easily become real combat that ranged over fields and through villages, destroying peasants' livelihoods and in many cases their lives. The 'little battle of Chalons' was an infamous tournament that evolved into a real battle, but it was by no means unique. Henry II prudently forbade tournaments in England and was a strong enough ruler to enforce the ban, which explains Young Henry's preference for the continent. The marches of France, Normandy and Flanders were the breeding ground of tournaments, precisely because they lay between the dominions of the Angevin king, French king and Count of Flanders and were not subject to strong control. It was not until the reign of Richard the Lionheart that tour-naments became legal in England, and he allowed them for the reason he allowed most things: he needed money, and sold licences for tournaments as a revenue enhancement project.

In the later Middle Ages criticism of the tournament was commonplace because it was thought to be decadent, sadly fallen from the purity of its origins in the 12th century, and indeed such criticisms became common even in the 13th century. However, despite the undoubted changes in the way tournaments were conducted, and their ultimate replacement by the more easily regulated joust, they served the same function in every period, as an aristocratic sport that provided training for warfare. Modern historians may dispute the utility of even the violent 12th-century tournament in preparing knights for actual warfare, but however distinct the tactics used in war may have been from those practised in tournaments, the latter still provided a dress rehearsal for warfare: the same armour and weapons were used, the warhorse had to be controlled under chaotic circumstances and the knight himself had to control his fear and become used to receiving and dealing blows.

There was another thread to the 12th-century tournament that is frequently ascribed to its 'decadence', and that is the presence of spectators and the incorporation of entertainment into the event. 14th- and 15th-century representations of the tournament or joust – notably King René's treatise on tournaments – always show spectators, particularly female spectators, watching and applauding. However, we learn from William Marshal's biography that ladies were present at the tournaments he attended, and that William entertained them by singing, at which he was famously accomplished, and that the knights and ladies danced. Minstrels were also present at these early tournaments and expected to be rewarded, and William gave a minstrel one of his captured horses on at least one occasion, which can have done no harm to his reputation.[34] This emphasis on the social aspect of the tournament as early as the 1170s flies in the face of later criticism that tournaments and jousts were empty social occasions remote from their original purpose.

William Marshal: The Perfect Knight

William Marshal served as the factual counterpart to the knights of Chrétien de Troyes's romances, and it is to his biography – the first biography of an 'ordinary' person (i.e. not a saint or a ruler) in medieval history – that we owe our knowledge of early tournaments and the rise of chivalry, as well as a great deal about Young Henry. William Marshal was also a key player in nearly a century of Angevin history, having made his first appearance as a child hostage in the civil war between Stephen and Matilda and ending his days as the most respected man in England and regent for Henry III after John's death. In between he served Henry II, became the tutor and companion of Young Henry, nearly killed Richard in a skirmish, and attempted to preserve John's kingdom when the king himself threw it away. William's rise to prominence came solely because of his prowess and chivalric behaviour, because he was the younger son of a nobleman and had to make his own way, and through his success in the new sport of tournaments he became wealthy and famous enough to marry an heiress, become an important baron and ultimately rule England as regent.

William's biography gives us details about how warfare and tournaments were conducted in the mid- to late 12th century, as well as aristocratic behaviour and customs. In the summer of 1167 William was knighted to participate in a battle between the forces of Henry II and Louis VII. Although William distinguished himself in the battle of Drincourt, he lost his horse and was too busy fighting to capture any horses or equipment himself. After the battle when the knights and commanders were feasting, the Earl of Essex teased William for not taking any booty, and William's lord declined to replace his horse to teach William the vital lesson that warfare was as much about taking prisoners and plunder as anything else. This reminds us that warfare in the 12th century was certainly violent and dangerous, but it was also a business proposition and method of making money.[35] For the participants, the dividing line between battles and tournaments was very fine and often non-existent.

That may have been acceptable to the aristocrats, but for everyone else warfare was horrifyingly brutal. The point of medieval warfare was to lay waste the opponent's land rather than to seek pitched battles. Destroying or seizing villages, crops, animals and supplies and slaughtering the peasants who worked the land strengthened the attacking army, weakened the opponent and undermined his right to rule. Although I have highlighted the growing administrative sophistication of the 12th century, fundamentally lordship was about providing protection, and a lord who couldn't protect his people was no lord at all.[36]

Even in a civil war or revolt where each side hoped ultimately to control the land being ravaged, the method of war was the same. As Count Philip of Flanders was said to have advised, 'This is how war is begun: such is my advice. First destroy the land.' Or as a 15th-century commentator put it more colourfully, 'War without fire is like sausages without mustard.'[37]

Here is the central myth of chivalry: the overtly Christian ceremony of knighting, the splendid trappings, decorated armour, deeds of valour for fair ladies and elaborate code of courtesy to other knights existed alongside – indeed, to disguise – the principal occupation of knights. This was to wage war, but since pitched battles were rare, 'waging war' meant pillaging and burning the countryside and murdering peasants. The aristocracy believed that if they followed this code of conduct between themselves, their appalling behaviour to non-nobles was simply an unfortunate side effect of war. The tension between ideal and reality would reach its breaking point in the Hundred Years War in the 14th and 15th centuries, with the participation of non-nobles in battles and consequential increase in the number of deaths, as well as the development of artillery that had to be operated by professionals and killed indiscriminately with no regard for rank. Although the aristocracy continued to participate in warfare, by the 15th-century knightly pageants and ceremonies had been definitively detached from actual warfare.

In the 12th century, when these ideals and contradictions were still being created, William Marshal was undoubtedly the embodiment of the perfect knight and became the 12th-century version of a millionaire sporting superstar. William's adventures in tournaments provide us with snapshots of 12th-century life as evocative as the images in the misericords of medieval cathedrals. At a tournament in Maine, William was attacked by five knights and managed to defeat them, but his helmet was turned around by a blow and he had to retire to have it rearranged. In an episode fit to inspire an Arthurian romance (and which in fact is very close to a scene in Chrétien de Troyes' *Lancelot*), William overheard two other knights questioning the identity of the knight who had fought best, only to realise they were talking about him when they recognized the device on his shield.[38] At a tournament in Champagne, William fought so well that he was awarded the top prize, but when the judges looked for him to make the award he was discovered with his head on an anvil while a blacksmith tried to remove his mangled helmet with tongs.[39]

This devotion to tournaments was not incompatible with military service, and early on William became embroiled in a feud that would haunt the Angevins for decades. In 1167 the turbulent Lusignan brothers led a revolt of Poitevin barons and William, now in the household of his uncle Earl Patrick of Salisbury, went to Poitou to assist in the operations against them. Henry II quickly subdued the castle of Lusignan and left Eleanor of Aquitaine under the protection of Earl Patrick while he went to meet Louis VII. Guy and Geoffrey Lusignan ambushed Eleanor and Patrick as they rode outside the castle one day, and although Eleanor escaped, the unarmed Earl Patrick was treacherously stabbed in the back and killed. William rushed to avenge his uncle but was also overcome after being attacked from behind. The Lusignans earned William's undying enmity for killing his uncle – and worse, the representative of their feudal lord – and compounded the insult by holding William captive without treating his wound, though William sufficiently charmed one of the ladies in the Lusignan household for her to send him bandages in a hollowed-out loaf of bread. Fortunately for William, Eleanor ransomed him and rewarded him generously for his loyalty and courage.[40]

On the strength of his military ability and friendship with Eleanor, in 1170 William was made Young King Henry's tutor in chivalry and head of his household knights. William's friendship with Young Henry gives us an insight into the life of the heir to the throne under a strong monarch, and how confining and frustrating the experience can be. Young Henry, despite being crowned as co-monarch with his father, was given no authority of his own in any of the Angevin domains.

Although from the 12th century onward knights would often emulate Arthurian romances in their tournaments, in 1182 William and Young Henry's relationship mimicked the story of Lancelot in deadly earnest. A rumour spread through the court that William and the Young King's wife Margaret were lovers, and William fell out of favour. On learning of the rumours, William offered to fight all comers over three days to prove his innocence, but like Lancelot, no one dared to challenge him.[41]

The Great Revolt: 1173–1174

Despite his important, though neglected, status as an early knight errant, Young Henry is most remembered by modern historians for the revolt against his father in 1173–74 in which he allied with Louis VII and was joined by his mother and brothers. The origins of the revolt were complicated. Henry had married Young Henry to Margaret of France and engaged Richard to her sister Alice (these were Louis VII's daughters by his second wife), and Geoffrey had married Constance the heiress to Brittany, but Henry needed a bride for his youngest son John. He arranged a marriage for John to the daughter of the Count of Maurienne, who ruled an alpine territory between Provence and Piedmont, in the hope that John – who was already called 'Lackland' because all his father's lands had been apportioned between his other brothers – might inherit the county.

The Count was happy for an alliance with the greatest monarch in Europe, but he rightly questioned what lands John would bring to the marriage. Henry decided to give John the castles of Chinon, Loudon and Mirebeau (which were traditionally allocated to Angevin younger sons like Henry II's brother Geoffrey[42]), but failed to take into account that the castles already belonged to Young Henry, and the Young King refused to relinquish them to his brother. Henry angrily insisted, and Young Henry, infuriated by this proof of how little power he, a crowned co-monarch, actually wielded, rose in revolt against his father and fled to Louis VII in whom he was sure of finding an ally.

Tellingly, Young Henry drew his brothers Richard and Geoffrey into his revolt, revealing that Young Henry was not the only one frustrated by Henry's refusal to share any of his power. William the Lyon of Scotland invaded northern England, and many Anglo-Norman barons also rebelled in what seems to be a massive reaction to twenty years of Henry's administrative reforms and codification of royal rights and privileges at the expense of the aristocracy. It is no surprise that Louis VII and William the Lyon chose to support Henry's sons, as they could hope for rich pickings on the Angevin borders if the revolt succeeded. The most shocking element of these events to contemporaries was that Eleanor of Aquitaine also decided to join her sons against her husband, and began the journey from Poitou dressed as a man so she could slip past her husband's troops to join her son in Paris. She was captured, and would remain imprisoned intermittently until Henry II's death in 1189. Contemporaries were shocked by Eleanor's action, and Ralph of Diceto declared that in a search through ancient and modern history he found more than thirty examples of sons rebelling against their fathers, but never of a queen rebelling against her husband.[43]

We have seen other women sidelined, imprisoned, exiled to convents and deprived of their rights. Yet in Eleanor's story, this is not the end. She was incarcerated and marginalized for fifteen years, but she lost none of her desire to rule or her will to endure. Eleanor survived her failed marriage to Louis and the scandal of the Second Crusade, which would have destroyed anyone else, and instead married the mightiest king in Europe and acted as co-ruler. Why she chose to rebel isn't known; she may have wanted her sons to have more of a role in ruling the Empire, or she may have believed their triumph would also allow her more power. Regardless, she failed in the rebellion, but was only eclipsed for a time before returning and becoming more powerful than ever.

Things looked bleak for Henry, yet he divided his enemies and easily defeated them one by one. Contemporary gossip said the revolt was Henry's punishment for Becket's death, and indeed Henry chose this moment to do formal public penance, going barefoot to Becket's shrine where he was publicly scourged and begged the saint's forgiveness.[44] It certainly worked, since almost immediately William the Lyon was captured as he attacked Alnwick Castle and was forced to perform homage to Henry, not only for his English possessions, but also for Scotland. Rather than shocking Henry into giving his eldest son and co-ruler more responsibility, this comprehensive victory merely confirmed Henry in his opinion that sharing power was too dangerous, and the Young King gained no advantage from the failed revolt. Legend said that the troubadour Bertran de Born stirred Young Henry to revolt, and this severing of the father from the son inspired Dante with one of his most arresting images: he depicted Bertran in the eighth circle of hell carrying a lantern made of his own severed head, suspended by the hair.[45] To the ever spiteful Gerald of Wales, the revolt was God's punishment of Henry for marrying another man's wife.[46]

If the sudden collapse of the revolt showed Becket's forgiveness of Henry II after his public penance, it seems the saint wasn't completely mollified: in 1179 Philip Augustus, the god-given sole heir to the throne of France, was dangerously injured in a hunting accident and seemed likely to die. His father Louis VII, although himself dying, dragged himself across the Channel to Becket's shrine and beseeched the saint, whom he had known personally, to save his son. Philip duly recovered and was crowned a month later, and would go on to cause Henry's downfall and destroy the Angevin Empire.[47]

After Eleanor's imprisonment, Henry openly acknowledged his mistress Rosamund Clifford, through whom Henry himself becomes a figure of folklore and has his moment as pantomime villain. Like most of the aristocracy in the Middle Ages, he took mistresses and had no shame in his adultery, despite the condemnation of clerics and the opprobrium heaped on women such as Eleanor if they were suspected of the same. Henry had at least two bastard children: Geoffrey, who became Archbishop of York, and William Longsword who became Earl of Salisbury.[48]

However, Rosamund Clifford was said to be Henry's great love, because after her death in 1176 he erected a splendid tomb for her in the convent at Godstow in front of the high altar. The tomb was still being treated with reverence in 1191 when St Hugh of Lincoln, appalled that a king's mistress should be openly venerated in a church, ordered that the tomb of this 'harlot' be moved outside.[49] Gerald of Wales in his malicious account of the revolt says that Henry, '... attributing his success like another Pharaoh not to divine mercy but his own strength, hardened his heart and returned incorrigibly to his usual abyss of vice, or rather, to an even worse one, since, going downhill things

can only deteriorate. And to mention only one thing, omitting the rest, he imprisoned Queen Eleanor his wife as punishment for the destruction of their marriage; his
adultery, previously hidden, now became open and blatant, not with a "pure rose" *rosa
munda*, falsely and frivolously named, but rather with an impure one.' Gerald's scorn
was not reserved for Henry alone, since he couldn't resist also alluding to Eleanor's
behaviour in Palestine during the Second Crusade, rejoicing in the unhappiness of her
children and then offhandedly accusing her of adultery with her father-in-law Geoffrey
Plantagenet as well.[50]

As for Rosamund, her mention in contemporary sources testifies to her importance,
but later legend would run riot in much the same way it did with Eleanor of Aquitaine,
and the two women would be drawn into each other's legends. Rosamund's name was
a gift to authors, since *rosa munda* means 'pure rose' in Latin, though freer translations
would also call her the 'rose of the world' (*rosa mundi).* The scene was set in Ranulf
Higden's *Polychronicon* of the early 14th century, in which – apparently purely based on
his imagination since no earlier source can be found for this tale – he accused Henry
II of 'misusing' Rosamund and locking her in a labyrinth at Woodstock to hide her
from Eleanor.[51]

A king imprisoning a fair maiden in a labyrinth is simply too good a story to resist,
and innumerable variations of the legend followed. Later writers would elaborate
Rosamund's prison into a garden maze, a tower in a labyrinth or in Thomas Delaney's
Ballad of Fair Rosamund, '… such a bower / the like was never seene. / Most curiously
that bower was built, / of stone and timber strong; / an hundred and fifty doors / did to
this bower belong: / And they so cunninglye contriv'd, / with turnings round about, /
that none but with a clue of thread / could enter in or out.'[52] All agreed that the reason
for Rosamund's imprisonment was Eleanor's hatred for her, since Henry truly loved
and wished to protect her. At the end of Delaney's ballad Henry must go to France
to put down the rebellion of his eldest son, and Eleanor 'with envious heart' goes to
Woodstock, tricks the knight guarding Rosamund into leaving the labyrinth, wounds
him and seizes the 'clue of twined-thread' that will guide her to her victim, where she
forces Rosamund to drink poison. Delaney was quite restrained since later authors
accused Eleanor of variously tearing out Rosamund's eyes, offering her a choice between
drinking poison or being stabbed and, most luridly, stripping Rosamund naked, roast-
ing her between two fires then letting her bleed to death in a hot bath.[53]

Philip Augustus and the Angevin Heirs

The revolt of 1173–74 had been the first real crisis of his reign, but Henry faced a new
enemy in his final years: in 1180 Louis VII died and his fifteen-year-old son Philip
became sole king of France. Philip had been crowned in 1179, attended by Young King
Henry, 'who humbly held one side of the crown on the head of the king of France, as

a sign of the submission he owed him', according to Rigord of St Denis.[54]

Louis suffers by comparison with his son, for Philip was the most successful medieval king of France and would be called Philip 'Augustus' in his own lifetime. The monk Rigord, who wrote Philip's biography, said Philip deserved this title even by 1193 since he had so 'augmented' the size of the royal demesne by taking over Vermandois and many other lands[55], but he would go on to conquer most of the Angevin continental territories, whereas Louis had always failed in his military endeavours (including the Second Crusade), and failed as a husband to Eleanor only to see her marry his bitterest rival. Eleanor's gibe, quoted by William of Newburgh, that Louis was more like a monk than a king[56] characterizes him, yet this conceals the fact that he and his father Louis VI laid the groundwork for Philip's successes by consolidating and ordering the French domains, and despite Louis's failures in his opposition to Henry II there was never any question that France itself was more secure during his reign. Perhaps a more fitting tribute is Walter Map's story that Louis, as an old man, could sleep alone in a wood without attendants because he was so beloved by his people. What other king could do this, Map asked?[57]

Henry II seems to have expected, and it seems an obvious plan to us, that his sons would take over the management of portions of his empire and work together to assist in its rule. Yet this is precisely the opposite of what happened, and in large part this was due to Henry's own actions. In the aftermath of the great rebellion of 1173–74, Richard became Duke of Aquitaine in his mother's right, and despite his youth gradually brought the rebellious southern lords to heel. Even the next son, Geoffrey, had been invested as Duke of Brittany in 1180 (with Chrétien de Troyes's Arthurian romance, *Erec et Enide*, specially written for the ceremony, performed as part of the celebration).[58]

This was in stark contrast to Young King Henry, who was a crowned king yet had no power whatsoever, making him increasingly unhappy with his lack of personal authority, and he searched for a solution. He asked Henry II to give him Normandy as his own province, but his father refused. In 1182, Richard faced a major rebellion in Aquitaine and Young Henry dutifully joined his father to quell the revolt, but his contact with the rebels suggested an interesting possibility: perhaps Aquitaine might be the arena for his ambitions, if he could only take it from Richard. This was a high-risk strategy since Henry II might choose to intervene on either side, but Young Henry received encouragement from his brother Geoffrey and a provocation from Richard.

Why Geoffrey should have chosen to incite one of his brothers against another is unknown, but contemporary chroniclers – whether based on information lost to us, or simply inventing a reason – had no doubts: it was because Geoffrey was a devious, evil character. Roger of Howden called him, 'Geoffrey, that son of perdition...that son of iniquity' and Gerald of Wales described him as 'overflowing with words, smooth as oil, possessed, by his syrupy and persuasive eloquence, of the power of dissolving the apparently indissoluble, able to corrupt two kingdoms with his tongue, of tireless endeavour and a hypocrite in everything.'[59]

More significantly, Richard fortified the castle of Clairvaux, which was technically in Anjou, and thus infringed on his brother's rights. The troublemaking troubadour Bertran de Born wrote a song to provoke the Young King:

> Between Poitiers and l'Ile Bouchard and Mirebeau and Loudun and Chinon someone has dared to build a fair castle at Clairvaux, in the midst of the plain. I should not wish the Young King to know about it or see, for he would not find it to his liking; but I fear, so white is the stone, that he cannot fail to see it …[60]

Probably because he knew matters were so fraught between his sons, Henry II decided to hold a Christmas court at Caen to celebrate the unity of his family. This was the greatest court ever held in Normandy, and in addition to his sons Henry was joined by his daughter Matilda and her husband, Henry the Lion, Duke of Saxony and Bavaria, and all the barons of Normandy, who were forbidden to hold their own courts. Henry attempted to defuse the tension between the brothers by having Richard turn the castle of Clairvaux over to Young Henry, and Geoffrey and Richard do homage to Young Henry to reinforce his seniority and perhaps satisfy his longing for greater power. Although Geoffrey willingly performed homage, the plan backfired spectacularly when Richard first refused, then agreed but only on the condition that Aquitaine would belong to him and his heirs forever, which condition Young Henry rejected because he had already undertaken to support the Aquitainian barons against Richard.[61] Henry attempted to reconcile his sons and wanted them to swear to a peace treaty, but such a peace had to include the barons of Aquitaine, and Geoffrey was sent to arrange this. He at once stirred up further trouble and Young Henry, on the pretence of going to smooth things over, joined the rebels. Richard had now had enough and also went to Poitou to prepare for war.

As was always the case with Angevin difficulties, their enemies were quick to exploit them. Raymond Count of Toulouse and Hugh Duke of Burgundy joined the Young King, Philip Augustus sent a party of mercenaries to join them, and the Lusignans and other barons also revolted. Things began to look as bleak for Henry II as they had in 1173–74 (though this time at least Richard was on his side), when Young Henry caught a fever and died on 11 June 1183. Though the rebellion had drawn on longstanding political issues, the proximate cause of this particular struggle was Young Henry, and with his death the rebel coalition disintegrated and the revolt was over.[62]

With Young Henry dead and Richard and Geoffrey established in their own lands, Henry attempted to solve the problem of John in the only way that might have succeeded, by making him lord of Ireland. Because Ireland had entered the Angevin Empire after Henry apportioned his lands to his elder sons (it had been overrun by the Norman lords of south Wales, led by Richard de Clare, known as 'Strongbow'), the others had no objection to John being given the lordship. In the aftermath of Young King Henry's death in 1183, a new division might quite easily have been reached.

Richard still ruled Aquitaine directly and became heir to everything else, Geoffrey could be content with Brittany and John could be given a land that had no connection to his brothers.

Henry attempted to implement this plan by sending John to Ireland in 1185. John was provided with a crown of peacock feathers from the pope for his coronation, but otherwise he was left to own devices, and told, like Richard in Aquitaine, that he must take the throne for himself. Chroniclers relate that John's expedition was a disaster, because he and his youthful companions alienated the Irish lords (by being childish enough to make fun of their beards) and were unable to win the respect of the Norman lords. Ultimately John and his party were driven out of Ireland. John's failure in Ireland left the division of lands after Henry II's death unresolved, and continued to stoke Richard's fears that his father might yet try to take away some of his patrimony to leave to John.[63]

Henry did exactly that, and made what he must have thought was a sensible suggestion: now that Richard was heir apparent to England, Normandy and Anjou, he told Richard to give Aquitaine to John, who would then do homage to him. Richard knew how Young Henry had been treated as heir; moreover, he had spent eleven years pacifying the duchy and felt a deep connection to it, so relinquishing it was unacceptable. Richard immediately fled to Poitou and told his father he would never give up Aquitaine.[64]

In his dealings with his sons, especially Richard, Henry lacked the penetrating insight with which he outmanoeuvred his other rivals. He had failed to see that keeping Young Henry waiting for the throne with no authority when his brothers had duchies to rule would be intolerable, and he failed to see that by giving Richard complete authority in Aquitaine he would create an attachment that meant the duchy was no longer a piece of the family patrimony to be moved from one son to another. When Richard refused to give Aquitaine to John, Henry told the sixteen-year-old John to go and take it.[65] Nothing demonstrates Henry's attitude towards his empire more clearly – how could he order one of his sons to lead an invading army into part of the Angevin domains, especially when the family had just put down a rebellion and their enemies were constantly circling and looking for an opportunity to break them apart? Henry simply didn't see this as anything other than a family difficulty and was unable to believe that the family could truly turn against each other. This despite the events of 1173–74, whose consequences were still being played out in Eleanor of Aquitaine's captivity.

John attempted to follow Henry's instructions and raided Poitou, joined by the ever meddlesome Geoffrey. However, over the last decade Richard had done exactly what Henry desired of him and created a ruthless military machine and efficient administration, and the invasion made little impact. As had become the norm since the time of Henry's struggles with Stephen, mercenaries formed the bulk of Richard's fighting force. We now hear of Richard's most faithful mercenary captain, Mercadier, who would be at his side until the moment of his death.[66]

Now came further evidence that Henry viewed all this as a game that he could call off whenever he liked, for in 1184 he summoned his sons back to England for a Christmas court where they were joined by Eleanor. This is the moment that was chosen for the play and film *A Lion in Winter*, and although we unfortunately know little about what happened, it must have been a moment of incredible tension and drama. Eleanor's presence is proof that Henry thought he should try a different approach, as he must have known that any appeal to Richard would have an infinitely greater chance of success if it came from her. Later events show that Henry persisted in his plan of reallocating the family domains between his three remaining sons, so he must somehow have tried to make this palatable to Richard, though he would fail utterly.

Henry then attempted to change the rules again. In 1185 he summoned Richard to Normandy and ordered him – quite legitimately – to surrender Aquitaine to its rightful ruler, Eleanor. Richard complied willingly, because this showed that Henry couldn't take Aquitaine from Richard by force, and the only way to deprive him of the duchy was to rehabilitate Eleanor. As duchess, Eleanor had complete authority to do whatever she liked, including leaving the duchy to Richard.[67]

Henry's abandonment of Aquitaine to Eleanor and Richard seemed to circumscribe Geoffrey's opportunities to cause mischief, so he took the usual route of disaffected Angevin sons and went to Paris. He and Philip Augustus became very close, as all the chroniclers commented – something worth remembering when we discuss Richard's relationship with Philip – and followed the fashionable pursuits of the time, including tournaments. It is a commonplace to say that medieval tournaments were incredibly violent and dangerous, but now we come to one of the examples always cited to prove the point: in August 1186 Geoffrey was trampled to death in a tournament.[68] This was a terrible shock, especially to Philip, and at Geoffrey's funeral in Paris Philip had to be forcibly restrained from throwing himself into the grave to be with his friend. Geoffrey's death might seem to have simplified the succession, but his wife was pregnant and subsequently gave birth to a son, Arthur (born at a high point of the Arthurian craze), who would play a significant part in the later Angevin story.

From having too many legitimate sons Henry was now down to two. The perception that the Angevins were in turmoil tempted the young French king to intervene personally for the first time, though nearly with disastrous consequences. In June 1187, Philip Augustus led an army to besiege the Angevin border fortress of Chateauroux, but Richard and John brought up a small force and managed to delay him. In what would become a long tradition of intelligence failures, Philip was unaware that Henry was approaching with a large army and found himself cornered. Henry – who had never fought a pitched battle in his long military career – was probably equally surprised when the French stood their ground, and the two armies prepared for battle. The arrival of a papal legate who begged them to arrange a truce provided a face-saving solution, and the kings agreed a two-year truce. Philip Augustus turned what could have been a catastrophe into another Capetian opportunity, for Richard joined the French king and went to Paris.[69] As the Angevins' feudal overlord, the French king was always the first choice for disaffected sons, and although Philip Augustus had no real authority in Normandy, Anjou or Aquitaine, if Richard as Duke of Aquitaine chose to enter into closer relations with his overlord there was little Henry could do to stop him.

Richard's relationship with Henry had not recovered from the difficulties over the succession, and now that Philip Augustus had shown himself willing to intervene with force, Richard could see the advantages of cultivating him. Once Richard arrived in Paris, he and Philip publicly demonstrated their closeness, just as Geoffrey and Philip had the previous year, and once again the chroniclers took pains to point this out. However, the language they used has proved confusing to some modern readers and given rise to a persistent legend about Richard.

Roger of Howden wrote of Richard's stay in Paris:

> Philip so honoured him that every day they ate at the same table, shared the same dish and at night the bed did not separate them. Between the two of them there grew up so great an affection that King Henry was much alarmed and, afraid of what the future might hold in store, he decided to postpone his return to England until he knew what lay behind this sudden friendship.[70]

The fact that Richard and Philip shared a bed immediately suggests to modern sensibilities that there was a sexual relationship, but in the medieval period most people, even royalty, shared beds at some point. In William Marshal's biography it is reported that Henry II and William Marshal shared a bed, and no one has ever suggested they were lovers. The point that Roger of Howden was making, and it is the same point that William Marshal's biographer intended, is that in a culture where beds were often shared, if a king shared a bed it was with someone who was particularly trusted and close to him. Chrétien de Troyes makes the same point in *Erec et Enide*, where Enide is so honoured by Queen Guinevere that when Erec is injured and has to sleep alone, 'not far away, beneath a coverlet of ermine, lay Enide and the queen'.[71]

Henry understood the point Richard was making, and it was that Richard as Duke of Aquitaine could have a relationship with his feudal overlord that didn't involve his father. Henry demanded that Richard return from Paris, and Richard indeed returned but only to seize the Angevin treasury at Chinon and begin fortifying the castles of Aquitaine.

Henry's reign was by any measure successful, but it is overshadowed by the events of his final two years, which were influenced yet again by the Crusades. In the summer of 1187, relations between Richard and Henry were at breaking point, and Philip Augustus had almost provoked a full-scale battle at Chateauroux. Yet an event thousands of miles away was about to transform the political landscape of Europe. On 4 July 1187, on the hills of Hattin, the army of Jerusalem was destroyed by Muslim forces led by Saladin, and within months Jerusalem itself fell to the Muslims. This catastrophe horrified Europe and had profound consequences for Richard.

Saladin and the Conquest of Jerusalem

The Angevin descendants in Jerusalem had not prospered since the fiasco of the Second Crusade. Outremer still had to cope with the rising threat of Nur ed-Din, and added to this were political difficulties in Jerusalem. Queen Melisende was still the rightful ruler of the kingdom, but now her son Baldwin III, who had been crowned as an infant, was old enough to want more power. From 1149 the relationship between Melisende and Baldwin broke down completely, with Melisende establishing an independent household and Baldwin having control only of Acre. Yet Baldwin was able to play the factions of the court skilfully against each other, and more importantly he held a trump card: he could lead military expeditions to defend the borders of the kingdom and Melisende could not. By 1152 Baldwin had consolidated his position sufficiently to demand that he be crowned sole ruler without Melisende. Although the Patriarch of Jerusalem correctly refused to perform this coronation, which would deny Melisende her rights, Baldwin simply crowned himself. Now the kingdom was divided between the two, with Baldwin taking the north and Melisende retaining Jerusalem, but this was financially and militarily impractical. Baldwin demanded the entire kingdom, and marched against Melisende's fortresses. Melisende held out in Jerusalem, but at the spectre of civil war her supporters finally deserted her. Baldwin assumed full control of the kingdom and Melisende was sidelined for the rest of her life.[72]

This forms a fascinating parallel story to that of Matilda and Henry II. Despite her indomitable will and willingness to participate in the military struggles required to secure her kingdom, after her disastrous attempted coronation Matilda seems to have realized that she could never be accepted as queen in her own right and stood aside for Henry. However, contemporaries were clear that Matilda retained a great influence on Henry until her death, not least by giving him his name, as he was always called Henry 'Fitz-Empress'. Walter Map also says that she gave Henry advice about how to rule.

> She told him, 'he should spin out all the affairs of everyone, hold long in his own hand all posts that became vacant, collect the revenues of them, and keep aspirants to them hanging on in hope: and she supported this advice by an unkind parable: an unruly hawk, if meat is often offered to it and then snatched away or hid, becomes keener and more inclinably obedient and attentive'.[73]

Whether or not this was truly the advice Matilda gave him, this was certainly how Henry treated his courtiers, and more importantly his sons, with the results we have seen. This advice also illuminates Matilda's behaviour when she had captured Stephen and was preparing to take the throne. She refused to make sweeping concessions to those who switched sides – most importantly Stephen's brother, Henry of Blois, the Bishop of Winchester – and she believed it was more important to stress her own authority and that everything proceeded from her as queen, even at the risk of alienating her own supporters. This insistence on royal rights is something we will see with Henry, but Matilda, either because she chose the wrong time to make these assertions, or because a male-dominated society simply would not accept these claims from a woman, was unsuccessful in her own right.

Her greatness was still recognized. Matilda died on 10 September 1167, and her tomb in Bec Abbey in Normandy bore the epitaph 'Here lies Henry's daughter, wife and mother: great by birth, greater by marriage, but greatest by motherhood.'[74] Although this definition of Matilda through the three Henrys who were her father, first husband and son does her a disservice, it does elaborate a truth, because even if she could take no credit for her father being a king or her first husband being an Emperor, her son became a king only through her efforts to preserve her claim in the most hostile of circumstances.

Yet Melisende, in a much stronger position as a crowned monarch in her own right, in a kingdom that officially recognized female succession, was essentially deposed by her son. The justification for this was that the marcher kingdom of Jerusalem had to have a military leader, and only a man could fulfil this role. Melisende behaved entirely appropriately by insisting on her rights yet also being willing to share power with first her husband and then her son, but Baldwin would not accept this. The injustice is apparent, and unlike Matilda, Melisende was not trying to do something unprecedented. These were the realities of 12th-century power, and even in kingdoms that officially recognized female succession, women's right to rule was under constant threat, usually from members of their own family.

Melisende died in September 1161, and was buried relatively obscurely at St Mary Josaphat (near the tomb of the Virgin), rather than with the other kings in the Church of the Holy Sepulchre, or at the Dome of the Rock, whose canons she had patronized. Although she may have requested this herself, Baldwin may also have been behind this in a final, mean attempt to minimize his mother's achievements. It is unfitting that so powerful a figure didn't take her place with the kingdom's other rulers, but history certainly remembers her more than Baldwin, who himself died in early 1163 and was buried in the Church of the Holy Sepulchre. Baldwin III had many military and diplomatic successes to his credit, and it was said that both the Christian and non-Christian population of Jerusalem mourned as his body passed, but his treatment of Melisende was unquestionably shabby.[75]

This is in contrast to Melisende's younger son Amalric, who remained loyal to her in the conflict, and succeeded Baldwin III. Amalric's succession was not undisputed and numerous oddities attended it. He was required to separate from his wife Agnes of Courtenay on the grounds they were too nearly related and he had not received

the appropriate dispensation when they married in 1157, a condition that must have
come from the Patriarch and suggests clerical opposition. However, their two children
Sibylla and Baldwin were confirmed in their legitimacy, and Amalric had another
daughter, Isabelle, from his second marriage. Amalric was then crowned 'suddenly'
in the words of William of Tyre, as though his accession had to be pushed through
against opposition. Nevertheless Amalric was also a fairly successful king, although his
reign witnessed a new and fatal preoccupation with the conquest of Egypt, which had
descended into chaos.[76]

Nur ed-Din was not idle while his enemies were distracted, and he continued to
put pressure on the rulers of Damascus. This led to the Damascene alliance with the
Christians being renewed, which simply alienated the ordinary citizens of the city. Nur
ed-Din arrived before Damascus in 1154 prepared to begin a siege, but instead the city
was delivered to him by residents who preferred to submit to his rule. He responded
by promoting Sunni institutions like schools, mosques and courts and was swiftly recognized in the region as the model Muslim ruler, valiant in war and wise in peace. By
creating a united Syria he also posed the gravest threat to the Crusader States yet seen.

One consequence of the great respect Nur ed-Din inspired in the Muslim world
was that refugees from more chaotic regions sought his help. In 1163, after yet another
vicious series of coups in Egypt, the losing claimant fled to Nur ed-Din and requested
his intervention. Nur ed-Din had previously been reluctant to intervene in Egyptian
affairs, but now Amalric invaded Egypt to take advantage of the chaos, and though
his attack failed, Nur ed-Din must have feared an extension of Christian power into
Egypt. One of Nur ed-Din's most trusted vassals, Shirkuh, requested permission to
launch an Egyptian expedition. Shirkuh was allowed to proceed, and may already have
had in mind the creation of an independent Egyptian state for himself and his family.[77]
Shirkuh's force, which included his nephew Saladin of whom we will hear so much
shortly, occupied Egypt, provoking a response from Amalric.

Amalric, who had now married Maria Comnena, the great-niece of the Byzantine
Emperor, and established what he thought would be an irresistible alliance, tried to
conquer Egypt in 1168. Shirkuh repulsed Amalric's attack, and in his position as the
defender of the country definitively seized Egypt for himself. Shirkuh was fairly old by
this point and died a few weeks later, leaving Saladin as the ruler of Egypt.[78]

Discussions of the Crusader States involve figures like Nur ed-Din, Saladin (or Saleh
ed-Din, in its original form) and many others not mentioned here like Asad ed-Din,
Shams ed-Din and Usul ed-Din, so it is worth a quick comment about their names.
In fact, these are not names but Arabic titles. The 'ed-Din' portion means 'of the faith'
and is preceded by various poetic terms – Nur ed-Din means 'light of the faith', Asad
ed-Din means 'lion of the faith', Shams ed-Din 'sun of the faith', Usul ed-Din 'pillar
of the faith' and Saleh ed-Din 'righteousness of the faith'. This was a popular naming
convention throughout the period, but only Saleh ed-Din became sufficiently famous
to have had his title absorbed into Western culture today as Saladin.

As these were titles, all these rulers had personal and family names as well. Saladin's name was Yusuf, and in the Arabic style he was also known as the 'son of Ayub'. Ayub had been a trusted lieutenant of Nur ed-Din like his brother Shirkuh, and he joined Saladin in Egypt after the conquest. Saladin and his family's success in conquering Egypt, Yemen and Jerusalem led to a relatively short-lived dynasty that is referred to as 'Ayubbid'.

It is a commonplace of Crusader history to attribute the success of the First Crusade partially to the disunity of the Muslim world in the late 11th century, and then trace the rise of increasingly powerful Muslim rulers – Zengi, Nur ed-Din and Saladin – who united the region and reconquered most of the Crusader States. The progression usually also leads, either implicitly or explicitly, from Zengi, the local strongman who was murdered when drunk, to Nur ed-Din, a military hero and model of piety who inspired respect, culminating with Saladin, the legendary hero, Islamic scholar, paragon of chivalry and conqueror of Jerusalem.

Yet it is a mistake to assume that the Muslim world was inherently any more or less religious than the Christian, or that Muslim rulers as a group were any more or less eager to put aside their personal ambitions for religious reasons. When Nur ed-Din rose to power, Damascus, rather than throwing open its gates to him as a willing participant in a grand Muslim alliance, instead allied with the Christian King of Jerusalem to preserve its independence. Similarly, when Saladin took control of Egypt, tension immediately arose between him and Nur ed-Din precisely because Saladin was more interested in creating an Ayubbid state than joining Nur ed-Din to attack the Crusader States.

Saladin's actions in Egypt were unequivocally dynastic. After restoring Egypt to the obedience of the Sunni caliph in Baghdad (who was conveniently remote), Saladin initiated military expeditions into Libya, Nubia and, most significantly, Yemen, where his brother Turan Shah conquered the region and set up another Ayubbid state. What Saladin did not do was attack the Crusader States. He participated in a few desultory campaigns against them in conjunction with Nur ed-Din, but each time he broke off operations on the basis that Egypt was still too insecure for him to remain absent. Relations between Nur ed-Din and Saladin deteriorated to the point where armed conflict seemed inevitable, but Nur ed-Din's death in May 1174 spared Saladin this unpleasantness.[79]

Nur ed-Din was notable as the figure who united Syria and, more importantly, showed the power that could be unleashed if a strong military leader was also a respected religious figure. He was certainly known and respected by Christians not only in the Holy Land, but even in France: in *Yvain*, Chrétien de Troyes has Kay mock other knights by saying that when they are full of food and wine 'each one is ready to slay Nor-adin'.[80]

Nur ed-Din's death might have been welcomed by the Christians, but two months later Amalric died, leaving as king his thirteen-year-old son Baldwin IV. Worse, after his coronation it became clear that Baldwin had leprosy. The court quickly dissolved into factions, including one joined by the ubiquitous Lusignan brothers Aimery and Guy, who had been expelled from Poitou by Richard the Lionheart and were seeking their fortune in Outremer, with a success beyond their wildest dreams. Baldwin was unable to marry, so his sister Sibylla was now the focus of courtly intrigue. Sibylla had been married to William Marquis of Montferrat, but he had died leaving her with a posthumous son, the future Baldwin V.

With all major power brokers in the Holy Land, and many from elsewhere, putting forward candidates as Sibylla's new husband, Baldwin IV feared he would be deposed, and decided to act decisively by marrying her to Guy of Lusignan. Guy quickly became one of the most powerful figures in the kingdom, and when Baldwin's health deteriorated in 1183, Guy became regent, although he subsequently fell out with Baldwin and was removed from power. When Baldwin IV died in 1185 and the child Baldwin V died in 1186, the kingdom was thrown into crisis. The factions divided between Sibylla and Guy on one hand, and Isabelle, the daughter of Amalric and Maria Comnena, on the other. Sibylla was victorious, and after being crowned Queen of Jerusalem, she herself crowned Guy as king.[81]

In comparison with the chaotic situation in Jerusalem, Saladin had smoothly consolidated his authority after Nur ed-Din's death. He occupied Damascus in 1174 and married Nur ed-Din's widow in 1176, achieving recognition from the caliph in Baghdad as the ruler of Egypt and Syria. In 1176 another event favourable to Saladin took place, when the army of the Byzantine Emperor Manuel Comnenus was annihilated by the Seljuk Turks, and all of Anatolia fell to them. The Crusader States were now completely encircled by Muslim states at a time when they lacked strong leadership.

Aleppo and Mosul remained in the hands of Nur ed-Din's family, and Saladin directed his energy against them for the next ten years, further proving that the Muslim states were not monolithic and quite happy to fight against each other. This gave the Crusader States a brief breathing space during the political turmoil of Baldwin IV's reign, but Saladin inexorably expanded his power, taking Aleppo in 1183 and allying with the Seljuks to bring Mosul into his political orbit by 1185. By 1187 he was ready to achieve his stated goal of retaking Jerusalem.[82]

After being provoked by Christian attacks on pilgrims travelling to Mecca and a raid on the coast of the Red Sea, Saladin gathered a large army from all his possessions and invaded the kingdom of Jerusalem. Guy of Lusignan managed to unite the Franks and raise a large force in response, and took the field to oppose him. The only sensible strategy would seem to be for the Christians to avoid a pitched battle and shadow Saladin's force to minimize the damage it could do, until it inevitably broke up under the pressures faced by armies in all pre-industrial societies. In this respect, Guy had an advantage, precisely because Jerusalem was an embattled outpost with a relatively small Christian population; this meant his much smaller army was essentially professional, so if he could avoid a battle it could hold together longer than Saladin's essentially feudal force. Saladin knew this and wanted to draw the Franks into battle, and contrary to the seemingly obvious delaying strategy, Guy marched through the arid Galilean hills to attack.

One of the reasons for Guy's decision may have been related to, of all things, the murder of Thomas Becket. Since Becket's murder in 1172 Henry II had transferred considerable sums to the Templars and Hospitallers, which he planned to use in a projected Crusade. However, Henry was clear that this money was not a gift and was to be kept for him until he used it or took it back, so none of it could be spent without his permission. In 1187 the Master of the Templars had used these funds to hire mercenaries for the army against Saladin, and it is possible that he and Guy were forced to seek an outright victory or face the disgrace of having stolen Henry II's money.[83]

In the end, they faced a much worse fate. The army only managed to reach the two hills known as the Horns of Hattin before being surrounded by the Muslim forces. Guy and his army were trapped on the hills without water, and were forced on 4 July 1187 to attack and try to break free. With few exceptions, the Christian army was killed or captured by Saladin's forces, leaving no one to protect the Crusader States. Saladin famously treated most of his captives kindly, courteously offering Guy a cool drink after the battle, but pointedly executing the Templars.[84]

This was a catastrophe for the Crusader States. Saladin was virtually unopposed as he took one town after another, and Jerusalem fell on 2 October. Only Tyre, Tripoli and Antioch remained of the Crusader States. If Becket's death had shocked Europe, the loss of Jerusalem was worse, as it produced an effect equal and opposite to that which had greeted the success of the First Crusade nearly a century before.

Henry II's Final Years: 'Shame on a Conquered King'

A new Crusade was obviously required. Preachers began to cross Europe, some using visual aids showing a Saracen knight trampling on Christ's tomb and crying out over the shame of this violation.[85] Richard the Lionheart was the first prince north of the Alps to take the cross, and Henry II and Philip Augustus joined him, though Philip had already expressed his dissatisfaction that Richard was going on Crusade without having married his sister Alice. This ongoing conflict would be resolved in a quite unexpected way once the Crusade started.

Richard was also suspicious of Henry's motives, not least because John had not taken the cross and there was a nagging suspicion that Henry might try to make John his heir to England, Normandy and Anjou. Henry was unwilling or unable to reassure Richard on this point and, if the story is true, still faithful to his mother's advice to tease the hawk rather than let it eat. Henry even refused to confirm Richard as his heir. This proved to be his fatal mistake, because Richard was too forceful a character to tolerate this. Furthermore, Richard's attempt to forge a feudal relationship with Philip that did not involve his father had been successful.

Skirmishing broke out in the borderlands between the Angevin Empire and France, with each side occupying territory claimed by the other or its allies. Philip made various offers to end the strife, but Henry and Richard, now with diverging interests, could not agree. Richard then approached Philip directly again and offered to have the dispute judged by the French court, a step that would mark the final break with his father. A new peace conference was arranged at Bonsmoulins in November 1188, but Henry II was shocked to find that Richard and Philip arrived together. Philip offered to return all the lands he had taken if Richard married Alice and Henry recognized Richard as his heir. Henry naturally refused to accept any interference from Philip in the way he managed his kingdom, but Richard now demanded that Henry publicly recognize him as his heir. When Henry once again refused to speak, Richard reportedly said, 'Now at last I must believe what I had always thought was impossible.'[86]

Richard was now committed to taking the inheritance his father seemed unwilling to give him. He immediately performed homage to Philip for all the lands he held in Aquitaine, as well as Normandy, Anjou and Maine. Although a truce was agreed, Henry, Richard and Philip all began to prepare for war. When Henry held his Christmas court at Saumur many stayed away, preferring to pin their hopes on Richard. Henry fell ill and failed to attend a peace conference in January 1189, but his enemies believed he was stalling and proceeded to ravage his lands.

These continuing delays to the Crusade irritated the pope, who sent a legate to arrange another conference so the dispute could be judged by a panel of archbishops. When the meeting finally convened at La Ferté-Bernard near Le Mans, Philip and Richard had a list of demands: Richard must be allowed to marry Alice; Richard must be recognized as heir; and, most importantly, John must take the cross, as Richard refused to go on Crusade unless John went with him. Henry still refused, and the legate threatened to place France under an interdict unless Philip came to terms. Philip remained unmoved and the conference ended without result.[87]

Henry returned to Le Mans, but Philip and Richard suddenly attacked the castles of Maine and quickly captured part of the county, then marched on Le Mans itself. Henry, now in his last illness, retreated towards Normandy, but Richard pursued him and caught up with his rearguard, commanded by William Marshal. William later delighted in telling the story that when Richard, who had left his armour behind for the long ride, came up to threaten the king's men, William turned and rode straight at him with his lance lowered. Richard suddenly understood his danger: '"God's feet, marshal!" cried Richard with his wonted oath, "slay me not! I have no hauberk." "Slay you! no; I leave that to the devil," retorted William, plunging his spear into the horse's body instead of the rider's.' Richard was left in the dust while Henry escaped.[88]

Henry now seemed to understand that he was dying, and he suddenly turned back to Anjou to die in his homeland. He went to Chinon with a few retainers and did nothing while Richard and Philip overran Maine, and Tours fell on 3 July 1189. With this proof that all was lost, Henry dragged himself to a last meeting with his son and

Philip, who dictated severe terms including an indemnity of 20,000 marks, a requirement that all Henry's vassals in England and the continent must swear allegiance to Richard and a condition that if Henry did not appear at Vézelay to start the Crusade by Lent 1190, all his vassals were to transfer their allegiance solely to Philip and Richard. Henry had no choice but to agree, but Gerald of Wales reports that when Henry was required to give Richard the kiss of peace to ratify the agreement, he whispered in his son's ear, 'May I only be suffered to live long enough to take vengeance upon thee as thou deservest!'[89] It was not to be.

Henry was carried back to Chinon in a litter and died two days later, deserted by everyone except his bastard son Geoffrey. His tragic death excited much commentary among contemporaries, and all chose to dwell on the fact that the once strongest ruler of Europe was brought low by his son – the biblical story of David and Absalom was frequently invoked – and died alone and friendless, thus forming the perfect example of how God could humble the mightiest. John's role in the crisis gives an early indication of his character: despite the fact that his father's difficulties were in large part due to his desire to provide for John, once it became clear who would win the conflict John deserted his father and joined Richard. The news that John had betrayed him was said to have caused Henry's death; when he saw John's name on a list of rebels, he was said to have cried, 'Is it true that John, my heart, John, whom I loved more than all my sons, and for whose gain I suffered all these evils, has forsaken me?' Then he turned to the wall and fell into a coma, dying the next day. This sounds like later commentary, but in a more realistic version, Henry's last words are given as, 'Shame, shame on a conquered king.'[90]

Henry's body was carried to Fontevraud, where Richard went to see it. Roger of Howden claimed that when Richard entered the room, Henry's body bled from the nose 'as though his spirit was angered by his approach', one of the earliest references to the idea that a body bleeds if its murderer approaches. This was a popular idea at the time, because it is also recorded by Chrétien de Troyes in his nearly contemporary romance *Yvain*, which is the first literary reference to the legend. There was certainly a feeling that Richard had caused his father's death, and whether through guilt or simply to show proper respect to his own lineage, Henry seems to have been the first king to be buried in his royal regalia.[91] His effigy at Fontevraud lies alongside those of Eleanor of Aquitaine and Richard himself, displaying an Angevin harmony in death that was decidedly lacking in life.

Thus ended the reign of Henry II. When he died he was in a civil war with his son and had been driven out of his birthplace of Le Mans, but he was one of the greatest English kings, and ruler of so much else besides. We still live with many of the legal, judicial and administrative reforms begun in his reign, but more importantly he emerges from the 12th century as a fully rounded, knowable character, and I have great affection for him.

CHAPTER 5 – THE ANGEVIN EMPIRE II: THE ARBITER OF EUROPE

T HOUGH MANY (PROBABLY MOST) modern historians think Henry II was the better king, it is his son Richard I the Lionheart who has remained alive in the popular imagination. Partially this is due to his connection with the completely fictional story of Robin Hood, which didn't develop as a folk tale until the 13th century and was only associated with Richard's reign by the Scottish historian John Major in 1521.[1] But Richard's fame is grounded in reality and he was most famous in his own day for his Crusade. Though the Crusade was seen as a failure by contemporaries because it failed to recapture Jerusalem, from a military point of view it accomplished a great deal because Richard captured Cyprus and consolidated the Christian hold on the coastal cities of the Holy Land, which ensured the survival of the Crusader States for another century.

Richard is indisputably the great romantic hero of all the Angevins. Once again we look at an Angevin name, but it presents no difficulties. Richard was first called 'Lionheart' by his contemporary Ambroise, who wrote a history of Richard's Crusade and applied the epithet to him at the moment he reached the siege of Acre. Later legends grew up around his name, as with every aspect of Richard's life, and a 13th-century romance related the story of Richard reaching down a lion's throat to rip out its heart and then eat it, but these were openly acknowledged to be fantasy. Richard also codified the heraldic representation of England, as it was the device on Richard's second great seal, the three lions passant, that became fixed as the arms of England to this day.[2]

Although Richard is often portrayed as the perfect knight, his reputation has not always been unblemished. Some of these problems began in the 12th century when Philip Augustus established a propaganda factory to blacken Richard's name,[3] largely to compensate for his own undistinguished behaviour on the Third Crusade, and Richard was also deeply unpopular with Victorian historians who could not forgive his neglect of England in favour of his 'French' lands. Some modern historians too have chosen to see Richard as the embodiment of the reckless warrior with no administrative ability and no concern aside from war, but these claims have mostly been refuted, and in any event we must evaluate Richard in the context of Angevin kingship.

We have already seen a great deal of Richard since he became Duke of Aquitaine at a young age and played an active part in the Angevin Empire throughout the 1170s and 80s. Yet he remained somewhat in his father's shadow – as so many did – until the tumultuous final years of Henry's reign, when he then emerged quite forcefully in his own right. His two overriding concerns were the Third Crusade and the battle against Philip Augustus to defend Normandy, Anjou and Aquitaine, and these two causes involved him constantly in the stuff of legend: travel around the Mediterranean, sieges, battles, diplomacy, capture and being locked away in a remote castle.

Although Richard inherited the Angevin Empire in dramatic circumstances, it is worth noting that no previous king had ever inherited both England and Normandy, much less the rest of the Angevin possessions, without opposition. One of the most critical aspects of kingship, which Henry II and Richard notably possessed and John notably lacked, is the ability to choose reliable ministers and delegate authority. Richard knew who his strongest supporter was, and his first order was for the release of Eleanor of Aquitaine from her imprisonment, upon which she immediately began to govern England with Richard's full authority. Richard gave the traditional order for all prisoners to be released from their jails, and it allows us, unusually, to hear Eleanor's voice, for when she implemented the order in England, she said that she carried it out with pleasure because she knew the delight of being freed after long captivity.[4]

Richard then dealt with other supporters and possible enemies. Despite accusing William Marshal of trying to kill him when he was pursuing Henry II on his desperate flight from Le Mans, Richard immediately forgave the Marshal and rewarded him with the hand of the Irish heiress Isabelle de Clare plus the earldom of Pembroke. William Marshal, the penniless knight errant, was now rich beyond his dreams and an earl as well, though he would later rise higher still. Henry II's bastard son Geoffrey – of whom Henry was reported to have said, 'this is my true son; the others are bastards', a statement certainly borne out by the circumstances of Henry's death – had made no secret of the fact that he harboured political ambitions, but Richard neatly countered this by forcing Geoffrey into holy orders and making him Archbishop of York.[5]

Richard wanted to begin his Crusade without delay, but there were many things for the new king to attend to, not least his coronation, and he had to go to England. The first account of the English coronation ceremony is Roger of Howden's description of Richard's coronation on 13 September 1189. Roger recognized that the key moment was the anointing, for as we have seen with King Stephen, being God's anointed representative was one of the most mystical qualities of kingship. Richard stripped to his breeches and shirt to expose his chest, and Baldwin Archbishop of Canterbury anointed his head, chest and hands. Richard was then dressed in ceremonial robes, crowned by the Archbishop – though characteristically he picked up the crown himself, the crown Matilda had brought back from Germany, and handed it to Baldwin – and sat enthroned during the mass. We even have the coronation anthem performed at the ceremony, which announced, 'The age of gold returns / The world's reform draws nigh / The rich man now cast down / The pauper raised on high.'[6] Incidentally, we also have the anthem performed at Philip Augustus's coronation as co-ruler with his father in 1179; it is by Walter of Chatillon and called *Ver Pacis apperit*, 'The springtime of peace / opens the bosom of the earth'. Interestingly the tune to this anthem was also used in a song by the troubadour Blondel, of whom we shall hear more.[7]

Our delight in the survival of so much information about Richard's coronation must be tempered by the later events. A banquet at Whitehall Palace followed the ceremony, but this was tragically marred when a party of Jews arrived to bring gifts to the new king and they were attacked, and some killed, by a mob outside the palace. This riot spread to the City of London where more Jews were killed and their houses burned down. Though Richard had the rioters arrested and some of them hanged, and he sent letters to the shires to prevent further outbreaks of violence against the Jews – because he viewed them as a valuable source of revenue – the Crusading fervour of Richard's early reign led to more unrest. This culminated in the attack on the Jews of York in March 1190 when around 150 men, women and children either committed suicide to escape the fanatical mob or were massacred.[8] This recalls the events of the First Crusade when Jews were routinely attacked; the religious belief that motivated the Crusades included a fanaticism that led to the wanton slaughter not only of Muslims, but also Jews and other Christians.

For the Crusade dominated everything. Richard needed men, ships and, above all else, money to pay for the expedition, and he pursued this single-mindedly. Arranging transport to the Holy Land would always create difficulties – most notably on the Fourth Crusade – but Richard was the first king able to requisition his own fleet. We speak glibly of Angevin activities in England, Normandy, Anjou and Aquitaine as though they were one entity, but this disguises the fact that the Angevin Empire was actually a maritime Empire that could only exist through constant cross-Channel traffic. As master of ports including Portsmouth, Dover, Cherbourg, La Rochelle and Bordeaux, the Angevin king controlled more ships than any other power in northern Europe.

It is this fact that is responsible for a fleeting appearance by one of the only regions of Europe usually untouched by Angevin activity: Scandinavia. When Richard was in captivity in the Empire, Philip Augustus toyed with the idea of attacking England, but to do this he needed ships. In August 1193, Philip married Ingeborg, sister of the Danish king, Cnut VI, to form an alliance with a maritime power, and one that even had a distant claim to the English throne. Although modern historians have usually scoffed at the idea that Philip actually meant this as a threat, contemporary chroniclers such as Roger of Howden and William of Newburgh explicitly stated that this was Philip's aim.[9]

The outcome of Philip's Scandinavian policy was farcical: after one night of marriage Philip repudiated Ingeborg and sent her to a convent, then attempted to have the marriage annulled on the grounds of consanguinity. Although Philip failed to procure the annulment, in 1196 he married Agnes of Meran anyway, leading to a ten-year rupture with the papacy just as his relations with the Angevins entered their most critical phase. Modern historians generally assume that Philip was somehow physically repulsed by Ingeborg or that there was a catastrophic sexual problem between the two, whereas French chroniclers like Rigord and William the Breton say that sorcery was involved. The modern view that something profoundly odd happened on the wedding night has left many historians searching for ever more fantastic explanations, although one historian has pointed out Roger of Howden's much more prosaic explanation: with Richard's release from captivity imminent and the Danes failing to honour their promises about providing a fleet, Philip simply put Ingeborg aside in hopes of making a more useful marriage alliance with someone else. Philip's plan had backfired spectacularly, as his failed marriage to Ingeborg caused problems for the next twenty years and contributed in large part to his dismal reputation – both to contemporaries and modern historians – as a terrible husband.[10]

Richard's own marital problems and their solution would be played out on the Crusade itself, and for that Richard needed his ships and money to pay for them. He began a sale of offices and benefits on an unprecedented scale: Roger of Howden reports that Richard put everything up for sale, most notably requiring sheriffs to buy back their offices, but also selling back the Scottish king's homage and licensing tournaments in England for the first time. Gerald of Wales said the king was 'like a robber always looking for something to steal'.[11] Once again, Richard's subjects had no idea how much more stringent these exactions would soon become.

The Third Crusade

We know a great deal about Richard's Crusade because Roger of Howden, a royal clerk, travelled with the army and not only left a vivid account of events until his departure from the Holy Land in August 1191, but also included many original documents. The Norman minstrel Ambroise also left a verse account of the Crusade, which nicely complements Roger's account since Ambroise had no access to royal councils but could give a good idea of what life was like for the ordinary soldiers. The Third Crusade is for many reasons the most notable of the Crusades besides the First. It falls at the midpoint of the Crusading movement and was also the last Crusade to achieve any success. More importantly, it was led by the three most prominent rulers of the time: Richard, Philip Augustus and the Emperor Frederick Barbarossa. The 'Crusade of the Three Kings' was the greatest military expedition ever undertaken from Europe, and with the added incentive of recapturing Jerusalem it assumed an unprecedented importance.

Richard had taken the cross in 1187 and Philip Augustus in January 1188, and the Third Crusade finally got under way in 1190. After the catastrophe of the Second Crusade and even the quite unpromising early events of the First Crusade, it is a refreshing change to read about a Crusade that was well organized. Richard's journey was a model of logistics, and in addition to progressing smoothly to the Holy Land, Richard also made important political and military settlements along the way that shaped Mediterranean history for centuries. Philip Augustus also reached the Holy Land with ease, but one significant calamity was the death of Frederick Barbarossa when he drowned crossing a river in Asia Minor. Frederick was a towering figure in the 12th century, but sadly he has little place in this history and died just at the moment when he might have played a bigger role. However, his death would have enormous consequences for Richard and all subsequent Angevins, as we shall see.[12]

The Crusade officially began when Richard and Philip Augustus joined forces at Vézelay and set off on 4 July 1190, the third anniversary of Hattin. The two armies divided at Lyon, not because of any conflict, but simply because it was too difficult to find supplies for such a large force. Richard had also sent a fleet of over 100 ships from England to meet him at Marseilles and transport his army to the Holy Land, whereas Philip Augustus hired ships from Genoa for transport. Amusingly, in the 14th-century story cycle the *Decameron*, the rather cold-blooded Philip is supposed to have chosen Genoa as his port of embarkation because he was overcome with lust for the wife of the Marquis of Montferrat after hearing of her beauty, although as is typical in the *Decameron*, she dissuaded him through an adroit stratagem and a devastating snub.[13] Unfortunately Richard's ships had not yet arrived when he reached Marseilles: they had paused to massacre the Jewish and Muslim population of Lisbon and then sack the city (to widespread disgust), so Richard sent part of his army to the Holy Land in hired ships while he sailed to Sicily with the remainder. Richard arrived in Messina with matchless style in a brightly painted galley bedecked with shields and standards, and Richard himself stood on a platform to be welcomed by cheering crowds.[14] However, Sicily was not the most unproblematic place to pause on the way to the Holy Land.

Sicily had been in a state of turmoil since the death of King William II in 1189. William's heir was his aunt Constance, who was married to Frederick Barbarossa's son and heir Henry of Hohenstaufen. Barbarossa had attempted to restore imperial domination of the towns of northern Italy, much to the dismay of the papacy, which had been establishing its political authority over central Italy. The spectre of Henry of Hohenstaufen as Emperor and also King of Sicily in right of his wife was terrifying to the pope, whose political power in Italy might be destroyed by such a concentration of German might. The pope thus conspired with the Sicilian barons, who also disliked the thought of having the Emperor as their king, and the crown instead passed to William's illegitimate cousin, Tancred of Lecce.

What made the situation of direct concern to Richard was that his sister Joan was William II's widow. Joan's dowry should have been returned to her on William II's death, but instead Tancred had seized it and imprisoned Joan. If that weren't enough, William II had also bequeathed money and galleys to Henry II to use in the Crusade. Henry had died before William, though the news hadn't reached Sicily in time for William to alter his will, but Richard felt that as Henry's heir he was still entitled to the legacy.

Richard's relationship with Tancred was already extremely precarious when matters were complicated by trouble between the Greek population of Messina and the Crusaders. After a Greek assault on the Crusaders' lodgings, Richard launched an attack on the city and captured it. Philip Augustus opposed this attack by Crusaders on a Christian city, but once the city had been taken he demanded that his banners be placed on the city walls so he could take a share of the spoils, as had been the agreement for all the towns taken by the Crusade. Planting banners on the walls was a very important symbol, as Richard would later learn to his cost.[15]

Faced with a Crusade on his doorstep that showed no hesitation about attacking him, Tancred immediately agreed to return Joan's dowry. The political situation took another turn, for it was now that the shocking news arrived that Frederick Barbarossa had drowned in Asia Minor. Henry of Hohenstaufen was now destined to be Emperor, and like everyone else Richard had no wish to see him add Sicily to his other possessions. Richard accepted Tancred's overtures and agreed to support him against the Hohenstaufen, and proved his friendship by – rather casually – giving Tancred King Arthur's sword Excalibur, which he had brought from England.[16]

Richard now produced a revelation of his own that probably ended the Crusade's chances for success and set in motion the events that would dominate the rest of his life. Eleanor of Aquitaine arrived in Sicily, and accompanying her was Berengaria of Navarre, whom Richard had agreed to marry. This was a shocking humiliation for Philip Augustus, whose sister Alice was still – after decades of waiting – officially Richard's fiancée. Even in their final negotiations with Henry II, Richard and Philip had been demanding that Alice be married to Richard, but now Richard refused to marry her, and even worse claimed that she had been seduced by Henry II and borne him a child.

Philip must have had a fair idea that Richard wouldn't marry Alice after all the delays, but to have her replacement arrive in Sicily so she could be publicly discarded and accused of bearing Henry II's illegitimate child was beyond insulting. Philip's biographer Rigord of St Denis claims that Philip's hatred of Richard stemmed from Richard's treatment of Alice, and though the Angevins and Capetians were always going to be rivals, this incident particularly poisoned Philip's relations with Richard. Philip was forced to recognize that Alice's engagement was broken, and a treaty was agreed to set out the relationship between the two kings and how to restore Alice's dowry, but this injected a sour note into the Crusade – which was already reeling from the loss of Frederick Barbarossa – and essentially guaranteed that the two kings would not work together to recapture Jerusalem.[17]

Next to a figure like Eleanor of Aquitaine anyone might have struggled to make an impression, but we know very little about Berengaria. Perhaps her most vivid moment comes in fictional form, though mercifully it is largely forgotten today. In Cecil B Demille's *The Crusades* of 1935, Berengaria was portrayed by Loretta Young, and she summed up the importance of the Crusade by exhorting her husband, 'You gotta save Christianity, Richard, you gotta!'

What we do know about Berengaria is that she and Richard never had children, and that with his Crusade, year-long captivity and then constant warfare against Philip

Augustus, he didn't spend much time with her. This is enough to suggest that Richard had no interest in his wife, which is used as further proof that he must have been gay.

I have alluded to this when we discussed the report that Richard and Philip Augustus were so close that 'the bed did not separate them', but now is the time to look at all the evidence. The earliest reference to Richard's homosexuality comes from a book written in 1948. Certainly none of Richard's contemporaries thought he might be homosexual; in fact, all the 13th-century sources condemned him for his insatiable desire for women. What is taken as the proof of Richard's sexual orientation is that a hermit rebuked him for his sins in 1195 and told him to 'remember the destruction of Sodom', and to return to his wife whom he had been avoiding. The sin of Sodom, sodomy, has a very specific meaning in modern usage, but in the Middle Ages the destruction of Sodom was believed to be because of general sexual licence, not any specific sexual acts. Thus the hermit's warning was probably a condemnation of promiscuity, not sleeping with men.[18]

In the 20th or 21st century, a warning to abandon 'the sin of Sodom' and return to his wife, plus the fact that he had no children but had shared a bed with Philip Augustus, seems to some people sufficient evidence to confirm Richard's sexual orientation. The truth is that we have absolutely no way of knowing what Richard's sexual orientation was. The fact that contemporary sources say nothing about Richard having inappropriate relationships with men but quite a lot about his inappropriate relationships with women – including the fact that he had a bastard son called Philip, who was given a lordship in Cognac – strongly suggests that he was heterosexual. Yet he did have close friendships with men, such as the mercenary Mercadier and the troubadour Blondel, so who knows?

When the Crusade finally left Sicily, Berengaria's ship was driven in a storm to Limassol in Cyprus, which had been captured by Isaac Comnenus, a renegade Byzantine who called himself Emperor and had entered into an agreement with Saladin. When Richard appeared in pursuit of his fiancée, Isaac attempted to oppose his landing, but Richard routed his forces. Richard then met Isaac to negotiate, and in Ambroise's account of the Crusade we have perhaps the best description of how Richard looked when he appeared in his full majesty:

> The king went in regal state, attired in a tunic of rose-coloured samite and a mantle 'bedight with small half-moons of solid silver set in rows, interspersed with shining orbs like suns'; his head was covered with a scarlet cap; he was girt with a well-proved sword 'with a golden hilt, a silken belt, and a finely chased scabbard edged with silver'; his spurs were golden (or gilt), and he was mounted on a Spanish horse of great beauty as well as of a size befitting a rider of such lofty stature; 'his saddle was red, studded with little golden and bright-coloured stars, and having on its hinder part two golden lion-cubs rampant, and as if snarling at each other.'[19]

Richard and Berengaria were married at Limassol on 12 May 1191 and Berengaria was crowned Queen of England, and perhaps Richard hoped that he might address the troublesome problem of producing a legitimate heir before facing Saladin. It was at this moment that Richard reconnected with the political and military travails of the Holy Land, surprisingly in the person of Guy of Lusignan. But how had the king of Jerusalem come to be in Cyprus?

In the years since the fall of Jerusalem that it had taken to prepare the Crusade, events had taken an astonishing turn. Guy of Lusignan had been captured at Hattin and remained Saladin's captive as the Crusader cities fell in quick succession. Modern historians believe that Saladin could have taken all the fortified coastal cities if he had attacked them first, ending any hope of survival for the Crusader States, but instead he chose the more politically and emotionally satisfying target of Jerusalem. Its capture gave him enormous prestige, but meant that he didn't turn to the heavily fortified city of Tyre until November 1187, when his exhausted soldiers faced the prospect of a winter campaign that must have seemed anticlimactic in the wake of Jerusalem's fall.

Tyre was ruled by Conrad of Montferrat, brother of Queen Sibylla's first husband, William of Montferrat. Conrad had prepared the city well for the siege and after a desultory couple of months Saladin finally abandoned his attack and went away. Conrad of Montferrat became a hero to the Christians as the leader who stood up to Saladin and actually managed to drive him away. With Guy still in captivity, Conrad was the most prominent leader remaining, and he naturally enough assumed control of the Christian defences. It seems that some, not least Conrad himself, felt that this should go even further and he should take Guy's place as king.

Saladin, presumably with full knowledge of the effect his action would have, released Guy of Lusignan in the summer of 1188 but only on the condition that Guy swore not to take up arms against him. Guy immediately found a priest to absolve him of this oath, and rushed to Tyre to assume command of the remaining Christian forces, but Conrad of Montferrat refused to recognize any allegiance to him or even his title of king. Conrad justified his actions by saying that he was waiting for the kings of France and England and the Emperor to arrive, and they could decide who would rule the kingdom. Guy was left with an impossible situation – a king without a kingdom and pitifully few soldiers to rely on.[20]

Guy needed a base of his own, and in an action whose foolhardiness outweighed his behaviour at Hattin, Guy decided to lay siege to Acre, which Saladin had captured. Acre was the key port of the Holy Land and had been its richest city, and its garrison alone numbered twice Guy's army. Guy had no hope of taking the city, yet he did have two things: a fleet of ships from Pisa had come to fulfil a Crusading vow and the potential of a naval blockade greatly increased the siege's threat; and this act of mad, suicidal resistance provided a focus for efforts to recapture the Holy Land. The scattered remnants of the Christian armies and, more importantly, the Crusaders who began to drift across the sea to fulfil their vows had a place to meet and concentrate their efforts. Guy began the siege on 28 August 1189 and Crusaders were already arriving by September.

Proof that Guy had recaptured his position of authority came when even Conrad of Montferrat had to join the siege of Acre as the focus of Christian activity. Saladin had now realized the potential threat and managed to gather an army, and although he led an attack on the besiegers that killed many of them, he was unable to dislodge them. Every day brought more individual Christian reinforcements from all over Europe, and it was reported that the Emperor Frederick Barbarossa was en route with a large army. Interestingly, Saladin wrote to the Muslims of Morocco and Spain in an attempt to organize a counter-Crusade, but with no success. Yet he still managed to blockade the Christian camp so that the besiegers were besieged in turn, and he broke the naval blockade.[21]

What was worse for the Christians, Sibylla and her two daughters from Guy died in an epidemic in autumn 1190. Although Guy of Lusignan was still king, he now had no connection to the royal family, and in the opinion of many, no right to the throne. Conrad of Montferrat made what he thought was a master stroke by arranging for Sibylla's younger sister, Isabella, to be divorced and then marrying her himself, though her divorce was invalid and Conrad himself had a wife, so the marriage was doubly bigamous as well as incestuous. Despite these problems, Conrad believed that as Isabella's husband and thus the nearest male to the royal line his claim would be accepted. In the face of this farce, the majority of the Christians believed that they should wait for the Crusading armies to arrive so the three greatest rulers in Europe could settle the matter.

Unfortunately the three armies were completely independent of each other. Frederick Barbarossa of course had died, and although his army continued the journey, Philip Augustus was the first leader to arrive in Acre and he immediately intervened in the fraught political situation. Philip opposed Guy of Lusignan's attempts to remain king of Jerusalem, and in the face of such opposition it was natural for Guy to seek an ally in Richard. Guy, and others, also made the point that the dynasty in Jerusalem was in fact Angevin, and a younger branch of the family headed by Richard and so subject to him.

Guy joined his brother Geoffrey and they went to Cyprus to see Richard. Richard was willing to put aside the old rivalries between Angevin and Lusignan; as we have seen, the feudal relationship worked both ways, and despite their turbulent past, as Duke of Aquitaine Richard owed the Lusignans his protection. Richard in his customary way had seen the big picture and realized that no attempt to hold the Holy Land could succeed without naval support, and Cyprus could provide an ideal base. Richard divided his fleet to sail around the island and take its fortresses, and he sent Guy to capture Isaac. The Cypriot fortresses were no more match for Angevin siegecraft than the castles of France or England, and the island quickly fell to Richard. Guy failed to capture Isaac, but Richard held Isaac's daughter hostage, and Isaac quickly came to terms. Isaac agreed to surrender on condition that he was not put in irons – an insult to his supposed imperial majesty – and Richard agreed, then clapped the former Emperor in chains made of silver.[22] Richard gave Cyprus to the Lusignans, providing a vital base for future Crusades and to serve as a support to the Crusader States, and was finally free to proceed to Acre.

With the arrival of Philip Augustus and Richard and their Crusading armies, plus the German forces that had continued despite Frederick Barbarossa's death, the siege of Acre reached its climax. Saladin knew that if he could defeat the Christian armies here the Crusade might fail, but in the end the task was beyond him. His armies were too fractious and exhausted, and the Crusaders were too numerous.

The siege of Acre was a turning point for the Crusader States, which might so easily have been swept away entirely after Saladin's victory at Hattin. It lasted so long that participants compared it to the siege of Troy,[23] and in the end the Christians were victorious. Had the port remained in Saladin's hands, the Crusader States would have ended, but Acre's capture secured a Christian foothold in Outremer until 1291.

The circumstances of Acre's capture also had a profound influence on Richard's reign. When the city was taken, the victorious Christians placed their banners on the walls. As Barbarossa was dead, the remaining German contingent was led by Leopold Duke of Austria, who planted his banner to stake a claim to the spoils, but Richard's men tore the banner down, as Leopold had no right to join the other leaders. Leopold was justifiably furious, not only because this denied the Germans what he believed was their rightful share, but also because he had fought so heroically.[24] According to legend, the Austrian flag actually derives from this, as Leopold's shirt was soaked in blood after the fighting, and when he removed his belt there was a white stripe in the middle. This red-white-red banner became his personal device and eventually the Austrian flag.[25]

Leopold did not forget the insult at Acre. When Richard returned from the Crusade, he faced a difficult choice because most of the lands on the way to England were under the control of rulers hostile to him. He chose the land route and passed through Vienna, where he was captured by Leopold, who then sold him to the Emperor Henry VI, initiating Richard's long captivity as we will discuss below.

Despite the victory at Acre, Richard chose not to attack Jerusalem. The city was too exposed and would put his army at risk for no strategic advantage, as it would almost certainly be lost again as soon as the Crusaders left. But this meant that despite Richard's achievements in retaking Acre, later defeating Saladin at the battle of Arsuf and stabilizing the coastal cities, which guaranteed the survival of the Crusader States for another century when all seemed lost, his Crusade was still a failure. Saladin suffers from a similar problem: he was (and is) criticized for failing to recapture all the Crusader States, and his failure allowed the Christian states to remain for another century. Historians point out the reasoning behind Saladin's decisions and how ultimately his conquests did end the Crusader States, albeit after his death, but this is irrelevant. Saladin conquered every Christian possession except Tyre and was expected to end the Crusader States for good, but for whatever reasons, good or bad, he failed to do so. Richard's undisputed success gives the lie to any claim that he was a poor ruler, but his undisputed failure to retake Jerusalem means his Crusade failed, whatever revisionist attempts to salvage success may be offered.

Nevertheless, Richard's adventures still leap off the page. When Saladin captured Jaffa and only the citadel still held out, Richard appeared with a squadron of galleys to relieve the garrison. According to Saladin's secretary Baha ad-Din, Saladin believed Richard wouldn't be able to land, but Richard did, in his galley '... painted all red, with a red canopy on the deck, and a red flag'.[26] Baha ad-Din might not have noticed or been interested, but presumably this red flag carried the device of the three lions that would be familiar to us today.

Richard's small force now camped outside Jaffa and Saladin realized that if he brought his army up he might destroy them. Richard formed the Crusaders into a compact line, and after repeated failures to break the Crusader ranks, the entire Muslim army abandoned the attack. Baha ad-Din was present, and he and others relate the incredible story of how Richard taunted them:

> The Arab historians relate that in one of the intervals between these futile charges Richard rode alone, lance in hand, along the whole front of the Moslem army, challenging it to fight, and not a man came forth to meet him; according to one account, he ended by stopping his horse midway between the two hosts, asking the Moslems for some food, and calmly dismounting to eat what they gave him ... In vain the Sultan rode up and down among them, promising them splendid rewards for one more charge ...[27]

Here is truly a moment from a Hollywood film, yet we have no reason to question Baha ed-Din's story.

A King's Ransom

Part of Richard's legend is his captivity in Austria on his return from the Crusade. Philip Augustus had left the Crusade earlier, pleading illness, though it was widely known that he was preparing to attack Richard's lands and he was accused of cowardice. Philip ignored this criticism, instead building up alliances with Richard's enemies like Emperor Henry VI (the opponent of Richard's brother-in-law Henry the Lion of Bavaria) and Raymond of Toulouse. This closed off most of the Mediterranean coast to Richard, and as he was returning in winter it was considered too dangerous to return to England by ship. Richard ultimately decided to sail up the Dalmatian coast to Venice, and then attempt to reach Henry the Lion's protection.

This is yet another highly romantic tale. Richard and a few companions disguised themselves as pilgrims and made their way north, choosing a more easterly route to avoid the highest mountains. This brought them to the lands of Leopold of Austria, who had not forgotten his treatment by Richard at Acre. Later reports give more and more fanciful accounts of how Richard came to be captured – the supposed pilgrims were said to have spent money on a lavish scale that aroused suspicion, or Richard was said to have hidden in a kitchen and pretended to be turning the spit for roast meat, but was betrayed by a ring that was obviously too valuable to be owned by a servant. In whatever circumstances, he was captured sometime before Christmas 1192 and imprisoned in the castle of Durnstein.[28]

The most romantic tale of all is based on this imprisonment. After Richard's disappearance, the minstrel Blondel is said to have travelled around Germany searching for him. Blondel went to each castle and sang a song known to Richard, and finally outside Durnstein he heard Richard singing the next verse from a tower. The story dates from the 13th century and doesn't seem to be true, but it is too compelling to ignore. Blondel was known to be a troubadour at Richard's court, and may even have been a spy for him,[29] but there is no evidence that Blondel was the person who discovered Richard's whereabouts. In fact, Richard's captivity was a cause célèbre around Europe, with the pope excommunicating Leopold for capturing a Crusader, and Richard's officials making contact with him to receive his instructions.[30]

Leopold passed Richard on to Emperor Henry VI, who entered into complicated negotiations with Richard, but also with Philip Augustus, for the terms of his release. Philip immediately told John, who promptly went to Paris to do homage for all the Angevin continental lands in hopes of usurping the throne. John then tried to seize castles within England while Philip attacked Normandy. However, Richard's loyal officials defended the realm against John, and although various border regions of Normandy were lost, for the most part the duchy held out. It was clear though, that Richard desperately needed to get back, and he was prepared to pay an enormous ransom for his release. The negotiations dragged on through 1193, but it became clear that Richard would be returning. On hearing that Richard had reached an agreement with the Emperor, Philip sent a message to John saying, 'Look to yourself; the devil is loose.'[31] Although Philip and John offered Henry VI more money to keep Richard than he would receive in ransom, in February 1194 Richard was released for the sum of 150,000 marks.

Although Richard used his time in captivity to form alliances with German princes that would serve him later, he also used his enforced idleness – like King René, when he was a prisoner in Dijon, or the great 15th-century captive Charles of Orleans in the Tower of London – to engage in cultural pursuits. We possess a song reputedly written by Richard when he was in captivity called 'No one who is in prison':[32]

> English and Normans, man of Aquitaine,
> Well know they all who homage owe to me
> That not my lowliest comrade in campaign
> Should pine thus, had I gold to set him free;
> To none of them would I reproachful be –
> Yet – I am prisoner here!

....

And they, my knights of Anjou and Touraine –
Well know they, who now sit at home at ease,
That I, their lord, in far-off Allemaine
Am captive. They should help to my release;
But now their swords are sheathed, and rust in peace,
While I am prisoner here[33]

It cannot help but delight us that Richard embraced his heritage as the grandson of troubadours by composing songs himself. This is of particular interest since the late 12th century was a key moment in western music when polyphony began to supersede plain Gregorian chant, although this was condemned by conservatives such as John of Salisbury as 'the wanton and effeminate sound produced by caressing, chiming and intertwining melodies, a veritable harmony of sirens'.[34] The Angevin empire facilitated travel between diverse regions and we have already seen that troubadours such as Bertrand de Born were in England. Limoges in the heart of Richard's duchy of Aquitaine was the most famous centre of 12th-century music, and its library still contains early religious music and troubadour lyrics. Richard loved the new music, and when the clerks of his royal chapel were singing in the choir, he would urge them with his hand and tell them to sing louder.[35] Even on his Crusade Richard indulged his passion for music: during one of his meetings with Saladin's brother al-Adil, Richard asked if al-Adil could arrange for him to hear Arabic singing, so a woman was brought in who played on the guitar and sang, to Richard's delight.[36]

These stories make Richard's character come to life as vividly as his father's. There are many records of his direct speech that leap off the page and let us hear how he spoke. We know Richard's favourite oath, 'By god's legs [or feet]' as reported by William Marshal (a less blasphemous echo of Fulk Nerra's 'By God's souls'). The legendary Angevin rage shared by Henry, Richard and John was also complemented in Henry and Richard by a capacity for fun (and isn't it interesting that the humourless John was the only Angevin failure?). Gerald of Wales says Richard mocked the supposed Angevin descent from the fairy Melusine by saying that no one should be surprised if he lacked all human feeling since he was descended from the devil. When Fulk of Neuilly presumed to give him a sermon about his three 'wicked daughters' (pride, avarice and sensuality), Richard responded that he would marry them off respectively to the Templars, Cistercians and Benedictines.[37]

The Battle for Normandy and Richard's 'Unromantic' Death

On Richard's return from captivity, he immediately began a whirlwind of activity to recapture lost possessions and protect his domains. Most famously, he constructed

Chateau Gaillard, whose ruins above the Seine at Les Andelys are one of Richard's most enduring monuments. Despite being a ruin, Chateau Gaillard gives us the most complete idea of what Richard viewed as the perfect castle, because it was built all at once in the incredibly short time of two years. As we have seen, Geoffrey Plantagenet and Henry II were master castle-takers, and in the 12th century professional engineers with extensive siege trains were able to take most castles. Chateau Gaillard was meant to redress the balance. It incorporated all the innovations from the castles of the Crusader States, which were the most advanced of the time, and its elliptical keep and interconnecting outworks were meant to counter 12th-century advances in siegecraft by removing any 'dead areas' where enemies could mine the walls or launch projectiles.

The massive castle and attendant outworks and fortifications were built at a cost of around £11,500, which was a huge expense when compared with the £7,000 Richard spent on all his other castles throughout his entire reign, or the £8,250 spent on Dover castle between 1164 and 1214.[38] To accomplish this, Richard brought the full force of his formidable character to bear on the workmen. William of Newburgh reports that the king was so committed to the project that 'if an angel had come down out of the sky to bid him stay his hand, he would have got no answer but a curse'.[39]

Richard's statements about the castle demonstrate his pride in it. The name Chateau Gaillard means 'saucy castle', showing Richard was very well aware how offensive – in both senses of the word – it would be to Philip, and this jesting nickname quickly became the name it was known by.[40] Richard also claimed that the design of the castle was so perfect that he could have held it against an assault even if its walls were made of butter.[41] Did this massive investment in time and money pay off? Chateau Gaillard was intended as a forward base for Richard's aggression against Philip Augustus, but this potential was never explored because Richard died shortly after it was completed, though the castle would have its day a few years later in John's desperate fight to defend Normandy from Philip.

Richard's death, as with everything about him, is a good story though a tragic one. Richard was campaigning against rebellious vassals in Aquitaine and besieging the castle of Chalus-Chabrol. His forces were far superior to those of the defenders and the castle's fall was inevitable. A lone archer on the battlements, defending himself from the arrows of Richard's army with a frying pan, continued to shoot at Richard's men in defiance. Richard, romantic hero to the last, stepped out from behind his shield to applaud the courage of the defender and was promptly shot in the shoulder. He tore the arrow out and said nothing to his men, but the wound festered and he was dead within days.

The anticlimactic death of such a famous hero has troubled many even now. The indefatigable historian John Gillingham responds to the criticism that Richard's death in a 'meaningless' siege of a minor castle was unworthy of a legendary hero by arguing that suppressing rebellion and maintaining the integrity of the Angevin Empire was the most important task Richard faced, rather than a meaningless nuisance. Richard died performing the very essence of his role as an Angevin king, protecting the unity of his domains.[42] This is correct, but Gillingham misses or ignores the point: Richard was a hero-king and Crusader, described by his chroniclers as invincible and invulnerable, and to die from an infected wound inflicted during a minor siege is a sorry end to the legend. The fact that he was dispatched by an arrow fired by a mere foot soldier is deeply unsatisfying.

It is a tribute to Richard that legend tries to finish the tale in a fitting way. In Roger of Howden's version of the story, the archer is named Bertrand du Gurdon, and after the castle falls all the defenders are slaughtered except for Bertrand, who was brought before Richard as he lay on his deathbed. Richard asks what wrong he has done to Bertrand that he should kill him (obviously Richard thinks besieging the castle and swearing to hang the garrison doesn't count). Bertrand replies, 'With your own hand you killed my father and two brothers, and you intended to kill me. Take your revenge in any way you like. Now that I have seen you on your deathbed I shall gladly endure any torment you may devise.' Chivalrous to the end, Richard forgives Bertrand and orders him to be released, and although in some versions of the story he leaves peacefully, others report that Mercadier, Richard's faithful mercenary captain, tracked him down and flayed him alive as punishment for his crime against a hero.[43]

Contemporaries were besotted with Richard, and not just in Europe. Joinville, the chronicler of Louis IX's Crusade, noted that even fifty years after Richard's death Muslim women in the Holy Land would tell their crying children, 'Hush, or King Richard will get you.'[44] Modern historians have not always been as complimentary, and from the 19th century it has been common to criticize Richard as a poor administrator who neglected England, and his Crusading glory is tarnished by his failure to recapture Jerusalem. For generations what was considered his worst offence by British historians was that he spent only six months of his ten-year reign in England. Even considering his two years on Crusade and year in captivity, this seems rather low (Henry II spent a similarly small proportion of his reign in England, but he reigned for thirty-five years so the difference doesn't seem so stark). Of course Richard viewed England as only part of his realm, and it is this that was his gravest offence for British historians writing in a nationalist tradition. Equally, Richard was traditionally ignored by French historians as a foreign king, despite the fact that he ruled a large part of France.

Richard, strangely, also suffers because of John. Though in almost every respect Richard is compared favourably to John (and may gain too much from the comparison), the fact that John lost the Angevin Empire so quickly demeans Richard's efforts to defend it. John's failure makes Richard's work on the continent seem pointless. The absorption of the Angevin Empire by France seems inevitable and Richard's time wasted, but this isn't true, and if John had been a better ruler and the Empire had lasted another generation or more, Richard's groundwork might have been better appreciated.

Richard's death on 6 April 1999 (at a house still standing in Chinon, if one believes the plaque on the building) precipitated a crisis in the succession, since John was the last legitimate son of Henry II, but Arthur, son of John's deceased elder brother Geoffrey Duke of Brittany, had an equally good or better claim to the throne. Later in the 13th century the laws of primogeniture were settled in the form in which they remain today, namely that the line of succession always passes through the elder line, and the son of an elder brother inherits before a younger brother. In 1199, however, especially when the kingdom was under such extreme threat from Philip Augustus, there was no reason to prefer a youth to an adult who had already held, albeit in an undistinguished manner, important responsibilities. Furthermore, this only concerned the English throne and the rights to Normandy and Anjou. Aquitaine still belonged to Eleanor, and her presence undoubtedly provided substantial support for John. Despite the challenges he faced, there was no reason to believe that John's fight to preserve the Angevin Empire was unwinnable, yet within five years John had lost most of his Empire, including Anjou itself.

CHAPTER 6 – THE FALL OF EMPIRES

I N 1200 THE STRUGGLE between the Angevins and Capetians entered its final phase, ending with the unravelling of the Angevin Empire, but the 13th century also witnessed other phenomenal changes including the collapse of other empires. The specific disintegrations that most concern us are three. In 1204, Philip Augustus completed the conquest of Normandy and the Angevin Empire collapsed swiftly afterwards. In that same year, Constantinople was captured, seemingly ending the Byzantine Empire – and by extension marking the final end of the Roman Empire – but astonishingly this defeat came at the hands of a Christian army mustered for the Fourth Crusade, which turned against the greatest Christian city in the world. Finally, the Holy Roman Empire, so revitalized by the successes of Frederick Barbarossa, reached a new peak under Emperor Frederick II, but within a generation this edifice too was virtually destroyed. Even more shockingly, the forces opposing the Holy Roman Empire were again Crusaders summoned by the pope, and they were led by an Angevin. Although that tale will be told more fully in the next chapter, the origins of that conflict can be set out here.

First, we must return to the Angevin Empire, and John, the last king of England to be called 'Angevin'. John's reign is completely defined by his loss of the Angevin continental domains. Everything proceeds from this: his entire reign was spent raising money to pay first for the unsuccessful defence of Normandy and Anjou and then to raise forces to regain them. He had no other concerns, from the moment of his accession when Philip Augustus began operations against Normandy, to his final assault on France, which led to the battle of Bouvines on 27 July 1214. The failure at Bouvines proved so deadly a blow that the barons' revolt followed swiftly on and John was forced to agree to the limitations to his power enshrined in Magna Carta, but even worse was a French invasion of England that ended with John's death as a fugitive in his own realm. John's reign was certainly eventful, but as with Henry II and Richard, since he will be more familiar to English readers I will focus specifically on his relationship with the Angevin Empire.

John is one of the most recognizable English monarchs for several reasons: he was the only English king to bear that name; he assumed his place in legend as the chief of the villains opposed by Robin Hood; and he is notorious as one of the worst kings ever, even if the reasons for this are hazy. His terrible reputation began in his own lifetime, and he was comprehensively defamed by the St Albans chroniclers Roger of Wendover and Matthew Paris, who blackened his name whenever possible. Matthew Paris sums it up by repeating a contemporary's famous verdict, 'Foul as it is, Hell itself is defiled by the foulness of John'.[1]

Yet modern historians have adopted another view. John's star rose considerably in the 20th century when he was praised for administrative innovation and hailed as the first bureaucrat-king presiding over a modern state. Either implicitly or explicitly, this praise for John is always to some degree in opposition to Richard as the mindless Crusader knight, brilliant at warfare but useless otherwise, off having adventures and neglecting his kingdom. Richard and John are inextricably linked because both concentrated almost entirely on the struggle against Philip Augustus to preserve the Angevin Empire, and praise for one becomes criticism of the other. On the face of it there should be no discussion, because Richard successfully defended the Empire even though he spent years outside the kingdom on Crusade and in captivity, whereas John lost it within a few years. Nevertheless the point has been made that Richard's extraordinary demands on his subjects to raise money for a Crusade and then pay his ransom left them bankrupt, and there were no resources remaining for John to use in the defence of the realm.

John's life was turbulent from start to finish. He was born in 1167, and his brothers had already been given responsibility for various parts of the Angevin Empire while he was still a child. He would have been aware of the great revolt of his brothers in 1173–74 without having any possibility of playing a role, and by the time he was old enough to be given any responsibility his brothers were well established in their various domains. John was Henry II's favourite because he was the youngest, and although it was inadvertent, John caused Henry's downfall when Henry's attempt to redistribute his lands to include John prompted Richard's final, successful rebellion against his father. John's disastrous attempt to become lord of Ireland in 1185 is one of the main proofs of his ineptitude, and it does demonstrate all the character flaws that would later blight his reign – arrogance, indecision and tactlessness. The fact that John was eighteen at the time might be some excuse, but in response it is always observed that Richard became Duke of Aquitaine – much larger and possibly even more turbulent than Ireland – from the age of fifteen and Philip Augustus took the throne at fifteen. John's behaviour in the last revolt against his father also tells considerably against him, as does his treachery when Richard was on Crusade.

A Disputed Succession

When Richard died, John acted swiftly. Richard – somewhat surprisingly, given their history – had finally designated John as his heir, but although influential, this was not decisive because their nephew Arthur had an equally good claim. John rode immediately to Chinon to seize the Angevin treasury. This is worth remembering, because later in his reign it is consistently John's indolence and inability to take decisive action that is blamed for his failures. Equally vital to John's success at this point was the fact that in the absence of any legitimate children of Richard's, Aquitaine immediately reverted back to his mother Eleanor. She swiftly did homage to Philip Augustus to confirm her rights, then passed the duchy to John and made a tour of Aquitaine and Poitou to secure it in his name. A huge portion of the Angevin Empire was now firmly claimed for John, including Anjou itself. John almost immediately left Anjou because he needed to be accepted as duke of Normandy and crowned as king of England, which seemed vital, but here lay the seeds of his downfall.[2]

Although John had made the first move, the succession was still in the balance. Arthur's mother, Constance of Brittany, asked Philip Augustus to take her son into his protection and she also summoned Breton troops to help secure the throne for Arthur. They seized Angers, and in the Angevin capital on Easter Sunday (18 April) a group of barons from Anjou, Maine and Touraine accepted Arthur as their lord, claiming that this was justified by their established customs. The critical fortresses of Chinon and Saumur had been surrendered to John so he still had a base from which to make a recovery, but this immediate defection of Anjou to Arthur shows that John's position was much more precarious than it first seemed.

Interestingly, after being such a thorn in the side of Richard, the Lusignan family (Hugh, Ralph and Geoffrey) became strong supporters of John and harassed Poitou and Anjou on his behalf.[3] John went to Le Mans but the garrison refused to allow him entry, and he narrowly escaped being captured as Philip Augustus's troops marched on the city. The seismic shift in political alignment is demonstrated by the Angevin heartland immediately abandoning John, and although John would continue to assert his rights to Anjou until 1214, in 1199 the history of Anjou and the Angevins had already begun to move decisively away from the dynasty in England.

In the debates about the relative rights of John and Arthur, we are fortunate again that William Marshal, as one of the chief barons, was a key figure in deciding the succession. Naturally William remembered the moment he learned of Richard's death vividly, and his discussion with Hubert Walter, the Archbishop of Canterbury:

> It was late at night, and the Marshal was going to bed. He dressed immediately, and went to the priory of Notre Dame-du-Pre, on the other side of the river, where the archbishop was staying. The archbishop, seeing the late hour of the visit, guessed its cause. 'The king is dead,' he cried. 'What hope remains to us now? There is none, for, after him, I can see no successor able to defend the kingdom. The French will overrun us, and there will be no one to resist them.'
>
> 'We must choose his successor at once,' said the Marshal.
>
> 'In my opinion we should choose Arthur.'
>
> 'Ah, sire, that would be a bad thing,' replied the Marshal; 'Arthur has bad councillors, and he is proud and passionate. If we put him at our head he will

cause trouble, for he has no love for the English. There is Count John; he is the next heir to the lands of his father and brother.'

'Marshal,' replied the archbishop, 'do you really mean this?'

'Yes, sire. It is right; the son is nearer the land of his father than the nephew is.'

'Marshal, it shall be as you wish. But I warn you that you will never repent of anything as you will repent of this.'

'So be it; it is my view all the same.'[4]

Perhaps it is not surprising that William, relating the story when John's son Henry III was established on the throne, emphasized his support for John, but William's recollection of his views does seem to have been indicative of the rest of the Anglo-Norman aristocracy, for despite the loss of Anjou and Maine, John was quickly invested as Duke of Normandy in Rouen on 25 April and crowned King of England at Westminster Abbey on 27 May. The point has also been made that William Marshal was quoting from established Norman law that succession should pass from one brother to another rather than to the son of an elder brother.

Although John's inheritance of the throne of England depended on the English barons, and Aquitaine was secure, a change of rulership in the rest of the Angevin domains was subject to Philip Augustus's approval as feudal overlord. Indeed, when John later demanded to know why Philip had invaded his lands, Philip's excuse was that John had been invested as Duke of Normandy without his permission. John offered to do homage for his lands if Philip would recognize his title, but Philip refused unless Anjou, Maine and Touraine were given to Arthur.[5]

It is striking that in these early days John acted quickly, decisively and with complete success, in marked contrast to what would happen later. When Philip attacked Normandy in September 1199, John ignored him and struck at Anjou, the heart of Arthur's support. William des Roches, the leading baron of Anjou, was Arthur's key supporter, and Philip had recognized him as constable of Anjou, Maine and Touraine to keep him onside. However, the disputed succession had plunged Anjou into a civil war and John, already king of England and duke of Normandy, was on hand with a large army, so William began to reconsider. Philip had also offended him by invading Maine and destroying a castle William claimed was in his jurisdiction. It is noteworthy that it was Philip who was alienating his own supporters through thoughtless actions and arrogance, constantly two steps behind John's decisive and well-thought-out attacks. William offered to reconcile Arthur and his mother Constance to John and make peace with the Bretons, and by the end of September this had been accomplished. Philip was left with nothing, and after agreeing to a Christmas truce and having a productive meeting with John in January 1200, he agreed to recognize all John's claims in May with the Treaty of Le Goulet.

Although Philip recognized John as heir to all the lands held by his father and brother, there was a high price. The terms of the treaty were sealed by a marriage alliance between Philip's son Louis and John's niece, Blanche of Castile, the daughter of his sister Eleanor, and for her dowry John gave Blanche many of the disputed lands in the Vexin (the border territory between Normandy and France) that had so long been a cause of conflict between France and England. Blanche and Louis were still children, so Philip would take custody of Blanche and her dowry until the marriage, just as Henry II held Alice's dowry through the long years of her engagement to Richard. Philip also insisted that John recognize Arthur as heir to Brittany and respect all his rights, and accept the homage of various other rebellious vassals without punishment. John further agreed to pay 20,000 marks as a 'relief' for inheriting Richard's lands. It was not uncommon for a lord to demand a relief from his vassal for the right to inherit, but the confidence to make the demand and the power to enforce it were a good indication of a lord's status, and neither Henry nor Richard had been asked to pay a relief. Henry and Richard had recognized Philip as their nominal overlord for their French possessions, but this authority now seemed much more tangible.[6]

Interestingly, the monk Gervase of Canterbury recorded that it was now, after this treaty, that some people began to call John 'Softsword' because he seemed to prefer peace to war. John had by no means been defeated and had rather been quite successful in the face of considerable upheaval over the succession, so Gervase's comments are puzzling.[7]

We know that the Angevin continental possessions were under enormous pressure at the end of Richard's reign, but in 1200 John seemed to have the initiative. There was still the problem of Arthur as a rival claimant to the throne, but it was unlikely he could threaten John in England, and John's claims to Normandy and Anjou had been recognized in the treaty of Le Goulet. This seemed a strong position from which to assert his authority, yet it was John's own action that precipitated a crisis.

'It must be witchcraft': John's Disastrous Defence of Normandy

Philip Augustus was already seeking appeals from unhappy Angevin vassals and incrementally undermining the Angevin position, and John now gave him a perfect weapon. John decided to discard his wife Isabella of Gloucester as the marriage was childless, and in 1200 he married Isabella of Angoulême, an important heiress in Aquitaine. This could have been a clever strategic move, which would help stabilize the vital link between the two pieces of the Angevin Empire that had been so unstable in the past, and continued Richard's strategy of establishing better links with the southern portion of the Angevin domains. However, the main problem with the marriage was that Isabella was already engaged to Hugh of Lusignan's son (also named Hugh and known as Hugh 'le Brun'), and John forced her to break the engagement. Medieval chroniclers reported that, rather than being a strategic decision, John did this because he was besotted with Isabella of Angoulême's beauty and threw away everything for this passion. In fact, we have no need to choose between the options, and perhaps this episode is a striking example of John's strengths and weaknesses. The Angoulême marriage can be seen as a sensible strategic move, but the manner in which John undertook it, alienating key local figures and ignoring the consequences also demonstrates his fatal flaws.[8]

Within a day of Isabella's engagement to Hugh being broken, John was betrothed to her, and within a week they were married at Chinon. When Hugh protested to John about this violation of his rights, he received only abuse. Hugh appealed for satisfaction to Philip Augustus as his and John's overlord, and the dispute dragged on for some months with John manifesting his displeasure against the Lusignans in a variety of ways. It was while events between Philip and John were at this difficult state that preparations began for the Fourth Crusade, and it became clear that Richard's former allies, the Count of Flanders and other regional figures, were preparing to leave. This may be the reason Philip had initially sought an accommodation with John in 1200; he may have been waiting until his troublesome vassals were safely in the eastern Mediterranean.

John was ultimately summoned to Paris to defend himself. John refused to appear in Philip's court on the basis that the Duke of Normandy was exempt from such appearances, but Philip responded that it was as Duke of Aquitaine and Count of Anjou that John was being summoned. John still refused to appear so he was declared to be in rebellion and all his lordships in France were forfeited. Philip was clearly stretching his authority as a feudal lord by declaring John stripped of Normandy, Anjou and Aquitaine for this offence, and even if he claimed that he was seizing John's lands to coerce his obedience, by the terms of feudal law he should have restored the confiscated possessions to John's heir after a year and a day.[9] Yet none of this mattered: Philip could declare John's possessions forfeit, but it meant nothing if he couldn't take them, and conversely if John had been able to defend his lands it would have made no difference that Philip Augustus had declared them forfeit.

It was now that Arthur, aged sixteen and old enough to participate in the struggle, reappeared. Philip knighted him and received his homage for Brittany, Anjou, Maine and Aquitaine, and he seemed determined to renew his claims against John. Arthur went to Tours, where he joined forces with the Lusignans and all the other leading rebels against John. They learned that Eleanor of Aquitaine was at the castle of Mirabeau between Angers and Poitiers, and Arthur besieged the castle with a force of around a thousand men.[10]

John was at Le Mans and received word from William des Roches that his mother was in danger. At this moment, John lived up to the legacy of his father and brother and produced what had become the typical Angevin response to such circumstances: to move so swiftly that he appeared as if by magic when his enemies least expected it. With incredible speed he led a force to Mirebeau and completely surprised the besiegers. Eleanor had been driven to the keep and the besiegers had taken the outer walls of the castle, but John's forces utterly routed them, appearing at dawn and herding their opponents through the narrow streets and capturing more than 200 knights and barons, including Arthur himself and the Lusignans. John wrote to the English barons to report the victory:

> Know that by the grace of God we are safe and well and God's mercy has worked wonderfully with us … we heard that the lady our mother was closely besieged at Mirebeau, and we hurried there as fast as we could … And there we captured our nephew Arthur … and all our other Poitevin enemies who were there, being upward of 200 knights, and none escaped. Therefore God be praised for our happy success.[11]

This was a triumph on the scale of Poitiers in the Hundred Years War, and John loaded the captives with chains and sent them to various prisons in Normandy and England. Philip Augustus retired through Normandy with his army, causing mayhem along the way, but it was still a retreat.

At this moment, when John seemed to have triumphed on a scale even Richard would have envied and made himself secure, he once again brought about his own ruin, and this time it was irreversible. The difficulty seems to have been with William des Roches, the seneschal of Anjou who had first supported Arthur but had subsequently been a key supporter for John, and had in fact masterminded the assault on Mirebeau that led to Arthur's capture. William had explicitly demanded that any decisions about how to treat the captives or conduct affairs in Anjou be discussed with him. John ignored this agreement and reportedly treated the prisoners cruelly. Shortly after, rumours that Arthur had been murdered began to circulate, and although they don't seem to have been true at this point, they further damaged John's reputation in Brittany, Anjou and Touraine, and hinted at the trouble that might come if Arthur were killed.

William des Roches defected back to Philip, taking key barons from Poitou with him, and within months John's position in Anjou and Touraine had collapsed. William des Roches captured Angers and once again Aquitaine was cut off. The Lusignans joyfully stirred up trouble in the south while Philip Augustus again prepared to move against Normandy. He was assisted by the fact that the Norman barons began to defect en masse as well. William Marshal described an 'epidemic of treachery', and as everything crumbled around him John seemed incapable of formulating a response. The chroniclers still believed it was because of infatuation with his new wife: Roger of Wendover, amongst others, criticized him for spending too long in bed with Isabella and idling away hours at the dining table.[12]

Modern historians have sought other explanations, speculating that John was prone to depression or other forms of mental illness that prevented him from acting. This may be true, but perhaps it's enough to say that John was simply unequal to the enormous task he faced. He wasn't a good king, as many others before and after him weren't strong rulers. He had demonstrated this time and again, in his failure to make good his lordship in Ireland, his clumsy handling of the marriage to Isabella and his treatment of William des Roches. He would show it again later in his reign when the English barons became disaffected. Another element of John's personality may have been plain exhaustion. Even Henry II was worn out by the constant movement required to maintain the empire, and if John finally couldn't summon the energy to face the incessant strain of ruling such vast territories, we may feel a tiny glimmer of sympathy with him.

Another fact that must be considered, and has been raised by modern historians to explain the stunning speed of the collapse, is the exhaustion of taxpayers in Normandy and England. Richard's wars, Crusade, ransom and prodigious expenditure on Chateau Gaillard and other castles may have brought the Angevin Empire to breaking point. Gerald of Wales thought so, and commented that John had brought his tyrannical methods from England to bear on Normandy, alienating the barons. John – and we mustn't forget, Henry II and Richard before him – had to solve the problem of adapting the feudal host to long periods of warfare overseas, an insoluble problem when knights were only required to serve for forty days. All the Angevins relied extensively on mercenaries, who were detested by nobles and common people alike. Although we have seen how close Richard was to Mercadier, John's relationship with his mercenaries was even closer, and as his trust in the nobility waned he began to appoint mercenaries to high positions in his government. This was anathema to the nobles and further eroded their trust in John.[13]

Finally, there is evidence that the cross-Channel nobility with large landholdings in both England and Normandy were a much smaller class by 1200 than they had been two generations earlier in the civil war between Matilda and Stephen. Once Geoffrey Plantagenet had conquered Normandy, these cross-Channel nobles were a great source of support for Matilda because they would lose their English possessions if Stephen triumphed. They would presumably have fought for John on the same grounds, since there was never the slightest hint that he would lose the English throne. Yet either as an unintended consequence or by design, Henry II and Richard's policy of weakening the great barons resulted in many fewer nobles with such cross-Channel possessions, and so a large class of landowners with a vested interest in keeping England and Normandy together no longer existed. There were still some nobles in this category, most notably William Marshal, and this goes far to explain his support for John.

Perhaps the most important factor of all was that John was unable to bring security, leading to a sense that all the money his subjects paid was being wasted. John's mercenaries didn't help, and William Marshal's biographer commented that one of the reasons the people of Normandy abandoned John was because one of his captains, Louvrecaire, 'maltreated them, and pillaged them as though he were in an enemy's country'.[14] With no security, punitive taxes and a government run by mercenaries, there is a sense that the Normans had no motivation to remain loyal, especially when the Capetians had consciously created an image as wise rulers. Philip Augustus played on this, and perhaps the barons felt that Philip would be a less rapacious master than Henry II, Richard and John.

Philip Augustus appears as the villain when we look at things from an Angevin point of view, and his plots against Henry II with Geoffrey and Richard create an unfavourable image of his character from the moment he took the throne. There is also a lingering distaste associated with his behaviour on the Third Crusade, where his actions in Sicily and ultimate abandonment of the Crusade seem mean and cowardly. His subsequent efforts to grab Angevin territory while Richard was away and then bribe Richard's captors not to release him may have been crafty politically, but must always seem quite shabby in comparison with Richard's military exploits and romantic escapes. However, after 1200 Philip's patient and inexorable military pressure in contrast with John's lethargy and incompetence begin to reverse this image, and the feeling grew that the Capetians treated their subjects better than the Angevins did.

When John did take action, the results were as is often seen when inherently weak people attempt to show strength – bullying instead of firmness, impulsiveness instead of decisiveness, stubbornness instead of resolution. This is displayed most notoriously in John's treatment of Arthur. Philip Augustus, fortunate as always in the tools the Angevins placed in his hand, had taken up Arthur's cause enthusiastically, just as he had done previously with his 'best friends' Geoffrey of Brittany and Richard the Lionheart when they stirred up trouble against Henry II, and indeed with John himself against Richard. In every treaty with John, Philip mentioned Arthur and his rights, and insisted that his protection of Arthur's feudal rights was one of the main motivations of his attacks on John.[15] Sometime before Easter 1203, Arthur disappeared from the castle in Rouen, never to appear again. The rumour immediately spread that he had been murdered by John, and this was accepted by contemporaries, as it is by modern historians, as what must have happened.[16] John's reputation never recovered from this stain.

Philip Augustus barely had to change his rhetoric, and he now called for vengeance for Arthur rather than restoring his rights, and John's position swiftly collapsed. Philip followed the roll call of important cities and castles that have become so familiar in earlier chapters, and after consolidating his hold on Angers, Le Mans and Tours, he also took Saumur (Chinon and Loches would follow). He then turned to Normandy and in summer 1203 took the key fortress of Vaudreuil. This was catastrophic for John, especially because the castle surrendered as Philip was approaching and before he had actually begun the siege. This caused local outrage as there was a perception that the garrison contained many English knights who had no interest in defending Normandy. John released an extraordinary open letter in which he claimed to have ordered the garrison to surrender, in what has been assumed to be an attempt to pretend he had some kind of strategy, but this only served to undermine confidence in him further. It is clear that morale was all-important, since Henry II had spent enormous sums on repairing all the castles in his domains and Richard had continued this work, meaning that Normandy's defences were in excellent repair and would have been expected to hold out.[17]

Contemporaries commented on John's indolence and seemingly serene assertion that he would take back all the conquered fortresses; some attributed this to witchcraft, or again to his uxoriousness. There is evidence that John had sent an envoy to the pope and expected papal intervention to stop Philip's attacks, as it was well known that Innocent III strongly favoured peace so that more knights could join the Fourth Crusade. Yet although he argued eloquently for peace on the basis of the ruin and suffering caused to the people of Normandy, Innocent made it clear that he could not arbitrate in matters of feudal law between the two kings, and Philip Augustus, who had feared the consequences of papal ire even if it had not made him change his behaviour, now redoubled his efforts in Normandy.

John attacked Brittany in an attempt to lure Philip away from Normandy, but Philip was not drawn and all John did was antagonize the Duke of Brittany and further damage his reputation. John's actions seem increasingly aimless, and after futilely touring the remaining border fortresses of Normandy, he finally decided to return to England. Although this was ostensibly to gather money and reinforcements, there seems to have been a feeling in Normandy that John would not return, and essentially this sealed the fate of the duchy. William Marshal, who again was a key player in these events, told his biographer how John's retreat was accomplished:

> The king stayed but a short time at Rouen, and announced his intention of going to England in order to ask aid and counsel of his barons; then, he said, he would return without delay. But he took the queen with him, which made many fear he would stay in England until it was too late. On the first night he slept at Bonneville, not in the town, but in the castle, for he suspected treason ... He commanded the Marshal and those in whom he felt most confidence to be ready in the morning before daybreak; and so the king left without taking leave while he was supposed to be still asleep; and when his departure was discovered he was seven leagues away ... it was quite clear that they could not look for a speedy return.[18]

Philip now settled down for the siege of Chateau Gaillard, and although already all seemed lost, if Philip had been delayed too long there might have been a chance for John to recover. More importantly, as modern historians point out, Chateau Gaillard was Richard's project and Richard's masterpiece. This siege was Philip's final battle with Richard, four years after Richard's death.

Philip's forces had previously appeared before the castle and begun preparations for the attack, and John had launched an audacious combined land-and-river-based attack to foil the besiegers, but despite the soundness of the plan, it was mistimed: the boats coming up the river arrived too late, giving the French time to defeat first the land forces and then in turn the boats. This failure meant that Philip's forces had invested

Chateau Gaillard when John left Normandy at the end of 1203, so he was turning his back on what must have been the most important siege of the campaign.

John's claim that he had only returned to England to gather additional men and materials does seem to be true, for early in 1204 he was still organizing the defence of Normandy and sent reinforcements to the castles along a defensive line in western Normandy to protect it against invasions from the south. This did nothing for Chateau Gaillard in the east, but John might have been forgiven for putting his faith in Richard's engineering skill and believing that the castle could hold out for many months. John was preparing his return when the castle fell on 6 March 1204.[19]

Given that Chateau Gaillard was considered at the time to be the greatest fortification ever built, incorporating all the military developments pioneered by the Crusader castles in the east, which Richard had had plenty of time to study, its fall was shocking. Modern historians predictably turn this, as everything else, into a judgement on Richard versus John. First, the facts: the castle fell because of a design flaw. Despite its elliptical form, which gave completely open sight lines for the defenders to send missiles against the attackers, it turned out that there was one tiny blind spot that afforded protection to the besiegers and allowed them to force their way in. This has variously been described as a tiny bridge connecting the inner to the outer keep or the privies, though inevitably Gillingham finds a comment from William the Breton saying the flaw was because of additional work done by John when he added a chapel to the castle, thus spoiling Richard's perfect military design and causing the disaster. There is no clear consensus amongst contemporaries as to why the castle fell. If it had held out longer, John might have gained sufficient time to organize a return to Normandy, but given the scale of disaffection with his rule and John's loss of such significant portions of his domains, I find it hard to believe that Chateau Gaillard could have saved Normandy.[20]

Regardless, Chateau Gaillard did fall, and another event that caused equal damage to John occurred a month later: Eleanor of Aquitaine died. Despite her advanced age she had remained a stalwart of Angevin authority, and indeed she had secured Aquitaine for John at his accession when so many other regions were slipping away. Eleanor was quite simply the key figure in the creation of the Angevin Empire. Henry II was only heir to the Anglo-Norman kingdom and the county of Anjou, but Aquitaine provided an enormous, culturally different region that doubled the Angevin possessions. Moreover, Eleanor's relationship with her sons, especially Richard, shaped the latter part of Henry's reign and all of Richard's.

Eleanor's death caused yet another feudal complication between John and Philip when John could ill afford it, not to mention the emotional impact – which must have been considerable – on John of losing his mother and suffering another disaster on top of Chateau Gaillard. John did not return to Normandy, and in May Philip Augustus swept through the duchy, leaving Rouen behind as an isolated fortress and bypassing the defensive line John had established, in order to take Caen, Argentan and other major cities. Rouen surrendered in June 1204, and Normandy was lost. Philip had already secured Anjou, Maine and Touraine, and the Angevin Empire effectively ended, though not the English king's continental possessions, since Gascony remained under John's control.[21]

The Fourth Crusade

As catastrophic as the end of the Angevin Empire was for John, 1204 saw another conquest with even more profound consequences than the annexation of Normandy by France, and which was certainly more shocking: the capture of Constantinople by the Fourth Crusade. Although the first three Crusades had met with varying fortunes, there were still Crusader States in the Holy Land and a sense that Jerusalem could be recaptured, and the Crusading ideal remained at the heart of both papal policy and the dreams of the European aristocracy.

No one in Western Europe was yet reconciled to the loss of Jerusalem, and throughout the 1190s plans for a new Crusade had been under way. One of the stumbling blocks to a new Crusade was the death struggle between the Angevins and Capetians that prevented two of the most powerful states in Western Europe from participating. Emperor Henry VI had been interested in preparing a new Crusade, partially to expunge the memory of his father Frederick Barbarossa's ignominious death on the way to the Third Crusade, but also because as King of Sicily he was ideally placed to impose his will on the eastern Mediterranean.

Although Henry did not organize an 'official' Crusade with papal approval, a number of German Crusaders did go to Acre. The Germans quickly became embroiled in the complicated politics of the Crusader States and performed poorly on the occasions when they faced Muslim armies. Henry VI's death late in 1197 removed any impetus behind their involvement and they returned home. Their only lasting accomplishment, and it was an important one, was the foundation of the order of Teutonic Knights in 1198. The Teutonic Knights were a distinctively Germanic order and attracted knights from a region that did not traditionally provide members to the Templars or Hospitallers. Their statutes were modelled on the Hospitallers, and as we will see, long after the Crusader States in the Holy Land were gone, they were a major force in the politics of Germany and Eastern Europe.[22]

Given the relatively haphazard activity of the Germans, the feeling that a new Crusade was needed persisted. Of note is that from the outset this Crusade was aimed at Egypt. Richard the Lionheart's experience had shown clearly that Jerusalem could not be held in isolation, and there was a widespread realization that only by 'striking at the head of the serpent', in Egypt, could the Holy Land be regained. Although there was a consensus on this point among political and religious leaders, to ordinary Crusaders the idea that a Crusade could be divorced from the concept of a pilgrimage to the Holy Land would prove difficult to accept, and many who took the cross for the Fourth Crusade insisted on going to Syria, with profound consequences for the mission. With one bizarre exception, there would never again be a Crusade to the Holy Land, and subsequent Crusades were always directed at Egypt, Tunisia or closer to home. As we will see, sufficient numbers of knights were able to overcome this prejudice to allow Crusades within Europe to flourish, but there is no question that Crusades outside the Holy Land never had quite the same glamour as the first three.

We possess one of the best sources in Crusading history for the Fourth Crusade, the account of Geoffrey of Villehardouin, Marshal of Champagne, who was one of six envoys appointed to arrange the logistics of the expedition. Geoffrey's account is patently a justification of the decisions that led to the Fourth Crusade's outcome, but it is no less valuable because of this, and takes the form of a classical tragedy where each decision – which seemed inevitable at the time – led inexorably to horrific consequences.

Geoffrey's first task was to arrange transport for the army. By the beginning of the 13th century there was one obvious place to look for ships, and this was Venice. We have come across Venice from time to time before, but only as one among a number of other maritime powers such as Genoa and Pisa. Yet its power had been growing and it had strong trading relationships with the Byzantine Empire – to which it had once been subject – and more controversially with Egypt. Venice was also beginning to extend its dominion along the Adriatic, but it was the Fourth Crusade that established Venice as a great power.

Geoffrey of Villehardouin and others were sent to Venice to hire sufficient ships to transport the army, and by doing so inadvertently doomed the Crusade. Geoffrey says that the Venetians were quite clear about how much the expedition would cost, and the Crusaders undertook to pay a fixed amount per soldier and per horse if the Venetians provided the ships. Because the Venetians had to build the ships before the Crusade began, Geoffrey and the other envoys guaranteed a fixed number of Crusaders and agreed the final price in advance.[23]

This is where everything went wrong, because over the course of the year allowed for the Crusaders to assemble in Venice, various groups decided to travel via alternate routes. Many went to Syria in direct opposition to the planned attack on Egypt, showing the resistance to a purely military basis for the Crusade and the desire to include a pilgrimage to the holy places. Geoffrey's frustration emerges when he decries those who went to Syria, 'where, as they must have known, they could do nothing worth while', rather than join the main attack on Egypt. Worse, every Crusader who didn't turn up in Venice was another person not contributing to the agreed fee, and when the deadline in 1203 arrived there wasn't anywhere near enough money to pay the Venetians. Geoffrey is scathing about all those who chose alternative means of transport, though it must have been difficult for ordinary Crusaders to comprehend that if they didn't travel via Venice, the Crusade would fail. Geoffrey also noted that more people sailed directly to Syria from Marseilles than ultimately went to Constantinople, so what is seen as the 'real' Fourth Crusade was in fact a minority group. Since all those who went to Syria were slain or returned home without accomplishing anything of note and the smaller party captured Constantinople and founded a Latin Empire in Greece, naturally it is justified to call the Crusade to Constantinople the true Fourth Crusade.

Geoffrey emphasizes at every step that the Venetians were acting in accord with agreements that the Crusaders had formally sworn to uphold, but his contemporaries and many modern historians choose to see Venice as the villain in the piece. This is perhaps best expressed in John Ruskin's thundering indictment, when he says that the reader seduced by Venice's ancient power and beauty might be surprised to discover that:

> ... while all Europe around her was wasted by the fire of its devotion, she first calculated the highest price she could exact from its piety for the armament she furnished, and then, for the advancement of her own private interests, at once broke her faith and betrayed her religion.[24]

Certainly there was a touch of opportunism in the Venetians' behaviour. With a large, well-armed force now at their disposal, the Venetians offered to delay full payment of their fee if the Crusaders would help them recapture the city of Zara (modern Zadar, in Croatia, a place we will begin to encounter frequently), which had been seized by the Christian king of Hungary. The terms were that the Venetians would then transport the Crusaders to Egypt without having been paid in full, but the Crusaders would have to make good the deficit from plunder. This raises the question of why the Venetians didn't simply transport the Crusaders to Egypt in exchange for future plunder, rather than also requiring them to attack another Christian ruler, but Geoffrey didn't find their request unreasonable. Pope Innocent III took a different view, and made it absolutely clear that a Crusade had no business intervening in an essentially commercial dispute between two Christian powers over a maritime city.

There was considerable disagreement among the Crusaders about how to respond to the Venetian offer, but the Doge Enrico Dandolo, in a masterstroke of public relations, publicly took the cross in St Mark's and encouraged the rest of the Venetians to do so as well, thus joining their fate to that of the Crusaders after Zara had been taken. We forget the atmosphere of the Crusades at our peril, and despite the undoubted readiness of the Venetians to use the Crusade for their own aims, the Crusading army would genuinely have believed it was doing God's work, and the willingness of the Venetians to join in impressed the Crusaders. They duly went to Zara and took the city without much difficulty.

At this point came another unexpected development: Alexius, son of the deposed Byzantine Emperor Isaac Angelos, approached the Crusaders and offered to give them a huge amount of money and considerable support in men, ships and supplies for the Crusade if they would help him return his father to the throne. He also agreed that the Greek Orthodox church would return to the obedience of Rome, a goal of the papacy for centuries. With hindsight, the idea that a Crusade should be turned against Constantinople to intervene in its internal politics can only seem misguided, if not ridiculous, but at this point the Fourth Crusade was bankrupt and had lost a substantial part of its strength, so we can perhaps understand why its leaders saw accepting Alexius's offer as the only possible way of succeeding. Anyway, they had already intervened in one petty dispute between Christian powers and captured a Christian city, so why not another?

The Crusader army now attacked Constantinople to overthrow the usurper and restore Alexius and his father to power. Despite the nearly impregnable fortifications of this, the greatest city in the Christian world, and its overwhelming advantage in manpower, something of the situation in Constantinople can be discerned by the fact that after the first attack by the Crusaders – in which the remarkable Doge Enrico Dandolo, although blind and nearly ninety, stood in the prow of a Venetian galley holding the banner of St Mark, and was carried to the shore with the first wave of attackers – the usurper quickly abandoned the city to his rival.

Isaac Angelos was released from prison and restored to the throne, and Villehardouin was part of the delegation that went to him and presented the terms of the agreement with his son. These do seem rather onerous, as recorded by Villehardouin:

> The terms are as follows: First of all to place the whole of this empire under the jurisdiction of Rome, from which it has long since broken away; further, to give 200,000 silver marks to the army and a full year's supply of provisions to men of all ranks; to convey 10,000 men, in his own ships to Egypt, and keep them there at his own expense for a year; and, during his lifetime, to maintain, at his own expense, a company of 500 knights in the land oversea, to keep guard over it.[25]

Isaac commented that he didn't see how the terms could be met, but accepted that as he owed his empire to the Crusaders he must agree to them, and duly agreed, witnessed 'by oath and by charters with gold seals affixed'. He and his son were crowned with great splendour and did begin to pay some of the money due, while the Crusaders settled into their camps and acted as tourists until the time came to depart.

Villehardouin's account vividly gives a sense of the morass into which the Crusade was sinking, and the endless complications that beset them. Alexius now told the leaders of the Crusade that he was still resented by the Byzantines because he had returned to power through the support of the Crusade, and he was also unable to fulfil all the terms of the agreement because things were not yet settled enough for the full revenues of the empire to be collected. He therefore suggested that the Crusaders stay in Constantinople until the following Easter (it was now late August) at his expense, as well as renewing the contract with the Venetian fleet (which would expire in about a month) for another year at his expense, all of which would allow him to consolidate his hold on the throne and bring in enough money to pay his debts to them. They could then continue the Crusade on a sound financial footing and with the Byzantine support that had been promised.

Alexius's analysis of the situation was almost certainly correct, but it caused great discord among the Crusaders. Many of the ordinary soldiers complained that all this was taking far too long, with the Crusade first capturing Zara, then Constantinople and now being expected to act as a mercenary force for the new emperor for another year. Villehardouin and his party strongly advocated accepting the new agreement, since from an organizational point of view the Crusade had no possibility of success unless it had sound finances and a fleet that could attack Egypt. We see here, in the early 13th century, the sharp divide that had developed between the idealistic, mystical view of the Crusades that advocated simply turning up in the Holy Land and trusting God to take care of the details – which, after all, had worked brilliantly on the First Crusade – and the practical view, founded on the limited success or outright failure of the Second and Third Crusades as well as the loss of Jerusalem, that these were military expeditions that must be adequately funded, supplied and supported.

Villehardouin's party prevailed, and a new contract was agreed. Alexius undertook a successful tour of the empire with Crusader support to receive the submission of all his subjects. Although things remained tense in Constantinople between the Greeks and Latins – and a huge fire that destroyed much of the city, and for which the Latins were blamed, didn't help – the situation seemed stable.

However, Alexius's payments to the Crusaders dwindled and gradually stopped. Villehardouin attributed this to pride and ingratitude, though it could just as easily have been from lack of resources. Of course, the Crusaders could not daily look at the richest city in Christendom and believe that its emperor lacked funds, so they duly sent another delegation that informed Isaac and Alexius that if they did not honour their agreement the Crusaders would attack the city. Naturally the Byzantines were furious at this insult, and a new conflict began. This dragged on for months without either side gaining the advantage, causing discontent in the city. Any student of Byzantine history will be prepared for what followed, because Isaac and Alexius were overthrown by yet another usurper; Isaac died and Alexius was murdered. Now Constantinople was in complete turmoil and the Crusaders felt justified in attacking to force compliance with the terms of their agreement.

After bitter fighting the Crusaders broke into the city once again and caused great slaughter among the inhabitants, as well as another huge fire that according to Villehardouin destroyed more houses than in any three of the greatest cities in France. They sacked the two main palaces and 'Geoffrey de Villehardouin here declares that, to his knowledge, so much booty had never been gained in any city since the creation of the world.'[26]

Villehardouin is unapologetic about the business arrangements that underpinned the attack. It was agreed that once the city was conquered one of the Crusaders would be chosen as Emperor, and he would take one quarter of the Empire. The remaining three-quarters would be divided between the Crusaders and the Venetians. This division would have considerable resonance for the Venetians, who forever after called themselves the rulers of 'one quarter and one half of the Roman Empire'. This seems a little too neat, and again many modern historians argue that the Venetians must have planned the attack on Constantinople all along. However, we must remember we are in an age before secularization, and there was no distinction between the religious goals of the Crusade and the prosaic mechanisms that were used to fund it. The Crusaders saw no inconsistency in being materially rewarded for their participation in a Crusade and the Venetians saw no hypocrisy in being paid for their services.

And handsomely paid they were. The Crusaders plundered Constantinople comprehensively, and Venice gained huge wealth from the conquest and considerably enhanced its trading position in the eastern Mediterranean, providing the basis for its virtually unchecked expansion until the late 15th century. Even today, the eastern wall of the great council chamber in the Doge's Palace in Venice shows the story of the Fourth Crusade in a series of 16th-century paintings, since later Venetians were never in doubt about the origins of their city's success.

From a religious point of view, Constantinople was best known for its unmatched collection of relics. Villehardouin said there were as many relics in Constantinople as in all the rest of the world, and most of these were seized by the Crusaders. Christ's Crown of Thorns eventually made its way to Paris after being sold to Louis IX in 1239 (Louis built the Sainte Chapelle, perhaps the most beautiful medieval church still in existence, to house it), and the treasury of St Mark's in Venice is stuffed with the relics seized on the Fourth Crusade.

Even more impressively, the Venetians took secular memorials of the Roman Empire, most notably the four horses that stood for centuries above the entrance to St Mark's (they have been replaced by replicas, but the original horses still inspire awe in the museum). Other items such as the four porphyry Tetrarchs on the corner of St Mark's next to the entrance of the Doge's palace and the classical columns said to be from Acre are dotted around the basilica. JG Links, author of arguably the best travel book written about Venice, *Venice for Pleasure*, put it perfectly when he said that the Venetians treated St Mark's as their mantelpiece where they put the souvenirs of their conquests around the Mediterranean.

It had been agreed before the attack that the choice of Emperor should be between Baldwin Count of Flanders and Boniface Marquis of Montferrat, and Baldwin now became the first Latin Emperor of Constantinople.[27] Contemporaries were in no doubt that the Fourth Crusade had been worthwhile and celebrated the scale of the victory. The troubadour Raimbaut de Vaqueiras wrote:

… Never did Alexander or Charlemagne or King Louis lead such a glorious expedition, nor could the valiant lord Aimeri or Roland with his warriors win by might, in such noble fashion, such a powerful empire as we have won, whereby our Faith is in the ascendant; for we have created emperors and dukes and kings, and have manned strongholds near the Turks and Arabs and opened up the roads and ports from Brindisi to St George's Straits [the Bosphorus].

By us will Damascus be assaulted, and Jerusalem conquered, and the kingdom of Syria liberated for the Turks find this in their prophecies.[28]

The emphasis is on Constantinople as a stepping stone for retaking the Holy Land, not an end in its own right, which the Crusaders do genuinely seem to have believed.

However, the new empire did not flourish, and within a year the Emperor Baldwin had been captured by the Bulgarians and died in prison, and Boniface of Montferrat was killed in battle in 1207. The Latin settlers did reach an equilibrium with the other powers in the region, resulting in (roughly) a Latin Emperor controlling only Constantinople, the Duke of Athens controlling northern Greece and the Prince of Achaea controlling southern Greece. The Latins had only taken Constantinople and the Peloponnese, and the Greeks crowned their own Emperor based in Nicaea who controlled lands along the coast of Asia Minor, and a Greek despot of Epiros controlled northwestern Greece and Macedonia. Finally, the Venetians held key Greek ports such as Negroponte, Modon and Corfu and would extend their hold over various ports and islands over the course of the next two centuries.

These new Crusader States in Greece and the Aegean proved something of a distraction and an embarrassment. As with the original Crusader States, they were desperately short of manpower and needed new Crusaders to replenish their numbers. Papal attempts to interest the largest source of Crusaders, France, by calling the Greek territories 'New France' in 1224 failed to attract much support. In fact, the Latins called Greece 'Morea', derived from the word for 'mulberry', said to be because of the shape of the Peloponnese. The new territories quickly devolved into petty principalities squabbling with each other and their neighbours, and there we will leave them for fifty years until they were drawn into the Angevin orbit.

The Battle of Bouvines, Magna Carta and the Fall of King John

While the new Emperor and other Latin rulers were trying to establish themselves in Greece, King John was trying to come to terms with the loss of his own empire. Perhaps owing to the ease with which Philip had conquered Normandy and Anjou, and the wave of disloyalty that had guaranteed this, John initially most feared that Philip would invade England. He began what we can first properly call an English 'navy', organizing the Cinque Ports and his own ships into the first coherent fleet, supervised by a dedicated official, William of Wrotham. When the invasion didn't materialize – and of course Philip had absolutely no feudal right to attack John in England, though in ten years a French invasion would become a reality – John simply shifted his preparations into his own invasion to retake Poitou, again demonstrating that he had by no means accepted the loss of his continental possessions.

The consequences of this policy were even harsher financial exactions on his kingdom and a further increase in centralization that began to seem like tyranny. John was forced to limit his activity to England and Ireland, which made him the first king since 1066 to be so confined. Though Gascony still belonged to him, the lack of contiguity made it a much less significant factor in English politics than Normandy had ever been. This creates the false impression that John was more active in administration than his predecessors, because the better organized English records survive in greater number and we have a higher percentage of material remaining for his reign. Yet there can be no doubt that John's administration had to be more focused on England. Had he succeeded all might have been forgiven, but his military failure – the fact that his rapacity resulted in no gain – tipped the kingdom into rebellion.

Because if John had not given up, the situation among the barons was markedly different. Years of continuous warfare had taken a toll and the barons were fed up. When John gathered the feudal host at Portsmouth in May 1205 to invade Poitou, an acrimonious council of barons ultimately refused to go, and the expedition was cancelled (although a small force under John's bastard son and brother did go to Poitou to conduct desultory operations).[29] As we have seen, all medieval kings, though perhaps especially the Angevins, had realized that the old feudal host based on individual knights serving for a set number of days with limits on where they would travel was hopelessly outmoded in a new era of international warfare. John began formalizing a system whereby out of every ten knights who owed service, nine would commute their obligation into money to support the tenth who would serve for as long as and wherever the king needed him. These were the first tentative steps towards standing professional armies.

In 1206 John was able to launch a successful expedition across the Channel, securing Gascony and invading Anjou and ultimately taking Angers. This symbolic retaking of the Angevin homeland should have been significant, but Philip Augustus sent a force towards Anjou and John was unable to maintain his position, largely due to the fact that his Poitevin subjects were reluctant to take the field against Philip Augustus, who was their ultimate overlord and given recent events in Normandy and Anjou might well become their actual master quite soon. Although John was unable to maintain his position in Anjou, 1206 stabilized the situation considerably after the disasters of 1204 and 1205. This confirmed to John that regaining his empire was a possibility and he began preparing for an attack on a scale that had not been seen since Richard's force for the Third Crusade, and it is this that defined his legacy.[30]

From the beginning John planned a pincer movement on Philip that would involve an English invasion of Poitou and a simultaneous northern invasion from an allied Flemish and German force. John patiently built a series of alliances with the count of Flanders and the count of Boulogne, amongst others, in the Low Countries, but the key to the plan was John's relationship with his nephew Otto of Brunswick, a contender to be Holy Roman Emperor. This compares well with – and can be seen as a direct extension of – the coalition Richard constructed to immobilize Philip, and reminds us that John was not without diplomatic skill, at least with people who did not live under his rule.

As an aside, Otto of Brunswick was also known as Otto of Welf, and the Hohenstaufen line of Emperors such as Frederick Barbarossa, Henry of Swabia and later Frederick II were from southwestern Germany and had an important centre at the castle of Waiblingen. As Giovanni Villani documents in his Florentine chronicle of the 14th century, the enormously destructive conflict between the papacy and the Hohenstaufen in Italy that ripped the peninsula apart for the next 600 years began with the struggle between these two factions, and they became known as 'Guelfs' (Welf) and 'Ghibellines' (Waiblingen).[31]

As with most political parties the two factions quickly evolved and became identified with many other issues in each community, but this is their origin. Throughout the 13th and into the 14th century the Guelfs and Ghibellines endlessly fought within Italian cities, and for our purposes the most important point is that the Guelfs were generally aligned with the papacy and the later Angevin kingdom of Sicily and Naples, whereas the Ghibellines supported the imperial party, particularly the Hohenstaufen.

It had taken more than seven years for John to prepare his forces, and even then their mood was precarious as the barons were no more reconciled to long service abroad than they had been in 1205. Philip Augustus then made a bold decision: he decided the time was finally right for his invasion of England, and he marched into Flanders to seize appropriate seaports. This galvanized John's Flemish allies to fight against the French, and John's meticulous preparations for his own navy demonstrated their value. In 1213 John and his allies sent a fleet of 500 ships that caught the French ships unawares at Damme (the port for Bruges) and destroyed virtually the entire French fleet. This was the first in a series of critical English naval victories in the Middle Ages that would also shape the course of the Hundred Years War. Philip's invasion of England was stillborn and John now had the initiative for his own invasion.

As was frequently to become the case with grand military plans launched by Angevins (notably Charles of Anjou), John's strategy was hindered by a Crusade. This was the Albigensian Crusade against the heretics of southern France, particularly those in the lands of the count of Toulouse. Raymond VI of Toulouse was actually an Angevin kinsman, because he had married John's sister. John supported Raymond and had undertaken to send military support to him in 1213, but as we know John faced difficulties raising troops to fight his own battles, never mind those of an in-law who was the target of a Crusade. Raymond and his ally the king of Aragon were defeated by the Crusaders at the battle of Muret in 1213, and so in turn were unable to provide any support to John, which might have tipped the balance in his favour in 1214.[32]

John landed at La Rochelle in 1214 to launch the reconquest. Proof that this was part of a larger strategy for reconstituting the Angevin Empire came when John immediately went south on a tour of Aquitaine that allowed him to demonstrate his authority to potentially wavering vassals and judge the degree of support available to him. This public display of power was meant to impress Philip but also to draw him southward and leave him exposed to the attack from the north being prepared by Otto of Brunswick. John then threatened Philip's southern border by capturing Nantes in a victory resounding enough to drive William des Roches from Angers, and John occupied the Angevin capital again in June 1214. John's strategy proved sound and Philip had advanced southward to meet him, but realising the danger from Flanders he returned north and left his son Louis to meet John. John had superiority in numbers and was desperate to fight at the castle of La Roche aux Moines, but once again the chroniclers report that John's Poitevin vassals were unwilling to fight the son and heir of their liege lord, and John was forced to retreat. In the summer of 1214 this left him sitting impotently in La Rochelle trying to construct a more reliable army for a final showdown with Philip.

Of course that showdown did occur, but John was not involved. Philip's correct assessment of the situation allowed him time to return to Flanders to meet Otto's invading force at the bridge of Bouvines, and on Sunday 27 July Philip won an overwhelming victory that secured his augmented kingdom and broke John's power for good. It made Philip a French national hero, and despite all the previous reports of timidity and the stain on Philip's reputation for leaving the Third Crusade early, it also made him a more successful military commander than Richard the Lionheart.[33]

We know the consequences of Philip's victory for John. The English barons had been restive since the loss of Normandy and Anjou in 1204 and defied John on several occasions since. Philip marched south after Bouvines and John agreed a truce with him in September, returning to England in October. The barons were now openly in revolt. This was not only the result of John's military defeats but also a direct result of the Angevin Empire. England's position as a literal island of stability in the turbulent Angevin Empire made it by default the source of funding for royal projects, and by 1214 the situation was intolerable, most immediately because of John's repeated failures, but ultimately also because of the behaviour of Henry II and Richard.

Indeed, one of the rallying cries of the rebel barons was a return to the 'good old law' of the time of Henry I. Although there would certainly have been an element of nostalgia in harking back to a time before any of the current barons had been alive, there was definitely a sense that Henry II had instituted new policies, new laws and a new direction for the monarchy. There was also a solid basis to this nostalgia, because the huge increase in the availability of written documents in the 12th century gave barons access to collections of the laws of Edward the Confessor and Henry I and the coronation charter of Henry I, which had now been translated into French, the language of the nobility.[34]

Despite attempts by John to send the dispute for arbitration to the pope, which was probably just a delaying tactic, the barons renounced their fealty to John on 5 May

1215 and appointed Robert fitz Walter their leader.[35] Although John had been preparing for the revolt and his castles were well defended, the rebels managed to seize London, which instantly gave them a notable success and a kind of legitimacy. Within a month it was clear to John that he had to sue for peace, and the accommodation he reached with the barons was sealed by Magna Carta, issued between 19 and 24 June 1215. Copies were made to be circulated around the kingdom, of which four survive.

On the one hand Magna Carta has been seen as the foundation of English democracy, guaranteeing equal treatment for all under the law and government only by consent of the governed, but on the other it is a solidly feudal document that also has many specific provisions that applied only to John. This is not a contradiction, since by the very act of limiting the monarch's authority in specified ways Magna Carta achieved a broad and abstract definition of limited government, even if its actual provisions were quite narrow and specific. One that is often noted is the specific call for John's 'foreign' counsellors to be removed. These 'foreigners' were mainly Poitevins, and it is telling that these inhabitants of the former Angevin Empire could be seen as aliens.[36]

When John died little more than a year after the issuance of Magna Carta, the document might have become an irrelevance. However, the circumstances of John's death with the kingdom both embroiled in a civil war and having been invaded by the French meant that Magna Carta became a rallying point for the English barons, and was reissued in the name of the nine-year-old Henry III as a way of proving that the provisions of Magna Carta were more than a specific attack on John and did seek to be the 'law of the land'. The charter's definitive reissue in 1225 enshrined it as the governing contract between the king and his people, and this was what gave Magna Carta its lasting importance, and established it as the fundamental document that laid the foundation for English democracy.[37]

John's final year of life was disastrous even by his standards. In August 1215 John received papal sanction to repudiate Magna Carta, as it had been imposed on him under duress, and the civil war began again. The barons still held London, but otherwise John was in a strong position since he possessed the most important castles, and he was supported by great feudal lords such as William Marshal and Ranulf Earl of Chester who had significant fighting forces. In opposition, the barons could portray themselves as fighting to defend Magna Carta and the rights of the governed against a tyrant. This moral advantage was somewhat diminished by the fact that the rebel barons also invited Philip Augustus's son Louis to invade England to support the rebellion.

Innocent III took a dim view of this interference and excommunicated Louis, but the French invasion, so long feared but never materialising, finally became a reality. In May 1216 Louis landed in England. John had been preparing his response for some time, but in one of the very few English naval failures of any period, his ships were wrecked in a storm and couldn't stop the French departing Calais. Although John had an army in Kent awaiting Louis, he chose to retreat to Winchester. The French followed and took the city.

The rebels failed to capitalize on this early success. Although Alexander II, the king of Scotland, now invaded from the north and personally joined the French at their siege of Dover castle, where Alexander did homage to Louis, he was not able to bring his full army south because of John's energetic activity around the midlands and especially his attempts to relieve the siege of Lincoln castle, which blocked the Scots from joining the French. John had certainly not given up, and by October 1216 the situation was at a stalemate with the French holding the southeast, rebel barons holding the north and London, and John controlling the rest of the country. Neither side seemed capable of defeating the other, much as in the civil war between Matilda and Stephen, and John's presence at Lincoln kept his foes divided.[38]

When John was on his way back to Lincoln after being received in the town of Lynn, one of the most iconic moments of his reign occurred: his baggage train was caught in the high tide in the Wash and entirely lost, including his money and jewels. This was more a humiliation than a substantive blow, but it highlights the desperation and bad fortune that marked John's last days. Roger of Wendover's *Flores Historiarum* ('Flowers of History'), written around 1230, describes the lost loot as 'treasures, precious vessels, and all the other things which he cherished with special care'. Ralph of Coggeshall's *Chronicon Anglicanum* describes it as 'his chapel with its relics … and diverse household effects'. Another source describes the king's 'princely carriage and furniture'.[39] It was also noted at Henry III's coronation that some of the royal regalia had been lost in this disaster, though the crown of Edward the Confessor had been kept safe at Westminster Abbey. Records of the time show that the king was moving round the countryside at quite a rate – sometimes as much as thirty-seven miles a day – which suggests that he was not accompanied by a large baggage train, since that would have been extremely sluggish. Nevertheless, some people still believe John's treasure lies beneath the mud and continue the search for it. One thing is certain: the 'King John Cup' in the museum in King's Lynn dates to c1340 and didn't belong to John, though it is one of the best examples of 14th-century enamelling techniques.

It was not clear how long the civil war would drag on, but fate intervened. John had been ill for some months, and on 19 October 1216 he died at the Bishop of Lincoln's castle of Newark. Hostile chroniclers were delighted to note the last days of such a bad king, with parts of his kingdom held by rebels or invaders and his continental empire mostly lost. John's son and heir was only nine years old, and a minority was always disruptive.

Yet it was precisely Henry III's youth that saved the kingdom. If the problem was simply that John was a tyrant, well, he was gone. Rebels were now rebelling against a child who had never done them harm, and they were assisting French invaders. All the royalists needed was a strong leader to make this point and lead the fightback, and it was at this moment that William Marshal stepped forward for the crowning achievement of his long career.

Despite their differences, John had appointed William as the first of his lay executors; William's biography elaborates this by having John say dramatically on his deathbed: 'Sirs, for God's sake beg the Marshal to forgive me, and because I am surer of his loyalty than that of any one else, I beg you to entrust to him the guardianship of my son, for the land will never be held by anyone except with his help.'[40] Although William had preserved his obligations to Philip Augustus for the land he held in Normandy, there had never really been any question of his loyalty to the English throne, despite John's insinuations to the contrary, and his leadership was critical to the English recovery.

William seized the moral high ground by reissuing Magna Carta and proving that the rebel barons had no real cause for dissatisfaction, and he was supported in this by the papal legate, nullifying the fears raised by Innocent III's repudiation of the charter. Innocent himself had also died in 1216, helping to clear the way for compromise. In addition to winning the battle for hearts and minds, Henry III's supporters had tangible success in the summer of 1217. The French had taken East Anglia and moved north against Lincoln, but they were comprehensively defeated by royal forces. Next, England's navy defeated a French fleet near Dover, cutting off Louis's support and potential reinforcements.

This marked the end of the French invasion; Louis was forced to agree a treaty and withdraw, and the rebel barons made peace. William Marshal, having saved the kingdom (according to his biographer), prepared to die in 1219 surrounded by his family, and he called on the papal legate to protect Henry III. His work done, William took the vows of a knight Templar on his deathbed, and was buried in the Temple Church in London, where his effigy, although damaged in the Blitz, can still be seen.

Emperor Frederick II: Wonder of the World

The Angevin Empire had collapsed and the Byzantine Empire had been seized by Latin invaders, so now we must turn to the Holy Roman Empire. The story revolves around perhaps the most fascinating character of the Middle Ages, the Emperor Frederick II. Frederick defies superlatives. Even in his lifetime he was called *stupor mundi*, the wonder of the world. His position as heir to Hohenstaufen power in Germany and the kingdom of Sicily would always have made him a pivotal figure in European history, and his actions as Crusader and Crusaded against, restorer of Jerusalem and enemy of popes, make him more interesting still, but his personality – irreverent, brilliant, multilingual, intellectually curious – exercises a fascination that endures across more than seven centuries. Who but Frederick could simultaneously have been called the Messiah, the Anti-Christ and the eternal Emperor who will return to save Germany? How many medieval figures (who aren't Angevins) leave even one memorable saying, much less a joke? Frederick reputedly said, 'Of the three great holy men of the three great religions – Moses, Jesus and Mohammed – only one of them got what he deserved.' This is still mildly shocking in our secular times, but how would this have been received in the 13th century? Dante duly consigned Frederick to the sixth circle of hell with the other heretics.[41]

Frederick inherited the throne of Sicily as an infant, was declared of age in 1208 when he was fourteen, and became Emperor in 1218. In return for the support of Pope Honorius III in becoming Emperor, he had promised to surrender Sicily to his own infant son and immediately go on Crusade. We have seen that the Fourth Crusade attracted serious criticism and was characterized as a perversion of the Crusading ideal, but it was the Crusades involving Frederick II that marked the real low point in Crusading history.

At the Fourth Lateran Council, the twelfth great council of the church and the most important of the Middle Ages, Pope Innocent III had called for yet another new Crusade, again to be directed against Egypt. Innocent died in 1216 before the Crusade was launched, although preaching was well under way and many people had taken the cross.[42] The Fifth Crusade, which led to a failed attack on the Egyptian city of Damietta, was enough of a threat to frighten the Ayubbid sultan of Egypt into offering terms.[43] One of these was the return of Jerusalem to the Crusaders in exchange for leaving Egypt unmolested.

The Crusaders were aware that from a military point of view this would be a mistake since, as had been known since Richard the Lionheart's time, Jerusalem could not be held without controlling a substantial hinterland around it. It is interesting that the Crusaders never considered accepting this offer, and again raises the question of what a Crusade was *for*. Was it to return Jerusalem to Christian rule? Yes, but apparently only by military means, and the Fourth and Fifth Crusades had shown that the means of securing Jerusalem might involve an attack on somewhere else entirely. The Albigensian Crusade and Fourth Crusade showed that maybe the principal aim of the Crusades was fighting against Christianity's enemies whoever they were, not just Muslims. We are now a step closer to the modern sense of a Crusade as an uncompromising attack against something that is believed to be wrong, no matter what or where. Yet these are abstract considerations. The Crusades also had the specific goal of supporting the Crusader States in Outremer, and it was this practical, strategic thinking that made a deal impossible. Securing free passage for Christian pilgrims to Jerusalem would do nothing to help Acre and Antioch.

Needless to say Frederick failed to surrender Sicily after becoming Emperor, and like many kings before him, including Henry II of England, he showed no haste in preparing for his promised Crusade. His lack of participation in the Fifth Crusade contributed to its failure, since the Crusade had no leader on the spot who could make binding decisions that would be respected by the king of Jerusalem, the pope and all the other figures with an interest in the region. This all changed when Frederick himself became the king of Jerusalem, though in a quite convoluted fashion.

The legal situation in Outremer remained as it was at the time of Fulk of Anjou and

Melisende, in which women could inherit the throne, although a queen's consort was also recognized as king. The current king was John of Brienne, the penniless younger son of a family in Champagne, who had become king through marrying the reigning queen. Outremer's barons were scrupulous in recognizing where the true claim to the throne lay, and as John's wife was dead he was now only regent for their daughter Yolanda (also known as Isabelle), who was fourteen and thus ready for marriage. Following the usual pattern, John of Brienne went to Europe looking for an appropriate husband for her. The Master of the Teutonic Knights seems to have been the instigator of the scheme to marry her to Frederick, and with the pope's support John agreed to the union. This infuriated Philip Augustus, since as we have seen the French king traditionally arranged matches for the rulers of Jerusalem, but it was too late. John of Brienne must have been forgiven, as he was at Philip Augustus's deathbed on 14 July 1223 and received a large donation to support the states of Outremer.[44]

Frederick II married Yolanda in November 1225, but things went wrong almost immediately. Although John had agreed to the marriage on condition that he would retain the regency until his death (and he was in his 70s at this point, so the condition would not have seemed unreasonable, although in fact he lived for another twelve years), Frederick immediately repudiated the agreement and proclaimed himself king, additionally seizing the money Philip Augustus had given John to support the kingdom. Frederick now had a much greater stake in promoting an expedition to the Holy Land. John of Brienne showed a penchant for becoming involved in lost causes, as after losing the kingship of Jerusalem he moved to the doomed Latin Empire of Constantinople and became Emperor for the last eleven years of his life. His daughter was not so lucky. Frederick treated Yolanda callously, allegedly seducing her cousin immediately after their wedding and then sending Yolanda to become part of his harem in Palermo. In 1228 she provided Frederick with a son, Conrad, who was now heir to Jerusalem, but she died six days after his birth when she was still only sixteen. Just as with John of Brienne, to the punctilious barons of Outremer this now meant Frederick was regent for Conrad, rather than king in his own right.[45]

Pope Honorius III had been Frederick's tutor and always retained a fundamental stock of goodwill for his former pupil, but Honorius died in 1227. His successor Gregory IX had no such patience, and threatened Frederick with excommunication if he did not proceed with the planned Crusade immediately. He initially met with no resistance from Frederick, who viewed a Crusade to the Holy Land as nothing more than an expedition to make good his claim to the kingdom of Jerusalem.

Of course Jerusalem itself had been under Muslim control since 1187, but there was still a 'kingdom of Jerusalem' that consisted of the rump of the old Crusader States centred on Acre. Why would Frederick want this insignificant and imperilled kingdom? Rampant acquisitiveness has been the hallmark of most of the rulers we've encountered, but what was Frederick hoping to gain? He was in his prime by 1228, and as Holy Roman Emperor and King of Sicily he may have felt that his position as the most powerful figure in Europe would be enhanced by the glamour of leading a successful Crusade.

What is clear is that Frederick took a completely pragmatic view of the Crusade, and believed that its goal was recapturing Jerusalem by whatever means. When he arrived in the Holy Land he found his Muslim adversaries perfectly amenable to negotiation, and without any bloodshed he negotiated the return of Jerusalem to Christian rule, on condition that Muslims were still free to come and go in the city. To us, this may seem a sensible approach to resolve over a century of religious warfare, but it horrified Frederick's contemporaries, and the pope promptly excommunicated him.

Frederick's relationship with the papacy never recovered, and by 1247, this Crusader and King of Jerusalem was being described by the pope as 'the limb of the Devil, the servant of Satan, the miserable precursor of Antichrist' and had been deposed.[46] We can see that the root of the conflict between Frederick and the papacy was Frederick's dominion over northern Italy as Emperor and southern Italy as king of Sicily, which was a direct threat to the pope's authority, but the ideology of the Crusades poisoned things further. This bitter conflict between Emperor and pope had numerous long-lasting consequences, but for us what is most important is that the papacy would consider the extermination of Frederick II and his descendants as a Crusade, unleashing decades of warfare and leaving the imperial throne vacant for more than sixty years. The Holy Roman Empire never fully recovered, losing its power in Italy but becoming a fairly successful Central European state.

It was this conflict that drew Sicily into the Angevin orbit, but first we must consider how the Angevin lands were absorbed by the Capetians and how this launched the career of Charles of Anjou.

CHAPTER 7 – CHARLES OF ANJOU: LORD OF THE GREATEST PART OF THE WORLD

W<small>E HAVE SEEN THE</small> debates over whether the 'Angevin Empire' of Henry II, Richard I and John deserves this appellation, and we know that creating an empire was never their intention, but in the 13th century there was an Angevin who consciously set out to create an empire. Although Charles of Anjou nearly succeeded, the ultimate failure of his attempt to establish a Mediterranean empire provoked a full-blown Mediterranean war that effectively ended the Crusading movement and nearly destroyed the papacy. Despite this, Charles did create an Angevin state in Naples that lasted until 1435 and shaped Mediterranean politics throughout the period. In doing so he participated in (or caused) the most important events of the later 13th century: the extinction of the Hohenstaufen Emperors; two Crusades against Muslim states and countless others against fellow Christians; and finally the Sicilian Vespers, the repercussions of which echoed for centuries. Moreover, although his career was one of constant strife and his government was characterized by legendary rapaciousness, he was the brother of Louis IX of France, later Saint Louis, one of the great figures of the Middle Ages and a crucial supporter of Charles's schemes.

Firstly, who is Charles of Anjou and how is he an Angevin? Charles was the youngest son of Louis VIII and Blanche of Castile, so he was the grandson of Philip Augustus, but also the great-grandson of Henry II and Eleanor of Aquitaine. That might qualify him for inclusion in this book by descent, but of course there is a much more important factor, indicated by his being named Charles 'of Anjou'.

Philip Augustus, after his great victory of Bouvines, faced the problem of absorbing the Angevin domains into the French kingdom. This process was ongoing when he died in 1223 and his son Louis VIII became king. Louis VIII's brief reign (1223–1226) at first seems almost a footnote in medieval French history, but it had an enormous impact on France's future. Louis himself was a notable warrior, not only invading England with some initial success, but also capturing La Rochelle and significantly stabilizing Capetian control of Poitou. The Capetians faced a situation analogous to that of Henry II and had the problem of administering their extensive territories, particularly those taken from the Angevins and annexed through the Albigensian Crusades, which might be expected to resent French rule.

Because he was blessed with an abundance of sons, Louis decided to divide some of the new lands between them, and set this plan out clearly in his will. This was similar to the strategy Henry II had used, with the attendant difficulties we have seen, but Louis's formal creation of 'apanages' for the younger French princes was more successful and became the standard for the French royal family. The heir to the throne, the future Louis IX, would be crowned in his father's lifetime, and like Young King Henry he was not included in the partition. The Capetians tended to be better at involving their heirs in ruling France and didn't face rebellions like Henry II, though this may be because they usually died young enough that their heirs didn't face such a long period outside power as had Young Henry and Richard the Lionheart.

Of Louis's younger sons, Robert would take the county of Artois, his mother's dowry; Jean would take Maine and Anjou; and Alphonse would receive Poitou. Assigning these apanages also raised the princes to the same status as the five great feudatories of France – the Dukes of Burgundy, Aquitaine and Brittany and the Counts of Flanders and Champagne – and as all of these were independent of the king, the creation of three new and presumably loyal peers would balance their influence.[1] Strikingly, the duchy of Normandy, which had always been the most powerful of the states that were technically vassals of the French king, remained in the king's possession until the 14th century when it was finally considered safe to give to a royal son.

However, French possession of the former Angevin Empire was by no means secure. When Philip Augustus died in 1223, there were murmurings in England that Normandy should be reclaimed from its 'illegal' French occupation and an English embassy to Paris formally demanded that the duchy be returned, but Louis VIII publicly asserted his right to keep Normandy.[2] Louis went further, and in 1224 invaded Poitou, which was still a debatable land between English-controlled Gascony and newly French Anjou.

Poitou might have been expected to remain subject to England, since before his death King John had engaged his daughter Joan to Hugh of Lusignan, son of Hugh 'le Brun' who had previously been engaged to John's wife Isabelle of Angoulême. Isabelle spectacularly overthrew these plans when she returned to Angoulême, broke her daughter's engagement and married Hugh herself in 1220.[3] She showed no more loyalty to her son Henry III, as she and Hugh allied with Louis VIII and helped him secure Poitou, then attacked Gascony in 1225. This attack failed because Louis VIII was again distracted by the ongoing Albigensian Crusade and went on to die at Avignon in 1226, seemingly leaving Poitou ripe for an English fightback. However, Louis's widow Blanche of Castile became regent for the young Louis IX, and showed herself more than equal to the task of managing the kingdom, and secured treaties with England and with Hugh and Isabelle to stabilize the region.

Blanche engaged her son Jean to the Count of Brittany's daughter in 1227, and gave control of Angers and Le Mans to the count until the marriage occurred. However, in 1229 the count defected to Henry III and raised the spectre of an Angevin reconquest of their homeland. We must remember the precariousness of Capetian control in this period. The king of France was a minor and Henry III was very interested in taking back the lands lost by his father; Henry might have restored the Angevin Empire when he launched an invasion in 1230 in conjunction with the Bretons. Although Henry's fleet landed safely and he held court at Nantes, Isabelle and Hugh's solid adherence to France kept the rest of Poitou from joining Henry, and he returned to England having accomplished nothing.[4] Henry would soon discover that the only thing worse than having his mother oppose him was having her on his side.

After being abandoned by Henry III, the count of Brittany was swiftly defeated by Louis IX, who regained control of Anjou and Maine by 1234. Louis's brother Jean had died in 1232, so Anjou and Maine passed into the royal domain. Louis gave Le Mans as a wedding present to his wife in 1234 and it seemed that the counties would be absorbed into the kingdom, putting an end to 'Angevin' rulers. Louis was active in the region, most notably rebuilding the castle of Angers to produce what is largely the building that we see today.[5]

Now that his brothers were old enough, Louis IX honoured his father's wishes and granted them their apanages. Robert duly acquired Artois in 1237 and Alphonse was granted Poitou in 1241, but this formal investiture of Alphonse with Poitou provoked an uprising by Isabelle and Hugh of Lusignan. Henry III supported his mother and step-father by launching an invasion of the Saintonge, and his alliances with the count of Toulouse and kings of Aragon and Castile might have made this a real threat to France. Instead, the revolt was a pitiful affair. Henry had no support for the project from England, and his Gascon and Lusignan allies did nothing. Worse, Isabelle seems to have instigated the revolt without proper consultation, since Hugh quickly rejoined Louis IX and led the French armies against the count of Toulouse. Isabelle was disgraced and retired to Fontevraud, where she died in 1246 and is commemorated by a serene effigy at odds with her turbulent life.[6] Henry had to slink back across the Channel, and this ignominious failure disposed him towards a final peace with Louis IX in 1259, in which he recognized Capetian possession of Normandy, Anjou and Poitou. With Louis's support, Alphonse's management of Poitou would have no further difficulties.

Where does Charles of Anjou figure in this? Charles was born either in 1226 or perhaps posthumously in 1227, and was the only son to survive to adulthood who was born after Louis VIII took the throne. In the arcane hierarchy of royalty, being born to a reigning king rather than an heir apparent brought extra status, and Matthew Paris claimed that Charles 'was inclined to give himself airs as one "born in the purple"'[7] (a nice dramatic irony, since this title – *porphyrogenitus* – originated in the Byzantine Empire, which Charles would later plan to conquer). However, Charles was the youngest son and Louis had stated clearly that only the elder sons would receive apanages and his younger sons should go into the church.

Charles doesn't appear in the records until 1237 when he was at Robert of Artois's court, but by then it must have been clear that he would not be going into the church. With Jean dead, there were now only three princes remaining to support Louis IX:

Robert, Alphonse and Charles. Louis VIII's will had made plans to allocate three apanages, and Louis IX may have been thinking of making Charles Count of Anjou throughout the late 1230s and early 1240s. The brothers were very different in temperament, as neatly encapsulated by the chronicler Thomas of Tuscany: 'two brothers Louis and Alphonse were mild and peaceful, while the other two, Robert and Charles were men who were energetic, vigorous in body, strong in arms and very warlike'.[8]

However, in 1246 everything changed, when Charles made his mark on the European stage by marrying Beatrice of Provence and becoming Count of Provence. Provence had never been part of France, being rather a part of the Holy Roman Empire, though the Emperors hadn't controlled it for centuries and it had been held by a branch of the ruling family of Aragon (and this passing of Provence from Aragonese control was not forgotten – after Charles lost Sicily to the Aragonese in 1282, their own 'loss' of Provence would be mentioned in subsequent negotiations). The previous count, Ramon-Berengar, died in 1245 leaving four daughters, who famously all became queens. Three sisters had already married well: Margaret married Louis IX, Eleanor married Henry III and Sanchia married Henry's brother Richard of Cornwall, the future king of the Romans. For this reason, Ramon-Berengar had decided to leave his entire inheritance, which included the counties of Provence and Forcalquier, to the youngest daughter, Beatrice. Since Beatrice's elder sisters were the queens of France and England and wife to an English prince with extraordinary wealth, and they had already received handsome dowries, one might have thought they would be content to see Beatrice inherit Provence and Forcalquier. If so, one would be foolish – as we have seen many times, most medieval rulers fought for every inch of land to which they felt entitled, and the more they had the more rapacious they became. Beatrice's sisters were furious to be denied their inheritance, and were supported by their mother, who clung to the county of Forcalquier despite having no legal claim to it.[9]

These family rifts would play out in the future, and in 1245 the main question was who would marry the fourteen-year old Beatrice and become Count of Provence. Multiple rivals of more and less importance came forward, including Raymond VII of Toulouse and Conrad the son of Emperor Frederick II. In the aftermath of the Albigensian Crusade, France had a significant stake in the south, but the recent skirmishes in Poitou and Gascony had involved Henry III's allies the count of Provence and the kings of Aragon and Castile, who showed themselves to be an increasing threat. Provence could not be allowed to pass to the Emperor, a Spanish prince or southern baron, so Louis IX and Blanche of Castile proposed Charles of Anjou as Beatrice's husband, and they trumped their rivals by obtaining papal support.

In 1245 Pope Innocent IV was at the Council of Lyon seeking support for the deposition of Frederick II, and he particularly wanted Louis IX's backing. Papal consent for the Provençal marriage was thus the price for Louis's support, and Innocent was willing to pay it. The agreement was concluded quickly, and Beatrice and Charles married in January 1246 in Aix.[10]

Dante famously believed that all Italy's problems could be traced to this marriage, since it launched the French on their Italian adventures and created 'that sick weed... that overshadows every Christian land, so that it's rare to strip good fruit from it'. Dante portrays Hugh Capet as a penitent soul in Purgatory lamenting the horror he unleashed on Europe, which all began with Charles of Anjou:

> Until that splendid dowry of Provence deprived my blood of any sense of shame, they didn't do much good – nor much great harm. There, there began, with violence and with lies, their course of plunderings.[11]

Given the prolonged warfare between Philip Augustus and the English kings, and Louis VIII's participation in the Albigensian Crusade that annexed much of the south to France, it is hardly fair to say that Capetian 'plundering' started with Charles, but Dante's viewpoint was firmly fixed on Italy. It certainly is fair to say that Charles of Anjou may have been more easily enticed into Italy because he was count of Provence, and French involvement in the peninsula would last for another three centuries.

Despite Charles becoming Count of Provence, in the same year Louis gave him the deceased Jean's apanage of Anjou and Maine and knighted him. Louis was noted for being scrupulously fair, so perhaps he had already promised Anjou and Maine to Charles and honoured the arrangement. Louis seemed perfectly comfortable increasing Charles's territories to this extent, and in fact he also facilitated Alphonse's annexation of the Limousin and acquisition of the county of Toulouse by marriage. Having his brother in Toulouse from 1249 considerably aided Charles in his struggles in Provence, and he and Alphonse each also inherited one third of Avignon.[12]

As Count of Anjou and Maine, Charles 'of Anjou' now had the name that he would retain for the rest of his life, the Angevin name he would give to dynasties in Naples, Hungary and Poland. Yet he was also Count of Provence, which would remain an Angevin possession until the 15th century. It might be more appropriate for Charles to be called 'Charles of Provence', given that it was his first title, and he certainly retained a deep affection for Provence for the rest of his life, devoting much more time to it than he did to Anjou. Furthermore, the 'Angevin' kings of Naples would retain Provence long after Anjou was ceded to their Valois cousins in France. Why did the name 'Angevin' stick to Charles and his descendants?

The reason is, as previously mentioned, that Provence wasn't actually part of France, though today it may seem the very epitome of *la France profonde* and the most stereotypically French of provinces. Provence wound its way through the Angevins of Naples and back to the Dukes of Anjou, only becoming part of 'France' in the late 15th century. Charles was a French prince to his core – in fact, he would be criticized for how French he remained, years after he had become King of Sicily – and he was known by one of the great titles of France, like Anjou, not a foreign title such as Count of Provence. Also, Charles became Count of Provence in right of his wife Beatrice, and although he happily used her title, he must have preferred the title that belonged to him personally. Charles was always known as Count of Anjou before becoming King of Sicily, and his French identity was critical to him, most notably in his coat of arms, the Capetian gold fleurs-de-lys on a blue background differentiated with a red 'label' across the top. The heraldic practice of 'differencing' arms of various members of the family was introduced to Italy by Charles of Anjou, spreading French heraldic customs with his conquests.[13] This Angevin device can be seen on some of the most striking artworks to survive from the 14th and 15th centuries, and appears again and again in the coats of arms of various European dynasties.[14]

Perhaps because he was the youngest son who never expected to inherit anything, Charles seemed obsessed with acquiring as much territory as possible. What is so extraordinary about Charles is the energy and ambition he showed from the moment he stopped being the landless youngest son of a deceased king in 1246 until his death in 1285. Like his great-grandfather Henry II, he simply never stopped.

Charles built his empire step by logical step and progressed very naturally from one project to the next, never stopping long before undertaking a new challenge. He was probably still a teenager, and certainly no more than twenty, when he became Count of Provence and Count of Anjou in 1246, and he immediately implemented the methods of government he would later use in Sicily. He sent French administrators to Provence to curb local liberties and restore comital rights that had been usurped, and created a central administration and treasury to maximize his revenues from the county. These important activities were curtailed, however, when Louis IX launched his Crusade in 1248 and Charles accompanied him. It would not be the last time Charles's plans were seriously disrupted by his brother's Crusading zeal, and the troubadours in Provence were loud in their condemnation of him for neglecting his duties in Provence to embark on a futile endeavour.[15]

Louis IX's Crusade Against Egypt

Louis's first Crusade was notable for a number of reasons. He created the new port of Aigues-Mortes, which still exists in its medieval splendour, to launch the Crusade, since ports such as Nice and Marseilles technically belonged to the Empire, even if they were now ruled by Charles of Anjou. As has been stated so many times, Crusades were as much financial and logistical enterprises as religious, and achieving political or economic goals was not incompatible with Crusading. Charles of Anjou had already brought Provence from the orbit of Aragon to France, and by founding Aigues-Mortes Louis now blocked coastal access to Montpellier, a possession of the king of Aragon and the second greatest city in the south after Toulouse.[16]

The fleet that set off from Aigues-Mortes arrived in Egypt uneventfully, and we have a detailed account by Louis's close companion Jean de Joinville that gives us many striking anecdotes about Louis and Charles of Anjou. Despite later criticism, it was an opportune moment to attack Egypt. The earlier Damietta Crusade had shown the logic of striking at Egypt, though it also demonstrated the difficulties in attacking a well-organized state rather than individual castles or cities. However, the political situation in the Holy Land was about to shift dramatically, with the collapse of the successor dynasties to Saladin and the rise of an extraordinary new power, the Mamluk sultanate in Cairo.

The Crusade was initially successful. When the ships arrived, Louis leapt from his galley like Richard the Lionheart and waded through the surf to establish a beachhead, and the Crusaders went on to drive back the Egyptian army and take the city of Damietta. They secured this as a strong base, and since the sultan was ill and in fact would soon die, there was little coordinated resistance as the Crusaders audaciously marched up the Nile towards Cairo with every hope of success.

Yet this quickly turned to disaster. When the Crusaders reached the city of Mansourah, due to the fatal recklessness of Robert of Artois (although Charles himself was also described as attacking recklessly and being 'mad with rage'), the ill-disciplined attack became bogged down and the Crusaders, including Robert, were slaughtered in the narrow streets as the Egyptians hurled burning logs onto their heads. The attack on the Crusaders was organized by the young 'Mamluk', or slave soldier, Baibars, who would one day become sultan of Egypt himself and drive the Christians from the Holy Land for good. The Crusaders lingered for some time at Mansourah in an attempt to regain momentum, but illness devastated the army, and by the time Louis decided to retreat it was too late. He nearly achieved an amazing result anyway, since as the Crusaders began their retreat the chaotic government in Cairo offered to give Louis the city of Jerusalem if he would withdraw from Egypt. This reaffirms the political situation that we saw previously when Frederick II took Jerusalem without a fight: as the Crusaders themselves realized, Egypt was the most important state in the region, and the Egyptians would be perfectly willing to surrender Jerusalem – symbolically important but expendable in political and military terms – in exchange for peace.

Louis suggested that Charles of Anjou or Alphonse of Poitiers remain as a hostage to guarantee the treaty, but the sultan refused the offer, saying only Louis himself would be an adequate hostage. Unfortunately for the Crusaders, disease decimated the army and their situation deteriorated so dramatically during the negotiations that any deal became irrelevant. The entire army was captured and many were killed. Damietta was still under the control of Louis's queen, Margaret of Provence, who arranged a treaty whereby Louis and the army would be released in exchange for Damietta and a large ransom. After incredible hardship, the king was released and sailed to the Holy Land, where he remained for some years in an attempt to bolster the situation in the Crusader States.

Joinville gives horrific descriptions of the suffering the French endured in Egypt, the disease that ravaged them and the constant fear after their capture that they would be killed. Yet this pales into insignificance beside the experience of the Queen of France, who gave birth in Damietta while all this was going on. She too was in constant terror and Joinville reports that she had an elderly knight stay in her room to protect her, and she instructed him to kill her if the Egyptians should take the city. Her new son was named Jean, but Joinville says he was known as 'Tristram', after the unfortunate Arthurian hero, because the circumstances of his birth were so horrific. When the Queen heard that the Pisans, Genoese and other merchants were about to abandon the Crusade, she called them in and dramatically appealed to them, saying that if they wouldn't stay for her sake, they should at least have pity on the infant before them.[17]

As the defeated Crusaders sailed to the Holy Land, Joinville notes one of the most striking episodes about Charles. Louis was naturally upset by the failure of the Crusade and the death of his brother Robert. Louis plaintively said that if Robert were alive he would have come to see Louis, and not avoided him as Alphonse of Poitiers was doing. Louis then complained that Charles of Anjou was also avoiding him, and asked where he was. On being told that Charles was below deck gambling, 'Weak as he was through illness, his Majesty tottered towards the players. He snatched up dice and boards, flung the whole lot into the sea, and scolded his brother very soundly for taking to gambling so soon.'[18]

The Charles we see on the Crusade seems to be a completely different person from the future King of Sicily, who is universally described as cold, aloof, unapproachable, methodical and calculating. Brave to the point of rashness, unable to control his temper, lacking in seriousness to the extent that he played dice whilst sailing away from the utter defeat of a Crusade – who was this? It suggests that Charles, who was only twenty-two when he went on the Crusade, changed his entire personality under the pressure of imposing his authority on Provence, then on conquering Sicily and beginning the never-ending cycle of acquisition and warfare that would mark the rest of his life. This gives considerable definition to the somewhat flat impression we have of Charles later in his life. If Joinville is correct – and we have no reason to doubt him, since he spent years on Crusade with Charles and clearly had a great deal of contact with him – and Charles was a rash and undisciplined young man, what an effort of will it must have taken to produce such iron control later in life. His ill temper could sometimes still come out in the harsh reprimands he gave to officials who failed him, but his entire later life was spent in an effort of repression and control that never slipped. Charles can already be seen as a tragic figure because of the Sicilian Vespers and the catastrophes that attended his final years, but on a psychological level this denial of everything he was seems even sadder.

Once in the Holy Land, Louis held a council of all the barons including his brothers and Joinville, because Blanche of Castile had written to request his urgent return, saying that there was no truce with England and the entire realm was in peril. All the barons except Joinville advised Louis to return to France, though the barons of Outremer pointed out that the Crusader States would be in desperate straits if he departed. Joinville says that he alone of the French barons counselled Louis to remain, and Louis did decide to stay. The king's brothers did not: 'The king, it is said, ordered his brothers to return to France; but whether this was at their own request or by his wish I cannot really say.'[19] Charles and Alphonse risked suffering the same stigma that adhered to Philip Augustus after leaving the Third Crusade, but in fact this was not the case: both had behaved too well during the actual fighting, and there certainly was a perception that the Crusade was over. They also went on Louis's next Crusade, though this did far more damage to Charles's reputation than leaving Acre. Although Alphonse and Charles both entreated Joinville to take care of the king, he was unusually caustic in his description of Charles's departure: 'When the Comte d'Anjou saw that the time had come when he must embark, he showed such grief that everyone was amazed. All the same he went back to France.'[20]

On his return, Charles turned to Provence and resumed the methodical organization of the county that would be the hallmark of his rule, both here and later in Italy. Provence was the laboratory of state building where Charles implemented all the procedures that would later be enacted on a larger scale in Sicily and southern Italy. There were striking similarities between the situation Charles found in Provence and what he would later encounter in Sicily. Charles brought a French mindset and a team of French lawyers, and he was determined to enforce all his rights. The Capetians had been through the crucible of competing against and finally conquering the Angevin Empire, and Henry II's empire and the Anglo-Norman kingdom it sprang from were the most bureaucratically advanced states in Europe. The Capetians had been forced to maximize the revenue from their limited possessions, and they had learned from Henry II to insist on every right due to them. Provence, technically part of the Empire and previously ruled independently by a cadet branch of a Spanish kingdom, was not a place accustomed to obsessive adherence to the law. The counts of Provence had ruled with a light hand, and the cities of Arles, Avignon and Marseilles did not even form part of the county and were used to managing their own affairs.

When Charles went on Louis IX's first Crusade, the three cities formed a defensive alliance against him and the rest of Provence revolted as well. Charles was gone for three years, but when he returned he quickly took control of Provence and defeated the cities one by one. He treated the rebels leniently, and when he was again called away for several years on Louis's business (this time because Blanche of Castile had died and he became co-regent of France), the situation remained relatively stable. His mother-in-law actually proved the chief cause of trouble, as she refused to surrender Forcalquier and incited others to resist Charles. Charles resolved the situation through diplomacy, helped markedly by the fact that the Dowager Countess was Louis IX's mother-in-law as well, so Louis felt an obligation to help resolve the dispute. The Dowager finally did relinquish Forcalquier, but only on the condition that she received a stipend for the rest of her life, and this was paid by Louis.[21]

Although he could not have known his future and how he would become engaged in ongoing wars for control of the entire eastern Mediterranean as King of Sicily and

Jerusalem, Charles's determination to use all his resources to the full would prove useful in the future. Maritime cities such as Genoa, Venice, Pisa and to an extent Marseilles dominated Mediterranean trade, but Charles established an arsenal and shipyard in Nice in 1251 to support his ambitions along the Ligurian coast. This foundation flourished and the Niçois navy participated in Charles's later campaigns. Provence, more than Anjou, became the keystone to Charles's lands, providing a steady income (particularly from a monopoly on salt exports on the Rhone) and a constant supply of administrators throughout his reign. Provence remained a solid source of support for the Angevins long after Charles's death, a mutually beneficial relationship that allowed the Provençals access to lucrative opportunities in southern Italy and the other Angevin domains.

Throughout the later 1250s Charles built on his territory in Provence with methodical legality, obtaining the submission of local lords such as the Count of Ventimiglia and the Bishop of Gap, and extending his authority along the coast and into Piedmont. Once into what we now think of as Italy, Charles patiently formed alliances with one town after another, building a path from Provence into northern Italy by way of Cuneo, Alba and Asti. In the absence of a Holy Roman Emperor, Charles was becoming an Italian potentate to be reckoned with a decade before he became an Italian king.[22]

The Sicilian Question

I have referred several times to the fact that Charles became King of Sicily, but how did this happen? As we know, the beginning of the 13th century was chaotic, with the war between the Angevins of England and the Capetians reaching its climax with the collapse of the Angevin Empire, John's excommunication, the barons' revolt and a French invasion of England; the conquest of the Byzantine Empire by the Fourth Crusade; the vicious Albigensian Crusade in southern France; and a power vacuum in the kingdom of Sicily and the Holy Roman Empire. This situation stabilized in the 1220s and with a period of peace between France and England and the succession of Frederick II both to the throne of Sicily and as Holy Roman Emperor, it might have been expected that the situation in Europe would stabilize. Precisely the opposite happened. The devastating conflict that erupted between Frederick II and the papacy shattered Italy and left the Holy Roman Empire in disarray for decades, and as the popes actively sought to overthrow first Frederick, then his son Manfred, gradually France, the Empire and the Spanish kingdoms were drawn into centuries of conflict. The key event in this was the French invasion of southern Italy, an invasion led by Charles of Anjou at the invitation of the papacy.

Charles's invasion was at the instigation of a series of fairly short-lived popes, who nevertheless worked together towards a policy that would end with the near destruction of the papacy itself. This policy of 'papal monarchy' had been developing since the late 11th century, and culminated in the early 13th century. Pope Innocent III was a lawyer trained at Bologna, the leading law school in Europe, and he falls neatly into the line of monarchs such as Henry II and Charles of Anjou who had a meticulously legalistic sense of their rights and authority and were doggedly determined to uphold them. Although Innocent did not claim universal political authority, he did claim absolute power within the Church and by extension the power to enforce any of the Church's rights within the secular sphere. The centralization of political power in France and England played its part in this process, since the newly powerful administrations in Westminster and Paris were able to promulgate papal authority as effectively as their own. Secular leaders had borrowed sophisticated papal administrative techniques to consolidate their power, but now the papacy reaped the benefits, since if a king were willing to disseminate papal commands within his kingdom – the 'Saladin Tithe' or the Inquisition – he could do so much more easily and successfully. The papacy had also learned from its secular counterparts in Anglo-Norman England and Capetian France, and consciously reorganized the papal administration on monarchical lines.[23]

More importantly, Innocent was applying these methods as a secular ruler himself. He had formally established the papal states in central Italy, a block of land that had been left to the papacy by the Countess Matilda of Tuscany in 1115, possession of which was finally recognized by Otto of Brunswick, the Angevin ally and contender for the imperial crown, in 1209.[24] This confirmation of the pope as a secular lord with a territory that must be ruled, taxed and defended forever compromised the authority of the papacy and had a poisonous legacy. Innocent, although not claiming abstract authority over all the lands of Christendom, was also the feudal overlord of the kingdoms of Sicily, Aragon and Hungary – and later England – which had been given into his care, and he was as scrupulous in retaining the papacy's rights in this regard as in every other. Innocent's theoretical framework of papal power was hugely influential with his successors, and their attempts to make these theories a reality led directly to the Italian wars of the Angevins in the 13th century.[25]

The popes of the 13th century were now unapologetically concerned with Italian politics. Frederick II died in 1250, but he had been married three times and left two legitimate sons as well as several bastards. Frederick's heir was Conrad, son of Yolanda of Brienne, who took his father's lands in Germany and also had a legal right to Sicily and Jerusalem. Conrad was elected king of the Romans (the title of the Emperor-elect before his coronation) and moved into Italy to take up the rest of his inheritance, though the turbulent politics in the peninsula made this difficult. Frederick II's will had appointed his bastard son Manfred as Prince of Taranto, which gave him control of southern Italy and a mandate to secure the territory for Conrad. Sicily was held peaceably by another Hohenstaufen retainer, but Manfred sent his own agents and attempted to take over the island as well. These signs of Manfred's ambition were just as disturbing to Conrad as to the pope, and Conrad swiftly intervened. He reappointed his own loyal deputy in Sicily and reduced Manfred's formal power on the mainland, though he still had to fight for another year to assert his authority over centres such as Naples.

Securing the Empire and Sicily would make Conrad just as much a threat to the papacy as his father had been, and the pope was determined to thwart him. In August 1252, the pope sent a legate with a letter to Henry III's brother Richard of Cornwall offering him the kingdom of Sicily. The legate was also provided with a copy of the letter addressed to Charles of Anjou if Richard refused. Richard famously did refuse, saying it was 'like being offered the moon on condition that one unhooked it from the sky'.[26] The legate then went to Paris to make the same offer to Charles, who was interested, but naturally had to consult his brother Louis IX.

Louis was in the Holy Land when news of the pope's offer was relayed to him, but he was disturbed by the pope's scheming and saw no reason that Conrad, Frederick's legitimate son and the rightful heir to Sicily and Jerusalem, should be deposed. Blanche of Castile as regent of France was also horrified by this attempt to launch a holy war against a papal enemy for purely political purposes and wanted no part of it. Whatever his personal feelings may have been, Charles couldn't accept the offer in opposition to his mother and brother. Although he deliberated until October 1253, ultimately he refused as well.[27]

Pope Innocent IV now put forward William of Holland as an opposition candidate for Emperor and William was elected as a rival king of the Romans, but this was of limited value. The pope's attempts to divide Conrad's inheritance and stir up trouble against him failed, and relations between Conrad and the pope deteriorated swiftly. By January 1254 Conrad was accusing the pope of usurpation and heresy, and the pope responded by excommunicating Conrad in February.[28] Once again the pope attempted to launch a Crusade against the Hohenstaufen, and once again it met with either vague repugnance or outright hostility, with Blanche of Castile threatening to confiscate the lands of anyone in France who participated.

Despite the initial failure of the pope's scheme to find a replacement for Conrad, the pope had succeeded in piquing the interest of one person, and that was Henry III. Although Richard of Cornwall had refused to become involved (having even greater ambitions of his own), Henry III thought that obtaining a throne for his younger son Edmund (still a child) would be a worthy project. The pope was desperate to replace Conrad, and events moved quickly. By May 1254 the pope had written letters referring to Edmund as 'King of Sicily' that were to be delivered by his legate, who would arrange the final terms of the agreement.

Now there was another stunning reversal in the negotiations: Conrad fell ill and died in May 1254, even as the letter offering his throne to Edmund was en route, and the legate refrained from delivering the letter until the situation could be assessed. Conrad had married Elizabeth of Bavaria, and she had remained in the Empire with their two-year-old son Conradin, who was now the legitimate heir to Sicily and Jerusalem. The titles of Emperor and King of the Romans were elective, and would not automatically pass to a minor, though as a Hohenstaufen Conradin could hope one day to succeed. This meant there was a vacancy at the head of the Empire, and now Richard

Francia
990–1031

- National boundary of France c. 1000
- French Royal Domain c. 1031
- Fiefs of the Crown
- Fiefs of the Duchy of Aquitaine
- Church lands
- Other territories owing nominal allegiances to the King
- ⚑ Archibishopric
- ⚑ Bishopric
- ✝ Abbey

English Channel

County of Flanders

Thérouanne

Arras

Co. of Ponthieu

Co. of Vermandois

Co. of Beauvais

Co. of Valois

Rouen

Bayeux

Lisieux

Coutances

Avranches

Dukedom of Normandy

Co. of Vexin

St Denis

Paris

Reims

Châlons

Chartres

County of Champagne

Dukedom of Brittany

Co. of Rennes

County of Maine

Co. of Orleans

Co. of Gatinais

Sens

Troyes

Langres

Co. of Auxerre

Co. of Nantes

Co. of Anjou

Co. of Blois

Tours

Touraine

Co. of Sancerre

Dijon

Besançon

Nantes

Bourges

Co. of Arcouin

Co. of Bourges

Co. of Nevers

Duchy of Burgundy

County of Poitou

Poitiers

Co. of Deols

Co. of Bourbon

Cluny

KINGDOM OF GERMANY

Duchy of Lorraine

County of le March

KINGDOM OF BURGUNDY

Bay of Biscay

Co. of Santonge

Angoulême

Limoges

County of Limousin

Clermont

Co. of Forez

Anse

Lyon

Vienne

Tarantaise

Co. of Perigord

County of Auvergne

Bordeaux

Duchy of Gascony

Co. of Rodez

Co. of Toulouse

Embrun

Auch

Toulouse

March of Gothia

Arles

Aix

Nice

Narbonne

Marseille

NAVARRE

Ribagorza

Mediterranean Sea

CALIPHATE OF CORDOVA

County of Barcelona

Barcelona

The Angevin Empire
1150–1214

Growth

Areas inherited by Henry II in 1150–54

Areas acquired by Henry II's marriage to Eleanor of Aquitaine in 1152

Areas acquired by conquest or diplomacy

Areas acknowledging Henry II as overlord

Areas claimed by Henry II

Collapse

French territory retained by John in 1214

Battle site

N

0   100 km

100 miles

EARLDOM OF ORKNEY

SCOTLAND
Perth
St Andrews
Edinburgh
Berwick

Warkworth
Harbottle
Newcastle
Wark
Galloway
Carlisle
Durham
Appleby
Brough
Richmond
Thirsk
Lancaster
York
Malzeard
Pontefract
Axholme
Stockport
Conisbrough
Peak
Lincoln
Chester
Duffield
Nottingham
Rhuddlan
Tutbury
Mountsorrel
Norwich
PRINCIPALITY OF WALES
Shrewsbury
Leicester
Bungay
Bridgnorth
ENGLAND
Huntingdon
Framlingham
Builth
Coventry
Warwick
Orford
Cardigan
Northampton
Colchester
St David's
Hereford
Oxford
Pembroke
Carmarthen
London
Bristol
Windsor
Rochester
Canterbury
Salisbury
Dover
Exeter
Winchester
Chichester
Boulogne
Southampton

Carrickfergus
Ulster
Armagh
Connacht
Meath
Clontarf
Athlone
Dublin
IRISH CHIEFDOMS
Leinster
Limerick
Cashel
Munster
Wexford
Waterford
Cork

SCOTLAND

North Sea

Irish Sea

Celtic Sea

ATLANTIC OCEAN

English Channel

HOLY ROMAN EMPIRE

Flanders
Tournai
Bouvines 1214
Brabant

Channel Islands
Barfleur
Bayeux
Caen
Argues
Eu
Drincourt
Amiens
Aumale
Vaudreuil
Rouen
Vermandois
Gournay
Gisors
Reims
Normandy
Evreux
Chateau Gaillard
Argentan
Alencon
Nonancourt
Paris
Champagne
Avranches
Pontorson
Verneuil
Dol
Fougeres
Belleme
Catinais
Troyes
Brittany
Maine
La Ferte-Bernard
Mayenne
Rennes
Le Mans
Sable
Orleans
Vannes
Anjou
Vendome
Nantes
Angers
Touraine
Blois
FRANCE
Ancenis
Tours
Ste Maure
Saumur
Loches
Bourges
Chinon
La Haye
Issoudun
Nivernais
Loudun
Preuilly
Poitou
Parthenay
Mirebeau
Burgundy
Vouvant
Poitier
Lusignan
Bourbonnais
La Rochelle
Niort
Le Marche
Marcillat
Clermont-Ferrand
Tailebourg
Limoges
Saintes
Angoueme
Limousin
Pons
Chateauneuf-sur-Charente
Auvergne
Perigueux
Le Puy
Perigord
Bordeaux
Aquitaine
Argenais
Cahors
Rodez
Agen
Nimes
Gascony
County of Toulouse
Armagnac
Auch
Toulouse
Bayonne
Narbonne
Bearn
Bigorre
BEARN

NAVARRE

Bay of Biscay

The Expansion of Hungary, 1370-1470

Hungary 1370

Hungarian Vassels with date of Hungarian Suzerainty

Hungarian provinces under occasional vassel rule

TEUTONIC ORDER

Stettin

Berlin

Poznan

Warsaw

POLAND
*in personal union
with Hungary
1370*

HOLY

Prague

ROMAN

Cracow

GALICH-
LODOMERIA

Lvov

LITHUANIA

Kiev

EMPIRE

Kassa

Galich

Vienna

Pozsony

AUSTRIA

Buda

Fehérvár

HUNGARY

Várad

Kolozsvar

GOLDEN
HORDE

Suceava

Bala

MOLDAVIA

STYRIA

Zagreb

Pecs

Temesvár

Brasso

VENETIAN
REPUBLIC

Belgrade

Ozora

Szöréby

WALLACHIA

Târgoviste

to Genoa

Zara

BOSNIA
1365

1358
Lazar

1365
Stratsimir

Bulgarian States

DOBRUJA

Black
Sea

PAPAL
STATES

Cattaro

SERBIAN

Sofia

BYZANTINE
EMPIRE

Manfredonia

STATES

LOCAL

Naples

Bari

Taranto

KINGDOM
OF
NAPLES

Salonica

OTTOMAN EMPIRE

Constantinople

RULERS

BYZANTINE
EMPIRE

MEGALOVACHIA

Aegean

SARUHAN

DUCHY
OF ATHENS

Sea

AYDIN

PRINCIPALITY OF
ACHAIA

France in 1477

Capitan houses
- Valois-Alençon
- Valois-Anjou
- Valois-Orléans
- Dunois (Orléans)
- Valois-Angoulême
- Bourbon
- Bourbon-Vendôme

Other houses
- Foix
- Armagnac
- Albret
- Other

House of Burgundy
- Burgundy
- Burgundy-Nevers

Royal domains

- English possessions
- Ecclesiastical states
- Free Imperial cities
- Other

L. : Lordship
V. : Viscount
C. : Count
M. : Marquisate
D. : Duchy
K. : Kingdom
B. : Bishopric
Arch. : Archbishopric

NORMANDY

Duchy of BRITTANY

Duchy of ALENÇON

C. of MAINE

Duchy of ANJOU

TOURAINE

C. of BLOIS

D. of ORLÉANS

Paris

CHAMPAGNE

VALOIS

Duchy of NEMOURS

BERRY

County of NEVERS

Duchy of BURGUNDY

County of BURGUNDY

Duchy of BOURBON

POITOU

AUNIS

SAINTONGE

C. of LA MARCHE

C. of ANGOULÊME

V. of LIMOGES

PÉRIGORD

V. of TURENNE

FOREZ

Duchy of AUVERGNE

VELAY

GÉVAUDAN

DAUPHINÉ

Duchy of SAVOY

GUYENNE

L. of ALBRET

C. of ARMAGNAC

County of RODEZ

LANGUEDOC

County of PROVENCE

Principality of ORANGE

County of VENAISSIN (Papal States)

Marquisate of SALUZZO

Kingdom of CASTILE

K. of NAVARRE

Kingdom of ARAGON

ANDORRA

ROUSSILLON

County of FLANDERS

County of ARTOIS

PICARDY

County of HAINAUT

Duchy of BRABANT

Duchy of LUXEMBOURG

Duchy of LORRAINE

Duchy of BAR

SWISS CONFEDERATION

The castle at Angers.

Fulk Nerra haunted by the ghosts of his victims.

Melisende's psalter.

Jerusalem, from King Rene's Book of Hours.

Chinon.

Fontevraud.

Richard the Lionheart's and Isabelle of Angouleme's effigies at Fontevraud.

Chateau Gaillard.

Charles of Anjou's effigy at St Denis.

Conradin's memorial
at Santa Maria del
Carmine.

Robert the Wise.

Castel Nuovo, Naples.

Petrarch's house, Arqua Petrarca.

Tomb of Jadwiga,
Wawel Cathedral.

Tomb of Ladislas,
San Giovanni Carbonara,
Naples.

King Rene's Book of Hours, office for the dead.

Motif from King Rene's chivalric romance.

of Cornwall, who had rejected the offer of invading Sicily as too ambitious, directed his considerable resources towards achieving this prize.[29]

Conrad's will had appointed agents to administer Sicily and southern Italy for Conradin, but in a bizarre twist Conrad also placed Conradin in the pope's care and begged Innocent IV to safeguard his rights. This gave the pope an opportunity to prove that, however much he may have disliked Conrad or believed him unfit to rule, he still supported rightful succession and the rule of law and would not persecute an innocent infant. Innocent declined this opportunity.

Although Conrad's will made it clear who should rule the kingdom of Sicily, Manfred remained on the scene, and he was an attractive figure to those who wanted to see a Hohenstaufen prince rule immediately without having to wait for Conradin to reach maturity. The pope, as feudal overlord, insisted that the kingdom be put under his own control, and Manfred submitted to him in return for recognition of his rights as Prince of Taranto. With the pope acknowledging Conradin's future claim on the kingdom and Manfred in agreement with the pope, the situation might potentially have remained stable.

Yet the pope was either being deceitful or he failed to communicate with his subordinates. The pope sent an army under his nephew to receive the submission of all the parties in southern Italy, but when this demand was made there was no reference to Conradin's rights, instantly arousing the suspicion of those loyal to the Hohenstaufen. Papal agents also occupied parts of southern Italy that rightfully belonged to Manfred. Manfred, either equally duplicitous or reacting very quickly to the pope's apparent betrayal, rushed to seize the kingdom's treasury held at Lucera. Lucera was a historical curiosity that caused considerable tension between the papacy and the Hohenstaufen, because it had been settled by Muslims deported from Sicily by Frederick II. Frederick's goal had been to cut the Muslim community off from contact with North Africa, but to retain their services as soldiers and weapon-makers. This policy was successful and the community at Lucera remained loyal to the Hohenstaufen, but this tolerance for Muslims in Italy disturbed the papacy. Manfred's quick action at Lucera allowed him to deprive the papal army of funds, and it dissolved, leaving Manfred virtually unchallenged in southern Italy.[30]

Innocent IV was at Naples when he heard of this complete defeat, and he swiftly reopened negotiations with Henry III. Once again he offered the eight-year-old Edmund the throne, though now with a caveat that Conradin's future rights must somehow also be respected. However, Innocent himself died in December 1254. His unrelenting hostility to the Hohenstaufen, which made him willing to scheme with foreign princes to overthrow legitimate rulers and excommunicate his political enemies, was not unprecedented, but critics of the papacy see his pontificate as a low point. He certainly set in motion a train of events that would change Italian history forever and launch the Angevins on their European adventures.

An absolutely vital component to bringing off the Sicilian conquest was lasting peace with France, and Henry III was determined to accomplish this. He negotiated with Louis IX to agree a permanent peace between the two kingdoms, resulting in the Treaty of Paris of 1259. This acknowledged the possession of Normandy, Anjou, Maine and Poitou by the French king and that Aquitaine belonged to the English king, but Henry definitively accepted that he was Louis's vassal for this territory. It is fitting that the unfinished business involving the collapse of the Angevin Empire was resolved as part of the Sicilian affair that would launch the next great Angevin dynasty and an attempt to form another empire. Proof that Henry III was sincere in this renunciation is that he had a new seal made in England discarding old Angevin titles, as the existing seal still said 'King of England, lord of Ireland, duke of Normandy and Aquitaine and count of Anjou', with an image of the king on his throne holding a sword. Henry's new seal said 'Henry, by the grace of God, king of England, lord of Ireland and duke of Aquitaine' and showed the king on a Gothic chair holding a sceptre. The old seal was destroyed at a ceremony in the king's chamber at Westminster on 18 October 1260, officially recognizing the end of the Angevin Empire.[31]

Despite this, the English barons insisted that the king could not commit the kingdom to a costly foreign war without the consent of a parliament, and Henry was forced to agree to hold a parliament at Oxford. This produced the 'Provisions of Oxford' that became the rallying point for the barons' war in the 1260s, forging another key link in the chain of English democracy. Although ultimately the barons gave grudging support to the Sicilian invasion, the new pope, Alexander IV, recognized that Henry III would never be in a strong enough position to carry off the invasion, and in December 1258 he issued a bull formally revoking Edmund's title as king and releasing Henry from his obligations. The pope had received about £40,000 from England, so he had not done badly.

As his enemies fell into disarray, Manfred's position was flourishing. After discomfiting the papal forces in 1254, Manfred had sent to Bavaria where Conradin was living with his mother's family, and obtained recognition as regent on behalf of the infant prince. Alexander IV had sent another mercenary army south to unseat Manfred and incited the Sicilians to declare themselves an independent republic under papal authority, but in an atmosphere of constant betrayal and uncertainty, Manfred blockaded and starved the papal army into submission, procured the deaths of his other rivals and offered himself as the saviour of the kingdom. Sicily preferred this to an uncertain future under papal control, and by 1257 Manfred controlled the entire kingdom of Sicily. When a rumour, perhaps started by Manfred, spread that Conradin had died, Manfred had himself crowned king on 10 August 1258 in the cathedral at Palermo.[32]

Within four years of Conrad's death, another Hohenstaufen king was in complete control of Sicily and southern Italy, and the papal position was deteriorating inexorably as Manfred built alliances with anti-papal interests in Rome, Tuscany and Lombardy. After traditionally pro-Hohenstaufen Siena decisively defeated traditionally pro-papal

Florence at the battle of Montaperti in 1260, Manfred was the greatest power in Italy, and in the pope's words, he had 'imitated his father's evil actions from his early years, and we have seen how much further he has gone in savagery'.[33] The pope was completely isolated in Rome with no army to help him, and as Manfred consolidated his hold in Italy, Alexander IV must have been thinking that Manfred might ultimately gain the Holy Roman Empire as well. This was not the only empire on Manfred's mind though, since the Latin Empire of Constantinople was in its death throes and the Emperor Baldwin II was touring Western Europe seeking assistance.

The End of the Latin Empire of Constantinople

There were several successor states of the Byzantine Empire after its conquest by the Fourth Crusade. On the Latin side, these were the nominal Latin Empire ruled by Baldwin II (essentially only two-thirds of the city of Constantinople, since the Venetians ruled one third of the city); the Duchy of Athens, an area in central Greece ruled by the La Roche family with a capital at Thebes; and the Principality of Achaea, consisting of the Peloponnese or 'Morea', ruled by Geoffrey of Villehardouin's successors. On the Greek side, there was a small but rich state centred on Trebizond on the Black Sea coast and ruled by a successor to the Comneni; the land ruled by the Despot of Epirus, a successor to the Angelus Emperors overthrown by the Fourth Crusade, which included the northwestern part of Greece between Albania and the Gulf of Corinth; and most importantly, the Empire of Nicaea, whose ruler called himself Emperor and had captured all the territory up to the outskirts of Constantinople and beyond into Thessalonica, and seemed on the verge of recapturing the capital itself.

Frederick II had supported the Emperor of Nicaea as an ally against the pope, but Manfred recognized that opposing the Nicaeans would make him the de facto champion of the Latins, and the pope might find it embarrassing to continue his vendetta against the potential saviour of the Latin Empire. Manfred married Helena, the daughter of the Despot Michael of Epirus, and received Corfu and several towns on the coast as her dowry. Michael had married his other daughter to the Prince of Achaea, thus all the pieces were in place for an Epirote-Latin alliance against Nicaea.[34]

The Emperor in Nicaea was now the highly skilled general Michael Palaeologus, who in 1259 sent a force against Epirus that defeated the Despot's army and seized some of his territory. The Despot Michael now called on his allies, and an impressive coalition formed consisting of the Despot's forces, a strong contingent of heavily armed horsemen from Manfred, a large force from Athens and Achaea led personally by William Villehardouin, and various other contingents provided by Latin and neighbouring rulers assembled in Epirus. They ranged themselves against the Nicaeans on the plain of Pelagonia, where they had the advantage of numbers. However, for reasons that are not clear – the most common story given was that the Achaeans insulted the beautiful wife of the Despot Michael's son – the Epirotes quarrelled with the Latins and withdrew overnight, leaving Manfred's troops and the Achaeans alone to face the Nicaeans the following morning. In the resulting chaos the Nicaeans attacked and completely defeated the Latin force, capturing William of Achaea and most of the Frankish lords on the battlefield.[35]

Baldwin II realized this complete Nicaean victory could spell his doom and appealed to Manfred and the pope for help, but Manfred was too busy tightening his grasp on Italy and the pope was too busy inciting opposition to Manfred for either to respond. Baldwin agreed a truce with Michael Paleologus to last until August 1261, though neither side was likely to consider it binding if it became inconvenient.

Then an astonishing event occurred. In July 1261 Michael Paleologus sent a small army to resolve some trouble on the border with Bulgaria, and instructed the soldiers to pass by Constantinople and make a show of force. When the army arrived before the city they met a Greek villager who told them that most of the city's garrison and the Venetian fleet were away trying to a capture an island in the Black Sea. He further offered to show them a secret underground passage into the city. On the night of 24 July a few men entered the city and opened the gates to the rest of the army, and by the morning of 25 July Constantinople had been taken. Although the Venetian fleet and garrison returned later in the day, they were driven off, and Baldwin II only just managed to row out to meet them to avoid capture. The Latin Empire was finished and the Byzantine Empire returned to Constantinople.

A courier rushed to tell Michael Palaeologus about the miraculous event, and Michael formally entered Constantinople on 4 August 1261, following the traditional imperial processional route through the city to Hagia Sophia. Although he was crowned a few days later at Hagia Sophia and the Byzantine Empire would survive for almost 200 more years, it was now only a phantom of what it had once been and the scars of the Fourth Crusade still lay on the city. A contemporary Greek source describes what Michael Palaeologus found when he arrived:

> Then indeed you might have seen that the Queen of Cities was a vast field of desolation, full of rubbish and heaps of stones: some buildings were destroyed and little remained of others gutted by the great fire. For the violence of the flames had often consumed its beauty and its most potent decoration since the time that it had first been menaced with the slavery of the Latins. They had taken so little care in imposing that subjugation that they destroyed it in every way, day and night. For it was as if the Latins despaired of the possibility that they could keep possession of it forever; God, I believe, in secret words told them what the future would be. … The first and special occupation of the emperor was therefore that he should at once cleanse it and restore order to the confusion that had prevailed by propping up the churches that had not completely collapsed and filling the empty houses with inhabitants.[36]

Michael also lost no time turning the screw on Frankish Greece, and offered to ransom William Villehardouin in exchange for the three key fortresses of the Peloponnese. Guy the Duke of Athens was the highest-ranking lord not in captivity, and he summoned a parliament to consider the offer. This was the famous 'Ladies' Parliament', so called because almost all the Frankish lords had been captured at Pelagonia and their wives ruled their lands. Although Guy questioned the wisdom of accepting the terms, the Princess of Achaea insisted that they be accepted and the other women agreed. The exchange was made and William and the other lords were released.[37]

Although Constantinople was lost to the Franks, Michael Paleologus was unable to capitalize on his success. An expedition against Epirus was defeated, and Duke Guy and Prince William were able to resist attacks on their territories. Although the Latin Empire of Constantinople was gone, the Frankish land of Morea also endured for another 200 years, and unsurprisingly would one day become Angevin.

The Angevin Invasion of Italy

Manfred, despite the defeat of the force he sent to Pelagonia, was not inconvenienced by the disasters in Greece. He was still firmly in control of Corfu and the important city of Durazzo (modern Durres, in Albania) on the Dalmatian coast. Further, he warmly welcomed the exiled Emperor Baldwin II to his court and pledged to help him regain his Empire. Manfred offered to send an expedition to recapture Constantinople that would then continue on to the Holy Land as a Crusade, if only the pope would agree to a truce with him, and he asked Baldwin to intercede with the pope on his behalf. This put the pope (now Urban IV, after Alexander IV's death) in an awkward position. The papacy must remain committed to the restoration of the Latin Empire and the reunion of the Latin and Greek churches, and more importantly, Urban had been the Patriarch of Jerusalem and he had only come to Europe to seek help for the increasingly beleaguered Crusader States when he was unexpectedly elected pope. Yet even with a new pope, the papacy's antipathy to Manfred was still too great for any attempt at reconciliation. After visiting the pope, Baldwin proceeded to Paris to seek Louis IX's help in reconciling the pope and Manfred, but Louis still viewed Manfred as a usurper and also refused.[38]

England, France, Italy, Germany, the Spanish kingdoms and Greece were now caught up in the struggle between Manfred and the papacy. Henry III's brother Richard of Cornwall and Alfonso X of Castile were vying to become Emperor, and Richard had been elected King of the Romans (Emperor-elect). Manfred had also concluded a marriage alliance with James of Aragon, thus ensuring that the ruling houses of most of Western Europe were now involved. This is what put the Angevins so firmly at the heart of Europe for 200 years, and this is why the Angevin story touches almost every aspect of European history.

In 1262, the pope again had to seek a saviour. Ten years after the first offer was made to Richard of Cornwall the papacy had gained a substantial sum of money from Henry III, but no material aid in deposing Manfred. The English barons had made it clear that England would provide no further assistance. The Empire was still highly unstable, and although it did have a ruler in the form of Richard of Cornwall, in truth he was a compromise candidate who never actually commanded any power in the Empire. The Spanish kingdoms might have been an option, but James of Aragon was allied to Manfred and Alfonso of Castile was still trying to claim the Empire despite the election of Richard of Cornwall. That left only France, which had become the traditional bastion of the church and would likely have been Urban's preferred choice anyway.

Urban sent a legate yet again to Paris to offer the throne of Sicily to a French prince. Louis IX had promised his support to Henry III for Edmund's candidacy, and he was also aware that Conradin was the legitimate heir to the kingdom. Yet he did not refuse outright. He declined the offer on behalf of himself and his heirs, but when it was suggested that the offer might be made once again to Charles of Anjou, Louis did not object.

Urban IV was on the verge of renewing the appeal to Charles, but paused when Baldwin II came to him again to beg for help restoring the Latin Empire, as well as bringing another letter from Manfred promising to assist Baldwin. Despite believing that Manfred was a usurper who should be deposed, Urban did take into account Baldwin's position, and he did carefully consider whether it might not be better to allow Manfred to stay in power if he was going to launch an assault on Constantinople to restore the Latin Empire. More importantly, Urban was fully aware of the threat to the Crusader States posed by the Mamluk dynasty who now ruled Egypt. They had defeated even the Mongols in 1260, and were the most organized Muslim state since the time of Saladin. Putting aside his animosity towards Manfred, and instead of continuing with the plan for an invasion of Sicily, Urban called for a new general Crusade to the Holy Land. He went further, summoning Manfred to appear before him by the end of November 1262, when presumably the two might be reconciled.[39]

Although Urban is a more attractive figure than Innocent IV or Alexander IV, because he did genuinely seem to have the interests of all of Christendom at heart, he too was caught up in the impossible political situation in Italy. Further, there were too many parties involved now to avoid misunderstandings, delays and miscommunications. For example, Louis IX was fervently in favour of a general Crusade and wrote to the pope to approve of the attempt to reconcile with Manfred, a vote of confidence that might have confirmed Urban in this course of action. Yet Louis's letter was delayed (Steven Runciman suggests it was a plot by Charles of Anjou!), so when Urban did begin negotiating with Manfred he still had too many misgivings, and ultimately relations between the two broke down again. Even while the discussions were in progress, Urban sent his legate to renew talks with Charles of Anjou. We can't be sure that Manfred was negotiating in good faith, but Urban definitely appears duplicitous.

By 1263, Baldwin was in Paris exhorting Louis IX to support the Crusade and end his opposition to Manfred, but the pope had already informed Louis that no reconciliation with Manfred was forthcoming, and that for the Crusade to succeed Manfred must be deposed. In May, Charles of Anjou was also in Paris and Louis officially approved his involvement in the papal scheme. Moreover, the pope had begun negotiating with Michael Paleologus for the unification of the Eastern and Western Churches without the restoration of the Latin Empire in Constantinople, cutting off at the roots any influence Baldwin may have had. The net was tightening around Manfred, and Baldwin became aware of the situation. In July, he wrote to alert Manfred of the pope's treachery and urged him to send an envoy to Paris to detach Louis from the scheme. Baldwin also cleverly suggested that Manfred send a separate message to Queen Margaret, as it was clear that she disliked Charles of Anjou and might be willing to use her influence to stop any scheme beneficial to Charles.

Baldwin's letter had catastrophic consequences for Manfred. The letter was intercepted by the Podesta of Rimini, who sent it to the pope. Urban saw at once how damaging it would be, and forwarded the letter to Louis. The idea that Baldwin, a deposed Emperor who was living off Louis in Paris, should be intriguing with Manfred behind his back outraged even the saintly Louis. He was even more annoyed by the suggestion that his wife's hatred for Charles of Anjou might be used to influence him. Louis now supported the Sicilian scheme fully and the pope finalised the agreement, which included steep tribute payments and various limitations on Charles's power, in a bull issued on 26 June 1263.[40]

Some near contemporaries like Giovanni Villani, the 14th-century Florentine chronicler, said the real reason Charles accepted the papal mission to conquer Sicily was because of his wife, who was jealous that her three sisters were queens and she was only a countess:

> She pledged all her jewels and invited all the bachelors-at-arms of France and of Provence to rally round her standard and to make her queen. And this was largely by reason of the contempt and disdain which a little while before had been shown to her by her three elder sisters, which were all queens, making her sit a degree lower than they, for which cause, with great grief, she had made complaint thereof to Charles, her husband, which answered her: 'Be at peace, for I will shortly make thee a greater queen than them', for which cause she sought after and obtained the best barons of France for her service, and those who did most in the emprise.[41]

This flies in the face of everything we know about Charles's character, and is a typical medieval slur against the avariciousness and flightiness of women, who were always accused of being a bad influence, going back to Adam and Eve. As we know, the pope's 'Sicilian Business' had been in progress for more than ten years, and Charles was under consideration from the beginning. As a Crusader who had distinguished himself militarily and a strong ruler who had shown administrative and diplomatic skill in taking over Provence, Charles was an obvious choice.

Once news of the agreement spread and it became clear that an invasion might actually take place, the pro-papal Guelf and pro-Hohenstaufen Ghibelline forces in each Italian city sprang into action. Manfred's adherents tried to have him appointed Senator of Rome, so in response the Guelfs offered the title to Charles. This explicitly violated Charles's agreement with the pope, which stated that he must not accept any other office in Italy, and Charles was quick to reply that he would not accept it without papal approval. However, the eruption of unrest in Italy was a real threat to the pope, and Charles pressed for a renegotiation of the agreement. Not only should he be allowed to hold the office of Senator, he wanted a reduction in the tribute owed to the pope, permission to accept offices and titles in Italy as long as he was willing to relinquish them on the pope's request, a provision that if he or his descendants became Emperor, Sicily should pass to the next heir in his line, and – critically – that the throne should pass to his female as well as male heirs.

The pope had little room for manoeuvre, since his position had deteriorated quickly in 1264. Manfred and his agents imposed Manfred's authority over Tuscany and the regions around Rome, encircling the pope and preparing the way for a full-scale invasion from Naples. Papal rhetoric reached its most hysterical pitch yet, with Urban IV saying that Manfred was 'plunging his savage hands into the bowels of the Church', and even more shockingly, using Muslim troops in his preparations for war:

> For behold the heathens have entered the inheritance of the Lord, they are polluting and profaning the churches and other sacred and pious places ... Behold the followers of the law of Mahomet daring to invade and shake the Church, the bride of Christ, and the Catholic Faith, in their very foundations ... Continually they attack the vicar of Christ, the successor to the prince of the apostles, the rector of the Faith, the father of all Christians, the pilot of Peter's bark.[42]

In the 'political' Crusades against Frederick II and Manfred (and others), the rhetoric of the 'normal' Crusades against the Holy Land was still used. Faced with this apocalyptic scenario, Urban agreed to all Charles's terms. An unpopular levy on the French clergy was also raised to support the invasion, and Urban even intervened with Queen Margaret, securing her consent that she wouldn't do anything to hinder Charles.

As was so often to happen with Charles on the verge of a great campaign, there was a sudden dramatic change: Urban IV died on 2 October 1264. This could have thrown the whole plan into disarray if a new pope failed to ratify the updated terms of the agreement, but Charles took bold action. He was already in Provence preparing his forces, and he undertook a course of action which seems to have been designed to impress his potential enemies with his resolution and ruthlessness. Although his position in Provence had been fairly secure for some time, the previous year he had imprisoned several nobles and rich merchants who had been involved in treasonable activities or otherwise opposed him. He suddenly had them publicly executed in Marseilles and confiscated their property. He then openly continued his preparations for the invasion, which would make it difficult for a new pope to stop the proceedings.

This was seen as a distinct possibility, since many cardinals had already expressed disquiet about the proposed overthrow of Manfred, and an evenly divided College of Cardinals could easily have chosen a new pope who would decide to call off the invasion. Manfred was aware of what was happening, and chose to withdraw his forces to avoid frightening the cardinals into supporting Charles. This turned out to be the wrong course of action, since after months of deliberation the College elected a French cardinal who had formerly been the chief adviser to Alphonse of Poitiers. The new pope, Clement IV, supported the agreement with Charles and swiftly approved his appointment as Senator of Rome, urging him to come to Italy as quickly as possible. The cardinals and pope were now residing at Perugia, as Rome was too dangerous for them.[43]

Charles's preparations were nearly complete. He had built a network of alliances throughout northern Italy and secured the neutrality of Genoa, a former ally of Manfred, so that his army could pass from Provence to Italy. As the situation in Rome was desperate, and Manfred could easily have launched an attack on the city, Charles took a few hundred men and sailed from Marseilles to Ostia. This was not without peril, since Manfred was allied to the naval power of Pisa, whose galleys were patrolling the sea. Villani reports that Charles's ships were scattered in a storm and he was driven into the Pisans' port, but when Manfred's vicar in Pisa attempted to capture Charles, the Pisans rose up against him and refused to open the city gates until he returned certain of their fortresses to them, and Charles had time to escape.

He arrived in Rome on 23 May 1265, one day before Manfred wrote a letter that attempted alternately to flatter and threaten the citizens of Rome to accept him as their Emperor without reference to the pope. Charles was welcomed by the citizens, and crassly moved into the papal palace at St John Lateran, but when the pope complained he then moved to the Senatorial palace at the Capitol.[44]

Manfred was initially pleased by this development, because Charles had only a small force and Manfred had been preparing an attack on Rome for some time. Nevertheless, Charles was formally invested as Senator on 21 June and King of Sicily on 28 June. Manfred's supporters in and around Rome began to defect to Charles as they sensed he might be the ultimate victor. Manfred marched into central Italy and threatened Rome, but Charles and his small force took up a strong position against him, and Manfred feared treachery from his local allies too much to risk a battle. Manfred then inexplicably gave up the campaign entirely and returned to his heartland of Apulia. Villani says Manfred believed that his Ghibelline supporters throughout Tuscany and Lombardy would protect the route into Italy, and Charles's army would not be able to force its way through the Alps.

Charles was now an established power in central Italy, with unwavering papal support and a hint of glamour from this early success against Manfred, but he still needed to raise enormous sums of money to prepare an army to drive Manfred out of Sicily. He now suffered a reverse where he least expected it: Louis IX refused to provide any more money from France to support the invasion, since he wanted to use all his resources on a Crusade to the Holy Land. Even Alphonse of Poitiers only provided a small sum, and the French clergy were resisting demands to pay the money they owed. The pope was already heavily indebted to bankers in Tuscany, but he and Charles raised additional huge loans, especially in Florence and Siena, using church property and plate as security. Florence was to become intimately involved in the Sicilian business, and one of the chief reasons for this was that the city had bet heavily on Charles of Anjou's success and would lose all the money given to the pope if Charles failed.

Charles gambled that he now had enough money to pay his troops for a sufficient time and ordered the army to set off. This was precisely the risk run by the previous papal forces sent against Manfred, and both times the papal armies had melted away from lack of pay. This time things were different: the army had a seasoned military commander who was not a hired soldier, but a prince personally committed to the success of the expedition, and who had involved many other nobles from France and Provence.

The army assembled at Lyons and set off across the Alps in early October 1265. Chroniclers reported that it consisted of 6,000 horse, 600 mounted bowmen and 20,000 infantry, and although these numbers must be exaggerated, it was clearly a substantial force. Now Charles's patient diplomacy of the previous ten years bore fruit, as the army could pick its way from ally to ally across northern Italy. Even some Ghibelline towns defected to Charles, and there were rumours of bribes to some of the governors to allow the French army through (for which Dante placed at least one of the leaders in hell to rue his behaviour). By January 1266 the army had arrived in Rome.[45]

Charles already bore the title King of Sicily, but on 6 January 1266 he and Beatrice of Provence were crowned in St Peter's in a ceremony presided over by five cardinals (Clement IV was still too fearful to leave Perugia). In all this time, Manfred had done little. Charles had moved extremely quickly and Villani says that Manfred was furious that his allies in the north had allowed Charles's army to cross the Alps, but his inactivity still seems incredible. Charles was the opposite: he immediately led the army from Rome on 20 January and soon reached the border of Manfred's kingdom.

Manfred finally responded to the news that the Angevin army was approaching, and marched his own army to the border to await them at Capua. Villani now reports a famous encounter. Manfred sent ambassadors to seek a truce with Charles, and Charles reportedly replied in French: 'Go and tell the Sultan of Nocera [Lucera] for me that today I will send him to hell or he will send me to paradise.'[46] This reply reminds us that, although the impact of religious sanctions may have been diminished by overuse, Manfred was excommunicated, and the war against him was a papally sanctioned Crusade. Moreover, Hohenstaufen patronage of the Muslim colony at Lucera allowed Charles and the pope to portray this Crusade as a war of Christians against Muslims, which was basically inaccurate, but contained a grain of truth that papal rhetoric could magnify.[47] The battle cries the two sides used during the battle are especially telling: Charles's forces cried 'Montjoie', the name of the hill from which the Crusaders first saw Jerusalem as well as Charlemagne's battle cry, whereas Manfred's troops used the much less compelling cry 'For Swabia'. Charles had positioned himself as the instrument of God in a holy war against evil, and whether he won or lost the battle he had no doubt that he was on the right side.

For the moment Charles seemed more likely to gain a spiritual reward than an earthly one. Manfred held the stronger position, and his nephew also had a force further north that was marching down to meet him. Charles was too quick for them, and outflanked Manfred by passing a string of Manfred's castles whose garrisons either did nothing or defected to Charles. Manfred moved his army to the city of Benevento, where Charles arrived on 25 February. The amazing feat of getting the army from Lyon to Italy in winter had come at a cost: the Angevin army had suffered in the cold and supplies were low, and Manfred's force was protected behind a river. Manfred's strategy would seem to have been simply to wait for his nephew to join him and then overwhelm the Angevins, who would only get weaker as time passed.

Yet this is not what Manfred did. The endless treachery of his garrisons may have made Manfred suspicious of his own army, or perhaps Charles's army seemed to be in such a bad state that Manfred thought it wouldn't put up much resistance. Villani says that Manfred decided to attack before the Angevin army had time to rest, though he says that this was a poor choice because the Angevins had no food or money to buy more, so they would have starved if he had left them. Either way, Manfred brought his army across the river and attacked on 26 February.

Both armies were divided into three groups with a reserve, but Manfred's army was more disparate, being composed of a contingent of German horsemen in newly developed plate armour, Muslim archers and light cavalry, northern Italian mercenaries and the army from his own kingdom. Manfred initially had the best of the battle, especially when the German cavalry's plate armour proved to be impregnable to the French swords. But then Villani reports that the French discovered a weakness: if they struck at the German horses, they could bring down the knights and then stab with their daggers through chinks in the armour. The Germans were beaten, and although Manfred brought up his reserve in a counterattack, various contingents began to flee or desert him.

Villani praises Manfred for choosing to 'die as a valiant lord, who would rather die in battle as king then flee with shame', and Manfred indeed plunged into the battle with a small force. He seems to have exchanged his coat with a lieutenant to avoid capture, which Villani spins into a story about Manfred's crest of a silver eagle prophetically falling off just as he entered the fray. There was great slaughter, and Manfred was killed.

Charles took the city of Benevento and captured many of Manfred's leading captains. Manfred himself was discovered on the battlefield three days later by a camp follower, who threw his body on an ass and rode to the French camp crying 'Who buys Manfred?' When the identity of the corpse was verified, many of the French felt that Manfred should be given a proper funeral, and Charles replied that he would have done so willingly, if only Manfred hadn't been excommunicated. Instead, Manfred was placed in a grave by the bridge of Benevento and each soldier laid a stone on it to build a cairn.[48]

Charles of Anjou, King of Sicily

Charles was now master of the kingdom, and rode into Naples with his queen on 7 March. He had met no resistance in taking over the rest of Manfred's possessions, and Sicily, the Muslim colony at Lucera and Manfred's navy all surrendered without further armed struggle. Charles also captured Manfred's wife and children. Manfred's wife and sons died in prison, though his daughter Beatrice was freed in 1284 and married the Marquis of Saluzzo. Manfred's daughter Constance was already married to King James of Aragon, which would have enormous implications for Charles in the future. Even Manfred's closest allies made their peace with Charles, and there were no immediate reprisals. The only blot on the conquest was that Charles's army had sacked Benevento, a papal city, which particularly irritated the pope. After months of marching through the Alps and down through Italy it is not surprising that the army felt entitled to take what they wanted from Benevento, but this action was a sour note in what had otherwise been a remarkably smooth exercise in regime change.

In fact, what is most striking about Charles's victory is how quickly the transition from Hohenstaufen to Angevin rule proceeded. Charles did not despoil the new kingdom to reward his supporters, and he was scrupulous in establishing procedures for his tax collectors to ensure they weren't abusive. He left many of Manfred's officials in place, and he quickly set up an effective administration.[49]

Perhaps this is where he went wrong. We have already seen the resistance Henry II met in England when he increased the efficiency of royal administration. 'Efficient administration', 'order', 'effective royal authority' – all these may sound like good things, but in a kingdom that had gone through a period of disruption and then Manfred's lackadaisical rule, the new regime must have seemed harsh, meddling and oppressive. Charles also had massive debts to Tuscan bankers and owed punitive tribute payments to the papacy, so however well supervised his tax collectors were, they were still making enormous demands on Charles's subjects, and ordinary people are never enthusiastic about the efficiency of tax collectors.

Charles was also a Capetian by birth, and adhered to the austere French model of kingship. This was in notable contrast to Manfred and Frederick II, though it is fair to say that most of our descriptions of Manfred are coloured by his tragic end, and he is described by Dante and others as practically perfect: blond, handsome, gentle of aspect, valorous, joyous and virtuous. The jolly youth who loved nothing more than to go hunting on his estates in Apulia is the perfect foil to the remote, militaristic, serious conqueror that Charles had become. Of course Manfred had also spent his time hunting instead of properly preparing to meet Charles's invasion, so there was a downside to this happy indolence.

Yet even Clement IV almost immediately began to complain, without any sense of irony, that Charles's methods of fundraising were too oppressive and he was hearing bad reports of him. Clement finally wrote to Charles that his subjects found him 'neither visible nor audible nor affable nor amiable'.[50] There may have been a degree of unreality in the expectations of the Sicilians and southern Italians of what a strong king would do. Frederick II had too many other obligations and ambitions to be an oppressive ruler – at least early in his reign – and before him there had been more than thirty years of unrest since the death of 'Good King William'. No one alive had any recollection of what this mythical 'good kingship' would look like.

Hindsight has shaped views of Charles, and since he ultimately faced a revolt over his oppressive taxes he was traditionally portrayed as grasping and unsympathetic. More recent studies, though, have considerably modified this image and shown his chivalric education as well. He wrote poems in Provençal and inventories of his library in Naples shows his interest in medicine and chivalric stories. Charles also had a reputation for loving tournaments, and Ptolemy of Lucca said that Louis IX was happy to see him go off to Italy in 1265 because he would stop disturbing the peace with them.[51] The strain of preparing the invasion of Italy certainly didn't curb his love for the sport: Andrew of Hungary reports that during the Italian campaign, Charles defied the warnings of his men and challenged a Neapolitan professional at a tournament. He entered the lists with him and was overthrown, breaking his ribs, causing the Neapolitan to rush from the field for fear of reprisals. Charles had to be led to his tent by his son, but declared that he would return to the combat as soon as he could get to his feet. Adam de la Halle said of him – in a description very similar to what was said about Henry II a century earlier – 'Under arms he had so good a figure, he was stronger and more compact than a bird in its feathers, and more assured on his horse than in the tower of a castle'.[52]

In 1266 Charles seemed to carry all before him. With Manfred's death the Ghibelline cause collapsed in northern Italy, and with the Empire still irrelevant, Charles moved in. The Ghibellines also fled Florence, and Charles was elected Podesta of Florence and Lucca. He made a ceremonial entry into Florence in May 1267, then conducted a five-month siege of the fortress of Poggibonsi to break the power of Siena and Pisa. He was now King of Sicily with a kingdom extending up through southern Italy nearly to Rome. He had stepped down as Senator of Rome and appointed his supporter Henry of Castile in his place, but he was the elected ruler of Florence and Lucca and his seneschal administered Piedmont and Lombardy. Aside from a few isolated cities (notably Venice and Genoa), by the end of 1267 Charles ruled most of Italy.[53]

Italy was only the start, as Charles now set in motion the wide-ranging military and diplomatic activity that gives credibility to the argument that he was trying to create nothing less than a Mediterranean Empire that would include Greece, Constantinople and the Holy Land. He sent troops to seize Corfu and the mainland fortresses that had been the dowry of Manfred's Queen Helena, who was the daughter of the Despot of Epirus, and established a foothold in Albania and Greece. When the disgraced Emperor Baldwin II returned to Italy – now that he had burnt his bridges with Louis IX – to meet the pope and beg for assistance to retrieve his throne, naturally he was referred to Charles. Clement was being slightly disingenuous, as he was also negotiating with Michael Paleologus in Constantinople for a reunion of the Latin and Greek churches without the restoration of the Latin Empire, but he seems to have had little hope of this proceeding and was happy to involve Charles in another potential invasion of the eastern Mediterranean.

Although Baldwin was reconciled with Charles, it was at a price: he formally confirmed Charles in possession of Helena's dowry; he ceded his nominal authority over the Principality of Achaea to Charles along with sovereignty over most of the islands in the Aegean (aside from those ruled by Venice and a few Baldwin was allowed to keep); he granted Charles one-third of any territory in the former Latin Empire he reconquered; and, most importantly, Baldwin's son and heir Philip was to marry Charles's daughter Beatrice, with the proviso that if Philip died without heirs the claim to the Latin Empire would pass to Charles. Charles in turn agreed to provide an army of 2,000 knights to serve for one year in the reconquest of Constantinople for Baldwin. Although this kind of provision was standard, especially in anything to do with the Crusades, and Manfred had promised the same, it is striking that Charles was now committed to conquering Constantinople, and if he succeeded there was a distinct possibility that the Latin Empire might pass to him.[54]

Charles also sent envoys to the Mongols, hoping they might prevent the Byzantines from allying with the Turks to resist him. Sadly we have no idea what message his envoys brought and how the Mongols replied, though they seem to have been cordial. The Mongols were not averse to seeking an alliance in the West to gain assistance against the Mamluks of Egypt, and Charles would have further dealings with them.[55]

In this great burst of diplomacy Charles made one final overture, the most important of all. Despite Charles's great victory over Manfred, one cloud above his success was the death of Beatrice of Provence in May 1267. If Beatrice had yearned to be a queen to match her three sisters, she had achieved her goal, but she held this status for only just over a year, and she never had the opportunity to join her sisters and enjoy their recognition of her new rank. Charles was besieging Poggibonsi when she died, but he found time to contact King Béla IV of Hungary and suggested marrying Béla's daughter Margaret. This was rejected because she had vowed to become a nun, and she was also rumoured to have disfigured herself to avoid marriage. Although Charles looked elsewhere for a wife for himself, he suggested that his heir Charles of Salerno and his daughter Isabella should marry Marie and Laszlo, the children of Béla's heir István. The double wedding was concluded, and although Charles could not have relied upon this outcome, the alliance would bring an Angevin dynasty to Hungary by the beginning of the 14th century.

Why was Charles interested in Hungary? There were two reasons. Hungary in this period was a vast kingdom that included Transylvania, Slovenia, Croatia and Dalmatia, and thus was Charles's neighbour across the Adriatic. Further, the Arpad dynasty of Hungary was the holiest in Europe with numerous saints in its ancestry, including three holy kings. Charles was already beginning to promote the sanctity of his family, the *beata stirps*, or 'holy lineage' that would come to characterize the – completely inter-twined – dynasties in France, Hungary and Naples. Louis IX was known in his own lifetime to be a saint, and Charles consciously sought to link the prominent religiosity of the Capetians with the saintly pedigree of the Arpads. Again, this would succeed beyond his wildest dreams since the Angevin ruling families of Naples and Hungary would themselves produce saints within the next century.[56]

After being rejected by the King of Hungary's daughter, Charles was more success-ful in Burgundy, and he married Margaret of Burgundy in 1268. Charles seems to have been a good husband to both Beatrice and Margaret, and there are no reports of any royal mistresses or bastards. Margaret outlived Charles and would return home to find much greater fame for establishing a hospital in Tonnerre, where the splendid 13th-century building still stands, than for being Charles's wife.

Charles was now completely in the ascendant in Italy and was expanding his domains unchecked in every direction. Or so it seemed, but the Hohenstaufen were not finished. Conradin was the heir to Sicily, and he was now fifteen. If Manfred is eulogized as the perfect handsome prince, Conradin the brilliant teenager is even more lauded. He had been raised by his mother, Elizabeth of Bavaria, and she had powerful relatives. Although they lived fairly quietly in Bavaria, no one had forgotten Conradin and what he represented.

'The Empire Strikes Back'

Despite the seemingly easy acceptance of Charles's rule in Italy, by the end of 1266 many of Manfred's former supporters had crossed the Alps and joined Conradin, who was ready, even at this young age, to take the opportunity offered him. He held a diet at Augsburg in October 1266 and announced that he would launch an invasion of Italy the following summer. Even as Charles was mopping up resistance in Tuscany and carrying out the long siege of Poggibonsi, Conradin was raising an army and preparing to cross the Alps. Two years after Charles's great victory at Benevento, as Martin Aurell wryly puts it, the time had come for the Empire to strike back.[57]

Although Charles himself seemed oblivious or indifferent to the Hohenstaufen threat, the pope was aware of the danger. By the end of 1266 he had threatened to excommunicate anyone who worked to make Conradin emperor or even received his agents. This was the background to papal acceptance of Charles's domination of Italy, since Charles had explicitly renounced plans to hold other offices in Italy and yet now he held numerous titles and was systematically reducing the cities of Tuscany. Although the pope warned Charles that he was spending too long in Tuscany and there were potential problems in Sicily and the south, Charles stubbornly remained before Poggibonsi throughout the summer of 1267.

Conradin's army set off for Italy in September 1267. He had lived at the castle of Hohenschwangau with his Bavarian relatives, the (rebuilt) castle where Mad King Ludwig would grow up in the 19th century steeped in medieval fantasies, and go to an equally tragic end. Conradin first issued a strident manifesto condemning Manfred as a usurper and the pope for his meddling, and he had other agents promoting his cause. Also in September 1267, they raised a revolt in Sicily, and much more importantly, and foreshadowing the conflict that would define Angevin rule in Naples for decades, a force from Tunis led by Frederick of Castile invaded the island. The two brothers of King Alfonso of Castile, Frederick and Henry, were as active as those other royal brothers Richard of Cornwall and Charles of Anjou himself. Henry of Castile had become Senator of Rome with Charles's backing, and Frederick had fought for Manfred at the battle of Benevento and was currently in the service of the Muslim emir of Tunis. As Frederick attacked Sicily with a Tunisian force, Henry betrayed Charles and declared his support for Conradin, receiving his envoys in Rome in a formal procession with the Hohenstaufen banners flying.[58]

Even as Charles triumphantly imposed his will on Tuscany, Conradin arrived in Italy and the revolt was spreading from Sicily throughout southern Italy. Modern historians have criticized Charles for lingering in Tuscany for nearly a year while the revolt spread, but there was a strategic reason for his actions. Tuscany was the richest area in Italy and the basis for Charles's finances, as well as traditionally being the strongest political unit that supported the papacy. If Tuscany were destabilized, Charles's finances and the position of the papacy could unravel very quickly. We should also keep in mind geographical considerations: Charles must have felt that controlling the centre of the peninsula by dominating Tuscany would do him more good than removing himself to the south and abandoning the north to Conradin. He had the example of what had happened only two years before. Manfred had remained in the south while Charles established himself in Rome and brought his army into Italy unopposed, and this had proved disastrous. Charles's strategy clearly emerges, which was to impose his authority in the middle of Italy and support the Guelfs of Tuscany, which would block Conradin's passage south and potentially threaten Conradin in the north by inciting Guelf resistance in traditionally Ghibelline cities. The danger was that Charles sat in the middle between a growing revolt in Sicily and the south and a hostile army in the . north, and he risked being crushed between the two.

Conradin and his army were in Verona by October 1267, probably hoping that Charles would go south to deal with the revolts and allow them to move towards Rome, but they waited there for three months, vindicating Charles's strategy. Charles was aware of Conradin's presence, and we might ask why Charles didn't go north to meet Conradin at once. Charles is known to have considered this option, but it would have involved a winter crossing of the Apennines into hostile territory, where his army might easily be harried by enemies without ever getting near Conradin.

This jockeying for position carried into 1268, and finally in March Charles returned to the south, first receiving formal recognition as imperial vicar of Tuscany from the pope. Conradin had left Verona in January, though the Duke of Bavaria and many of the other Germans in his army declined to accompany him further and returned home. Charles's efforts in Tuscany seemed to have succeeded in blocking the way south as Conradin now went west to Liguria, but he found a ship to carry him to Pisa, and this traditional Angevin enemy welcomed him warmly. Over the next month Ghibelline forces poured in to support him, showing that his activity in key cities such as Verona and Pavia had paid off.

Worse, Conradin's arrival in Tuscany showed how superficial Charles's victory had been. Poggibonsi immediately expelled its Angevin garrison and went over to the Hohenstaufen. Siena, mortal enemy of the Angevin ally Florence, also welcomed Conradin and was promised rewards for its support. All of Tuscany was crawling with Ghibellines, and although an attempt on Lucca was blocked by the Angevin force Charles had left behind, the Angevins were later surprised and routed. Conradin now had a credible army and marched south from Siena to Rome. On the way, Conradin marched past Viterbo where the pope resided, and legend says that the pope sat at the window of a high tower watching him pass and praying that the lamb was being led to the slaughter.[59]

Conradin arrived in Rome at the end of July, and he received a rapturous welcome. The Senator Henry of Castile presided over the ecstatic celebrations and the historian Saba Malaspina described the people of Rome decked in flowers and dancing in the streets as if a Golden Age had come. Everywhere Conradin went, Angevin support seemed to melt away as if Charles no longer existed. Yet there still had to be a final confrontation with Charles, so on 14 August Conradin and his ever increasing army set off south to complete the conquest.

Charles had besieged the Muslim city of Lucera in an attempt to cut off support for Conradin, but when he heard that the Hohenstaufen army was on the move he broke off the siege. The road to Naples was well defended by Angevin forces, so Conradin was heading southeast towards Apulia where Hohenstaufen support was stronger. Charles waited on the road to Apulia to block this advance and camped not far from the town of Tagliacozzo.

Conradin knew Charles's position, so he manoeuvred his army to meet Charles on the plain of Scurcola, where his heavy cavalry might have an advantage. On 22 August, Charles drew his force up to meet Conradin, and the two armies settled on either side of the river Salto to prepare for a battle the next day. Conradin's army was probably slightly larger, numbering about 6,000 compared to the 5,000 troops led by Charles, but it was also much more recently raised and disparate, whereas the troops Charles led had been together continuously for nearly two years.

Each army was divided into three groups as at Benevento, but each side also used a variety of stratagems. Villani links this to Charles's disadvantage in numbers, and gives credit for directing Charles's army to the Chamberlain of France, Erard of Saint-Valery, who was returning from the Holy Land and had joined Charles. The Angevin troops were led by Henry of Cousances, who wore Charles's insignia to act as a decoy, and guarded the bridge over the Salto with a division of Provençal and Italian knights, supported by a second division of French knights. The third detachment, led by Charles and Erard, hid behind a hill to wait in ambush.[60] They were joined by William of Villehardouin, who led a detachment of 400 knights from Morea, a rare example of Angevin hegemony over Greece proving beneficial, although by the 14th century the main Angevin attitude towards their lands in Greece was boredom.

Conradin also had three detachments, the first of Spanish cavalry and Ghibellines from Rome led by Henry of Castile; the second of Ghibellines from Lombardy and Tuscany; and the third of German troops led by Conradin himself. Henry of Castile led the assault, and attacked the bridge over the Salto. However, he had also sent half his force south to a ford, so that they might cross the river unnoticed and attack the Angevin army from the flank.[61]

In the event, both tricks were completely successful. While Henry of Castile engaged the Angevin army at the bridge, the Ghibellines who had crossed at the ford took the second Angevin detachment by surprise and launched a devastating attack. In the chaos, the first Angevin corps fell back from the bridge and Henry of Castile's force crossed the river. The Angevin army was routed. Henry of Cousances, dressed in the king's surcoat, was mistaken for Charles and killed, and the royal banner was captured. The Angevin army disintegrated and fled, pursued by Henry of Castile and a large part of his army, while the rest began to plunder the Angevin camp. Conradin crossed the bridge to savour his victory, and his detachment also broke up to take a share of the plunder.

All of this was witnessed by Charles of Anjou and his hidden reserve force. Charles at first considered intervening to try and turn the tide, but Erard of Saint-Valery coun-selled patience. As appalling as the slaughter was, Erard predicted that if they waited, Conradin's army would lay down their arms to plunder the Angevin camp, and that would be the moment to attack. This is precisely what happened. Conradin's forces began to disperse to collect the spoils of war, and when they saw that Conradin was almost alone, the Angevins struck. It took a moment for Conradin to realise that a new Angevin force was attacking, and by then it was too late. The Angevins easily defeated the few remaining German and Ghibelline troops, and Conradin and his bodyguard fled up the road to Rome.

Henry of Castile and his substantial force now realized what was happening and turned back to meet Charles. They outnumbered the Angevins and included a large number of German knights in plate armour. Yet they had been fighting all day and their horses were tired from pursuing the stragglers from the initial Angevin defeat. They also had to cross a considerable part of the plain in full view of Charles and his troops, who had plenty of time to prepare. As they charged towards the Angevins, Charles, with admirable sangfroid, drew his army up to meet them but instructed the men to remove their helmets so they could cool off and rest before the battle started.

Erard of Saint-Valery, who had already saved the day once, intervened again. Erard led half the army away in a feigned retreat, as if they were afraid of the superior Hohenstaufen force, and for the third time in the battle a stratagem worked. Despite Henry of Castile's warning that it might be a trick, the Hohenstaufen army divided to attack the Angevins separately, and when Erard of Saint-Valery suddenly turned back to rejoin the fight, the Angevins gained the advantage. In the August heat the cavalry, especially the Germans in their plate armour, were exhausted from their previous exertions, and they either fled or were killed.

Villani makes an interesting point that is analogous to the situation when the Angevins faced Germans in plate armour fighting with Manfred at Benevento. He says:

> Then was the battle fierce and hard; but the Spaniards [i.e. the Germans led by Henry of Castile] were well armed, and by stroke of sword might not be struck to the ground, and continually after their fashion they drew close together. Then began the French to cry out wrathfully, and to take hold of them by the arms and drag them from their horses after the manner of tournaments; and this was done to such good purpose that in a short time they were routed, and defeated, and put to flight, and many of them lay dead on the field.[62]

He explicitly links the techniques developed in tournaments with a practical use on the battlefield, supporting the justification for tournaments that had been made since their origin. We will remember that Charles was said to have loved tournaments, and what could be perceived as his misspent youth seems to have served him well at Tagliacozzo.

Now Charles had gained a complete victory, and that night he wrote to the pope to rejoice in the most flowery style:

> Humbly I offer you, most merciful father, as well as the most holy Roman Church, the sweet incense of a joy long awaited by all the faithful of the world, begging that the father, 'arising and eating of his son's game' [Genesis 27:31], might pay his debt of gratitude to the Most High, and that both the father and the mother might henceforth find respite from their labors.[63]

Despite the bloody business of warfare, feints and counterattacks, Charles had not forgotten that this was a Crusade to exterminate the 'race of vipers', and he had no doubt that he was doing God's work. In the letter he accused Conradin and his army of seeking a way into the kingdom 'through which they might secretly enter and join forces with the Saracens'. Although the Muslims at Lucera almost certainly would have supported Conradin, this adds a misleading religious dimension to the struggle as a justification for a holy war against the Hohenstaufen. Charles then gave an account of what happened on the battlefield that ignored his own near defeat, and concluded triumphantly:

> Indeed, the slaughter of the enemy there was so great that what happened to other persecutors of the Church on the fields of Benevento can hardly be compared to it. At the time this letter is written, immediately following the victory, I cannot be certain whether Conradin and the Roman senator Henry fell in battle or were able to escape. I can tell you that the senator's horse, which fled without its rider, was captured by my men. Therefore, Mother Church should rejoice and let out a cry of praise on high to him for mercifully providing so great a triumph, one obtained by the efforts of his warriors. For now it appears that Almighty God has put an end to her troubles, and freed her from the ravenous jaws of her persecutors.[64]

Charles commemorated the victory by founding the abbey of Santa Maria della Vittoria at Scurcola.

Henry of Castile fled to a monastery, where he was captured and turned over to Charles. Conradin fled first to Rome. There he found that the lieutenant left by Henry of Castile was no more trustworthy than Henry himself had been: he had heard of the battle and barred the gates of the Capitol against Conradin. Rather than risking the roads north where the triumphant Guelfs would be watching, Conradin and his companions headed for the coast and attempted to find a ship to take them to Genoa, but they were recognized by the local lord and imprisoned. Charles's agents swiftly appeared to take possession of them, and they were transferred to Naples where they were imprisoned in the Castel dell'Ovo.

The situation was a repeat of what Charles had already faced in Provence. There he had shown mercy at first, but when faced with further revolts he executed the ringleaders. After Benevento he had been scrupulously fair to Manfred's supporters, but having witnessed how practically all of them defected the moment Conradin arrived in Italy, he immediately executed some of the leading Ghibelline nobles while contemplating the fate of Conradin and Henry of Castile. The kings of France and England begged for clemency for Henry, which was given, though he spent twenty-three years in prison. Conradin was different.

Matthias von Neuenburg, writing in the 14th century, says that when Charles wrote to Pope Clement asking what to do with Conradin, Clement advocated Conradin's death, saying, '*Vita Conradini, mors Caroli; vita Caroli, mors Conradini*' (life to Conradin, death to Charles; life to Charles, death to Conradin).[65] Charles must have understood that he would never be safe while a legitimate Hohenstaufen heir remained, but as he would repeatedly show, he believed in scrupulously following the law, or at least appearing to do so. Conradin was formally put on trial and charged with treason for invading the kingdom, and naturally he was found guilty. A scaffold was erected in Naples on the site of the current Piazza del Mercato, and Conradin was publicly beheaded on 29 October 1268.

This execution violated contemporary customs and caused shock around Europe. Even though he condemned Conradin with a formal trial, Charles's reputation was permanently stained by this action. His contemporaries condemned him for it and Villani linked this crime to Charles's later misfortunes:

> Yet because of the said judgement King Charles was much blamed by the Pope and by his cardinals, and by all wise men, forasmuch as he had taken Conradino and his followers by chance of battle, and not by treachery, and it would have been better to keep him prisoner than to put him to death. And some said that the Pope assented thereto; but we do not give faith to this, forasmuch as he was held to be a holy man. And it seems that by reason of Conradino's innocence, which was of such tender age to be adjudged to death, God showed forth a miracle against King Charles, for not many years after God sent him great adversities when he thought himself to be in highest state, as hereafter in his history we shall make mention.[66]

Conradin is buried in the church of Santa Maria del Carmine near the marketplace where he was executed. Charles of Anjou magnanimously placed a grave marker for him, though this was subsequently lost and only rediscovered in the 19th century. That slab, and another explaining the circumstances in which it was recovered, are displayed unobtrusively in the chapel of the miracle-working image of the Madonna del Carmine, which completely upstages them. Fortunately for Conradin, Crown Prince Maximilian of Bavaria erected a much more substantial memorial in the nave in 1847: this is a suitably romantic statue of Conradin with inscriptions and reliefs commemorating the 'last of the Hohenstaufen'. A German friend of mine (who is something of a Swabian nationalist) remarked that it is unusual to see a Bavarian celebrating a Swabian, but we have seen Conradin's Bavarian connections and his association with Hohenschwangau, and it is fitting that Mad King Ludwig's father should so honour him, also neatly locating him in the current of 19th-century doomed German romanticism.

With Conradin dead, in the words of a troubadour, Charles would now be 'lord of the greatest part of the world'.[67] As he described himself in a peace treaty he made with Siena in 1271, he was now 'most glorious king of Sicily, Duke of Apulia, Prince of Capua, Senator of Rome, count of Anjou, Provence and Forcalquier, vicar-general of the Roman empire in Tuscany through the Holy Roman Church'. He would also take the title King of Albania and become King of Jerusalem. Yet this creation of almost a second 'Angevin Empire' created powerful enemies, and Charles's vaulting ambition also exposed him to risks.

CHAPTER 8 – THE WHEEL OF FORTUNE: THE SICILIAN VESPERS AND THE NEW ANGEVIN KINGDOMS

THE CONFLICTS WE HAVE seen between Charles and Manfred, then Charles and Conradin, had so convulsed Italy that there was much work to do to restore order. On top of that, Clement IV died a month after Conradin's execution, certainly with misgivings over the death of the teenager. Although the cardinals met to elect a new pope, there were too many divisions between the French and Italian parties in the college of cardinals to reach an agreement, and it took nearly three years to reach a decision. During this time Charles was the only power in Italy, and he used his position to the full.

Charles was again elected Senator of Rome for ten years, and he had already been confirmed as imperial vicar of Tuscany. Although Charles did not often visit Rome or Tuscany, he was quite active in ruling them through his officials. In Tuscany, Charles's agents joined the Florentine Guelfs and together they defeated Siena decisively and isolated Pisa by land. Charles then concluded an agreement with the Genoese to isolate Pisa from the sea and finally brought the Pisans to terms. By 1270 Charles controlled all of Tuscany, and he appointed a governor for Florence. In Rome, he struck coinage in his own name, stabilized the finances and reformed the judiciary, and the citizens of Rome erected a statue of Charles in gratitude for his stable government.

This statue by Arnolfo di Cambio is probably not an entirely accurate portrait of Charles, but it must be based on his appearance and is considerably more realistic than other royal statues from the 13th century. If we consider the images available of Louis IX, Charles's statue gives us a much more immediate sense of his appearance. The way Charles is represented is also instructive. He is portrayed seated, as a judge, rather than standing as kings usually were. The statue specifically commemorates Charles as a bringer of justice to the chaos of Italy, and fits him into a line of lawgivers stretching back to ancient Rome – literally, since the statue is carved from a piece of ancient architectural moulding.[1] The statue is in the Capitoline Museum in Rome and to stand before it is a vivid reminder of how far Charles had travelled in status from being the landless youngest son of the French king. It also gives us a psychological insight into Charles, as Robert Brentano comments: 'Arnolfo's imaginatively plain, strong statue of him on the Capitol is great in the way he was great. It is full of powerful authority.'[2]

Charles needed all of that authority to maintain his position. Although he held

Tuscany, Rome and Piedmont securely, Lombardy was dominated by Ghibellines, and various foreign powers such as Alfonso of Castile and Peter of Aragon displayed an interest in the region. Sicily and the Muslims at Lucera were also still in open revolt. Lucera was only taken in August 1269, and it took until 1270 for Sicily to be brought under control. Many of the enemy leaders were beheaded in Naples as Conradin had been, reinforcing impressions of Charles as brutal and inflexible, acting against the custom of the time to execute those who opposed him.

In the midst of this turmoil Charles continued to look for new arenas of expansion. He had already gained feudal authority over William of Achaea, but he now demanded that William marry his eldest daughter Isabelle to Charles's second son Philip, with a provision that if Isabelle died without issue Achaea should pass to Charles himself. This disrupted a proposed marriage alliance between Isabelle and the eldest son of Emperor Michael Paleologus that might have reunited the Latin and Byzantine Empires and, theoretically, brought greater stability to the region and given the Byzantine Empire a stronger position against the Turks. Numerous Angevin critics in the mould of Dante see this as another example of the 'sick weed' of Capetian and Angevin acquisitiveness spreading over Europe and causing untold damage.[3]

Charles had agreed to launch an attack on Constantinople on behalf of the Emperor Baldwin, but of course Conradin's invasion put paid to that. The agreement had certainly not been forgotten, and by the summer of 1270 Charles was preparing an armada to attack the Byzantine Empire. He stated that he wanted to help Baldwin and the doge of Venice recover their rights in Constantinople, and began preparing all his ships for the invasion. We have seen how intimately the question of the Latin Empire was bound up with Crusading, and indeed the justification for the Fourth Crusade attacking Constantinople in the first place was largely because it would be a formidable staging post and ally for any attack on the Holy Land, and a support for the few remaining and desperately imperilled Crusader States. It would not be possible to launch an attack on Constantinople if it would clash with a Crusade, and unfortunately for Charles, Louis IX was planning just that.

Louis IX's Crusade Against Tunis

If the execution of Conradin is a stain on Charles's reputation, he is accused of the much worse crime of perverting the course of Louis IX's second Crusade. This Crusade, directed against Tunis, would turn out to be yet another disaster and caused the death of Louis himself. Joinville, still a good friend of Louis's, certainly opposed the expedition, but not because of its destination:

> I considered that all those who had advised the king to go on this expedition
> committed mortal sin. For at that time the state of the country was such that

there was perfect peace throughout the kingdom, and between France and her neighbours, while ever since King Louis went away the state of the kingdom has done nothing but go from bad to worse.

It was besides a great sin on the part of those who advised the king to go, seeing that he was physically so weak that he could neither bear to be drawn in a coach, nor to ride – so weak, in fact, that he let me carry him in my arms from the Comte d'Auxerre's house, where I went to take leave of him, to the abbey of the Franciscans. And yet, weak as he was, if he had remained in France he might have lived for some time longer, and have done much good, and carried out many fine projects.[4]

Thus the accusation that someone manipulated Louis into the attack on Tunis contains the implication that that person also effectively killed Louis.

That a Crusade failed is unremarkable, but what is the basis for accusing Charles of somehow hijacking Louis's Crusade? It is simply the choice to attack Tunis, which seems odd considering a Crusade had never been directed here before, and it would do nothing to help the Crusader States or strike at their real enemies, the Mamluks of Egypt, whose systematic conquest of the Holy Land and recent taking of Antioch were the primary concern in the West.

The story of the Crusade is brutally simple. Louis and his army set out from Aigues-Mortes on 1 July 1270, and arrived in Tunis on 17 July where they established a camp to wait for Charles of Anjou. Disease broke out in the camp and many died, including Louis's son Jean 'Tristram', who had been born in Damietta twenty years before on the previous Crusade. Charles's fleet was in the Adriatic to prepare for the assault on Constantinople, so it took more than a month for him to sail back around Sicily, and he finally arrived on 25 August to be told that Louis had died that morning.

Charles worked with Louis's son, the new king Philip III, to pick up the pieces of the Crusade. They attacked Tunis and defeated the emir's army. On hearing that an additional Crusading army under Prince Edward of England was on the way, the emir sought a peace treaty. He would pay the expenses of the Crusaders (one-third of which went to Charles), restore his tribute payments to the King of Sicily, allow merchants from Sicily free access to the city, release all his Christian captives and exile political refugees hostile to Charles. This was agreed on 1 November 1270 and the Crusade was over.[5]

The simplicity of the events around this four-month Crusade reveals why the conspiracy theory about Charles is so compelling. Louis launches a misguided Crusade against an irrelevant enemy and tragically dies. If we ask who benefitted from the attack on Tunis, the answer is Charles. The emirs of Tunis since the 12th century had paid tribute to the kings of Sicily, but after Manfred's death the emir stopped these payments. Tunis had also harboured Charles's enemies like Frederick of Castile and had served as a base for them to attack Sicily and foment rebellion. Charles of Anjou then arrives and makes a settlement that benefits him financially and politically, and the Crusade ends. As in so many cases, we have a contemporary source, the ever hostile Saba Malaspina, who stated in 1285 that Charles convinced Louis to attack Tunis for his own gain: 'wishing to go to that country and desirous of extirpating by the force of others the serpent from his cave, Charles had acted adroitly to lead such an important army against Tunis'.[6]

Although there is no other direct evidence to support this theory, the attack on Tunis is so odd that it cries out for an explanation. Among modern historians, Runciman entirely accepts Saba's accusation, and bolsters this position by highlighting criticism of this Crusade launched by – amongst others – the Crusaders led by Prince Edward. They asked why, instead of trying to capture Tunis, Charles and the Crusaders had instead agreed a treaty that benefitted Charles, and then ended the Crusade. The conspiracy theory also presupposes that Louis could not be talked out of the Crusade (which would have suited Charles better), and so if there had to be a Crusade, in Runciman's words, Charles decided 'it would be against Muslims whose conquest would be of direct advantage to him'.[7]

Villani actually gives a perfectly valid reason for attacking Tunis. He says of Louis and his advisers:

And believing it to be the better course they determined to go against the kingdom of Tunis, thinking that if it could be taken by the Christians they would be in a very central place whence they could more easily afterwards take the kingdom of Egypt, and could cut off and wholly impede the force of the Saracens in the realm of Ceuta, and also that of Granada.[8]

But he also repeats criticism of Charles, especially that Charles stopped the Crusader army from capturing Tunis, which would have meant it would be divided between all the parties involved in the Crusade, and instead arranged tribute payments for himself. This was duly punished:

Others blamed King Charles, saying that he did it through avarice, to the end he might henceforward, by reason of the said peace, always receive tribute from the king of Tunis for his own special benefit; for if the kingdom of Tunis had been conquered by all the host of the Christians, it would have afterwards pertained in part to the king of France, and to the king of England, and to the king of Navarre, and to the king of Sicily, and to the Church of Rome, and to divers other lords which were at the conquest. And it may have been, both one cause and the other; but however that may have been, when the said treaty was concluded the said host departed from Tunis, and when they came with their fleet to the port of Trapani in Sicily, as it pleased God, so great a storm overtook them while the fleet was in the said port that without any redemption the greater part perished, and one vessel broke the other, and all the belongings of that host were lost, which were of untold worth, and many folk perished there. And it was said by many that this came to pass by reason of the sins of the Christians, and because they had made a covenant with the Saracens through greed of money when they could have overcome and conquered Tunis and the country.[9]

Saba Malaspina accuses Charles of hinting to Louis IX that the Emir of Tunis could be converted, thus deceiving him into sending the Crusade against Tunis. Runciman masterfully twists the story:

Charles skilfully directed King Louis's attention to Tunis. He pointed out how valuable the control of Tunis would be for an attack on Egypt and the Muslim East. He indicated that Mustansir [the Emir of Tunis] was trembling on the brink of adopting Christianity but was afraid of the opposition of his generals and his imams. A slight show of force would enable him to defy them and make up his mind for himself. It is doubtful whether Charles really believed in the convertibility of the Tunisian king. But it would suit him to have a docile client ruling in Tunis; and it would suit him still better to conquer the country and add it to his Empire.[10]

The accusation that Charles diverted the Crusade does not entertain the possibility that Louis himself chose a target that could benefit from his brother's rule in Sicily. The single most important development in Crusading in the 13th century was its expansion into places other than the Holy Land – Constantinople, Egypt, southern France, Italy, the Baltic, Spain and, in this case, Tunisia. There had been a definitive break from the idea that a Crusade by definition included a pilgrimage to Jerusalem, so Louis's decision is not as extraordinary as some would claim. Based on their previous relationship, it also seems clear that Louis was not so easily swayed by his brother as this position assumes.

As the Crusade limped home the disasters continued. In addition to the shipwrecks suffered by the fleet, as the French army made its way back through Italy the new queen of France was killed in a riding accident. Alphonse of Poitiers survived the Crusade, but his health was so damaged that he died in 1271. Unsurprisingly, Charles tried to claim Alphonse's apanage, which now included all of Aquitaine except Gascony, plus Toulouse and part of Provence. This would have given Charles more land in France than the king, and the Parlement of Paris refused his claim.[11]

Complications in the East and West

Although Louis's second Crusade had interrupted Charles's plans, within another year he was ready to proceed again. Charles consolidated his position in Dalmatia, and his son Philip married the heiress to Achaea in May 1271. In February 1272, momentously, Charles declared himself King of Albania, but just when he seemed poised to dominate the east he allowed himself to be drawn into a war with Genoa. This seriously undermined his position in northern Italy and occupied his fleet and manpower.[12]

Even worse for Charles, the entire political balance in Europe also changed quickly. On the way back from the Crusade, Philip III of France insisted on stopping at Viterbo to encourage the cardinals to elect a new pope, and Charles accompanied him, bringing the authority of two kings to bear. The cardinals finally reached a compromise, and in September 1271 elected an Italian, Tebaldo Visconti, but one who had spent most of his career north of the Alps and had been in Palestine when he was elected. He took the name Gregory X.

Gregory immediately set out his priorities, one of which was to resolve the chaos in the Empire. Richard of Cornwall, although never Emperor, remained King of the Romans and while he lived no one else could be elected to the title. Fortunately for Gregory, Richard died in April 1272. Having had enough of foreign princes who sought the Empire as a prize rather than a German prince who might actually rule, Gregory skilfully saw off the claims of various contenders and made it clear to the electors that they should choose a German ruler. They were careful not to choose anyone too power-ful, and settled on Rudolf of Habsburg, the Landgrave of Alsace, who was respected and rich, but not a particularly notable figure. This marked the entrance on the his-torical stage of a family who would one day dominate much of Europe and surpass even the Angevins in the breadth of their possessions (though I would note that on the extinction of the Habsburg dynasty in Spain in the 18th century, who should become king but the Duke of Anjou, to this day providing the coat of arms of Spain with an inset shield showing the arms of Anjou. *Plus ça change* ...). Rudolf was elected King of the Romans in October 1273. Villani notes that since the former Duke of Austria had been executed with Conradin by Charles of Anjou, Rudolf gave the title to his son Albert, establishing the Habsburgs in Vienna and incidentally adding to Angevin ubiquity by having them (inadvertently) launch the Habsburgs in their future capital.[13]

Gregory summoned a council at Lyons in 1273 to ratify all these policies and, more importantly, declare a Crusade to rescue the desperately imperilled Crusader States. He invited most of the kings of Europe, including Charles, but the only one who attended was James of Aragon, who quickly became disillusioned with the pope's schemes and left, and the idea of a Crusade was stillborn. The pope also invited leading theologians to put forward reasons for the Greek church to submit to Rome, including the most famous of all, Thomas Aquinas. Thomas was from southern Italy, and resided in Naples, where he had encountered Charles of Anjou and been critical of him. When Thomas, who was already ill, died not far from Naples on his journey to the council, gossip suggested that he had been poisoned, and more particularly that he had been poisoned by Charles of Anjou.[14]

Dante absolutely believed this and laid the crime at Charles's door in the *Purgatorio*. This begs the question of why Charles wasn't placed in hell if he were a murderer, though Dante couldn't quite consign the king who had been the main papal champion to the Inferno. There is no evidence whatsoever that Charles did poison Aquinas, and there was no reason for him to do so. It is only another example of how myths swirled around the Angevins and any significant event or crime came to be laid at their door.

Gregory was more successful in achieving the union of the Greek and Latin churches. Michael Paleologus was desperate for support and, ignoring the distaste for this policy by practically everyone else in the Greek world, decided that he would agree to the union. His representatives accepted the form of the Creed used in the Latin church and the primacy of Rome, though in a somewhat vague way and with enough reservations that the union seemed more of a formality than a reality. Still, it was a triumph for Gregory. It was also a considerable complication for Charles, who could not now attack the newly reconciled Greek Emperor in the guise of a Crusade. Gregory arranged a truce between Charles, the titular Latin Emperor Philip and Michael Paleologus, which was agreed for a year in 1275. Although this forestalled Charles from any assault on Constantinople, the truce did not cover Greece or Albania, and in 1274 Michael Paleologus had attempted to conquer Achaea.[15]

At the Council of Lyons Gregory had also secured support for Rudolf of Habsburg as King of the Romans. As Charles's war with Genoa spiralled into a general northern Italian war with the Ghibellines, rather than receiving papal assistance he instead faced a prospective Emperor with real power who would resume imperial authority over northern Italy, Tuscany and Provence. The situation infinitely worsened when Margaret of Provence, widow of Louis IX and mother of King Philip III, wrote to Rudolf and again claimed that she had been denied her share of the inheritance of Provence. The pope's chief aim was to keep Rudolf and Charles on friendly terms, so he discouraged Rudolf from acting on this request, but it underlined the difficulties a strong Emperor could make for Charles, as would soon be demonstrated.

Charles was now hindered on all sides and must have been annoyed that the new pope's policy should disadvantage him so much. Fortunately for him, the promotion of one of Gregory X's policies actually worked in Charles's favour. After Conradin's death, there had been a disputed succession to the crown of Jerusalem, and the losing contender, Maria of Antioch, had gone to Lyons to request the pope's assistance. The throne had been taken by the Lusignan king of Cyprus, Hugh III, on the grounds that the 'kingdom', which now consisted only of the beleaguered city of Acre plus a few coastal towns and castles, needed a military leader. The pope convinced Maria to sell her claim to the kingdom to Charles since it was no use to her, and Charles was much better able to launch an expedition to support Acre than she was. More importantly for the pope, having such a direct interest in the Holy Land should prompt Charles to rescue Acre rather than attack Constantinople. Although Gregory died in January 1276, an agreement was finally reached in March 1277 and Charles took the title King of Jerusalem.[16]

Charles sent a small force to Acre to demand recognition of his claim. Aside from growing Mamluk power in Egypt, the main problem with the pitifully small Crusader States was that they were in a position of constant feud between the Templars and the Hospitallers as well as the Venetians and the Genoese. Hugh III had abandoned the ungovernable kingdom and gone back to Cyprus, but as he was still king, Charles's representative had no right to demand the kingdom's submission. The Templars and the Venetians supported Charles's claim, and after Hugh III refused to respond when asked for instructions, the barons officially recognized Charles as king.

The new pope, Innocent V, was sympathetic to Charles and confirmed him as Senator of Rome and imperial vicar in Tuscany, though Rudolf of Habsburg complained that it was his right to grant this title. However, since Rudolf had still not become Emperor, he was in no position to antagonize the pope. Innocent promptly died and another new pope was elected, who died before he was even consecrated. Next, John XXI was elected and reigned just long enough to confirm Innocent's policies, namely that Charles remained Senator and vicar of Tuscany, and that Rudolf was forbidden to come to Rome for his coronation until arguments over imperial sovereignty in various bits of Italy had been resolved. Rudolf was fully occupied with affairs in the Empire, and was gradually building the block of power in Austria and eastern Germany that would be the foundation of Habsburg fortunes, so he was content for the moment to leave Italy alone. John was then killed in a bizarre accident when the roof of a newly built wing of the papal palace in Viterbo collapsed on him, and a new pope, the Roman Nicholas III succeeded.

He immediately had to deal with what in one sense was a petty land squabble, but in another struck at the heart of Italian politics. Margaret of Provence again approached Rudolf of Habsburg, this time to arrange a marriage alliance between his son Hartmann and Edward I of England's daughter Joanna. The couple were to be given the old imperial domains of Arles, Vienne and, most importantly, Provence, dispossessing Charles of Anjou. This was completely unacceptable to Charles and risked a major conflict with the Empire, but the pope navigated a way through the difficulties. Fortunately for Nicholas, Hartmann died. Nicholas then made a counter offer, that Charles should keep Provence after doing homage to Rudolf, but that his grandson Charles Martel should marry Rudolf's daughter Clementia, and this couple should take the Kingdom of Arles.[17]

Nicholas further asked Charles to give up the Senatorship of Rome and the vicarate of Tuscany, as he had previously agreed. This went a long way to sorting out relations between Charles and Rudolf, though it reduced Charles's standing in Italy. However, it might also free him to deal with matters in the east.

Although there was officially a truce between Michael Paleologus and Charles while the union of the churches agreed at the Council of Lyons took effect, it only stopped Charles attacking Constantinople, and Michael repeatedly sent forces against Albania, Achaea and Athens, as well as his local Greek rivals. The Byzantines didn't win any overwhelming victories, but they gained control of the sea and were putting increasing pressure on the Latin states. In 1278 the deaths of William of Achaea and Charles's son Philip meant that Achaea reverted to Charles, and he sent a vicar to rule in his name.

The time now seemed right for a final push against Constantinople. Charles initially planned to launch the attack from Durazzo and take the Via Egnatia, the old Roman road to Constantinople. He sent a commander with a considerable army to besiege the Byzantine stronghold of Berat nearby, but by 1281 Michael Paleologus had heavily defeated the Angevin force and driven them back to Durazzo. This is what determined Charles to launch a seaborne attack on Constantinople.[18]

In a replay of the Fourth Crusade, Charles agreed a treaty with the Venetians to provide the fleet to reconquer Constantinople. As the Crusaders had found in 1204, the costs of preparing such a fleet were enormous and Charles pushed his subjects to the limits to pay for the new campaign. Given the failed land assault in 1281 and the costs of defending Achaea, Charles's revenues were stretched to breaking point. From the point of view of his subjects, his reign had been one of constant warfare and the heavy taxes imposed to pay for it. He had already faced a massive revolt in Sicily and southern Italy when Conradin invaded, in which members of the Castilian royal family had been involved. Now everything came to a head, in the event that would define Charles of Anjou forever.

The Sicilian Vespers

The 'Sicilian Vespers' is the name given to a revolt that began in Palermo in 1282 and rapidly spread throughout Sicily and into southern Italy, nearly toppling Charles from power, though ultimately after Charles's death the Angevin dynasty remained and ruled a truncated kingdom from Naples. The causes of the revolt are complex and disputed. Certainly Sicily, and the rest of Charles's domains, had been punitively taxed and were fed up with the financial burdens forced on them by Charles's endless Crusading and expansionist policies. Sicily itself had also retained a distinctive identity and constantly harked back to the days of Frederick II's charismatic court based in Palermo and even further to the days of 'Good King William' in the 12th century.

There was more to the story than Sicilian dissatisfaction. The royal houses of Castile and Aragon have repeatedly been involved in Charles of Anjou's story, and it may be that Aragon, in conjunction with Michael Paleologus, formed a grand coalition of Charles's enemies to bring him down. Manfred's daughter Constance had married Peter, the heir to Aragon, and Peter became king in 1276. His interests overlapped with Charles in Sardinia and Tunisia, and Hohenstaufen supporters definitely went to Aragon to meet Constance. A legend quickly arose that John of Procida, a doctor who had been Frederick II's personal physician, then served Manfred and joined Conradin, and was now chancellor of Aragon, was the mastermind behind the plot. Legends tell of him travelling around the Mediterranean disguised as a Franciscan, bringing bribes from Michael Paleologus and distributing them to rebel Sicilian barons, and rallying the Ghibellines across Italy.[19]

It is a fabulous story in both senses of the word – a disguised agent patiently building up a network of support, the imperilled Byzantine Emperor using guile and bribes to overcome military force, and most importantly of all, the revenge of the Hohenstaufen. Certainly Hohenstaufen loyalists had gone to Aragon, and there are suggestions that there genuinely was an attempt by Charles's various enemies to join forces and find some way to resist him. However, there is an overall lack of evidence, plus a few distinct pieces of contradictory evidence, and the 'grand conspiracy' led by John of Procida seems to be a romantic fiction.

Villani can't quite make up his mind whether the Vespers arose because of an organized plot by John of Procida or if the revolt grew from an incident when a French knight insulted a Sicilian woman, so he includes both:

> In the year of Christ 1282, on Easter Monday of the Resurrection, which was the 30th day of March, as had been purposed by M. John of Procita, all the barons and chiefs which had a hand in the plot were in the city of Palermo for Easter, and the inhabitants of Palermo, men and women, going in a body, on horse and on foot, to the festival at Monreale, three miles outside the city (and as those of Palermo went, so also went the Frenchmen, and the captain of King Charles, for their disport), it came to pass, as was purposed by the enemy of God, that a Frenchman in his insolence laid hold of a woman of Palermo to do her villainy; she beginning to cry out, and the people being already sore and all moved with indignation against the French, the retainers of the barons of the island began to defend the woman, whence arose a great battle between the French and the Sicilians, and many were wounded and slain on either side; but those of Palermo came off worst.
>
> Straightway, all the people returned in flight to the city, and the men flew to arms, crying, 'Death to the French.' They gathered together in the market place, as had been ordained by the leaders of the plot; and the justiciary, which was for the king, fighting at the castle, was taken and slain, and as many Frenchmen as were in the city were slain in the houses and in the churches, without any mercy … This plague spread through all the island, whence King Charles and his people received great hurt both in person and in goods.[20]

This middle ground seems most persuasive: Charles's enemies were in contact with the Aragonese and there had been attempts by the court of Aragon to stir up resistance to Charles in Sicily, and when a local revolt was sparked by an incident between Angevin forces and local people, the rebellion quickly gained momentum. What is also true is that Peter of Aragon had prepared his own fleet, ostensibly for a Crusade against Tunis, and was ready to capitalize on Angevin problems in Sicily.

The aftermath of the revolt also showed that there were much longer-standing problems in the island than the actions of Charles of Anjou. Modern historical analysis has shown repeatedly that in most cases Charles was continuing Hohenstaufen financial policy and was no more rapacious than Frederick II, but this was irrelevant when the Sicilians were actually protesting against decades of financial oppression. The Vespers can just as easily be seen as a continuation of the fall of Frederick II, who had also come unstuck through having too many distractions in the rest of Italy and had been forced to be too demanding in Sicily.[21]

Although academics engage in somewhat dry disputes about the cause and implications of the revolt, it has gained an emotional resonance and is still viewed as an early popular outcry against oppression. A thrilling representation of this is Verdi's opera *The Sicilian Vespers,* which has little grounding in fact and focuses on a family drama and romance, although it does make John of Procida a substantial character credited with organizing the plot. However, it is a powerful work that has much to say about opposing tyranny and the anger of an oppressed people.

After the rebellion began in Palermo, it spread quickly through the west and centre of the island, with only Charles's administrative centre of Messina remaining under Angevin control. Soon, however, it too went over to the rebels and the portion of Charles's fleet for the Constantinople expedition moored there was destroyed. Messina elected its own officials to replace the Angevins, one of whom was Bartolomeo di Neocastro, who wrote a history of the revolt that is one of our best sources. There was great loss of life among the French, with thousands being killed.

Although at first not wanting to believe that the revolt was serious, the loss of his fleet at Messina brought home to Charles what was happening since it now ended any chance of attacking the Byzantines. Villani, who often claimed to know Charles's exact words though writing fifty years later, says that Charles cried: 'Lord God, since it has pleased you to ruin my fortune, let me only go down by small steps.'[22] This is exactly what happened.

Whether there was a conspiracy against him or not, Charles still had allies. The pope – yet another one, Martin IV – excommunicated the rebels in Sicily and anyone who supported them, plus Michael Paleologus and the Ghibellines in northern Italy. Philip III of France was quick to support his uncle, and immediately remonstrated with King Peter of Aragon, whom he had suspected of designs against Sicily for some time. A force from France and another from Provence joined Charles, as well as a contingent from Florence. In July, Charles and his army landed near Messina. Several attempts to storm the city failed, but the citizens of Messina knew they were in desperate danger. The Sicilians now contacted Peter of Aragon, who had taken his 'Crusading' fleet to Algeria and was waiting for the right moment to intervene.

Now was the time, and Peter formally agreed to aid the Sicilians and restore his wife Constance, Manfred's daughter, as the rightful queen of Sicily (with himself as king). He landed at Trapani and then brought an army overland towards Messina while his fleet followed around the northern coast of the island. Charles faced the prospect of a pitched battle with the knowledge that the Aragonese fleet would cut him off if he lost, since his own fleet was cobbled together from the remains of his own navy plus hired

Genoese, Venetian and even Pisan ships that were unlikely to put up much resistance to the Aragonese. He chose to retreat back across the strait of Messina and wait for reinforcements.[23]

Intermittent skirmishes between the two forces dragged on for months with no knockout blow, while both sides tried to rally their allies. The pope had excommunicated Charles's enemies, but more importantly Philip III of France sent troops and money, and threatened an invasion of Aragon itself. Peter's allies had their own troubles, as Castile had fallen into civil war, Rudolph of Habsburg would never jeopardize his coronation as Emperor by intervening and risking excommunication, and Michael Paleologus died at the end of 1282, secure in his reputation as the reconqueror of Constantinople and having foiled an attack from the West. Edward I of England initially professed neutrality and expressed a wish for peace in Europe, but then surprisingly became involved in the war.

Late in 1282, Charles made an unexpected proposal for breaking the deadlock: he suggested that he and Peter meet in single combat and the winner would take Sicily. Even in the 13th century this method of resolving a conflict seemed quaint and foolishly romantic, but Peter accepted the proposal and serious negotiations began. Quickly it was decided that instead of single combat between Charles, now elderly by medieval standards at the age of fifty-five, and his younger rival (Peter was forty), each king would choose 100 knights to accompany him, and the two sides would fight on 1 June 1283 at Bordeaux. As Gascony belonged to Edward I, this was seen as neutral ground.[24]

Staking everything on this combat seemed incredibly foolish for Charles. Even if Charles believed right was on his side and God would never allow him to lose this judgement in battle, it was not his place to test God, as the pope pointed out. Edward I was similarly dismissive. There is always the possibility that Charles never intended to go through with the combat, as it was not uncommon for this kind of suggestion to be made. The party who issued the challenge would have the moral high ground if the enemy refused, and even if both sides agreed to the combat, negotiations would usually drag on so long that there would be many opportunities to call it off. This may have been Charles's goal all along. By issuing the challenge he might take the heat out of the war in Sicily, and by diverting attention and resources to Gascony he could draw the conflict back onto the mainland and into the sphere of influence of his allies in France.

Early in 1283 Charles left his son Charles of Salerno as regent, and traveled to Paris to prepare for the combat. Charles of Salerno held a parliament in southern Italy and issued a series of reforms and proposals for improving government in the kingdom, showing both that the rebels had legitimate concerns and that the Angevin government was willing to respond to them. Despite this, Peter of Aragon consolidated his position in Sicily. Queen Constance arrived with their children, and a parliament in Messina confirmed that while on Peter's death Aragon would go to Peter's eldest son Alfonso, his next son James would inherit Sicily. John of Procida became chancellor of the kingdom and Roger of Lauria, of whom we will hear much more, became Grand Admiral of the fleet. Peter then returned to Spain and by May was proceeding to Bordeaux for the combat.

The great trial by battle turned into a farce. Edward I was forbidden by the pope to have anything to do with it, but he allowed his seneschal to prepare a battlefield. Charles was accompanied by Philip III and they arrived in Bordeaux with great splendour and ceremony, whereas Peter chose to arrive quietly. On the day of the combat, for which no particular time had been arranged, Peter and his knights went to the battlefield early in the morning, and on finding themselves alone issued a statement that Charles had failed to appear and that Peter was the winner. They then left. A few hours later Charles and his company also appeared on the battlefield, declared that Peter had failed to appear and claimed victory. They then each left Bordeaux.[25]

The battle for Sicily might have remained a local problem, but the pope and king of France were already involved. This escalated the conflict into a more general European war and inevitably with the papacy involved, a Crusade. Peter of Aragon was already excommunicated, and the pope declared that an attack on Peter and the Sicilian rebels would carry the full Crusading indulgence. Twenty years after the papacy organized the invasion to replace Manfred, the template was in place. Peter's vassals were released from their obedience to him, and he was to be replaced with another prince. This would be Philip III's younger son Charles of Valois, who, like Charles of Anjou, would dispossess the excommunicated king and found a new dynasty. Regardless of the fact that the proposed Crusade was unpopular with many in France, including Philip IV, the heir to the throne, to others it looked like another attempt to extend Capetian domination outside France. Philip III officially announced on 2 February 1284 that his son Charles of Valois had accepted the kingdoms of Aragon and Valencia from the pope.

While this distraction played out, Charles of Salerno continued to organize the Angevin response to the Sicilian Vespers. Although he received a large loan from the pope, he also had to borrow money from the Kings of England and France as well as banks in Florence and Lucca. We have already seen that the pope and Charles of Anjou were heavily indebted to Tuscan bankers for the initial attack on Manfred, and this further involvement of the banks in the affairs of the Angevins would have lasting consequences for the European economy in the 14th century.

Charles of Salerno used the newly raised funds to fit out a Provençal fleet that went to the relief of Malta, where the Angevin garrison was blockaded by the Aragonese. The Aragonese admiral Roger of Lauria demonstrated his superiority and almost entirely destroyed the Angevin fleet, then mounted a brazen attack to capture the islands of Capri and Ischia within sight of Naples, and then used his control of the islands to blockade Naples itself. Unaware that Charles of Anjou was on the way with reinforcements by land and sea, and in violation of his father's explicit instructions to avoid any conflict with Roger of Lauria, in May 1284 Charles of Salerno launched an attack on one of the islands to break the blockade, only to stumble into a naval battle with Roger's fleet and suffer an overwhelming defeat. The entire Angevin force and Charles of Salerno himself were captured, and panicked riots broke out in Naples and across the remaining Angevin dominions.[26]

Although Charles of Anjou arrived a day later with a new fleet from Provence and restored order to his territories, the scale of the disaster could not be denied. Charles wrote to the pope and reassured him that he had ample forces to carry on the fight, but he could only manage inconclusive operations in southern Italy while Roger of Lauria continued to harry the coast. The entire kingdom seemed to be slipping away. Charles settled into winter quarters to prepare for a renewed attack on Sicily in 1285, in conjunction with the French Crusade against Aragon, but his health had begun to deteriorate.

On 7 January 1285, Charles died. Most of his empire was lost and his only surviving son and heir was a prisoner, yet to the end he remained convinced of the justice of all his actions. Villani gave his dying words, pointedly relating Charles's speech in French in his Italian chronicle: 'Lord God, as I truly believe that you are my Saviour, thus I pray to you, that you have mercy on my soul; as I took the kingdom of Sicily more to serve the Holy Church than for my own profit or other gain, forgive me my sins.'[27] Villani also provided an epitaph:

This Charles was the most feared and redoubted lord, and the most valiant in arms, and of the most lofty designs, of all the kings of the house of France from Charles the Great to his own day, and the one which most exalted the Church of Rome; and he would have done more if, at the end of his life, fortune had not turned against him.[28]

Charles truly was a conqueror on a scale unseen since Charlemagne, operating on a wider stage than William the Conqueror, but in the end his accomplishments were ephemeral. Although he founded a lasting dynasty in Naples, the calamities of his last years mean that he is remembered either as a tragic figure or a savage oppressor who got what he deserved, neither evaluation quite hitting the mark.

Charles had calmly made his will and left detailed instructions for the succession. He begged the pope to protect the kingdom, and if Charles of Salerno died in prison or were never released, his grandson Charles Martel would inherit all his possessions. Robert of Artois, son of the Robert of Artois who died in Egypt on St Louis's Crusade, was to serve as regent. Although Charles seemed to have lost almost everything at the time of his death, in fact many of his achievements would live on.

Charles was buried in the cathedral in Naples in a grand marble tomb, though this sadly is no longer extant. Fittingly for a ruler who was consistently criticized in his Italian kingdom for being too French, he has several monuments in Paris. The *rue du Roi-de-Sicile* in the Marais is so named because Charles's townhouse was once in this street, though the house itself passed to Charles of Valois when he married Charles's granddaughter. Charles's heart was also sent for burial at the Dominican convent of St

Jacques in Paris, and the casket that held it was inscribed 'the heart of the great King Charles who conquered Sicily'.[29] Margaret of Burgundy's heart was buried with Charles in 1309, and Charles's great-granddaughter Clementia of Hungary commissioned a proper tomb in 1326. Although this was destroyed in the French Revolution, Charles's effigy was moved to St Denis where it still lies with the kings of France. It is appropriate that he should be memorialized in this way, with an effigy among the French kings and his statue on the Capitol in Rome, and if his tomb in Naples is gone, the Castel Nuovo and the cathedral itself serve as his memorials in the city.

The Crusade Against Aragon

Although Charles was dead, the war continued, and Philip III invaded Aragon under a Crusading banner. This Crusade was infamous, even more than the Fourth Crusade and the Crusades against Frederick II and Manfred in Italy, and met with particular odium. Consider the facts of the case: a Christian king of Aragon was involved in a war with the Christian king of Sicily after being invited by the citizens of the island to pursue a claim to the throne by his wife, and on this basis the pope declared a Crusade so the Christian king of France could invade his neighbour's kingdom. This could not but leave a bad taste in everyone's mouths and the 'Crusade' was seen by many as nothing more than a straightforward war of conquest by France on behalf of the Angevins, who themselves were no more than French invaders who had taken Sicily from one rightful ruler and murdered another in the form of Conradin.

For the pious, the outcome of the Crusade fully demonstrated its dubious moral basis. Although Philip managed to take the important city of Girona, this was only after a siege lasting the entire summer, and by the time the city fell in September the army and Philip himself were ravaged by illness. Worse, Philip was relying on a French fleet to resupply the army and secure his lines of communication, and in the war of the Vespers there is literally only ever one outcome to naval engagements: Roger of Lauria appeared with the Aragonese fleet and completely destroyed the French ships. Aragonese troops cut off the French supply lines, and Philip was forced to retreat. On 5 October Philip died at Perpignan, 'fleeing and disgracing the lilies', as Dante aptly put it.[30]

This would seem to be a complete triumph for Aragon and the outlook for the Angevins was grim, but on 10 November Peter of Aragon died as well. The year 1285 saw the clearing of an entire generation of participants in the conflict, with the deaths of Charles of Anjou in January, Pope Martin IV in March, Philip III in October and Peter in November. Although the situation remained highly confused and the conflict would drag on for nearly another 200 years, the first sharp phase of the war did begin to subside as all the participants came to terms with a new generation of leaders and a new division of power in the Mediterranean.

Of course the new Angevin 'King of Sicily', Charles II 'the Lame', was a prisoner in Aragon. Sicily was lost, parts of southern Italy had revolted or been occupied by the Aragonese, Albania was gone except for outposts such as Durazzo, and Achaea was threatened by the resurgent Byzantine Empire. The scale of the catastrophe was such that we might not have expected anything to survive from Charles of Anjou's attempt to build an empire. Yet Angevin fortunes recovered everywhere, and Charles of Anjou's descendants would add another two crowns, and indeed a central European empire, to their possessions. The much less well-known figure of Charles II can take credit for restoring Angevin fortunes, and if he did not create a vast Mediterranean empire, nevertheless he did create a stable southern Italian state that endured for more than a century.

Angevin Naples

The Angevin kingdom centred on Naples, which had become one of the largest and most dynamic cities in Europe under Angevin rule. Considering that the Neapolitan Angevins are probably the most famous of all the Angevin dynasties, and Naples remains one of the most fascinating cities in Europe, it is worth looking at it in more detail as a character in the story.

Naples is an ancient Greek city: the Greeks named it 'Neapolis', the 'New City', which it was when they founded it in the 7th century BC, and it flourished under the Romans, where the nearby resorts of Baiae and, infamously, Capri, were the playgrounds of Emperors and the wealthy. Although Naples was an important centre under the Hohenstaufen and Frederick II founded its notably secular university, it was Charles of Anjou's decision to establish it as his capital instead of Palermo that really made its fortune. The Angevin imprint on the city was immediate: Charles of Anjou built the new castle still known as the Castel Nuovo or *Maschio Angioino* ('Angevin Keep'), and which still dominates the city.

This supplanted the existing castles of the Hohenstaufen at the Capuan Gate, which Villani says Charles found 'too German', and the castle of *Salvatore a mare di Napoli*, universally known as the Castel dell'Ovo or 'Castle of the Egg'. The basis for this name is rather marvellous. According to medieval legend, the Roman poet Virgil was also a powerful magician, and he had ended his days in Naples. The castle was built near the cave where he practised his enchantments, and a magical egg was said to be buried beneath the castle that would prevent it from being captured. The 14th-century French chronicler Jean Froissart believed the legend and wrote, it 'is one of the strongest castles in the world, and situated as it were by enchantment in the sea, so that it is impossible to take it but by necromancy or by the help of the devil'.[31]

The castle needs no such fantastic story to be one of the most remarkable places in Europe. It sits on the island of Megara, which is the mythical site where the body of the siren Parthenope washed ashore (she, of course, flung herself into the sea and died after failing to seduce Odysseus with her song). Greek settlers from Cumae founded Neapolis on Megara in the 7th century BC, and it was a flourishing, and still very Greek, city throughout the Roman period. The Roman general and legendary epicure Lucullus built his villa on Megara, so as if the island hadn't witnessed enough (real or fantastic) events, it was also the site of Lucullus's spectacularly decadent banquets, including the one where in the absence of sufficiently important guests Lucullus entertained himself. The Emperor Nero made his debut as a singer in the theatre at Neapolis and performed there several times, though an earthquake during his first performance rather obviously foreshadowed the outcome of his artistic endeavours.

All this gives the Castel dell'Ovo a striking location in the sea, connected to the mainland by a causeway. Sadly it is mostly empty now and used for exhibitions, though it is open to the public and an atmospheric stroll on the battlements is a must on any visit to Naples. Under the Angevins it was in constant use as a lodging place for visiting dignitaries or a prison for important captives, and also served as their treasury.

The foundation of the Castel Nuovo had the effect of shifting the centre of gravity in the city from the eastern gate to the seafront, where it remains today. Although Naples retains its geometric arrangement of Greek streets and the Roman names for them, the *decumani* and the *cardini*, the Angevins would have a profound impact on the structure of the city. In addition to building the Castel Nuovo and many monasteries and churches, they also added rambling new quarters that made it more like other medieval European cities, and it had a population of about 60,000 in 1315. Naples became one of the cultural capitals of Italy, and its links with Florence meant that almost all of the important literary and artistic figures emerging from Florence spent time in Angevin Naples.

Resolving the 'War of the Vespers'

First the Angevins had to recover their shattered position in Italy and have their king released from prison. One of the prime movers in this recovery, surprisingly, was that quondam Angevin, Edward I of England. This was despite Edward's disgust at the outcome of Louis IX's second Crusade, and perhaps the part Charles of Anjou played in that outcome. When he heard of Charles of Anjou's death, Edward sent Charles II's young sons a message of encouragement, and more pertinently he sent 800 ounces of gold to Charles II's wife Marie, and envoys to visit Charles himself in his Aragonese prison.[32]

Italy was in such chaos following the Vespers that Provence became the de facto capital of the remaining Angevin state. The barons and bishops of Provence met to organize a response, and they wrote to Edward I begging him to intervene to obtain Charles II's freedom. The reason that Edward, rather than the king of France, was consulted, was of course because Philip III was too busy invading Aragon on his disastrous

Crusade and then dying, and the new king Philip IV was understandably somewhat disgusted with the entire business. Edward received another plea from Charles II's three sons Louis, Robert and Ramon Berengar; they sent a heart-rending letter begging for his help, describing themselves as virtual orphans and begging the 'great king' to show pity. Most pathetic of all, they explained that the letter was sealed by the Archbishop of Aix because they had no seal of their own. Edward responded with a letter addressed to his 'beloved cousins', and it was largely due to his efforts that Charles II was eventually freed in 1289. Unfortunately for the boys, the agreement to release Charles depended on his three sons taking his place in prison in Aragon, where they remained for some years.[33]

Charles II's captivity meant that the kingdom was technically ruled by the pope for four years after the death of Charles of Anjou. Martin IV initially refused as feudal overlord to accept that Charles of Anjou could leave the kingdom to Charles II, and although he accepted Charles of Anjou's appointment of Robert of Artois as regent, he made it clear that this was on behalf of the pope, not the captive Charles II. There was a diplomatic logic to this beyond the pedantic point that the pope ultimately ruled the kingdom: by disinheriting Charles II the pope deprived him of the status that made him valuable as a captive, which might have hastened his release.

Martin IV died in March 1285, and although the new pope Honorius IV showed more flexibility than Martin, he was also adamant that Sicily could not be taken (again!) by conquest. This proved awkward for Charles II, who was continually negotiating from his prison and seemed open to the idea of surrendering Sicily to Aragon, only for the pope to forbid any notion of such an arrangement. Edward I then brokered a deal in which Charles would be exchanged for three of his younger sons, pay a huge fine and undertake to reach a final arrangement over Sicily that was acceptable to Aragon, the papacy and France within three years. If he failed to do so, Provence – which the Aragonese pointed out had been taken from them by the Angevins – would revert to Aragon. This deal was at first vetoed by Philip IV of France, who could not accept the loss of Provence; a telling indication that the king of France now viewed the Mediterranean coast as pertaining to France, not Aragon. However, on the provision of guarantees and money from Edward I, this agreement was finally accepted in October 1288 and Charles II was released on condition that he went to Paris to obtain Philip IV's consent, and that he did not take the title King of Sicily, given that the island was ruled by the King of Aragon's brother. There was one other positive event in 1288, which was that Charles Martel and Clementia of Habsburg had a son, Charles Robert, known as 'Carobert', the future king of Hungary.[34]

Unfortunately for Charles, the other parties to the agreement still proved inflexible. Philip IV arrested the Aragonese ambassadors who came to Paris with Charles, and refused to accept the terms. When Charles arrived in Italy, the pope promptly arranged his coronation as King of Sicily in violation of the agreement. This ceremony was per-formed at Rieti on 29 May 1289, and provides us with the complete order of service for the Angevin king's coronation. The details of which cardinal stood where and which prayers and psalms were read is interesting in its own way, but not terribly revealing. What does stand out is the way the coronation ceremony reinforced the Angevin king's complete dependence on and subservience to the pope. This was most strikingly represented after the ceremony when Charles led the pope on horseback back to his palace.[35]

To end the War of the Vespers, a flurry of marriage contracts was meant to draw France, Sicily and Aragon together. Dynastic marriages were the usual method of cementing treaties between states, especially when they'd been at war, but the attempt to impose harmony on the Capetians, Angevins and Aragonese through the force of marriage reminds me of couples who suddenly turn to marriage in an attempt to demonstrate commitment, only to reveal how far apart they really are and precipitate greater conflict. The obsessive intertwining of the three dynasties did reduce the amount of open warfare, but it also meant they would be trapped within a cycle of destruction for the next 200 years.

Worse, the ruling family of Aragon had split, with one branch on the throne of Aragon and another taking the title Kings of Majorca and variously claiming Sicily, Sardinia and Corsica. James I of Aragon had divided his inheritance between two sons, making Peter III king of Aragon and James II the king of Majorca. What would already have been complicated three-way negotiations were thus made worse by a fourth party that was further involved in a bitter family struggle.

Charles II married his son Robert Duke of Calabria to Yolanda of Aragon, and his daughter Blanche to James II of Aragon. Another marriage was much more significant, since on 18 August 1290 he married his daughter Margaret to Charles of Valois, with Anjou and Maine as her dowry to compensate the Valois for giving up their claim to Aragon from the disastrous Crusade of Philip III. The Angevin homeland was separated from Naples and would pass to yet another new branch of the family, as always with far-reaching ramifications. The Neapolitan Angevins did receive the French portion of Avignon in return, giving them full control of this important city, which in the 14th century was about to become even more significant.[36]

1290 was also the year of a remarkable coup for the Angevins: King Ladislas IV 'the Cuman' of Hungary died without heirs. His mother was a Cuman, the Turkish nomads who had played a significant role in eastern European politics and were also a source for the 'Mamluk' slave soldiers who ruled Egypt, and Ladislas was said to have abandoned his Angevin wife and lived a pagan life with a Cuman mistress. Through Ladislas's sister Marie of Hungary, who was married to Charles II, a claim passed to their eldest son Charles Martel. This was not straightforward, since the Hungarians had crowned one of Ladislas's other relatives, Andrew III 'the Venetian', as their king, though the pope supported the Angevin claim. When Charles Martel died in 1295 his claim passed to his young son Carobert, who would be crowned several times in a variety of locations, but was finally recognized as King of Hungary in 1310.[37]

One of the keys to the Angevin resurgence was the multitude of Charles II and Marie's offspring. The later Neapolitan Angevins would be plagued by the failure to produce children who lived to maturity, perhaps not surprisingly given their near Habsburgian penchant for marrying their cousins, but Charles II and Marie of Hungary had at least thirteen children. The sons, about whom we know more, included Charles Martel who died in 1295 as titular king of Hungary; Louis of Toulouse who died in 1297 as an acknowledged saint and was canonized in 1317; Robert the Wise who succeeded as king of Naples in 1309; Ramon Berengar who died in 1305; Philip of Taranto who became titular Emperor of Constantinople, Prince of Achaea and Prince of Taranto; and John of Gravina and Durazzo, whose children intermarried with Robert's descendants and later produced two kings and the last queen of Naples.[38]

The Fall of Acre and Plans for a New Crusade

On top of the turmoil of the War of the Vespers, King Henry of Cyprus appeared in Acre in June 1286 to pursue his claim as King of Jerusalem. The city went over to him willingly and the Angevins were expelled, although Charles II technically retained the title of king and continued to use it. This accomplished little since the Mamluks took Acre and completed the destruction of the Crusader States in 1291, though the empty title King of Jerusalem continued to exist and was held by the Angevins for most of the next 200 years.

As titular King of Jerusalem, Charles II attempted to rally a response, and although he failed utterly to produce an effect in the Holy Land, he set in motion a chain of events that gained Corfu, Albania and the duchy of Athens for the Angevins, along with confirmation of the title of Prince of Achaea. Charles I's dream of taking over the Byzantine Empire for his descendants may have failed, but Charles II ruled or influenced a considerable portion of Greece. Although he is completely overshadowed by his father in historical terms, it is worth noting that Charles II was almost as ambitious as Charles of Anjou and established a more durable legacy.

Charles II also had his part to play in the Crusading movement, though he did not participate in overseas Crusades like his father. In addition to leading the pope's Crusades against their mutual Christian enemies, Charles II took his obligations in the Holy Land seriously. When Pope Nicholas IV requested guidance on how to respond to the loss of Acre, Charles prepared a detailed proposal, known as the *Conseil du Roi Charles II*, on how to recapture the Holy Land through a general Crusade. Although Charles drew on ideas put forward in previous tracts by Fidenzio of Padua and Ramon Lull, his ideas were far in advance of any yet advanced by a potential commander.

In line with the Crusade of Louis IX, Charles recommended that a combined fleet and army, supported by alms and tithes from all of Christendom, should be sent against Egypt. As had been noted by others, Charles thought the expedition would fail unless there were an economic boycott that would weaken the Mamluks. Also in line with previous discussions going back to the Council of Lyons in 1274, and which had involved Charles of Anjou, Charles II recommended that the Templars and Hospitallers be united. For many years they had been a divisive influence in the Crusader States because of their squabbling and fierce independence, which meant they refused to serve the commanders of Crusading armies. Charles also went beyond previous plans by suggesting that the newly combined orders be led by a prince of royal blood who would become King of Jerusalem. He further had in mind a concept of the Crusading force as a unified army, even detailing the uniform they would wear. Finally, Charles understood that this would be an ongoing commitment, and recommended that once recaptured, the new state would need to be defended by a permanent army of 2,000 knights and settled by colonists from the Italian maritime republics.[39]

Nothing came of Charles's plans, but this idea that the Crusade could only succeed if it were well organized by a prince who would unite the military orders and found a new kingdom was compelling. Although there is no direct evidence of influence, it is striking that these same ideas were taken up by the essayist Pierre Dubois in his *Recovery of the Holy Land*. This was the most comprehensively thought-through explication of such a project, and in it Pierre also stated that the King of Sicily would be willing to give up his title as King of Jerusalem to the leader of the new army, which implies familiarity with Charles's treatise.[40]

Pope Celestine V: 'il gran refutto'

The close Angevin ties to the papacy meant Charles II was bound up in the events of the brief pontificate of Celestine V. As an antidote to the line of overtly political popes of the 13th century and after a two-and-a-half-year interregnum, the cardinals decided that the notable holy man Pietro Morrone should be elected pope in July 1294. Charles knew Pietro and had visited him earlier that year, and Charles Martel was with the group who went to Pietro's hermitage at Mount Maiella to inform him that he was pope. Pietro announced that he was too old and infirm to go far for his consecration, so he went to the Castel Nuovo in Naples and arrived in November.

Pietro's life as a hermit may have given him the aura of sanctity, but he seems to have been completely unprepared for the job of pope. He did manage to create twelve cardinals, including five from France, and assigned tithes in France and England to Charles to carry on the war against Aragon. By December, however, Celestine was persuaded to renounce the papacy, according to one legend when the cardinal Benedetto Gaetani pretended to be God and whispered down the chimney to Celestine that he must resign. Resign he did, the first pope ever to do so (though not the last, as we have seen so recently). This abdication was termed *il gran refuto* by Dante, when he consigned Celestine to hell for failing in his duty. The cunning Benedetto Gaetani was then elected pope as Boniface VIII, and although he did rescind most of Celestine's acts, he permitted the twelve new cardinals to remain.

Upon his abdication Celestine hoped to return to life as a hermit, but Boniface VIII could never allow a former pope to remain free. Celestine was first put under guard, but after escaping for a few months he was confined to the tower of Castel Fumone, and died on 19 May 1296. Naturally his followers believed that he had been ill-treated or even murdered, and the Colonna family were quick to revive these rumours a few years later when they came into conflict with Boniface VIII. These allegations came into the hands of Philip IV of France, who used them aggressively against Boniface in his own conflict with him, and Philip continued to blacken Boniface's name even after his death in 1303. Philip then pressed Boniface's successor Clement V for Celestine's canonization as a further way to demean Boniface. Clement V agreed in hope of reconciling with the French king, but he carefully stressed that the investigation was an inquiry into the miracles of Pietro Morrone as a holy man, not Celestine V as pope. St Pietro Morrone was duly canonized in 1313, and the fact that he was canonized by Boniface's successor at the instigation of Boniface's mortal enemy Philip IV was lost on no one.[41]

This canonization showed that not everyone saw Celestine in the same terms as Dante. Charles II founded a religious house at Aversa dedicated to him, and the Angevin knight Giovanni Pippino da Barletta commissioned the church of San Pietro 'Maiella' (named after Pietro's hermitage on Mt Maiella) in Naples in his honour. San Pietro Maiella is considered a significant example of Angevin architecture in Naples and gives its name to a music conservatory, though I suspect most passersby – including me! – aren't aware of the connection to Celestine/Pietro Morrone until they enter the church and read about its history.

Carobert's Accession in Hungary

It took more than ten years for Charles II and his sons fully to escape the consequences of his capture by Roger of Lauria in 1284. The proximate cause of the princes' release was the death of Charles Martel on 5 August 1295, and the three princes were released soon after. Naples was now faced with a similar succession question to that of England after the death of Richard the Lionheart 100 years before: should Charles II's heir be Charles Martel's son Carobert (son of the elder brother) or one of Charles II's younger sons? Although Charles II would live until 1309, the Angevins resolved the issue quickly, and in the same way it had been in England. Charles II acknowledged Robert as his heir on 13 February 1296, which must have seemed more palatable at the time since the child Carobert was now titular king of Hungary. Yet even though Boniface VIII quickly approved the decision on 27 February and excluded Carobert from the throne of Naples, Robert would be plagued by questions over the legitimacy of his rule from the remarkably successful Hungarian branch of the family founded by Carobert.

The initial circumstances of Carobert's claim to Hungary were not auspicious. Andrew III 'the Venetian' had taken the throne in 1290, but faced significant resistance to his rule. In particular, the lords of Croatia and Dalmatia, neighbours of the Angevins across the Adriatic, came out in favour of Charles Martel, and after his death transferred their support to Carobert. Andrew struggled to impose his authority, particularly in the south.

In August 1300, the twelve-year-old Carobert, like another Henry II, went to Dalmatia to take up the struggle personally. He was conducted across the Adriatic by Juraj Šubić, scion of perhaps the most important family in Croatia, the counts of Bribir. They controlled Split and many other important cities along the coast, also extending their power inland to control an essentially independent principality in Croatia and Bosnia. Charles II had recognized Pavao Šubić (brother of Juraj) as *ban* of Croatia in 1292, a not particularly valuable grant when we consider that Charles II had no authority over Croatia, but given that the Šubićs were powerful enough to dominate the area themselves there was no harm in obtaining recognition of their power from the king of Naples. This arrangement was much more beneficial to the Angevins, since throughout the 1290s the Šubićs had consistently recognized first Charles Martel, then Carobert, as the rightful kings of Hungary in opposition to Andrew III. When Carobert and Juraj arrived in Split, they were received by Pavao Šubić, who then conducted the young king to Zagreb. This solid support from the Šubićs was the critical local basis of Carobert's bid for the throne. He then also had an incredible stroke of luck, since Andrew III died on 14 January 1301 leaving no children.[42]

The other key factor to Angevin success in Hungary, naturally, was the support of the papacy. Boniface VIII supported Carobert's claim, and instructed the Hungarian clergy to give him their backing. This would have the advantage for Boniface of strengthening papal authority in Hungary, where it had been somewhat tenuous in the past. Despite this clerical support and the support of the Šubićs, Carobert was still not accepted by the barons of Hungary. As we saw previously with both Henry I and King Stephen in England, one way of cementing a claim to the throne was simply by being crowned in spite of other claimants, which afforded an intrinsic status that could overwhelm rivals. Carobert adopted this approach.

There were very specific requirements for a king of Hungary's coronation. The ceremony could only be performed at the cathedral of Székesfehérvár by the Archbishop of Esztergom, using the crown of St Stephen, or it would be invalid. Carobert was in luck, because Gregory Bicskei, the Archbishop-elect of Esztergom, was a supporter of Boniface VIII and willing to perform the ceremony. Unfortunately the crown of St Stephen was not in his possession and Székesfehérvár was not considered safe, so in 1301 Gregory conducted the coronation in Esztergom with a provisional crown. Although this coronation was not accepted as legitimate by most, Carobert dated his reign to this date.[43]

With Andrew III dead, a new claimant appeared in the form of Wenceslas, son of King Wenceslas II of Bohemia. He was preferred by the Hungarian barons, and in a potentially devastating blow for Carobert, he too adopted the coronation strategy. Wenceslas was crowned at Székesfehérvár with the crown of St Stephen on 27 August 1301, but the ceremony was performed by the Archbishop of Kalocsa. Civil war broke out, with the Habsburgs of Austria and most of the clergy backing Carobert, and the barons backing Wenceslas. Rising Habsburg power showed the wisdom of Charles II's alliance with them through the marriage of Charles Martel and Clementia of Habsburg, and Carobert benefitted greatly from this support by his mother's family. By 1304 Carobert was successful enough for many of the barons to take his side, and Wenceslas retreated to Bohemia, taking the holy crown with him.

Although Carobert and his Habsburg allies invaded Bohemia in turn, the situation reached something of a stalemate. Again Carobert benefitted from a fortunate death, that of Wenceslas II, and Wenceslas III now succeeded to the throne of Bohemia and renounced his claim to Hungary. He passed his claim to Otto of Bavaria, grandson of Béla IV of Hungary through his mother, and Otto retained the Holy Crown. Otto was able to get the bishops of Veszprém and Csanád to crown him in Székesfehérvár on 6 December 1305, but since the Archbishop of Esztergom still supported Carobert the coronation was rejected and Otto failed to mobilize the barons.

Despite this new rival, Carobert steadily built up his power base, capturing Esztergom in 1306 and Buda in 1307. More importantly, in 1307 Otto was captured and the Holy Crown was seized from him, though it remained in the hands of Carobert's opponents. Carobert was again acclaimed as king in Buda on 10 October 1307 and at a diet in Pest on 27 November 1308, and further crowned in Buda by a papal legate in 1309, but none of these procedures fulfilled the necessary requirements. Only in 1310 did he finally obtain the Holy Crown, and on 27 August 1310 he was crowned in Székesfehérvár, by the Archbishop of Esztergom, with the Holy Crown. It was just as Carobert finally cemented his position as king of Hungary that the Angevins of Naples also reached their peak, after the steadying reign of Charles II.[44]

Charles II's Cultural Legacy: Naples and the *Beata Stirps*

Charles II presided over what would become the settlement between the Angevins and Aragonese over Sicily. This was the Treaty of Caltabellota in 1302, which recognized Sicily as an independent kingdom for the lifetime of Frederick III, though he was only allowed to use the title 'King of Trinacria', an ancient name for the three-cornered island, and the Angevins would continue to call themselves kings of Sicily. Charles II's son Philip of Taranto was released from a Sicilian prison and Charles agreed to pay a tribute of 100,000 ounces of gold. Sicily was meant to revert to the Angevins after Frederick's death, but unsurprisingly this didn't happen, and the Angevins and Aragonese would fight over the island throughout the 14th century.[45]

Still, Charles did secure peace in his own lifetime, allowing him to consolidate and expand the cultural life of Naples to make it one of the most vibrant cities in Europe, as well as the courtly centre of Italy in the early and mid-14th century. Boccaccio has his heroine in *Fiammetta* condemn Florence as bristling with arms and filled with 'greedy, proud and envious people' compared with Naples, which is 'contented, peaceful, flourishing, liberal and subject to a single ruler'.[46] This slightly misses the mark, as all that Florentine money and political agitation produced the profound intellectual and artistic ferment we call the Renaissance. Moreover, although much of the artistic life of Naples still relied on French craftsmen, there was also an influx of Florentine artists (as well as bankers), which contributed significantly to Naples's intellectual life. We would be wrong, however, to say that Naples was in some way parasitic on Florence. Through its combination of influences particularly from France and Greece, Naples had a distinctive intellectual life; for example, Naples was the only European court where Greek was systematically studied in the mid-14th century, a century before the Renaissance proper.[47]

Charles commissioned the single most important medieval object in Naples today, and one of the outstanding artistic achievements of any period, the silver reliquary of San Gennaro. It is a masterpiece of medieval metalwork and enamelling, as in addition to the astonishing portrait bust itself (rumoured without any foundation to depict a member of the Angevin ruling family, or slightly more plausibly, a contemporary bishop), the shoulders of the bust are covered with Angevin coats of arms and precious and semi-precious stones.[48]

The bust was created by four French silversmiths in 1303–04 to celebrate the millennium of San Gennaro's martyrdom, and it was designed to hold the ampule of San Gennaro's blood, which to this day miraculously liquefies three times a year (on 19 September, the day of his martyrdom; 16 December, commemorating his patronage of Naples; and the first Saturday in May, celebrating the transfer of his relics). Or at least it should, because if the blood fails to liquefy, catastrophe will strike, as evidenced by the miracle's failure in 1939, and as in fact happened on 16 December 2016, which could be considered entirely appropriate given some of the events of 2016.

Although all medieval rulers were religious patrons to a greater or lesser extent, the Neapolitan Angevins starting with Charles of Anjou were the first dynasty to make the idea of their 'holy lineage' (*beata stirps*) a key component of the legitimacy of their rule. The first important family saint was naturally Louis IX, brother to Charles of Anjou. Charles personally provided testimony to support Louis IX's canonization, and the actual event in 1297 was a huge boost for the Angevins, now represented by Charles II.[49]

Charles II was known for his piety in a way that strangely eluded Charles of Anjou, the multiple Crusader, brother of a saint and right arm of the papacy. Charles II discovered the remains of Mary Magdalen in 1279 at St Maximin in Provence, and he was instrumental in establishing her cult in Provence as a major religious centre. According to one chronicler he helped to dig up her relics with his own hands: 'he tore off his royal vestments, helping to remove the earth with his bare hands, sweat pouring profusely from him'.[50] The Magdalen became associated with the Angevins, and to this day her shrine in Provence is a notable site. More importantly, Charles's own son Louis of Toulouse was widely known to be a saint at the time of his death in 1297, even though Charles wouldn't live to see him canonized in 1317.

Louis's sainthood was a direct consequence of the Angevin wars with Aragon. After Charles II's capture, his release was arranged in exchange for his sons Louis, Robert and Ramon Berengar, who were held in the fortress of Cuirana for seven years. They were accompanied by their tutor, Francis le Brun, who was a 'Spiritual' Franciscan, a believer in Apostolic poverty. Louis's instruction by Francis from the age of fourteen to twenty-one had a great impact, and when in 1295 a treaty was arranged between Aragon and Naples that was meant to be sealed by Louis's marriage to the king of Aragon's sister, it was discovered that he had taken a vow of celibacy. On the death of his elder brother Charles Martel, Louis could have become heir to the throne, but he refused and stated his intention of becoming a Franciscan. At the Castel Nuovo in Naples in 1296 he formally renounced his claim to the throne in favour of his brother Robert.[51]

Although Charles II was prepared to allow his son to choose his spiritual over his political obligations, he was still required to do this in an appropriately aristocratic style. Louis wished to become a Franciscan friar, but his father insisted that he become a bishop and procured the wealthy see of Toulouse for him. Louis went to Rome to be invested by Pope Boniface VIII, but demanded that if he accepted the bishopric he must also be allowed to become a Franciscan. Boniface allowed Louis to be received into the Franciscan order secretly on Christmas Eve 1296, but required him to conceal his habit beneath his episcopal robes.

Louis maintained this secrecy for a month, but on 5 February 1297 he received the pope's permission to celebrate mass at Santa Maria Aracoeli – the great city church of Rome that now belonged to the Franciscans – and publicly reveal himself as a member of the order. In what has been called the most dramatic scene in 13th-century Rome,[52] at the end of Mass Louis publicly removed his bishop's robes and revealed his Franciscan habit to a huge crowd. A king's son and heir, and bishop, openly renouncing so much pomp and authority in the heart of the Christian world had, and has, a profound resonance, and when Louis died in August 1297 his canonization came swiftly after in 1317.

The Death of Pope Boniface VIII: The 'Colonna Slap' and the Babylonian Captivity of the Church

Unlike Louis, there was no question that Boniface VIII fully embraced the power of the Church and believed that the time had come for the pope to wield secular power directly and openly. During the papal jubilee of 1300 when Rome was crowded with pilgrims from all over Europe who had come to expiate their sins, Boniface appeared on the balcony at the Vatican and openly brandished two swords: these were the 'two swords' of secular and religious authority that he unsubtly claimed for himself. This was particularly offensive to Philip IV of France, now the most powerful ruler in Europe, who presided over an intensely centralized and wealthy state. In the following years Boniface pushed his claims over the Church in France too far, and in 1304 Philip sent Guillaume de Nogaret and other henchmen, including the infamous Sciarra Colonna (member of one of Rome's most powerful families), to the papal palace of Anagni to convince the pope to modify his claims. Philip made it clear that he wasn't too particular about the methods of persuasion they used.

The armed men burst into the elderly pope's bedchamber and manhandled him, culminating when Sciarra dealt the pope the 'Colonna Slap', which passed into legend. When Boniface died shortly after, presumably from shock, there was a rerun of the Becket situation for Henry II, though Philip IV (probably much more culpable than Henry II had been) did not attract quite the same opprobrium. Notably, Charles II backed Boniface VIII in this incident, straining his relationship with Philip IV.[53]

In the aftermath the papacy fell into confusion, and after the brief pontificate of Benedict IX, the French and Italian cardinals were unable to agree on a new pope. The cardinals finally elected the Archbishop of Bordeaux, who avoided Rome, where he would have been at the mercy of the Colonna, eventually settling in Avignon and leading to the sixty-seven-year 'Babylonian Captivity' of the papacy, when a series of French-speaking popes ruled from the Provençal city.

Although as we have seen Provence wasn't part of France, the series of French popes in Avignon were regarded by everyone else in Europe as tools of the French king, and part of that was their support for the 'French' Angevins of Naples. There was a solid basis for this in the behaviour of the first Avignon pope, Clement V, who although French-speaking, as Archbishop of Bordeaux was a subject of the king of England and so might have been expected to maintain his independence from France. Sadly for him, Edward I of England was far too involved in trying to conquer Scotland and had no time to support the pope.[54] Instead the popes turned to the Angevins of Naples, who became their chief supporters, although by the mid-14th century the Angevins were much more reliant on papal support for their survival than vice versa. This relationship between the Avignon popes and the Angevins (in Naples and elsewhere) would provide the political architecture for the 14th century, and the background to some of the most momentous events of the Middle Ages.

CHAPTER 9 – THE ANGEVINS OF NAPLES AND HUNGARY: THE KING OF SERMONS AND THE HARLOT QUEEN

WITH CHARLES MARTEL AND Louis of Toulouse dead, and Carobert now King of Hungary, in 1309 Charles II's third son Robert the Wise succeeded to the throne of Naples. Robert was born in 1278 and initially educated in Provence, where contemporaries particularly commented on how closely the education of the Angevin royal children matched that of the French royal household. Of course this came to an end in 1288, when Robert and his brothers Louis and Ramon Berengar were sent into captivity to replace Charles II, and the boys were educated by the Franciscan tutor Francis le Brun, who instilled a deep piety and devotion to the Franciscans in all three princes.

The Franciscan tutor was competent as well as pious, because Robert's religious fervour was underpinned by genuine learning. His education formed the basis for the most famous aspect of Robert's reign, and indeed the one that gave him his name, 'the Wise'. He demonstrated this in his public examination of Petrarch to prove his worthiness to be the first poet laureate since Roman times, as well as his delivery of hundreds of public sermons and authorship of at least two theological treatises. Despite tales of Richard the Lionheart correcting a bishop's Latin, Frederick II writing a treatise on hawking, Louis IX engaging in theological debates and Alfonso the Wise of Castile commissioning astronomical tables, we have not seen a true scholar king before Robert who produced such a copious body of work. Kings were still largely seen as military leaders, and there was suspicion about a king who was too pious or learned, a prejudice to which Robert was not immune.

Yet although critics such as Dante mocked him as 'King of Sermons', he was not an ineffective king. He saw off two major threats from the Empire, and repeatedly attempted – with some minor successes – to retake Sicily. In addition to this skirmishing over Sicily, there would also be proxy wars between the Angevins and Aragon in various areas of the Mediterranean: for example in Greece, where companies of Catalan mercenaries centred on Athens had repeated conflicts with Angevin deputies in Morea; and in Genoa, where the city's Guelfs, particularly the Grimaldi family (who still rule Monaco), struggled against local Ghibellines supported by the Visconti of Milan.[1]

The first great crisis of Robert's reign was the invasion of Italy by Henry VII of Luxembourg. Henry was elected King of the Romans in 1309, with the support of Pope

Clement V, as the papacy had finally realized that the power vacuum in the Empire dating back to the deposition of Frederick II was just as bad for Italy as for the Empire itself. However, this was awkward for the Angevins, whose dominance of Tuscany and other parts of Italy would be threatened by a reigning Emperor, as well as Guelfs throughout Italy whose Ghibelline rivals would receive imperial support.

Thus Henry's journey to Rome for his coronation was a military expedition that was viewed as an invasion, and an Angevin army led by John of Gravina advanced to block him. Although there was no military confrontation, the Angevin army prevented Henry from reaching St Peter's and he had to be crowned at the Lateran, on 29 June 1312, although the pope was not present and three Ghibelline cardinals performed the ceremony. As Emperor, Henry responded to the Angevin attempts to block his coronation by summoning Robert to appear before him for trial as a treasonous vassal, and when Robert refused he was declared a rebel on 26 April 1313. Henry was also negotiating for a marriage alliance with King Frederick of Sicily, and there was a danger Robert could be encircled.

Although Robert had sent a military force to Rome to impede Henry's coronation, he personally responded to Henry's attempt to depose him in exactly the way that we would expect him to, by having jurists prepare legal opinions showing why Henry's position was invalid. Robert's scholars prepared glosses on the law code promulgated by Frederick II in the 13th century, the *Constitutions of Melfi*, demonstrating that Robert was not subject to the Emperor and thus could not be deposed by him. They went further, and attacked any Emperor's claim to universal jurisdiction by saying that the kings of Sicily were sovereign in their own realm exactly as the Normans and Frederick II had been; that in any event the Roman Empire itself had no right to rule others through conquest; and regardless of all that, all imperial rights had been ceded to the pope in the Donation of Constantine, the 4th-century document in which (allegedly) the Emperor Constantine ceded dominion of the empire to the pope. Robert put a personal twist on this argument in a letter to the pope, pointing out that all emperors since Domitian (who reigned from 81–96) had harmed the church (putting the first Christian Emperor Constantine in an interesting position), and as the Germans were barbarians, the Holy Roman Empire should be dissolved. Although Henry VII died on 24 August 1313 and the conflict ended, Clement V, perhaps thinking better of his support for Henry, accepted these arguments and issued a bull in March 1314 declaring that there was no basis for imperial claims of universal dominion.[2]

After Clement V's death in 1314, Robert promoted the candidacy of Jacques Duèze, who had administered Provence for the Angevins, served as chancellor of Naples from 1305 and been Robert's personal counsellor until his accession in 1309. Jacques duly became pope in August 1316 with the name John XXII, and Robert maintained a close relationship with him. This papal connection proved extremely beneficial to the Angevins and in fact Robert spent 1319–1324 in Provence to be near the pope.

John XXII canonized Louis of Toulouse in 1317 and would canonize Thomas

Aquinas in Robert's presence in 1323, and he appointed Robert vicar of all imperial territories in 1317. However, despite the two men's long friendship there was also tension, because the ideal of apostolic poverty as practiced by the extreme 'Spiritual' wing of the Franciscans, and which had troubled the papacy throughout the 13th century, offended the notoriously venal papal court in Avignon. John XXII condemned the Spirituals, and burnt four of their members at the stake in May 1318. The Angevins had traditionally supported the Spirituals, and as we know Robert's early education and affection for Louis of Toulouse made him particularly attached to the order. Given Robert's later actions, it may be that one of his reasons for choosing to live near the pope was an attempt to influence his opinion about this vexed question. Robert's position as a philosopher king and champion of apostolic poverty by no means reduced his interest in royal magnificence, and he enjoyed making a show. When he began his move to Avignon in 1318, the list of his attendants includes 236 names, including chamberlains, knights, squires, constables, surgeons, barbers and 'custodians of the royal cup'.[3]

Robert maintained close connections to Florence at a time when it was fighting its Ghibelline enemies, particularly the Visconti of Milan, who would dominate the north of Italy throughout the 14th century. Robert was in Florence in 1310 organizing resistance to Henry VII, and he was offered the signory for five years from 1313. Although not a warrior himself, like the future Charles V of France Robert did not shy away from military conflicts. When the Ghibelline lord of Pisa invaded Tuscany in 1314, Robert sent his brother Philip of Taranto with an Angevin army to resist him. The Angevins were heavily defeated at Montecatini in August 1315, and another of Robert's brothers, Peter of Eboli, was killed in the battle. Although Florence urged Robert to avenge his brother, he failed to respond, leading the furious Florentines to accuse him of leaving Tuscany to be overrun. Robert brokered a peace between the Tuscan cities in 1317, but Florence was now suspicious of him, and particularly believed that his vicar was interfering with the city's republican institutions. Despite this, Florence did not end Robert's signory until 1321, but it did so on quite bad terms.

This was a poor choice, since the warlord Castruccio Castracane now invaded Tuscany, taking Pistoia in May 1325 and defeating a Guelf army and taking Fiesole in the hills above Florence in September. The Visconti were also on the move, attacking Bologna at the same time. Florence and Bologna now appealed for Robert's help. Robert's response is telling, since he preached a sermon to the ambassadors about the story of Joseph, and how his arrogant and ungrateful brothers had to beg for his help in Egypt after they had wronged him. Florence again offered Robert the signory, and he sent his only son Charles of Calabria to rule the city.[4]

Another threat now arose in the form of Ludwig of Bavaria, who became a candidate for Emperor in 1322. Ludwig chose the traditional Ghibelline alliance in Italy and thus opposed the pope, so he attacked John XXII's position on apostolic poverty. Although Robert himself held a different view from the pope, he entered the fray in 1322 with his first religious treatise, on the theme of poverty. Ludwig's position hardened and he declared the pope to be a heretic in May 1324, though as we would expect only Ludwig's allies accepted this condemnation.

Ludwig and his army entered Italy in 1327, and Florence was justifiably fearful of his intentions. The Angevins also had cause to be worried, as the memory of Conradin lived on in the Empire: Matthias von Neuenburg reports that when Ludwig passed the castle in which he believed Conradin had been beheaded (mistakenly, since he was executed in Naples), he had it razed to the ground.[5] Robert seemed to believe that allowing Ludwig a free hand in Tuscany would keep him from invading the Angevin kingdom, which is quite a hard-nosed calculation for the 'King of Sermons', and Charles of Calabria was recalled from Florence to defend the border. Despite Charles's generally good reputation elsewhere, this decision was met with fury in Florence, and undermined Angevin standing in the city. Giovanni Villani commented that if Charles hadn't left Florence the city would have risen against him and expelled him, and Florence would not accept another Angevin vicar until 1342.

Ludwig reached Rome on 7 January 1328, and despite abandoning Tuscany, Robert opposed this advance just as he had that of Henry VII, and in the same way, by sending his brother John of Gravina with an army to Rome to block the coronation, but John was defeated. We do now get a very clear sense that Robert, although perfectly prepared to use military power, preferred not to lead the armies himself and delegated authority to his brothers or son. This type of kingship, where a wise king would devote himself to managing the kingdom and let other more suitable commanders lead his armies, is one that we will see again with Robert's near contemporary, Charles V of France, who resembled Robert in many ways.

Ludwig was crowned Emperor in Santa Maria Maggiore on 17 January 1328, and followed his condemnation of John XXII by declaring his deposition on 18 April and appointing a Spiritual Franciscan as anti-pope Nicholas V on 12 May. Although John XXII was not seriously threatened, these actions do demonstrate that the Empire was returning to its levels of influence of the 12th century, when Emperors frequently appointed their own candidates as rival 'anti-popes'. Ludwig also declared Robert a rebel on the grounds that the Emperor somehow had authority over him, but this had no basis and Robert would only be threatened if Ludwig actually found sufficient military power to attack directly. As we would expect, a Crusade was duly declared against Ludwig, though this similarly had little impact.[6]

Despite Florentine unhappiness with his policies, Robert the Wise used Ludwig's invasion as another opportunity to emphasize the holiness of his lineage. Giovanni Regina, a Dominican preacher closely connected to Robert's court, gave a sermon in April 1328, when Charles of Calabria was leading the army to defend the border against Ludwig, in which he remarked upon *beata stirps*. He noted that like Robert, Charles of Anjou had fought the enemies of the church and Saint Louis was part of the Angevin lineage, and especially that Robert's own brother Louis of Toulouse was a saint.[7]

Charles of Calabria, despite Villani's caustic comments, had a generally positive reputation with contemporaries, and when he suddenly died of illness in November 1328 it was a serious blow for Robert. Charles had ruled the kingdom when Robert resided in Avignon from 1318–24, and he had taken the lead in the fight against Ludwig. Like many princes who died young, Charles was perhaps credited with more virtue than he actually possessed, but the chroniclers are fairly unanimous in their praise of him. The chronicler known as the 'Roman Anonymous' says of Charles of Calabria: 'He was a very judicious man and said, "King Charles our great-grandfather acquired and maintained this realm through military prowess, my grandfather through generosity, my father through wisdom. Therefore I want to maintain it through justice." Strenuously did the duke strive to serve highest justice.'[8] The *Chronicle of Parthenope* also reports that when Charles ruled the kingdom during Robert's absence, he put a bell outside the royal castle that anyone could ring, whereupon he would appear and render justice to them.

In the midst of Ludwig of Bavaria's invasion, Robert now faced trouble from an unexpected quarter when John XXII betrayed him. John, like all popes, was deeply troubled by the disturbed condition of Italy and hoped to find a stable solution. Given recent Crusades against Genoa, Venice and the Visconti of Milan, it was clear that none of the existing powers in northern Italy was to his liking, and John never supported the utopian dream of a united Angevin kingdom of Italy. Who was left? John opposed Ludwig of Bavaria's invasion, so the Empire was not a possibility. Despite the catastrophe of Philip the Fair and Boniface VIII's conflict, France was once again home of the 'most Christian' king as well as being perceived as the most powerful state in Europe. John therefore approached the current French king, Philip VI, and proposed that he should rule a 'kingdom of Lombardy' as the papal champion in northern Italy, basically taking over the old imperial role.

Yet as was so often the case, events overtook the pope. Even as these discussions were underway in 1330, King John of Bohemia, son of the former Emperor Henry VII and a potential rival to Ludwig, began his own campaign in Italy. He quickly took the signory of Brescia in 1330, and by 1331 he was lord of most of Lombardy. This drove Ludwig back to the Empire, an undeniably good result for Robert, but also had an unexpected consequence: the pope's plan for a 'kingdom of Lombardy' had now almost come to fruition, only with a different ruler. John XXII was in a different mould to the popes of the 13th century and didn't fall into a vendetta as his predecessors had against the Hohenstaufen. Instead the pope adroitly pivoted and recognized John of Bohemia as overlord of Lombardy, leaving Philip VI and Robert out of the equation.

John of Bohemia was aware of the pope's initial plan with Philip VI, so he in turn began negotiations with Philip to arrange a division of northern Italy between them and then seek the pope's approval. John XXII willingly joined these discussions, and as had happened before, talk of dividing the old imperial possessions in northern Italy quickly extended to comprise the 'kingdom of Arles', including Provence. The pope now agreed that John of Bohemia would rule the kingdom of Lombardy and Philip VI would rule the kingdom of Arles, completely betraying Robert in both Italy and Provence.

The one seemingly unchanging truth about Italian politics since the 1260s, the singularity of purpose between the pope and the Angevins, was thus overturned. Although technically assigning these new 'kingdoms' to other rulers would not dispossess Robert of anything, in fact it would deliver a fatal blow against Angevin authority. This led to an equally unprecedented political move: Robert gathered his Guelf allies and formed a previously unthinkable alliance with the Ghibelline cities of the north to resist 'whoever comes to trouble the peace in Italy, including the Empire and the Church.'[9]

In the midst of this complicated situation, something utterly extraordinary happened. On the Feast of All Saints in 1331, John XXII began a sermon in Avignon in which he – quite casually – asked if saints really saw God immediately when they arrived in heaven, or if they would have to wait until Judgement Day. John developed this theme in another sermon and again challenged the doctrine of the 'Beatific Vision', essentially espousing heretical views himself.[10]

A potential imperial invasion of Italy, the church riven by a spiritual monastic movement, Guelfs and Ghibellines joining forces (like lambs and wolves, as the chroniclers said) and now a heretical pope. It did seem to be the end of days. The theological basis for this consternation over John XXII's views was that so much church doctrine was underpinned by the Beatific Vision. The entire cult of the saints depended on the idea that saints were with God in heaven and could intercede with him, otherwise there would be no point in praying to them.

Robert intervened in a characteristic way, asking the pope if he could rebut this scandalous opinion, and he produced a treatise in two parts on the Beatific Vision. This is a fairly standard theological work, but it does demonstrate Robert's erudition, and suggests that Petrarch's description of him in his *Letter to Posterity* as 'the only monarch of our age who was the friend at once of learning and of virtue'[11] wasn't idle flattery. Robert marshalled an impressive array of authorities to support his position, and divided the treatise into sections where he set out scholastic arguments (the saints on earth see God, Moses and Saint Paul saw God on earth, therefore the saints must also see God in Heaven) and drew heavily on the work of the recently canonized Aquinas, whose canonization he had been instrumental in securing. More interestingly from our point of view, he then included a section where he drew on pre-Christian philosophers to show that the most ancient human traditions supported his opinions, citing Seneca, Apuleius, Aristotle, Macrobius and Boethius within the first paragraph. Appealing to pagan philosophers is not so surprising, but he then referenced Avicenna and Algazel, showing a quite unexpected openness to Islamic thought. Robert concluded by appealing to Virgil's *Eclogues* and *Georgics*, but then disarmingly admitted that he didn't have the original works with him, so people with better memories would have to find the exact references.[12]

We have seen royal authors before and will see them again, but the level and quality of Robert's output is unique. This raises the question of whether he really did write the works attributed to him, but a recent modern editor (M. Dykmans) argues persuasively that he did. Dykmans notes that the treatise on the Beatific Vision and Robert's treatise on Apostolic Poverty have a similar idiosyncratic style; there aren't any reasonable candidates at Robert's court who were available to write both; and that the treatises are clearly written by a layman, with a personal quality that suggests Robert himself was the author.[13] Robert duly sent his treatise on the Beatific Vision to John XXII, who received it cordially. More importantly, Robert's ambassadors who carried the treatise to Avignon also negotiated with the pope and managed to achieve a reconciliation.

By June 1333 Robert's Italian league had succeeded: John of Bohemia gave up his plans to rule a northern Italian kingdom, and he withdrew from Italy. Not coincidentally, Angevin support for the Spiritual Franciscans also waned, John XXII ended his persecution of the Spirituals and the traditional papal-Angevin alliance was restored. John XXII, who was nearly ninety, died in 1334 and the episode was at an end.

The events surrounding John of Bohemia and Philip VI should put paid to the idea that the Neapolitan (or indeed the Hungarian) Angevins were 'French' in the way that Charles of Anjou had been. The Angevins were independent and, in this case, actually opposed to France. Even after the failure of his plot, Philip VI would still buy the rights to the signory of Lucca from John of Bohemia, prompting Robert to lodge a formal protest at this intervention in Italy. Certainly Petrarch and Boccaccio viewed Robert and his successor Johanna as 'Italian' rulers and did not see them as foreign, and on this occasion the Angevins were acting against their traditional papal and French alliances.[14]

Interestingly, during the first conflict between Emperor and Angevin, some of Robert's supporters began to agitate for Robert to become king of a united Italy, and this idea would reappear. The most famous example came in 1335–36 with the *Regia carmina*, a sumptuously illuminated manuscript paean to Robert prepared by the people of Prato in which a personification of Italy tells Robert that he must take her into his protection for her own safety. This is followed by personifications of Rome and Florence also pleading for his rule, as Rome has been deserted by the pope and Tuscany doesn't have a king. The document was circulated in at least five copies, of which three survive, the best being the British Library copy with a stunning portrait illumination of Robert, which given its idiosyncrasies seems to be a good likeness. Robert's gaunt face and prominent nose resemble Charles of Anjou's portrait statue, and the background of fleurs-de-lys ties him to the Capetians in a way that was perhaps unwarranted.

The *Regia carmina* also lauds Robert as the sole hope of the entire world, not just Italy, because of his role as King of Jerusalem. Robert treasured this title, as would his descendants and other Angevins down through King René, because, empty though it was, it was such a resonant title that it gave its holder priority over other monarchs. Robert did accept that some duties came with the title, and he wrote to the sultan of Egypt to ensure safe conduct for Christians travelling to the Holy Land, and he joined in the general correspondence to the Mongol Khans and other Tatar leaders exhorting them to convert to Christianity. What he did not accept was any role as a leader of Crusades. When the pope called for a general Crusade in 1333 with the support of France, Venice and Cyprus, Robert agreed to provide sixteen ships, but when the expedition actually began in 1334 he only provided two. Although the Christian fleet did defeat a Turkish fleet in the east, nothing else came of the expedition and it returned having accomplished almost nothing. Still, given the situation Robert had just faced with invasions of Italy by Ludwig and John of Bohemia, it may have been too ambitious to expect him to send much support.

The timing of the *Regia carmina* is interesting, coming after Robert's conflict with the Emperor, and in light of the pope taking the side of Robert's opponents. The *Regia carmina* alludes to this, saying that Robert is the true saviour of Italy precisely because he led an alliance of the Guelfs and Ghibellines to oppose a papally sanctioned invasion by a foreign power. This is an explosive idea, but one which gained little momentum as Robert reconciled with the pope and seemed to have no interest in promoting his own leadership of Italy.[15]

That said, Robert was still interested in building Angevin power in northern Italy and the Alps. At this time, the ruler of the Dauphiné, Umberto II, was childless and had enormous debts, and was looking for someone to buy his realm. The Dauphiné is the region centred on Grenoble, west of Piedmont and north of Provence, and thus would have meshed well with Robert's territories. Unfortunately Robert was unable to afford the 20,000 ounces of gold Umberto II needed. In 1349 Umberto eventually found a buyer in Philip VI of France, and one of the conditions of the sale was that the heir to the French throne would take Umberto's title and be known as the 'Dauphin', a condition that was honoured until the end of the French monarchy.[16]

In terms of his personality, it is easy to sneer at Robert as Dante did, and call him the 'King of Sermons', more fit for preaching than to wear a sword. Certainly his sermons are tedious to read and do not suggest he was the most engaging personality. Yet if we step aside from his intellectual activity for the moment and look at his cultural interests, he fits very well in the long line of Angevin patrons. It was Robert who commissioned Giotto to decorate the chapel at the Castel Nuovo, and although the paintings are no longer extant, a 14th-century poem describes the decorations, which showed pairs of illustrious men and women from the Bible and antiquity. Giotto is the most recognizable name today, but Robert also commissioned the Sienese master Simone Martini to paint the magnificent and profoundly propagandistic panel of Louis of Toulouse enthroned in majesty and crowning Robert, now in the Capodimonte Museum. Robert patronized other artists, such as the Tuscan Tino da Camino, who produced six royal tombs, and the Roman Pietro Cavallini who decorated Santa Maria Donna Regina with frescoes celebrating Angevin rule.[17]

Besides the Simone Martini panel, the most magnificent object to survive from Robert's reign is the Bible of Malines, now in Louvain, which the Neapolitan artist Cristoforo Orimina painted in the style of Giotto, again celebrating Angevin rule and explicitly setting out Robert's dynastic connections and legitimacy. It is one of the best and most striking illustrations of the Angevin dynasty, depicting the entire family in three bands across the frontispiece, showing Charles I, Charles II and Robert with their wives, children and heirs set out clearly to demonstrate the succession. The bible was commissioned as a present for Robert's granddaughter and heiress, Johanna, and her husband Andrew of Hungary, son of Carobert and so a potential rival, and their marriage was meant to unite the two dynasties, with the results we will see below.[18]

Robert was also associated with the two greatest composers of the 14th century. Marchetto da Padova, a music theorist whose work was fundamental in establishing modern tuning and time notation, dedicated his *Pomerium* to Robert and was employed in the royal chapel. Philippe de Vitry, author of the treatise *Ars Nova*, which gave its name to the musical style of the period, composed a motet glorifying Robert and giving him all the virtues, of which the first letters of each line spell 'Robertus'. As with the visual arts, so too with music: the usually foreign artists who worked for Robert would return to their native cities and spread Robert's fame as a learned patron.[19]

However, Robert's reputation for wisdom and literary merit really rests not so much on his own literary production, impressive as it was, but because of his relationship with Petrarch. Petrarch has been described as the 'first celebrity', and the Fontaine de Vaucluse, where he lived and first wrote his sonnets about his idealized love, Laura, was a tourist attraction even in the 14th century. He was the most famous private citizen of his day, as well as being described as the 'last of the Troubadours' and 'the originator of modern literature'[20], and these descriptions are justified. He had a profound and lasting cultural influence through his use of the vernacular in a literary context, his pioneering use of sonnets, his conception of history and his coining of terms such as the 'Dark Ages' to describe the period between the fall of Rome and his own enlightened times. Perhaps most enduringly, it is believed that the italic script still used in printing today was based on his handwriting.

As the preeminent literary figure of the day, Petrarch was invited to Rome to be crowned with laurel as the first poet laureate since Roman times, but he modestly asked to be examined first to prove he was worthy of the honour. For Petrarch, there was only one candidate qualified to perform the examination, and that was Robert the Wise, though Robert's position as a king who could dispense lucrative patronage would not have been lost on Petrarch.[21] Petrarch was probably also partial to the Angevins because they were the rulers of Provence, and in one of his first letters around 1325 he commented that Sicily 'now lies under the dominion of a hostile ruler, or tyrant, as I might say'[22], i.e. the house of Aragon. In 1341, Petrarch went to Naples and was publicly examined by Robert for three days in a piece of theatre that did more for Robert's subsequent reputation than Petrarch's. Despite this revival of Roman tradition fitting very neatly into the origins of humanism and the Renaissance in the 14th century, it should be noted that the form of the examination was actually quite close to a medieval degree ceremony for academics. As for Robert's qualifications for performing the examination, Petrarch later remarked that although Robert was well versed in theology, philosophy and the sciences, he showed little interest in poetry or classical literature.

Robert's own writings consist of sermons and his two theological treatises. His critics accused him of having only superficial learning, and there is some evidence for this, since he had a Franciscan friar prepare a summary of Aristotle for him, and this seems to be the basis for his references to Aristotle in his sermons, rather than a profound understanding of his own. Yet this may be unfair, since a comment in a manuscript of Paolino da Venezia's *Historia satyrica* says that Robert read and annotated the text himself. Paolino also says that on the basis of the information contained therein, Robert 'spoke to foreign ambassadors about their homelands as if he had been there, wherefore they rightly marvelled at his wisdom', confirming that Robert actively cultivated his reputation for wisdom and liked to show off his knowledge.[23]

There can be no question that he had a genuine love of learning. He had an official scriptorium and provided lodging for a team of copyists, and we know that he commissioned many works to be copied for the royal library, some of them relevant to Angevin interests. For example, Robert acquired the *Gesta Francorum*, the account of the First Crusade; a history of Robert Guiscard, his predecessor in southern Italy; and Marco Polo's book about the wonders of China, which Robert had copied and lavishly illustrated. He continued Charles of Anjou's and Charles II's commitment to the improvement of the university in Naples, and he invited many other leading scholars besides Petrarch to work in Naples.[24]

One reason Robert could afford to commission literary works and other luxury items for the court is notable. Villani reports that when he was crowned in 1309, Robert 'was entirely acquitted of the loan which the Church had made to his father and grandfather for the war in Sicily, which is said to have been more than 300,000 ounces of gold'.[25] It is not coincidental that at a time when the papacy was in turmoil, with its resettlement in Avignon and the potential renewed prosecution of Boniface VIII by Philip IV, that the pope would choose to offer an inducement to his staunchest supporter, the Angevin king of Naples who was also the ruler of Avignon.

Robert may have provided stable and secure rule for Naples, but one group of Angevin possessions was in complete disarray: Morea and Albania. The complicated history of the Balkans only impinges on Angevin history occasionally, but an outline of events is important for a few key future developments, and some familiar players such as the Byzantine Empire and the kingdom of Aragon will make an appearance.

Angevin Rule in Morea

Charles of Anjou concluded marriage alliances for his children that, in addition to bringing Hungary into the Angevin orbit, also brought Morea and a claim to the Latin Empire of Constantinople to the Angevins. The Latin Empire should have been irrelevant after the Byzantines recaptured the city in 1261, but it still carried a tangle of rights in mainland Greece and the islands that the Angevins wanted to pursue. This had long-ranging consequences, because it forced the newly re-established Byzantine Emperors to look west rather than east, and to their cost they neglected matters in Anatolia. By 1300 most of Anatolia was controlled by Turkish tribes, and the future conquerors of Constantinople, the Ottoman Turks, were growing in power throughout the 14th century.

The Angevins first acted as suzerains of the principality of Achaea and the duchy of Athens, and did not directly rule Greece. However, after Isabelle the Princess of Achaea (daughter of William of Villehardouin) made an imprudent marriage in 1301, and her husband pillaged Achaea for his own benefit, in 1302 Charles II named his son Philip of Taranto direct ruler of Achaea. Philip had another local connection, having married Ithamar/Tamara, daughter of the Despot of Epirus (the region between northwestern Greece and Albania, which had a Greek ruler), and her dowry brought fortresses in Epirus to add to Philip's nominal rights as suzerain of Achaea, Corfu and his meagre possessions in Albania.

A new power that burst on the scene in 1303 was a group of Catalan mercenaries. Their behaviour prefigures that of the mercenary companies that would appear during the Hundred Years War and prove so damaging to France and Italy, though they were more successful. A group of 6,500 Catalans was hired by the Byzantine Emperor to fight the Ottomans in Anatolia, and achieved some success. As was inevitably the case, their pay fell into arrears, and they divided into three separate companies that began to ravage areas of northern Greece. Despite one of the bloody ambushes at a dinner that are such a feature of medieval history (and reminiscent of scenes from modern Mafia films when enemies are murdered in restaurants), which removed one of the Catalan captains, the companies remained in Greece and their power grew.

They were next hired by Charles of Valois, widower of Robert the Wise's sister Margaret. Charles had now married Catherine of Courtenay, daughter of Charles of Anjou's sister Beatrice and her husband Philip of Courtenay, and carried the claim to the Latin Empire. With the support of the pope, Venice, the Serbs and the Catalan mercenaries, Charles of Valois invaded Greece in 1308, at which point the Catalans promptly deserted him. Catherine of Courtenay died in 1309 and Charles's claim to the Empire passed to his daughter Catherine of Valois-Courtenay (who married Philip of Taranto from the Neapolitan Angevins, as discussed below), and Charles returned to France where the Valois would be compensated for losing the non-existent Latin Empire of Constantinople by inheriting the very real throne of France.[26]

The Catalans were then hired by the Duke of Athens, but once again they turned on their master, and this time took Athens and ruled the duchy for themselves from 1311–1388. They invited Frederick of Sicily to be their overlord to give them legitimacy, and Frederick accepted, making his son titular Duke of Athens and sending a viceroy, but having little else to do with them. This new Catalan state formed part of a chain of Catalan-Aragonese possessions stretching from Barcelona and including the

Balearics, intermittently Sardinia, Sicily and now Greece. The kings of Aragon would seem to have created the Mediterranean Empire that Charles of Anjou so coveted, though in reality each Catalan state was independent and they had little connection with each other, and the Catalan companies in Greece were eventually driven out.[27]

Charles II finally made his son Philip of Taranto Prince of Achaea in 1307, but Philip almost immediately returned to Italy and left his Greek possessions to be governed by bailiffs. In 1309 he accused his wife Tamara of Epirus of adultery and imprisoned her, where she died, which would seem to have weakened his position in Greece. However, Philip now married Catherine of Valois-Courtenay, his first cousin's daughter, and heiress to the Latin Empire. She had broken off an engagement to the Duke of Burgundy's brother to marry Philip, so the disappointed suitor was married to Isabelle of Villhardouin's daughter Matilda and became Prince of Morea very briefly, before dying – or perhaps being murdered by the Angevin agents in Achaea who resented his presence – in 1316. Philip decided to bring Morea back to the Angevin fold, and forced Matilda to marry his brother John of Gravina. Matilda refused to accept the marriage, and was forced by the Angevins to leave Greece in 1318, with John of Gravina keeping Achaea.

Robert the Wise's policy in the east always seemed to be one of benign neglect, and he left members of his family to sort things out. This did not mean that he was unaware of the value of these territories, and in 1311 he proposed giving Achaea and Durazzo to Frederick of Aragon in exchange for Sicily, perhaps because the Angevins were not currently ruling Achaea directly. Robert offered Philip of Taranto 70,000 ounces of gold to recompense him, and the proposal was promoted by the Angevins until 1316, although Frederick never really seems to have considered accepting it.[28]

Philip of Taranto died in 1331, and his right to Achaea plus Catherine's claim to the Latin Empire passed to their son Robert of Taranto. John of Gravina objected to this counterclaim to what he viewed as his territory of Achaea, but he was persuaded in 1332 to sell Achaea to Robert of Taranto. John was given Durazzo in return, and this territory gave its name to John and his descendants, the Dukes of Durazzo, who would become the rulers of Naples in 1382.

Before leaving Greece, John had undertaken military operations against various Byzantine territories, which required a great deal of money. As usual, John raised loans with Florentine bankers, in this case from the house of Acciaiuoli. The security for his loans consisted of several fortresses, and when John left Greece he ceded them to the Acciaiuoli, who duly took charge of them and became increasingly active in Greece. They proved more effective than most other powers by virtue of having enough money to hire mercenaries.[29]

Catherine of Valois-Courtenay maintained a much keener interest in Greece than her husband or brothers-in-law, and in Naples she began to work with the representatives of the house of Acciaiuloi. In particular she befriended Niccolo Acciaiuoli, who managed the fortresses in Greece forfeited by John of Gravina. Niccolo was knighted in 1335 and received additional territory in Achaea, where he and his family would become the dominant power on behalf of the Angevins until the 1360s. However, Niccolo played an even more important role in Naples, of which we will hear more shortly.

The story of Morea takes us beyond Robert's reign, when the history of Naples and Hungary became completely intertwined, so we must catch up with Hungarian affairs, where Carobert's reign had also flourished. Hungary will loom so large for the Angevins in the 14th century that we must take a moment to consider its history. The situation in Hungary in the late 13th and early 14th centuries was shaped by the Mongol invasions of the 13th century.

Hungary and the Mongols

The Mongols burst on the scene in the 13th century, and if they were like nothing that Europe had experienced in the memory of anyone living, they were very much like the repeated waves of invasions at the end of the Roman Empire, and which had continued with the Magyars themselves, who after terrorizing southern Germany and northern Italy had settled down to form the kingdom of Hungary.[30] However, the Mongol Empire was so vast and the Mongols themselves had become so sophisticated through their long contact with China, that they conducted themselves as conquerors rather than nomads. It was their practice to send an ultimatum to each new land before they attacked, demanding its inhabitants' submission. King Béla IV of Hungary received such an ultimatum, and although he would later be criticized for not preparing for the onslaught that followed, other rulers such as Frederick II had also received these communications from the Mongols and ignored them.

Béla was not as lucky as they were. The Mongols invaded in 1241, with one group attacking Poland and defeating all the forces ranged against it, then moving on to Hungary to join the rest of the Mongol army. Béla led his own army to meet them, and given the mobile nature of the Mongols, he chose to surround his force with carts to limit potential avenues of attack. The Mongol commander Batu contemptuously described how the Hungarians 'closed themselves in a narrow pen in the manner of sheep'; the Mongols surrounded them and slaughtered the Hungarian soldiers with arrows.

Béla escaped from the battle and tried to rally support, but the conflict between Frederick II and Pope Gregory IX meant no one in the Empire or Italy had any interest in helping him. The Mongols were unopposed in Hungary and inflicted unimaginable devastation: 'In this year', noted an Austrian annalist under the year 1241, 'the kingdom of Hungary, which had existed for 350 years, was destroyed by the army of the Tatars.'[31] They continued their conquest in 1242, but then something utterly inconceivable happened: the Mongols simply left. The Mongol Great Khan Ögedei, who succeeded Genghis Khan, had died at the end of 1241, and when this news reached the Mongols in Hungary they were required to return to Mongolia for the election of a new Great Khan.

Although the Mongols had gone, Béla would not risk being caught unawares again. Hungary had not had a social structure like that of other countries in Western Europe before the 13th century. Noble status in Hungary had never been linked to military service, and so ideals of knighthood, castle-holding and chivalry had not developed as in France or England. In Hungary, noble status was attained by owning land freely rather than as a tenant of another, so many of the 'nobles' in Hungary would simply have been considered wealthy peasants in the rest of Europe. This lack of a firmly established class of soldiers had been one of the reasons for the defeat by the Mongols, and the lack of castles had also hindered resistance after the battle. Béla initiated a programme of castle building and distributed additional land to nobles on condition that they provide military service, thus establishing a class of knights as in the rest of Europe. This is analogous to what we saw in Anjou and other border lands in the 10th and 11th centuries, when land grants were made to local leaders so they could build fortified positions and defend their borders against the Normans, creating local strongmen like the Count of Anjou.

Naturally this policy in Hungary led to the same situation that it had in France in the 11th century, and England during the civil war between Matilda and Stephen: royal authority waned as local leaders firmly ensconced themselves in their fortified manors and castles, and by the 14th century were asserting their independence. Like Louis VI or Henry II, Carobert reasserted royal rights and began to reclaim revenues and estates, and entered into a protracted war with his nobles. Although he had already faced ten years of struggle merely to be crowned, Carobert faced another decade of intermittent warfare before finally prevailing against the nobles in 1323. As a sign of his victory, Carobert founded a new royal residence at Visegrad to isolate him from the turbulent people of Buda. Carobert recognized that 1323 was his pivotal year, and manufactured a new seal and revoked previous grants to confirm that his authority was now supreme.[32]

The Reign of Carobert

Now that he was secure, Carobert needed an heir, but this proved surprisingly difficult. Carobert's political outlook was illustrated by his marriage alliances, particularly his close alliance with Poland, which began as early as 1306 when he sent military assistance to the Polish king even before his own uncontested rule. The sources vary considerably on whom Carobert married and when, but he seems to have married Mary of Galicia in 1305 or 1306; Mary of Bytom from Poland in around 1311; Beatrice of Luxembourg, daughter of the Emperor Henry VII and sister of John of Bohemia, before February 1319; and finally Elisabeth of Poland on 6 July 1320. Carobert had no children with his first two wives and Beatrice died in childbirth in November 1319, but he had five sons with Elisabeth: Charles and Ladislas who died young, followed by the future Louis the Great, Andrew and Stephen. The sources are less interested in his daughters, but there seem to have been two, Anne and Catherine.[33]

It was in the reign of Carobert, despite his abundance of sons, that a custom arose for the benefit of those who had only daughters: 'masculinization'. In Hungary, in many cases women were excluded from inheritance. Under Carobert, when there were no male heirs, it was established that the king could use his plenitude of powers to declare a female to be male, and allow her to inherit. This practice would become very important in the generation after Carobert, when Louis the Great had only two daughters: when they inherited the throne they would become 'kings' rather than 'queens'.[34]

As in Italy, Angevin rule introduced French chivalric culture to Hungary. Carobert welcomed foreign knights into his household, which he modelled on French lines. He also founded the Order of Saint George in 1326, which seems to be the first chivalric order anywhere in Europe. These knightly orders first appeared in the 14th century and ranged from confraternities like Carobert's, which seems to have been simply a group of knights organized to hold jousts, to political organizations like the Garter in England, the Golden Fleece in Burgundy, and the Angevin orders of the Knot, the Ship and the Crescent, which explicitly formed connections between a monarch and potential supporters.

The statutes of Carobert's order are still in the National Archives of Hungary, and emphasize the brotherhood of the members as exemplified by their participation in tournaments. Carobert held the first tournament in Hungary in 1318 and regularly hosted tournaments throughout his reign, under the aegis of the Order of St George. Since Hungary did not have a history of chivalry and tournaments, Carobert was able to avoid the disruptive effects of the early tournaments in France and England, instead forming a 'team' of knights who accompanied him to tournaments and jousts, which created a loyal nucleus of supporters. In Hungary, tournaments have none of the negative connotations they sometimes had in other countries, instead forming a mechanism for introducing chivalric culture into Hungary to provide coherence for its military class and vital support for a new dynasty. Carobert recognized the importance of this, and at his funeral in 1342 his body was accompanied by three knights bearing his arms for war, tournaments and jousts.[35]

Carobert was able to entertain on a lavish scale because gold mines were discovered in Hungary in the 1320s. The profits of these mines allowed Carobert to become the first ruler north of the Alps to issue a gold coin, the florin, which was based on the coin produced in Florence and in circulation by 1326. Like his Italian cousins, Carobert also invested in imagery to demonstrate his legitimate rule. A mural in the church of Szepeshely in Slovakia shows the Virgin crowning Carobert, an image strikingly similar to Simone Martini's painting of Robert the Wise being crowned by Louis of Toulouse.

Carobert also commissioned the beautiful golden orb marked with his arms, now in the National Museum in Budapest, as part of his royal regalia.[36] Hungary now became the largest producer of gold in Europe, and the role of this wealth in the impending struggles between the Hungarian and Neapolitan Angevins would be vital.[37]

Carobert was no less ambitious than any other Angevin, and as soon as he was secure in the Hungarian heartland he immediately turned to securing his wider possessions and becoming a regional powerbroker. This was desperately needed, since Hungarian territory faced aggressors on all sides, but he was not particularly successful. Although Bosnia always remained loyal to the Angevins, Carobert launched several expeditions against Serbia in an attempt to make good his title 'King of Serbia', without success. The cities of Croatia and the Dalmatian coast that had been so vital to him obtaining the throne, and that had remained loyal to him under the Šubićs, who kept the region stable throughout the civil wars and instability of his early reign, were now lost to Venice.

As we know, Zara had been seized from Hungary by the Fourth Crusade, and although Innocent III excommunicated the Venetians over this and made them pay reparations, the city had been formally ceded to Venice shortly after. Zara's strategic position as the best port on the Croatian coast and also the logical termination of trading routes into central Europe and to Constantinople gave it an economic importance that made it the lynchpin of Adriatic policy for any power that wished to control the region. Although controlled by Venice since the Fourth Crusade, in 1310 Pope Clement V placed Venice under an interdict for the sack of Ferrara, and the people of Zara took this opportunity to revolt and beg for help from the Šubićs. Pavao took Zara in 1311, but died the following year and his son Mladen II was chosen count of Zara in 1312.

Over the next decade Mladen increased his control over the coastline, but his growing power alienated some, even of his own family. Initially Carobert was in no position to intervene, but by the early 1320s his position in Hungary was secure enough for him to consider the Adriatic coast. He supported a coalition against Mladen led by the ban of Slavonia, and in 1322 Mladen was defeated. Carobert then generously called to mind the services rendered to him by Mladen's father Pavao, and welcomed Mladen to his court in Visegrad. Unfortunately for Hungary, in the absence of a Šubić overlord, most of the Croatian and Dalmatian coast quickly fell to Venice. Wallachia, although it had recognized Carobert as king, also transferred its allegiance to Bulgaria.[38]

Carobert was unwilling to accept any losses to his territory, and launched a punitive expedition against Wallachia in 1330. After achieving nothing, Carobert began a retreat only to be ambushed and trapped in the valley of Posada on 9 November. The Wallachians spent four days slaughtering the Hungarian army, and Carobert himself only escaped by exchanging clothes with the loyal knight Dezső Hédervári. Dezső's self-sacrifice passed into legend and became one of the great romantic events of Carobert's reign that has often been retold and depicted. It was equally famous at the time, and a processional cross in the British Museum that must date from shortly after the event depicts Dezső's heroism.[39]

We are notably short of such episodes for Carobert and indeed for his son Louis the Great, because there is a dearth of chronicles in 14th-century Hungary. Although there is archival material to provide a chronology, we lack the anecdotal evidence that brings characters to life, aside from such vital romantic episodes. The tale of Dezső Hédervári is uplifting and heroic, but the other dramatic story of Carobert's reign is much darker.

After his marriage to Elisabeth of Poland, Carobert remained close to his father-in-law, Władysław Łokietek (Władysław the Short or 'Elbow-High'). After being defeated by the Teutonic Knights, in 1329 Władysław sent his heir Casimir to request help from Carobert. Whilst in Visegrad, the nineteen-year-old Casimir allegedly seduced one of Queen Elisabeth's ladies-in-waiting, Claire Záh. On 17 April 1330, Claire's father Felician Záh was welcomed into the dining room where the royal family were eating, but drew his sword and attacked the king and queen, wounding them both before being killed by the guards. Carobert took a terrible vengeance, which the Italian Franciscan who chronicled his reign made the centrepiece of his chronicle. Felician Záh's children were tortured to death, except for Claire, whose lips and fingers were cut off, then she was dragged through various cities of the realm by a horse. All other members of the Záh family to the third degree were executed, and those to the seventh degree were condemned to lose their property and become serfs. The pursuit of the Záh clan continued for many years.[40]

This event is shocking and overshadows everything else we know about Carobert. However, although it is documented elsewhere that Carobert executed the entire Záh clan, we do only have one source that provides any motive for the killings, and this is openly hostile to Carobert. The Franciscan chronicle is the only source attributing Záh's attack on the king and queen to the dishonouring of his daughter by Casimir, and given that Felician had initially opposed Carobert's bid for the throne there may have been another explanation for the pursuit of the Záh family. Regardless of the motive, the ferocity of the persecution of the Záhis is well attested and, fairly or not, allows us to judge Carobert's character.

The cruelty of Carobert's actions against the Záhis foreshadows the behaviour of Louis the Great when he avenged his brother Andrew's death, part of a catastrophic war between the Hungarian and Neapolitan Angevins that blighted the kingdom of Naples for decades. These events involved Robert the Wise's successor Johanna, and we must first see how Robert's plan to unite the Hungarian and Neapolitan branches proved a complete disaster.

Queen Johanna I of Naples

When discussing Richard the Lionheart, it can be difficult to make a sober analysis of his reign because we are frequently in the realm of breathless adventure. Sadly for Queen Johanna, the situation is similar, but for her any objective analysis of her reign is superseded by the numerous slanders about her and her tragic end. Even the strongest ruler might fade into the background behind the cataclysmic events that occurred during Johanna's reign: the Black Death, the first major battles of the Hundred Years War and the invasion of Italy by the mercenary companies it spawned, and the Great Western Schism when rival popes in Avignon and Rome tore Christendom apart, bringing Johanna down with them. Yet this does not happen, because Johanna was a strong character who, although sometimes acted upon by events, usually maintained her own agency and was always bolstered by an unshakeable belief in her right to rule.

Johanna's reign is overshadowed and – for contemporary and many modern historians – completely defined by one event, the murder of her first husband Andrew of Hungary. This happened only two years after her accession to the throne, when she was still a teenager, and rapidly brought about her exile, loss of her kingdom to a Hungarian invasion and remarriage to an Angevin cousin. The story of Andrew's murder kicks off and illuminates the dynastic struggles that would last until the end of Angevin rule in Naples, and would be worth examining in detail even if it weren't so fascinatingly lurid.

The background to the story was the question of Robert the Wise's right to the throne. Carobert's successor Louis the Great firmly believed his, elder, line of Angevins should rule Naples. Robert's heirs were his granddaughters Johanna and Maria, and his plan to address the problem was to have Maria marry Louis, and Louis's younger brother Andrew marry Johanna. Robert proposed the marriage between Johanna and Andrew in 1333, and Carobert was delighted to accept. Carobert personally brought Andrew to Naples in 1333 and the two children (Joanna was seven and Andrew five) were betrothed in September.

Contemporaries endlessly stress that Andrew and his Hungarian attendants were outsiders in Naples, and were perceived as gauche and uncultured. Although this may have been due to Andrew's personality, it also seems to show that within two generations the Angevins of Hungary had become quite different from their Neapolitan cousins. Considering Andrew lived in Naples from the age of five, it seems unlikely that he would have been too linguistically or culturally isolated, unless this was by choice. This is precisely what some historians do claim, and Petrarch noticed that Andrew was marginalized and taunted by others at court.

Johanna and Andrew were married before Carobert's death, which occurred on 16 July 1342. On the accession of Louis the Great to the throne of Hungary, relations between the kingdoms deteriorated when Louis began marriage negotiations with the King of Bohemia's daughter despite his engagement to Johanna's sister Maria. Robert seems to have responded to this by emphasizing Andrew's role as Johanna's consort rather than king of Sicily in his own right.

Robert died in 1343 when Johanna was seventeen and Andrew fifteen. The succession in one sense went smoothly, as Johanna was clearly Robert's heir, but her sex and youth meant a struggle for control of the kingdom began at once. There were numerous people who believed they had a right to the throne itself, or at least a say in who held it: the pope, the Hungarians and the Taranto and Durazzo branches of the royal family. Robert had also confused matters by stipulating that neither Johanna nor Andrew would come into their inheritance until the age of twenty-five, not the usual age of majority at eighteen, and appointing a ruling council led by his widow Sancia of Majorca and consisting of his trusted advisers.

None of the factions was happy with this arrangement. The pope felt it usurped his rights as overlord of the kingdom, and corresponded directly with Johanna as queen instead of with the council. Johanna's cousin Charles of Durazzo acted more decisively by secretly marrying – perhaps by force – Johanna's sister Maria, who was only thirteen and engaged to King Louis of Hungary, as well as being second in line to the throne.

It was clear to all that there was great instability in Naples and that factions were vying for control of the kingdom. No less a source than Petrarch wrote to one of Robert's former secretaries expressing great concern over Johanna and Andrew, fearing that their positions – for he viewed Andrew as king – would be usurped.[41]

Petrarch's comments reflect the tension in Andrew's position: as Johanna's husband he was in some sense king, and to many there was no such thing as a king-consort; if Andrew was king then he was entitled to rule. This was antithetical to the position set out in Robert's will, which was that Andrew should always retain the title of king, but political power belonged solely to Johanna. This is borne out by Johanna's correspondence with the pope, in which she sets out her views quite clearly and makes it plain that Andrew is not to be treated as her co-ruler.

By 1344, the disorder in Naples's government was such that the pope sent a legate to govern the kingdom. He also began to press for Andrew's coronation and recognition as king, a position Johanna rejected in the strongest terms. She neatly countered Clement's arguments about Andrew's right to rule by stating that she, as the rightful queen and Andrew's wife, as well as having attained her majority while Andrew was still a child, was best placed to look after Andrew's interests.

This argument seems to have worked, and by summer 1345 things seemed to be improving and, more importantly, Johanna was known to be pregnant. However, on 28 July Sancia died, and with her any notion of the royal council having any control of the kingdom. Factional strife in the court burst out anew, with rumours that Johanna was having numerous adulterous affairs, including with her cousin Louis of Taranto. Contemporaries such as Donato degli Albanzani, a friend of Boccaccio, also reported that Johanna's retinue mocked Andrew and treated him cruelly.[42]

Against this backdrop – and after having received 100,000 gold florins from the Hungarians – the pope again demanded that Andrew be crowned, anointed and recognized as co-ruler, and he sent a legate from Avignon for this purpose. In Naples, this was clearly not wanted, and all the clergy and nobility swore that if Johanna died in childbirth, they would not recognize Andrew as king.

The Murder of Andrew

Even as the papal legate made his way to Naples, Johanna and Andrew went to Aversa, where they and the rest of the court stayed at the royal hunting lodge, and matters came to a horrifying conclusion. The story is minutely recorded by many contemporary sources, and we know every detail of the murder except who was actually responsible. The events were as follows.

On the night of 18 September 1345, as Andrew went to bed, he was informed that a messenger had arrived from Naples who wanted to speak to him urgently. Lured out of his room, Andrew was then seized by assassins who brutally gagged him, mutilated and murdered him, then threw his body from a balcony into the garden, where it was immediately discovered by his Hungarian nurse who raised the alarm. So sensational a murder was quickly embroidered by many sources, but there is good contemporary evidence for what happened. Pope Clement himself wrote to a cardinal and described the murder like this, based on 'the reports of many':

> Immediately he was summoned by them, he went into the gallery or promenade which is before the chamber. (Then) certain ones placed their hands over his mouth, so that he could not cry out, and in this act they so pressed the iron gauntlets that their print and character were manifest after death. Others placed a rope round his neck, in order to strangle him, and this likewise left its mark; others (I must leave this sentence to the Latin) ...

This is Welbore St Clair Baddeley's translation from 1897, and he then coyly reverts to Latin and consigns the next sentence to a footnote. The unprintable detail is that others seized Andrew and dragged him by his genitals in a way that left clear marks, and Clement says he had this from people who said they saw it themselves. The rest of Clement's report is scarcely less horrifying. After mutilating Andrew's genitals:

> ... others tore out his hair, dragged him, and threw him into the garden. Some say that with the rope with which they had strangled him they swung him, as if hanging, over the garden. Some (also) got him under their knees ... and we heard that this likewise left external traces. It was further related to us that they intended to throw him into a deep well (even as St. Jeremy was thrown into a pit), and thereafter to give it out he had left the kingdom.... And this they would have carried out had not his nurse quickly come upon the scene.[43]

Much more pertinently, we have Johanna's own account of the murder from a letter she wrote to her allies in Florence:

> An unutterable crime, a prodigious iniquity, a sin inexpiable, hateful to God and

horrifying to mortality, perpetrated with inhuman ferocity and the shedding of innocent blood, by the hands of miscreants, has been committed on the person of our hitherto lord and husband.

On the 18th of this month, our lord and husband, late at the hour of retiring, would have gone down to a certain garden adjoining the gallery of our palace at Aversa, unwisely and unsuspecting, boy-like rather (as often, both there and elsewhere, at doubtful hours, he was wont to do), taking no advice, merely following the rash impulse of youth, not permitting a companion, but closing the door after him. We had been awaiting him, and owing to his too long delay, had been some time overtaken by sleep. His nurse, a good and respected woman, took a light to search anxiously (for him), and at length discovered him close to the wall of the said garden, strangled. It is impossible for us to describe our tribulation. And albeit from the vile perpetrator of this unheard-of crime is sought by stern justice done (already) whatever can be extracted or ascertained [she refers to Tomasso Mambriccio, who had already been executed for the crime]; nevertheless, viewing the atrocity of his deed, the severity must be considered mild.... He carried out his outlandish crime with the aid of a menial who is not yet caught. The villain adduced for motive of his setting on, that he had brought upon himself the punishment of death by designing against our former lord and husband ...

When, therefore, we find ourselves, in consequence of such a disaster, environed by perplexities, it is our trust, relying on God, Holy Church, and our faithful subjects and allies, that the guidance of divine mercy and the grace of God's pity will not be lacking to us. (Dated at Aversa, on September 22, under our secret seal.)[44]

Johanna's account is notable for scrupulously observing the proprieties (referring to Andrew as her 'lord and husband') while at the same time getting in a merciless dig at Andrew's immaturity and 'boy-like' behaviour. She expressed her horror at the crime, but she also made it plain that Andrew was not fit to be king. She was more diplomatic when she wrote to Andrew's brother Louis the Great of Hungary: 'I have suffered such intense anguish by the murder of my beloved husband, that, stunned by grief, I well-nigh died of the same wounds.'[45]

She was wise to justify herself in this way, because the crime caused horror throughout Europe. Petrarch best expressed the shock everyone felt over the death. He lamented at how quickly Naples had changed and what had happened at 'unhappy Aversa', writing that he wished Andrew had been killed by 'a sword, or another manly way, so that he was killed by the hands of men, not torn by the claws and teeth of wild beasts'.[46]

There were abundant factions in the court who might have desired Andrew's death before his coronation, and the fact that Andrew was lured from the very room he shared with Johanna, yet she claimed to be sleeping and know nothing about the crime, was highly suspicious. The people of Naples immediately blamed Johanna, and various chroniclers and commentators also believed the queen was responsible, either person- ally or through acquiescence. Johanna herself, in the elliptical reference quoted in her letter above, accused Tommaso Mambriccio, Andrew's chamberlain, of carrying out the murder, but even if this were true, Tommaso could only have been acting at the instigation of others. The Hungarians blamed the Angevin royal family in general, not surprisingly, considering that the central problem of the court was whether or to what extent Andrew would be king alongside or instead of his Neapolitan cousins, and they had a vested interest in removing him.

The Hungarian branch of the family were quick to make the connection between Johanna's presumed involvement in the murder, her alleged immorality and the funda- mental illegitimacy of Neapolitan Angevin rule. Elisabeth of Hungary, Louis the Great and Andrew's mother, was the early standard bearer for the Hungarian position. She wrote numerous letters to Pope Clement and by summer 1346 had explicitly accused Johanna of the murder, and further demanded that she be deposed and Naples given to Louis the Great.

Elisabeth, and numerous contemporaries seizing on similar arguments, drew on a long and inglorious literary tradition about female rulers, female morality and the inherent 'danger' of uncontrolled female sexuality. The most striking image in this arsenal is that of the 'she-wolf' (*lupa*), which was also slang for a prostitute. Boccaccio wrote an allegorical poetic account of a pregnant she-wolf representing Johanna who murdered the prince 'Alexis', and the term had already been applied to Isabella, the wife of Edward II of England. The tradition would culminate with Shakespeare's con- demnation of Margaret of Anjou, Angevin wife of Henry VI, who became the most notorious she-wolf in English history and literature. The accusations against Johanna quickly and inevitably linked the murder to immorality and other sexual crimes, and contemporaries described her as the 'harlot-queen' and gave detailed accounts of her multiple partners in adultery as well as her personal involvement in the murder.[47]

The pope, however, stood by Johanna, and the factions within Italy that tended to support the pope generally accepted her innocence. This was an interesting historical juncture, since Clement repeatedly insisted on his rights as overlord of Naples, and if he had decided to condemn Johanna and remove her from the throne, he could have given the kingdom to Louis the Great (as Louis frequently requested) and perhaps spared the kingdom much turmoil. On balance, it seems probable that Clement truly believed in Johanna's innocence, since nothing in his later behaviour suggests that his support of her was opportunistic, and supporting Louis would likely have been the easier option.

Clement was genuinely interested in punishing the murderers, so he sent com- missioners to Naples with judicial authority. Tomasso Mambriccio had been executed before they arrived, and much more importantly Charles of Durazzo took it upon himself to arrest many of Johanna's friends and supporters, including even Robert the Wise's illegitimate son Charles of Artois. By the summer of 1346, the papal delegates had arrived and they swiftly began a reign of terror. No one believed that Tomasso Mambriccio was solely responsible, and it was rumoured that his tongue had been cut out before his execution to prevent him naming anyone else. Now Johanna's servants and even members of the royal family like Charles of Artois's own son were publicly tortured, broken on the wheel and finally burnt at the stake.[48]

Charles of Durazzo had attempted to stay ahead of events by hosting the inquiries in his own palace, and it was he who had executed Tomasso Mambriccio so quickly (before he could implicate Charles?), but as fear mounted of a Hungarian invasion he needed another suspect. He joined those who sought to shift suspicion to Johanna, and she became a virtual prisoner in the Castel dell'Ovo. In light of his marriage to Johanna's sister, Charles certainly had an eye on the possibility that he could become king of Naples if Johanna were imprisoned or removed from the throne, but he seems to have underestimated the Hungarian threat and failed to realize that Louis the Great had the same idea.

Johanna had given birth to a son in December 1345, which would have seemed to be a cause for celebration and to provide stability for the dynasty. She sent an envoy to Hungary with the news, but the response was this chilling statement from Louis:

> Your former ill-faith, your impudent assumption of the government of the kingdom, the vengeance you have neglected to take, the excuse made for it, all prove you to have been accessory to the death of your husband. Be sure, however, that none ever escape retribution for such a crime.[49]

Louis had now joined his mother in explicitly linking Johanna's 'usurpation' of the kingdom to her guilt for Andrew's death, and it was clear that she would need to marshal support for herself and her son. She had named him Charles Martel, after Carobert's father and Louis the Great's grandfather, but this reference to his right of descent through the Hungarian line, as well as through Johanna, probably only inflamed Louis's belief that Johanna should be deposed. Louis was marshalling his forces and gathering support in central Europe and Italy for an invasion, but where could Johanna look for help?

The Hungarian Invasion of Italy

Johanna may have formed a plan very early on, for only weeks after Andrew's death a petition was sent to the pope requesting dispensation for her to marry her cousin Robert of Taranto. Naturally when this became known, it was taken by some as evidence of Johanna's guilt, since she was attempting to replace Andrew with indecent haste. There are two points to bear in mind: first, that the origin of the petition isn't clear and it may have been sent at the instigation of Robert, rather than Johanna; and second, as is stressed repeatedly in any study of medieval relationships, marriage – and most especially royal marriage – was a political and financial arrangement with no basis in romance or any notion of 'love'. True, remarrying only weeks after a previous husband had been murdered would be in bad taste, but as Johanna's kingdom was in turmoil and facing a Hungarian invasion, she desperately needed political support, and neutralizing her cousins of Taranto, potentially her most dangerous enemies, through a marriage alliance was a sensible approach.

The pope refused permission for Johanna to marry Robert, but in a move that does appear to be part of a carefully calculated strategy, either by Johanna or the Tarantini, Robert's younger brother Louis of Taranto now came to the fore. Louis commanded a body of Neapolitan troops and had been asked to come to Naples to restore order, and it was now proposed that Johanna marry him instead. Charles of Durazzo in turn barred the city gates against Louis, because clearly he still believed he could claim the throne if Johanna were deposed, and her marriage to Louis of Taranto would provide a significant stumbling block to his ambitions.

Contemporary rumour had smeared Johanna's name with accusations of adultery even before Andrew's murder, and now these only increased. She had allegedly had adulterous affairs with both Robert and Louis of Taranto (amongst many others), so her enemies looked on her attempts to marry one of them as proof of her infidelity. Application was made to the pope for dispensation for Johanna to marry Louis, which again was refused. The maelstrom of Angevin family politics seemed to reach its most chaotic moment now, with all the branches, represented by Johanna, Louis of Taranto, Charles of Durazzo and Louis the Great of Hungary openly vying for the throne. Louis of Taranto successfully entered Naples in spite of Charles of Durazzo, and by August 1347 he was living with Johanna in the royal residence. They ignored the pope's refusal to sanction their marriage, and on 22 August they married privately.

We can never know the true circumstances of their marriage, but contemporaries found the liaison highly irregular, variously criticizing the union as adulterous, illegal, immoral and incestuous. That the marriage was wrong everyone agreed, but who was responsible? Although many continued to accuse Johanna of murdering Andrew so she could marry her adulterous lover Louis, others criticized Louis as the instigator of the irregular marriage. Domenico da Gravina went so far as to accuse the family of Taranto of scheming to marry Johanna, with the brothers Robert and Louis competing for her hand. He even suggests that Louis may have raped Johanna to force the marriage, a course of action that had already been and would again be used against Johanna's sister.[50] Johanna's rapid remarriage was the last straw for Louis the Great, and he finally launched his invasion of Italy.

Louis was involved in a war over Zara, that perennial bone of contention between Hungary and Venice since the time of the Fourth Crusade. The papacy was constantly in conflict with Venice in the 14th century (there had even been a Crusade against the Venetians), and there was a risk for Johanna that the pope would seek an alliance with Louis the Great, who had extended his realm to the shores of the Adriatic and could be a useful ally. Indeed, Louis had been writing to the pope constantly in the aftermath of Andrew's murder seeking Johanna's condemnation and deposition, and the pope may have been tempted to agree. However, Louis had already angered the pope by his support for the Emperor Ludwig of Bavaria, and now he ended any hope of papal favour by reaching an agreement with the Venetians. They, aware of Louis's main priority, offered to transport his army across the Adriatic if he would abandon the siege of Zara, and Louis accepted. One detachment of the Hungarian army had already invaded, and now the main body arrived in force. Louis himself made a progress through the peninsula, being feted in Padua, Mantua and even traditionally pro-Angevin Florence, where Villani – convinced of Johanna's guilt – approvingly described the banquets and celebrations.

Although Louis of Taranto led a small force to attempt to resist the Hungarians, he had no success, and it was plain that Naples would fall. Johanna was now pregnant with Louis's child, and decided to flee. She would seek protection with the pope, but the sea journey to Provence was too dangerous for the infant Charles Martel, so she left him with the papal legate. She ordered the city to surrender to Louis the Great to avoid being sacked, and on 16 January 1348 she took ship to Provence.

Louis of Taranto challenged Louis the Great to single combat, but it seems to have been the Hungarian king who found a way to avoid the challenge without even the farce that Charles of Anjou and Peter of Aragon went through. It was clear enough that there would be no resistance to the Hungarian invasion, so Louis the Great would have been foolish indeed to accept such a challenge. As all the Angevin allies fell away, Louis of Taranto, advised by the increasingly influential Niccolo Acciaiuoli, decided to join Johanna in Avignon, and the two left Naples. This was portrayed by many chroniclers as cowardice, especially on Louis's part, and it tainted his reputation when he did return to Naples.[51]

Louis the Great, now at Benevento, received the submission of Robert of Taranto and Charles of Durazzo, who had decided to try their luck remaining in the kingdom and blaming Johanna for the murder. Louis received them graciously, and they accompanied him to Aversa where he wished to see the place of his brother's death. It was here that Louis took his vengeance on the man he blamed for the murder. Giovanni da Bazzano – who argued that Charles of Durazzo was innocent of the crime – described the scene in detail, with Louis demanding to be shown the balcony from which Andrew was thrown, then furiously turning on Charles of Durazzo and murdering him, then throwing his body from the balcony in a parody of Andrew's death.[52]

Louis's savage action alienated the Neapolitan nobles, who refused to support him when he declared himself king. Louis's actions in Naples did not seem to be those of someone who believed he was assuming his rightful throne or planned to reign for long, as he persecuted locals and relied upon Hungarian and German supporters for his new administration rather than forming relationships with Neapolitans.

Louis's actions certainly offended the pope, whose authority over Naples had been flouted, and he now publicly denounced Louis as well as taking more practical measures. Petrarch himself carried papal instructions to the northern Italian cities to refuse Louis passage should he attempt to leave the peninsula.

Johanna was delayed in Provence and arrived in Avignon just after Louis of Taranto, and shortly before the Black Death. One of Petrarch's correspondents – amongst others – declared that the plague was a physical manifestation of the queen's iniquity.[53] Johanna's situation was desperate, since she was widely believed to have murdered Andrew and she would require not only papal belief in her innocence, but full papal backing with monetary and military support to regain her throne. Fortunately for Johanna, there never seems to have been any doubt about Clement's support for her, and she was received at the papal court and allowed to defend herself in a closed papal consistory before the pope and cardinals, leading to Clement's public declaration of her innocence.

One reason for Johanna's warm reception at the papal court was financial. Florentine bankers were heavily involved in financing Charles of Anjou's conquest of Sicily and had subsidized the Angevins ever since, to their detriment under Robert the Wise and Johanna. They also funded the papacy, and one of the important banking houses was that of the Acciaiuoli, whose scion Niccolo rose to power through his work in Greece for Catherine of Valois-Courteney, where he managed the claims of the Tarantini with great success, and he was now Louis of Taranto's chief supporter.[54] The fact that Niccolo was securing lucrative contracts for Florentine merchants in Naples that would help them recoup some of the losses suffered under Robert and Johanna, and secure future funding, would have substantially improved Johanna's prospects should she return to power, and must have been a factor in Clement's decision to back her rather than Louis the Great.

Another financial consideration was more pertinent. As we know, Avignon belonged to the Angevins, but as it had been the residence of the papacy for several decades, the popes were eager to secure it for themselves. In May, Clement arranged to buy the city from Johanna for 80,000 florins, providing her with money to fund her return to Naples, and the pope with outright ownership of his home. Niccolo may have been behind this arrangement, and even if Johanna and Louis proposed the deal themselves, Niccolo would certainly have organized the complex financial arrangements it required.

Johanna quickly cleared herself of the murder charge, but she had still married Louis without papal consent, which she required as a papal vassal, or the dispensation required because they were cousins. Clement was well disposed towards Johanna, but Louis's connections to the Acciaiuoli must also have been a factor in the swift approval given to Johanna's choice of him as her new husband. It would also have been behind Clement's decision on 30 March to award Louis, like Fulk Réchin before him, the Golden Rose as the leading figure at the papal court on the fourth Sunday in Lent.[55]

Lest Niccolo be seen as a sinister *éminence grise* whose influence and power at the Neapolitan court are somehow unsavoury, it is worth noting that Niccolo's son Lorenzo had remained in the Regno (as Angevin southern Italy was known) and led a highly successful resistance to the Hungarians from the castle of Melfi. When it was announced in May 1348 that Johanna and Louis would return to Naples to reclaim their throne, Lorenzo was instrumental in working with the Neapolitan nobility, and the mercenary forces they employed, to secure the Regno for them. His actions were certainly more effective militarily than anything Louis of Taranto had done to oppose the Hungarians, though perhaps this is uncharitable given that Louis had been a vital support to Johanna in Avignon, even if it were only to secure his own power as her husband. Niccolo also rallied the Guelf allies of the Angevins in northern Italy, particularly Florence, which as we have seen had flirted with Louis the Great when he arrived in Italy.

The Black Death

Johanna and her allies were active in organizing opposition to Louis the Great and preparing for her return to Naples, but her greatest assistance came from the single biggest disaster of the Middle Ages, the Black Death. The great plague first appeared in Sicily in October 1347 and spread through the Regno, and although it did not end the invasion, it drove Louis the Great back to Hungary for a time. He kidnapped Johanna's son Charles Martel from the papal legate and took him to Hungary, earning him further opprobrium and accusations of cruelty, especially when the baby died shortly after arriving in Hungary. As Charles Martel was Andrew's son – despite some of Johanna's detractors arguing that he was the product of one of her many adulterous affairs – there is no reason to believe Louis bore responsibility for his death, aside from having snatched him from his home to die in a foreign land.

Estimates of the plague's death toll are one-third to one-half the population of Europe, with some regions more affected than others, but the entire continent was stricken. There are numerous contemporary accounts of the plague, many of which were rhetorical exercises rewriting descriptions of previous plagues, but it is clear that the plague was horrific. Perhaps the most notable was by Boccaccio in his introduction to the *Decameron*, where his description of unburied corpses and families turning on each other is largely taken from an account of a plague written by Paul the Deacon in the 8th century, although it may also be accurate:

> I say, then, that the years [of the era] of the fruitful Incarnation of the Son of God had attained to the number of one thousand three hundred and forty-eight, when into the notable city of Florence, fair over every other of Italy, there came the death-dealing pestilence ...

... in men and women alike there appeared, at the beginning of the malady, certain swellings, either on the groin or under the armpits, whereof some waxed of the bigness of a common apple, others like unto an egg, some more and some less, and these the vulgar named plague-boils. From these two parts the aforesaid death-bearing plague-boils proceeded, in brief space, to appear and come indifferently in every part of the body; wherefrom, after awhile, the fashion of the contagion began to change into black or livid blotches, which showed themselves in many [first] on the arms and about the thighs and [after spread to] every other part of the person, in some large and sparse and in others small and thick-sown; and like as the plague-boils had been first (and yet were) a very certain token of coming death, even so were these for every one to whom they came ...

The condition of the common people (and belike, in great part, of the middle class also) was yet more pitiable to behold, for that these, for the most part retained by hope or poverty in their houses and abiding in their own quarters, sickened by the thousand daily and being altogether untended and unsuccoured, died well nigh all without recourse. Many breathed their last in the open street, whilst other many, for all they died in their houses, made it known to the neighbours that they were dead rather by the stench of their rotting bodies than otherwise; and of these and others who died all about the whole city was full ...

The consecrated ground sufficing not to the burial of the vast multitude of corpses aforesaid, which daily and well nigh hourly came carried in crowds to every church,—especially if it were sought to give each his own place, according to ancient usance,—there were made throughout the churchyards, after every other part was full, vast trenches, wherein those who came after were laid by the hundred and being heaped up therein by layers, as goods are stowed aboard ship, were covered with a little earth, till such time as they reached the top of the trench.[56]

Certainly many people felt that the world was coming to an end, and troops of flagellants took to the streets trying to atone for the sin that could cause such divine vengeance, in some cases becoming violent anti-clerical and anti-governmental mobs.

Yet it is also striking how ordinary life could go on in spite of the Black Death. Because of superior sanitation and cleanliness and generally more robust health, royalty were mostly spared, with only one monarch dying (Alfonso XI of Castile), and although many nobles and clerics did perish there was not complete institutional collapse. However, in such disordered circumstances Louis the Great was unable to sustain his domination of the Regno, and Johanna, Louis and Niccolo took advantage of this to return to Naples on 17 August 1348, where they formally entered the city with great pageantry and were met by welcoming crowds. There were many lasting repercussions from the plague, but administrative records trace the reinstatement of Angevin government in Naples with calm precision.

Johanna's Second Husband: Louis of Taranto

These records are not complimentary to Louis of Taranto. Although he, asserting himself as the military commander of the Regno by virtue of his maleness, took charge of driving the Hungarian forces from the kingdom, he met with little success. Italy was already being tormented by the mercenary forces that would ravage it for the rest of the century, and Louis employed the German commander Werner of Urslingen, who had been an Angevin ally during Johanna's Avignon exile, only for Werner to defect to the Hungarians. The independent forces commanded by the Neapolitan nobility and allied cities were much more effective, and in spite of Louis the Hungarian troops were gradually driven out, with the Regno largely secure by early 1349.[57]

His military inadequacy did not hinder Louis, with Acciaiuoli's support, from consolidating his position in the court. By mid-1349 he had assumed control of the government and Johanna begins to vanish from the records. Although Louis had not yet been crowned king, he was made Duke of Calabria and issued orders in his own name without reference to Johanna.

Johanna fought back by writing to the pope and her Provençal supporters, and a legate arrived to assert papal authority over the kingdom. This reiteration of papal sovereignty, aimed at Louis the Great and meant to put a final end to the Hungarian occupation, was also a means of controlling Louis of Taranto. Johanna also profited from the disparate nature of Angevin possessions, in that Provence and Forcalquier were not part of the Regno, and she appealed to her Provençal subjects for support.

Hugh des Baux, count of Avellino and member of a family that had been instrumental in governing Provence since the time of Charles of Anjou, brought a fleet of galleys under a papal flag and blockaded Naples, demanding that Louis of Taranto recognize that Provence was ruled solely by Johanna. A public declaration was also made that Johanna was a prisoner in the Castel Nuovo and Louis had tried to poison her, and Hugh was prepared to attack the castle to release her.

Hugh's intervention seemed highly effective, and he began negotiations with Louis the Great (who had returned to Italy when the plague subsided and was now at Aversa) for a final Hungarian withdrawal and a peace treaty. As usual, Louis of Taranto proved no match for a determined foe, and he abandoned his attempt to supplant Johanna. She now resumed control of Provence, appointed her own seneschal and wrote to the people of Marseilles to thank them for their loyalty and confirm that she alone ruled the county.

Hugh's treaty with Louis the Great stipulated that the Hungarian king would return to Buda and await a final pronouncement from a papal tribunal on Johanna's innocence or guilt in Andrew's murder; if she were judged guilty she would be removed from the throne, and if innocent Louis the Great would make peace with Naples. Johanna and Louis of Taranto were to accompany Hugh des Baux to Provence to confirm the arrangements made for governing the county, and presumably also to be near Avignon in case they felt the need to influence the papal tribunal.

However, Hugh des Baux, Johanna's apparent saviour, now showed his true colours. He let Johanna and Louis begin their journey to Provence but stayed behind. He then captured Johanna's sister Maria, widow of Charles of Durazzo, and forced her to marry his son Robert des Baux after, according to Matteo Villani, a forced consummation of the marriage. Bizarrely, Hugh then took ship with Robert and Maria and rejoined Johanna and Louis at Gaeta. Louis of Taranto boarded Hugh's galley, stabbed Hugh and threw him overboard, but similarly to Hugh himself, rather than being a help to Johanna, he used his position of strength to strip Johanna of her power again.

Louis appointed a new seneschal in Provence to take control of the county, then returned to Naples to be crowned jointly with Johanna at Pentecost 1352, giving official recognition to Louis's position as the kingdom's ruler and essentially overthrowing Johanna.[58] However, in an example of poetic justice that might have pleased Boccaccio, Louis's actions in seizing the kingdom immediately made him a lightning rod for criticism and allowed Johanna to be seen as a victim, not a murderess. Indeed, the papal tribunal had officially cleared her of Andrew's murder, although contemporaries such as Matteo Villani chose to see this vindication not as innocence, but proof that Johanna was a weak woman who had been influenced or compelled into evil rather than acting through 'corrupt intention'. This was possible because Johanna was no longer the monstrous husband-murderer and unnatural queen of 1345, but an oppressed wife with no political power.

That Louis was an incompetent and unworthy king was plain from the start. Villani tells the story of Louis's coronation and includes a bad omen:

> And after the coronation, the king rode through the city of Naples in royal vest-ments, mounted on a large and ponderous warhorse and escorted by his barons. As they were passing through the Petrucci gate on the street to the harbour, certain women, to do him honour and to celebrate, threw roses and perfumed flowers down to him through a window. The horse took fright and reared, and, while the noblemen who guided it struggled to bring it to the ground, the horse, which was heavy, broke the reins. King Louis, finding himself without reins astride the frightened horse immediately leaped deftly to the ground. And the crown fell from his head and broke into three pieces, losing three points … On this same day, one of his daughters died … Many people for this reason predicted dire things for the royal majesty.[59]

The kingdom that Louis seized was still in a difficult position, but one of Louis's first actions was to found an order of chivalry. This was not quite as frivolous as it might seem, since a chivalric order was a means of distributing patronage to the nobility and motivating a group of knights to defend the kingdom in its time of need. In 1353, Louis founded the 'Order of the Holy Spirit', better known as the 'Order of the Knot' from its insignia. There was a fashion for chivalric orders in the 14th and 15th centuries with a huge number being founded, including the Order of St George in Hungary (c1326), the Order of the Band in Castile (c1330), the Garter in England (1348), the Star in France (1351), the Golden Fleece in Burgundy (1430) and René of Anjou's Order of the Crescent (1448), but with the notable exceptions of the Garter and the Golden Fleece, most did not outlive their founders.

The Knot was based on the order of the Star, which Jean II founded to compete with Edward III's order of the Garter. The Knot was meant to consist of a group of 300 knights who would advise the king and protect Naples, but their chief goal was to be the reconquest of Jerusalem for the Angevins as its titular king. As with most chivalric orders this goal doesn't seem to have been taken very seriously, and the Knot served much more as a vehicle for chivalric pageantry, with explicit literary associations and conscious links to ancient Rome. Companions who distinguished themselves would be crowned with laurel like ancient Romans, and the headquarters of the order also had legendary Roman associations, since this was the Castel Dell'Ovo, or the castle of the *oeuf enchanté du merveilleux peril* as it was dramatically described in the statutes, playing up its reputed location near the cave where Virgil worked his enchantments and the legend of the magical egg. Like other orders, there would also be a book of adventures documenting the knights' activities, and apparently Niccolo Acciaiuoli actually began writing the book, because Boccaccio mocked him for it – 'he wrote in French of the deeds of the Knights of the Holy Spirit, in the style in which certain others in the past wrote of the Round Table. What laughable and entirely false matters were set down, he himself knows.'[60]

The Knot's most lasting legacy, and it is an impressive one, is that Louis commissioned a sumptuous illuminated manuscript of the order's statutes that survives in the Bibliothèque Nationale in Paris. Cristoforo Orimina illuminated the manuscript, which has a complex and highly specific iconographical programme designed to emphasize Louis's right to rule and his divine status as king, and demoting Johanna to a subordinate position. This is shown strikingly in the frontispiece, which depicts the Trinity enthroned in heaven with Louis and Johanna kneeling before them. Louis is on the right in the position of honour, and Louis wears a larger crown than Johanna and is flanked by an attendant holding a winged Angevin banner. Further illuminations in the manuscript show Louis ruling alone, receiving homage, dispensing justice and presiding over tournaments and banquets.[61]

Given the turmoil attending Johanna and Louis's reign, their previous flight from the kingdom and struggle to regain the throne, their reign saw one completely unexpected victory. Seventy years after the Sicilian Vespers, Niccolo Acciaiuoli was committed to the reconquest of Sicily, and despite the continued failures of Charles II and Robert the Wise to make any headway in this regard, under the troubled reign of Johanna and Louis the Angevins finally achieved limited success.

Not unexpectedly, the divided Aragonese dynasty that separately ruled Sicily, Aragon and Majorca had gone through its own vicissitudes in the intervening decades, and Sicily lacked military and political leadership. Acciaiuoli solicited the support of disaffected nobles in the island, then led Angevin forces across the strait to take Messina. Louis of Taranto joined him, and after somewhat desultory sieges of Palermo and Catania they managed to take control of portions of the island. Although the Angevins never controlled the entire island, their position was secure enough for Johanna and Louis to be crowned in Messina in October 1356. They entered the city in triumph and the coronation was attended with appropriate pomp, but no one, and most certainly not Johanna and Louis, would have believed that they were truly in a position to make good their claim to the island. However, if they lacked the reality of power in Sicily they did succeed in securing the phantom. In the peace treaty with Frederick of Aragon it was reaffirmed that he would never again call himself King of Sicily, instead continuing to use the title 'King of Trinacria' as confirmed in the Treaty of Caltabellota. Johanna and Louis secured their empty titles Queen and King of Sicily, and also ensured that when later rulers took the thrones of both Trinacria and Sicily – i.e. the actual island of Sicily and the so-called Kingdom of Sicily based in Naples – the kingdom would become known as the 'Kingdom of the Two Sicilies'.

In addition to his success in Sicily, Niccolo defeated the brothers Louis and Robert of Durazzo (younger brothers of the murdered Charles of Durazzo) and drove them to Provence, where they took up with a mercenary company, that of the 'Archpriest' Arnaut de Cervole, and attacked Avignon. Niccolo also arranged the marriage of Johanna's sister Maria to Philip of Taranto, Louis's brother. Maria had procured the murder of Robert des Baux, the hated husband who had forced marriage on her through rape, but her freedom was of short duration, and this new marriage to Philip guaranteed a Taranto interest in the succession, as Louis and Johanna's two daughters were now dead and Maria and her surviving daughters were the heirs to the throne.

As Louis's grip on the throne tightened his lack of ability became apparent. The Regno was still impoverished, divided and increasingly subject to attacks from the mercenary companies spawned by the Hundred Years War, and although anyone might have struggled to manage all these difficulties, Louis signally failed to deal with them. More importantly, he fell out with Niccolo Acciaiuoli, who had the ability to address the Regno's problems but now lost royal backing. There was violent dissent from the nobility and Louis was drawn into conflicts with various nobles and communities within the kingdom. However, as Louis became a stereotypical 'bad king' so Johanna's reputation continued to rise. Once Louis proved himself to be unfit, Johanna was transformed from the usurping murderess into the rightful queen who had been supplanted and whose return was longed for.

Johanna too chose to illustrate this in an artistic programme comparable to Robert the Wise's use of paintings emphasizing his ties to Louis of Toulouse, or Louis of Taranto's illustration of his authority in the statutes of the Order of the Knot. Although Louis had driven her from government, Johanna participated in the traditional queenly role as a patron of religious foundations, and at the church of Santa Maria dell'Incoronata she commissioned a fresco cycle of the sacraments.

Each of the sacraments is illustrated with an event from or connected to Johanna's life, and it is clearly her life that is being celebrated, not Louis of Taranto's. *Baptism* is represented by the baptism of the late Charles Martel, *Confirmation* by Johanna's daughters receiving the rite, *Holy Orders* by the consecration of Louis of Toulouse, *Marriage* by the wedding of Johanna to Louis of Taranto, *Communion* by Johanna receiving the sacrament with a group of women and *Extreme Unction* by Louis himself receiving the sacrament (showing that the work was completed after his death). The iconographic programme displayed in the Incoronata shows Johanna wresting back control, perhaps initially in a symbolic sense, although this would soon become real.[62]

Fortunately for Johanna, Louis died in 1362 and she reclaimed control of her kingdom. Johanna benefitted from a change in the papacy, since the decline in her fortunes had in part been due to the loss of Clement VI's protection, as Innocent VI (1352–62) did little to support her, and his reign coincided exactly with Louis of Taranto's supremacy. Innocent died in the same year as Louis, and the new pope Urban V (1362–70) had been the papal legate sent to Naples in 1362 on Louis of Taranto's death, and thus had already been instrumental in restoring Johanna to power before he succeeded to the throne of St Peter.

The Angevins were still a large and troublesome family, but Louis of Durazzo, the last of his generation from that branch of the family, also died in 1362, leaving only a young son, the future Charles III. Johanna brought him to be raised in the royal household, though he repaid this by later overthrowing and murdering her. The only other direct rivals for the throne were Philip and Robert of Taranto, and since Philip was married to Johanna's sister Maria he was a considerable threat. Maria had four daughters who were also claimants to the throne, and this tangled inheritance would cause problems for the rest of Johanna's reign, until Charles III of Durazzo eventually emerged as the winner. This again was through mortality, as Robert of Taranto died in 1364, Maria in 1366 and Philip of Taranto in 1374.

However, Johanna in her final years, as well as Charles of Durazzo and his descendants, would not be unopposed, and surprisingly their main competition would come not from the Hungarian Angevins as it had previously, but from yet another new Angevin dynasty springing from Anjou. To understand the rise of this 'Second House' of Anjou, we must first look at what had happened in France during the reigns of Robert and Johanna, and the vital role the final Angevin dynasty played in the affairs of Naples and Hungary.

CHAPTER 10 – PLANTAGENETS AND ANGEVINS

A T THE BEGINNING OF the 14th century, France was the largest and most stable state in Europe, but it was not without its problems. In the aftermath of the disastrous Aragonese Crusade that ended with the death of Philip III of France and a war between his successor Philip IV and Edward I of England, France needed money. The richest body in the medieval world was of course the Church, and Philip was drawn into conflict with Pope Boniface VIII as we have already seen, but he also began trying to assert his authority against the rich towns of Flanders. This culminated with a massacre of the flower of French chivalry by Flemish weavers at Courtrai in July 1302, one of the most shocking military defeats in French history, though it would not bear this title for long. Courtrai prefigured future defeats, because mounted French knights heedlessly charged into battle against low-born enemy foot soldiers, only to blunder into a series of ditches where they were thrown from their horses and 'speared like fish'.[1] The defeat at Courtrai seriously weakened Philip, and once again put pressure on him to raise additional funds.

The Curse of the Templars

If the surviving fragment of the Angevin Empire in Gascony would be one cause of the Hundred Years War, another was even more dramatic: the curse of the Templars. By the early 14th century, there may still have been a king of Jerusalem, the Angevin Charles II, but the loss of Acre in 1291 had ended the Christian states in the Holy Land. Despite repeated calls for a new Crusade to reestablish the Crusader States, after nearly a century of toxic political Crusades against Christian enemies of the pope and the Angevins, the chances of an actual military expedition being mounted were minimal.

However, if the Crusader States had vanished, the three great institutions spawned by the Crusades had gone from strength to strength: the orders of the Templars, the Hospitallers and the Teutonic Knights. The three military orders had taken dramatically different paths. Only the Hospitallers remained true to their original purpose, and continued to be militant monks fighting the Turks from their new base on Rhodes. They would lose Rhodes to the Ottomans and move their base to Malta, where after resisting one of the most brutal sieges in history in the 16th century, they would evolve and endure to the present day as the Knights of St John of Malta.

The Teutonic Knights have a complicated reputation. They initially remained a Crusading force, but directed their zeal against the pagan peoples living near the Baltic. They were heavily involved in the political development of central Europe because, exactly as the first Crusaders did, they established a new state in the conquered territory. This cannot help but be bound up with the ethnic dimension of the knights, since they were mostly German and their conquests were viewed as German conquests. We have seen that most of the other Crusaders and military orders were largely French, but for modern historical reasons this is not viewed as so problematic. One important factor in establishing the reputation of the Teutonic Knights for a modern audience was Sergei Eisenstein's 1938 film *Alexander Nevsky*, where his depiction of the Russian hero's victory is portrayed in straightforward terms as a victory of heroic Russians against the evil German Knights, who are even adorned with swastika motifs.

The Templars had augmented their military role by becoming a leading force in banking, simply because potential Crusaders would deposit money with their local Templars to prepare for their Crusade, meaning every major city now had a 'Temple' that was a storehouse for vast sums. The Templars quickly learned to lend this money out, and by the early 14th century rivalled the Italian banking houses in their wealth. Inevitably this caused the resentment always directed at moneylenders, but unfortunately for the Templars it also coincided with the loss of Acre in 1291.

Some asked what purpose the Templars served, now that there were no Crusader States for them to defend. Worse, the Templars were criticized by many for their role in Acre's fall, since their constant strife with the Hospitallers was well known. The opprobrium that attached to William of Beaujeu, the Master of the Templars at the time of Acre's fall, was also connected to his earlier support for Charles of Anjou's claim to Jerusalem in opposition to King Hugh of Cyprus, since this further complicated the politics of the city at the time of its gravest crisis. Despite the fact that William of Beaujeu died in the fight to save Acre, these accusations would be remembered when the order was attacked by Philip IV of France.[2]

Philip IV is one of the most fascinating and least attractive (despite his name, Philip 'Le Bel', the Handsome) characters of the 14th century. Like all monarchs, Philip constantly needed money, and he was deeply in debt to the Templars, who were most numerous in France although they were a Europe-wide institution. After his damaging conflict with Boniface VIII and military defeat in Flanders, it would be useful for Philip to have an enemy that the 'most Christian king' could oppose, and he now launched a full-scale attack on the Templars and confiscated their property. As he had with Boniface VIII, Philip couched this attack in religious and moral terms, accusing the Templars of heresy, sodomy and witchcraft. In 1307 he ordered the arrest of all the Templars and their examination under torture.

Unsurprisingly, all manner of shocking crimes were confessed, most notably around the initiation ceremonies for new candidates. These coalesced into a standard group of claims: that initiates renounced and spat on the cross; received the 'kiss of shame' from the order's preceptor on the mouth, navel and anus; and that there was an idol of a man's head revered by the order. These kinds of accusations – of a head that foretold the future, black cats, deviant sexual practices – had been seen before, and would return again and again in trials for witchcraft. It is difficult to analyse them. Certainly in an all-male military fraternity, the fact that the initiation rites and other behaviour may have had a homoerotic dimension is not impossible, but there is no evidence to suggest that the Templars were guilty of the crimes attributed to them.[3]

Outside of France, Philip was criticized for his actions against the Templars, and in other kingdoms, such as England, the Templars were not all arrested. But Philip compelled the newly elected pope, Clement V, to support him by threatening to reopen the case of Boniface VIII and resurrect the (very similar) claims about his sorcery, heresy and sodomy, as well as accusing the Templars of having 'betrayed the Holy Land' when Acre fell.[4] After a series of trials and confessions, the Templars were suppressed throughout Europe. Knights who confessed their 'crimes' and sought absolution would be spared, although they would remain imprisoned, but those who refused to confess would be burnt at the stake as heretics.

The Master of the Order, Jacques de Molay, first denied the accusations, then confessed under torture, recanted his confession before the pope and then admitted the crimes again under further torture. As a result he would be allowed to live, but in 1314, when called to make his final admission of guilt, he repudiated his confession and insisted on the Order's innocence. He was sentenced to death and burnt at the stake on 18 March 1314 in Paris. Legend says that as the flames began to rise around him, Jacques de Molay called down a curse on his persecutors, condemning the pope and the French king to death within a year, and the extinction of the French royal line.[5]

The Templar curse was supremely effective. Pope Clement V and Philip IV, although neither was particularly old, were both dead within months. Philip had three sons, yet each died along with their own sons, and they suffered further lurid scandals such as the imprisonment of their wives for adultery and the murder of one. The rapid turnover in succession introduced some challenging constitutional issues for the French court.

Philip IV was succeeded in 1314 by his son Louis X. Louis died in 1316, leaving a young daughter, Jeanne, and a posthumous son, Jean I, who lived only a few days. Louis's brother, Philip Count of Poitiers, asserted a similar argument to King John in England or Robert the Wise in Naples and advanced his own candidacy over that of Jeanne, though because she was female rather than only because of her youth. He succeeded as Philip V, but when he died in 1322 leaving only a teenaged daughter, the logic of his own path to the throne precluded her from succeeding. His brother Charles succeeded as Charles IV, but reigned for six years and died in 1328, again leaving only a daughter, though his wife was pregnant. If the child were male, he would succeed, but when she proved to be a daughter, the direct male line was at an end.

Philip IV and his sons may have been dead, but Philip's daughter Isabelle and her son were very much alive. The only problem was that Isabelle had married Edward II of England and her son was King Edward III. Worse, in 1326 Isabelle and her lover Roger Mortimer had led an invasion of England to deprive Edward II of power, and Isabelle was widely believed to have ordered Edward's murder in 1327. The French barons had decided that they would not allow a woman to succeed, but Isabelle argued that her son Edward should be able to inherit via his mother's claim. The French now had to decide whether they wanted to allow the king of England to take the French throne, which unsurprisingly they did not.[6]

With the precedent already established that female succession was forbidden, the barons and prelates of France asked the scholars of the University of Paris to delve into the past to 'discover' that their ancient forebears, the Salian Franks, allowed neither female succession nor succession through the female line. On the basis of this 'Salic law', Isabelle and all her progeny were excluded from the throne, as would be all succession in the female line in the future.

With Philip IV's descendants dead or excluded from the succession, who was next in line? Who else could it be but the Count of Anjou. Philip IV's younger brother, Charles of Valois, had as we know married King Charles II of Naples's daughter Margaret, and received Anjou and Maine as her dowry, but he kept his own title. His son Philip of Valois was also Count of Anjou when he was chosen to become King Philip VI of France in 1328, but because their first title was to Valois, the new line of kings is known as 'Valois' and not 'Angevin'.

With the deposition and murder of Edward II in 1327, it was no time for the English royal family to take over France, however strong their claim might appear. Yet Edward III proved to be of a different calibre than his father, and he quickly revitalized royal power, though as Duke of Aquitaine he had grudgingly paid homage to his cousin Philip VI. A further complication was that the French had renewed their alliance with Scotland, and each country promised to support the other if attacked by England. After the Scottish defeat at Halidon Hill in 1333, Philip VI sent a French fleet into the Channel to threaten England in 1336. As tensions mounted, the old conflict over English territory in France arose again, and Philip VI formally confiscated Aquitaine in 1337. Edward III responded by declaring war on France as his father and grandfather had, but also advancing his own claim to the throne, and in 1340 he adopted the title 'King of France' and quartered the lions of England with the lilies of France on his arms. The Hundred Years War had begun.[7]

The Hundred Years War: Crécy and Poitiers

A few points are worth considering first. England had been through a punishing series of wars in the late 13th and early 14th centuries, occupying Wales and nearly conquering Scotland, before the shattering defeat at Bannockburn in 1314 secured Scottish independence and threw the English monarchy into crisis. In these wars the English discovered new types of warfare and weapons, most notably the longbow in Wales. These were the experiences that served the English so well in the Hundred Years War.

On the other side, France was unquestionably the biggest, wealthiest and most powerful state in Europe. Yet this is slightly misleading. Although France was huge and had expanded nearly to its modern boundaries, the perception of French dominance was based to a considerable extent on French cultural and linguistic hegemony over Europe, which is not quite the same thing as real power. Angevin Italy was 'French' and was perceived by contemporaries as an example of French dominance, but it was not part of France and did nothing to help during the Hundred Years War. Apanages such as Burgundy would become independent and, by the 15th century, actually antagonistic to 'France', with devastating effects. The ruling class in England itself was French in language and culture well into the 14th century, though not coincidentally in the 14th century, as English national identity began to solidify, so too did the English language. So if France was not a paper tiger, at the same time – as would be brutally revealed very soon – it was not the military behemoth that most believed it to be.

The stage was set for the century of military conflict that would engulf France, but as we are about to encounter a new, and final, line of Angevins, we must trace their origins. They are known as the 'Second House' of Anjou, following the 'First House' founded by Charles of Anjou. Obviously this ignores the existence of the counts of Anjou whose history we traced from the 9th century until the time of King John, but this is how most modern historians classify them.

When Philip of Valois became king of France, his county of Anjou became a royal demesne and remained so under his son Jean II (Jean 'le Bon', the Good). Jean made his second son Louis Count of Anjou in 1350, but didn't formally cede the county to him as an appanage until 1360. At that time the county was elevated to a duchy, making Louis the first Duke of Anjou. In 1361 Maine was added to the duchy, and other familiar names were added over time, such as Loudon in 1367, Touraine in 1368, Chinon in 1370 and Mirebeau in 1379. The arrival of Louis gave new life to Anjou: members of the First House had never really lived there, but despite their foreign expeditions, the dukes of the Second House usually did reside in Angers or Saumur.[8]

Analysing the conflict from an Angevin perspective will give us a different view of the Hundred Years War, and as we would expect, the Angevins were so intimately involved in events that focusing on them will give us a good account of what happened. Although some of the Angevins still exhibited a knack for avoiding major battles (think of Fulk Réchin and the First Crusade, King John and the Battle of Bouvines) and they missed out on Crécy and Agincourt (fortunately for them), Louis I fought at Poitiers in 1356. More importantly, Louis I was regent of France from 1380–82, and Louis II, Yolanda of Aragon and King René were intimately involved in all aspects of French government in the 15th century.

In the absence of French Angevins in the early part of the war, which coincided with the reign of Robert the Wise and Johanna I in Naples and Carobert in Hungary, we can summarize it by focusing on a few key issues. Both sides sought allies, and the Holy Roman Empire was drawn into the conflict. Edward had an early success, when in 1337 he gained an alliance with Emperor Ludwig of Bavaria by means of a large bribe. Ludwig had given up his designs in Italy, and although still excommunicated, he gave Edward the right to summon imperial subjects outside of Germany to join him in the war, though this amounted to little. Philip VI also allied with a former Angevin opponent, John of Bohemia, who was now – and forever after – known as 'Blind King John'. He had lost his sight, probably due to disease, around 1336, though some contemporary sources claimed his blindness was caused by being poisoned in Italy, an early example of Italy's reputation as a land of intrigue, poison and murder. John brought a contingent of knights and fought personally at Crécy, but otherwise, like Ludwig, he had little impact on the struggle.[9]

When the war began in earnest, Edward's strategy became clear: he began extended chevauchées, ravaging the French countryside and trying to cause as much pain as possible to force Philip to grant him outright sovereignty in Aquitaine. None of his actions look like an attempt at conquest. The crushing victories of Crécy in 1346 and Poitiers in 1356 were completely unexpected, and left the English in the embarrassing position of having achieved much more than they anticipated and being unsure what to do about it.

The great contemporary historian of the early part of the war is Jean Froissart, who worked for both the French and English, and so generally had access to good information for both sides. He also had an interest in Naples, and noted that 'Robert the king of Sicily', known as a great astrologer, had warned Philip VI at the start of the war that he would only find misfortune if he fought the English, another example of 'great wisdom' in the medieval period being nearly synonymous with sorcery.[10] Modern historians somewhat churlishly criticize Froissart's work for its breathless tone and focus on deeds of chivalry and derring-do, but he is an invaluable resource, not in spite of, but because he indulges his bias in favour of valour and rousing quotes to the full.

His account of the battle of Crécy is a perfect example. The French arrived late in the day and in some disorder, as various parts of the force arrived at different times. Philip VI, seeing the English in a strong position, was advised to wait until the next day to fight and accepted this advice, but the mass of the army was pushed forward by later arrivals until they drew too close to the English line and were forced to engage. Philip tried to retrieve the situation and ordered an attack. This was to be led by a group of professional Genoese crossbowmen, using the weapon that, until the 14th century, was the premier piece of battlefield artillery. As the Genoese advanced, they were soaked by a heavy rain shower that damaged their weapons – Froissart throws in a solar eclipse and an ominous flock of crows for good measure – and before they could get close enough to the English to do any harm, the English longbows, with a much greater range and quicker rate of fire, annihilated them. The Geneose tried to flee, but the French knights, infuriated by what they saw as the cowardice of these mercenaries, rode them down and attacked. The French were attacking uphill, into the setting sun and into the hail of arrows from the longbows, and suffered massive losses.

Some of the French did reach the English lines and there was fierce fighting. Froissart reports the most glamorous and touching moments of the battle. Edward III's sixteen-year-old son, Edward the Black Prince, led a division and was sorely pressed, but when a messenger went to Edward III to request help, the king replied, 'Let the boy earn his spurs for I am determined that all the honour and glory of the day be given to him.' Blind King John also managed to fight, instructing his companions to lead him to the front so that he might 'strike one stroke with my sword'. His company tied their horses together by the reins so that they wouldn't lose each other in the press, and they did reach the front: Froissart reports that they were all killed and the next day they were found in a group, with their horses still tied together. The Black Prince was said to be so impressed by John's bravery that he took John's badge of three ostrich feathers and his motto, 'ich dien' or 'I serve', for his own, and it remains the Prince of Wales's motto to this day.

As wave after wave of French knights charged even after night fell, and were slaughtered, some finally began to leave the battlefield, including Philip VI. The English army included detachments of non-noble Cornish, Welsh and Irish light infantry or 'knifemen', who, as 'low-born villeins', asked for no quarter in battle and gave none. They dispatched all the injured French knights where they lay, meaning that the battle was vastly more deadly than medieval battles tended to be. Froissart claims that Edward III was 'greatly exasperated' that the knifemen killed so many French nobles, who might otherwise have been held for ransom. Be that as it may, Crécy was an iconic victory that heralded something of a military revolution. The tactics Edward used had not been seen outside the British Isles and had overwhelmed what was, rightly or wrongly, perceived to be the most powerful army in Europe.[11]

The consequences of Crécy were perhaps not as striking as one might expect. The English army went on to besiege and finally take Calais, which the English would hold for more than 200 years. A separate force was sent to Aquitaine, and consolidated the English position there when the French army under the Duke of Normandy, the future Jean II, retreated on hearing of the catastrophe at Crécy. More importantly, the Scots invaded England in October 1346 in support of France, only to be heavily defeated at Neville's Cross near Durham, and their king David II was taken prisoner and sent to the Tower of London. England's northern frontier was now secure, and Edward III could concentrate on the war with France. However, as we reach the end of the 1340s we know what is coming, and in 1348 the Black Death arrived in France, spreading to England the same year and ravaging both countries, along with the rest of Europe, until the end of 1349.

Perhaps not quite as significant as the Black Death, but still an important factor in the events of the late 1340s and early 1350s, was Edward III's financial situation. Edward had borrowed heavily from the largest banks in Europe, the Florentine houses of the Bardi, Peruzzi and Acciaiuoli. Despite the victory at Crécy, the enormous expenses of the war were too much and Edward repudiated his loans. The Florentine banks were already in difficulty after their massive loans to the papacy and the Angevins of Naples, and this latest setback caused the collapse of all three houses, essentially ruining Florentine banking until the rise of the Medici, who operated on a greatly reduced scale.[12]

Philip VI died in 1350 to be succeeded by his son Jean II, and it was in this year that Jean's younger brother Louis became Count of Anjou. Both England and France were still recovering from the Black Death and Edward III was struggling to raise funds, but by 1355 he was ready to revive the campaign. Edward the Black Prince was sent to Aquitaine to begin another devastating chevauchée, and in 1356 he launched a raid that reached the city of Tours, though he was unable to take it. Jean II led an army to intercept him, and the Black Prince tried to elude the French and return to Aquitaine with his swollen baggage train.

However, on Sunday 18 September 1356, the French army finally caught the English near Poitiers. As they prepared for battle, a papal legate begged the French not to attack because of the Truce of God, and Jean II agreed against the advice of his Marshal and others, allowing the English additional time to prepare.

Just as at Crécy, the English were arrayed in a favourable position with orchards and hedges shielding their flanks. The Earl of Douglas, who led a Scottish contingent with the French army, advised the French knights to dismount for the attack, sound advice since horses were much more vulnerable to arrows than the heavily armoured knights. This shows that the French did learn from their defeats and attempt different tactics, which would finally bear fruit, though not for many decades.

Although the result of Poitiers was even more overwhelming than Crécy, the battle itself was a more straightforward affair. The French attacked and suffered heavy losses from the arrows, but the division led by the Dauphin reached the English line and engaged them. The Dauphin, the future Charles V 'the Wise', was very much in the bookish mould of Robert the Wise, yet he acquitted himself well at Poitiers and would prove to be a remarkable king. Accompanying him in the front line were his brothers, the seventeen-year-old Louis of Anjou and the sixteen-year-old Jean, who would become the renowned aesthete the Duke of Berry. This first attack was driven back and threw the next division into confusion. Jean II saw the army faltering and flung his own division, the strongest, into the battle. The French now seem to have regrouped, but the Black Prince launched a reserve force into Jean II's flank. The French army disintegrated under the attack and Jean II and his last son, the fifteen-year-old Philip the Bold, future Duke of Burgundy, were surrounded. Jean II was asked to surrender, and according to Froissart, courteously replied that he would prefer to surrender to the Black Prince himself, and this being accepted he and Philip were escorted to the prince.[13]

One of the barons killed at Poitiers was Robert of Durazzo. The Durazzo branch of the Neapolitan Angevins was becoming quite active against Queen Johanna in this period, but their unwavering hostility to Louis the Great over the murder of Charles of Durazzo directed some of their energy away from her. Robert of Durazzo went to the French court, where he was knighted, in hopes of receiving French support for a challenge to Louis the Great to a trial by combat to avenge his brother's death. He never achieved this, instead serving the French king at Poitiers where he met his death.

To face another such disaster only ten years after Crécy and six years after the Black Death was a heavy blow for France. The Dauphin Charles took over the kingdom in his father's absence, but popular unrest over the cost of the war led to uprisings by the bourgeoisie in Paris, and even the peasants rebelled in the movement known as the *jacquerie*. Tired of being the victims of English raids and receiving no protection from the king, large numbers of peasants rose against their lords, and quickly stories spread of rape, pillage and murder across northern France.[14]

The peasants were not alone. As we know, in the Middle Ages there were not yet professional national armies, so after Poitiers the English and Gascon mercenaries and foreign troops who had fought for the Black Prince were left to their own devices. Released from English service, these men – many of whom were knights – became the 'Free Companies', the mercenary armies that would plague France and Italy for the next few decades. Although they were essentially bandits who ravaged the countryside, burned villages and extorted ransom money from towns in return for not sacking them, they were also professional armies at a time when states lacked them, and the companies would flourish because they were routinely employed by both sides in the war.

The Dauphin himself enlisted the support of Arnaut de Cervole, known as the 'Archpriest', who led the most notorious of the Gascon companies, in a design against Queen Johanna. In 1357 the Archpriest invaded Provence and attacked Avignon, and he was definitely in contact with Johanna's enemies Louis of Durazzo (father of Charles III of Durazzo who would eventually overthrow and murder Johanna) and the powerful des Baux family. Pope Innocent VI wrote to the Dauphin complaining that attacks were being made on Provence in the Dauphin's name and possibly even at his command, and he reminded the Dauphin that Provence belonged to Johanna. The Dauphin naturally disavowed the actions of the Archpriest, who was entertained lavishly by the pope and then given a huge ransom to take his army elsewhere.[15]

As this turmoil engulfed France, what had happened to the captive King Jean II? Jean was entertained royally by Edward III, and after riding through London on a white horse as part of the Black Prince's triumphal procession, he was installed in the Savoy Palace. Despite the impeccable treatment of the king, the treaty that Edward III proposed is striking. Edward demanded no less than the restoration of the entire Angevin Empire to England – Normandy, Anjou, Maine and Poitou were to be added to Aquitaine – plus additional territory all the way to Calais, all with full sovereignty and in addition to a heavy ransom. Jean accepted the treaty in 1359, and this attempt to turn the clock back to 1200 is an astonishing result. Despite Jean II's agreement, the treaty was sent to Paris where the Dauphin and his council rejected it.

Proof that England had essentially won the war came when Edward III retaliated by invading France at the end of 1359 with the goal of being crowned king of France in Reims. However, Reims was prepared for a siege and the English were unable to do more than make a military demonstration. The English moved on to Paris in early 1360 and were equally unable to take the city, but their ability to march through the countryside with impunity is remarkable. The Dauphin Charles showed his mettle by refusing to be drawn into another disastrous battle and holding his nerve in the well-fortified cities, until Edward III was forced to make another proposal.

This was the Treaty of Brétigny, and its terms were still quite harsh for France. Calais and an expanded Aquitaine comprising around one third of France were ceded outright to Edward, plus a huge ransom of three million écus. However, Edward renounced his claim to the throne, and also gave up his claim to Normandy, Anjou, Maine and Touraine. This treaty would be the framework for all activity in the war for the next few decades when both sides jockeyed for position. After the treaty was agreed, Jean II was released and allowed to return to France, but only in exchange for hostages, and these hostages included his son Louis of Anjou.[16]

Louis joined a group of forty hostages including Jean the future Duke of Berry, the Duke of Orleans, the Duke of Bourbon plus other nobles and notable knights. They were forced to live in England at their own expense, though this did not prevent many of them from living lives of extreme luxury. Although we hear of them being guarded, the conditions of their captivity seem no more onerous than those of Jean II. Indeed, they seem to have moved between England and newly English Calais with only their word as their guarantee, as we would expect for knights of the most chivalrous kingdom in Europe. Louis of Anjou, who had recently married Marie of Blois-Penthevieres in July 1360, was even given permission to visit his wife in Boulogne. He then broke his word and refused to return to Calais.[17]

On the one hand this is a shocking breach of knightly etiquette, but on the other we have seen countless examples of knights, nobles and kings breaking their word whenever it suited them, particularly at times of war, and there was always a good reason and they were always able to find a clergyman to absolve them of whatever oath they were breaking. We don't have specific information about Louis being absolved, but no opprobrium seems to have attached to him for this faithlessness.

One person, however, took these matters very seriously, and that was Jean II. Now that one of the hostages had broken his word, and more importantly, given that the ransom payments were grossly in arrears, Jean made what is seen as the extraordinary decision to return to captivity. Jean is heavily criticized by modern historians, with justification, for this behaviour. We have seen other kings captured in battle, and their absolute priority was to gain their freedom so they could return to their kingdoms, which were usually in turmoil during their absence. Not so Jean II. There was never any question of Jean being ill-treated in England; quite the contrary, as Edward III took this opportunity to show to the full how wealthy, cultured and chivalrous the English court was. Naturally Jean was enchanted, and although he had returned to his devastated kingdom, he seemed to feel no need to remain there. In January 1364 he returned to his welcome confinement in England, and died shortly after in April, said by some to have been so indulged with banquets and feasting that it caused his death. Although he seems a jolly chivalrous figure, Jean II was simply a bad king and his willingness to leave his son to pick up the pieces makes him an unattractive character.

His death was a blessing for France, who now in Charles V 'the Wise' had a king who proved more than a match for Edward III. Charles steadily reversed the consequences of France's catastrophic defeats in the war, and also addressed problems such as the Free Companies. One means of dispersing the companies was to send them to war elsewhere. They were happy to work for the highest bidder, and frequently found themselves supporting both sides in a war at various times. Under the guise of a Crusade against the Moors of Granada, Charles organized an expedition to Spain to intervene in a civil war between Pedro the Cruel and Enrique de Trastamara. This was led by the Breton knight Bertrand du Guesclin, who would become the most famous knight in France and remain a chivalric hero into modern times. After initial French success overthrew Pedro and installed Enrique on the throne of Castile, the Black Prince intervened, and Castile became the battleground in a proxy war between England and France. A second battle, at Najera in 1367, reversed the previous result with the Black Prince victorious, du Guesclin captured and Pedro the Cruel restored to the throne. Also participating in the battle was Queen Johanna's estranged third husband, James IV of Majorca.

Although the English candidate was successful, the defeat at Najera was of little consequence to France, and as would often be the case, was something of a win-win for Charles V. He had rid France of a substantial number of mercenaries, and after Pedro repudiated his debts to the Black Prince, the victory turned into a financial disaster for the English in Gascony. Within two years du Guesclin was back in Spain and defeated Pedro the Cruel at the Battle of Montiel in 1369. Enrique of Trastamara murdered the captive Pedro after the battle and took the throne, resulting in a Castilian–French alliance that would prove highly beneficial to France.[18]

The Black Prince's position, and his health, deteriorated rapidly after the Battle of Najera. Aquitaine was financially crippled, and as resistance to the Prince's rule grew, disaffected nobles appealed to Charles V as their overlord for redress. By the terms of the Treaty of Brétigny this should not have been possible, as Aquitaine was now held freely by the English king, but the terms of Brétigny had never really been met by the French and they now repudiated the treaty. Charles V summoned the Black Prince to Paris to answer the charges against him, and when he failed to appear Charles declared the duchy forfeit in May 1369 and resumed the Hundred Years War.

Despite this aggressive stance, Charles maintained his successful strategy of avoiding open warfare, instead harrying the English troops. Du Guesclin now led the fight, being named Marshal of France in 1370, and won a series of victories. By 1375 the

French had recovered all their territories except Gascony and Calais, nullifying the terms of the Treaty of Brétigny and nearly restoring the situation to what it was before the war. The Black Prince, his health broken, returned to England and died in 1376, followed by Edward III in 1377.[19]

The Wheel of Fortune had turned again, and after the victory at Poitiers seemed to have won the war for England, now France was in the ascendant. However, both France and England would very soon enter periods of dynastic turmoil as a consequence of bad kingship, and more importantly for our purposes, the Second House of Anjou would intervene directly in the affairs of Naples and enter into a conflict that endured until the extinction of the Angevin line.

CHAPTER 11 – THE SECOND HOUSE OF ANJOU AND THE ANGEVINS OF NAPLES/HUNGARY

NAPLES HAD SURVIVED THE turmoil of Andrew's murder and the Hungarian invasions, and after the death of Louis of Taranto in 1362 Johanna regained control of her kingdom. Neither of Johanna's two subsequent husbands was considered king, and from 1362–1380 she reigned alone. Tangible evidence of this is that after 1362 Johanna issued all her coins with only her own image. Although numismatics is not always the most thrilling topic, Johanna's representations on her coins are revealing. After Louis's death, Johanna's coins bestow on her all the attributes of sovereignty, including defending the kingdom. From 1370 her coins portrayed her holding a sword as well as a sceptre, and after 1372 she was also shown wearing a coat of mail.[1]

Unfortunately, at the time of Louis of Taranto's death Johanna was still only in her mid-30s, and she needed to remarry. It would have been very difficult for any reigning queen to resist societal pressure to marry, but Johanna also faced a succession crisis. As we saw, Charles Martel had died young and her daughters Françoise and Catherine had both also died by 1362, and the lack of a direct heir exposed Johanna to continued pressure from the Taranto, Durazzo and Hungarian branches of the family that might ease if she had a child.

Naturally the Pope Urban V became involved, and he advocated a marriage to Philip of Touraine, youngest son of Jean II of France, which Jean himself was keen to promote as a means of taking control of Naples. Johanna cordially refused, and stated in a letter to Jean that she had learned from bitter experience not to marry anyone so nearly related to her, as this was one reason for the early death of her children. Even if this were an excuse, it shows an awareness of how dangerous the Angevin policy of intermarriage was.

Johanna's Third Husband: James of Majorca

Instead, Johanna chose to marry James IV of Majorca, a great-nephew of Robert the Wise's wife Sancia (who was Robert's second wife, and thus not a direct ancestor of Johanna). James is a tragic figure, since he spent his younger years as a captive at the court of his uncle Pedro IV the Ceremonious of Aragon, and rumour said that he had been kept in an iron cage, with consequences for his mental health that we will see. In 1362 James had escaped from Barcelona and fled to Naples, where he arrived just in time for Louis of Taranto's death and Johanna's availability for marriage. The union was agreed in December 1362 and the marriage took place early in 1363.[2]

James was an unthreatening choice since he was only titular king of Majorca, which was ruled by Pedro IV, and he was younger than Johanna, being only around twenty-seven at the time of their marriage. The terms of the marriage were clear: he was excluded from the succession and defined as Johanna's consort, and although he was granted the title Duke of Calabria to make him the highest-ranking nobleman in the Regno, he held no other titles. Although Urban V hadn't given his consent and had still been pressing for the French marriage when Johanna chose James, he accepted her decision without complaint since he too felt James was a good choice. Urban's view of arrangements at the court are clear, since his correspondence to Naples was addressed to Johanna alone or referred to James as 'King of Majorca'. More pertinently, in April 1363 the pope wrote to Louis the Great of Hungary informing him that he was expected to respect the marriage.

If there was some hope that Johanna's third marriage would prove lucky for her, this was quickly dashed. She became pregnant, but miscarried in 1365 and had no more children. Worse, James proved to be in a similar mould to Andrew, finding his subordinate position at court a humiliation, and insisting on participating in the Regno's government and attending councils and private meetings. This in itself is not surprising, but James's behaviour went beyond dissatisfaction at not being Johanna's equal and seemed more like insanity. James exhibited violent behaviour (which Johanna said was connected to the cycles of the moon), blasphemed and had temper tantrums. When Johanna dared to oppose him he was publicly violent to her, and she described in letters to the pope that he physically attacked her and publicly accused her of murdering Andrew and having many lovers. Twenty years later, the slurs about Johanna's supposed adultery and murder of Andrew were still used to attack her.[3]

We have abundant correspondence from Johanna to the pope describing James's actions, and lest this be seen as propaganda from Johanna to force James into a subordinate position, her statements are corroborated by the letters of the Archbishop of Naples, Pierre d'Ameil. Regardless of the degree of James's mental instability, it is also a sad fact that his use of physical violence against his wife was only notable because he was attacking a reigning queen in public: domestic violence by husbands against wives was accepted as a fact of life, even if the church condemned it.

Johanna's response demonstrates her character, as she defended herself from James's physical violence in Naples and methodically elaborated her legal position in letters to the pope, the clergy and the nobles to reinforce James's subordinate position. Her success is demonstrated by the fact that James soon left the kingdom, presumably to everyone's relief. He had an interesting subsequent career, joining the English side in the Hundred Years War, and as we saw he fought with the Black Prince in Spain. In 1368 James was captured at Burgos by Enrique of Trastamara, the French candidate in the Spanish war, and Johanna paid a large ransom to release him, though no doubt she would have preferred him to remain a captive. He finally died in 1375.

The succession was now the most pressing issue, and Johanna's sister Maria and her daughters were next in line. Maria's children were known as Johanna, Agnes, Clementia and Margaret 'of Durazzo', as they were the children of her first husband, Charles of Durazzo. After Maria ordered the execution of her second husband and rapist Robert des Baux, she had married Philip of Taranto, younger brother of Johanna's husband Louis. Philip of Taranto, together with the courtiers and papal agents in Naples, was keen to resolve the succession, and was hoping to arrange a marriage for Johanna, eldest daughter of Maria.

When it became known that Frederick III of Sicily's wife had died, Queen Johanna, supported by the pope, began negotiations for Frederick to marry the younger Johanna and resolve the interminable war between Naples and Sicily. This led to disputes between the Queen and Young Johanna, complicated by the involvement of the pope, Maria, Philip of Taranto, Frederick of Sicily and others. The episode finally ended when Young Johanna concluded a different marriage without papal dispensation for consanguinity, leading the pope to bar her formally from the succession to Naples in 1370, and putting her cousin, the younger Charles of Durazzo, another step closer to the throne. Not coincidentally, in January 1370 Charles had married Young Johanna's sister Margaret, potentially uniting the two lines. Charles's prospects were looking better all the time, since at this point he was also the heir presumptive to the throne of Hungary.[4]

This period of struggle to secure the succession coincided with Johanna's personal rule and a period where her previous reputation as the 'Harlot Queen' began to improve. Most striking were her relationships with the saints Birgitta of Sweden and Catherine of Siena, which were seen by many contemporaries as bizarrely out of step with her reputation as a murderess and harlot.

The 'Black Legend' that swirls around Johanna even rears its head in this case, because there is a story that Johanna had an affair with Birgitta's son Karl during their visit to Naples. Karl had left his wife in Sweden, and once in Naples he is said to have formed a liaison with Johanna. Karl then died in Naples, and a lurid detail of the story is that Birgitta prayed for his death because she couldn't stand to see him living in sinful adultery with Johanna. This is another horribly damning account of the harlot queen and her insatiable lust.

Yet the story comes from Margareta Clausdotter, from the life of Birgitta she wrote 100 years later. It comes in the context of showing how Birgitta was so holy that she preferred to see her children die rather than sin.[5] Thus the story is not about Johanna, but about Birgitta and Karl. The fact that Margareta chose the 'harlot queen of Naples' to illustrate Karl's sin and Birgitta's holiness is based purely on Johanna's later reputation, and possibly confusion with Queen Johanna II, rather than any evidence. Whatever the truth about this relationship, after Birgitta died in 1373 Johanna actively promoted her canonization, which came in 1391.

After Birgitta's death, Johanna began to correspond with a new saint, Catherine of Siena. Their relationship had a different tone, in that Birgitta had seen herself – and been accepted by Johanna – as a spiritual adviser, and Birgitta frequently rebuked Johanna in harsh terms for her perceived sins. Catherine, who was younger than Johanna, corresponded with her on more equal terms, and was primarily interested in enlisting Johanna's support for a Crusade. Catherine and Johanna's relationship was intimately bound up with their relationships with the pope, and in this sense was not as exclusively spiritual as Johanna's relationship with Birgitta had been. The pope was interested in supporting Constantinople against the Ottomans, as he had a clear sense of the future of the eastern Mediterranean, and Johanna, as Queen of Jerusalem, was active in the campaign, as was St Catherine.[6]

Although it seemed that the age of the Crusades had passed, and the kingdoms of the West were busy fighting amongst themselves, those in the east were aware that the Ottoman Turks were a powerful new enemy interested in expanding their territory at the expense of neighbouring kingdoms. Hungary was on the front line of this threat, and when finally in 1396 a Crusade was launched against the Ottomans, Hungary was instrumental in organizing it. By then Hungary had passed from Angevin control, and we must examine how this happened.

King Louis the Great of Hungary

Louis the Great succeeded Carobert as king of Hungary in 1342 at the age of sixteen, and perhaps his youth explains the extremity of his response to his brother's murder three years later. Although our encounters with Louis so far have shown only his savagery in Italy, if we try to look at events objectively and not favour either the Neapolitan or Hungarian Angevins, the Hungarian Angevins were justified in their claim to the Neapolitan throne, and Louis certainly had a right to be outraged by Andrew's brutal murder. In the early days after Andrew's death, it is not surprising that Louis and Andrew's mother Elisabeth took the lead in negotiations with the papacy, since she had gone to Naples in 1343 after Robert the Wise's death to monitor the transfer of power from Robert to Johanna and – if she had her way – Andrew. We should also remember the youth of the parties involved, as at the time of Andrew's murder Louis was still no more than nineteen, Johanna was eighteen and Andrew was seventeen.

Although the pope remained committed to Johanna's right to rule and never seems to have considered deposing her in favour of Louis, the crises that Johanna faced, her uncanonical marriage to Louis of Taranto and the power and influence of the Hungarian court might have begun to tell if Louis had tried further diplomacy. Instead he invaded, summarily executed Charles of Durazzo in January 1348 and claimed the throne for himself. Within three months the Black Death had driven him away, which was not something he could have prepared for, but by September 1348 Johanna had returned on a wave of popular outrage against the brutality shown by the Hungarian troops. Despite Johanna's return, Hungarian forces still occupied parts of the Regno, and Louis himself returned in May 1350 and reoccupied Naples, forcing Johanna to flee to Gaeta. Yet Louis's reputation in the Regno never recovered, and by the end of 1350 he had been forced to withdraw once again.

If his Italian campaigns do him no credit, Louis's activity in Croatia and Dalmatia was much more successful. Louis was already at war with Venice at the time of Andrew's murder, because Zara had overthrown the Venetians and returned to Hungarian control. The Venetians besieged the city and Louis's rescue attempt was repulsed in July 1346. Venice ultimately took Zara in 1348, but Louis was now focused on invading the Regno, so he agreed an eight-year treaty with the Venetians. As we have seen, his relations with the Venetians improved remarkably, to the point where Venetian ships carried Hungarian troops across the Adriatic for the invasion.

This peace was not renewed, and Louis had used the time to prepare an altogether more ambitious plan. In 1356, with the support of Pope Innocent VI, the Emperor Charles IV and the city of Padua, Louis invaded the Venetian mainland provinces and attempted to force the Republic to terms. Louis was defeated, and again had to seek peace, but events now moved quickly. Throughout 1357 the cities of the Dalmatian coast, including Zara, expelled the Venetians and placed themselves under Louis's protection. In 1358 Venice was forced to cede the entirety of Dalmatia to Hungary, and the doge officially resigned the titles Duke of Dalmatia and Croatia that the Venetians had held for more than 300 years.

To some in Hungary, Louis's Mediterranean ambitions were a distraction that drew him away from his proper duties in his kingdom. Certainly Louis's invasion of the Regno and his repeated attacks on Venice drew him away from Hungary, but the Hungarian kings considered Croatia part of their kingdom, and Louis was no more wrong to focus on this part of his domains than Richard the Lionheart had been to spend most of his reign in his French territories.

Louis's victory over Venice particularly benefited trade for Venetian rivals. Louis granted Dubrovnik (or Ragusa, as it was known at the time) autonomy, and it began its development as an independent city-state. Furthermore, Louis's amalgamation of all the territory from the Adriatic coast, through Hungary and into Poland, once he became its king, united the area from the Baltic to the Adriatic as a single trading block, protected by royal fortresses and under a central administration. The economic possibilities were enormous, and the merchants of Florence – always closely connected to Angevins whether in Naples or Hungary – exploited this potential to the full.[7]

Although he was now supreme on the Dalmatian coast, Louis remained committed to limiting Venetian power. In 1373 he sent assistance to Padua in a war with Venice, and although this expedition failed, in 1378 he joined Genoa in what was an outright attempt to destroy Venice. The Republic was besieged by the Genoese, and after several naval defeats and a land-based attack by Louis, seemed likely to be conquered. A Venetian fleet that had been campaigning in the eastern Mediterranean returned in the nick of time and defeated the Genoese, relieving the city, but Venice had to pay an indemnity to Genoa and in the Treaty of Zara in 1381 confirmed Hungarian rule of Dalmatia.

The wealth and luxury of the Hungarian court left a tangible mark on Zara, and the silver reliquary chest donated by Louis's wife Elisabeth to the church of San Simeon is an outstanding example of 14th-century metalwork. The chest is decorated with plaques showing historical events, such as the entry of Louis the Great into Zara when he finally took the city; the death of Elisabeth's father, Stjepan Kotromanic, the ban of Bosnia who gave considerable support to Louis; and the life of St Simeon himself.

Louis's court was known as an intellectual centre, and despite Petrarch's waspish suggestion that Louis should pay more attention to his Latin style than his greyhounds, Louis clearly did like books, and he seized Robert the Wise's library when he captured Naples, and took it back to Hungary. Louis's copy of the *Secretum Secretorum* is now in the Bodleian Library, and he commissioned the *Illuminated Chronicle*, one of the best and most beautiful sources for Hungarian history. He also founded the first Hungarian university, at Pécs in 1367.

We have no portrait of Louis, but John Kukullei described him in 1390 – after his death, and not particularly helpfully – as being of medium stature with fleshy lips, and a 'proud regard' that was a sign of his authority.[8] It was also shortly after his death that a foreign chronicler referred to him as 'the Great', which given the vicissitudes of Hungarian history in the 13th century seems fair for someone who presided over such significant territorial expansion.

Louis maintained Carobert's relationships with his central European neighbours, but his closest relationship was with King Casimir of Poland, also known as 'the Great', and early in his reign he was acknowledged as Casimir's heir. When Casimir died on 5 November 1370, Louis was crowned king of Poland twelve days later and initiated the Angevin period in Polish history.[9]

The Angevin Succession in Hungary and Naples

Like so many others, Louis failed in the primary responsibility of a ruler and was unable to secure the succession. Louis and Elisabeth had no children for seventeen years, and Louis recognized his younger brother Stephen as his heir until Stephen's death in 1354. Stephen's son John was then recognized as the heir to both Hungary and Poland, but he too died in 1360. This prompted the arrival in the Hungarian court in 1364 of Charles of Durazzo, nephew of Charles of Durazzo whom Louis had murdered in 1348.

Because Johanna also had no surviving children and her sister Maria died in 1366, the succession in Naples should naturally have passed to Maria's children. Maria had four daughters, but as we saw the eldest (Johanna) was disqualified after her unsanctioned marriage, Clementia had died in 1363 and Agnes had renounced her rights to the throne, leaving only Margaret, the youngest. In 1370, Louis the Great and Johanna agreed that Charles of Durazzo should marry Margaret, once again looking towards a union of the Hungarian and Neapolitan thrones. As Louis also inherited the throne of Poland in 1370, there was the potential for a new 'Angevin Empire' stretching from the Baltic to the Adriatic, and including Italy and Provence.

These plans were disrupted when Louis and Elisabeth were suddenly blessed with three children: Catherine in 1370, Maria in 1371 and Hedwig in 1374.[10] Despite his renunciation of the crowns of Sicily and Jerusalem when his war with the Neapolitan Angevins ended, now that he had children of his own Louis remembered his claim, and chose to forget about Charles of Durazzo. He betrothed his eldest daughter Catherine to Louis of Orleans, second son of Charles V of France, and offered the kingdom of Naples and the county of Provence as her dowry despite the fact that Johanna was very much alive and the ruler of both territories.

It was now, in 1376, that Johanna married her fourth husband, Otto of Brunswick, a seasoned soldier whom she undoubtedly chose because he could lead a military response if necessary. Otto of Brunswick was one of the papacy's main supporters, and Johanna's marriage to him after James of Majorca's death in 1375 was an act of support for the papacy, and a way for the papacy to support her. James of Majorca's death had another consequence, since his sister and heir Isabelle of Majorca, Countess of Roussillon and Cerdagne, chose Duke Louis I of Anjou as her own heir. In 1376 she ceded Louis her rights to Achaea, Morea and the Latin Empire, giving him the ancillary claims that went with the throne of Naples, and putting him in a prime position to be Johanna's heir even if she resented his attempts to seize her throne.[11]

It is intriguing to consider where the negotiations between Hungary and France would have ended, but two events intervened. First, Catherine of Hungary died in 1378. Second and more importantly, the Western Great Schism in the papacy erupted. In previous struggles between Johanna and Louis the Great, the unshakeable support of the papacy had been the key to Johanna's survival and ultimate success in retaining her throne. After 1378, relying on the papacy was an altogether different proposition, and required the extraordinary choice of which pope.

The Western Great Schism

Returning the papacy to Rome had been advocated by many figures, including Petrarch and Birgitta of Sweden, and when Urban V decided to visit the city in 1367 Johanna sent ships to escort him. In 1368 she attended his court, and when he awarded the Golden Rose (to the most eminent person attending the papal court on the fourth Sunday in Lent), it was to Johanna, the first woman to be so honoured, and this despite the fact that Peter I of Cyprus and his son were there. The situation was especially tense because both Peter and Johanna claimed the titular throne of Jerusalem, and Peter had been crowned king in 1359 despite Johanna's claim. Nevertheless, Johanna joined the line of Angevins such as Fulk Réchin, Louis of Taranto and Niccolo Acciaiuoli who had received the Golden Rose. However, Urban's residence in Rome was brief and he returned to the safer environs of Avignon in 1370.

Urban's example proved decisive though, and in 1376 Pope Gregory XI, despite being old and infirm, decided the time had come to move the papacy back to Rome for good. This was despite the opposition of the French cardinals – who were now the majority of the college – and many who argued that at such a critical time in the Hundred Years War it was the pope's duty to remain nearby to help negotiate. Gregory was obdurate and arrived in Rome in January 1377, dying there in March 1378. Now there had to be a new election, and with the French cardinals divided on whom to elect and the Roman people in an uproar, rioting in the streets and demanding that a Roman be elected to the throne of St Peter after so many French popes, the cardinals were deadlocked. As a compromise they finally decided on the Archbishop of Bari, a Neapolitan who took the name Urban VI. However, he soon proved high-handed and divisive – or outright insane, if the French cardinals were to be believed – and the cardinals determined to overthrow him. The cardinals appealed to Charles V and the University of Paris for sanction to depose him, and although they wisely refrained from giving a definitive opinion, the cardinals elected the cardinal Robert of Geneva as Pope Clement VII.[12]

Despite Johanna's predisposition to support the pope's return to Rome, Urban VI chose to attack her, stating that a woman should not rule and threatening to depose her. This forced Johanna and the renegade cardinals into each other's arms, and after being driven from Rome Clement VII took refuge in Naples. Johanna became the first monarch to recognize Clement VII as pope, on 31 October 1378, though this was disastrous for her reputation and ultimately her crown. Although France and the political entities generally favourable to France – Aragon and Castile, Leon, Scotland and Cyprus – supported Clement, most of Italy was solidly behind Urban. When Johanna allowed Clement to lodge in the Castel dell'Ovo, the people of Naples rioted and Clement was forced to flee to Avignon, where he established his court in June 1379.

The Schism was a real crisis for Johanna, because Urban VI promptly excommunicated her, at precisely the time Louis the Great had re-emerged as a threat. Of course Johanna had the support of Clement VII, and it was he who now suggested that she adopt Duke Louis of Anjou as her heir. Although Clement still needed Johanna, France, and by extension Louis of Anjou, were his most vital allies, and French interests were always more important to him. This was shown most strikingly when, before Johanna adopted Louis, Clement proposed creating a new kingdom in Italy to reward Louis for his support. This was to be the 'kingdom of Adria' that Clement wanted to create from a constellation of papal territories in central Italy, which obviously were currently held by Urban, and weren't Clement's to offer. The new kingdom would have consisted of Ravenna, Ferrara, Bologna, the Romagna, Massa Trabaria, the March of Ancona, Perugia, Todi and the duchy of Spoleto. Most notably, Clement copied the bull offering this new kingdom to Louis directly from the bull that had granted the kingdom of Sicily to Charles of Anjou, entirely appropriately, given that if there were ever a case of 'offering someone the moon if only he could unhook it from the sky', this was it.[13] This notional new kingdom died a quiet death when Clement was able to convince Johanna to adopt Louis as heir to the throne of Naples, which had the advantage of actually existing.

Although Johanna had struggled throughout the 1360s and 70s to maintain her independence in the face of encroachment from France and Louis himself, she now had little choice. She adopted Louis, emphasizing his remarkable qualities and the fact that they were ultimately from the same family. This adoption would form the basis for the Second House of Anjou's claim to Naples, one which would later be reinforced by another adoption, of King René by Queen Johanna II, and would embroil Anjou and then France in Italian affairs for the next 150 years. Such an adoption was considered unusual at the time, and Honoré Bonet in his *Tree of Battles* questioned whether Johanna even had the right to pass her kingdom to an adopted heir. In the French chronicles, Louis's acceptance of the claim to Naples was portrayed as a generous act designed to support Johanna, childless and beset by enemies. This was patently false, as Louis had previously tried to wrest Provence from Johanna and the adoption was purely political in purpose.

Urban in turn offered Louis the Great the throne of Naples, but Louis, perhaps remembering how much he was loathed in the Regno, decided to put his support behind Charles of Durazzo. Urban duly branded Johanna a heretic, deposed her through his authority as her suzerain, and summoned Charles of Durazzo from Buda to replace her. In 1380 Charles led a Hungarian army into Italy, and he was crowned King Charles III of Sicily in Rome on 1 June 1381. Johanna retaliated by publishing the articles of adoption and making it known that Louis was her successor, but Charles marched on Naples.

Although Otto of Brunswick led an army to defend the Regno, he was defeated and Charles took Naples on 16 July 1381. Johanna and Otto were besieged in the Castel Nuovo for nearly two months waiting in vain for Louis of Anjou's arrival, but Johanna was finally forced to submit on 2 September and was imprisoned. Louis's failure to do anything to rescue Johanna when Charles of Durazzo imprisoned her suggests that he was only interested in taking the kingdom for himself, rather than assisting Johanna. Yet perhaps it is unfair to criticize him too much, since Charles V of France had died on 16 September 1380, and Louis became regent for the eleven-year-old Charles VI, which contributed to the delay. In fact, Louis's eventual departure from France to go to Naples could be seen as a dereliction of his duty to France.[14]

The Death of Queen Johanna

Johanna's deposition and later murder are a key part of the 'Black Legend' of the Neapolitan Angevins that has also led them to be called the 'Accursed Kings of Naples',

like the '*Rois Maudits*', the accursed progeny of Philip IV. The cycle of murder, retribution and usurpation sparked by Andrew of Hungary's death is perhaps most tragically
represented by Johanna, though it did not end with her. Her reputation never recovered
from Andrew's murder, and contemporaries attributed her death to the violence she had
initiated. The chronicler Dietrich von Niem, who wrote a chronicle of the Schism, noted
that Otto of Brunswick's brother was executed in the same place Conradin had been
executed by Charles of Anjou, another example of Angevin violence against Germans
continuing through the 14th century.[15]

When Louis of Anjou learned of Johanna's defeat, he became more active and sent
representatives to Naples, but it was too late. Clement VII and Louis made a great
show in Avignon of preparing an expedition to rescue Johanna, always identified as
Louis's 'mother', and Louis was created Duke of Calabria, the title of the King of
Sicily's heir. This mission was consciously associated with Charles of Anjou's original
conquest of the Regno and called a Crusade, but despite all this rhetoric Louis didn't
set out until June 1382, by which time Charles of Durazzo was well established in the
Regno. Charles was not blind to the theatrical element of kingship, and he had been
crowned again in Naples on 25 November 1381 with his wife Margaret and their son
Ladislas, emphasizing their unification of two claims to the throne and the fact that
the succession was secured. Ladislas was created Duke of Calabria as the 'real' heir to
the kingdom in opposition to Louis of Anjou.[16]

Louis of Anjou's delay in setting out was fatal to Johanna. She had been imprisoned
since September 1381, and on 27 July 1382 Charles announced that she was dead.
Charles claimed that she had died of natural causes, but most sources state that he
murdered her. Because she had been excommunicated by Urban VI, Johanna was not
entitled to a funeral or Christian burial. She had prepared a tomb for herself in the
church of Santa Chiara near the tombs of Robert the Wise and Sancia of Majorca, but
she was not allowed to be buried there and the location of her grave is unknown. Her
sister Maria, who had died in 1366, was instead reburied in Johanna's tomb in honour
of her position as Queen Margaret's mother. Johanna's undeniably troubled reign ended
with her in a sense being erased from history, with the 'Anjou-Durazzo' line claiming
descent from Charles II through John of Gravina-Durazzo, and from Robert the Wise
through Maria, not Johanna.

Johanna has a considerably more vivid afterlife than many medieval figures.
Froissart gave a long account of her life and tribulations, but converted the story
into something resembling an Arthurian legend. The highlight came when Charles
of Durazzo besieged Johanna and Otto of Brunswick in the Castel dell'Ovo and
employed a sorcerer who used marvellous enchantments to compel them to surrender.
Froissart also described Louis of Anjou's meeting with the sorcerer who had helped
Charles: the wizard tempted Louis with an offer to betray Charles and capture the
castle through a demonic enchantment, but Louis remained pious and the sorcerer
was beheaded.[17]

As is so often the case, Johanna's reign was fixed by a few key studies, and these judgements are then repeated by most modern historians. Although in one case a Victorian biographer, Welbore Baddeley St Clair, exonerates Johanna from murdering Andrew, his reasoning – that she was simply too beautiful, virtuous and generally lovely to be guilty of a crime – probably works against her and modern historians are tempted to be too harsh. They certainly don't mince words: one of the leading historians of the papacy describes Johanna as 'infamous, dissolute and incompetent'; the editor of St Catherine of Siena's correspondence calls Johanna 'licentious, violent, and fickle, an opportunist of the first degree'; and the biographer of the early humanist Coluccio Salutati calls her 'a licentious and indolent queen, committed to bedroom intrigues'.[18]

This flies in the face of an outstanding 14th-century source that unfortunately, much like Baddeley St Clair, seems to do more harm than good by being too positive. Boccaccio's prolific output included a work entitled *On Famous Women,* which provides brief biographies of a variety of women from antiquity down to his own age, and Johanna is the centrepiece of the work. This is most likely because Boccaccio would have liked Johanna to be a patron, and he says in his introduction that he first planned to dedicate the book to her, but since he feared the greater light might eclipse the lesser, he dedicated the work to Lady Andrea Acciaiuoli in Florence and instead devoted his final chapter to Johanna's reign. This describes Johanna as so perfect that his words almost seem ironic, but his fundamental message that she overcame 'the grim ways of her husbands', internal struggles with her family and foreign invasion 'with her lofty and indomitable spirit' seems an accurate assessment of her reign. As well as its fulsomeness, the sincerity of the work is undermined by Boccaccio's previous scathing allegorical denunciations of Johanna as Andrew's murderer.[19]

Johanna almost seems to play hide and seek with us in the available sources. We have fantastic accounts like that of Froissart and more informed, but still hyperbolic, accounts like that of Boccaccio, but we also have her letters about Andrew's murder in which we hear her own words and we get a distinct sense of her personality, and her later correspondence with Saints Birgitta of Sweden and Catherine of Siena also gives us an insight into her thoughts, feelings and the kinds of friends she chose for herself. At other times, notably during her marriage to Louis of Taranto, she almost disappears, obscured behind her husband until finally and most tragically she literally disappears, imprisoned, deprived of her throne and murdered by Charles of Durazzo.

Charles III of Durazzo

Charles III of Durazzo was now King of Sicily, and he is known as Charles 'the Peaceful' or 'the Short'. Given that his great-grandfather was Charles the Hunchback, the second name is not surprising, and the epithet 'the Peaceful' demonstrates a historical truism about royal names: any ruler known as the 'the Peaceful' is a disaster. It also seems quite unwarranted given the way Charles took the throne of Naples, but his later actions will explain it.

Paradoxically, given the tumult at the end of Johanna's reign, the accession of Charles III marked a return to the expansionist policies of Charles of Anjou. Charles III became the greatest power in Italy, and similarly to Robert the Wise was hailed by leading humanists as the new master of Italy. He also made contact with various cities in Provence and began steps to take the county back from the Dukes of Anjou. More importantly, he had an interest in Hungary.

Louis the Great's success in backing Charles of Durazzo for the throne of Naples was about to backfire spectacularly. With his health deteriorating, the pious Louis retired from public life and died on 11 September 1382 at Trnava. He was buried at Székesfehérvár with Carobert and other Hungarian kings, and he had left instructions for his eldest surviving daughter Maria, who was eleven, to succeed him, with his wife Elisabeth as regent. It would seem to be a supreme irony that after all Louis's efforts to overthrow Johanna, he himself should be succeeded by a woman, although through 'masculinization' Maria succeeded as king, not queen. Maria was crowned on 17 September, but there was unrest among the nobility over being ruled by a woman, and they sent word to Charles of Durazzo asking him to take the throne.

At the end of 1382 Charles of Durazzo was in no position to concern himself with Hungary, because Louis of Anjou had invaded Naples in June, ostensibly to avenge Johanna's death, but of course mainly to take the Neapolitan inheritance that he had coveted for years. Louis's army was compared to the army of Xerxes in its pomp and magnificence, and included the retinue of Amadeus, the 'Green Count' of Savoy, who travelled with lavish paraphernalia and livery in his trademark colour, but Louis faced grave political disadvantages that put him in a very difficult position.

Most importantly, the papal schism meant that virtually all of Italy was enemy territory, even Guelf states like Florence that were traditional Angevin allies. Florence retained the services of Sir John Hawkwood to keep Louis's army away, and with the necessity of avoiding Florence and Rome, Louis was forced down the east coast of the peninsula where his army was harried by various enemies rather than receiving a welcome. Although Louis did succeed in conquering the eastern part of the Regno, Charles of Durazzo, like his namesake Charles V in the Hundred Years War, simply refused to be drawn into battle, and Louis was forced to wait in Bari and Brindisi for additional funds and troops from France. Unfortunately for Louis, though perhaps appropriately given the consequences of his delay in assisting Johanna, the reinforcements from France simply took too long to arrive. Louis died of a fever on 20 September 1384 at Bari and his army disbanded. He was succeeded by his young son Louis II of Anjou.[20]

Charles of Durazzo now re-established his authority in the Regno, formed an alliance of Provençal cities to dispossess the seven-year-old Louis II of Anjou of the county and finally had time to consider his invitation to take the throne of Hungary. Hungary was now suffering from the claims to multiple thrones that had seemed such a part of Louis the Great's greatness. Louis had succeeded Casimir the Great as king of Poland, and his heir Maria should have inherited the throne as well. However, the Polish council refused to accept a ruler who did not live in Poland, leading the regent Elisabeth to consider an invasion. This was a poor option when Hungary itself faced a potential invasion by Charles of Durazzo, so Elisabeth decided to send her second daughter Hedwig to Poland instead, where she was eventually accepted as 'King Jadwiga'. Elisabeth also repudiated Maria's betrothal to the future Emperor Sigismund in favour of a French alliance, in hopes that this would provide support to Louis of Anjou and help him depose Charles of Durazzo. Louis's death in 1384 put paid to that plan, and Charles's position quickly improved.

Invited by the Hungarian nobles to take the throne, Charles landed in Dalmatia in September 1385 and marched on Buda. Elisabeth returned to the original plan and married Maria to Sigismund in October, but now Charles of Durazzo entered Buda in peace, without an army, and at the invitation of his supporters convened a diet to choose the kingdom's ruler. Charles was chosen by an overwhelming majority, forcing Maria to abdicate and Sigismund to flee to Prague. Charles was crowned King of Hungary on 31 December 1385, and his assumption of power by consent earned him the sobriquet 'the Peaceful'.

This union of the Neapolitan and Hungarian crowns was incredibly short-lived. Charles's stroke of genius in arriving without an army and taking the throne through a peaceful elective process was now revealed as a piece of completely misguided optimism. Elisabeth rallied her supporters behind the scenes, and on 7 February 1386, thirty-nine days after his coronation, Charles was kidnapped and carried to Visegrad, where he died a prisoner on 24 February, a fitting end for the man who deposed Johanna.[21]

The Female Kings of Hungary and Poland

Elisabeth formally claimed the Hungarian throne again on behalf of Maria, and recalled Sigismund. The region of Neapolitan support in the south of the country and Dalmatia rebelled and invited Charles's young son Ladislas to take the Hungarian throne as well. Elisabeth bizarrely showed herself to be as naive as Charles had been, and she took Maria to face the rebels in an attempt to calm the situation. Instead, the rebels killed Elisabeth's escort on 25 July 1386 and sent their heads to Charles's widow in Naples, and Elisabeth and Maria were imprisoned in the Archbishop of Zagreb's castle of Gomnec. Sigismund now took control of Hungary as regent, and made a bold attempt to rescue Elisabeth and Maria in January 1387. This failed, and in retaliation Elisabeth was strangled in front of her daughter.

Sigismund returned from his failed rescue attempt and decided to take over the kingdom himself as Maria's husband. This required approval from the barons, which was obtained, but when Sigismund was crowned at Székesfehérvár on 31 March 1387, it was as an elective king rather than a hereditary monarch, an important constitutional development. Pressure from the Neapolitan Angevins was reduced when Charles of Durazzo's widow Margaret was expelled from Naples in 1387 in favour of Louis II of Anjou, and she took her heir Ladislas to Gaeta for safety. Although Ladislas would eventually take the throne of Naples, the way was now clear for the dukes of Anjou.

Maria was liberated from her prison by a Venetian fleet in June 1387 and crowned as ruler in her own right. This coronation led to an interesting dispute that would clarify the linguistic and philosophical conception of a reigning queen. When Maria was crowned, the archbishop of Esztergom and the bishop of Veszprem argued over who should perform the ceremony, because it was the archbishop's role to crown the king and the bishop's role to crown the queen, i.e. the queen-consort who was married to the king. The fact that the archbishop prevailed demonstrates again that Maria was 'king', the ruler of the kingdom.

Although Maria's position was officially recognized in this way, in practice Sigismund ruled as king and she essentially acted as queen-consort. Maria died after a riding accident while pregnant in 1395, and although Hedwig and her husband launched an invasion from Poland to claim the throne for themselves, they were repulsed, and although Hungary would be successfully ruled by Sigismund, it had passed definitively from Angevin control.[22]

Angevin rule in Poland was brief, lasting only twenty-nine years with Louis the Great and Hedwig reigning as kings of Poland, but it was quite significant. As we have seen, the origins of Angevin rule in Poland came through Carobert's support for Władysław Loktiek, who was Duke of Łęczyca and finally became King of Poland in 1320. Carobert married Władysław's daughter Elisabeth, and Władysław's son Casimir the Great agreed in 1339 that if he died without male heirs the throne would go to one of Carobert's sons. Although Casimir was married multiple times and had several children, these were all daughters and most of them predeceased him, and when he did finally have sons they were from a later marriage of questionable legitimacy, meaning Louis the Great remained his heir apparent.

However, Casimir was concerned about the fact that Louis himself had no male heirs, and began to incline towards his grandson, Casimir Duke of Pomerania, son of his daughter Elisabeth who had died in 1361. Had Casimir the Great lived longer, it seems likely that Louis wouldn't have ruled Poland after all, but Casimir was injured in a hunting accident – that constant royal peril – and died soon after on 5 November 1370. Louis immediately hurried to Poland when he heard Casimir was dying, but arrived after Casimir's death, and the Polish nobles seemed likely to support Casimir of Pomerania. Fortunately Louis was accompanied by his mother Elisabeth, from whom his claim to the throne originated, and together they dispossessed Casimir of Pomerania and Louis was crowned king of Poland on 17 November. Louis left Poland

and Elisabeth ruled in his name supported by a council led by the bishop of Cracow. To secure the future succession of Louis's daughters, Elisabeth and Louis made various concessions to the nobles, which permanently weakened royal power in Poland.[23]

In 1380, after ten years of regency, Elisabeth died, but there was a smooth transition to a new regency council of three nobles, still led by the bishop of Cracow. All seemed to be going well for Angevin rule in Poland, but the country was about to be drawn into the turmoil that overtook Hungary. In July 1382, as part of his general withdrawal from public life as his health failed, Louis the Great sent Maria's husband Sigismund to Poland and forced the nobles to do homage to him. Sigismund was still in Poland when he learned that Louis had died on 4 September 1382, and he attempted to take the Polish throne outright. Louis had intended for Maria to inherit Poland, but the Polish nobles were unwilling to accept Maria's husband instead of her, and when Sigismund learned that there was also opposition to her succession in Hungary, he left Poland to help her secure what was viewed as the primary throne.

In the turmoil that resulted, many nobles still supported the Angevins, but called for Hedwig to be sent to Poland to rule instead of Maria. Initially the regent Elisabeth, Louis the Great's widow, refused to send her young daughter to Cracow, but by March 1384 she was informed that if Hedwig did not arrive by Pentecost then Poland would choose another king. Elisabeth sent Sigismund to mediate, but he was rebuffed, and in September the nobles formally met to choose a new king. This galvanized Elisabeth, who finally relented and sent Hedwig to Cracow. She arrived on 13 October 1384 and at the age of ten was crowned on 15 October.[24] Like her sister, Hedwig was 'king' rather than queen, but unlike in Hungary there was no need for a process of 'masculinization'; instead, Poland was much more pragmatic and simply called the ruler of the country king, whether a man or a woman.

As king, Hedwig, or as she was now known, Jadwiga, faced a variety of problems. The most pressing, inevitably, was marriage. She had been betrothed to William of Austria, a Habsburg prince, and there is some confusion in the sources as to whether the marriage had actually occurred or not. The Angevins maintained that Jadwiga had only been betrothed to William of Austria, and as she was only ten at the time of the betrothal, it seems reasonable to suppose that whatever form of ceremony had taken place, Jadwiga was not in any meaningful sense married to William. Certainly this was the view in Poland, leaving Jadwiga available to marry a more useful prince.[25] The Habsburgs steadfastly maintained that the marriage had taken place, and prosecuted Jadwiga in ecclesiastical courts culminating in the papal court in Rome in 1387. Although the pope supported Jadwiga, Habsburg sources labelled her a bigamist, and such accusations were being made against her even in the mid-15th century when she was long dead.

A nagging problem for Poland had always been the presence on its eastern border of Lithuania, the only remaining pagan state in Europe. This made it a target for European invaders, specifically the Teutonic Knights, who had been Crusading there for centuries. The constant attacks by the Knights had nearly destroyed Lithuania as an independent state, and the Lithuanians needed an ally. Their situation was now sufficiently dire that they were willing to consider conversion to Christianity to end the Crusades against them. The Lithuanians had close ties to their Orthodox Russian neighbours and a conversion to Orthodox Christianity might have been natural, but if the goal of the conversion were to forestall attacks by the Teutonic Knights, then this would have been a poor choice: we have seen repeatedly that Latin Christians, and especially Crusaders, viewed Orthodox Christians as schismatics. The Lithuanians instead chose Poland and Latin Christianity.

Naturally any agreement would be concluded by a marriage alliance, and a treaty between Poland and Lithuania cemented by the union of Jadwiga and a Lithuanian ruler was proposed. This marriage of a Christian ruler to a pagan prince is a relic from another time and seems utterly peculiar in the late 14th century, yet it would be a great success. The marriage was arranged between Jadwiga and Jagiello, the Grand Duke of Lithuania. The transaction proceeded briskly, and the Lithuanian envoys arrived in Cracow in January 1385. Jagiello would have to meet fairly severe demands: he would be baptized before the wedding along with his attendants, and then the entire population of Lithuania would have to convert. More importantly, Lithuania would become part of Poland, and there were various other territorial and financial requirements.

Although Jadwiga was still only eleven, and the envoys sought approval from her mother, Elisabeth reputedly left the final decision to Jadwiga herself. Her choice to agree to the marriage is viewed as a noble act facilitating the conversion of the Lithuanian people, and was key to her later sainthood. Although Jadwiga had agreed to the marriage, the arrival of William of Austria in Poland insisting that Jadwiga was already married to him threatened to derail proceedings. We are not entirely sure how this was resolved, though given the lack of information it seems most likely that William was simply ignored and sent away.

However, the story of the child Jadwiga piously agreeing to marry the middle-aged Jagiello to spread Christianity may be a little too neat. Viewed objectively, it is much more likely that Elisabeth agreed to the marriage and Jadwiga had no choice. In the mythology that surrounds her, there is a sense that Jadwiga was 'sacrificed' to convert the Lithuanians, and such a 'human sacrifice' obviously has myriad references in Christian tradition. The question is whether Jadwiga, as a saint, sacrificed herself, or Elisabeth made the decision to sacrifice her. Another tradition sheds some light on this, because there is a different story: Jadwiga actually loved William of Austria and deplored the thought of marrying Jagiello. William came back to Poland to carry her away, and when he was resisted, the child Jadwiga is said to have taken an axe and tried to smash through the gates of Wawel castle to free herself, though to no avail.

Polish envoys then went to Lithuania to secure Jagiello's agreement with all the terms, which was done in August 1385. Jagiello arrived in Cracow on 12 February 1386, and he was baptized on 15 February with the name Władysław. The couple were married on 18 February, and they were both crowned – and both as 'king' – on 4 March in Wawel cathedral, inaugurating the most splendid era in Polish history, which although known as the 'Jagiellon', is rooted in Angevin Poland.[26]

Jadwiga then became known for her religiosity in several notable ways. The Teutonic Knights, in one of the actions that would cement their unsavoury reputation, claimed that Jagiello's baptism was fake and continued to attack Lithuania. Jadwiga was the guarantor of her husband's sincerity, and she negotiated with the Knights to make peace. Further, Casimir the Great had founded the university of Cracow in 1364 as part of a wave of university foundations in central Europe, but he intended it to focus on creating diplomatic and administrative staff, so there was an emphasis on law. In 1397, Jadwiga secured the Roman Pope Boniface IX's agreement to renew the university and create a faculty of theology, with a special mission to create clergy to work on the evangelisation of newly Christian Lithuania. At the same time, Jadwiga endowed a Lithuanian college at the university of Prague for similar reasons.

Although it was a very traditional role for a queen-consort – and Jadwiga was forced into the role of consort despite her right to rule as king of Poland – to be a religious patron, Jadwiga was particularly committed to the spiritual life of Poland. She adopted the device of two entwined 'M's to symbolize the value she placed on both the active life of Martha and the contemplative life of Mary. The intellectual Henrik Bitterfeld dedicated a work on the active versus contemplative life to her, and she had a large library of mainly religious and theological works. An illustration of her intellectual life can be found in Warsaw, where her psalter with parallel columns in Latin, Polish and German survives. Other personal items that survive are her 'rational' in the treasury of Cracow cathedral, and most importantly, a splendid rock crystal vessel in the Grünes Gewölbe in Dresden decorated with her arms. This was designed as a gift to Wawel cathedral, but Jadwiga died before it could be presented and it found its way into the collection of Augustus the Strong, duke of Saxony and later king of Poland.[27]

Jadwiga's life had been full of intellectual and religious activity, but as both king and queen of Poland she was required to continue the dynasty. On 22 June 1399, she gave birth to a premature daughter who was christened Elizabeth Bonifacia, since Pope Boniface IX had been enlisted as her godfather, but Jadwiga died after a few days and the child died after three weeks. Jadwiga was aware that she was dying from the difficult pregnancy, and requested that all her valuables be sold to fund the university of Cracow that she had re-established. Her wish was granted, and in 1400 Jagiello issued a formal act reopening the university, where the Angevin arms are still displayed over the gateway.

After Jadwiga's death, she was popularly believed to be a saint and a cult sprang up around her almost immediately in the 15th century. Although this was not made official until Pope John Paul II canonized her in 1997, her tomb occupies a prominent place in Wawel cathedral and has always been a significant shrine. It has a beautiful early 20th-century effigy in white marble that fittingly sets her apart from the other monarchs buried in the cathedral. Jadwiga joins the other Hungarian and Angevin saints of the *beata stirps*, but is also fully embraced as a Polish national saint. This is apt, since in addition to achieving the conversion of the Lithuanian nation to Latin Christianity through her marriage, which was of great significance to the Catholic Church, her later actions to defend the validity of the Lithuanian conversion as well as establishing and reestablishing educational foundations had lasting significance in Poland and beyond.[28]

The death of Jadwiga and her daughter marked the end of Angevin Poland, although Władysław Jagiello founded one of the most important dynasties in the country's history and was succeeded by his son from a subsequent marriage. A similar situation arose in Hungary, where the turmoil that marked the end of Angevin rule had dire consequences.

Since 1389 the Ottoman Turks had been operating close enough to the Hungarian border to cause constant skirmishing, and Sigismund was deeply worried about defending the kingdom. He attempted to organize a Crusade against the Ottomans in 1395, and sent messengers throughout Europe and even to the Mamluks in Egypt to seek allies. The pope approved the Crusade in 1396, and a large French force led by the Duke of Burgundy joined a Hungarian force to invade Bulgaria in August of that year and besiege the fortress of Nicopolis. The Ottoman sultan led a relief force, and the Crusaders were overwhelmingly defeated on 25 September 1396. Sources said that this was due, inevitably, to the indiscipline of the French knights. Froissart gives the story in great detail, and after explaining how the French knights ignored the warnings of the Hungarians, describes the defeat:

> The lords of France were so richly dressed out, in their emblazoned surcoats, they looked like little kings; but, as I was told, when they met the Turks, they were not more than seven hundred, which sufficiently shewed the folly of the measure; for, had they waited for the hungarian army, that consisted of sixty thousand men, they might, perhaps, have gained a victory, but, through their pride and presumption, was the whole loss owing; and it was so great, that never since the defeat at Roncesvalles, where the twelve peers of France were slain, did the French suffer so considerably.[29]

Sigismund himself survived the defeat and fled by ship to Constantinople, only returning to his kingdom in 1397, but the disastrous Crusade made his position somewhat precarious, and he was overthrown by a coalition of nobles in April 1401. Ladislas of Naples was considered as a replacement, and although Sigismund regained control of the kingdom, Ladislas was already committed to the project and sent troops to Dalmatia in 1402. The southern barons returned to their traditional loyalty to the Neapolitan Angevins and revolted, and Ladislas went to Zara, where he was crowned King of Hungary by a papal legate in August 1403. Sigismund quelled the revolt and Ladislas was forced to return to Naples in November, although Ladislas appointed a supporter as Duke of Split and ruled parts of the Dalmatian coast, and Sigismund never fully regained control. Ladislas maintained tenuous control of the Adriatic coast until 1409, at which point his fleet was defeated, and he then ceded all his claims and rights in Dalmatia to Venice.[30]

The continuing struggle between the Hungarian and Neapolitan Angevins had only resulted in the loss of Dalmatia to both, erasing the gains of Louis the Great, and Hungary was now an embattled frontier province constantly harried by the Ottomans. To help mobilize supporters, Sigismund adopted the same course as many of his contemporaries and founded a chivalric order, which had possibly the most bizarre consequences of any of the 15th-century orders. Sigismund founded the Order of the Dragon, and although he awarded membership to figures such as Alfonso and Ferrante of Naples who will soon play a large part in our story, most members were local military leaders. One was a Wallachian warlord named Vlad, who became known as Vlad 'the Dragon' or, in Romanian, Vlad *Dracul*. His son was Vlad *Tepes*, 'the Impaler'. The legendarily diabolical cruelty of Vlad Tepes was conflated with the more sinister name of his father (*dracul* also means 'the devil' in Romanian) to, finally, give us the name 'Dracula'.[31] Sigismund himself went on to considerably greater things and will reappear decades later in the story of King René, but first we must go back to Anjou and the final line of Angevins.

Louis II of Anjou and Yolanda of Aragon

After the untimely death of Louis I in the Regno, his successors in the Second House of Anjou continued the fight for Naples with greater success. In addition to the dukes of the Second House – Louis I, Louis II, Louis III and René – there is a figure who is equally important, and takes her place in the line of remarkable Angevin queens: Yolanda of Aragon. Her marriage to Louis II made her titular queen of Sicily, and not only did she do more to establish the Angevins of the Second House in Naples than anyone else, she also – through the marriage of her daughter to the future Charles VII of France – became the de facto leader of France at its lowest point in the Hundred Years War.

We have seen that the situation in Naples was chaotic, with outright war between the Angevins of Naples and the Second House of Anjou, who had seized Provence. Although the Neapolitan Angevins clung to power for a few more decades, the Second House continued the struggle in each generation. After Louis I's death in 1384, his widow Marie of Blois-Penthièvre led the fight to take Naples from Charles of Durazzo for her seven-year-old son Louis II. However, the 'League of Aix', a coalition of cities formed by Charles of Durazzo to retake Provence for Naples, had succeeded in taking the entire county except Marseilles. Marie fought back by going to Avignon and having Clement VII recognize Louis II as the rightful Count of Provence, then pawned her gold and silver plate to raise an army, which she mobilized against the League of Aix. Had Charles concentrated on Naples and Provence, he might have restored them to the Kingdom of Naples, but the fatal lure of Hungary led him to his death in 1386, leaving the child Ladislas as his heir (Ladislas and Louis II were the same age, both being born in 1377). This crippled Neapolitan power in Provence, and by the end of 1387 Marie and Louis II had entered Aix in triumph.

The Valois kings were also active in opposing the Neapolitan Angevins in favour of the Second House, and this continued under Charles VI. Marie sought French royal backing for Louis II's claim to Naples, and this was formally recognized when Louis II and his brother Charles were knighted at St Denis by Charles VI in May 1389. On All Saints Day 1389, at the age of twelve, Louis II was crowned King of Sicily at Avignon by Clement VII in the presence of Charles VI.[32]

In August 1390 a Provençal fleet appeared at Naples, besieged and captured the Castel dell'Ovo and established Louis II's rule in the city. Ladislas and his mother remained in an impregnable castle at Gaeta, where naturally they had the support of the Roman pope. Although Louis II resided in Naples, and for the next nine years he and his supporters attempted to build alliances throughout the Regno, he could never establish firm support for his 'foreign' regime.

One problem was that a new Spanish pope in Avignon abandoned the Avignon papacy's traditional support for the Second House, and another was that Ladislas was growing older and more accomplished as a warrior, a career in which he would excel. As the two boys matured, Ladislas worked against Louis II throughout the 1390s, culminating on 10 July 1399 when Ladislas captured Naples and took the throne for himself. Louis II, abandoned by the barons of the Regno, was fortunate to have Provence and Anjou to fall back on, although he was essentially a foreigner having spent so long in Naples. He now needed to marry and perpetuate the dynasty of the Second House.[33]

Not unexpectedly, the continuous intertwining of Angevin and Aragonese in the Mediterranean produced a great marriage that set the stage for the final battle between the two dynasties in the next generation. In 1381, Louis I of Anjou had proposed that his two sons marry the future Juan I of Aragon's two daughters to form an alliance with the lord of Sicily and Sardinia before he attempted to take Naples, but there was no interest. After Louis I's death Charles VI revived the request for Yolanda of Aragon to marry Louis II, but Yolanda herself refused the match. She wrote to the king to explain that she had only been eleven when the match was previously discussed and her wishes had not been consulted, but she now categorically refused. She was still only fifteen and this was an unusually strong position for a young woman to take. It was an early demonstration of the character Yolanda would show throughout her time as duchess of Anjou and queen of Sicily.[34]

Throughout the remainder of the 1390s Marie of Blois-Penthièvre periodically renewed the marriage proposal to the Aragonese court, but Yolanda's resistance remained, and the matter progressed no further. The situation changed in 1399 when

Louis II was expelled from Naples by Ladislas, and he returned to Provence. Louis took up the negotiations on his own behalf, and either because she now had some sense of his character, or because she had gained a new appreciation of the advantages the match might provide, or possibly – though unlikely given her character – because she gave in to pressure from her advisers, in 1400 Yolanda finally agreed to marry him.

As Yolanda journeyed to Arles for the wedding, Louis enacted a chapter from a courtly romance. Yolanda set out from Zaragossa with her entourage, and Charles of Taranto, Louis's brother, met her at Perpignan to escort her to Arles. Yolanda and Louis had never met, and Louis decided that he would secretly go to Montpellier to catch a glimpse of his bride. He mingled in the crowd as Yolanda made a grand entrance into the city, and, unsurprisingly in this type of story, he was so captivated by her beauty that he went back to Arles to await her official arrival, congratulating himself on the match. That said, other chroniclers such as Juvénal des Ursine did describe Yolanda as 'one of the most beautiful creatures one could ever see', so perhaps the story is true.[35]

The wedding itself was conducted in the archbishop's palace, and one striking note was the decoration: the tapestry of the Apocalypse, which had been commissioned by Louis I from Hennequin de Bruges, and which is still the glory of the castle at Angers, was sent to Arles for the occasion. This is the largest tapestry in the world, comprised of six panels, each measuring six metres high and 23.5 metres long, making the complete work 140 metres long. As well as being the oldest surviving tapestry in France, it is one of the supreme artistic accomplishments of the Middle Ages, and takes its place beside other iconic examples of Angevin cultural production.[36]

Yolanda was fortunate in her marriage to Louis II in that she had remarkably comfortable accommodations. Although the castle at Angers remained the military building completed by Saint Louis, with only the addition of a great hall by Louis I to house the Apocalypse Tapestry, the court would frequently travel by boat from Angers to Saumur. Louis I had used Saumur as a residence and remodelled the castle, but after Yolanda received Saumur as part of her dowry she turned it into one of the most beautiful chateaux (as we will call residences, rather than military buildings) on the Loire. We know exactly what it looked like, since Saumur was used as the image for the month of September in the *Trés Riches Heures* of the Duc de Berry. This was commissioned in 1413, and thus shows the building at the time of Yolanda and Louis II. The chateau today still looks exactly like the image – but this is because it was restored in the 1930s, and the restoration was based on the image in the *Trés Riches Heures*.

The court was peripatetic in another way, since Louis II divided his time between Anjou and Provence. This was practical, since the revenue of Provence was twice that of Anjou, with the tax, or *gabelle,* on the salt works at Hyères and Toulon bringing in considerable funds. The journey from Angers to Tarascon, where the court resided in Provence, took seven to eight weeks and so must have caused considerable discomfort. Nevertheless, residing as they did at Tarascon or Aix in the winter and spring, and Angers or Saumur in the summer and autumn must have been pleasant. Despite the genuine horror and destruction of the Hundred Years War, we see a generation in Louis I and II of Anjou, King Charles V and the Duc de Berry who began to live with quite an unparalleled degree of luxury, and this would only increase in the 15th century for their children and grandchildren.

Louis II also had a windfall in 1404 that helped him maintain his magnificent lifestyle. When Marie of Blois-Penthièvre was dying, she called Louis to her and told him a secret: she had always kept hidden savings of 200,000 écus, which she would now give to him. Louis was astonished and asked why she had never given him the money before, when he had needed it so desperately in Naples; she said it was because she had always feared he would be captured, and she never wanted him to have the shame of having to find a ransom elsewhere.[37] The wisdom of this plan would soon be revealed, when Louis's son King René would be financially ruined by a huge ransom.

Origins of the French Civil War

As for the Hundred Years War, this seemed to have ground to a halt by 1380. Under the guidance of Charles V and Bertrand du Guesclin, the French had recaptured all their territory except Calais and Gascony, and the situation was basically as it had been before the war. The illness that had characterized the last years of Edward III and the Black Prince had sapped the energy of the English for fighting, and Edward's successor, Richard II, was in an entirely different mould to Edward III or his namesake Richard the Lionheart. Richard II sought harmonious relations with France but was unable to maintain stability in his own kingdom, and was deposed and murdered in 1399.

The man responsible for Richard's murder, Henry IV, was unsurprisingly a more bellicose figure. He was keen to renew the war in France, since military success would help legitimize his reign, and foreign adventures were always a useful means of occupying restive knights. Despite these plans, Henry IV was largely preoccupied with solidifying his grasp on power and was not able to make headway. Things would be very different for his son Henry V.

Although Richard's reign was troubled, France after Charles V and du Guesclin was in no stronger a position. Charles VI succeeded to the throne in 1380 at the age of eleven, and Louis I of Anjou became regent, only to leave France to pursue his Italian kingdom, where he died in 1384. The Dukes of Berry and Burgundy, Louis's brothers, plus the Duke of Bourbon, now became the most influential and powerful men in the kingdom. The Duke of Berry quickly turned his attention towards his love of collecting books and artworks and furnishing palaces, and took little interest in the affairs of the kingdom, leaving the Dukes of Burgundy and Bourbon to rule for Charles. The Duke of Burgundy, Philip the Bold, who had already made his mark at the battle of Poitiers at the age of fifteen, dominated the regency and remained in power until Charles VI assumed his majority at the age of twenty in 1388.

France seemed to be stronger than it had been for decades, but in 1392 it became clear that Charles VI was subject to fits of madness. These episodes would continue for the rest of his reign, some lasting for weeks and some for months. His wife Isabeau of Bavaria remained with him despite the trauma of his illness, although she was treated very badly by him when he was mad. They still had eleven children, notably the Dauphin Louis of Guyenne (note his title, specifically alluding to Gascony or 'Guyenne', the land held by England) born in 1397, and the future Charles VII who was born on 22 February 1403.

Charles VI's madness devastated France. Inevitably factions split the court, with Philip the Bold preferring peace with England to benefit the wealthy trading cities in Flanders that formed part of his domains. A new figure, Charles VI's brother Louis of Orleans, now became increasingly important, and Louis saw war with England as the best way to bolster royal power. A key battleground in the royal court was the position of the 'Marmosets', wizened low-born counsellors from the time of Charles V who remained highly influential. Philip the Bold detested them as non-nobles, whereas Louis of Orleans wanted to use their experience to implement policies that would increase royal revenue. When Charles VI was sane, he trusted Louis of Orleans and followed his advice, but during his bouts of madness Isabeau of Bavaria favoured Philip the Bold and his policies gained ground.

Despite the divisions in the court, Philip the Bold was competent and his periods of ascendancy were not detrimental to the kingdom. France was also fortunate, because England too was in turmoil under the divisive rule of Richard II and ultimately saw a change in ruler, when Henry IV overthrew Richard. France's luck changed though, because Philip the Bold died in April 1404 and was succeeded by his son John 'the Fearless'. John's bellicosity and rudeness pushed Isabeau into the arms of Louis of Orleans – literally, if contemporaries are to be believed – and Louis consolidated his grip on power, as he was now dominant whether the king was sane or mad. He and Isabeau planned to cement his power by marrying his eldest son Charles to the king's daughter Isabelle, which infuriated John the Fearless.[38]

On the evening of Wednesday 23 November 1407, Louis of Orleans was with the queen when a messenger arrived summoning him to the king. As Louis went through the dark streets towards the Hotel St Pol, he was ambushed and brutally murdered, with 'his brains spilling out onto the pavement'. The assassins then set fire to a house to cause a distraction, and fled. Louis II of Anjou lived nearby and was the first to be alerted to the crime. He took charge of the response, summoning the provost of Paris to begin an inquest and bar the city gates so the assassins could not flee.

At the funeral the following day, all the royal dukes were pallbearers, including John the Fearless, who was the only duke to dress in full mourning attire. The provost of Paris discovered that the murderers were Burgundians, and John fled, taking the murderers under his protection. Louis of Orleans's widow, Valentina Visconti, cried out for justice, and the royal uncles of Anjou, Berry and Bourbon met the Duke of

Burgundy. John the Fearless was unrepentant, claiming that his actions were for the good of the crown, and in the interests of peace the other dukes accepted this. John the Fearless was restored to favour in 1408, but then Valentina Visconti and Louis's son Charles, the new Duke of Orleans, gained control of the council and banished John.

John then marched on Paris and the other dukes fled to Tours. After months of turmoil, Louis II brokered a peace in March 1409, and at the cathedral of Chartres, the king, the Dauphin and the princes of the blood reconciled with Burgundy. John the Fearless used this as an opportunity to consolidate his power in Paris, and executed the chief of the 'Marmosets'. This provoked a reaction from the party of Orleans. They fought back and by 1413 had retaken Paris and were in the ascendant throughout the kingdom.[39] This was a particularly dangerous time for France, since the accession of the new king of England, Henry V, in 1413 marked the arrival of the most formidable enemy France would face.

Agincourt

Henry V was a remarkably forceful character and the greatest military commander of the age. However, there is something unappealing in his stern inflexibility and ostentatious religiosity; in fact, something very similar to Charles of Anjou. Henry was certainly as ambitious as Charles, and he explicitly set out to reclaim the old Angevin Empire as well as make good Edward III's claim to the French throne, and he had substantially greater resources in his base of England than Charles had found in Anjou and Provence. In Henry, all of this combined to show how successful a gifted soldier with unlimited ambition could be.

This was especially true when he faced an enemy as fragmented as France now was. John the Fearless had not given up, and attacked Paris unsuccessfully in 1414. His rivals retaliated by threatening to invade Burgundy and depose the duke, and both sides now began to negotiate with Henry V. John the Fearless was prepared to cede Gascony to Henry with some additional lands, but Henry countered by demanding the full settlement from the Treaty of Brétigny plus recognition of his claim to be king of France. At this point, the Burgundians were horrified by the idea of putting the English king on the throne of France, and refused.[40]

Charles VI's advisers offered Henry full sovereignty of Aquitaine and to pay the balance of Jean II's ransom, but Henry toyed with them, continuing the negotiations but asking for more, not less, at each meeting. By summer 1414 Henry's demand was for Aquitaine, plus Normandy, Anjou, Maine, Touraine, Poitou and Ponthieu, and he threatened to invade if this were not accepted. The trap was sprung, as Henry had always planned an invasion and had merely been stringing the French along and deepening the divisions between the two factions.

Henry's decision to resume the war was popular in England, perhaps as a symbol of resurgence after the debacle of Richard II's reign, as well as a sign of growing national consciousness. Parliament granted Henry generous subsidies for the war, and additional funds were forthcoming from the church and the laity.[41]

When Henry sailed for France on 11 August 1415, he had a well-armed armada, an impressive artillery train and a coherent strategy. First he besieged and took the port of Harfleur, which would become the forward base for his march on Paris and eventual conquest of France. Harfleur proved difficult to take and the siege dragged on until the city finally surrendered on 22 September, and probably a third of Henry's army had died in battle or from disease. Henry wasn't ready to continue the attack until 6 October, and he planned a long march to Calais, which would allow him to pillage Normandy and demonstrate his own power and the impotence of France with its mad king and feuding nobility.

Henry was unaware that the French knew his location, and a French army was on the march. This included most of the great nobles of the royal party and some even of the Burgundians. The Dauphin at the time, Louis of Guyenne, was not allowed to participate given his father's condition, and the Angevins were also absent; Louis II was debilitated by illness and would die in 1417, and Louis III and René were too young, at the ages of twelve and six respectively. This was fortunate for them. The French pursued the English army until they finally caught up with them on 24 October near the village of Agincourt and blocked the road to Calais. Although the English were heavily outnumbered and had been marching for many days in pouring rain with short provisions, and were exhausted and hungry, they had no choice but to prepare for battle. The situation was so desperate that even Henry thought better of fighting, and offered to give up Harfleur if he were allowed to continue to Calais, but the French countered with a demand that he give up all his claims in France except Gascony, and Henry refused.

The English army at Agincourt was arranged very much as at Crécy, protected by woods on either side and facing the French across a ploughed field that after days of rain was a sea of mud. The French remained in good order and refused to charge into the muddy field, so Henry had his archers advance within bowshot and began firing at the French army. Under the hail of arrows the dismounted French knights did finally advance and actually reached the English line, killing a few of the English knights before being overwhelmed.

Now began the catastrophe. The remaining French knights continued to advance, creating irresistible pressure from the back although the front line were losing their footing and being crushed down into the liquid mud. The English were now standing on piled French bodies, continuing to cut down the French knights as they pressed forward and died by their thousands. What stands out is not that the French were unable to learn new tactics, as they had tried different approaches since Crécy, but that without any form of artillery to counter the English longbows, once battle was joined the French were always sucked into a death zone of close-packed bodies where the pressure from advancing troops drove them into disaster, and only after the new gunpowder-based artillery became more important would the French advantage in this arena help turn the tide in their favour.

Despite the massive loss of life on the French side, many nobles were also captured. At one moment in the battle there was a panic among the English when they thought they were being attacked from the rear, and Henry ordered most of the captives killed, including by setting alight a tent where many nobles were held, and this slaughter of knights who had surrendered would remain a stain on Henry's reputation. Some captives survived and were taken back to England, including Charles of Orleans, heir to the murdered Louis of Orleans. Charles languished in the Tower of London for twenty-five years, time he spent writing poetry that made him a noted literary figure. It also meant that the party opposed to the Burgundians would be led not by the house of Orleans, but by Louis of Orleans's father-in-law, the Count of Armagnac, meaning that the two sides in the approaching French civil war are referred to as Burgundians and Armagnacs.

Henry V returned to England to be met with wild rejoicing and various forms of celebration, including the specially composed 'Agincourt Carol'. He wasted no time on celebrations though, and instead used the popularity for the war generated by this great victory to raise new funds and equip another force, this time one bent on conquest. Henry returned to France in the summer of 1417 and swept through Normandy, conquering most of the duchy by the middle of 1418, though he only took Rouen after an incredibly bitter siege that ended early in 1419.[42]

English Supremacy in France

France was now in a terrible state. The Armagnac party had been decimated at Agincourt, and the Dauphin Louis of Guyenne, although he hadn't participated in the battle, had died shortly after. The future Charles VII was now the Dauphin, and although Louis of Guyenne seems to have been an unappealing figure, at the time Charles was even less well regarded. It would have taken an enormously strong character to bring the two sides together or somehow rise above the factional politics, and Charles was not such a character. Unfortunately for France, rather than attempt to reconcile the parties, each side thought only of how it might destroy its rivals.

Sigismund of Luxembourg, still King of Hungary and now King of the Romans (though he wouldn't be crowned Emperor until 1433), returns to our attention, because he had taken it upon himself to end the Western Great Schism. Various attempts to end the rival papacies in Rome and Avignon had done nothing to resolve the conflict, and instead had only produced a third pope. Sigismund, committed to fighting the Ottomans and thus hoping to secure solid papal backing and a new Crusade after the disgrace of Nicopolis, tried to broker peace between England and France, and travelled to England in 1416 to meet Henry V. He was unsuccessful in securing peace, although Sigismund did form an alliance with Henry, and was made a knight of the Garter. Ultimately his support for the Council of Constance resulted in the election of pope Martin V in 1417 and the retirement or deposition of his rivals, ending the schism.[43]

John the Fearless of Burgundy also began overtures to Henry at this time, and seemed to be contemplating a full alliance with the English against the hated Armagnacs. The struggle between the two sides continued, with the Burgundians driving the Armagnacs from Paris in 1418, but Henry's complete conquest of Normandy by 1419 seems to have given John pause, and he opened discussions with the Armagnacs to consider the possibility of joining forces against the English.[44]

On 10 September 1419, the Dauphin and the Armagnacs invited John the Fearless to a meeting at Montereau, ostensibly to make peace and form a united resistance to the English. Instead, when the party met on a bridge to begin the negotiations, and reputedly at a signal from the Dauphin himself, John the Fearless was murdered. This transformed the factional strife into open civil war, and the prospect of a Burgundian alliance with Henry V made a complete English victory in the Hundred Years War a real possibility. This was well known at the time, and remembered subsequently:

> A century later a Carthusian monk, who was showing François I the mausoleum of the Dukes at Dijon, picked up John's broken skull and commented, 'This is the hole through which the English entered France.'[45]

The new Duke of Burgundy, Philip the Good, now cast his lot entirely with the English. The Burgundians and English went to Troyes, where Charles VI was based in opposition to his own son, and the terms of the agreement were finalized in the Treaty of Troyes. Henry would marry Charles VI's daughter Catherine, and was proclaimed Charles VI's heir, after Isabeau of Bavaria declared that the Dauphin was a bastard and unable to inherit.[46]

This was particularly threatening to the current Angevin dukes, as Henry V had appointed English agents to control Normandy, and he began granting French titles – including Duke of Anjou – to his followers in anticipation of the lands they would conquer. With English control of Normandy, Anjou was directly in the firing line. However, the Angevins had other concerns, as after Louis II's death in 1417 Yolanda of Aragon went to Provence from 1419–1423 to undertake the negotiations that led to Louis III becoming heir to Sicily.

The Dauphin had been engaged to Marie, the daughter of Louis II and Yolanda, in 1413, and the marriage was concluded in April 1422 at Bourges, sealing the unity of the Angevins and the crown. It is notable that when Yolanda was in Provence and unable to influence Charles, his fortunes remained at a low ebb, and only began to improve in the 1420s when Yolanda returned to Anjou and acted as his counsellor. It was Yolanda who essentially provided the backbone of French opposition to the English and support for the Dauphin, at least until Joan of Arc galvanized French resistance. Yet although Joan was unquestionably important, her meteoric rise in some ways obscures the patient work of Yolanda of Aragon to restore the kingdom, and Joan gets the credit for a French resurgence that owed at least as much to Yolanda.

King Ladislas and Queen Johanna II of Naples

Yolanda was free to return to Anjou because the situation in Naples, after considerable turmoil, had turned to her favour. After the Second House had been driven from Naples, King Ladislas went considerably further towards uniting Italy under his own rule than anyone since Charles of Anjou. He occupied Rome and captured almost all the papal states in central Italy, given him control of more than half the peninsula. By 1409 the (short-lived) pope Alexander V was so concerned that he formed an alliance with Florence and Siena. They now invited Louis II to join them and their condottiere Muzio Attendolo Sforza, ancestor of the Sforza dukes of Milan, to drive Ladislas from Rome, then conquer Naples. Unable as ever to resist the lure of Naples, Louis II raised an army and went to Italy.

The plan succeeded and the allies captured Rome, but once the papal and Tuscan objectives had been satisfied, they were indifferent to Louis's goal of capturing Naples, and Louis was forced to return to Provence to seek help. Charles VI continued the Valois tradition of supporting the Second House, and gave him 200,000 francs. This allowed Louis to retain Muzio Attendolo Sforza, and together they invaded the Regno and defeated Ladislas at Roccasecca in May 1411, although they were unable to take Naples. This was Louis's last attempt on the Regno, and by August he was back in Provence after developing the illness that would ultimately kill him in 1417. This was particularly unfortunate for the Second House, because Ladislas had died suddenly of illness in 1414 and there might have been an opportunity for them in Naples, but Louis II was too ill and the future Louis III was only eleven.[47]

Although he certainly had ambition, Ladislas struggles to make an impression in the midst of the other Angevin kings of Naples, except in one respect in which he outshines them all: his tomb. In the church of San Giovanni Carbonara in Naples, Ladislas has a chapel dedicated to his stupendous tomb, which unlike the tombs in Santa Chiara wasn't badly damaged in the Second World War. The tomb is also a monument to his sister and successor, Johanna II, since she commissioned it, and although buried elsewhere she appears seated in majesty next to Ladislas. The design was inspired by the tomb of Robert the Wise in Santa Chiara, and it has the form of a triumphal arch of several registers, with Ladislas and Johanna portrayed seated on a throne at the central level, and an equestrian portrait of Ladislas at the top. The church as a whole is a treasure trove of 14th- and 15th-century sculpture and painting, with Ladislas's tomb the highlight. It is only a few minutes' walk from the cathedral, yet it is somewhat

overlooked, which is a shame because it gives a much better sense of the craftsman-
ship that went into the Angevin tombs than the somewhat battered examples in the
better-known Santa Chiara.

After Ladislas's death, Johanna II assumed the throne as the last of the Neapolitan
Angevin line. Johanna had been born in 1373, and was thus forty-one at the time of
her succession and without children. Fascinatingly, she had been married to none other
than William Duke of Austria, the rejected fiancé (or husband) of her cousin Jadwiga,
the Angevin ruler of Poland. As we know, William had insisted that his marriage
to Jadwiga was valid, and he only married Johanna in 1401 after Jadwiga's death.
Given what we know about the history of Hungary, Poland and Naples, this move by
William to become king-consort of Naples must also have been an attempt to renew
his claim to the throne of Poland. It was only his purported marriage to Jadwiga that
gave William any claim to Poland, but the death of Jadwiga and her infant daughter in
1399 meant that Jagiello, reigning as King Władysław II, was without heirs and his own
hold on power looked tenuous. William must have believed that the throne of Naples
would be an excellent position from which to meddle in Poland – or Hungary – if the
opportunity arose. However, William had little time to make good his plans. In 1404
he was drawn into a succession dispute in Austria, where he died in 1406.[48]

Her brief marriage to William had not produced any children, and as heir apparent
and then queen, Johanna II needed to build support in the kingdom, especially given
Ladislas's penchant for military campaigns that might cause his death at any time. Here
is where Johanna's reputation suffers, since legend now credits her with a succession of
lovers and 'favourites', incidentally linking her to – and confusing her with – Johanna
I as a 'harlot queen'. Johanna II certainly did appoint various officials who were, inevitably, male. Yet as we saw with Queen Melisende, a female ruler's trusted advisers tend
to be called 'favourites', and are also frequently assumed to be lovers. We remember
Louis of Taranto's dependence on Niccolo Acciaiuoli, yet Niccolo is never described as
Louis's 'favourite' (or indeed lover) by modern historians, whereas of course Niccolo was
assumed to be the lover of Catherine of Courtenay when she entrusted him with the
management of Morea. The fact that Johanna was a widow and had close male advisers
was considered sufficient evidence that she had many lovers.

The 'Black Legend' then runs riot, and Johanna II is accused of behaviour more
appropriate to a fairy tale or – not coincidentally – Roman Empresses such as Messalina
or Agrippina. A brief internet search quickly shows the common opinions, and searching for 'Giovanna II Napoli' brings up the most lurid details: Giovanna the dissolute,
the hunter of men, the insatiable, Giovanna of the hundred lovers, mad queen Giovanna
the eater of men – the list goes on. Perhaps the most notorious stories tell of the 'baths
of Queen Giovanna': when tired of her lovers, Johanna had a trap door through which
she would drop them into the sea, where they would be devoured by crocodiles.[49]

It is impossible to evaluate these stories, other than to dismiss most as obviously
fanciful, and to consider again the ways in which female rulers are judged. Most

male rulers had mistresses and illegitimate children, and although certainly some are called 'dissolute', I cannot think of a male ruler described as 'insatiable' much less 'the devourer of women'. The fact that there is a double standard is no surprise. Yet the larger point is that criticism of female rulers is usually not limited to the facts of their rule, and instead other, usually sexual, slurs are immediately applied. To put it another way, Ladislas had no more peaceful or successful a reign than either Johanna I or Johanna II, yet he is always evaluated, somewhat boringly, solely on the meagre evidence of his political and military actions.

Muzio Attendolo Sforza was not the only famous condottiere active in the Regno, as Bartolomeo Colleoni also began his career fighting in Naples. Colleoni went on to become the captain-general of Venice and one of the greatest commanders of the 15th century, and he modestly left money in his will to commission the equestrian statue of himself by Andrea del Verrocchio that stands outside San Zanipolo in Venice, one of the great Renaissance statues (along with Donatello's statue of the condottiere Gattamelata outside the Basilica of San Antonio in Padua). This is of interest for a particular reason: on the marble base of Colleoni's statue are plaques with the Colleoni coat of arms, which includes the Angevin arms. Johanna II is said to have given the young Colleoni the right to carry her arms, and naturally he was also said to be one of her lovers. However, it was King René who in a letter sent from Angers on 14 May 1467 granted Colleoni and his legitimate issue the right to bear the Angevin arms and add 'd'Anjou' to his name. This shows again how the existence of the Angevin arms on Colleoni's statue and the knowledge that he worked for Johanna II are spun into another slanderous story.[50]

Once Johanna had actually taken the throne, the succession was a critical concern, as was her widowed state. As with Johanna I, even when a reigning queen was probably too old to have children, it was necessary for her to marry. Johanna II considered the traditional alliances with Aragon or France, and in 1415 married Jacques de Bourbon, the Count of La Marche. He had participated in the ill-fated Nicopolis Crusade in 1396 and would have been known to Sigismund of Luxembourg, but otherwise had little to recommend him. Johanna attempted to preempt the problems Johanna I had faced with her husbands, and Jacques was explicitly barred from becoming king, though he would be given the title Prince of Taranto.

Yet Jacques behaved exactly as Louis of Taranto and James of Majorca had towards Johanna I. He executed Johanna II's chief minister (and reputed lover) Pandolfello Piscopo and imprisoned Muzio Attendolo Sforza. He then imprisoned Johanna too and tried to seize the kingdom. Fortunately for Johanna, her patient work establishing her power before Ladislas's death had given her substantial support among the Neapolitan nobles, and they rose up against Jacques and freed Johanna.

Johanna found a new adviser (naturally always described as her 'favourite' and lover) in Sergianni Caracciolo, and together they excluded Jacques from the rule of the kingdom. Johanna remained uncrowned in this period, since no doubt Jacques had prevented this in the years of his dominance if he could not be crowned with her, and Johanna herself probably avoided the ceremony when Jacques was still in the Regno since it would effectively have given him a better claim on the throne. Despite this, Jacques claimed to be king and quartered his arms with those of Naples, but was finally expelled from the Regno in 1419 and never troubled Johanna again (he became a Franciscan monk and died in 1438). However, their marriage was never dissolved, and neither would marry again. It may well have been a relief to Johanna to be prevented from finding yet another husband, but this would mean that every male adviser in her subsequent reign would be considered to be her lover.

Johanna was finally crowned on 28 October 1419, but this still left the problem of the succession, which was of particular concern to the pope as overlord of the kingdom. It is notable that now we can say 'the pope', rather than 'one of the popes', because the Council of Constance had finally resolved the Western Schism and confirmed Martin V as undisputed pope in 1417. Johanna's story now becomes very confusing. Martin V officially recognized Louis III of Anjou as Johanna's heir on 4 December 1419, but this seems to have been without the consent of Johanna herself. The choice of a representative of the Second House, given the recent history of Ladislas and Louis II, can only have been meant to threaten Johanna. She retaliated by looking to the most obvious ally: if the papacy and France supported Louis, then she would turn to the house of Aragon, in the person of Alfonso V, king of Aragon and Sicily.[51]

Things became even more complicated, since Louis III was only sixteen and Yolanda of Aragon was highly sceptical about the papal plan, given that Louis I and II had both died as a consequence of fighting for Naples. Nevertheless, Yolanda went to Provence in 1419 and began negotiations to ensure Louis III's safety should he go to Naples. In particular, she required an exchange of Neapolitan hostages who would stay in Provence until Louis had taken the crown. This was arranged to Yolanda's satisfaction, and in 1420 Louis III joined Muzio Attendolo Sforza in an invasion of the Regno.

Johanna was not idle, and concluded her agreement with Alfonso V, who launched a counter-invasion of the Regno in 1421. Alfonso was the mature and powerful king of several wealthy kingdoms with an unmatched fleet, whereas Louis III was a boy completely dependent on the condottiere Sforza and the pope. When the pope decided to stop funding Louis, and Sforza switched his support to Alfonso, the matter seemed to be finished, with victory for Johanna and Alfonso.

Once established in Naples, Alfonso behaved exactly as the other king-consorts and heirs had. In 1423 he arrested Caracciolo and attempted to overthrow Johanna, who was besieged in the Castel Capuano. She appealed to Sforza, who supported her as the rightful queen, and they ransomed Caracciolo. Johanna now went to Aversa to consider her options, and reached a surprising conclusion: she repudiated Alfonso V and adopted Louis III as her heir. Her calculation must have been that as an isolated boy, Louis would present considerably less of a threat than Alfonso. Louis could expect no help from France, which had been virtually conquered by England in the Hundred Years War, and Johanna and Caracciolo could keep him in check.

With everyone ranged against him, Alfonso was now forced to leave the Regno. He attacked Louis III's city of Marseilles on his way back to Aragon, and spitefully stole the skull and other bones of Louis of Toulouse, removing them to the cathedral of Valencia, where they – along with the Holy Grail, another gift to the city from Alfonso V – remain. In 1956 some of the bones were returned to Marseilles, but the relics of Louis, the most important Angevin saint, remain in enemy territory, albeit in a kingdom that would also be claimed by the Angevins.[52]

Naples desperately needed stability, and Johanna had finally achieved it. Louis III was made Duke of Calabria, and retired to his estates there. With Louis III we can only conclude that the boundless Angevin energy had briefly subsided, as he seemed content to live in southern Italy and wait to succeed Johanna, although there are unverified tales that he joined his brothers René and Charles on their campaigns with Joan of Arc.

The situation remained stable for around ten years, but Johanna was troubled again near the end of her reign. Her seneschal Sergianni Carraciolo was murdered in 1432, though he achieved a kind of immortality with his spectacular Renaissance tomb, which lies behind that of Ladislas in San Giovanni Carbonara and forms part of the Angevin necropolis.

Louis III was of little help and did not even succeed Johanna, since he died of malaria in 1434. He had married Margaret of Savoy in 1431, but as she was only eleven, the couple had no children in their brief time before he died. Louis III's death meant that his brother René was now Duke of Anjou and heir to Naples, along with a truly bewildering array of other claims, not to mention being a key figure in the climactic years of the Hundred Years War. It is fitting that the history of the Angevins should end with him.

CHAPTER 12 – KING RENÉ AND QUEEN MARGARET

LIKE HIS BROTHER, FATHER and grandfather, René was titular King of Sicily and Jerusalem, and although he ruled Naples for only around four years, he continued to use his royal titles until his death at an advanced age. He also inherited a claim to the throne of Aragon through his mother, and sent his son to make it good. More important than these nominal titles were René's real possessions of Anjou, Provence, Lorraine and Bar. Yet René stands out from the other members of the Second House of Anjou for many reasons besides his territorial ambitions. He was at the centre of all the key developments of the 15th century: the conclusion of the Hundred Years War including Joan of Arc's extraordinary career; Italy's position as birthplace of the Renaissance as well as being Europe's main battleground; the final extinction of the Crusading ideal in practical terms; the transformation of chivalry into a formalized, highly decorative form of aristocratic entertainment; and the coalescence of France into something like its modern form.

King René marks the end of the long Angevin story that began in the 9th century with the first Angevin counts, and saw Angevins rule over large parts of France, England, Sicily and southern Italy, Jerusalem, Hungary and Poland. This story comes to a close almost too neatly, because René's daughter, Margaret of Anjou, married Henry VI of England, reuniting the Plantagenet and Angevin lines that had diverged in 1204. That the Plantagenets lost their throne in the Wars of the Roses in which Margaret was one of the main participants, leading to her immortality as Shakespeare's 'She-Wolf of France', at almost exactly the same time as René's line failed and Anjou was finally absorbed by France, is fitting. In England, the end of the Plantagenet dynasty is taken as a convenient dividing line between the medieval and modern, and though there is considerable continuity between 15th- and 16th-century English history, it is undeniable that Tudor government and culture seem to operate in a different world from that of the Plantagenets.

Many historians writing in English denigrate René as a failure, and it is indisputable that he did fail in his attempts to rule Naples, although in this he was not unlike his father and grandfather. I have argued consistently that failure as perceived by contemporaries *is* failure, and this is certainly the case with René's political activities. Yet paradoxically some modern historians use René's cultural achievements to emphasize his political inadequacy, rather than considering them in their own right. The image of the aesthete writing his chivalric romances, holding his elaborate tournaments and pageants and commissioning glorious works of art while he loses his throne and is utterly ineffective in politics is simply too neat a juxtaposition to overlook. However, Louis I and Louis II are never held to this standard, and they both failed to make good their claim to Naples. It is only *because* René was such a significant figure in the cultural life of the 15th century that his political and military failings are magnified.

Margaret would have a similar experience of political struggles followed by desperate military conflict, which saw her husband and son murdered and Margaret herself imprisoned. René failed in his bid for Naples, but seems to have glided through the rest of his life happily enough in a whirl of pageantry and artistic achievement. Margaret's defeat in a much more bitter conflict was not so lightly forgotten.

The Hundred Years War: French Resurgence

First, the Angevins had to weather the English attempt to conquer Anjou. René was born in 1409, and in 1419 assumed the role of heir to the first of his possessions, the duchy of Bar. He inherited this claim through Yolanda of Aragon's mother Yolande of Bar, since her two brothers had been killed at Agincourt and the current Duke, the Cardinal Louis, was naturally unmarried. In the same year René married Isabella of Lorraine, heiress to the duchy of Lorraine, and the young couple lived at her father's court at Nancy. At this time, René would have had no thought of inheriting Anjou or a claim to Naples, and defending Anjou fell to Yolanda of Aragon and his older brother Louis III.

In the aftermath of the Treaty of Troyes, Henry V initiated an invasion of Anjou. Fortunately for Yolanda, the Dauphin's forces, aided by a Scots detachment, were victorious against Henry's brother the Duke of Clarence, who was killed at Baugé on 22 March 1421, finally stopping the English advance after Agincourt. Much more importantly, Henry V himself continued campaigning, but contracted a fatal illness and died on 31 August 1422. He left a nine-month-old son, Henry VI, but critically the poor mad Charles VI, whose malady had done so much to injure France, did the one thing that could save his kingdom: he lived two months longer than Henry V and died on 21 October 1422. This was of paramount importance, since although Henry V had been recognized as Charles VI's heir, he had never been crowned king of France. Although Henry VI would later be crowned – in Paris, not in Reims – it would be argued that Henry V had no right to pass his claim to his son, and Henry VI had no right to be king of France.

Henry V had appointed his brother John Duke of Bedford as Regent of France for the young Henry VI, and Bedford was a formidable commander. In 1424 Bedford was formally created Duke of Anjou and Maine to encourage him to conquer the counties, and after the English won another crushing victory at Verneuil in 1424 they overran Maine. The Earl of Salisbury, one of the greatest English commanders in the war, besieged Le Mans in July 1425 and on 10 August the city fell to English artillery. Anjou itself was now subject to attack.

Louis III was in Naples and Yolanda had been charged with the defence of Anjou, for which purpose the Dauphin gave her 30,000 francs per year.[1] Yolanda turned to diplomacy and repeatedly tried to form an alliance with Brittany to block further English expansion. The treaty of Saumur on 17 October 1425 finally sealed the alliance, and the Duke of Brittany's brother Arthur of Richemont was drawn out of an alliance with Burgundy to support the Dauphin. Although the Angevins had no way of knowing it, they had seen the high point of English conquests. Just when the English seemed to carry all before them, strife in the council governing on behalf of Henry VI forced Bedford to return to England, and for several years he was unable to concentrate on France. Maine would be held by the English for another twenty years and there would be raids on Anjou, but the situation slowly began to improve for the Dauphin, and Yolanda of Aragon was instrumental in this fightback.

One key component was the appearance of able commanders after decades of squabbling, incompetent leaders whose antics demoralized their troops. In addition to Yolanda herself are some of the more colourful figures in the war: Dunois, the Bastard of Orleans, who was an illegitimate son of Louis Duke of Orleans, murdered by the Burgundians; the mercenary captain Etienne de Vignolles, always known as 'La Hire' or 'The Fury'; the fabulously named Poton de Xaintrailles, whose conduct was so impressive that Sir Thomas Malory mentioned him by name twice in the *Morte d'Arthur*; and the above-mentioned Arthur de Richemont, the future Duke of Brittany, whose switch from supporting the Burgundian party to the Dauphin was due to the patient diplomacy of Yolanda of Aragon. Despite their presence, the Dauphin's uninspiring leadership and low morale generally still sapped any resistance to the English, and some kind of inspiration was needed.

The turning point came, of course, at the siege of Orleans in 1429. After the capture of Maine, the English were still poised for a final push south to drive the Dauphin from Bourges and possibly win the war entirely, and the Dauphin was considering fleeing to Scotland to avoid capture. The English commanders, the Duke of Bedford and the Earl of Salisbury, disagreed on the best means of achieving this. Bedford preferred to attack Angers, as the conquest of Anjou and the defeat of Yolanda of Aragon, mainstay of the Dauphin, might have been the knockout blow that the English had hitherto failed to deliver. Salisbury disagreed, and advocated capturing Orleans, which he believed was a more significant city and better sited geographically for the final surge across the Loire. Salisbury won the argument, and in1429 the English began the operation that would change everything.

Orleans was a large and heavily defended city, with the garrison outnumbering the besiegers, and the English troops were unable to surround the city completely. Nevertheless, with their artillery and their air of invincibility, they made good headway and captured some of the city's outworks. Here came the first disaster, when a shot fired from the battlements freakishly killed the Earl of Salisbury, despite his sheltering in a tower. If it seemed that God had finally withdrawn his favour from the English, more proof was quickly to come.[2]

Joan of Arc

In the village of Domremy, which was situated between Bar and Lorraine and thus in René's future domains, a peasant girl called Joan began to hear voices telling her to rescue France. They were very specific about her mission: she should raise the siege of Orleans and have the Dauphin crowned at Reims. Although initially met with scepticism, Joan convinced the garrison commander at Vaucouleurs to send her to Chinon with an escort so that she could make her case to the Dauphin. She was also summoned to meet Duke Charles of Lorraine at Nancy, where she exhorted him to give up his mistress and specifically asked him to send his son-in-law René to escort her to Chinon. It was not yet time for René to join Joan, though this would happen soon.[3]

The Dauphin was mockingly called the 'King of Bourges' because that was one of his centres of power, but in fact he moved around frequently and it is not coincidental that the iconic Angevin castle of Chinon would now take centre stage. Chinon, although it had been the treasury of Anjou and was the place where Henry II died, is perhaps best known today for the role it plays in Joan's story. The castle is a ruin, but the room where Joan met the Dauphin is still mostly extant and it is quite moving to stand in the place where she began to fulfil her mission.

That story is dramatic. Joan was taken to an upper chamber lit by torches, and as a first test for her, the Dauphin stood in the midst of the other courtiers to see if she could identify him. Despite his legendarily unprepossessing appearance, Joan unerringly went to him and hailed him with the epithet she would always use, as the 'Gentle Dauphin'.[4] Either now, or later during her religious examination in Poitiers, Joan was also examined by Yolanda of Aragon to see if she were truly a virgin, which she was.

Joan now underwent weeks of religious interrogation in Poitiers to prove she wasn't a witch and that her claim to be on a divine mission was true. There was a diabolical undercurrent associated with the Dauphin's court (which would reach a spectacularly gruesome climax some years later), so fears about the source of Joan's inspiration were not unreasonable. Even when John the Fearless had been killed in 1419, his hand had reputedly been cut off before his burial to stop him 'raising the devil'. This practice had occurred with others close to the Dauphin, who claimed they had sold their right hands to the devil, and only if the offending hands were cut off would they be spared damnation. Joan, whatever we think about the nature of the voices that guided her, had no part in this kind of satanism and quickly proved this to her examiners.

She also dictated the extraordinary letter to the English commanders that survives in various versions:

Jhesus Maria. King of England, and you, Duke of Bedford, calling yourself
Regent of France; William de la Pole, Earl of Suffolk; John Lord Talbot, and you,
Thomas Lord Scales, calling yourselves lieutenants of the said Bedford … deliver
the keys of all the good towns you have taken and violated in France to the Maid
(*Pucelle*) who has been sent by God the King of Heaven … Go away, for God's
sake, back to your own country; otherwise, await news of the Maid, who will soon
visit you to your great detriment.[5]

No reply from the English survives, and we can only assume that they found the letter
absurd. They were about to discover to their cost that it was not.

Joan did not simply go to Orleans and raise the siege herself; instead, she was allowed
to accompany the relief force that Yolanda of Aragon had organized some time before
to rescue the city. Still, the presence of Joan gave the army hope that had been lacking
during their years of defeats, and Joan's genuine piety and insistence that the soldiers
attend mass and not swear gave them a sense of mission. Joan was not in any sense in
command of the army, and many decisions were being made without consulting her
– to which she would respond with considerable anger when she found out – but Joan
was most important simply in being herself and inspiring the army.

When an assault was finally launched on one of the fortifications held by the
English, Joan was in the front line, and although she was wounded in the shoulder, she
continued to fight and the English were defeated. Joan had dramatically fulfilled the
faith put in her, and when the English soon after abandoned the siege and retreated, it
seemed that the tide of the war had finally turned. Shortly afterwards, at Joan's urging
the Dauphin's forces attacked a (considerably smaller) English army at Patay and won
their first significant victory in years.

Many of the commanders now wanted to attack Paris or consolidate territorial
gains along the Loire, but Joan was committed to having the Dauphin crowned at
Reims. This was an incredibly dangerous mission, since Reims and all the territory
around it were under Burgundian control. Yet Joan convinced the Dauphin, and the
army advanced through Champagne receiving the surrender of one town after another
through negotiation, showing that the allegiance of many towns to the Burgundians
was quite tenuous.[6]

On 17 July 1429, the Dauphin was crowned in the cathedral at Reims and formally
became Charles VII. Joan played a prominent role in the ceremony, as did Gilles de
Rais, a wealthy Cenomannian lord who had been notable at Orleans and formed a close
relationship with Joan, and who now became Marshal of France. René is reported to
have participated in the coronation, though this is unclear, but after the coronation he
definitely joined the group of nobles in Joan's entourage.[7]

Unfortunately, the coronation was the high point of Joan's career and things began
to go wrong for her. She now insisted on attacking Paris, a move opposed by a faction
around Charles VII who were assiduously trying to detach the Duke of Burgundy from

his alliance with the English and feared antagonizing him. Joan prevailed, and a force that included René as well as the other main commanders – Gilles de Rais, La Hire, the Bastard of Orleans and Poton de Xaintrailles – launched a somewhat foolhardy and underprepared attack on the city. They failed and Joan was wounded again (René took her to his residence in Chapelle Saint-Denis to recover), and now the aura of invincibility that surrounded her finally began to fade.[8]

In early 1430 Joan continued to campaign with mixed success, until on 24 May at Compiègne she was dragged from her horse by a Burgundian soldier and captured. The English were ecstatic and bought her from the Burgundians to be taken for trial in Rouen. Charles VII, frequently accused of having abandoned her, did send forces to attack Rouen, but they were unsuccessful and don't seem to have been very committed to the attack. Certainly Joan caused a great deal of discomfort even among her supporters, who were never quite sure of the basis of her power. She was also detested by some of the other commanders, who could not bear that this young girl – who was seventeen when she raised the siege of Orleans – with her claim of divine inspiration could appear and upset all their plans, and worse, challenge their influence. There is no question that some in Charles's court were happy at her removal, especially as she had already changed the momentum of the war and they felt no more need for her.[9]

There is no space here to go into the details of Joan's trial, which produced numerous depositions and reports that give us a wealth of detail about her life and actions, and her death at the stake in the marketplace in Rouen on 30 May 1431, but she was subsequently exonerated by the pope and canonized in 1920. Although her entire public career, from her arrival in Chinon until her death in Rouen, had lasted only two years, for most people today she is probably the best-known figure in the Hundred Years War. Historians take pains to state that Joan did not 'win' the war for the French, and some argue that her career was a failure since she failed to take Paris and didn't accomplish much militarily beyond raising the siege of Orleans, which in any event had been planned by others before her appearance. All this may be true, but what is also true is that before Joan, the English armies had been virtually invincible, and had they taken Orleans there is no reason to believe they wouldn't also have taken Anjou and driven the Dauphin from Bourges. By whatever means, Joan changed the momentum of the war. More importantly, she secured the coronation of Charles VII, which was absolutely vital to healing the breach between the Armagnacs and Burgundians and turning Charles VII – almost in spite of himself – into a leader who could win the war. This was her true accomplishment.

King René's Early Career

When he joined Joan in the attack on Paris, René at the age of twenty finally became involved in the war. He immediately established his profile as an English enemy, because his uncle Cardinal Louis of Bar had done homage to Henry VI as king of France, and also claimed to have done so on behalf of René as his heir. René quickly repudiated this and wrote to the Duke of Bedford to defy him in highly courteous, but very definite, terms.[10] René was already in a difficult position with neighbouring Burgundy, and his open avowal of Charles VII did not help matters.

René might be blamed for not doing more to help rescue Joan, but in fact he had a legitimate excuse. Cardinal Louis had died in 1430, making René Duke of Bar. On 25 January 1431, Duke Charles of Lorraine also died, making Isabelle of Lorraine duchess, and as her husband René should have been duke of Loraine. However, Antoine de Vaudémont, a son of the previous duke's younger brother, took a course we have seen so frequently, and denied that the duchy could pass to a woman. The duchy broadly supported Isabelle and René, and in April René demanded a formal submission from Antoine or he would confiscate his property. Antoine refused, and in May René attacked the town of Vaudémont, but in the meantime Antoine had secured aid from the Duke of Burgundy and was in turn attacking Bar.

This was possibly the most fateful moment of René's life, which influenced everything that followed. On 2 July 1431, René met the combined Vaudémont-Burgundian army at Bulgnéville and suffered a disastrous defeat, René himself being wounded and captured. René was sent to the Duke of Burgundy, as Yolanda of Aragon's standing at court and his near relation to Charles VII made him a valuable hostage. Philip of Burgundy demanded an enormous ransom and the renunciation of Lorraine, and negotiations dragged on for nearly a year. René was eventually released in April 1432 in exchange for his sons Jean and Louis.

René had failed in battle, but now that he was free he found greater success with diplomacy. Lorraine, like Provence, was not part of France and belonged to the Empire. René appealed to his feudal overlord, who was none other than King Sigismund of Hungary, crowned Emperor in 1433. In 1434 Sigismund duly ruled in favour of Isabelle and René, and their title to Lorraine was confirmed.[11]

Unfortunately for René, this only offended Philip of Burgundy and he demanded that René return to prison, famously sending him a message that consisted of a single word: *return*.[12] Philip was perfectly within his rights to hold René until he paid his ransom, proving Marie of Blois's wisdom in holding back a large sum until her death in case Louis II needed to be ransomed, and René had enormous difficulty raising the money. Although Philip had acted lawfully, contemporaries believed it was unusual and unfair to hold a 'prince of the blood' of France without allowing him to pledge his word and leave prison in order to raise his ransom (presumably forgetting that René's grandfather Louis I had immediately broken his word in a similar situation).

Of more note was the fact that Philip treated René quite cruelly, which again was contrary to the practice of the time. René was held in a tower in the castle of Dijon under close guard, and when the Milanese ambassador visited him he was surprised to find that René was held under such harsh conditions, noting also that René had a long beard, turning him almost into the caricature of a neglected prisoner.[13]

It is not at all clear what would have happened to René had not outside events moved very quickly. At the end of 1434, René's brother Louis III died in Italy, and René was now Duke of Anjou and Count of Provence. Months later, Queen Johanna II also died, having designated René as her heir, making him King of Sicily and Jerusalem as well. Johanna's sad story is summed up most poignantly by her tomb, on which was written: 'Here lies the body of Joanna II by the grace of God queen of Hungary, Jerusalem and Sicily, of Dalmatia, Croatia, Bavaria, Serbia, Galicia, Lodomeria, Romania, Bulgaria, countess of Provence, Forcalquier and Piedmont.'[14] All these titles were completely empty and she reigned only in Naples, and even there not undisputedly. Even more pitifully, a fire in 1757 destroyed the church where she was buried and not even her tomb survives. Perhaps the most accurate epithet of all for Johanna II is from a biography of 1980 that calls her the 'queen of straw', a powerless figure buffeted between rival factions with little authority of her own.

From his position as son of Yolanda of Aragon, brother-in-law of Charles VII and Duke of Lorraine and Bar, René had now become a king twice over, plus ruler of an additional duchy and the county of Provence. This only made him more valuable as a hostage and Philip demanded a greater ransom, but fortunately for René, 1435 was a momentous year for another reason. After constant negotiations with Yolanda of Aragon among many others, Philip of Burgundy was ready to make peace with Charles VII and the Armagnacs. There was a peace conference at Arras between Charles VII, Philip and the English, but English inflexibility over Henry VI's rights as king of France was the sticking point. Charles VII would have considered letting Henry hold Normandy and Gascony as his vassal, but the English refused to countenance any acknowledgement of Charles as king of France. The conference ended without agreement between the three parties, only for Charles and Philip immediately to make their own agreement, and Philip recognized Charles as king.

This was the death knell for the English in France, but it also meant Charles VII had considerable influence in securing René's release. This was accomplished, but not without sweeping concessions. By the treaty of Lille of 1437, René agreed to pay Philip 400,000 écus and cede Philip some of his lands that bordered Burgundy and Flanders. Inevitably there was a marriage alliance, and René's heir Jean of Calabria married Philip's niece Marie of Bourbon. She brought a dowry of 150,000 écus, of which two-thirds went towards René's ransom, and René would owe instalments of 100,000 écus in May 1437 and1438, and a further 100,000 when he took his throne in Naples. René also agreed to a marriage alliance between his daughter Yolande of Bar and Ferry de Vaudémont, son of René's rival Antoine, to unite the claimants to Lorraine.[15]

This latter marriage was a great success, because Ferry de Vaudémont became a key ally and would serve René and Jean of Calabria faithfully until he died in 1470 on the campaign to conquer Aragon. Yolande of Bar, about whom we know little, does have an interesting cultural presence, since Tchaikovsky's final opera, *Iolanta*, is about her.

The opera is based on the play by the Danish poet Henrik Hertz, *King René's Daughter*, in which René is a gentle and loving father who, somewhat bizarrely, protects his blind daughter by keeping her blindness from her so it won't make her unhappy, and houses her in a beautiful garden until a suitor can be found who won't reveal to her that she is blind. Entirely unexpected in an operatic setting is the ending, when Iolanta's blindness is cured and she marries Ferry de Vaudémont. The opera's determinedly upbeat tone and happy ending are a pleasing grace note to the undoubtedly positive moments of René's long reign.

King René in Naples

Sadly René had no such happy ending in reality. Alfonso of Aragon had never forgotten his adoption by Johanna II, and in the turmoil of her final years Johanna first re-adopted Alfonso, then repudiated him again in a final testament of 1435 in which she spoke compellingly of his ingratitude and obnoxious behaviour, and definitively adopted René as her heir before she died.[16] René could do nothing from his Burgundian prison, and Alfonso immediately attacked Gaeta in May 1435 and then seized the key castles in Naples. However, the possibility of Aragonese domination of Naples, and thus most of Italy, as well as their other possessions in the Mediterranean, threatened Genoa, and a Genoese fleet defeated Alfonso at Ponza on 5 August and captured him. Now both claimants to the throne were in prison, but Isabelle of Lorraine arrived in Naples in October 1435 and took charge of the kingdom, although the Aragonese continued to hold the Castel Nuovo and the Castel dell'Ovo. As was so often the case with prisoners, the Genoese had no use for Alfonso and gave him to the Duke of Milan, Filippo Maria Visconti.

This is another example used by René's detractors to show how ineffective he was. René languished in prison for years and did nothing but produce beautiful paintings on the walls of his cell (so the story goes), whereas Alfonso charmed Filippo Visconti to the point where he joined forces with the Aragonese and worked to put Alfonso on the throne of Naples.[17] This version of the story is highly misleading, because it ignores the fact that Alfonso and Filippo had been allies for many years, only recently being at odds. From the moment he was placed into Milanese custody, Alfonso was treated as a guest, not kept in the harsh conditions René found in Dijon. Filippo was only one player in an incredibly fluid situation in Italy and needed support desperately, whereas Philip of Burgundy was the most powerful prince in France and needed nothing from René. The situations could not be more different, and it is no surprise that there were different outcomes. Alfonso was released without paying a ransom and resumed his fight for Naples with Milanese support, whereas René was crippled financially. One positive note was that the pope backed René, and as overlord of the kingdom recognized his claim over Alfonso's.[18]

René was finally released in February 1437, but before going to Naples he raised as much money as possible in Lorraine, Bar and Anjou. Yolanda of Aragon took charge of Anjou and Provence, and René formally ceded Maine to his younger brother Charles, on condition that he reconquer it from the English.[19] Although it was currently irrelevant since Maine was under English rule, it is notable that René was already allowing the breakup of the 'greater Anjou' that had been in existence since the time of Fulk V in the early 12th century.

René and Jean of Calabria arrived in Naples in May 1438. By July, René was ready to launch a campaign against Alfonso, who still held the major castles of Naples. Another blow to René's cause was the fact that Francesco Sforza, the son of Muzio Attendolo Sforza who had been such a support – intermittently – to Johanna II and Louis III, offered to help René, but the Neapolitan commanders refused to work with him and so Sforza cheerfully supported Alfonso instead. Despite this, René was able to take the Castel Nuovo and the Castel dell'Ovo, and by 1439 controlled Naples completely.

Despite these victories, the outcome seemed inevitable for a very simple reason: René had no money, and Alfonso was wealthy. Alfonso was able to buy mercenary armies, the essential component of 15th-century warfare, and René was not. Why was René unable to find any allies against Alfonso? Part of the problem was the same one that Charles of Anjou had faced, which was that René was unequivocally French. The small Italian powers were too afraid of possible French interference in the peninsula to want René on the throne of Naples. Despite similar fears about Aragonese domination of the Mediterranean, Alfonso seemed a safer option.

By August 1440, René was aware that his position was crumbling, and although he managed to hold on for another two years, on 1 June 1442 Aragonese agents in Naples opened the gates to Alfonso's forces. René desperately fought them in the streets, but to no avail, and by October 1442 all was lost. René returned to Provence and Alfonso sacked Naples, only making his formal entry into the city on 26 February 1443, which is commemorated by the triumphal arch he installed on the Castel Nuovo, literally imposing himself on the 'Maschio Angioino'.[20] A pathetic but brilliant touch by Alfonso was that the frieze on the triumphal arch, which shows his victory procession in Naples, has him seated on a throne with King René's captured mantle draped over the back.[21]

Henry VI's Angevin Marriage

René by no means gave up the fight after Alfonso took the kingdom, although on his return to Provence in October 1442 he almost immediately heard of the death of Yolanda of Aragon. She had lived nearly long enough to see her tireless work in support of Charles VII reach fruition.

In the aftermath of the relief of Orleans and Charles VII's coronation, and despite Joan's execution in 1431, French morale was at a high. The English retaliated by arranging

Henry VI's coronation as king of France at Notre Dame in Paris on 16 December 1431 (he had been crowned king of England in 1429), but this backfired spectacularly. The king's uncle, Cardinal Beaufort, arranged the coronation and mismanaged it so badly that it became a factor in the defection of the Burgundians and permanently alienated the Parisians. Beaufort committed every possible mistake: the coronation service was performed according to the English rite rather than the French, the Bishop of Paris was given only a minor role and no prisoners were pardoned or taxes abolished. The overriding impression was of meanness, and the chronicler known as the Bourgeois of Paris reported that 'Paris had seen merchants' marriages which had been "of more profit to the jewellers, goldsmiths and other purveyors of luxury than this coronation of a King, with all its jousts and Englishmen."'[22] Henry and his advisers immediately departed Paris, leaving the French in no doubt that he was not really their king.

As importantly, the Duke of Bedford died in 1435, just before Philip of Burgundy finally repudiated the English alliance. Bedford had a genuine love for France and was well respected in Normandy, one factor in the duchy's willingness to remain under English control for so long. The loss of Bedford and the Burgundian alliance was a fatal blow to the English presence in France, and in February 1436 the Dauphin's forces entered Paris.[23] Although turmoil erupted in Normandy and there was skirmishing throughout the duchy, the English commanders, notably John Talbot, the Earl of Shrewsbury, known as the 'English Achilles', who was the final great English commander in the war, withstood the onslaught.

Still, the English found themselves in the same situation as King John when he had tried to defend Normandy, or King René in Naples: there was simply no money. England had grown tired of paying for the endless war, especially as for years there had been no iconic victory with its associated plunder and ransoms. In large part due to King John's initial loss of the Angevin Empire and his son's attempts to retake it, Parliament in England now had a significant say in how their money would be spent. There was no benefit in the war for English taxpayers, and although they now considered Normandy as part of English territory and would be horrified when it was finally lost, they were not willing to subsidize its defence.

Thus René's return in 1442 came at a good moment for France, though joining in the final years of the Hundred Years War was a distraction from his goal of retaking Naples. Although they had not made much headway in Normandy, the French now attacked Gascony, foreshadowing the war's conclusion when England would lose not only its gains in the war (except Calais), but the lands it held before the war began. Worse for the English, they in turn were discovering the difficulties of being ruled by a mentally incompetent king. Henry VI was now twenty, and it had become clear that he had much more in common with his mad grandfather Charles VI than his father, the hero Henry V. Exactly as had happened in France, the court was split into factions, which would ultimately lead to civil war.

In 1444 the situation was so desperate that the English sought a truce, and as

Henry VI was of the right age, the obvious solution was a marriage alliance. France was willing to listen, since it now had the upper hand and could demand significant concessions. The natural course of action would be to marry Henry to one of Charles VII's daughters, linking the warring factions directly. However, Henry still claimed to be king of France, and Charles would never consent to form a marriage alliance with a usurper who failed to renounce his claim. Both sides still desired a peace treaty, so the bride would have to come from a different family.

René's daughter Margaret of Anjou fulfilled the requirements perfectly. René's status as titular king of Sicily and Jerusalem, as well as all his other titles both real and nominal, gave Margaret the proper rank to marry a king. Forming an alliance with Anjou, a contested border land adjacent to English Normandy, was attractive to the English. Finally, René was essentially penniless despite his high-flown titles, and the lack of a substantial dowry rendered Margaret less threatening than a more substantial heiress might have been. Margaret's dowry in fact consisted only of 20,000 francs and a worthless Angevin claim to Majorca and Minorca. More importantly, she renounced any rights to Angevin territories, since the death of René and her brothers might have allowed Henry VI to claim them. René was Charles VII's brother-in-law, and René's brother, Charles of Maine, was Charles VII's closest companion. The Angevin connection to the crown thus remained very strong, and it is not surprising that Charles VII would look to Anjou for the marriage alliance with England. It is also not coincidental that the concession France sought from the English would be the return of Maine to the Angevins.

The marriage was concluded in May 1444 at the cathedral in Tours, at a ceremony where the earl of Suffolk acted as proxy for Henry VI, and would be followed by a two-year truce. Margaret then made a procession through Normandy, and was hosted at Rouen by Suffolk's wife Alice Chaucer, granddaughter of the author, whose rise to the nobility showed the social mobility available for clever people in the 15th century. Margaret finally arrived in England in April 1445 and was formally married to Henry in person.[24]

King René's Culture Wars

One reason for the delay was that Margaret first attended the wedding celebrations of her sister Yolande to Ferry de Vaudémont in Nancy in February 1445. This was marked by the first of the three great tournaments that René held from 1445–1449, and far from being an example of René's frivolity or lack of seriousness, this was absolutely central to his political programme. René is one of the greatest cultural figures of the 15th century, but we must look in more detail at the purpose behind this activity.

René was involved in a high-stakes cultural war with Philip the Good of Burgundy and Alfonso the Magnanimous of Aragon. In this context, his chivalric romances, tournaments, pageants and, most importantly, his chivalric order, were the opposite of useless luxuries; rather they were essential components in his assertion of his right to rule and his bid for support from other nobles. Philip the Good held many tournaments, as well as establishing the chivalric Order of the Golden Fleece in 1430, which are always taken as demonstrations of his power and authority, and it was with this that René had to compete.

René had earlier shown his ability to use this kind of propaganda in Naples. On 31 December 1441, although René had lost almost all the Regno besides Naples itself to Alfonso, he held an elaborate pageant in the Castel Nuovo. This was based on a dialogue by the Roman poet Lucian, in which Scipio Africanus, Hannibal and Alexander the Great appeared at the gate to the Elysian Fields, and argued before King Minos about who was the greatest warrior. Victory went to Scipio Africanus, the conqueror of Hannibal. The moral to the tale was revealed to the audience, which was this: Alfonso was an old man who fought against the Church in the way that Hannibal had fought against Rome, but René was young, prudent, just and a friend of truth and the Church.[25] It is easy to argue that René should have been organizing the defence of Naples instead of holding pageants, but that it precisely what he was doing. The only way to defend Naples was to muster the Neapolitan nobles, and by allegorically demonstrating his superiority to Alfonso, René was making his pitch for their support.

For his daughter Yolande's wedding in Nancy, René held a tournament where he jousted dressed as Godfrey of Bouillon. There could hardly be a more resonant figure: Godfrey was the only near contemporary among the 'Nine Worthies', but much more importantly he was recognized as the first king of Jerusalem (though he had refused to be crowned), a title now held by René; he had been the duke of Lorraine, another title now held by René; and he was a hero of the First Crusade. This was relevant because, although we have not heard much about Crusades since Nicopolis in 1396, the current pope was calling for a Crusade and Philip the Good of Burgundy had expressed interest. René's appearance as Godfrey of Bouillon, and the appearance of Charles VII – who also attended the wedding – under the arms of the Lusignans, heroic Crusaders and kings of Jerusalem and Cyprus, was a direct riposte to Philip. Both René and Charles VII were unwilling to undertake any Crusade with the Hundred Years War ongoing (though René owned a copy of Joinville's *Life of Saint Louis*, and was obviously interested in the movement), but their iconography at the tournament was a response to Philip's Crusading credentials.[26]

Philip doesn't seem to have taken offence – or perhaps he didn't take the point – since in July 1445 he released René from the rest of his ransom, amounting to 80,600 écus, meaning that René had paid just over three-quarters of his initial ransom.[27] This was not a bad bargain for Philip, and as René was now the King of England's father-in-law as well as the King of France's brother-in-law it did no harm to Philip to make this concession. René was finally out from under the crippling ransom payments that had dogged him for ten years, and although he would remain chronically short of funds, at least now his revenues could be directed towards his own projects instead of into Burgundian coffers.

These projects were René's further great tournaments, and that they were part of a political programme is demonstrated by their locations: the first had been in Lorraine, the next was in Anjou and the last in Provence. For his tournament in Anjou in June 1446, René held the *Emprise de la Joyeuse Garde* at his mother's favourite chateau of Saumur. 'Joyeuse Garde' was Sir Lancelot's castle where the lovers Tristram and Iseult met and thus had an explicitly erotic theme, and the tournament duly included a wooden castle guarded by real lions from René's menagerie.[28]

We know that René was already drawn to the unusual; even in 1429 before he gained any of his titles and was only heir to Bar, he was served by a dwarf jester known as *'petit fou'* ('little fool') and a servant from Morocco, who gained considerable (and unwelcome) attention as he walked through the streets of Metz.[29] René went on to employ another dwarf known as Triboulet, who is commemorated in a medal by the notable Renaissance sculptor Francesco Laurana (who sculpted Alfonso V's triumphal arch in Naples), and also in an extraordinary manuscript illumination showing René sitting despondently with the recently deceased Triboulet, who lies in a coffin wrapped in his shroud as the Grim Reaper enters the room. René was known to be fond of wearing 'Moorish' clothes and armour, and continued to be attended by many Moorish servants later in his reign.[30] René's passion for all things Moorish extended to Moorish dancing, which some sources say he introduced to Europe; it swept through European courts and thence to England, where it became 'Morris' dancing.

René's love for the exotic particularly extended to animals, and his menagerie at Angers was known to contain four lions as well as leopards and ostriches. The city of Florence offered him one of its lionesses in 1442, and a keeper was killed by a lion in 1463. Accounts mention a dromedary at Angers, and René's tailor in Provence was known to have prepared costumes for René's monkeys, for an elephant and for 'another beast, called "the tiger"'.[31]

We can see by the variety and intensity of his interests that, despite the undoubted political impact these actions would have had, this was part of René's character. Although he was not the host, René participated in, and was the champion of, the *'Emprise de la gueule de dragon'* (the *Enterprise of the Dragon's Mouth*) near Chinon in June 1446, where he dressed in black and carried a black shield covered in gold tears, a tribute to his younger son Louis who had just died. Such theatricality may strike us as unfeeling, but René lived his life very publicly and this kind of display would have been his tribute to a beloved son.

When René held his third great tournament, the *Pas d'armes de la bergiere* (*Passage of arms of the Shepherdess*), at Tarascon in Provence, on 3 June 1449, he highlighted the presence of his son-in-law Ferry de Vaudémont, who took the top prize, as a means of integrating the next generation from Lorraine into his wider territorial ambitions. This was much more a pageant than a tournament, with a shepherdess tending sheep outside a cottage and two knights dressed as shepherds defending her.[32]

The End of the Hundred Years War

These tournaments took place during a truce in the Hundred Years War, after Le Mans and the rest of Maine were surrendered by the English in 1448, and the truce had been continued until 1450. Charles VII had used the time since the initial truce in 1444 wisely, establishing the first standing army in France and giving France its first military advantage in the war. Previously, well-organized English troops – who had to be organized because they were crossing the Channel to another country – had been opposed by scratch levies defending their homes or thrown into the field without much stake in the outcome, but now the French forces were properly managed. They had also finally found an artillery solution to counter the English longbows, in the form of superior cannon and the first type of handguns, which although still clumsy could be effective when used from behind walls. We know the reason for the new French superiority in artillery: the Bureau brothers, Jean and Gaspard, professionals who had worked their way up in the French administration, had created an efficient artillery force capitalizing on all the recent technological advances.[33]

When hostilities resumed, René was in the forefront. The English broke the truce in early 1449 and Charles launched an invasion of Normandy. Now the previously loyal Normans knew they had nothing to hope for from England – which was well on its way to a civil war – and many surrendered to the French immediately. On 10 November 1449, when Charles VII ceremonially entered Rouen, René was on his left and Charles of Maine on his right. An English attempt at a counterattack was brushed aside at the Battle of Formigny in April 1450, and by August the capture of Caen and Cherbourg meant Normandy had been entirely retaken, leaving the English nothing except Calais and Gascony. René took a great deal of credit for the success in Normandy and was at the height of his power and influence.[34]

Public opinion in England was outraged by the loss of Normandy; as early as January 1450 Parliament had accused the Duke of Suffolk of treason and he was murdered as he tried to flee to Calais. Jack Cade raised a rebellion in Kent and entered London in July, though this was crushed by a force that included many of the former captains from Normandy. Worse was to come, as the French moved directly from Normandy to Gascony. By the end of 1450 many cities had fallen, and Bordeaux was captured in June 1451, essentially securing Gascony for France.

Yet this last outpost of the old Angevin Empire had no particular allegiance to France, and some resented the French invasion. Lord Talbot led a force to Gascony in late 1452, and the English retook Bordeaux and much of the county. Charles VII sent an army to meet them, and on 17 July 1453 Talbot led part of his army against a French artillery encampment near Castillon commanded by Jean Bureau. It was the opposite of Crécy and Agincourt: the English launched a frontal attack on a well-defended French position and were slaughtered by the French guns. Talbot was killed, the English army disintegrated and Bordeaux surrendered on 19 October 1453.[35]

This was not the only momentous event of 1453. The Byzantine Empire, fatally weakened by the Fourth Crusade and which had been threatened by the Ottoman Turks for so long, was now in dire straits and consisted of little more than Constantinople itself. The Ottomans were ready for the final assault and in the spirit of Fulk Nerra had planted aggressive forward fortifications to cut off the Bosphorus from the north and strangle the city, notably the 'Fortress of Europe' (*Rumeli hisarı*, also known as *Boğazkesen*, which can mean the 'strait-cutter' or also the 'throat-cutter'), one of the most impressive castles remaining in Europe. Needless to say, the frantic appeals to western leaders by the last Byzantine Emperor in the years leading up to the Empire's fall were futile: France and England were in no position to help, Italy was in chaos and most of the other western powers were involved in these disputes one way or another. After a prolonged siege, on 29 May 1453 the Ottomans took the city, ending the Byzantine Empire.

1453 is the traditional date given for the end of the Hundred Years War, although the English monarchs continued to claim the throne of France and bore the French fleurs-de-lis on their arms until 1802. England retained Calais until 1558 and monarchs down to Henry VIII intermittently launched raids to 'retake' their kingdom. For our purposes, the most important consequence of the war's end was the turmoil into which it threw England, and its impact on Margaret of Anjou.

Origins of the English Civil War: Lancaster and York

It was already clear that Henry VI was not a competent king, but defeat in the Hundred Years War put a new level of pressure on the English court. Henry VI's gentleness, unworldliness and pliability were constantly remarked upon by contemporaries, qualities eminently unsuitable for a king. We remember that Eleanor of Aquitaine accused Louis VII of being more like a monk than a king, but Louis managed to remain politically effective as well as pious, whereas Henry VI failed in every duty of a monarch. That put Margaret in an interesting position. She had been raised in Anjou, where King René's wife and mother administered the duchy during his imprisonment, and she knew that her mother had gone to Naples to establish René's claim to the throne and rule the kingdom for him until his release from prison. For a queen to play a role as regent would not seem unnatural to her, should it be required. The situation in England was about to require this, and much more, as two powerful relatives began to compete for control of the government.

The first was Edmund Beaufort, Duke of Somerset. Henry VI's own line came through Edward III's son John of Gaunt, Duke of Lancaster, but Somerset was also a descendant of John of Gaunt through the retrospectively legitimized offspring of his later marriage to Katherine Swynford. Somerset was thus part of the royal family, but not a direct rival to Henry. More importantly, Somerset had been involved in the French wars, and though he had personally surrendered Rouen to the French and was implicated in the widely perceived mismanagement of the war, he was intimately connected to royal government.

The second player was Richard Duke of York, who in 1448 adopted the name 'Plantagenet' to link himself to the 12th-century kings of England, though oddly through their forebear Geoffrey Plantagenet, rather than one of the kings. It is entirely unclear why Richard chose this name rather than any other, or why this nickname for Geoffrey, which was attested in the 12th century, had gone unremarked for 300 years only to re-emerge now. Dr John S. Plant has suggested that the name might have had obscene connotations referring to Geoffrey's procreative powers, so it might have remained as a familiar term to describe him, but not in polite circles or written sources, which was why it vanished from the records for so long only to reappear in a less prudish time.[36] Linking oneself to a previous dynasty was not unusual, and we have seen how the Angevins of Naples adopted this strategy and named two sons Charles 'Martel' in reference to Charlemagne's grandfather.

Yet if Richard sought to connect himself to the previous English monarchy through a name, which name could he use? Henry I, Henry III, Edward II and Edward III didn't have widely used epithets. William 'the Conqueror' was no use, and William II 'Rufus' and Edward I 'Longshanks' (or 'Hammer of the Scots', also unhelpful) had names based on physical characteristics. That left the Angevins, but Henry II was 'FitzEmpress', Richard was 'the Lionheart' and John was 'Softsword' or 'Lackland'. Richard of York wasn't the son of an Empress, John had only pejorative names and calling himself 'Lionheart' would seem presumptuous rather than impressive. If the name Plantagenet were still known, it might have been the only name from the old Angevin dynasty available to him.

Why did Richard particularly wish to link himself to an earlier dynasty? He was descended from Edward III from both his mother and father, making him closer to the throne than Somerset, so why would he need to boost his royal credentials? The only reason would be to assert his claim, not over Somerset, but over Henry VI himself. By appealing back to the Angevins, Richard may have been emphasizing his claim of descent from a family that had successfully ruled England and France, most notably the lands that had just been lost by the current incompetent king.

Margaret of Anjou in the 'Wars of the Roses'

In the initial contest between the two, Somerset emerged victorious, and the Duke of York retired to his estates while Somerset managed the king's affairs. By summer 1453 Margaret was finally pregnant after seven years of marriage, so there was some cause for optimism. There was even news that the English forces had recaptured Bordeaux, and there was now a possibility that after the disaster in Normandy England might be able to restore its position from before the Hundred Years War, with the addition of Calais. Of course that was not to be: Lord Talbot had been killed at Castillon in July and France was completely victorious by October 1453. In August, when Henry VI heard that Talbot had been killed and the war essentially lost, he fell into a catatonic state and became incapable of speech.[37]

This episode of madness, as it was considered at the time, although in some ways it did not really change the king's ability – or inability – to rule, was shocking and clearly had to be addressed. Matters were complicated, rather than helped, when Margaret gave birth to a son on 13 October. He was named Edward in honour of Edward the Confessor, and the presence of an heir threw up new permutations in the struggle for power. If Henry never recovered and died, Edward would become king, and a regent could then be appointed until his majority. But if Henry never recovered and lived, at what point could he be replaced by his son? What role might the queen play, now that her son was even more important than an heir would usually be, given his father's madness?

Margaret was not the only player in the drama. The Duke of York, on hearing of the king's incapacity, arrived in London in November and asserted his right to govern the kingdom. His success in overthrowing those who surrounded Henry was demonstrated by the arrest and imprisonment of Somerset. Yet it was not clear on what grounds he had done this, and he was not unopposed. In January 1454, Margaret publicly claimed her right to rule the kingdom in her husband's stead, publishing articles setting out the powers she would require to rule effectively. This was a bold attempt to take charge that must have owed much to Margaret's upbringing by Yolanda of Aragon and Isabelle of Lorraine, who both stepped forward when their husbands were imprisoned or absent. But the nobles vying for power formally rejected Margaret's claim, and instead in March 1454 instituted a council, led by York, to govern for Henry.

York immediately set in motion various plans for restoring stability to the kingdom, but the series of sudden unexpected events continued. On Christmas Day 1454, Henry VI suddenly awoke from his stupor and recovered his senses. There was general rejoicing, but in fact the king's recovery undermined the progress made by York and his council, since York was now removed from power and the council dissolved. Somerset was released from the Tower and the old factional infighting could resume. By February 1455 York had withdrawn again to his estates in the north, and the country seemed to be preparing for civil war.[38]

In the coming struggle, what most impresses us is Margaret's determination to keep Henry's government intact for her son. It is hard not to attribute Margaret's mental strength and single-mindedness to her early experiences, when she saw how King René, perhaps through too easygoing a character, lost his throne in Naples, and also how the determination and perseverance of women such as Yolanda of Aragon and Isabelle of Lorraine could triumph over the most difficult circumstances, most notably in winning the French throne for Charles VII.

However, others did not see Margaret in this way. As the struggle for the kingdom developed into a straightforward fight between Margaret on one side and the Duke of York on the other, Margaret's enemies were horrified – and even her supporters somewhat disturbed – by the way the queen began arrogating royal powers to herself. We can see that Henry was mentally incompetent, and Margaret was probably only doing what she believed was necessary to manage the kingdom. Yet this was politics, and in politics appearance is every bit as important as reality. Just as Matilda had been condemned for appearing arrogant and high-handed when she tried to make good her – perfectly legitimate – claim to the throne, now Margaret appeared to be overreaching her authority as queen. Worse, she also appeared, once again, as a woman who 'acted like a man', who showed a ruthlessness and determination that might have been praised in a man, but was viewed as 'unnatural' in a woman.

Events now began to move quickly. Somerset resumed control of the government and summoned the nobles to a council in Leicester in May 1455. York and his adherents, particularly the powerful Neville family from the north, believed this would result in a direct attack on them, and marched south. Somerset and the king, who were travelling north to Leicester, had only reached St Albans when they met York and his army. This turned into an armed confrontation, with York's army forcing its way into the town and widespread skirmishing breaking out, which resulted in victory for York and the death of Somerset and one of his chief supporters, Henry Percy, Earl of Northumberland, the most deadly rival of the Nevilles.

York was victorious and took possession of the king, who had sat quietly in the market square of St Albans as the battle raged around him. They returned to London, where York now seemed to be in the ascendant, but turmoil continued throughout the kingdom as the partisans of each side prepared to continue the conflict. In November 1455, York had himself appointed protector of the realm, but was forced out of the position by February 1456, unable to gain a consensus for this de facto regency.

Margaret then took the initiative, drawing on her support in the northwest and establishing a power base in Coventry. She summoned Henry VI to join her, and Margaret staged a formal ceremonial entry for her husband that emphasized the ability and right to rule of the entire family: Henry, Margaret and the young prince Edward. A great council then met in Coventry in October and attempted to reconcile all the parties. York and his supporters attended and swore a public oath of loyalty to the king, but now all the public offices were filled with Margaret's supporters, and a formal council was also appointed to manage Prince Edward's affairs, again packed with Margaret's men. Margaret could not forget that York had brought an army against the king and his followers at St Albans, and she seems to have been determined to crush him.

Another great attempt at reconciliation – a 'loveday' between the rival parties – was held in London on 25 March 1458, where York and the Nevilles accepted responsibility for those killed at St Albans and were formally forgiven, and Margaret took York's hand as they processed to St Paul's behind Henry to show that peace had been achieved. However, despite this pageantry nothing had really changed.[39]

By 1459, Margaret had again gone to Coventry with Henry and Edward and summoned a council, and when the Yorkists failed to appear, they were charged with treason. Both sides gathered their forces and there were skirmishes, but the reluctance of many of the Yorkists to take the field against a force carrying the king's banner undermined their cause, and the Yorkists left the country: the Duke of York to his estates in Ireland, and others, including York's son Edward of March, to Calais where the earl of Warwick commanded the English forces. A parliament held at Coventry in December condemned York, his sons and the earls of Salisbury and Warwick for treason and declared their lands forfeit. Margaret seemed to have won a complete victory, but this was only in theory. The only options now available to the Yorkists were to remain quietly in exile; surrender and be executed; or resume the fight, but this time with the explicit intention of overthrowing the king. They were quick to choose the latter.

The Earl of Warwick raised troops in Calais, and he returned to England in June 1460 accompanied by the Earl of Salisbury and Edward of March. They were welcomed in the southeast and London opened its gates to them, showing that despite Margaret's steely determination to fight for her husband and son, she had failed to gain wider support for her cause from the general populace. Although she still had considerable support in the north, the people of London and the southeast, perhaps more intimately connected to Calais and the disastrous events in France, were convinced that power had been wrested from an incompetent king and was being misused by Margaret and her supporters.

Now both sides took to the field in earnest. Warwick, Salisbury and Edward of March led their army north, and Margaret sent her army under the Duke of Buckingham, the new Earl of Shrewsbury (son of Lord Talbot who had been killed at Castillon) and Viscount Beaumont south, accompanied by the king himself, though as always he would take no part in events. The two forces met near Northampton on 10 July, and the Yorkists were completely victorious, killing the enemy commanders and capturing the king.

York himself now joined them, and he took events to their logical conclusion. On 10 October, he rode into London flying the royal banner, and formally claimed the throne in the great hall of Westminster. Yet just like Margaret, he had done what seemed to be the hard work of winning the war, but failed to gather the necessary support for his actions. The assembled nobles were not yet prepared to replace Henry VI, and they refused to accept York as their king. After urgent negotiations, they suggested a solution that we have seen on previous occasions: it was agreed that Henry VI would reign for his lifetime, then be succeeded by York, disinheriting Henry and Margaret's son Edward.[40]

Margaret refused to accept this defeat, and she still had plenty of supporters. The new Earl of Northumberland, the new Duke of Somerset and Jasper Tudor, Earl of Pembroke (and son by a second marriage of Henry VI's mother Catherine) were raising forces to defend her. The Duke of York was aware of this, and led his own troops north, hoping to consolidate his hold on power with another victory. This was not to be, since he was surprised by a superior force at Wakefield on 30 December 1460, and he was killed along with most of his men. The Earl of Salisbury was captured and executed. The heads of York, Salisbury and their two sons, who had fallen in battle with them, were impaled on the city gates of York as a warning to other rebels and a paper crown was put on the Duke of York's head, the only crown he would ever wear. As had happened so frequently in the Wars of the Roses, just when one side seemed to have a complete victory, events could dramatically reverse themselves in a single day.

Incredibly, these constant reversals continued, showing how evenly matched the two sides were, and more tellingly, how neither side could articulate a message that might have a broader appeal than to its own adherents. It also shows that neither side was monolithic, and the disparate groups that composed each faction would fight on even after a seemingly conclusive defeat. As Margaret marched south in triumph to celebrate York's defeat and death, Edward of March with another Yorkist army was defeating Jasper Tudor at Mortimer's Cross on the Welsh borders, a battle in which Jasper's father, Owen Tudor, ancestor of the Tudor monarchs, was captured and executed.

Warwick, who had raised yet another fresh army in London and was accompanied by Henry VI to give him legitimacy, rushed north to St Albans, hoping to defeat Margaret's forces under the Duke of Somerset and continue the Yorkist resurgence. Instead, the second battle of St Albans in February 1461 was a victory for Somerset, who also recaptured Henry VI. Margaret and her forces were still on course to capitalize on the death of the Duke of York and end the conflict, though Warwick himself had escaped.[41]

Now Margaret had only to enter London to claim her victory. But as had happened with Matilda, London proved the insurmountable obstacle for Margaret. Instead of welcoming Margaret and her army, the people of London were terrified of the city being sacked, and sent a delegation to negotiate. Margaret was unwilling to offer a full amnesty to her enemies in the city, and without such assurances the city refused to admit her. A stalemate ensued, and while this happened, Warwick and Edward of March were marching towards London in what must have seemed a forlorn hope when they set out.

Margaret finally decided to retreat rather than be trapped before the city, and in the final reversal of this phase of the war, her victorious army abandoned the field and the city welcomed Warwick and Edward. The Duke of York's son Edward, who at the age of eighteen was every inch a king – young, tall, handsome and successful in battle – was not one to waste this opportunity. Edward was escorted by joyous crowds to Westminster and crowned king on 4 March 1461. His claim to the throne was unquestionably valid, he was not personally implicated in the more unsavoury episodes of his father's career, and in London he was infinitely preferable to the queen, who was viewed as little better than a usurper.

Edward wasted no time, and pursued Margaret to end the conflict for good. Their two armies met at Towton in Yorkshire in what would become the bloodiest battle fought on English soil. Thousands died, but for once the battle didn't overturn the party currently in the ascendant. Edward was victorious, and Margaret, Henry VI and their son Edward fled to Scotland.[42]

From her exile in Scotland, Margaret first sought help from Charles VII (only to learn that he had died on 22 July 1461), then from his son King Louis XI. Although she was able to muster small forces, these were never a real threat to Edward IV. Margaret also discovered that her allies were more concerned with their own interests than supporting her. When the Scots and Louis XI (called the 'Spider King' because of his talent for spinning intrigues) decided it would be to their benefit to reconcile with Edward IV, they dropped Margaret and by the end of 1463 she had been completely abandoned.[43]

Although King René had been unable to help Margaret in England, he gave her the castle of Koeur in Bar as a residence for herself and her son. More important was who and what he was, because Margaret's most urgent task was raising funds to prepare for her return. Whatever one thinks about René's abilities, he was one of the best connected figures in Europe, and these connections were vital. A tantalising example of Margaret and René's activities can be seen in the 'Fishpool Hoard' in room 40 of the British Museum. This hoard of coins contains florins from many of the lands that supported Henry VI, as well as jewellery with the motto *en bon cuer* ('in good heart', but also a pun on Margaret's residence of Koeur), and it is most likely the product of Margaret's fundraising activities throughout her father's network of contacts in Europe.

Henry VI had remained at the Scottish court, but when the Scots made peace with Edward IV he was expelled, and in 1464 the utterly extraordinary situation arose of a deposed king wandering around the north of England as a fugitive. The Duke of Somerset was still in England and attempted to rally the Lancastrian supporters, but he was defeated in 1464 and executed. Henry was finally captured in 1465 and sent to the Tower of the London, though under easy circumstances, because Edward IV preferred to keep Henry alive rather than face the prospect of Henry and Margaret's son claiming the throne from France. The Lancastrians in England were essentially finished, but Margaret refused to concede defeat and continued in her diplomatic efforts, although she now bore more than a passing resemblance to her father as she schemed futilely to regain her lost kingdom.

King René: Chivalry and Warfare

Although he was a 'king without a kingdom', René had similarly not given up, and his prestige was at its high point in 1450, when he had participated in the reconquest of Normandy and held his great tournaments in Lorraine, Anjou and Provence. Perhaps most notably, René founded an order of chivalry in August 1448, the *Ordre du Croissant* or 'Order of the Crescent' (though there is an almost irresistible temptation to call it the 'Croissant' even in English). This has been portrayed by some as another example of René's preference for dressing up and playing chivalric games instead of tending to the 'real' business of managing his territories and retaking Naples. Superficially this can seem true: the point of a chivalric order was indeed for its members to dress in elaborate robes, wear the device of the order and attend meetings where they told tales of their military prowess and gathered them into a book of deeds. We have seen this before with Louis of Taranto's Order of the Knot, and indeed it continues to this day with the Order of the Garter in England.

The Crescent was a multi-layered symbol. It was immediately associated with Islam, fitting well with René's fascination for all things Moorish, and suggesting the Ottoman Empire and Jerusalem, but the crescent had also been used on Charles of Anjou's coins, so it had a link to René's lost kingdom in Naples. The order's motto was *Los en croissant*, which means both 'honour in the crescent' and 'increasing honour', suggesting that members would both gain honour from joining the order and should also work tirelessly to increase the honour and prestige of the house of Anjou. The patron saint of the order was the soldier-martyr St Maurice, the patron saint of Anjou to whom the cathedral in Angers was dedicated, and the order's chapel was in the cathedral, where it had annual meetings on St Maurice's feast day, 22 September.[44]

Yet there was much more to chivalric orders, as they were also diplomatic organizations and a means of cementing relationships, and the order's statutes required 'that all members swear loyalty to the Duke of Anjou and his legitimate heirs for as long as the Order exists'.[45] If we look at the members of the Order of the Crescent, although most were culturally French, they were from René's disparate territories and this was a useful means of bringing them together. Others were Neapolitans who had left Naples with René and continued in his service. There were only three properly 'foreign' members, but they are notable.

Johan, Count of Nassau and Saarbrücken, was a neighbouring prince and is generally assumed to have been admitted to the Crescent to shore up local support for Bar and Lorraine, although no other German princes were so favoured. However, Johan's mother was Elizabeth of Lorraine-Vaudémont (sister of René's old rival Antoine of Vaudémont and thus aunt of Ferry de Vaudémont), a noted literary figure who translated French chivalric romances into German. Johan had commissioned illuminated manuscripts of her works, making it much more likely that Johan and René had a literary association.[46]

The other two foreign members were Italian nobles: Jacopo Antonio Marcello, a prominent military commander in Venice, and Francesco Sforza of Milan. The timing of Francesco Sforza's appointment to the order, in 1449, is crucial: Filippo Maria Visconti had died in 1447 without heirs, and Alfonso of Aragon attempted to seize Milan and add it to his kingdom of Naples, but Sforza thwarted this plan and seized Milan for himself. Thus René's alliance through the Crescent with Sforza and the

Venetian commander was a means of consolidating an alliance against Alfonso.

This plan bore fruit by 1452. Alfonso allied with Venice against Florence and Milan, leading Sforza and Cosimo de Medici to request assistance from Charles VII, who naturally was more interested in finishing the Hundred Years War, but he offered to back an expedition led by René if Florence and Milan would help him conquer Naples. In April 1453, after the Florentines agreed to pay for the mission, René invaded Italy and drove the Venetians from Brescia by November, but he was now engaged in complicated diplomacy. He wanted the Milanese to help him attack Naples, rather than attacking Venice, which had formerly been René's ally and to which he was connected through Jacopo Marcello's membership of the Crescent.

Jacopo Marcello was a close friend of René's, and throughout 1453 he would send René some of the most precious manuscripts associated with the Angevins. These include the Greek text of John Chrysostom's first homily with a Latin translation (sent to show his sympathy for the death of Isabelle of Lorraine in February of that year) and an illuminated manuscript of the life of St Maurice as a tribute to the Crescent, one of the most magnificent works of 15th-century illumination. René sent another member of the order, Giovanni Cossa, to Venice to negotiate an alliance, but although he initially believed there was some chance of detaching Venice from Naples, he then discovered that the Venetians were supporting Alfonso in his plans to invade Tuscany.[47]

René declared war on Venice, but he was now betrayed by Francesco Sforza, who was worried about French aggression in northern Italy if René were successful in Naples. There was reason for this, because by now Charles VII had finished the conquest of Gascony, and France was free to look further afield for the first time in decades. The wisdom of Francesco's fears would be amply demonstrated, though not for forty years. Another complication was the fall of Constantinople, as Pope Pius II was now desperately – and belatedly – attempting to organize a relief mission and wanted all the combatants in Italy to stop fighting. In this impasse it became clear that René would get no support in his attempt on Naples, and in January 1454 he left Italy in disgust, although his son Jean of Calabria remained to make what he could of the situation.[48]

René followed up this disappointment in Italy by turning to a new field of chivalric endeavour, and he now produced the literary works that are his most lasting legacy. The most famous was also the first: the *Treatise on the Form and Devising of a Tournament*. This was written around 1451–52, and exists in an absolutely stunning manuscript in the Bibliothèque Nationale illuminated by Barthélemy van Eyck, who would produce numerous masterpieces as René's court painter. These are some of the most iconic images of the Middle Ages, showing richly caparisoned knights fighting and lavishly dressed ladies watching them, all in incredible detail. The complete manuscript can be viewed on *Mandragore*, the Bibliothèque Nationale's manuscript website.[49]

René had already held his great tournaments, so he was definitely an authority on the subject, but although René's events can be called 'tournaments' in the sense of great gatherings of knights with formalized combat, the actual form of combat at these events was the joust, which was easier to choreograph. For exactly this reason, the joust was much more common in the 15th century and further evolved into the *pas d'armes,* a scripted event often based on Arthurian legend, where an elaborate dramatic scene would be enacted that eventually included some kind of combat.

Thus René's treatise is in a sense a formal exercise, giving directions for a type of event that usually wasn't held, although René may have needed to codify the rules for tournaments because most people didn't know them. It is this that makes the treatise such a valuable source, because it provides minute detail about every possible aspect of the tournament: how to announce it, whom to invite, the equipment used by the knights, the preparations required at the venue and how to choose and reward the winner. René also elaborates the social function of the tournament, which was becoming paramount in the 15th century, not least as a consequence of the changes in warfare that we have already seen – the appearance of guns, the reliance on mercenaries and the rise in mortality in warfare. The position of knights in medieval society had changed radically, and the tournament (or joust) had become much more important as a means of asserting their social role than preparing them for battle. But this did not make it a worthless exercise, and it was not the case that nobles pining for a chivalric past were simply recreating it as fantasy.[50]

Gilles de Rais: The Legend of Bluebeard

One of René's former comrades from the glory years of Joan of Arc's campaigns provides a much better example than René of a fantasist wasting his life and property on ostentation, but the truly horrifying conclusion of his story prevents him from being compared directly to René. Gilles de Rais, who had been a Marshal of France and very closely connected to Joan of Arc in the siege of Orleans and Charles VII's coronation, had retired from military life in the 1430s and devoted himself to pursuits that do not seem so different from those of René. Gilles constructed a Chapel of the Holy Innocents where he personally supervised the decoration and designed robes and other decorative items. He produced a theatrical pageant, *Le Mistère du Siège d'Orléans,* which was on an astonishing scale and included hundreds of speaking parts and extras with lavish costumes, and was performed in Orleans and elsewhere for huge crowds who were given unlimited hospitality. Gilles essentially bankrupted himself on these projects, and had to sell of most of his property, and this seems to be partially responsible for his later behaviour.

Gilles became involved in the occult, particularly alchemy and the summoning of demons. We have seen that there was quite a bit of this diabolical interest around the Dauphin's court in the 1420s, but for Gilles we have detailed depositions about exactly what he did. The reason we have these is that Gilles also seems to have been a paedophile and serial killer, and he abused and murdered an unknown number of children, perhaps as many as 200. Gilles confessed in detail to the sexual assaults he performed throughout the late 1430s and how he murdered the children. The killings came to an end in 1440, when a violent dispute with a clergyman led to an ecclesiastical investigation that brought the crimes to light. At his trial, the parents of missing children in the surrounding area and Gilles' own confederates in the crimes testified against him. Gilles was condemned to death and hanged at Nantes on 26 October 1440.[51]

Gilles of course is known as 'Bluebeard', reputedly because he rode a grey Barbary horse known as a *Barbe bleu*, which can also be read as 'Bluebeard'. His story was later adapted by Perrault into the tale of the man who murdered his wives, which strangely is less horrifying than the actual events. Although in many ways Gilles served contemporaries as a standard cautionary tale about extravagance and waste leading to sin, the level of detail in Gilles's confession provides early information about sexual deviance and the psychology of a murderer. Needless to say, this has no connection to King René, and his chivalric pageants and the types of display he indulged in had a very different purpose.

King René's Other Literary Works

I think it is easy to see the potential political value of the Order of the Crescent and René's tournaments and jousts, but it is harder to argue that literary compositions such as his chivalric allegories and romances encouraged people to see him as a political or military leader. Not him, perhaps, but even if René now preferred to be an author, he had not given up Angevin political ambitions: he had simply shifted them onto his son Jean of Calabria. Jean remained extremely active in pursuing the various Angevin claims, and René could assist him by increasing his reputation and network of contacts.

A possible reason for René's decision to let his son pursue his claims was the death of Isabelle of Lorraine at the age of 44 in February 1453. Isabelle had ruled Naples when René was imprisoned in Burgundy and governed Anjou and Provence when René himself was clinging to power in Naples, and she had been a powerful figure in the mould of Yolanda of Aragon. She and René were clearly close, and on hearing that she was ill he rushed back from Provence to be with her when she died. As he had with his son, René expressed his grief in artistic terms by inventing the device of a bow with a broken string to symbolize his sadness, coupled with the Italian motto *Arco per lentare, piaga non sana* ('stilling the bow doesn't heal the wound').[52]

The duchy of Lorraine had belonged to Isabelle, and with her death Jean of Calabria became Duke of Lorraine. This was another reason for the changing of the guard, and René now does seem to have been content for Jean to continue the attempt to take Naples and pursue the other Angevin claims. René also married the twenty-one year-old Jeanne de Laval on 10 September 1454. We will recall that René and Isabelle of Lorraine had been betrothed and married very young, and the marriage had been arranged by Yolanda of Aragon. Although Isabelle and René do seem to have cared for each other, René's relationship with Jeanne was more tender. After his second marriage, with his acceptance of the futile political situation in Italy and the end of the Hundred Years War, which absolved him from the necessity of further military action, René finally allowed himself to indulge fully in the cultural pursuits that most interested him, and Jeanne participated in these.[53] Jeanne and René developed their own device, which would appear on the reverse of the medal René commissioned of Jeanne,[54] of two turtledoves wearing necklaces that tie them together. This charming device also appears in Jeanne's psalter.[55]

The manuscripts associated with René contain the most striking imagery of the period. Although the images from the *Treatise on Tournaments* are perhaps the best known today for their realistic depiction of knights, it is the illuminations – also by Barthélemy van Eyck – for René's chivalric romances that are the most visually stunning. In René's moral treatise, the *Mortification of Vain Pleasure* of 1455, in addition to the – very beautiful – portrayals of horses and carriages and knights besieging castles, we have the utterly extraordinary images of three richly dressed queens and a female bishop crucifying a heart and impaling it with a lance. Of course these are allegorical figures, but the images of a heart nailed to the cross are unlike anything else produced in the period.[56]

Even more direct in their appeal are van Eyck's illuminations for René's romance *The Book of the Love-Smitten Heart* of 1457. Again, there are representations of knights at *pas d'armes* that are almost certainly illustrations of the kinds of events René organized in reality, and more prosaically a long interlude where the arms are displayed of great heroes such as Hercules, Aeneas, Julius Caesar and Achilles, as well as the arms of Charles VII, Louis XI (as Dauphin), Louis of Orleans, the Duke de Berry, Philip the Good of Burgundy, Charles of Orleans and King René himself. Yet it seems these scenes are only prosaic to me: the mystical elements of the illuminations have prompted wild speculation by some, and René's connection with Provence, Jerusalem, chivalric orders and mysticism are an irresistible cocktail for conspiracy theorists seeking to identify custodians of lost knowledge. René is just as much a gift for the fantasy writer as Margaret of Anjou is for the dramatist, and René has been identified as one of the *illuminati,* or a keeper of lost secrets, explicitly so in *Holy Blood, Holy Grail.*[57] Perhaps this connection is not quite so tenuous as it might seem, considering that Wolfram von Eschenbach, in his seminal 13th-century grail romance *Parzifal,* stated that Parzifal's father was the 'king of Anjou'. Wolfram's story is wholly fantastic, and despite being the most popular vernacular romance of the time in Germany, there seem to have been no contemporary attempts to connect the 13th century or later Angevins to the grail legend.

Aside from this, René's story – which involves the figure of Love stealing the narrator's heart, which is then personified as 'Heart', a knight who is led by his squire 'Desire' – allows van Eyck to produce images and motifs of incredible originality. Heart's horse wears a caparison decorated with winged hearts and Heart himself wears a helmet with a winged heart, but at the end of the manuscript these are elaborated into images of various male and female personifications plucking hearts like apples from trees; gathering hearts in nets like birds; snaring hearts with lassoes; catching hearts in cages and pickling hearts in barrels.[58] There are simply no other images quite like this in the art of the 15th century. Yet despite these cultural achievements, René had not entirely given up on military exploits.

Jean of Calabria: Naples and Aragon

René was blessed with a long life, which was unfortunate in that he outlived his children, but also meant that he outlived his enemies. When Alfonso of Aragon died in June 1458, there was an opportunity for the Angevins to return to Naples. Alfonso left no legitimate children, and Aragon and Sicily went to his brother Juan, but Alfonso left Naples to his illegitimate son Ferrante I. However, Pope Callixtus III refused to recognize Ferrante as king, and Jean of Calabria, who was in Genoa, was in a strong position to oppose him.

By October 1459 Jean of Calabria had prepared a fleet and attacked Naples, then Puglia. Although he defeated the Aragonese on 7 July 1460 and wanted to press on to Naples, his Italian allies were more concerned with securing their own lands. Worse, the new pope, Pius II, was a determined foe of the Angevins and had formally invested Ferrante with Naples in October 1459 and pulled Francesco Sforza into an alliance against Jean. The Order of the Crescent now came into its own, and Jean admitted twenty-one Neapolitan nobles to the order in 1460 to secure their allegiance. Proof that this was taken seriously came when Pius II specifically attacked the Order, issuing a bull on 9 January 1461 formally dissolving the Crescent and releasing the members from their oaths.[59]

The conflict sharpened when Genoa expelled the French forces, and René himself brought a fleet to attack the city and support his son. There was confusion in the fleet, and after landing his forces René then sailed away and left them to be slaughtered. At best this revealed René as an inadequate general, but for some it was a stain on his reputation that almost seemed like cowardice. Jean of Calabria remained in the Regno after this reverse but was defeated on 18 August 1462 at the battle of Troia. The Angevins continued to have bad luck, since the death of Charles VII in 1461 deprived René of a constant friend, and Louis XI, whose relationship with his father had been remarkably poor, was disinclined to support friends of the late king. Margaret of Anjou's troubles in the same year were a further disincentive to Louis, as the Angevins now appeared to be mired in multiple lost causes. By the summer of 1464, Jean of Calabria left Italy, and the defeat of an Angevin fleet on 7 July 1465 at the Battle of Ischia essentially ended any Angevin involvement with Naples.[60]

These Angevin defeats take a striking place in the artistic and cultural fabric of the city, as Ferrante chose to commemorate his victories in a variety of ways. The most important is the *Tavola Strozzi*, a panoramic view of Naples that is the oldest depiction of the city and allows us to see the Castel Nuovo and many other buildings in their mid-15th-century detail. More visible are the great bronze doors of the Castel Nuovo, which Ferrante commissioned to complete his father's triumphal arch, and again imprinted on the surface of the Angevin castle representations of Angevin defeats.[61]

This reverse still did not end the dreams of the 'impossible heritage' and 'European destiny' of the Angevins. Although Angevin hopes in Naples had been dashed, there was now an opportunity for belated revenge on Aragon. Alfonso's bastard son Ferrante might have been secure in Naples, but Alfonso's successor in Aragon itself, Juan II, became involved in a protracted civil war in which the Catalonian estates rejected his kingship and called in several pretenders to oppose him. After the other candidates died, in 1466 the council sent ambassadors to Angers, where they invited René to become king through his descent from Yolanda of Aragon. René accepted the offer and was now titular king of Aragon on top of all his other titles, and he proceeded to take the arms of Aragon in his coat of arms and use the title 'King of Aragon' in future documents. Although René sent Jean of Calabria to conduct the military operations, he seems to have remained closely involved with the expedition and to have been active in diplomacy to help his son. Importantly, Louis XI also backed the adventure. In January 1467 the Angevin supporters invaded Catalonia, and on 31 August Jean of Calabria entered Barcelona.[62]

The Angevins had gained Louis XI's support, but this proved a double-edged sword, as they were now involved in royal diplomacy. In 1468 Louis XI recalled Jean to France to negotiate with the Duke of Brittany, and Jean left Ferry de Vaudémont to hold Catalonia. Jean returned in 1469, but by this time Juan II had made alliances with Burgundy and England and prepared his counterstroke. Modern historians don't take this Catalonian adventure very seriously, since with hindsight the Angevins don't seem to have had much chance of succeeding, but Jean held Barcelona for three years and there was every indication he might have remained. Unfortunately on 16 December 1470 Jean died suddenly, reputedly from poison, and Ferry of Vaudémont also died around the same time, leaving the Angevins leaderless.[63]

The Angevins suffered again from their surfeit of territories, since Jean's legitimate son Nicholas was now Duke of Lorraine, and in the deteriorating situation with Burgundy he could not make an attempt on Catalonia. Jean also had a bastard son, Jean II, who with René's support went to Barcelona in an attempt to revive the Angevin claim, but he lacked the resources to do anything significant. By early 1472 Juan II had surrounded Barcelona, and when he offered the council reasonable terms they submitted, and Juan made a solemn entry into the city to seal the Aragonese victory.[64]

Despite his earlier misfortunes, for René the years 1470–72 must have seemed the most painful. He lost his son Jean, his son-in-law Ferry of Vaudémont, Naples was long gone and the three-year Angevin kingship in Barcelona had ended in complete defeat. Little did he know that even worse would follow.

Margaret of Anjou and Louis XI

The Lancastrians in England may also have been all but exterminated by 1465 (although Jasper Tudor was still at large), but Margaret now found an ally in the most unexpected place of all. Edward IV owed his throne to the Earl of Warwick, but once established as king he began to resent his cousin's influence. Relations between the two men soured over a series of diplomatic disagreements, and by 1467 Warwick had left the court. More importantly, Warwick was an advocate of peace with France and had led negotiations with Louis XI, with whom he was on good terms. Edward IV was determined to form an alliance with the French enemy Burgundy, and Warwick took that as his signal to rebel, since he would have the support of Louis XI. However, Warwick and Margaret had been the bitterest of enemies for fifteen years, and Warwick saw no need for Margaret's assistance yet.

When Warwick did rebel, in July 1469, he took Edward completely by surprise, and although Edward attempted to raise an army he was defeated and captured. Yet Warwick was in a strange position: he was not claiming the throne for himself, he was not posing as a Lancastrian champion and it was not clear if he was claiming to rule on behalf of Henry VI or Edward IV. When a Lancastrian revolt did break out in the north of England, it was to oppose Warwick just as much as Edward IV, and Warwick had to take the extraordinary step of releasing Edward, because the Yorkist army would only fight behind their own king. The Lancastrians were quickly crushed and Edward IV returned to London and to his throne. He and Warwick attempted to reconcile for the good of the kingdom, but neither trusted the other. Warwick now schemed to put Edward's brother, George Duke of Clarence, on the throne in his place, but the plot was discovered in 1470, and Warwick and Clarence fled to France as rebels.[65]

Louis XI justified his nickname of the 'Spider King', and drew together the enemies of Edward IV to make them see the logic of working together. Louis convinced Margaret that Warwick was her only hope, and arranged a meeting of the queen and the earl at Angers. Margaret accepted Warwick's oath of allegiance, though she made him kneel for fifteen minutes for the privilege of her favour. They agreed that Warwick would go to England first and lead a revolt to restore Henry VI to power, then Margaret and her son Edward would return to England and Edward would become regent for his father.[66]

Once again a stunning military reversal came seemingly from nowhere. Warwick landed in England and marched against Edward IV, who had managed to alienate key supporters and was unable to muster much resistance. Edward fled to the Netherlands to request assistance from his ally the Duke of Burgundy, and England was left to Warwick. Henry VI was released from the Tower, and Warwick held the king's train as he was formally restored to power in St Paul's cathedral.

Then exactly the same thing happened in reverse. The Duke of Burgundy, initially somewhat reluctant to be drawn into the English civil war, became more forthcoming when he knew Warwick supported Louis XI, with whom Burgundy was at war. Burgundy provided ships and money for Edward IV, who landed in Yorkshire, then swept into London unopposed. On the same day that Margaret and her son Edward arrived in Weymouth, Edward IV led his forces against Warwick at Barnet. On 14 April 1471, Warwick was killed and Edward IV was victorious.

Margaret still had an army and attempted to join Jasper Tudor in Wales, but Edward IV intercepted her at Tewkesbury. The Lancastrian army was defeated on 4 May, and worse, Margaret's seventeen-year-old son Edward was killed in the fighting. Edward IV had finally won a complete victory, and Margaret was paraded through London as part of Edward's triumphal procession. The next day Henry VI was also dead, said to have died of natural causes, but widely believed to have been murdered on Edward IV's orders, as there was now no reason to keep him alive. Although even in a conflict as ugly and sanguinary as the Wars of the Roses we still have many examples of kings and other key players being captured on the battlefield and not executed, when the Lancastrians were utterly defeated, Edward IV seems to have had no compunction about killing Henry VI, now that his death would not release a more able heir onto the field of battle.[67]

Margaret was imprisoned in the Tower, and then at Wallingford, where she was placed in the care of Alice Chaucer, who had received her as a teenager in Rouen on the way to meet her destiny in England. Louis XI ransomed her in 1475 and allowed her to return to Anjou, but his price was that she reaffirm her relinquishment of any rights of inheritance to the duchy – given that her brothers were dead and René was sixty-six – sealing Anjou's fate to be reabsorbed by the crown.[68] Margaret returned to Anjou to live with René, surviving him by two years and dying in 1482. She was buried next to her father in the cathedral of Angers, joining him in the tomb (which René naturally had designed himself) showing a skeleton king losing his crown, a bitter testament to the vanity of both their hopes. She did not survive to see the death of Richard III in 1485 at Bosworth Field, which by ending the hated line of York and replacing the Plantagenets with the Tudors, truly ended Angevin rule in England.

Margaret divides opinion. It is just as easy to characterize her as an overbearing, ambitious and ruthless queen who used her power over her feeble-minded husband to dominate the government and bend English policy to her own aims, as to say that she was a woman of iron determination who attempted to maintain order in the kingdom despite her husband's incompetence and preserve the throne for her son, the rightful heir. These two views are not mutually exclusive.

Despite her perseverance and the undoubted success of some of her policies and actions, Margaret ultimately faced a tragic defeat, with her husband and son killed, her throne lost and her final years spent in obscurity. Yet her character and eventful life make her a gift for the dramatist, as Shakespeare was quick to see, and she is one of the most compelling characters in his history plays, albeit as a villain, making her one of the more recognizable characters from the Angevin story in the modern world.

As the 'She-Wolf' of France, she takes her place beside Lady Macbeth or Gertrude as a compelling and complex character, and although doubtless she would find this cold comfort, it is a not unfitting epitaph for her.

King René's Final Years: *Le Bon Roi René*

The dreadful events of the 1470s continued for the Angevins. René's illegitimate daughter Blanche of Anjou died in 1470, his brother Charles of Maine died in 1472, and worst of all, on 27 July 1473, came the death of his grandson Nicholas Duke of Lorraine, the son of Jean of Calabria. Nicholas died like his father, probably from poison, as he had broken off relations with Louis XI and was in the midst of marriage negotiations with the Burgundians, which seem to have been undertaken in opposition to King René.[69] Lorraine now passed to René and Isabelle's last surviving child, Yolande of Bar. She and Ferry de Vaudémont had a son, René II, and Yolande gave the duchy to her son, who took formal possession of it in Nancy on 4 August 1473.

The Second House of Anjou was in a succession crisis, especially as René II made it clear that he expected all of King René's inheritance, despite opposing his grandfather at every turn in favour of Louis XI. King René responded by making a will on 22 July 1474 that confirmed René II as Duke of Bar, which should be joined permanently to Lorraine, but making Charles II of Maine, his brother's son, the heir to Anjou, Maine and Provence.

This created an extremely complicated situation between Louis XI of France, René II of Bar and Lorraine, Charles of Burgundy and King René. On one hand, Charles continued to encroach on Lorraine and drove René II towards an alliance with Louis. On the other, Louis had seized Bar and Anjou, perhaps driving King René into an unlikely alliance with Burgundy. Although it is not entirely clear, King René does seem at least to have started negotiations with Charles of Burgundy for aid against Louis, and the price of this support was said to be Provence.

If true, this was nothing short of treason, and in April 1476 Louis XI summoned René before the *parlement* of Paris to answer charges for his dealings with Burgundy. Louis's intentions were quite clear: the apanage system of Louis VIII had finally broken down, and Louis XI was determined to have Anjou.[70]

In May 1476 Louis and René met in Lyon to reach an understanding, and Louis returned Anjou to René on 25 May with the provision that it would pass to Charles II of Maine on his death. Part of their understanding had also been Louis's ransoming of Margaret of Anjou from England. René seems to have been exhausted by the struggle with Louis XI, and without anyone to support him accepted any agreement that would allow him to spend the rest of his life quietly in Provence.[71]

René II, however, had chosen his allies well. René II declared war on Burgundy on 9 May 1475, and joined the League of Constance, a confederation of German and

Swiss towns opposing Burgundy. Although Charles of Burgundy invaded Lorraine in September 1475 and captured Nancy in November, he now began to suffer defeats at the hands of the Swiss – the astonishing new military power in Europe – and his power was waning. Vaudémont, part of René II's inheritance from his father Ferry, rebelled against Burgundy in April 1476 following a Burgundian defeat. Charles of Burgundy was known as *le Téméraire*, usually translated as 'the Bold' but equally validly as 'the Reckless', and he kept attacking the Swiss to avenge his defeats, and kept losing. On 2 March 1476 Charles was defeated by a Swiss army at Grandson, and when he attempted to avenge himself the Swiss defeated him again on 22 June at Morat. René II now swept back into Nancy on 6 October with Swiss support.

Charles lived up to his name and attacked again, although his army was now greatly depleted and it was the middle of winter. On 5 January 1477 he returned to Nancy, where he met the Swiss again, who were led by René II. The Burgundians were out-numbered and ill-supplied, and in another overwhelming defeat Charles was killed. Famously, Charles's naked, frozen body was only found two days later, and was so mangled and disfigured that it could only be identified by his long fingernails and his scars from old wounds. René II buried Charles honourably in Nancy, but after Charles's only child, Mary of Burgundy, married Maximilian of Habsburg and joined the family's fortunes to that great dynasty, Charles's body was removed to Bruges where his magnificent tomb survives.[72]

The struggle with Louis XI and tangential involvement in the Burgundian wars must have been an unwelcome interruption for King René, who from 1471 lived per-manently in Provence. It is this period of his life that led to his appellation of 'the good king' – *le bon roi René* – as his lifetime of chivalric pursuits was concentrated into a perfect rural idyll, with his court the epitome of culture and benign rule. Because he remained King René and his queen was Jeanne of Laval, there would later be confusion, and Queen Johanna I of Naples (who had always been known by the French form of her name, Jeanne, in Provence) became known retrospectively as 'Good Queen Jeanne', the great patron of the arts. Given everything that happened to Johanna, it is fitting that at least in Provence she is remembered fondly.[73]

René's rule was 'good' not just because he himself was a learned king. He included nobles and prelates on his councils and gave them some voice in the rule of the county, as well as regulating taxes. More importantly though, René's rule was consciously styled as a golden age. His pastoral poem *Regnault and Jehanneton* was the template for his court, and stories tell of him providing food for the sheep shearers at Aix and holding pageants at his parks and residence, with decorations and musicians.[74]

This musical involvement connects René to another great figure of the age, Josquin des Prez, perhaps the most important composer of the early Renaissance. Josquin is known to have been a singer in René's chapel in Aix until at least 1478, and after René's death he maintained his Angevin connection by moving to the Sforza court in Milan. It was in Italy that he produced the music for which he is justly renowned today, but it is fitting that his career started in the highly cosmopolitan environment of René's Provence.[75]

René's own artistic credentials began early in the cultured atmosphere created in Angers by Louis I and continued by Louis II and Yolande of Aragon, but he was exposed to an unprecedented variety of influences. In 1419, the eleven-year-old René went to the court of his uncle the Cardinal Duke of Bar and then to Lorraine, courts that were culturally and politically just as German as they were French. In the aftermath of Agincourt when France itself was practically annexed by England, Burgundy was the primary continental power politically as well as artistically, and René was in Dijon (though as a prisoner) in 1432 and then 1434–35, and also spent time in Brussels, the centre of Flemish art.[76] It may have been here that he formed an attachment to the van Eyck family, particularly Barthélemy van Eyck, who illustrated the most iconic manuscripts of René's works and worked for him from around 1445 until 1470.

The idea that René himself was a painter took hold from the late 15th century, and evolved into the story that René was trained by the great Jan van Eyck, then went on to produce various works of his own, beginning during his imprisonment in Dijon, but continuing throughout his life and even extending to the painting for his own tomb. Within eighty years of René's death, the essayist Michel de Montaigne could write:

> I saw today [in September 1559], at Bar-le-duc, that King François II had been presented, in memory of René, King of Sicily, a self-portrait that he himself had painted.[77]

There is not any direct evidence for this, and although contemporaries credited René with 'designing' many of the paintings and illuminations that would be created by members of his court such as Nicholas Froment and Barthélemy van Eyck, it seems more likely that René commissioned the works and perhaps described what he wanted, rather than playing a direct part. If there was a tension between the political and military duties of a king being incompatible with being too bookish or writing himself, there was a greater stigma attached to a king participating in the 'manual' arts like painting (and indeed Montaigne's essay cited above is in the context of Montaigne wondering whether it is as valid to draw a self-portrait with a pencil as it is to write one with a pen). If René was inspired by the brilliant artists around him to attempt drawing himself, lack of evidence prevents us from attributing any specific work to him, and the fact that he did employ Froment and van Eyck to produce such copious works suggests that he left painting to the professionals.

When I began discussions of the early Angevins I lamented the lack of any portraits until a much later period. We are now in this period and there are multiple portraits of René in oil, illumination, stained glass, sculpture, medals and even in a cameo. The only problem is that he seems to have been astonishingly unattractive, and can only be described as a *lump*. It is a shock to see the dashing, cultured, ideal patron of courtly

society appearing as he does, but I think in the end it makes him more endearing. His
most famous portraits are his diptych with his second wife Jeanne de Laval by Nicholas
Froment in the Louvre, Froment's *Triptych of the Burning Bush* in Aix-en-Provence
which shows René and Jeanne on the side panels, and the medals of René and Jeanne,
individually and together, by Francesco Laurana. Although much more visible, the
statues of René that stand in Angers and Aix-en-Provence are romanticized relatively
modern works that show his enduring impact in those cities.

With his brief rule in Naples and his other travels in Italy, René was the most
Italianized of all the French princes with the widest range of interests. To call him a
'Renaissance' prince perhaps misses the mark, though it is hard to see how he differs
substantially from figures such as Federigo da Montefeltro, Sigismundo Malatesta, the
Gonzaga, the Este and the Sforza. One difference is that he did not leave a single cultural centre like Urbino, Rimini, Mantua, Ferrara or Milan where we can see a coherent
body of his cultural production. More fatal is René's passion for chivalry: he can only
seem backward-looking with his treatise on tournaments, chivalric allegories and residence in fortified castles. Yet René had a library of books in Greek and patronized the
music of Josquin de Prez, and any Italian prince in this position would be hailed as a
paragon of modern taste.[78]

If we consider another fundamental dividing line between medieval and modern
Europe, the discovery of the New World, which forever changed European economics
and politics, the key name is Christopher Columbus. It is slightly shocking, but not
really surprising, that Columbus, the discoverer of the New World and the herald of
a complete rupture with the past, might have worked for King René. Yet Columbus
claimed in a letter that he had been hired by René to attack pirate bases in Tunisia, and
although there is some question about whether this is true, there are also claims that
Columbus was involved in the naval battles of Jean II against the Aragonese. It would
not be so odd for Columbus to be part of a court that contained the latest geographical
texts and maps (like those sent to René by Jacopo Marcello), even if he had to go to
Spain to find rulers with enough money to fund his voyages.[79]

René died on 10 July 1480. Although he chose to spend his final years in Provence,
he had always intended to be buried in Anjou next to Isabelle of Lorraine, and he had
made detailed plans for their tomb. This was inspired by the tombs in Santa Chiara,
and René himself is credited with the design – and formerly even for executing the
painting – which consisted of supine effigies of him and his wife in robes, and behind
them a painting of a mummified, enthroned skeleton king who had dropped his sceptre
and whose crown slipped from his head. This image of the *roi mort* was one that René
had used frequently as a *memento mori* in his manuscripts, and it is truly arresting.
Unfortunately the tomb itself does not survive, although drawings of it do. As with
Fulk Nerra, the grave beneath the tomb was opened in the 19th century, and in 1895
René and Isabelle's bodies were found intact, and given new coffins.[80]

Although by the time of René's death, Anjou and his first duchy of Bar were gone or slipping away, he had long since lost Naples and his children had died in bitter circumstances, with Margaret and Jean losing their own realms in England and Aragon, he seems to have led a contented and productive life. 'Le bon roi René', although taken as a study in failure by many modern historians, is significant for more than simply the crowns he claimed but never wore. Although he is sometimes used as an example of the foolishness of chivalry, portrayed as the stupidly chivalrous French knight who failed because he was no match for the ruthlessness of Italian politics, he is much more than a sad 'king without a kingdom'. His literary output, artistic commissions and participation in the Hundred Years War make him one of the most important – and interesting – figures of the 15th century.

After René's death, Angevin fortunes quickly declined. René II's bad relationship with his grandfather was carried over to King René's successor, and René II led a revolt in Provence against Charles II of Maine. Charles was only able to quell the revolt with help from Louis XI, who expected to take the county himself. Charles then died in 1481.

As had been arranged, Charles left Maine and Provence to Louis XI, who died on 30 Aug 1483, and the counties passed to Louis's successor Charles VIII. The Angevin claims to Italy were not forgotten, and whenever other Italian powers were in conflicts with Naples, they would revive the idea that the Angevins might be invited to reconquer the Regno. In 1483, René II led an army to Italy with some initial success, but when he heard about the death of Louis XI he returned to France to try to claim Anjou and Provence. René II was invited back to Italy again in 1488, but Charles VIII prevented him from accepting because the French king wanted to invade Italy himself using the Angevin claim.

With the main lines mostly extinguished, Naples in the hands of Aragon, Hungary and Poland passing to other families, England passing to the Tudors and Anjou itself in the possession of the French crown, the Angevin story is finished. Of course there were still Angevin descendants – René II's line of Vaudémont/Lorraine ruled for centuries and became the renowned house of Guise, including Mary of Guise who would give birth to Mary Queen of Scots – but we can no longer really talk of 'Angevin' ruling families. As the Angevins were the quintessential medieval rulers, perhaps this is appropriate, since the end of the 15th century is the beginning of the 'modern world', and rulers in the mould of King René no longer had a place.[81]

EPILOGUE

I N 1494 CHARLES VIII of France invaded Italy. This has frequently been claimed as the origin of 'modern warfare'[1] because Charles carried mobile cannons that allowed him to achieve stunning success quite rapidly. Yet the basis for Charles's invasion was his inheritance of the Angevin claim to Naples – the legacy of Charles of Anjou, which had cursed the Angevins for two centuries and now embroiled the French king. Though this might have given sufficient legitimacy to Charles's claim, he went further and also wrapped his enterprise in the mantle of a great Crusade against the Turks;[2] our old friend the Crusading ideal puts in another appearance, and although there would never actually be another Crusade, this ideal provided inspiration for characters as diverse as Henry VIII of England and François I of France throughout the 16th century.

So the Angevins have never been forgotten. The castles of Angers, Saumur, Chinon, Langeais and Loches, among many others, still maintain enough of their medieval form to remind us of all three lines of Angevin rulers, from Fulk Nerra to Charles of Anjou to King René. In England, Henry II, Eleanor of Aquitaine, Richard the Lionheart and John are well remembered in fact as well as fantasy, and the institutions perfected during their reigns are still with us for better (Magna Carta) or worse (bureaucracy and paperwork). The Angevins are perhaps most fondly remembered in Provence, where 'le bon roi René' and 'Good Queen Jeanne' presided over a golden age, even if there is some confusion over which Queen Jeanne is meant.

Naples retains the best and most impressive material remains of the Angevins: the Castel Nuovo or *Maschio Angioino*, the tombs in Santa Chiara and San Giovanni Carbonara, the frescoes in the Incoronata and the painting of Louis of Toulouse and Robert the Wise in the Capodimonte Museum. At the opposite extreme, Hungary has almost nothing left to commemorate the Angevins, since their tombs in Székesfehérvár were destroyed, although their gifts to Zara remain. Poland, although Angevin for such a short time, fares better and at least has the shrine to Jadwiga in Wawel cathedral.

These were their main territories, but all their other claims mean the Angevins crop up in other places, as with Charles of Anjou's statue in the Capitoline Museum in Rome and King René's coat of arms appearing in terracotta on the Pazzi palace in Florence, or indeed as the coat of arms of New College, Cambridge, which was re-established by Margaret of Anjou, who used her father's arms. In Germany bitterness about the execution of Conradin remained throughout the 19th century and is still remembered today.

The Angevin Empire even has echoes in the present, and it has been suggested that the Channel Islands form the last vestige of the Angevin Empire. More astonishingly, in 2012 the city of Angers somewhat facetiously claimed the British Crown Jewels as reparations for the harm done to the Plantagenets, though unsurprisingly without success.

What is most fascinating about the Angevins is their utter ubiquity: every important development of the Middle Ages, every important person and practically every realm encountered them in some way. Even if they did not succeed in becoming 'lords of the greatest part of the world', as was said of Charles of Anjou, making their acquaintance forms an introduction to the entire world of the Middle Ages, and I hope the time spent in their company has been enjoyable.

NOTES

Chapter 1

1. Norgate, Kate. *England under the Angevin Kings*, vol. 1, p98.
2. Norgate, vol. 1, pp27–28.
3. Dunbabin, Jean. *France in the Making 843–1180*, pp7–9.
4. James, Edward. *Origins of France*, p75.
5. Southern, R.W. *The Making of the Middle Ages*, p86.
6. Comnena, Anna, *The Alexiad*, Book XIII, chapter VIII.
7. Dunbabin, *France in the Making*, pp3–5.
8. Dunbabin, *France in the Making*, pp22–23.
9. Potter, David ed. *France in the Later Middle Ages*, p113.
10. Marchegay, Paul and Salmon, André, eds. *Chroniques d'Anjou*. Vol. 1, *Gesta Consulum Andegavorum et Dominorum Ambaziensium*. This will hereafter be known as the *Gesta* in the text without individual references.
11. Halphen, Louis. *Le Comté d'Anjou au XIe Siècle*, pVI. Fulk Réchin wrote his account in c1096.
12. Bachrach, Bernard. *State-building in Medieval France: Studies in Early Angevin History*, p3.
13. Bachrach, *State-building*, p4.
14. Norgate, vol. 1, pp126–32.
15. Bachrach, *State-building*, p3.
16. Bachrach, Bernard. *Fulk Nerra, the Neo-Roman Consul 987–1040*, p5.
17. Dunbabin, *France in the Making*, p24.
18. *Gesta*, p74; also Norgate p114.
19. William of Malmesbury, p130. Norgate also refers to this confusion, vol. 1, p114.
20. Dante, *Paradiso*, canto VIII, lines 82–3 and 139–48, pp75, 79.
21. Bachrach, *State-building*, p8 (in footnote).
22. Norgate, vol. 1, p140.
23. Hallam, Elizabeth M. *The Plantagenet Chronicles*, pp22–24.
24. Dunbabin, *France in the Making*, p 248.
25. Dunbabin, *France in the Making*, p175.
26. Southern, p82.
27. Halphen, pp210–12.
28. Norgate, vol. 1, pp147–48.
29. Halphen, p34.
30. Halphen, p68.
31. Halphen, p30.
32. Dunbabin, *France in the Making*, p185.
33. Dunbabin, *France in the Making*, p187.
34. Halphen, p130.
35. Norgate vol. 1, p155.
36. Bachrach, *Fulk Nerra*, p252.
37. Runciman, *History of the Crusades*, vol. 1, pp29–30.
38. Hallam, *The Plantagenet Chronicles*, p28.
39. Norgate, vol. 1, p168.
40. Halphen, p33.
41. Norgate, vol. 1, p166.
42. Halphen, p62, footnote 3.
43. Bachrach, *Fulk Nerra*, p76.
44. Halphen, pp62–63.
45. Salies, p46.
46. Norgate, vol. 1, p152.
47. Norgate, vol. 1, pp165–66, footnote.
48. Dunbabin, *France in the Making*, p132.
49. Michaud, pp60–61.
50. Salies, notes CXXXI and CXXXII.
51. Salies, p1.
52. Norgate, vol. 1, pp150–51.
53. Southern, pp81–86.

Chapter 2

1. Norgate, vol. 1, p170.
2. Norgate, vol. 1, pp174–75.
3. Dunbabin, *France in the Making*, p176.
4. Halphen, pp70–71.
5. Halphen, pp69–75.
6. *Plantagenet Chronicles*, p33.
7. Halphen, p56.
8. *Plantagenet Chronicles*, p33.
9. Norgate, vol. 1, p170 quoting Malmesbury.
10. Malmesbury, pp8–9,
11. Norgate, vol. 1, p171.
12. Malmesbury, p11.
13. *Plantagenet Chronicles*, p30.
14. Oman, *Castles*, p7.
15. Barker, Juliet and Barber, Malcolm, *Tournaments*, p15.
16. Douglas, David. *The Norman Achievement*, pp34–35.
17. Douglas, *The Norman Achievement*, p40.
18. Douglas, *The Norman Achievement*, p41.
19. Douglas, *The Norman Achievement*, pp53–55.
20. Douglas, *The Norman Achievement*, pp57–58.
21. Douglas, David. *William the Conqueror*, p228.
22. *Plantagenet Chronicles*, p33.
23. Marchegay, Paul and Salmon, André, eds. *Chroniques d'Anjou*. Vol. 1, *Fragmentum Historiae Andegavensis, auctore Fulcone Rechin*, p379.
24. Norgate, vol. 1, p216.
25. Halphen, p139.
26. Halphen, p144.
27. Halphen p150.
28. Malmesbury, p12.
29. Norgate, vol. 1, p229.
30. Malmesbury, p31.
31. Norgate, vol. 1, p229.
32. *Plantagenet Chronicles*, p36.
33. *Plantagenet Chronicles*, p37.
34. Malmesbury, p30.
35. *Plantagenet Chronicles*, p37.
36. Marchegay and Salmon, *Chroniques d'Anjou, Fulk Réchin*, pp375.
37. Halphen, p210.
38. Malmesbury, p66, note 4.

Chapter 3

1. *Plantagenet Chronicles*, p37.
2. Malmesbury, p13.
3. Norgate, vol. 1, p233.
4. *Gesta*, p151.
5. Warren, *Henry II*, p10.
6. Poole, A.L. *Domesday Book to Magna Carta*, p125.
7. Poole, p128.
8. Roziére, Eugène de. *Cartulaire de Saint Sépulcre*, pp17–18.
9. Runciman, *Crusades*, vol. 2 p24.
10. Runciman, *Crusades*, vol. 2, p39.
11. Runciman, *Crusades*, vol. 2, p388.
12. Runciman, *Crusades*, vol. 2, p116.
13. Seward, *Monks of War*, pp16–21.
14. Runciman, *Crusades*, vol. 2, pp150–51.
15. Runciman, *Crusades*, vol. 2, p144.
16. Martin, Therese. 'The Art of a Reigning Queen as Dynastic Propaganda in Twelfth-century Spain', Speculum vol. 80, p 1166.
17. Runciman, *Crusades*, vol. 2, p153.
18. Runciman, *Crusades*, vol. 2, p154.
19. Runciman, *Crusades*, vol. 2, p155.
20. Martin, 'The Art of a Reigning Queen', p1164.
21. Quoted in Martin, 'Art of a Reigning Queen', p1164.
22. Cormack, Robin and Maria Vassilaki, eds. *Byzantium: 330–1453*, pp299, 446.
23. Clanchy, M.T. *England and its Rulers 1066–1272: Foreign Lordship and National Identity*, p30.
24. Gillingham, John. *The Angevin Empire*, p8. This phrase 'tu felix [Austria] nube' would become much more famously associated with the Habsburgs, and in that context is attributed to Matthias Corvinus, the successor of the Angevins in Hungary, who amassed a famous library and was so well read that he may easily have known about the previous 12th-century reference.
25. Runciman, *Crusades*, vol. 2, p184.
26. Plant, p63.
27. *Plantagenet Chronicles*, pp46–48.
28. Marchegay, Paul and Salmon, André, eds. *Chroniques d'Anjou*, vol. 1, *Historia Gaufredi Ducis Normannorum et Comitis Andegavorum*, pp285–86.

29. Gillingham, John. *Richard the Lionheart*, p45.
30. *Plantagenet Chronicles*, p52.
31. *Plantagenet Chronicles*, pp53–54.
32. *Plantagenet Chronicles*, p47.
33. Warren, *Henry II*, p12, quoting Glanvill.
34. Warren, *Henry II*, p14.
35. Gillingham, *The Angevin Empire*, p14.
36. Norgate, vol. 1, p264.
37. Clanchy, p113.
38. Clanchy, p 116
39. Castor, Helen, *She-Wolves: The Women Who Ruled England Before Elizabeth*, p89.
40. Warren, *Henry II*, pp26–28.
41. Stafford, Pauline. 'The Portrayal of Royal Women in England, Mid-Tenth to Mid-Twelfth Centuries', in *Medieval Queenship*, p158.
42. Painter, Sidney. *William Marshall*, pp7–8.
43. Warren, *Henry II*, p28.
44. *Plantagenet Chronicles*, p74.
45. Boyle, David. *The Troubadour's Song: The Capture and Ransom of Richard the Lionheart*, p2.
46. Warren, *Henry II*, pp33–34.
47. Painter, p15.
48. Weir, Alison, *Eleanor of Aquitaine*, p8.
49. Dunbabin, *France in the Making*, p179.
50. Weir, pp11–12.
51. Gillingham, John. *Richard I*, p25.
52. Castor, *She-Wolves*, p135.
53. Weir, p32.
54. Weir, pp38, 43.
55. Tolhurst, Fiona. *Geoffrey of Monmouth and the Translation of Female Kingship*, pp3–4.
56. Weir, p45.
57. Gillingham, *Richard the Lionheart*, pp111–12.
58. Weir, p52.
59. Weir, p54.
60. Weir, pp67–68.
61. Weir, pp68–69.
62. Martin, 'Art of a Reigning Queen', p1164.
63. Runciman, *Crusades*, vol. 2, p210.
64. Weir, p74.
65. *Plantagenet Chronicles*, p78.
66. Runciman, *Crusades*, vol. 2, p266.
67. Weir, pp87–88.
68. Warren, *Henry II*, p223.
69. Weir, pp88–89.
70. Warren, *Henry II*, p46.
71. Weir, p90.
72. Warren, *Henry II*, p45.
73. Warren, *Henry II*, pp51–52.
74. Warren, *Henry II*, p53.

Chapter 4
1. Dunbabin, *France in the Making*, p336.
2. Quoted in Clanchy, p111.
3. Clancy pp114–15.
4. All three quotes from Norgate, p409.
5. *Plantagenet Chronicles*, p84.
6. Norgate, vol. 1, p410 and p422, quoting Peter of Blois.
7. Clanchy, p114.
8. Norgate, vol. 1, p411.
9. Warren, *Henry II*, pp207–8.
10. Henderson, Ernest F, trans and ed. *Select Historical Documents of the Middle Ages*, p22.
11. Clanchy, pp77–79.
12. Clanchy, pp80–82.
13. Gillingham, *Richard the Lionheart*, p31.
14. Harper-Bill, Christopher and Vincent, Nicholas, eds. *Henry II: New Interpretations*, p320.
15. Warren, *Henry II*, pp629–30.

16. Warren, *Henry II*, p234.
17. Warren, *Henry II*, p235.
18. Warren, *Henry II*, p232.
19. Warren, *Henry II*, p65.
20. Warren, *Henry II*, p65.
21. Gillingham, *Richard the Lionheart*, p28.
22. Warren, *Henry II*, p72.
23. Gillingham, *Richard I*, p38.
24. Weir, circa p154.
25. Gillingham, *Richard the Lionheart*, pp29–30.
26. Weir, p149.
27. *Plantagenet Chronicles*, pp108–9.
28. Kibler, William W. ed. *Eleanor of Aquitaine: Patron and Politician*, p69.
29. *Plantagenet Chronicles*, p116.
30. Warren, *Henry II*, p112.
31. Warren, *Henry II*, p113.
32. Barker and Barber, *Tournaments*, p23.
33. Malmesbury, p31.
34. Painter, p41.
35. Painter, pp20–21.
36. Gillingham, *Richard the Lionheart*, p118.
37. Gillingham, *Richard the Lionheart*, p118.
38. Painter, p24.
39. Painter, pp39–40.
40. Painter, p27.
41. Painter, pp31–49.
42. Warren, *Henry II*, p117.
43. Gillingham, *Richard I*, p43.
44. Warren, *Henry II*, p135.
45. Dante, *Inferno*, canto XXVIII, lines 118–142, p263.
46. Warren, *Henry II*, p119.
47. Baldwin, John. *The Government of Philip Augustus*, p6.
48. Weir, p179.
49. Warren, *Henry II*, p601, note, quoting Roger of Howden.
50. *Plantagenet Chronicles*, pp101–2.
51. Weir, p172.
52. Weir, p172. [and Thomas Deloney/Delaney download, also quoted in Plant Chronicles, p105]
53. Weir, p225.
54. Rigord, *La vie de Philippe II Auguste*, p23.
55. Baldwin, John W., *The Government of Philip Augustus*, p3.
56. Gillingham, *Richard the Lionheart*, p29.
57. *Plantagenet Chronicles*, p57.
58. Dunbabin, *France in the Making*, p348.
59. Gillingham, *Richard the Lionheart*, p90.
60. Gillingham, *Richard the Lionheart*, p91.
61. Gillingham, *Richard the Lionheart*, p93.
62. Gillingham, *Richard the Lionheart*, pp96–98.
63. Warren, *King John*, p36.
64. Gillingham, *Richard the Lionheart*, p100.
65. Warren, *Henry II*, p596.
66. Gillingham, *Richard the Lionheart*, p101.
67. Gillingham, *Richard the Lionheart*, p102.
68. Gillingham, *Richard the Lionheart*, p104.
69. Gillingham, *Richard the Lionheart*, p107.
70. Gillingham, *Richard I*, p84.
71. Chrétien de Troyes, Erec et Enide, p77.
72. Runciman, *Crusades*, vol. 2, pp272–73.
73. Gillingham, *Richard I*, p27.
74. Weir, p176.
75. Mayer, Hans Eberhard. 'Studies in the History of Queen Melisende of Jerusalem', pp169–70.
76. Runciman, *Crusades*, vol. 2, p295.
77. Holt, *The Age of the Crusades*, p47.
78. Holt, *The Age of the Crusades*, pp48–49.
79. Holt, *The Age of the Crusades*, pp51–52.
80. Staines, David trans. *The Complete Romances of Chrétien de Troyes, Yvain*, p264 (v581–646).
81. Runciman, *Crusades*, vol. 2, pp359–65.

82. Holt, *The Age of the Crusades*, pp54–56.
83. Runciman, *Crusades*, vol. 2, pp370–71.
84. Runciman, *Crusades*, vol. 2, pp373–75.
85. Gillingham, *Richard the Lionheart*, p111.
86. Gillingham, *Richard the Lionheart*, p120.
87. Warren, *Henry II*, p622.
88. Norgate, vol. 2., p261.
89. Norgate, vol. 2, p267.
90. Boyle, p65.
91. Gillingham, *Richard I*, p100.

Chapter 5
1. Gillingham, *Richard I*, p9.
2. Gillingham, *Richard I*, p8.
3. Gillingham, *Richard I*, p6.
4. Gillingham, *Richard I*, p105.
5. Gillingham, *Richard I*, p109.
6. Gillingham, *Richard I*, p108, noting that the CD is available: *Music for the Lionhearted King. Music to Mark the 800th Anniversary of the Coronation of Richard I of England*, Gothic Voices dir. Christopher Page, Hyperion CDA66336, 1989.
7. Boyle, p45.
8. Gillingham, *Richard I*, p109.
9. Benham, JEM. 'Philip Augustus and the Angevin Empire: The Scandinavian Connection', *Mediaeval Scandinavia*, pp37–42.
10. Benham, pp49–50.
11. Gillingham, *Richard the Lionheart*, p133.
12. Runciman, *Crusades*, vol. 3, p13.
13. Boccaccio, Giovanni, trans. GH McWilliam. *The Decameron*, Day 1, story 5, p48.
14. Norgate, *Richard the Lionheart*, p124.
15. Gillingham, *Richard the Lionheart*, pp152–53.
16. Gillingham, *Richard the Lionheart*, p159.
17. Gillingham, *Richard the Lionheart*, p160.
18. Gillingham, *Richard the Lionheart*, pp161–62.
19. Norgate, *Richard the Lionheart*, p146.
20. Runciman, *Crusades*, vol. 3, p18.
21. Runciman, *Crusades*, vol. 3, p23.
22. Gillingham, *Richard the Lionheart*, pp165–67.
23. Gillingham, *Richard I*, p3.
24. Runciman, *Crusades*, vol. 3, pp43–44.
25. *Heraldry*, p91.
26. Norgate, *Richard the Lionheart*, p250.
27. Norgate, *Richard the Lionheart*, pp254–55.
28. Boyle, p154.
29. Boyle, p176.
30. Gillingham, *Richard the Lionheart*, pp224–25.
31. Gillingham, *Richard the Lionheart*, p234.
32. Boyle, p199. The song can be heard on *The Cross of Red: Music of Love and War from the Time of the Crusades*, New Orleans Musica da Camera, Centaur (CRC 2373), 1998.
33. Norgate, *Richard the Lionheart*, p278.
34. Gillingham, *Richard I*, p31.
35. Gillingham, *Richard the Lionheart*, p33.
36. Norgate, *Richard the Lionheart*, p199.
37. Gillingham, *Richard I*, pp256–57.
38. Gillingham, Lionheart or Richard I, pp264–65.
39. Norgate, vol. 2, p380.
40. Norgate, vol. 2, p380.
41. Gillingham, Lionheart or Richard I, p264.
42. Gillingham, John. 'The Unromantic Death of Richard I', passim.
43. Gillingham, *Richard the Lionheart*, p13.
44. Joinville, *Life of St Louis*, p305.

Chapter 6

1. Clanchy, p192.
2. Warren, *King John*, pp49–50.
3. Gillingham, *The Angevin Empire*, p87.
4. Powicke, FM. *The Loss of Normandy*, p194.
5. Warren, *King John*, p53.
6. Warren, *King John*, pp54–56.
7. Warren, *King John*, p56.
8. Warren, *King John*, pp67–69.
9. Clanchy, pp186–87.
10. Powicke, *Loss of Normandy*, p223.
11. *Plantagenet Chronicles*, p274.
12. Powicke, *Loss of Normandy*, p234.
13. Warren, *King John*, p91.
14. Powicke, *Loss of Normandy*, p340.
15. Warren, *King John*, p96.
16. Powicke, *Loss of Normandy*, p457.
17. Warren, *King John*, p86.
18. Powicke, *Loss of Normandy*, pp248–49.
19. Warren, *King John*, p95.
20. Powicke, *Loss of Normandy*, p375, note – bridge was the defect; Warren, *King John*, p95; Gillingham, *The Angevin Empire*, p93.
21. Warren, *King John*, p96.
22. Seward, *Monks of War*, p36.
23. Villehardouin, pp34–35.
24. Ruskin, John. *The Stones of Venice*. In Rosenberg, John D, ed. *The Genius of John Ruskin: Selections from his Writings*, p142.
25. Villehardouin p75.
26. Villehardouin, p92.
27. Villehardouin, p95.
28. Lock, Peter. *The Franks in the Aegean*, p47, quoting J. Linskill's translation.
29. Warren, *King John*, p116.
30. Warren, *King John*, pp117–20.
31. Villani, Book V, section 38, p149.
32. Weiler, Björn K.U. with Rowlands, Ifor W eds. *England and Europe in the reign of Henry III (1216–1272)*, Chapter 4.
33. Duby, *Le dimanche de Bouvines*, passim.
34. Warren, *King John*, p226.
35. Warren, *King John*, p234.
36. Warren, *King John*, pp265–67.
37. Carpenter, D.A. *Minority of Henry III*, pp382–84.
38. Warren, *King John*, p253.
39. Warren, *King John*, p254.
40. Clanchy, p 201.
41. Dante, *Inferno*, Canto X, verse 119, p93.
42. Runciman, *Crusades*, vol. 3, pp122–23.
43. Runciman, *Crusades*, vol. 3, pp134–35.
44. Runciman, *Crusades*, vol. 3, pp146–47.
45. Runciman, *Crusades*, vol. 3, p149.
46. Housley, *The Italian Crusades*, p42.

Chapter 7

1. Dunbabin, Jean. *Charles of Anjou*, p12.
2. Powicke, *The Thirteenth century*, p87.
3. Powicke, *The Thirteenth century*, p89.
4. Powicke, *The Thirteenth century*, p95.
5. Vacquet, Étienne (editor). *Saint Louis et l'Anjou*, pp71ff.
6. Powicke, *The Thirteenth century*, p103.
7. Dunbabin, *Charles of Anjou*, p10. Although the term 'porphyrogenitus' is specifically Byzantine, the concept goes back at least as far as the 5th century BC. Herodotus in the *Persian Wars* (Book VII, Chapter 3) alludes to the fact that in Sparta a son born to a king after he took the throne had a superior claim to any previous sons.
8. Jehel, Georges. *Les Angevins de Naples*, p94.
9. Dunbabin, *Charles of Anjou*, p42.
10. Dunbabin, *Charles of Anjou*, p42.
11. Dante, *Purgatorio*, Canto 20, lines 61–65, pp187, 89.
12. Dunbabin, *Charles of Anjou*, p13.
13. Gardner, Julian. 'Seated kings, sea-faring saints and heraldry : some themes in Angevin iconography', *L'État angevin. Pouvoir, culture et société entre XIIIe et XIVe siècle. Actes du colloque international (Rome-Naples, 7–11 novembre 1995)*, pp120–21.
14. Dunbabin, *Charles of Anjou*, p9.
15. Aurell, *La Vielle et L'Epee*, pp161–62.
16. Abulafia, David. *The Western Mediterranean Kingdoms*, p47.
17. Joinville, p263.
18. Joinville, p265.
19. Joinville, p272.
20. Joinville, p274.
21. Dunbabin, *Charles of Anjou*, p47.
22. Dunbabin, *Charles of Anjou*, pp52–53.
23. Barraclough, *The Medieval Papacy*, p95.
24. Barraclough, *The Medieval Papacy*, p114.
25. Barraclough, *The Medieval Papacy*, pp115–16.
26. Runciman, *The Sicilian Vespers*, p57.
27. Housley, *The Italian Crusades*, p82.
28. Runciman, *The Sicilian Vespers*, p30.
29. Runciman, *The Sicilian Vespers*, pp64–65.
30. Runciman, *The Sicilian Vespers*, pp32–33.
31. Vale, *Origins of the Hundred Years War*, p56.
32. Runciman, *The Sicilian Vespers*, p35.
33. Housley, *The Italian Crusades*, p42.
34. Runciman, *The Sicilian Vespers*, p43.
35. Lock, pp87–88.
36. Barber, Malcolm, 'Western attitudes to Frankish Greece in the thirteenth century', *Mediterranean Historical Review*, vol. 4, issue 1, 1989, quoting Nicephorus Gregoras.
37. Lock, *Franks in the Aegean*, p305.
38. Runciman, *The Sicilian Vespers*, pp66–68.
39. Runciman, *The Sicilian Vespers*, p67.
40. Runciman, *The Sicilian Vespers*, p69.
41. Villani, Book VI, section 89, p193.
42. Housley, *The Italian Crusades*, pp44–45.
43. Runciman, *The Sicilian Vespers*, p83.
44. Runciman, *The Sicilian Vespers*, p85.
45. Runciman, *The Sicilian Vespers*, pp89–90.
46. Villani, Book VII, section 5, p205.
47. Housley, *The Italian Crusades*, p42.
48. Villani, Book VII, section 9, p213.
49. Runciman, *The Sicilian Vespers*, p97.
50. Runciman, *The Sicilian Vespers*, p98.
51. Dunbabin, *Charles of Anjou*, p201.
52. Jehel, pp98–99.
53. Dunbabin, *Charles of Anjou*, p83.
54. Dunbabin, *Charles of Anjou*, p93.
55. Jackson, Peter. *The Mongols and the West*, p168.
56. Gaposchkin, M. Cecilia. *The Making of Saint Louis: Kingship, Sanctity, and Crusade in the Later Middle Ages*, passim.
57. Aurell, p168.
58. Runciman, *The Sicilian Vespers*, p108.
59. Runciman, *The Sicilian Vespers*, p108.
60. Villani, Book VII, Section 26, p233.
61. See Runciman's brilliant account of the battle, *The Sicilian Vespers*, pp110–13.
62. Villani, Book VII, Section 26, p233.
63. *Medieval Italy, Texts in Translation*, ed Katherine Jansen, Joanna Drell and Frances Andrews, p135.
64. *Medieval Italy, Texts in Translation*, pp136–37.
65. Scales, Len. *The shaping of German identity: authority and crisis, 1245–1414*, p345.
66. Villani, Book VII, Section 29, p240.
67. Runciman, *The Sicilian Vespers*, p117.

Chapter 8

1. Dunbabin, *Charles of Anjou*, pp209–10.
2. Brentano, *Rome before Avignon*, p98.
3. Dunbabin, *Charles of Anjou*, p117.
4. Joinville, *Life of Saint Louis*, p346.
5. Dunbabin, *Charles of Anjou*, pp195–96.
6. Lower, Michael. 'Louis IX, Charles of Anjou, and the Tunis Crusade of 1270', in *Crusades: Medieval Worlds in Conflict*, p174.
7. Runciman, *The Sicilian Vespers*, p141.
8. Villani, Book VII, Section 37, p246.
9. Villani, Book VII, Section 38, p249.
10. Runciman, *The Sicilian Vespers*, pp141–42.
11. Dunbabin, *Charles of Anjou*, p39.
12. Dunbabin, *Charles of Anjou*, p119, 182.
13. Villani, Book VII, section 42, p255.
14. Dunbabin, *Charles of Anjou*, p147.
15. Runciman, *The Sicilian Vespers*, pp162–64.
16. Dunbabin, *Charles of Anjou*, p96.
17. Runciman, *The Sicilian Vespers*, p185.
18. Runciman, *The Sicilian Vespers*, pp195–96.
19. Runciman, *The Sicilian Vespers*, pp205ff.
20. Villani, Book VII, Section 61, p267.
21. Abulafia, *Western Mediterranean*, p79.
22. Runciman, *The Sicilian Vespers*, p220.
23. Runciman, *The Sicilian Vespers*, pp229–30.
24. Runciman, *The Sicilian Vespers*, pp236–37.
25. Runciman, *The Sicilian Vespers*, pp240–41.
26. Runciman, *The Sicilian Vespers*, pp247–48.
27. Villani, Book VII, Section 95, p274.
28. Villani, Book VII, Section 95, p274.
29. Dunbabin, *The French in Sicily*, p275.
30. Abulafia, *Western Mediterranean*, p86.
31. Froissart, Jean, *Chronicles*, vol. 2, Chapter CXLIX, p518.
32. *L'Europe des Anjou*, p50.
33. *L'Europe des Anjou*, p51.
34. Runciman, *The Sicilian Vespers*, pp264–66.
35. Dunbabin, *The French in Sicily*, p107.
36. Runciman, *The Sicilian Vespers*, p267.
37. Runciman, *The Sicilian Vespers*, p269.
38. *L'Europe des Anjou*, pp16–17.
39. Dunbabin, *The French in Sicily*, p201.
40. Dubois, Pierre. *De Recuperatone Terre Sancte: Traité de Politique Générale*, ed. Langlois, Ch.-V, passim.
41. Dunbabin, *The French in Sicily*, pp203–210.
42. Budak, Neven et Jurković, Miljenko. 'La politique adriatique des Angevins', *Les Princes Angevins du XIIIe au XVe Siècle: un destin européen*, eds. Noël-Yves Tonnerre et Élisabeth Verry, pp204-05.
43. Engel, p128.
44. Engel, pp129–30.
45. St Clair Baddeley, Welbore. *Robert the Wise and His Heirs, 1278–1352*, p23.
46. Quoted in *Decameron* pXXXIX.
47. Abulafia, *Western Mediterranean*, p153.
48. Leone de Castris, Pierluigi. *Ori, argenti, gemme e smalti della napoli angioina*, pp77–85. This is the catalogue to the exhibition of 2014 at the treasury of Naples cathedral, when the bust was reunited with a stunning collection of other 14th-century Angevin objects.
49. Carolus-Barré Louis. 'Les enquêtes pour

la canonisation de saint Louis — de Grégoire X à Boniface VIII — et la bulle Gloria laus, du 11 août 1297', *Revue d'histoire de l'Église de France*, Tome 57, No. 158, pp28–29.

50. Gardner, 'Seated kings, sea-faring saints and Angevin heraldry', pp120–21.
51. Welbore, *Robert the Wise*, p22.
52. Brentano, p259.
53. Dunbabin, *The French in Sicily*, p36.
54. Barraclough, p143.

Chapter 9

1. Abulafia, *Western Mediterranean*, pp139–40.
2. Kelly, Samantha. *The new Solomon: Robert of Naples (1309–1343) and fourteenth-century kingship*, pp195–98.
3. Kelly, p68.
4. Welbore, *Robert the Wise*, p134.
5. Scales, Len. *The shaping of German identity: authority and crisis, 1245–1414*, p345.
6. Kelly, pp81–82.
7. Kelly, p130.
8. Kelly, pp186, 189.
9. Kelly, pp87–88, quoting Léonard, *Angevins of Naples*.
10. Kelly, p88.
11. Petrarch, Francesco, trans. and ed. James Harvey Robinson and Henry Winchester Rolfe. *Petrarch: The First Modern Scholar and Man of Letters*, p71.
12. Robert d'Anjou, ed. M. Dykmans. 'La vision bienheureuse. Traité envoye au pape Jean XXII', *Miscellanea Historiae Pontificiae* pp74*–75*.
13. Dykmans, pp81*–82*.
14. Gilli, F.; Vauchez, A.; Arnaldi, G. 'L'intégration manquée des Angevins en Italie: le témoignage. des historiens', *Collection de l'Ecole française de Rome*, Vol 245, p27.
15. Kelly, p205.
16. Potter, p65.
17. *L'Europe des Anjou*, pp74ff.
18. Duran, Michelle M. 'The Politics of Art: Imaging Sovereignty in the Anjou Bible at Leuven', Academia.edu.
19. Kelly, p33.
20. *Old Provence*, vol. 2, p329.
21. Petrarch, ed. Robinson, p413.
22. Petrarch, ed. Robinson, p71.
23. Kelly, p49.
24. Coulter, Cornelia C. 'The Library of the Angevin Kings at Naples', *Transactions and Proceedings of the American Philological Association*, Vol. 75, 1944, pp143,149.
25. Villani, Book VIII, section 112, p390.
26. Lock, p106.
27. Lock, pp114–15, 119.
28. Kelly, pp209–10.
29. Lock, p130.
30. Jackson, *Mongols and the West*, p16.
31. Engel, p100.
32. Engel, p133.
33. Engel, p137.
34. *L'Europe des Anjou*, p176.
35. Barker and Barber, *Tournaments*, pp103–4.
36. *L'Europe des Anjou*, pp178–79.
37. Engel, p155.
38. Budak and Jurković, pp206-08.
39. The cross is beautifully enamelled and was made c1330; it is in room 40 of the British Museum. See also Engel, p135.
40. Engel, pp135–39.
41. Casteen, Elizabeth. *From She-Wolf to Martyr: The Reign and Disputed Reputation of Johanna I of Naples*, pp37–38.
42. Casteen, pp43–44.
43. Welbore, *Robert the Wise*, p344.
44. Welbore, *Robert the Wise*, pp345–46.
45. Welbore, *Queen Joanna*, p52.
46. Petrarca, Francesco. *Epystole familiares*, Biblioteca Italiana, Roma, 2004, Book VI, letter 5, 'Ad Barbatum Sulmonensem, de miserabili et indigna morte regis Andree'.
47. Casteen, pp53–54.
48. Welbore, pp388–89.
49. Welbore, *Queen Joanna*, p9.
50. Casteen, p102.
51. Welbore, *Queen Joanna*, p73.
52. Welbore, *Queen Joanna*, pp77–78.
53. Casteen, p49.
54. Casteen, p49.
55. Casteen, p80.
56. Boccaccio, Giovanni, trans. John Payne. *Decameron*, pp2–6.
57. Casteen, pp82–83.
58. Casteen, pp86–88.
59. Casteen, p108.
60. Keen, *Chivalry*, p 192.
61. Casteen, pp93–98.
62. *L'Europe des Anjou*, p119.

Chapter 10

1. Tuchman, Barbara, *A Distant Mirror*, p76.
2. Barber, 'Was the Holy Land Betrayed?', p41.
3. Seward, Desmond. *The Monks of War*, pp158–60.
4. Barber, 'Was the Holy Land Betrayed?', p35.
5. Tuchman, p44.
6. Allmand, Christopher. *The Hundred Years War*, p10.
7. Allmand, *The Hundred Years War*, pp12–13.
8. Reynaud, Marcelle-Renée. *Le temps des princes: Louis II et Louis III d'Anjou-Provence, 1384–1434*, pp18, 22. See also the full grant of Anjou to Louis I in Lecoy de la Marche, A. *Le Roi René: Sa Vie, Son Administration, Ses Travaux Artistiques et Littéraires d'après les documents inédits des archives de France et d'Italie*, vol 2, pp206-08.
9. Froissart, Jean. *Chronicles*, vol. 1, Chapter CXXVIII; p325; Seward, *Hundred Years War*, p35.
10. Froissart, *Chronicles*, vol. 1, Chapter L, p144.
11. Froissart, *Chronicles*, vol. 1, Chapter CXXVIII, pp324–26; Seward, *Hundred Years War*, pp64–66.
12. Allmand, *Hundred Years War*, p106; Seward, *Hundred Years War*, p33.
13. Froissart, *Chronicles*, vol. 1, Chapter CLXI, p437; Seward, *Hundred Years War*, pp86–93.
14. Froissart, *Chronicles*, vol. 1, Chapter CLXXVI, pp469–70.
15. Tuchman, pp163–67.
16. Seward, *Hundred Years War*, pp99–100.
17. Tuchman, p202.
18. Tuchman, p231.
19. Tuchman, pp264–65; 293–24.

Chapter 11

1. Casteen, p143.
2. Casteen, pp128–29.
3. Casteen, pp131–32.
4. Casteen, pp133–40.
5. Casteen, p168.
6. Casteen, pp166, 176.
7. Engel, p162.
8. Engel, p158.
9. Engel, pp164–67.
10. Engel, p169.
11. Reynaud, p24; Casteen, p148.
12. Casteen, p145.
13. Casteen, p212.
14. Casteen, pp198–203.
15. Casteen, p241.
16. Casteen, pp206-07.
17. Froissart, *Chronicles*, vol. 2, Chapter XCVI, pp301-04; Chapter CL, pp519–21.
18. Casteen, p123.
19. Boccaccio, Giovanni, translated Virginia Brown. *Famous Women (I Tatti Renaissance Library)*, Chapter 106.
20. Tuchman, pp399–409.
21. Engel, pp195–98.
22. Engel, pp199–201.
23. *L'Europe des Anjou*, pp239–40.
24. *L'Europe des Anjou*, p242.
25. Przybyszewski, Fr. Bolesław, trans. Bruce MacQueen. *Saint Jadwiga, Queen of Poland 1374–1399*, pp37, 41.
26. *L'Europe des Anjou*, p243.
27. *L'Europe des Anjou*, pp244, 242.
28. Przybyszewski, pp80–81.
29. Froissart, *Chronicles*, vol. 4, Chapter CI, p517.
30. Engel, p203.
31. Rezachevici, Constantin. 'From the Order of the Dragon to Dracula', *Journal of Dracula Studies*, vol 1, 1999, pp3–7.
32. Reynaud, Marcelle-Renée. *Le temps des princes: Louis II et Louis III d'Anjou-Provence, 1384–1434*, p19.
33. Kekewich, Margaret L.. *The good king: René of Anjou and fifteenth-century Europe*, p51.
34. Senneville, Gérard de. *Yolande d'Aragon: la reine qui a gagné la Guerre de Cent Ans*, pp26–27.
35. Lecoy de la Marche, A. *Le Roi René: Sa Vie, Son Administration, Ses Travaux Artistiques et Littéraires d'après les documents inédits des archives de France et d'Italie*, vol 1, pp24–25.
36. Senneville, p36.
37. Senneville, pp41–43.
38. Senneville, pp46–50.
39. Senneville, pp51–55, 58.
40. Allmand, Christopher. *Henry V*, pp48–49.
41. Seward, *Hundred Years War*, p156.
42. Seward, *Hundred Years War*, pp174–76.
43. Allmand, *Henry V*, p106.
44. Seward, *Hundred Years War*, pp170, 180.
45. Seward, *Hundred Years War*, p180.
46. Allmand, *Henry V*, pp145–56.
47. Kekewich, p52.
48. Abulafia, *Western Mediterranean*, pp195–96.
49. See for example: http://www.italiamedievale.org/personaggi/giovanna_II.html
50. Browning, Oscar. *The Life of Bartolomeo Colleoni*, p38.
51. *L'Europe des Anjou*, p35.
52. Kekewich, pp52–53.

Chapter 12

1. Lecoy de la Marche, vol. 1, p39.
2. Seward, *Hundred Years War*, pp209–10.
3. Sackville-West, Vita. *Saint Joan of Arc*, pp96–97.
4. Benedetti, Jean. *The Real Bluebeard: The Life of Gilles de Rais*, p68.

5. Sackville-West, p129.
6. Seward, *Hundred Years War*, p218.
7. Cordellier-Delanoue, pp63–64.
8. Lecoy de la Marche, vol. 1, p76.
9. Seward, *Hundred Years War*, pp219–20.
10. Lecoy de la Marche, vol. 2, pp219–20.
11. Kekewich, pp27–29.
12. Cordellier-Delanoue, p111.
13. Kekewich, p29.
14. Abulafia, *Western Mediterranean*, p196.
15. Kekewich, p31.
16. Lecoy de la Marche, vol. 2, pp213–16.
17. Kekewich, p56.
18. Abulafia, *Western Mediterranean*, p199.
19. Robin, Françoise. *La Cour d'Anjou-Provence. La vie artistique sous le règne de René*, p30.
20. Kekewich, pp59–66.
21. Cole, Alison. *Virtue and Magnificence: Art of the Italian Renaissance Courts*, pp62–63.
22. Seward, *Hundred Years War*, p223.
23. Seward, *Hundred Years War*, p235
24. Kekewich, p94; Castor, pp325–26.
25. Kekewich, p45.
26. Kekewich, pp97–98, 20.
27. Kekewich, p104.
28. Barker and Barber, *Tournaments*, p116.
29. Sackville-West, pp96–97.
30. Lecoy de la Marche, vol. 2, pp151–52.
31. Lecoy de la Marche, vol. 2, p252; Robin, p119.
32. Gautier, Marc-edouard, ed. *Splendeur de l'enluminure: Le roi René et les livres*. pp89–90; Tournaments, p116.
33. Seward, *Hundred Years War*, pp246, 257–58.

34. Lecoy de la Marche, vol. 1, p261.
35. Seward, *Hundred Years War*, p262.
36. Plant, passim.
37. Castor, p337.
38. Jacob, E.F., *The Fifteenth century: 1399–1485*, pp508-09.
39. Castor, p358.
40. Jacob, pp521–22.
41. Castor, pp373–74.
42. Castor, pp377–78.
43. Castor, p380.
44. Reynolds, Michael T. 'René of Anjou, King of Sicily, and the order of the Croissant', *Journal of Medieval History*, p128.
45. Reynolds, p148.
46. Classen, Albrecht, 'Authors, Translators, Printers: Production and Reception of Novels between Manuscript and Print in Fifteenth-Century Germany', in *Trust and Proof: Translators in Renaissance Print Culture*, edited by Andrea Rizzi, pp157–59.
47. Gautier, pp216–29.
48. Reynolds, pp155ff.
49. Search for manuscript 'Français 2692' or 'René d'Anjou' as the author: http://mandragore.bnf.fr/jsp/rechercheExperte.jsp
50. Reynolds, p126.
51. Benedetti, pp109–91, passim.
52. Lecoy de la Marche, vol. 1, p262.
53. Lecoy de la Marche, vol. 1, p302–3.
54. Mirnik, Ivan, 'The Laurana Medals', p6.
55. Gautier, p352.
56. Gautier, pp284, 296–97.
57. Abulafia, *Western Mediterranean*, p203.

58. Again, all viewable on Mandragore, search for Français 24399 or René d'Anjou as author: http://mandragore.bnf.fr/jsp/rechercheExperte.jsp
59. Reynolds, p157; Kekewich, p73.
60. Kekewich, pp74–75.
61. Cole, pp63–64.
62. Lecoy de la Marche, vol. 1, pp367–68.
63. Lecoy de la Marche, vol. 1, p378.
64. Kekewich, p222.
65. Castor, pp390–91.
66. Kendall, *Louis XI*, pp286–87.
67. Castor, pp398–400.
68. Kendall, p345.
69. Lecoy de la Marche, vol. 1, pp388–89.
70. Lecoy de la Marche, vol. 1, 400-01.
71. Kekewich, p235–36.
72. Kekewich, pp234, 239–40.
73. Casteen, p250.
74. Kekewich, p146.
75. Elders, Willem, trans. Paul Shannon. *Josquin Des Prez and His Musical Legacy: An Introductory Guide*, p22.
76. *L'Europe des Anjou*, p 259.
77. Gautier, pp120–21.
78. *L'Europe des Anjou*, p 260.
79. See for example: Irving, Washington, *History of the Life and Voyages of Christopher Columbus*, vol. 2, pp242–43.
80. Kekewich, p244.
81. Kekewich, p76, 244–46.

Epilogue

1. Black, Jeremy, *European Warfare 1494–1660*, pp37–38.
2. Black, p59.

BIBLIOGRAPHY

Primary:

Alighieri, Dante, trans. Allen Mandelbaum. *Inferno*. Bantam Books, 1980.

Alighieri, Dante, trans. and ed. Robin Kirkpatrick. *Paradiso*, Penguin, 2007.

Alighieri, Dante, trans. and ed. Robin Kirkpatrick. *Purgatorio*, Penguin, 2007.

Boccaccio, Giovanni, trans. GH McWilliam. *The Decameron*. 2nd edition, Penguin, 1995.

Boccaccio, Giovanni, trans. John Payne. *The Decameron of Giovanni Boccaccio*, Walter J. Black, Inc., New York, no date [c1886].

Boccaccio, Giovanni, translated Virginia Brown. *Famous Women (I Tatti Renaissance Library)*, New edition, Harvard University Press, 2003.

Camera, Matteo. *Elucubrazioni Storico-Diplomatiche su Giovanna I.a, Regina di Napoli e Carlo III di Durazzo*, Tipografia Nazionale, Salerno, 1889.

Chrétien de Troyes, trans. William Wells Newell. *King Arthur and the Table round, tales chiefly after the Old French of Crestien of Troyes*, vol. 1, Houghton, Mifflin, 1898. [For Erec et Enide.]

Chrétien de Troyes, trans. Staines, David. *The Complete Romances of Chrétien de Troyes*, Indiana University Press, Bloomington & Indianapolis, 1990. [For Yvain.]

Comnena, Anna, trans. and ed. E.R.A. Sewter. *The Alexiad*, Harmondsworth, 1979.

Comnena, Anna, ed. and trans. Elizabeth A. Dawes. *The Alexiad*, Routledge, Kegan, Paul, London, 1928.

Delisle, Léopold. 'Poèmes de Raimond Astruc et poésies sur Charles d'Anjou conservés dans le ms. 1008 de Saint-Gall', *Bibliothèque de l'école des chartes*, tome 77, pp405–414, 1916.

Dubois, Pierre. *De Recuperatone Terre Sancte: Traité de Politique Générale*, ed. Langlois, Ch.-V, Alphonse Picard, Paris, 1891.

Filangieri, Count Riccardo, trans. Arthur H. Leavitt and Salvatore D. Nerboso. *Report on the Destruction by the Germans, September 30, 1943, of the Depository of Priceless Historical Records of the Naples State Archives*, The American Archivist: Vol. 7, No. 4, pp252–255, October 1944.

Froissart, Jean, trans. Thomas Johnes. *Sir John Froissart's Chronicles of England, France and the Adjoining Countries, from the latter part of the reign of Edward II to the Coronation of Henry IV*, 4 volumes, Hafod Press, 1803.

Gerald of Wales, trans. Lewis Thorpe. *The Journey through Wales and the Description of Wales*, Penguin, London, 1978.

Hallam, Elizabeth M. editor. *The Plantagenet Chronicles*, First paperback edition, Papermac (Macmillan), London 1988.

Henderson, Ernest F, trans and ed. *Select Historical Documents of the Middle Ages*, George Bell and Sons, London, 1903. [Includes the *Dialogue of the Exchequer*.]

Housley, Norman. *Documents on the later crusades, 1274–1580*. Palgrave, 1996.

Jansen, Katherine L., Drell, Joanna, and Andrews, France, eds. *Medieval Italy: texts in translation*. University of Pennsylvania Press, Philadelphia, 2009.

Joinville, Jean de, trans. M.R.B. Shaw. 'The Life of Saint Louis', *Joinville and Villehardouin: Chronicles of the Crusades*,
Penguin, 1963.

Marchegay, Paul and Salmon, André, eds. *Chroniques d'Anjou*. Vol. 1. Chez Jules Renouard et Co., Paris, 1856. Contains works including *Gesta Consulum Andegavorum et Dominorum Ambaziensium* (Deeds of the Counts of Anjou and Lords of Amboise), *Historia Gaufredi Ducis Normannorum et Comitis Andegavorum, auctore Johanne Monacho Majoris Monasterii* (History of Geoffrey [Plantagenet] Duke of the Normans and Count of the Angevins, by John Monk of [Marmoutier]) and *Fragmentum Historiae Andegavensis, auctore Fulcone Rechin* (Fragment of the History of the Angevins by Fulk Réchin).

Musto, Ronald G., ed. *Medieval Naples: A Documentary History, 400–1400*. Historical Texts, Italica Press, New York, 2011.

Odo of Deuil, trans. and ed. Virginia Gingerick Berry. *De protection Ludovico VII in orientem (The Journey of Louis VII to the East)*, W.W. Norton & Company Inc, New York, 1948.

Petrarca, Francesco, ed. Stoppelli, Pasquale. *Epystole familiares*, Biblioteca Italiana, Lexis Progetti Editoriali, Roma, 1997. [Book VI, letter 5, 'Ad Barbatum Sulmonensem, de miserabili et indigna morte regis Andree'.]

Petrarch, Francesco, trans. and ed. James Harvey Robinson and Henry Winchester Rolfe. *Petrarch: The First Modern Scholar and Man of Letters: A Selection from his Correspondence with Boccaccio and other Friends, Designed to Illustrate the Beginnings of the Renaissance*, 3rd impression, G. P. Putnam's Sons, New York & London, 1909.

Petrarch, Francesco, trans. and ed. Mark Musa. *Selections from the Canzoniere and Other Works*, Oxford University Press, 1985.

Re, Giuseppe Del. *Cronisti e scrittori sincroni Napoletani editi ed inediti ordinate per serie e pubblicati*, vol. 2. Stamperia dell'Iride, Naples, 1868. Contains works including Saba Malaspina's *Rerum Sicularum historia (1250–1285)* and Bartolommeo di Neocastro's *Historia Sicula (1250–1293)*.

Rene d'Anjou, ed. M. le Comte de Quatrebarbes. *Oeuvres complètes du roi René avec une biographie et des notices*, 2 vols. Imprimerie De Cosnier Et Lachèse, Angers, 1845. Contains works including the *Traictié de la forme et devis d'ung tourney*, *La conquest de doulce Mercy par le Cueur d'amour espris*, and *Mortifiement de vaine plaisance*.

Rigord, traduite du latin par François Guizot and Romain Fougères. *La vie de Philippe II Auguste*, Editions Paléo, 2007.

Robert d'Anjou [Robert the Wise of Naples], ed. M. Dykmans. 'La vision bienheureuse. Traité envoye au pape Jean XXII', *Miscellanea Historiae Pontificiae*, Rome, 1970.

Roziére, M. Eugène de ed. *Cartulaire de l'église du Saint Sépulcre de Jérusalem publié d'après les manuscrits du Vatican*. L'imprimerie nationale, Paris, 1849.

Thuróczy, János; translated by F. Mantello. *Chronica Hungarorum / Chronicle of the Hungarians*, Indiana University. Research Institute for Inner Asian Studies, Bloomington, Ind, 1991.

Villani, Giovanni. *Villani's Chronicle: Being Selections from the First Nine Books of the Croniche Fiorentine of Giovanni Villani*, 2nd ed, Translated by Rose E. Selfe and edited by Philip H. Wicksteed M.A., Archibald Constable & Co. Ltd., London, 1906.

Villehardouin, Geoffrey, trans. M.R.B. Shaw. 'The Conquest of Constantinople', *Joinville and Villehardouin: Chronicles of the Crusades*, Penguin, 1963.

William of Malmesbury, trans. Joseph Stephenson. *A History of the Norman Kings (1066–1125)*, Llanerch Enterprises, 1989.

Secondary:

Abulafia, David. 'Venice and the Kingdom of Naples in the Last Years of Robert the Wise 1332–1343.' *Papers of the British School at Rome 48*, pp186–204, 1980.

Abulafia, David. *The Western Mediterranean Kingdoms 1200–1500: The Struggle for Dominion*, Longman, New York, 1997.

Allmand, Christopher. *Henry V*, Methuen, London, 1992.

Allmand, Christopher. *The Hundred Years War: England and France at War c.1300–c.1450*, Cambridge University Press, Cambridge, 1988.

Asbridge, Thomas. *The Crusades: The War for the Holy Land*, Simon & Schuster UK, London, Reissue edition 2012.

Aurell, Martin. *La vielle et l'épée. Troubadours et politique en Provence au XIIIe siècle*, Aubier, Paris, 1989.

Bachrach, Bernard. *Fulk Nerra, the Neo-Roman Consul 987–1040*, University of California Press, 1993.

Bachrach, Bernard. *State-building in Medieval France: Studies in Early Angevin History*, Variorum Reprints, 1976.

Bak, János M. 'Roles and Functions of Queens in Árpádian and Angevin Hungary (1000–1386)', *Medieval Queenship*, (Ed. J. C. Parsons), Sutton, Stroud, pp13–24, 1993.

Baldwin, John W. *The government of Philip Augustus: foundations of French royal power in the Middle Ages*, New edition, University of California Press, 1992.

Barber, Malcolm. 'Was the Holy Land betrayed in 1291?', in *Medieval historical discourses: essays in honour of Professor Peter S. Noble*, Ailes, Marianne J., Lawrence-Mathers, Anne and Le Saux, Françoise Hazel Marie eds., Reading, 2008, pp35–52.

Barber, Malcolm. 'Western attitudes to Frankish Greece in the Thirteenth century', *Mediterranean Historical Review*, Vol. 4, Issue 1, 1989.

Barbero, Alessandro. *Il mito angioino Nella cultura italiana e provenzale fra duecento e trecento*, Deputazione subalpina di storia patria, 1983.

Barker, Juliet. *Agincourt: The King, the Campaign, the Battle*, Abacus, 2005.

Barker, Juliet. *Conquest: The English Kingdom of France 1417–1450*, Harvard University Press, Cambridge, MA, 2012.

Barker, Juliet and Barber, Malcolm. *Tournaments: Jousts, Chivalry and Pageants in the Middle Ages*, Boydell Press, Woodbridge, 2000.

Barraclough, Geoffrey. *The Medieval Papacy*, First American Edition, Harcourt, Brace & World Inc, 1979.

Benedetti, Jean. *The Real Bluebeard: The Life of Gilles de Rais*, Sutton Publishing, 2003.

Benham, JEM. 'Philip Augustus and the Angevin Empire: The Scandinavian Connection', *Mediaeval Scandinavia* 14, pp37–50, 2004.

Black, Jeremy. *European Warfare, 1494–1660*, Routledge, London and New York, 2002.

Boulton, D'A.J.D. *The Knights of the Crown. The monarchical orders of Knighthood in later medieval Europe, 1325–1520*, Boydell Press, Woodbridge, 1987.

Boussard, Jacques. *Le Comté d'Anjou sous Henri Plantegenêt et ses fils (1151–1204)*, Volume 271 *Bibliothèque de l'Ecole des hautes études*, H. Champion, 1938.

Boyle, David. *The Troubadour's Song: The Capture and Ransom of Richard the Lionheart*, Walker and Company, 2005.

Brentano, Robert. *Rome before Avignon: A Social History of Thirteenth-Century Rome*, Basic Books, Inc, New York, 1974.

Browning, Oscar. *The Life of Bartolomeo Colleoni, of Anjou and Burgundy*, Printed for the Arundel Society, Chiswick Press, London, 1891.

Bruzelius, Caroline. *The Stones of Naples. Church Building in Angevin Italy, 1266–1343*, Yale University Press, New Haven, CT, 2004.

Budak, Neven et Jurković, Miljenko. 'La politique adriatique des Angevins', *Les Princes Angevins du XIIIe au XVe Siècle: un destin européen*, eds. Noël-Yves Tonnerre and Élisabeth Verry, Presses universitaires de Rennes, Rennes, 2015.

Carolus-Barré, Louis. 'Les enquêtes pour la canonisation de saint Louis — de Grégoire X à Boniface VIII — et la bulle Gloria laus, du 11 août 1297', *Revue d'histoire de l'Église de France*, Tome 57, No. 158, pp19–29, 1971.

Carpenter, D.A. *The Minority of Henry III*, Methuen Publishing Ltd, 1990.

Casteen, Elizabeth. *From She-Wolf to Martyr: The Reign and Disputed Reputation of Johanna I of Naples*, Cornell University Press, 2015.

Castor, Helen. *She Wolves: The Women Who Ruled England Before Elizabeth*, Faber & Faber, 2010.

Cevins, Marie-Madeleine. 'Société et vie culturelle en Hongrie sous les rois angevins', *Les Princes Angevins du XIIIe au XVe Siècle: un destin européen*, eds. Noël-Yves Tonnerre and Élisabeth Verry, Presses universitaires de Rennes, Rennes, 2015.

Clanchy, M.T. *England and its Rulers 1066–1272: Foreign Lordship and National Identity*, Fontana Press, London, 1983.

Classen, Albrecht. 'Authors, Translators, Printers: Production and Reception of Novels between Manuscript and Print in Fifteenth-century Germany', in Andrea Rizz ed., *Trust and Proof: Translators in Renaissance Print Culture*, Brill, 2017.

Cole, Alison. *Virtue and Magnificence: Art of the Italian Renaissance Courts*, Calmann and King Ltd, New York, 1995.

Contamine, Philippe. 'À l'ombre des fleurs de lis. Les rapports entre les rois de France Valois et les Angevins de Naples et de Provence (1320–1382)', *Les Princes Angevins du XIIIe au XVe Siècle: un destin européen*, eds. Noël-Yves Tonnerre and Élisabeth Verry, Presses universitaires de Rennes, Rennes, 2015.

Cook, Theodore Andrea. *Old Provence*, 2 vols., Charles Scribner's Sons, New York, 1905.

Cordellier-Delanoue, M. *René d'Anjou*, 8th ed., Alfred Mame et Fils, Tours, 1883.

Cormack, Robin and Maria Vassilaki, eds. *Byzantium: 330–1453*, Royal Academy of Arts, London, 2008.

Coulter, Cornelia C. 'The Library of the Angevin Kings at Naples', *Transactions and Proceedings of the American Philological Association*, Vol. 75, 1944, pp. 141–155.

Crouch, David. *William Marshal: Knighthood, War and Chivalry, 1147–1219*, 2nd edition, Routledge, 2002.

Davis, R.H.C. *A History of Medieval Europe: From Constantine to Saint Louis*, Longman, 1970.

Delorme, Philippe. *Blanche de Castille: épouse de Louis VIII, mère de Saint Louis*, Pygmalion, 2002.

Douglas, David C. *The Norman Achievement, 1050–1100*, 1st edition, Eyre & Spottiswoode, 1969.

Douglas, David C. *William the Conqueror: The Norman Impact upon England*, Methuen, London, 1964.

Duboscq, Guy. 'Le mariage de Charles d'Anjou, comte du Maine, et le comté de Guise (1431–1473)', *Bibliothèque de l'école des chartes*, tome 96, pp405–414, 1935.

Duby, Georges. *Le dimanche de Bouvines: 27 juillet 1214*, Gallimard, 1973.

Dunbabin, Jean. *Charles of Anjou: Power, Kingship and State-Making in Thirteenth-Century Europe*. Longman, New York, 1998.

Dunbabin, Jean. *France in the Making 843–1180*, Second edition, Oxford University Press, 2000.

Dunbabin, Jean. *The French in the Kingdom of Sicily, 1266–1305*, Cambridge University Press, New York, 2011.

Duran, Michelle M. 'The Politics of Art: Imaging Sovereignty in the Anjou Bible at Leuven'. uploaded on https://www.academia.edu/890773/.

Earenfight, Theresa. *Queenship in Medieval Europe (Queenship and Power)*, Palgrave Macmillan, 2013.

Elders, Willem, trans. Paul Shannon. *Josquin Des Prez and His Musical Legacy: An Introductory Guide*, Leuven University Press, 2013.

Elliott, Janis and Warr, Cordelia, eds.. *The Church of Santa Maria Donna Regina: Art, Iconography and Patronage in Fourteenth-Century Naples*, Ashgate, Aldershot, 2004.

Engel, Pál, *The Realm of Saint Stephen*, Tauris, London, 1999.

Epstein, S.R. *An Island for itself. Economic development and social change in late medieval Sicily*, Cambridge, 1992.

Field, Sean L. and Gaposchkin, M. Cecilia. 'Questioning the Capetians, 1180–1328', *History Compass* vol. 12, 2014, pp567–85.

Fine, John. *The Late Medieval Balkans: A Critical Survey from the Late Twelfth century to the Ottoman Conquest*, Reprint edition, University of Michigan Press, 1994.

Fügedi Erik, ed. Bak JM. 'Kings, Bishops, Nobles and Burghers in Medieval Hungary', *Variorum Reprints*, London, 1986.

Galasso, Giuseppe. 'Charles Ier et Charles II d'Anjou, princes italiens', *Les Princes Angevins du XIIIe au XVe Siècle: un destin européen*, eds. Noël-Yves Tonnerre and Élisabeth Verry, Presses universitaires de Rennes, Rennes, 2015.

Gaposchkin, M. Cecilia. *The Making of Saint Louis: Kingship, Sanctity, and Crusade in the Later Middle Ages*, Cornell University Press, Ithaca and London, 2008.

Gardner, Julian. 'Seated kings, sea-faring saints and heraldry: some themes in Angevin iconography', *L'État angevin. Pouvoir, culture et société entre XIIIe et XIVe siècle. Actes du colloque international (Rome-Naples, 7–11 novembre 1995)*, Collection de l'École française de Rome 245, p. 115–126.

Gautier, Marc-edouard (ed.). *Splendeur de l'enluminure: Le roi René et les livres*. Actes Sud Beaux Arts, Angers, 2009.

Gilli, Patrick. 'Culture politique et culture juridique chez les Angevins de Naples (jusqu'au milieu du xve siècle)', *Les Princes Angevins du XIIIe au XVe Siècle: un destin européen*, eds. Noël-Yves Tonnerre and Élisabeth Verry, Presses universitaires de Rennes, Rennes, 2015.

Gilli; F.; Vauchez, A.; Arnaldi, G. 'L'intégration manquée des Angevins en Italie: le témoignage. des historiens', *Collection de l'Ecole française de Rome*, Vol 245, Ecole française de Rome, pp11–34, 1998.

Gillingham, John. *The Angevin Empire*, 2nd edition, Arnold, London, 2001.

Gillingham, John. *Richard I*, Yale University Press, New Haven and London, 1999.

Gillingham, John. *Richard the Lionheart*, 2nd edition, Weidenfeld and Nicolson, London, 1989.

Gillingham, John. 'The Unromantic Death of Richard I', *Speculum*, vol. 54, No. 1. Jan 1979, pp18–41.

Halecki, Oscar, *Jadwiga of Anjou and the rise of East Central Europe*. Social Science Monographs, Boulder, Co., 1991.

Hallam, Elizabeth M and Judith Everard. *Capetian France 987–1328*, 2nd ed., Longman, 2001.

Halphen, Louis. *Le Comté d'Anjou au XIe Siècle*, A. Picard et Fils, Paris, 1906.

Harper-Bill, Christopher and Vincent, Nicholas, eds. *Henry II: New Interpretations*, The Boydell Press, Woodbridge, 2007.

Hébert, Michel. 'Le règne de Robert d'Anjou', *Les Princes Angevins du XIIIe au XVe Siècle: un destin européen*, eds. Noël-Yves Tonnerre and Élisabeth Verry, Presses universitaires de Rennes, Rennes, 2015.

Holt, P.M. *The Age of the Crusades: The Near East from the Eleventh century to 1517*, Longman, London and New York, 1986.

Housley, Norman. *The Italian Crusades: the Papal-Angevin Alliance and the. Crusades against Christian Lay Powers, 1234–1343*, Clarendon Press, Oxford, 1982.

Housley, Norman. 'King Louis the Great of Hungary and the Crusades, 1342–1382', *The Slavonic and East European Review*, Vol. 62, No. 2, pp192–208, April 1984.

Huizinga, J., trans. F. Hopman. *The Waning of the Middle Ages*, The Folio Society, London, 1998.

Irving, Washington. *History of the Life and Voyages of Christopher Columbus*, new edition, 2 volumes, Carey, Lea &

Blanchard, Philadelphia, 1838.

Jackson, Peter. *The Mongols and the West: 1221–1410*, Routledge, London, 2005.

Jacob, E.F. *The Fifteenth century: 1399–1485*, Oxford University Press, 1961.

James, Edward. *The Origins of France: From Clovis to the Capetians, 500–1000* (New Studies in Medieval History), Palgrave, 1982.

Jehel, Georges. *Les Angevins de Naples: une dynastie européene 1246–1266–1442*, Ellipses, Paris, 2014.

Jones, Chris. *Eclipse of Empire?: Perceptions of the Western Empire and its Rulers in Late-Medieval France*, Brepols N.V., 2007

Keen, Maurice. *Chivalry*, Yale University Press, New Haven and London, 1984.

Keen, Maurice. *The Penguin History of Medieval Europe*, Penguin, 1968.

Kekewich, Margaret L.. *The good king: René of Anjou and fifteenth-century Europe*, Palgrave Macmillan, 2008.

Kelly, Samantha. *The new Solomon: Robert of Naples (1309–1343) and fourteenth-century kingship*, Brill, 2003.

Kendall, Paul Murray. *Louis XI*, Sphere Books Ltd, London, 1984.

Kibler, William W. ed. *Eleanor of Aquitaine: Patron and Politician*, University of Texas Press, 1976.

Kiesewetter, Andreas. 'L'acquisto e l'occupazione del litorale meridionale dell'Albania da parte di re Carlo I d'Angiò (1279–1283)', *Palaver* 4 n.s., n. 1, Università del Salento, pp255–298, 2015.

King, Margaret. *The Death of the Child Valerio Marcello*, University of Chicago Press, Chicago, 1994.

Klaniczay, Gàbor. *Holy Rulers and Blessed Princesses: Dynastic Cults in Medieval Central Europe*, trans. Éva Pálmai, Cambridge University Press, Cambridge and New York, 2002.

Laborde, Léon de. 'Précédé de l'inventaire des bijoux de Louis, Duc d'Anjou, dressé vers 1360', in *Glossaire Français du Moyen Âge*, Slatkine Reprints, Geneva, 1975 (reprinted from Paris edition of 1872).

Le Goff, Guy ed. *L'Europe des Anjou: Aventure des princes angevins du XIIIe au XVe siècle*, Somogy éditions d'Art, 2001.

Lecoy de la Marche, A. *Le Roi René: Sa Vie, Son Administration, Ses Travaux Artistiques et Littéraires d'après les documents inédits des archives de France et d'Italie*, 2 vols. Librairie de Firmin-Didot Freres, Fils et Cc., Paris, 1873.

Léonard, Émile G. *Les Angevins de Naples*. Presses universitaires de France, Paris, 1954.

Leone de Castris, Pierluigi. *Ori, argenti, gemme e smalti della napoli angioina 1266–1381*, Arte'm, Napoli, 2014.

Lock, Peter. *The Franks in the Aegean: 1204–1500*, Longman, 1995.

Longnon Jean. 'Charles d'Anjou et la croisade de Tunis', *Journal des savants*, No. 1, pp44–61, 1974.

Lower, Michael. 'Louis IX, Charles of Anjou, and the Tunis Crusade of 1270', in *Crusades: Medieval Worlds in Conflict*, ed. Thomas F. Madden, James L. Naus, Vincent Ryan, Routledge, 2010.

Luce, Siméon. 'Louis, duc d'Anjou, s'est-il approprié, après la mort de Charles V, une partie du trésor laissé par le roi son frère?', *Bibliothèque de l'école des chartes*. tome 36, pp299–303, 1875.

Manikowska, Halina. 'La Pologne sous l'influence des Angevins de Hongrie', *Les Princes Angevins du XIIIe au XVe Siècle: un destin européen*, eds. Noël-Yves Tonnerre and Élisabeth Verry, Presses universitaires de Rennes, Rennes, 2015.

Martin, Therese. 'The Art of a Reigning Queen as Dynastic Propaganda in Twelfth-Century Spain', *Speculum* vol. 80, 2005.

Masson, Christophe. *Des guerres en Italie avant les guerres d'Italie : les entreprises militaires françaises dans la péninsule à l'époque du grand schisme d'Occident*, Collection de l'École française de Rome 495, École française de Rome, Rome, 2014.

Mayer, Hans Eberhard, trans. John Gillingham. *The Crusades*, 2nd edition, Oxford University Press, Oxford, 1988.

Mayer, Hans Eberhard. 'Studies in the History of Queen Melisende of Jerusalem', *Dumbarton Oaks Papers*, Vol. 26, 1972, pp93+95–182

Mérindol, Christian de. 'L'héraldique des princes angevins', *Les Princes Angevins du XIIIe au XVe Siècle: un destin européen*, eds. Noël-Yves Tonnerre and Élisabeth Verry, Presses universitaires de Rennes, Rennes, 2015.

Mérindol, Christian de. *Les Fêtes de chevalerie à la cour du roi René*, C.T.H.S., Paris, 1993.

Michaud, Joseph-François. *Histoire des croisades*, vol 1, Chez Ponthieu, Paris, 1825.

Mirnik, Ivan. 'The Laurana Medals', Zagreb, 1996, uploaded on http://www.academia.edu/30663114.

Monter, William. *The Rise of Female Kings in Europe, 1300–1800*, Yale University Press, New Haven, 2012.

Neubecker, Ottfried. *Heraldry: Sources, Symbols and Meaning*, Macdonald and Jane's, London, 1976.

Norgate, Kate. *England under the Angevin Kings*, 2 vols, Macmillan and Co., London and New York, 1887.

Ohnesorge, Christof. 'Les ambitions et l'échec de la seconde maison d'Anjou (vers 1380-vers 1480)', *Les Princes Angevins du XIIIe au XVe Siècle: un destin européen*, eds. Noël-Yves Tonnerre and Élisabeth Verry, Presses universitaires de Rennes, Rennes, 2015.

Oman, Charles. *Castles*, The Great Western Railway, London, 1926.

Painter, Sidney. *William Marshall: Knight-Errant, Baron, and Regent of England*, Medieval academy reprints for teaching, Reprinted Ed edition, University of Toronto Press, 1982.

Peraino, Judith A. *Giving Voice to Love: Song and Self-Expression from the Troubadours to Guillaume de Machaut*, Oxford University Press, 2011.

Plant, John S. 'The Tardy Adoption of the Plantagenet Surname', *Nomina*, vol. 30, pp57–84, 2007.

Poole, A.L. *Domesday Book to Magna Carta 1087–1216*, 2nd ed., Oxford University Press, 1955.

Potter, David ed. *France in the Later Middle Ages*, Oxford University Press, 2002.

Powicke, F.M. *The Loss of Normandy*, Manchester at the University Press, 1913.

Powicke, F.M. *The Thirteenth century: 1216–1307*, 2nd ed., Oxford University Press, 1962.

Prajda, Katalin. 'Trade and Diplomacy in pre-Medici Florence. The case of the Kingdom of Hungary (1349–1434)', in *Das Konzil von Konstanz und Ungarn*, ed. Barany, Attila, University Press, Debrecen, 2016.

Przybyszewski, Fr. Bolesław, trans. Bruce MacQueen. *Saint Jadwiga, Queen of Poland 1374–1399*, Veritas Foundation Publication Centre, 1997.

Reynaud, Marcelle-Renée. *Le temps des princes: Louis II et Louis III d'Anjou-Provence, 1384–1434*, Presses universitaires de Lyon, 2000.

Reynolds, Michael T. 'René of Anjou, King of Sicily, and the order of the Croissant', *Journal of Medieval History*, Volume 19, Issues 1–2, March–June 1993, pp125–161.

Rezachevici, Constantin. 'From the Order of the Dragon to Dracula', *Journal of Dracula Studies*, vol 1, 1999, pp3–7.

Robin, Françoise. *La Cour d'Anjou-Provence. La vie artistique sous le règne de René*, Picard, Paris, 1985.

Runciman, Stephen. *The Sicilian Vespers: A History of the Mediterranean World in the Later Thirteenth century*, 9th printing, Cambridge University Press, 2008.

Runciman, Steven. *A History of the Crusades*, 3 volumes, Folio

Society, London, 1997.

Rosenberg, John D, ed. *The Genius of John Ruskin: Selections from his Writings*, University Press of Virginia, Charlottesville and London, 1998.

Sackville-West, Vita. *Saint Joan of Arc*, revised edition, Michael Joseph Ltd, London, 1948.

Salies, Alexandre de. *Histoires de Foulques-Nerra, Comte d'Anjou*, JB Dumoulin, Paris and E. Barasse, Angers, 1874.

Scales, Len. *The shaping of German identity: authority and crisis, 1245–1414*, Cambridge University Press, Cambridge; New York, 2012.

Senneville, Gérard de. *Yolande d'Aragon: la reine qui a gagné la Guerre de Cent Ans*, Perrin, 2008.

Seward, Desmond. *The Hundred Years War: The English in France 1337–1453*, Atheneum, New York, 1984.

Seward, Desmond. *The Monks of War: The Military Orders*, The Folio Society, London, 2000.

Southern, R.W. *The Making of the Middle Ages*, The Cresset Library, London, 1967.

St Clair Baddeley, Welbore. *Queen Joanna I of Naples, Sicily, and Jerusalem, Countess of Provence, Forcalquier and Piedmont*. William Heinemann, London, 1893.

St Clair Baddeley, Welbore. *Robert the Wise and His Heirs, 1278–1352*, William Heinemann, London, 1897.

Stafford, Pauline. 'The Portrayal of Royal Women in England, Mid-Tenth to Mid-Twelfth Centuries', *Medieval Queenship*, ed. J. C. Parsons, Sutton, Stroud, pp143–67, 1993.

Staley, Edgcumbe. *King Rene d'Anjou and His Seven Queens*, Charles Scribner's Sons, New York, 1912.

Strayer, Joseph R. *The Albigensian Crusades*, University of Michigan Press, Ann Arbor, 1971.

Szakács, Béla Zsolt. *The Visual World of the Hungarian Angevin Legendary*, Central European University Press, 2016.

Tabacco, Giovanni, trans. Rosalind Brown Jensen. *The struggle for power in medieval Italy*, 1st edition, Cambridge University Press, 1990.

Tolhurst, Fiona. *Geoffrey of Monmouth and the Translation of Female Kingship*, Palgrave Macmillan, New York, 2013.

Tuchman, Barbara W. *A Distant Mirror: The Calamitous 14th century*, Ballantine, New York, 1978.

Turner, Ralph V. *King John*, Longman, London and New York, 1994.

Vacquet, Étienne (editor). *Saint Louis et l'Anjou*, Presses Universitaires Rennes, Rennes, 2014.

Vale, Malcolm. *The origins of the Hundred Years War: the Angevin legacy, 1250–1340*, New edition, Oxford University Press, USA, 1996.

Vitolo, Paola. 'Royauté et modèles culturels entre Naples, France et Europe. Les années de Robert et de Jeanne Ire d'Anjou (1309–1382)', *Identités angevines: Entre Provence et Naples, XIIIe-XVe siècle*, ed. Jean-Paul Boyer, Anne Mailloux & Laure Verdon. Publications de L'Université de Provence, 2016.

Vivarelli, Carla. '"Di una pretesa scuola napoletana": Sowing the Seeds of the Ars nova at the Court of Robert of Anjou', *The Journal of Musicology*, vol. 24, pp272–296, 2007.

Warren, W.L. *Henry II*, Methuen, London, 1991.

Warren, W.L. *King John*, 2nd edition, Methuen, London, 1978.

Weiler, Björn K.U. with Rowlands, Ifor W eds. *England and Europe in the reign of Henry III (1216–1272)*, Ashgate, Aldershot, Hants and Burlington, VT, 2002.

Weir, Alison. *Eleanor of Aquitaine*, Pimlico, London, 2000.

INDEX